D1358606

AN INTRODUCTION TO COMPARATIVE POLITICS

AN INTRODUCTION TO COMPARATIVE POLITICS

twelve nation states

Marian D. Irish
School of International Service
The American University

Elke Frank
Mary Baldwin College

APPLETON–CENTURY–CROFTS

Educational Division
Meredith Corporation

New York

Library of Congress Card Number: 70-184714

PHOTO RESEARCHER: **Ann Novotny**/Research Reports
345 Riverside Drive, New York, N.Y. 10025

PRINTED IN THE UNITED STATES OF AMERICA

72 73 74 75 76 /10 9 8 7 6 5 4 3 2 1

390-E-47757-5

This book was printed on recycled paper.

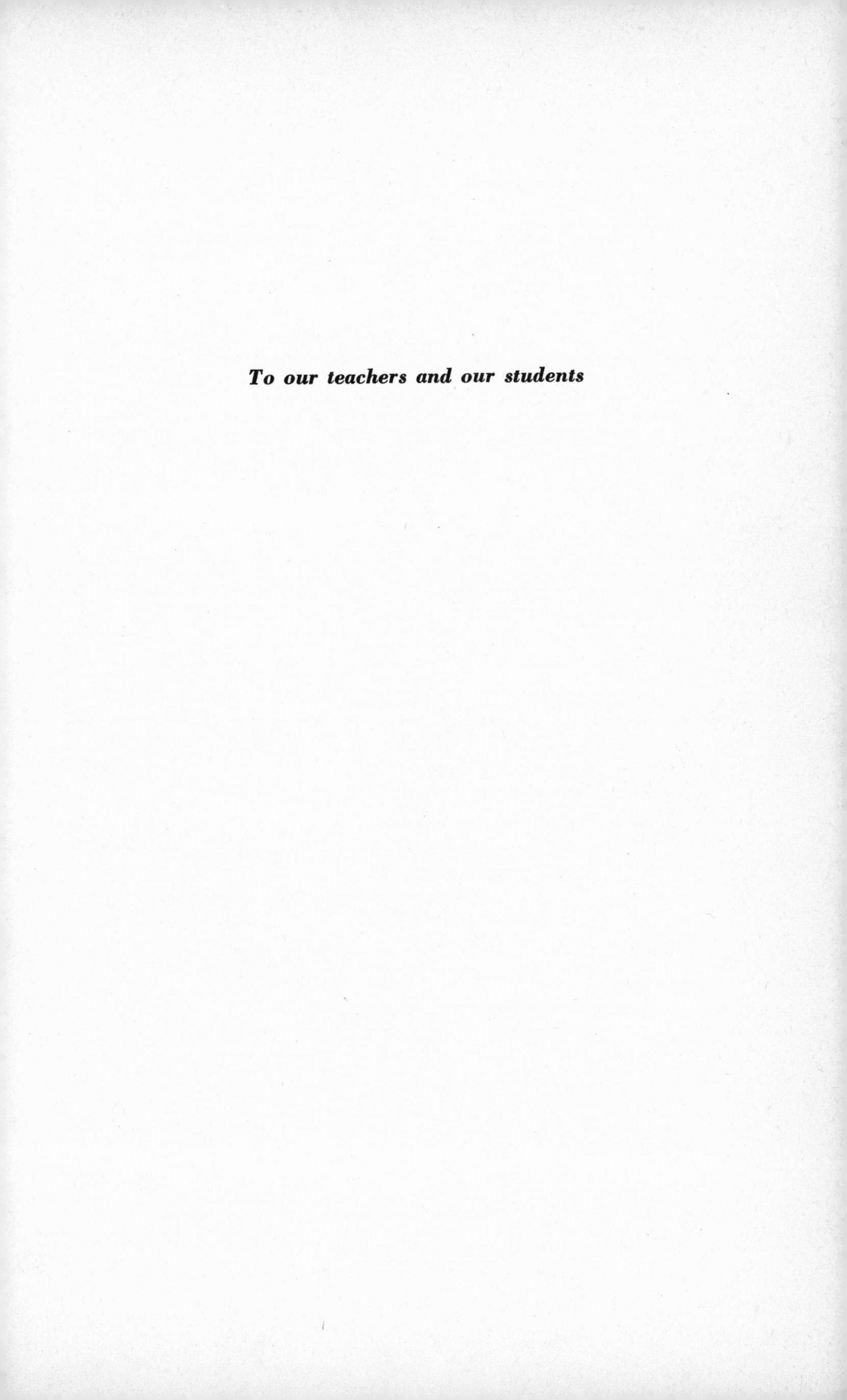

To our teachers and our students

CONTENTS

Chapter 10 **How Are Nation States Organized Institutionally? 247**

Chapter 11 **How Do Governments Operate? 285**

Chapter 12 **How Do Governors Govern? 315**

PREFACE

This book is the result of frustration and stimulation: Frustration because it is difficult to find textbooks in comparative politics that are truly comparative; stimulation because the theories of comparative politics in recent years have been many and fruitful; and more frustration because the various theories are used either to support abstract models or to serve as introductions to texts that still follow the conventional country-by-country approach. The countries selected are usually the same ones that have been used by students for generations: Great Britain, France, Germany, and Russia.

Many political scientists have broken away from the historical, constitutional, and descriptive studies that were traditional to the profession and have moved toward analytical frameworks which place the emphasis on political processes. The emergence of many new nations and states since World War II has turned the attention of scholars to more dynamic concepts of political systems that give them more leeway in explaining the differences between traditional and developing systems. And to advance our understanding of these emerging nations, some scholars have transformed myths and mystiques such as nationalism and statehood into more rigorous analytical schemes, focusing, for example, on the role of communication in social integration and political control.

The advances of theory in comparative politics, however, have largely taken the form of scholars speaking to scholars in the professional journals or in specialized monographs where they indulge in more model-building. Meanwhile, other political scientists who hold tightly to the course of objective fact-finding have been industriously extending the empirical bases, especially with survey research, and the results are a proliferation of statistical studies and data archives.

Undergraduate instruction generally is left to make its own synthesis between these two trends in the profession: on the one hand, abstractions and theoretical speculation, and on the other, systematic collection and interpretation of data about the real world. As we see it, however, the relevance of the one to the other is what makes political science meaningful and exciting.

In this text we try to synthesize theory and reality in a framework of comparative political analysis. Because the nation state is generally regarded as the principal actor on the world scene, we have chosen to examine twelve very different nation states to afford us a spectrum of empirical evidence on the behavior of political systems: the United Kingdom, the USA, Mexico, Colombia, the USSR, Turkey, the Federal Republic of Germany, Japan, Kenya, India, the Ivory Coast, and Israel. Our synthesis is derived from our own concept of the nation state as a political system, but we have borrowed freely from a wide variety of political theories now being developed and tested by our colleagues in political science. We think it important that undergraduates become familiar with the seminal and supporting literature in our profession. We have therefore included many footnotes, to open doors for students who seek new perspectives and new insights for understanding contemporary political man and woman.

We are not offering detailed country-by-country descriptions. We are, however, underpinning our theoretical discussions with cross-national data that serve to illustrate the common characteristics among, as well as the salient differences between, our twelve nation states. We prefer to avoid professional jargon, using, rather, the language of the lay citizenry, because politics is largely an activity of nonscholars. Political scientists, however, have developed a common technical vocabulary, and in this text we will use many of the basic terms which students need to know before they can read the professional journals. As we introduce these terms we shall provide explicit definitions in the Glossary.

This selective study of twelve nation states covers various stages in statehood and different stages in economic, social, and political development. It tries to differentiate between fundamental goals and operational goals and to distinguish between national interests and dominant interests. Further, it examines the role and function of the mass media and special interest groups in representative, totalitarian, and developing systems. It looks at competitive and noncompetitive party systems, observes election practices, and notes the linkages between those in authority and those who are governed. It assesses both structural and functional organization, especially the different roles played by executives, legislators, bureaucrats, and judges in various types of political organization. The overriding concern is how different governments operate; how they weigh the demands and supports of the people and determine who gets what within the system; how the governors govern; and what tools and techniques they use to obtain the consent of the governed or, at least, to secure compliance with authoritative decisions.

The study of comparative politics is a study of dynamics. The facts are ephemeral and the figures keep changing even as we write. The manufacture of a book takes time. We began writing this text in the spring of 1969, and as we slowly wended our way from Chapter 1 to Chapter 13, the course of events brought about many changes within each of our twelve nation states.

For example, national elections were held in 1969, 1970, and 1971 in Colombia, the Federal Republic of Germany, Kenya, Mexico, the Soviet Union, the United Kingdom, India, and the United States. In Chapters 8 and 9 we have briefly discussed how the election results may affect the government in those countries. Undoubtedly, we have missed events that may have had an even greater impact on the political system than a change in party fortunes or new names in the official hierarchy of authority.

In 1971, civil war in Pakistan escalated into war between India and Pakistan, with the Indian government supporting the Bengalese in East Pakistan. As this book went to press, the final outcome of the war was uncertain. Pakistan appeared to be defeated and dismembered. What had been East Pakistan was now proclaimed a new nation state, Bangladesh, under Bengali rule but still occupied by Indian troops. Whatever the outcome, however, the map of India which appears at the end of the text is outdated, because it still shows East and West Pakistan. The reader will have to do his own updating.

We have endeavored to explain rather than to evaluate. Inevitably, however, and especially when we discuss how political systems function—i.e., the impact of the system on the nation as a whole and on the members as individuals—our own value judgments are bound to enter into our conclusions. As political scientists we have tried to be objective with the evidence at hand. But we also believe that, in the final analysis, political scientists have an obligation to express their own convictions and judgments in the areas where they have done their homework; hence, our final chapter does include some appraisals, even though our evidence may not be entirely current or complete. Students who do their own digging for data—and find evidence to the contrary—are free to disagree with our conclusions.

We are indebted to the whole company of scholars whose names appear in footnotes throughout the text, in the Further Readings at the end of each chapter, and in the Selected Bibliography. Their research and findings have given us a broad base of intelligence. We are also indebted to numerous persons whose names do not appear anywhere in the text because their official positions in the government offices and embassies in Washington do not permit attribution. We wish to thank personally John D. Martz of the University of North Carolina and Samuel H. Beer of Harvard University, who read the manuscript in first draft and offered many helpful suggestions. We also wish to acknowledge the assistance of Michael Roskin, doctoral student in the School of International Service at the American University, who proofread the manuscript for us, compiled the appended Glossary, and prepared an accompanying Instructor's Manual. Most of all we want to express our appreciation for the valuable editorial guidance of Walter Green, whose sharp needling provoked us into upgrading the manuscript, and to Ernest Kohlmetz. Responsibility for the final manuscript including all shortcomings, errors of commission and omission, prejudices and predilections, rests jointly with the authors.

E.F., Staunton, Va.
M.D.I., McLean, Va.

INTRODUCTION

The dozen nation states compared here differ in terms of land area, strategic location in the world, demographic characteristics, historical environment, cultural characteristics, social structures, natural resources, economic development, degrees of political socialization, political attitudes, political institutions, and political behavior. All twelve examples are recognized and act as nation states in the contemporary world. As such, each is a political system motivated, organized, and operating so as to perform certain primary functions: to insure the survival of its people as a nation, as well as to maintain the territorial integrity and the political independence of the state; to provide domestic tranquility; to dispense justice according to the values of the society which the political system serves; and to assess and mobilize the resources of the state, determining who gets what within the system.

The use of real rather than model nation states introduces many practical difficulties which not infrequently confound the analysis. Every nation state is unique, and therefore none is really representative or typical. Whatever generalizations may be drawn from this selected sample are bound to be qualified by various exceptions. Moreover, what may be thought of as empirical evidence—the facts and figures with which we check out our hypotheses—sometimes turns out to be dated, defective, or uncorrelated. The figures are abundant, but they may also be unreliable in final analysis. Facts are usually what we perceive, but perceptions depend on vantage points. No doubt, our perceptions are conditioned by our upbringing in Western political democracy. But it is also certain that Russian, Arabic, African, or Asian citizens will not see us as we see ourselves and do not see themselves as we here record our views. So much for facts. One can only try to report and utilize them as he perceives them.

Dozens of other examples might have been chosen—there are about 150 nations in the world today. However, this particular dozen is representative of certain concepts which are germane to our overall comparative analysis:

The *United Kingdom* is the prototype of Western parliamentary democracy, a nation state that has evolved gradually, whose political institutions have matured through centuries. Here we find the cradle of the industrial revolution and can observe the development of the first modern industrial state, a small nation that created a worldwide empire on a business basis and subsequently survived the dissolution of that empire.

The United States of America, Mexico, and *Colombia* are the first new nations emerging in the late eighteenth and early nineteenth centuries from European colonialism in the Western hemisphere. Although each was strongly influenced by her mother country, each reacted quite differently to the indigenous culture. The United States of America developed into a highly urbanized, industrialized nation with a polyglot immigrant civilization showing little trace of the native culture. Mexico and Colombia, on the other hand, have fused their Spanish and Indian inheritances, albeit in different degrees; both are relatively underdeveloped with respect to modern industry and technology, although both have plans for progress. All three are constitutional republics, but with very different political behavioral patterns reflecting quite diverse historical and cultural environments.

The Union of Soviet Socialist Republics and *Turkey* demonstrate the transformation of traditional societies into modern political systems in the early decades of the twentieth century. They exemplify social and political engineering motivated by strong-willed personal leadership (Lenin and Stalin in the USSR, Atatürk in Turkey), accelerated by ideology (Marxism-Leninism in the USSR and nationalism in Turkey), and implemented through one-party control of the official governing system. We shall be concerned with the initial similarities but also with the salient differences, because the two countries now fall into quite different categories: the USSR is a superpower in world politics; Turkey is still a developing nation.

The Federal Republic of Germany and *Japan* were major world powers in the late nineteenth and early twentieth centuries. Both were economically devastated and their political systems completely destroyed by the end of World War II. Both have been reconstructed in the post-World-War-II period with outside economic assistance and political tutelage. Both have now surpassed their prewar economic status, a feat largely made possible by the fact that each was rebuilt upon a social base already technologically oriented. Both countries have a long history of strong cultural nationalism and an affinity for authoritarian political institutions. And both have been prompted from the outside to redesign their political systems on a democratic and representative model.

India, Kenya, and *the Ivory Coast* are newly developing nation states, emerging from the breakup of European empires in Asia and Africa after World War II. They illustrate the problems involved in transforming essentially traditional and agricultural societies into modern nation states. The caste system with its subcultures in India and tribalism in Africa pose various difficulties in political integration and the development of nationalism as a concomitant of statehood.

Israel is a unique example. It is a very old nation, its people scattered for centuries over the face of the earth but now turning back to an ancient promised land, and it is struggling to establish itself as a modern state. The problems of survival as an independent political system in a totally hostile environment are accepted as a challenge, but the acute strain is felt not so much within the system as in the rest of the world.

There is gathered here a great deal of cross-national data from such sources as the *UN Yearbook*, the *Statesman's Yearbook*, the *World Bank Atlas*, the *Statistical Abstract of the United States*, a variety of economic plans, and the holdings of numerous data banks. Also included is information garnered from embassies in Washington, interviews with numerous cultural and political officers, collected official handouts of many sorts, consultations with various country analysts in the Bureau of Intelligence and Research in the US State Department, the *Background Notes* of the US State Department, the *Basic Economic Data* series and other periodical and occasional publications of the Bureau of International Commerce in the US Department of Commerce, and the various pamphlets issued by the British Information Services, to mention just a few. Due references to the published materials appear in the footnotes, but much of the information obtained from interviews with officials is not attributable. The public records and the data available are not equally extensive, accessible, or current in this sample of nation states. Statistical information is by no means uniform, complete, or accurate. As is frequently pointed out in the text, the most meticulous quantitative analysis can be utterly misleading in substantive significance. Even so, with this caveat, full use is made of whatever facts and figures seem relevant, reliable, and accordingly useful as an objective base for comparative generalizations. The reader who wants to update this discussion or to give it more depth will have to do additional homework. One might begin with the *New York Times Index* and *Keesing's Contemporary Archives.*

The comparative study of these twelve nation states is organized around key questions, and the order in which the questions are raised determines the framework of analysis:

What makes a state?

What makes a nation?

What motivates a political system?

Who are the ruling elites in the system?

How do political opinions affect government?

How do political parties affect government?

How do elections affect government?

How are nation states organized—territorially?

How are nation states organized—institutionally?

How do governments operate?

How do governors govern?

DO NOT
ROSS
DEPT.

chapter 1

THE FRAME OF REFERENCE: twelve nation states

Both *state* and *nation* are old and familiar terms in the language of political science, but like so many terms that are old and familiar they are difficult to explain, because they have undergone so many shifts in meaning. Scholars, as well as statesmen, differ among themselves as to what exactly is a state, a nation, or a political entity in international relations. This is one explanation why the number of nation states is usually given as "approximately."

Bruce Russett, J. David Singer, and Melvin Small provide us with "an exhaustive list of the territorially based political units which are, have been since 1900, or are likely to become national political entities" [1]—over 250 entities whose populations exceed ten thousand. Note that they shy away from the old-fashioned term, *nation state;* their basic classifications are *independent* and *dependent* political entities. In the first category they include those states which have enjoyed some measure of diplomatic recognition, as well as effective control over their own foreign affairs and armed forces. In the second category they place colonies and dependencies, mandate and trust territories, and entities which had enjoyed independence until they were overrun and occupied by foreign military forces.

The list of "National Political Units in the Twentieth Century," which its authors hoped might help to discipline research in comparative politics and international politics, appears in the *American Political Science Review* (September, 1968). It is immediately followed by a number of critical com-

USA, parade watchers
(Ernst Haas : Magnum)

munications to the editor. One critic objects to the classical political-legal terms on which the classification of independent and dependent political entities is based. He argues that a behavioral approach to international relations calls for a more relevant criterion than "the age-old concern for sovereign status": an economist would consider cartels and common markets as members of the international system; a military strategist might include the National Liberation Front or the Yugoslav Partisans as national political entities. Another critic takes exception to the exclusion of ministates, "a state is a state irrespective of the population it controls. Population size describes no more than an attribute of a state (e.g., its importance) but does not bear upon its existence." The same critic also suggests that the entities which politically shape a world system would include a great deal besides states, "not only the United States and, say Dahomey, but also the State of California, the Royal Dutch-Shell Petroleum Company, the Ford Foundation, the World Bank, and the Roman Catholic Church."

TABLE 1–1
National Political Units in the Twentieth Century

WESTERN HEMISPHERE	*Independent*		*Dependent*		*Part of Larger Entity*	
Name	*From*	*To*	*From*	*To*	*From*	*To*
United States of America						
Mexico						
Colombia						
EUROPE						
United Kingdom						
West Germany		1945				
	1949					
			1945	1948 occ.		
USSR/Russia						
AFRICA						
Ivory Coast	1960			1960 col.		
Kenya	1963			1963 col.		
MIDDLE EAST						
Turkey/Ottoman Empire						
Israel/Palestine			1918	1923 occ.		1918
			1923	1948 man.		
	1948					
ASIA						
Japan		1945				
			1945	1952 occ.		
	1952					
India	1947			1947 col.		

SOURCE: Bruce Russett, J. David Singer, and Melvin Small, "National Political Units in the Twentieth Century: A Standardized List," *American Political Science Review* 62 (1968): 932–51. By permission of the American Political Science Association.

We think that Russett and his associates have done a tremendous job of compilation; we also agree with their critics that an authoritative definition of all the components in the international system might well include tens of thousands more items. Since, however, we are not primarily concerned with the international system, but rather with comparative politics and particularly with independent national political entities—we find the controversial tabulation a useful introduction to our study of nation states.

If you study this tabulation you will see that it gives us a start on comparative data about our twelve states. Five of the twelve were already nation states at the beginning of the twentieth century and have not lost that status in the seven decades since: the United States, Mexico, Colombia, the United Kingdom, and the USSR. Two of the states—West Germany [2] and Japan—were independent, but as a result of defeat in World War II were occupied by enemy forces and so must be classified as dependent during the period of occupation; both have since regained their sovereignty and are now counted as independent. Three of the states were colonies of Western powers at the turn of the century: India was the first of these to gain independence from the British Empire in 1947, the Ivory Coast declared its independence from the French Empire in 1960, and Kenya from the British in 1963. The status of Israel is more complicated. At the end of World War I the British government assumed responsibility for Palestine as a League of Nations mandate; Palestine then included both what is now Jordan and Israel; Jordan attained independence in 1946 and Israel in 1948.

Clearly such tidbits tabulated from political history do not answer our initial questions: What is a nation state? and How does it come into being? Russett's "Standardized List," for example, leaves blank the dates of independence for those national political entities which had already achieved statehood before 1900. Let us see if we can fill in the blanks and add some other pertinent data which will tell us more about the development.

THREE AMERICAN REPUBLICS

The United States of America

The United States celebrates its independence from the British Empire as July 4, 1776. But was the United States really independent from 1776 to 1783 while it was still fighting the Revolution? Does a unilateral Declaration of Independence create a state and give it the right "to assume among the powers of the earth the separate and equal station to which the Laws of Nature and of Nature's God entitle them"? To answer this question we need to look at the basic premises of international law and the prevalent practices among nations. Beyond the legal questions, moreover, are the more fundamental issues which relate to the creation of a nation. When did the British colonists begin to think of themselves as Americans? When the Continental Congress wrote the Articles of Confederation as a constitutional companion piece for the Declaration of Independence, it prescribed "a perpetual union" between the states. But in 1787, when they designed "a more perfect union," their instrument began with these significant words: "We the people of the United States." When did the citizens of Virginia and Massachusetts begin to think of themselves as a national community, as citizens of the United States, and how was the transfer of primary loyalty effected? [3]

The United States of America today is a far cry from the original thirteen united states. The total land area in 1790 amounted to less than nine hundred thousand square miles; today the area of the fifty states exceeds 3.5 million square miles; it spans the continent and includes the noncontiguous states Alaska and Hawaii. The population in the first census was less than four million; in 1968 the census clock ticked over two hundred million. The composition of the population in 1790 was 80 percent free, and 20 percent slave. Of the free population about 90 percent was of English-speaking, British stock. The colonists, then the immigrant pioneers, all but eliminated the native Indians; today there remain fewer than half a million Indians, most of them living on reservations. The blacks now comprise about 11 percent of the population; and the ancestry of the foreign white stock can be traced to just about every country, fewer than 15 percent to British stock. Certainly the United States is culturally one of the most pluralistic nations in the world; one homogeneous factor dominates, however—the English language.

All countries change, of course, and no country in the second half of the twentieth century remotely resembles its condition at the end of the eighteenth century. The remarkable thing about the United States is that it is still organ-

Mexico, schoolgirls view their heritage at the Museum of Anthropology
(Marc & Evelyne Bernheim : Rapho Guillumette)

ized, and operating, under the political system which its founding fathers designed at the end of the eighteenth century. The Constitution of 1787, the first and now the oldest written constitution in the modern world, is still the supreme law of the land in the United States. Constitutional law has been stretched by amendments, interpretations, institutional behavior, and popular understanding, but the pattern of government it prescribes—republican, federal, presidential, representative—still sets the outer limits for US decision-makers, national, state, and local.[4]

Mexico

For nearly three hundred years, Mexico was a Spanish colony. In the first decade of the nineteenth century, Father Miguel Hidalgo, a village priest, a Creole intellectual fired by the doctrines of the French Revolution, agitated for such reforms as emancipation of slaves, the return of lands to the Indians, and the end of tribute taxes to Madrid. He gathered an immense but ill-organized army of natives, and under the banner of Our Lady of Guadeloupe, stirred a religious insurrection. Hidalgo proclaimed the independence of Mexico on September 16, 1810, but independence would not be attained for many years. The Revolution of 1810 scarcely affected the everyday life of the people. Father Hidalgo himself was captured by the government forces, degraded by the Spanish Inquisition, and finally executed; but the fires of inde-

Colombia, La Ermita church, Cali (left) (Colombian Government Tourist Office)

Kenya, President Jomo Kenyatta (right) (Ian Berry : Magnum)

pendence which he helped to light were not quenched. The war for independence continued until the Republic of Mexico was established in 1822. Except for a brief interlude as an empire under the ill-fated Archduke Maximilian of Austria, 1865–67, Mexico has been a republic ever since.

The present constitution of Mexico, one of five since 1822, was written in 1917 and has been amended since then. So, when did Mexico become a nation state? When revolutions occur and the existing political system is rejected and replaced by one very different, does the state survive intact or is a new state created? International law offers some technical answers to questions of succession, but we will want to probe more deeply into the politics of a nation state if we are to understand what David Easton calls "stress on a system" or "those conditions that challenge the capacity of a system to persist." [5]

Of all the Latin American countries, Mexico has made the greatest material progress, since the Revolution of 1910, and especially since the 1940s. But national political development, despite all manner of official encouragement, has been agonizingly and disappointingly slow. Robert Scott, who has done an in-depth study of Mexico in transition, estimates that about a quarter of the Mexican people still have little or no awareness of the nation or its government, and only about 10 percent are participants.[6] Yet the constitutional structure modeled after that of the United States—federal, democratic, representative—calls for a high level of citizen participation. Why is it that

India, pilgrims at the Ganges (left) (Marc Riboud : Magnum)

Ivory Coast, the country's first car-assembly plant (right) (Marc & Evelyne Bernheim : Rapho Guillumette)

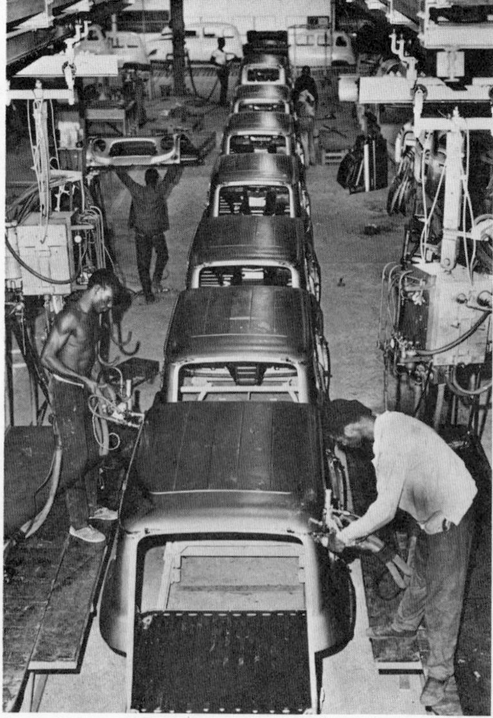

so many Mexicans think of themselves as consumers rather than producers, complying rather than demanding, within their own political system? What kind of infrastructure (communication and transportation systems) does it take to promote a more active sense of identity and common interest between the citizen and his government?

Colombia

What is now Colombia was founded as a Spanish colony—New Granada—in 1549, more than seventy years before the passengers of the Mayflower made the first political covenant in North America. In 1810, Bogotá, then seat of the viceroyalty of New Granada, declared its independence and in 1819 the Republic of Colombia was proclaimed. Through the nineteenth century the country was torn by nearly a hundred insurrections and civil wars, most of them over church-state questions. Endemic rural violence reached a climax in the first decade of the twentieth century, after which a kind of truce between the warring political elites brought about a condition of apparent stability that lasted nearly forty years. Students of Latin American politics in the early 1940s were characterizing Colombia as one of the most democratic and progressive countries in the Americas, definitely a mature nation state. Then came the period known as "the Violence," 1948–57, a period of political anarchy and social revolution without authoritative leadership or

United Kingdom, the Queen's coach
(George Rodger : Magnum)

any dominant ideology, a period of lawlessness, terrorism, and brigandage in which a quarter million people are said to have been slaughtered.[7] Later in this text we shall be considering concepts of legitimacy and what is implied in acceptance of authority and consent of the governed. Colombia will serve as a prime example that violence is a power factor in politics.

No doubt the politics of violence in Latin American countries derives in part at least from the Spanish political inheritance. Martin Needler, attempting to put Latin American politics in perspective, points out that "the central feature of the colonial legitimacy system in Latin America was that political power, like social status, depended on the acknowledgement of the rights of birth."[8] Authority came from the top down, by inheritance, and by God's grace. The wars of independence swept away the colonial system, but, as we have already observed with respect to Mexico, these wars were not social revolutions comparable to the American or the French. They did not result in replacing the concept of crown power with the basic doctrines of popular sovereignty. Consent of the governed, which was central to notions of legitimacy in the first new nation in North America, has not been an operational concept in Latin America. Constitutions formally patterned after that of the United States are generally regarded as statements of political aspirations rather than as fundamental law ordained and established by the people to govern the government. And in the absence of any set code for legitimating political power, much of Latin American politics has been a matter of loyalty to individual leaders and ruling families rather than respect for institutional

Turkey, past and present in Istanbul
(Henri Cartier-Bresson : Magnum)

authority. Moreover, the "legitimacy vacuum" has tended to promote the politics of violence that we have noted in Colombia.

The United States, Mexico, and Colombia were all discovered and colonized in the same span of European history, the sixteenth through the eighteenth centuries. In all three countries the native population was Indian. How did the European colonists react to the indigenous civilizations of the New World and what impact did the native people have upon the emerging new patterns of culture in the Western Hemisphere? We have already indicated what happened to the Indians in the United States; they were virtually eliminated. But the Spanish conquerors, for all their reputation for cruelty, were less thorough than their English counterparts, as the mixed populations of Colombia and Mexico today attest. In Colombia no more than 2 percent of the population today are pure Indian, and these are to be found only in isolated tribes; but more than half of the population are of mixed Indian and white blood; about 20 percent are white; and the remainder are Negroes or mixed black and white. In Mexico about two-thirds of the people are of mixed Indian and Spanish descent; a very small percentage are of pure Spanish or European ancestry; the rest are Indian. The language of the people in both countries is Spanish, although many Indians still speak their own languages.

To say the least, the interaction of Spanish colonialism with the indigenous civilization was a cultural shock to all involved. No doubt the Spanish concept of legitimacy in the colonial government added to the racial and religious complications. Perhaps, because the natives had so long been treated

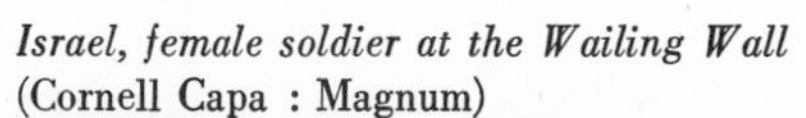
Israel, female soldier at the Wailing Wall
(Cornell Capa : Magnum)

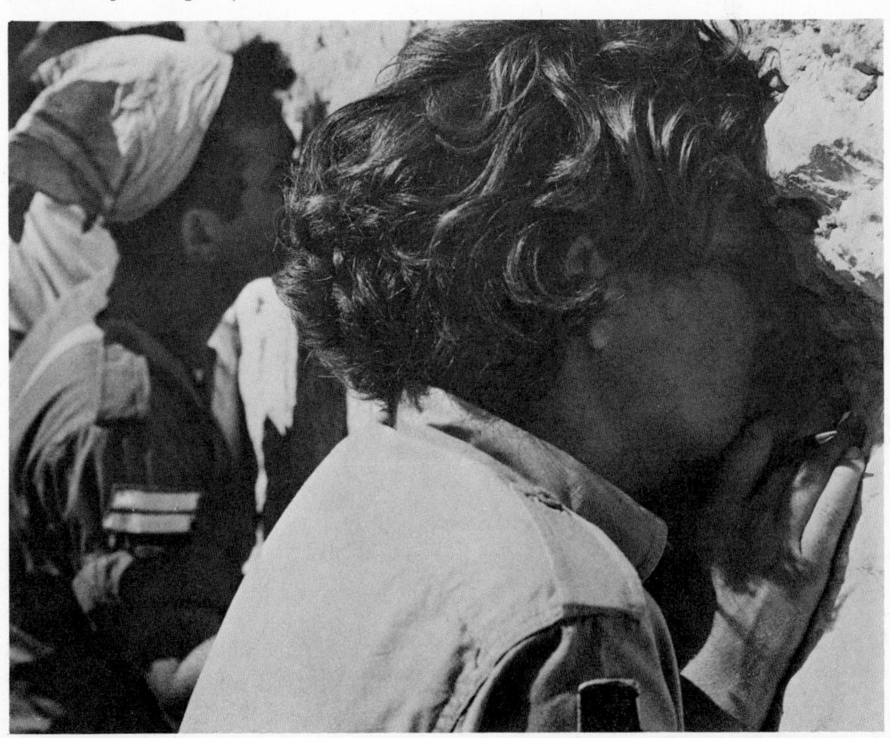

as inferior beings, it never occurred to them that they might have the right to rule. Mexican pride in its Indian heritage, for example, is of quite recent origin. Until the Revolution of 1910 Indians were expected to stay out of sight, and especially out of public places. Today the magnificent Museum of Anthropology in Chapultepec Park, Mexico City, gives the Mexican an understanding of "his own being—his own culture and personality—individual as well as collective" and is designed also "to eliminate prejudices against the indigenous races—both pre-Columbian and contemporary." [9]

Among the twelve states that we examine here, six have emerged from European colonialism: the United States, Mexico, Colombia, India, Kenya, and the Ivory Coast. All of them have experienced severe cultural shocks between the expatriate colonists and the indigenous populations. When we consider the problems of transition from colonial status to independent statehood we shall want to compare the British, Spanish, and French legacies within the new political cultures.

THREE EUROPEAN NATION STATES

The United Kingdom

Our three European examples—the United Kingdom, the Federal Republic of Germany, and the Union of Socialist Soviet Republics (USSR)—raise still

Japan, ironworks in Kyushu
(Henri Cartier-Bresson : Magnum)

more questions about the development of nation states. What birth date can we establish for the United Kingdom? Julius Caesar wrote about Britain in the fourth and fifth books of his *Gallic Wars*. Britain was there before the Roman legions came, saw, and conquered it; but it was still there long after the Roman Empire had served out its time in history. The Angles and Saxons invaded the island in the fifth century, fought and settled with the prehistoric Celts, and together they formed a kingdom. English schoolchildren read all about Alfred the Great who came to the throne in 871. The Danes and the Normans invaded England in the eleventh century; the Danish King Canute (1016–35) is reputed to have ruled the island as an English kingdom, accepting the customs, language, religion, and laws of the country. The Norman conquerors, however, introduced Norman ways and imposed many of them on Anglo-Saxon customs. Do we date the modern English nation state from 1066?

Note that our example is not England but the United Kingdom, which includes Wales, Scotland, and Northern Ireland. When was union officially, or actually, achieved? Wales was an independent Celtic kingdom in the period of Danish supremacy over England. To the north the Picts and the Scots also maintained a separate kingdom. Not till the thirteenth century did the English conquer Wales; in 1284 Wales was formally annexed to the realm of King Edward I. The same Edward dealt as harshly with the Scots as he had with the Welsh, but the Scots fought back more vigorously and for another three hundred years were able to forestall union with England. In 1707 a treaty

USSR, rally in Red Square (left)
(Burt Glinn : Magnum)

Federal Republic of Germany, Oktoberfest in Munich (right)
(Henri Cartier-Bresson : Magnum)

presented first to the Scottish Parliament in Edinburgh and then to the English Parliament in Westminster formed "an entire union" of the two countries. Thereafter, one king, one parliament, and one flag combining the crosses of St. George and St. Andrew marked the birth of Great Britain. But more important to the growth of Great Britain than these official acts of union was the Industrial Revolution, which would turn the British Isles into the foremost industrial power in the world by the end of the nineteenth century. We shall have a great deal to say about industrialization and its complementary characteristic urbanization when we attempt to measure modernization and development of other nation states. Suffice it here to point out that Great Britain headed the historic progression which got under way about the same time as the American Revolution.

And what about Northern Ireland which is also part of the United Kingdom? Like the Welsh and the Scots, the Irish were brought into the English kingdom by force. The story covers nearly a thousand years of bitter and often bloody history, beginning with the Anglo-Norman invasion of Ireland in 1170. From the early seventeenth century the English treated the Irish more or less as a conquered province. From 1800 to 1921 Ireland was an integral part of the United Kingdom. But the Irish never gave up fighting for emancipation. Economic ties between the Irish and the English could have been mutually rewarding but the unremitting brooding of the Irish over their historic wrongs against them demonstrates that repressed nationalism can outweigh economic determination. During World War I the Irish intensified their armed struggle to the point that the English finally acceded to the demands. The Anglo-Irish Treaty of 1921 established the Irish Free State as a British dominion with status identical to that of Canada and Australia in the then newly conceived British Commonwealth of Nations. At that time, however, six counties of Ulster preferred to keep their ties with the United Kingdom and were granted self-government within the kingdom. After World War II, during which the Irish remained neutral, the Irish Free State broke all constitutional lines with the British Commonwealth and on Easter Monday, 1949, formally declared Ireland to be an independent republic. Meanwhile the six counties of Northern Ireland retain, albeit uneasily today, their special political ties with the United Kingdom.

This capsule of very complicated British history points between the lines to all kinds of problems relating to our key question—Is the United Kingdom a nation state? Is it a nation? Who in the United Kingdom are English and what turned them into Englishmen? In the summer of 1971, as we write this chapter, the news headlines are featuring what almost amounts to civil war in Northern Ireland, with bitter fighting between the Roman Catholic and Protestant factions in the population and British troops called in to keep the peace by force. And Irish expatriates from Boston and New York are volunteering to join the religious war! We also read about Scottish nationalists and Welsh nationalists prone to violent political action. The latter almost succeeded in blowing up the royal train carrying the English Prince of Wales to his symbolic investiture at Caernarvon Castle, where he struggled to respond to part of the ritual in Welsh.

The Federal Republic of Germany

The Federal Republic of Germany adds different dimensions to our search for definitions that encompass both statehood and nationhood. At the turn of the century, *Germany* referred to the German Empire created on January 18, 1871, at the end of the Franco-Prussian War, in the Hall of Mirrors at the Versailles Palace. The German princes hailed William I, king of Prussia, as their emperor. The political unification of the German people came relatively late in European history. German nationalism as a cultural force was strong in the nineteenth century, but the creation of a union-state which meant Prussian hegemony was not wholly attractive to German princes and their subjects who had developed separate identities since the disintegration of the Holy Roman Empire. Aided, however, by the belated industrialization of the German economy in the late nineteenth century, Chancellor Bismarck ruthlessly and efficiently manufactured a nation state within the framework of the German Empire. By the first decade of the twentieth century, Germany was reaching for first place among the world's great powers, but the German Empire crumbled in defeat and disappeared in the last days of World War I.

The Weimar Republic which replaced the Empire was a delayed experiment with democratic and republican institutions and based on a constitution superimposed by the victorious Allies. It was not a success and in 1933 it was in effect dissolved by Adolf Hitler's National Socialist movement. The Third Reich was an even more unhappy experience for the German people; scheduled to last a thousand years, it ended after twelve years in holocaust and unconditional surrender, May 8, 1945.

From 1945 to 1948 what was left of the former German state was ruled by the American, French, British, and Russian military forces. Berlin was separately governed under a four-power arrangement. During this period Germany was not an independent state (Table 1–1). But when did it recover statehood, or attain new statehood? In 1948 the American, British, and French governments agreed to the calling of a Constituent Assembly to frame a new political system for the three Western occupational zones which had in the meantime been merged into a single economic unit. The assembly proceeded to draft the Basic Law for a Federal Republic while the three Western allies worked out the Occupation Statute which defined their residual powers in the proposed republic. The new government went into operation in September, 1949. During the following years, the Federal Republic developed an active association with the Atlantic Community and in recognition of this fact in 1954 the Western allies, acknowledging the full sovereignty of the Federal Republic, invited it to membership in both the North Atlantic Treaty Organization and the Western European Union. Subsequently the Federal Republic has been very active in the European regional organizations, especially within the framework of the European Economic Community (EEC, Common Market).

Now, what about Berlin and East Germany? Berlin, capital of the German Empire, the Weimar Republic, and the Third Reich, is still an occupied city. Bonn, chosen because of its nonpolitical identification with German culture, is the provisional capital of the Federal Republic.[10] West Germans claim West Berlin as an integral part of the Federal Republic, and the Basic Law of 1949 applies to the city. More important, West Berlin is of symbolic importance to the Federal Republic. The electoral laws require that the president be elected there; West Germans made it a point of national honor in 1969, despite East German protests, to select their third president in Berlin. East Berlin, on the other side of the Wall, is the capital of the German Democratic Republic. This "other Germany" (the GDR) also claims to be a sovereign independent state. Under Russian occupation, 1945–49, it emerged from occupation status simultaneously with the Federal Republic. The GDR is a Communist state, a volatile advocate of Eastern European political interests. The Berlin Wall, built by the East German government in the summer of 1961, symbolizes separation of the East and West Germanies—an enforced physical separation as well as an ideological partition. Both Germanies purportedly have reunification as a national goal. Anyone asking the question Will the real Germany please stand up? is bound to receive an ambiguous response; but this too is part of the German political tradition.

In this text we shall be discussing how a political system adjusts to its environment and responds to various demands and supports in order to insure its survival. When we look at the Federal Republic of Germany as a nation state we must keep in mind that the German political system is of relatively recent origin (1871). Moreover, three times in this century the German political system has totally collapsed—the German Empire, the Weimar Republic, and the Third Reich. Does the Federal Republic, as one of the reconstructed German states, appear to be a more viable system? What criteria should we use in testing viability?

The Union of Soviet Socialist Republics

The national anthem of the Union of Soviet Socialist Republics celebrates "an unbreakable union of free republics . . . forged forever by the Great Rus." The Great Rus refers to the medieval Russian state. The legal and political antecedent of the Soviet Union is Russia, which enters the annals of European history some time in the tenth century. Until the middle of the fifteenth century, however, most of Russia consisted of a number of principalities, many of them quite isolated from Western Europe, much preoccupied with fighting the Tartars. Modern Russia developed around the Grand Duchy of Moscow in the sixteenth century. Ivan the Terrible (1530–84) destroyed the Tartar power and established a despotic monarchy, a regime marked by violent and systematic terrorism as well as the beginnings of political stability. We note this technique of nation-building in some of our newest states today, a hard-line dictatorship, systematic violence used as a political tool, and enforced mass compliance.

The history of Russia under the czars is one of tyrannical monarchy, social oppression, economic backwardness—an agrarian society in which serfdom survived past the middle of the nineteenth century. (The ukase of Alexander II abolishing serfdom in Russia in 1861 came two years before President Lincoln's wartime emancipation of black slaves in the United States,

1863.) The absolutism of the czars was matched by apathy and political passivity on the part of the people, intermittently punctuated in the nineteenth century by acts of political violence, assassinations, and aborted revolutions, to which the government responded with increased terrorism. On the cultural side, especially in the nineteenth century, there was a great flowering of Russian music, literature, and arts among the elite. Industrialization, technology, and the sciences, however, made little impact on the Russian way of life until the beginning of the twentieth century. The czarist regime came to an end in World War I (March, 1917) with the establishment of a provisional government of moderately liberal persuasion which shortly thereafter collapsed when a small band of Marxists (Bolsheviks) successfully engineered the most consequential revolution of modern times.

The Bolshevik wing of the Russian Social Democratic party (which later became the CPSU, the Communist party of the Soviet Union) forcibly seized control of the Kremlin on November 7, 1917. Its leader, V. I. Lenin, who had returned from his exile in Switzerland in February, 1917, became head of the new government. It was Lenin who masterminded the designing and implementation of an entirely new political system, a socialist state of workers and peasants in which the principal political unit is the *soviet*, or "council." At Lenin's death in 1924, Joseph V. Stalin who had become general secretary of the CPSU in 1922—a position that gave him extraordinary opportunities to control the rank and file members of the party and to build an apparatus loyal to him—moved into position as absolute dictator.

Initially, as Lenin had envisioned it, the Russian Revolution was but the prelude to a worldwide revolution of workers and peasants. Stalin's regime turned to the establishment of socialism in one country. The major goal was to modernize the economy—to collectivize agriculture and to proceed with large-scale industrialization—so that the USSR by its own achievements could demonstrate to the world the superiority of the socialist, over the capitalist, system. Recognizing that the goal could not be approached without immense efforts, tremendous self-sacrifices, centralized planning, and massive implementation, Stalin resorted more and more to force and absolute control; under his rule the USSR became a totalitarian system. Further, to secure the country against imperialist attacks from the outside he built a mighty military machine, and to deter ideological subversion from within he used not only terrorist techniques of government but also the apparatus of the Communist party to channel all demands and to supply full support for the government.

This totalitarian government and one-party dictatorship which transformed the Great Rus into a modern industrial power in a little more than one generation has been a conspicuous model for other new states whose leaders are hard pressed to meet the rising expectations of their people. When we look at the role of political parties and the function they perform in channeling the demands and mobilizing the supports for the government, we shall find that the Russian example, the single-party dictatorship, has its attractions for developing nations whose leaders are in a hurry to modernize.

At the height of his dictatorship Stalin presented the Russian people with a modern written constitution. This Constitution of 1936, which was formally approved by the All-Union Soviet with much cheering and no debate, is still the basic prescription. This leads us to speculate on the significance of constitutions in the politicization of the people. Why does nearly every new state, including those far from the stage of constitutional government, feel impelled to publish a written constitution? Of the twelve states in our sample only the United Kingdom and Israel have not felt the urge, or at least have not deemed it necessary, to inscribe and enroll their political framework on paper.

In determining whether or not a national political entity is independent, Russett refers with deliberate vagueness to "some measure of diplomatic recognition." The Soviet system in its inception was so drastically different from the then current political institutions that some governments were inclined to withhold recognition. The United States, which had promptly recognized the provisional liberal government that had overthrown the czarist regime in March, 1917, continued to recognize that government in exile years after the Bolsheviks were in unquestioned control of the Kremlin. The United States admitted that Russia survived as a state but would not concede that the Communist government was based on consent of the governed. Recognition is a diplomatic nicety and a legal technicality; but what constitutes consent of the governed and whether a political system can long endure without popular consent are political issues which we need to explore further.

TWO MIDDLE EAST STATES

In the Middle East we have selected Turkey and Israel, two examples with very different backgrounds. By now, however, it must be obvious that every nation state is unique, like no other in the world. Every political system operates within its own environment and that environment is bound to be distinctive: in physical characteristics, historical experience, cultural values, and economic development.

Turkey

At the beginning of the twentieth century Turkey was the center of the Ottoman Empire, which extended from the Balkans through the Middle East to the borders of Egypt. The Turkish sultan claimed the title of *caliph*—"successor of Muhammed"—and, as such, temporal and spiritual head of all Islam. During World War I the Ottoman Empire was involved on the side of the Central Powers. Known as "the sick man of Europe" before the war, the Ottoman Empire did not survive military defeat. Internal wars wracked the country from 1919 to 1923. In 1921 a Grand National Assembly drafted a constitution for the Ottoman Empire which declared that all power belonged to the people. In 1922 the ancient office of sultan was abolished and in 1923 the Republic of Turkey came into being, replacing the political dominion of the Ottoman Empire, which had been greatly reduced in size.

Turkey's politics are Western-oriented, but only 3 percent of its territory lies in Europe, the rest in Asia. Since 1923 the Turkish government has been modernizing the social and economic environment as well as the political system. The present Constitution of Turkey, approved by popular referendum in 1961, is the third attempt of the Republic to establish a Western-style constitutional government.

Actually the political modernization of Turkey was begun before World War I. The Young Turk Revolution of 1908 was in essence a commitment to a new and nationalistic Turkey. But the hard and painful process of nation-building did not begin in earnest until the founding of the Republic in 1923.

Founding father of the Republic of Turkey was Kemal Atatürk. (He took that name in 1934—his original name was Mustafa Kemal. Kemal means "the perfect" and Atatürk means "father of the Turks.") Mustafa Kemal, who had participated in the Young Turk Revolution in 1908,[11] organized the Turkish Nationalist party after World War I, began to mobilize his own army, and finally set up a government of his own to oppose the sultan. Successful in the ensuing civil wars, he proclaimed the end of the sultanate in 1922. He was elected president of the Republic in 1923, reelected in 1927, 1931, and 1935, each time by a unanimous parliament. (This outmatched the record of George Washington, revolutionary leader of the American colonists who was twice elected president by the Electoral College, both times unanimously.) In our further observations on nation-building we shall have more to say about the differing roles of revolutionary leaders and founding fathers. For every nation has its heroes, and in the myths that grow up around them we can learn much about concepts of leadership and the popular bases of legitimate authority.

During Atatürk's dictatorial regime (officially 1923–38), Turkey underwent profound economic and social changes, not the least of which were the abolition of the caliphate and secularization of the state. The Ottoman Empire, as a theocratic state, had been dedicated to the advancement and defense of the faith of Islam. Noting that 98.9 percent of the Turkish people belong to Islam even today, we must be impressed by the valiance of Atatürk in daring to separate church and state.

The role of religion in building a nation and the place of the church in the structure of the state have been, and still are, significant problems in comparative politics. The church frequently serves as a political instrument in modern history: The Tudor monarchs created the Church of England as a national institution, the better to fend off the temporal as well as spiritual claims of the Roman papacy. The current title of the queen, *Defender of the Faith*, refers to her role as head of the Anglican Church. Likewise the Russian czars counted on the Orthodox Church to legitimize and give positive support to absolute rule, even to the point of collusion in oppression of the people. Religion can be the cause of great dissension among the people as it was between Catholics and Protestants in the German principalities during and long after the Reformation, as it still is in India between Hindus and Muslims, or in Northern Ireland between Roman Catholics and Protestants. The influence of traditional religion can obstruct the process of modernization as it did in Islamic Turkey or as it still does in Catholic Colombia. On the other hand, religion can be a constructive ingredient in the political culture as was Protestantism in the formative years of the United States, as Shintoism was in imperial Japan, or a force which helped to sustain the political integration as in Israel.

Israel

Religious identification is central to the national consciousness of Israel. The Jewish nation is perhaps the oldest in recorded history; its saga is familiar to us from the books of the Old Testament. Nevertheless Israel is one of the newest nation states, proclaimed as an independent sovereign republic May 14, 1948. It symbolizes the age-old dream of the Jews scattered across the world, to return to the homeland.

The modern return of the Jews to the homeland dates back to the 1880s, coincident with the pogroms and social oppression of Jewry in Eastern Europe. At the outset of this migration, about twenty-four thousand Jews lived in Palestine, out of a population of four hundred and fifty thousand. At first spontaneous, the movement was soon organized by international Jewry; the World Zionist Organization was founded in 1897 at Basle, Switzerland. The Basle Programme aimed "to create for the Jewish people a home in Palestine" and to achieve this aim it advocated systematic settlement of Palestine with Jewish agriculturists, artisans, and craftsmen. At the outbreak of World War I, the number of Jews in Palestine had reached eighty-five thousand, out of some seven hundred thousand inhabitants. These early settlers formed the nucleus of an autonomous Jewish community, the *Yishuv*, which still dominates the political system in Israel.

During World War I, the British foreign secretary, in a letter sent to Lord Rothschild, November 2, 1917, expressed the sympathy of the British government for "Jewish Zionist aspirations" and indicated its readiness to facilitate "the establishment in Palestine of a national home for the Jewish people." This communication, known as the Balfour Declaration, was regarded as a commitment to the Jews. After the war, when the League of Nations assigned Palestine as a mandate to the British government the assignment recognized "the historical connections of the Jewish people with Palestine" and "the grounds for reconstituting their national home in that country." The League also requested the British government as the mandatory power to designate "an appropriate Jewish agency" to advise it on the administration of Palestine and to assist it in development of the country. Forthwith the British government recognized the Zionist organization as "the appropriate Jewish Agency."

Britain's leeway as a mandatory power was complicated by the fact that Palestine had been part of the Ottoman Empire and the many Arabs of the Muslim faith still living there, the overwhelming majority of the population, violently resisted Jewish claims to Arab territory. The Balfour Declaration had explicitly recognized "the civil and religious rights of existing non-Jewish communities in Palestine." The Zionist organization mobilized a mass migration of Jews to Palestine in anticipation of political independence. Meanwhile British officials persisted in holding down immigration figures to what they considered the absorptive capacity of the mandate. When the German Nazis launched their all-out extermination policy upon the European Jewry and still the British persisted in restricting the entrance of refugees, the situation became intolerable. The Jewish *Hagana*, the volunteer defense army, waged guerrilla war as much with the British as with the Arabs in Palestine.

At the end of World War II, unable to resolve the tensions between the zealots of both faiths, the British were more than willing to relinquish their mandate. The Jews were outraged, however, when Jordan, also part of Palestine, was granted independence before the Jewish state was recognized. While the United Nations ineffectually grappled with the problem of how to partition remaining Palestine between Arabs and Jews, a solution which the Arabs adamantly rejected, Israel proclaimed its own sovereignty. First to recognize the new state was the United States, almost within minutes after the Israeli proclamation. President Truman announced de facto recognition; the Soviet Union went further with de jure recognition two days later. With such prompt endorsement by the two great powers of the world, Israel was launched as a new member in the community of nations. But the Arabs never have recognized the right of the Jewish nation to establish a homeland, much less to organize a sovereign state, in Arab territory. That war continues—.

The establishment of Israel as a state for the Jewish nation raises many questions not only in legal terms but also in basic international relations. When a people are integrated as a nation, can they expect as of right to achieve statehood? In a world where the real estate is already parceled out to existing states how does an aspiring nation go about getting territory it needs for a homeland? At first glance, the boundary lines for each state seem firmly drawn on the political map of the world. But if we look closely at the current state of international relations, we discover many disputed borders. The lines between Israel and its Arab neighbors are still unsettled and likely to remain so for some time to come, given the intransigence of all parties. If territorial integrity is a basic attribute of statehood, how do we explain away all the disputed borders on the political map?

The student of comparative politics can learn a lot about nation-building from the experience of Israel. The return to the homeland was only the beginning; the rest of the story deals with the determination of the Jews to make a success of their collective enterprise, to create a modern nation state and to secure its survival against all odds. The odds were—and still are—great. The land area is small with few natural resources; the population is also relatively small. The Yishuv, the original settlers, are now in a minority; the newcomers, more than half of them from Asia and Africa, many of them primitive people, have been difficult to assimilate. It is instructive to see how the Yishuv retains its hold on the political system, how the ideology and institutions of "labor zionism" serve to mold a national personality as well as to develop the economy, and how the army and schools are used to create a new and integrated society. But it is also instructive to discover how much outside assistance has been made available and from what sources.

TWO ASIAN STATES

Japan

In Asia, we have chosen two very different states, Japan and India. Japan is sometimes identified with the new nations, exemplifying a typical Western notion that industrial development and a technologically based society imply the establishment of a new political system. Actually Japan is a very old nation, a traditional society; but in terms of social and cultural patterns it is also very modern and certainly highly developed. Ranking sixth in size and fifth in population among the Asian states, Japan today stands first in industrial production, external trade, per-capita income, levels of literacy, and standards of education for the people at large. Its government is among the most stable and the most efficient in the world.

Probably no other people in our dozen states have been as homogeneous and unified from the beginning of their political history as have the Japanese. The continuity of the imperial institution from a prehistoric time is a remarkable phenomenon. According to ancient tradition, Japan was founded in 660 BC by the Emperor Jimmu, a direct descendant of the Sun Goddess and a direct ancestor of the present ruling dynasty. Conceding that what is known about the origin and early development of the imperial government is largely legendary, nevertheless Japanese records on the Empire date back to the seventh century AD. The role and functions of the imperial institutions changed frequently in the course of history, but still the fact remains that a single dynasty represented concepts of legitimacy and authority in the minds of the Japanese people for more than a millennium. Succession, sanctified by religious myth and ritual, gave a charisma to the Japanese emperor that made his office a crucial symbol of old Japanese nationalism.

The Westernization of Japan began in the mid-nineteenth century when Commodore Matthew Perry steamed into Tokyo Bay (1854) with eight US warships. Commodore Perry's mission was to secure trade concessions as well as privileges of provisioning and refuge for American ships. The mission was quite successful; as soon as Japanese officials realized the guns were pointed, no real violence was necessary. Within a short time, the British, Dutch, and Russians obtained similar arrangements and so perforce ended the long-time isolation of Japan from the Western world. Since then the Japanese people have been highly receptive to outside influences and eager to adopt (or imitate) what they consider to be the newest and best features of contemporary civilization. At the same time, however, they remain tenaciously aware of their own past and tremendously proud of their own culture. Even today the traditional ties are strongest in the basic social pattern.

The modern period of Japanese history is usually dated from the Meiji Restoration of 1868 when a group of nobles and warlords rallied round a new young emperor to assist him in the establishment of enlightened government. For decades this meant mostly the deliberate importation of European technology in industry, armaments, and politics. Politics followed the autocratic model of Chancellor Bismarck in the new German Empire. The Westernization of the Japanese political system may be largely attributed to Meiji *genro*, a ruling elite drawn from the merchant and military classes who acted as advisers to the emperor after 1890. It was a collective leadership for the most part institutionalized in the government bureaucracy rather than in the parliament or in the political parties. It provided a "high degree of stability, unity, and continuity" during Japan's political transformation into a modern nation state.[12]

The national goal of Meiji Japan was "to enrich the country and to strengthen the military." [13] We shall have more to say later about the coincidence of national goals with the special interests of the dominant groups in the society. Here we simply note in passing that the political merchants and the military bureaucrats who entrenched themselves in the Meiji power structure had a good thing going for themselves in the process of modernization. The course which they steered turned Japan into a strong industrial nation state; but it also took the Japanese people into four major wars within fifty years: the Sino-Japanese War of 1894, the Russo-Japanese War of 1904, the Sino-Japanese War beginning in 1937, and the Pacific War, 1941–45. The latter was all but fatal.

In 1945 a defeated and devastated Japan was occupied by military forces under the international control of the Allied powers with General MacArthur as supreme commander. One of the major political reforms of the occupation was to vest sovereignty in the people rather than in the emperor. The emperor, as prescribed in the Constitution of 1947, survives only as "a symbol of the state and of the unity of the people" and not as an institution of government. Moreover, the power of the military has been liquidated and military goals are constitutionally prohibited. On the other hand, the business community seems to have come out on top and again its members have managed to make economic prosperity the principal goal of the new nationalism in postwar Japan.

The first constitution of Japan, that of 1889, was the emperor's "gift to the people." Its second, and present, constitution was the gift of General Douglas MacArthur. The Constitution of 1947 was drafted in the government section of the supreme commander's headquarters, transmitted to the Japanese government, approved by the cabinet with some minor revision, submitted to the Diet (parliament) where it was approved with a few additional minor changes. The fiction that it emanated from the Japanese people is proclaimed in the Preamble: "We, the Japanese people, acting through our duly elected representatives in the National Diet. . . ." Not until April 28, 1952, when the treaty of peace with Japan was finally signed, did the Japanese people legally regain their rights of sovereignty. In comparative government, one is always tempted to begin with the constitutional prescription, the fundamental law. The Japanese Constitution of 1947, however, is not an indigenous political instrument; its American framers did a good job by American standards. But when we explore further the demands and supports of the Japanese people today we have to keep in mind that the Japanese government is still operating under a political system not of its own choosing or of its own making.

India

Unlike Japan, which has never been subject to Western conquest and settlement (except for the brief military occupation following defeat in World War II), India has been exploited by Europeans ever since the Portuguese conquest of Goa in 1510. British, Dutch, and French traders vied with each other for the lucrative Indian trade throughout the sixteenth and seventeenth centuries. Great Britain and France turned India into a battleground in the eighteenth century, each seeking to carve out an imperial domain. British rule in India dates from the military victory of General Robert Clive over the French forces in 1757. The vicissitudes of the Indian people as part of the British Empire is a long drawn out story: native insurrections, British concessions, Indian demands for self-government, and protracted tutelary steps on the part of the British government. Not until 1947, and then under great duress, did the British government relinquish its full dominion over India—and Pakistan.

India is the most populous nation in our sample of twelve; among the states of the world only the Chinese People's Republic includes more people. In 1966 India's estimated population was just under half a billion, and it has been increasing since at the rate of a million persons a month. The problem of devising a political system capable of governing such sheer numbers of people is compounded by the multitude of ethnic, linguistic, and religious groups as well as by the traditional, communal, and caste system. If Japan is one of the most homogeneous nations in the world, India is certainly one of the most heterogeneous.

One of the most difficult problems in securing Indian independence from British rule was the long-standing friction between Hindus and Muslims. Unable to resolve the problem, the British sought to alleviate the situation by recognizing the separate identity and statehood of two nations: India and Pakistan. As a result of this partition, about 85 percent of the people in India are Hindus, just under 11 percent are Muslims, but this still adds up to more than fifty million Muslims in India. Pakistan, originally consisting of two regions separated by the breadth of India, a thousand miles apart, comprised an almost solid concentration of Muslims, about 98 percent in West Pakistan, and 82 percent in East Pakistan.

Both India and Pakistan have been determined to maintain their respective territorial integrity and at the same time the domestic tranquility of each nation is threatened by religious and nationality disturbances that cross their boundaries. Racial differences in Pakistan, however, proved to be a more divisive force than any cohesiveness resulting from a shared religion. The people in East Pakistan, mostly Bengalese, and the people in West Pakistan, mostly Punjabis, had distrusted and despised each other throughout history. In 1970 when Pakistan held its first free elections in twelve years, the Bengalis went to the polls in such large numbers that they were able to capture a majority of seats in the National Assembly. West Pakistani politicians, faced with the prospect of Bengalese dominance in the national government or the secession of East Pakistan, chose a devastating military response. Millions of Bengalese fled across the border to exile in India where many of them died from starvation and disease.

The brutal civil war in Pakistan sparked an international conflict, for India was neither willing nor able to absorb some six million more Muslims into its predominantly Hindu culture. The final outcome of the India-Pakistan war was still uncertain at the end of 1971. With Indian military assistance, East Pakistan was separated from West Pakistan and proclaimed a new nation state, Bangladesh, under Bengalese rule, but Indian troops were still occupying the troubled area. Augmenting the disagreement between India and Pakistan is the initial and continuing dispute over who gets Kashmir, a relatively small territory between northwest India and northeast Pakistan, the population of which is predominantly Muslim, and the local rulers are Hindu.

The size of India—land area and population—make it potentially one of the great powers of the world. But size as well as a pluralistic society can be a tremendous handicap to a new nation state. When the thirteen American states on the Atlantic Coast joined in "a more perfect union" the authors of *The Federalist* [14] were most apprehensive that the vast territorial reaches might make a centralized government physically impossible. The advance of technology in the twentieth century—transportation by air and telecommunications—gives India an enormous advantage over the eighteenth-century nation-builders. On the other hand, the multilinguistic composition of the Indian people is a built-in barrier to communication which the English-speaking American colonists did not have to face. The Indian Constitution of 1949 makes Hindi the official language but only 30 percent of the Indians speak Hindi. For the time being English is also recognized officially but reluctantly since it is the language of colonialism. The total number of mother tongues in India is said to be over fifteen hundred and in the rural communities many people have not yet learned either Hindi or English. For purposes of formal communication and as the medium for public education, the Indian Constitution still recognizes fifteen languages.

Education in India is primarily the responsibility of the states. In some of the states primary education is both free and compulsory, but so far India's programs to raise the level of literacy have not been notably successful. Literacy is measured in the mother tongue, but even so less than one-fourth of the people are literate in any language. Although spoken English is still the principal language link for all India, less than 1 percent of the Indian people can read in English. English is the language of instruction in the universities, a medium of communication among the intelligentsia, the principal language for the national newspapers, but it is not the everyday language in the marketplace or at home. The highest level of literacy is around Madras, but there most of the people are illiterate in both Hindi and English. The overall illiteracy of the people creates tremendous problems in communication between the government and governed; moreover the multiplicity of languages severely limits the usefulness of many would-be participants in the political process who are unable to cross the linguistic barriers. Nevertheless the development of India as an integrated political community depends on what Karl Deutsch calls "the nerves of government," [15] an effective communication system between the governors and the governed. We shall have more to say about communications and nation-building in the next chapter.

Symbolism is always important in promoting or at least presenting a facade of national unity. One of the first official acts of the Constituent Assembly of India was the adoption of a national flag, July 22, 1947. The national flag is flown on all important government buildings in the national capital, in all the state capitals, in every rural district, the post offices, and tax collectors' offices in the remotest villages. The national anthem adopted in 1952 was composed by India's great poet philosopher, Rabindranath

Tagore; it was first sung in 1911 during an Indian National Congress session at Calcutta. National holidays include Republic Day, Independence Day, and Mahatma Gandhi's birthday.

New states tend to develop a cult of personality, a special veneration for the founding fathers that gives legitimacy to the institutionalizaion of their creative endeavors. Mahatma Gandhi, India's great political hero, presents a very different image from that of such founding fathers as George Washington, or Lenin, or Atatürk. *Mahatma,* meaning "great-souled one," suggests a more spiritual kind of leadership, a suggestion which the Mahatma himself deliberately fostered in his dress of loincloth and shawl, his abstemious way of living, and his frequent "fasts unto death" with which he extracted political concessions from British officials. It was Gandhi's campaign of massive nonviolent civil disobedience that wore down the morale of British officials and finally led to Indian independence. Ironically, Gandhi himself died by violence, assassinated at a prayer and pacification meeting in 1948 by a Hindu fanatic who resented the partition of India. According to Hindu custom, Gandhi's ashes were deposited in the sacred river Ganges. His protégé, Prime Minister Jawaharlal Nehru, swore to uphold the Mahatma's ideals in the building of independent India.

Nehru, leader of the Indian National Congress, India's oldest and largest political party, became India's first prime minister and minister of foreign affairs. Under his leadership India developed a relatively stable government, managed to steer a nonaligned course in the Cold War between the superpowers in the 1950s, and at the same time to act as one of the principal spokesmen for the Third World, the Afro-Asian bloc in international affairs. Indira Gandhi, Nehru's daughter, elected president of the Indian National Congress party, 1959–60, became prime minister in 1966.

Apparently Indira Gandhi has inherited some of the charisma and certainly much of the political skill of her father. When the party bosses in the National Congress picked her as prime minister following the death of Lal Bahadur Shastri, they were simply making use of her name and her family background to tide them over until the 1967 elections. Soon, however, the lady was making her own decisions and when it was time to recruit a winning candidate for the national elections, Indira Gandhi presented herself as the only figure in the party with an all-India appeal. After the 1967 elections, the prime minister began acting even more on her own and contrary to advice from her party leaders. In 1969, when the old-time leaders tried to offset her somewhat radical posture, e.g., nationalization of the banks (which had been a plank in the Congress party's platform for years) and to back a conservative candidate for the presidency, the prime minister selected her own candidate. Counting on her popularity with the rank and file, she flatly disowned the regular party candidate just five days before the election. The success of her strategy was attested by the election of V. V. Giri as India's fourth president. Following the India-Pakistan war of 1971, she emerged as India's modern version of Joan of Arc!

In Chapters 4 and 5 we shall consider at some length how ruling elites in new states determine the national interests. Most of them appear to put a high premium on modernization, meaning economic development. Mahatma Gandhi's great goals for India reached more toward intangibles, peace and freedom, rather than material things. He realized, however, that political independence alone could not bring peace and freedom to the Indian people unless and until they learned to live in tolerance with one another. For all its modest pretensions, Gandhi's preaching was intended to shake the very foundations of India's social system. As he viewed it, not only would Hindus, Muslims, Buddhists, and Christians all have to live and work together, the whole caste system would have to give way to a democracy based on the equal dignity of all human beings.

When we look at India's political system today, the temptation is to use the familiar language of its constitution. India's written constitution was adopted by a Constituent Assembly and came into force on January 26, 1950. It is a federal union with a mixture of presidential and parliamentary forms. The Directive Principles of State Policy "though not enforcable through courts of law" requires the state "to promote the welfare of the people by securing and protecting as effectively as it may a social order in which justice, social, economic and political shall inform all the institutions of the national life."[16] We must keep in mind, however, that a state does not always function according to its constitutional prescription, nor even according to the operational concepts of its ruling elite.

To understand how the political system of India actually governs, one must look at patterns of behavior in the villages as well as in the government houses in Delhi. More than 80 percent of the Indian people live in rural communities where a traditional caste system still prevails as a way of life and governance. Moreover, the castes are innumerable, with different kinds of social stratification occurring from one cluster of villages to the next. The English political scientist W. H. Morris-Jones writes:

> *Each caste is an exclusive endogamous group and no person is outside the system. Each caste is associated with a particular occupation or a limited range of occupations, the interdependence of castes and the exchange of services making for an organic unity in each village.*[17]

On a vast scale India faces the problem that confronts most new nations: how to cope with traditional patterns of behavior at the grass roots that belie the new national goals and operational concepts of its official policy-makers.

TWO AFRICAN STATES

The extent of the nationalist movement in Africa took the world by surprise. In 1955 there were just five independent states on the continent; at the beginning of 1960 there were seven; at the end of 1960, "the year of African independence," there were twenty-six; and in 1965 there were thirty-six. Our frame of reference includes two new nation states in Africa, the Ivory Coast and Kenya.

The Ivory Coast

A former French colony in West Africa, the Republic of the Ivory Coast entered the French Community as an autonomous member in 1958. Under the leadership of Felix Houphouet-Boigny, it became an independent republic in 1960. Houphouet-Boigny, a native African of the Baoule tribe, was four years old when the French subjected his tribe in 1910; not until 1917, however, was military control established completely. He graduated from the William Ponty School in Dakar in 1925, first in his class, and became a *médecin africain*, serving in the French colonial medical service. At the time he entered politics in the 1940s he was a wealthy planter, one of the richest Africans in the French colonies. His first wife was of royal Agni lineage on her mother's side and Senegalese on her father's side, which gave him extensive kinship ties with the traditional tribes. His education gave him social status and the fact that he was not European-schooled, like so many of the contemporary African leaders, made him appear, more than they, a true exponent of African nationalism. Note, however, that his early political successes were scored in Paris rather than in Abidjan. Elected to the first National Constitutent Assembly, he proposed the abolition of forced labor in Africa, a proposal that gained him great political capital at home, and with this political capital he bought his way, as it were, into the French political system, the first African to hold a cabinet position in the French government.

Aristide Zolberg calls "the old man" a master of ethnic calculus, referring to the skill with which he organized and manipulated the *Parti Démocratique de la Côte d'Ivoire* (PDCI).[18] When later we examine the function of political parties, we shall focus again on the PDCI: a mass-based party, tightly organized as a vanguard, somewhat modeled after the Communist organization, vertically controlled with Houphouet-Boigny at the apex of power, simultaneously fulfilling the functions of a tribal chief and acting as head of a modern nation on the make. Suffice it at this point to indicate that Houphouet-Boigny used his position as party leader first to bargain for economic advantages for his people within the French Community and finally, albeit reluctantly on his part, to take them out of the Community into political independence in 1961.

The political system of the Ivory Coast may be described simply and realistically as one of presidential politics reinforced by a single dominating party. Houphouet-Boigny, still unchallenged leader of the PDCI, is now president of the Republic, with no plans, constitutional or contingent, for a successor. The government is considered stable and conservative, with no strong bent toward ideology; in short, a good place for foreign investors to make a nice profit and at the same time to contribute to the modernization of a new nation. The government, i.e., Houphouet-Boigny, favors Africanization, though not at the expense of impeding economic development. The legacy of colonialism remains; control of the economy rests either with the government or foreign concerns, principally French. As yet there is no substantial commercial class or native pool of entrepreneurial skills; the people are predominantly rural mostly at subsistence level; the managerial class is almost wholly imported, both for the government bureaucracy and the business community.

The historic roots for Africanization were for the most part long ago eradicated, first by the Portuguese and then by the French. African kingdoms once ruled the area, but the Portuguese exploited the area as early as the sixteenth century for ivory and slaves. The French protectorate established in the mid-nineteenth century systematically suppressed the native population and extracted their natural resources for French consumption. When we examine the new nationalism of the twentieth-century states, we shall find anticolonialism a prime factor, but we also observe that in the strategic allocation of values, a political system may be persuaded, as in the Ivory Coast, to weigh economic development more heavily than anticolonialism. It may be interesting to examine the pattern of relationships between the colonial settlers and the native inhabitants before and after political independence, and to compare the French and British influence and activities in their respective colonies before and after the achievement of separate statehood.

Kenya

Kenya, a former British protectorate and colony, declared its independence on December 12, 1963. As in the case of the Ivory Coast, the precolonial history of the people is virtually lost; the ruins of the Zimbabwe culture found by early European visitors in the region of Kenya and Rhodesia point to a native civilization that was probably contemporary with the European Middle Ages. The Arabs are said to have developed a trade in ivory and slaves on the East Coast as early as the seventh century. When the Portuguese arrived in the latter part of the fifteenth century they found Indians and Chinese already on the spot doing business with the black natives. The British began explorations of the interior in the mid-nineteenth century, and in 1886 when the British and Germans marked off their respective spheres of influence in East Africa, the British took Kenya. British settlers began to arrive in the first decade of the twentieth century and in 1920 Kenya became a crown colony. After World War II, with escalating demands from both the white settlers and the natives, the British reluctantly set about preparing the colony for self-government.

Tribalism impeded initial moves toward nationhood and independence in Kenya (and in most African countries). Early in the 1950s a secret terrorist movement, known as the Mau Mau, was fomented among the Kikuyu tribe (about 20 percent of the population of Kenya). The Mau Mau revived primitive Kikuyu ceremonies in which murder played a prominent part. Some eighteen hundred Africans and thirty-six whites are said to have been murdered in the course of the Mau Mau activities. British efforts to suppress the Mau Maus turned into a full-scale military operation and thus the Mau Mau movement became identified with the cause of Kenyan nationalism. At any rate, Jomo Kenyatta, of the Kikuyu tribe, jailed by the British for his alleged leadership of the terrorist Mau Mau demonstrations—a connection which he denied—played the role of national martyr. When Kenya first attained independence, it chose to remain within the Commonwealth, with status similar to that of Canada or Australia. Kenyatta, released from jail in the new era, became the symbol of national independence. As head of the Kenya African National Union (KANU) party, he became Kenya's first prime minister. One year later when Kenya decided to secede from the British Commonwealth, Kenyatta became president of the new Republic.

Kenyatta, "probably the best educated Kenyan of his generation," [19] had studied and lived in England for seventeen years, was "the grand old man" of Kenyan, and indeed African, independence. But he had an equally well-known counterpart. Tom Mboya was more than a symbol—he personified a young and vigorous Africa, "the continent's closest equivalent to a Horatio Alger hero." [20] Born in 1930, into a family of illiterate laborers, of the Luo tribe (about 14 percent of the native population), Mboya rose to power and influence through the labor union movement. Despite his lack of formal schooling, Mboya became a successful labor leader before he was thirty; a frequent visitor to the United States and Europe, he enjoyed an international reputation as one of the most up-and-coming new African leaders. Despite violent disagreement between the Kikuyu and Luo tribes, their respective leaders Jomo Kenyatta and Tom Mboya worked together in the KANU party for national unification. Mboya served as minister of justice and constitutional affairs in the Commonwealth government and minister of economic planning and development in the Republic. It was in this latter post that Mboya was regarded as a key figure in the modernization of Kenya.

The assassination of Mboya in the summer of 1969 brought to the surface some of the seething undercurrents of tribalism in Kenya. Although Mboya himself had previously been regarded as something of a traitor by his tribe because of his political alliance with Kenyatta within the KANU party, his death stirred the Luos to threats of tribal vengeance against the Kikuyus. Actually it is difficult to measure African politics within the Western formula of who gets what, how, and where. The transition from tribalism to nationalism has only begun. It is hard to say whether the political parties of Kenya or the Ivory Coast—or in any of the new African states—are strongly rooted or still quite superficial, or whether they will ever perform the functions in their respective political systems that Westerners expect.

The reactions to Mboya's death in Nairobi show that tribalism is still a potent factor in African political culture. Tribalism may be a highly cohesive force in nation-building since it combines the ideal ingredients for community: common descent, common language, common customs, and religion. But when many different tribes vie with each other for special status and rewards within the new political system, or when tribal ties cross state boundaries that once marked colonial spheres of influence, then tribalism may play as destructive a role in newly emerging nation states as it did long ago in the struggles of European tribes so vividly illustrated in classical Western history. Democratic pluralism rather than one-party dictatorship, regionalism rather than nationalism, may yet provide the ultimate answers to African politics.

When we probe deeper into the problems of nation-building, the experience of Kenya as a former British colony, and the Ivory Coast as a former

French colony, should give us some illuminating data. How does a colonial power prepare a colony for self-government and how does the colony react to such preparation before and after attaining statehood? What ties do they choose to keep with the mother country? And what assistance does the mother country still offer after the colony has achieved independence? Both Kenya and the Ivory Coast are one-party states, with native tribal rulers determined to effect national unification and modernization whatever the cost. How does a traditional society respond to this sudden reallocation of values? What political instruments do the new ruling elites find most effective in determining national goals, mobilizing national resources, responding to different demands and varying supports, and withal functioning in the national interest?

These brief, and obviously much too simplistic, background notes on our selected twelve nation states must here suffice to establish our frame of reference. We turn now to a more theoretical discussion of what constitutes a state and how a nation is created. From here on we shall use our frame of reference merely to illustrate particular points. Since this text is an approach to comparative politics, we shall not attempt country-by-country accounts.

NOTES

1. Bruce Russett, J. David Singer, and Melvin Small, "National Political Units in the Twentieth Century: A Standardized List," *American Political Science Review* 62 (1968): 932–51.
2. Russett, et al. refer to the Cold War term *West Germany;* we prefer to use the constitutional title the *Federal Republic of Germany.*
3. See Seymour Martin Lipset, *The First New Nation: The United States in Historical and Comparative Perspective* (New York: Basic Books, 1963); also Karl W. Deutsch and William J. Foltz, eds., *Nation-Building* (New York: Atherton Press, 1966), especially Richard L. Merritt's chapter on "Nation-Building in America: the Colonial Years."
4. The historian Daniel Boorstin calls it the genius of American politics that the American people even today accept as a given, the notion that "we have received our values from the *past:* that the earliest settlers or Founding Fathers equipped our nation at its birth with a perfect and complete political theory, adequate to all our future needs." Daniel J. Boorstin, *The Genius of American Politics* (Chicago: University of Chicago Press, 1953).
5. David Easton, *A Framework for Political Analysis* (Englewood Cliffs, N.J.: Prentice-Hall, 1965), p. 90.
6. Karl W. Deutsch and William J. Foltz, eds., op. cit.; Robert E. Scott, *Mexican Government in Transition* (Urbana, Ill.: University of Illinois Press, 1959).
7. W. O. Galbraith, *Colombia* (London: Oxford University Press, 1966).
8. Martin Needler, "Putting Latin American Politics in Perspective," in John D. Martz, ed., *The Dynamics of Change in Latin American Politics* (Englewood Cliffs, N.J.: Prentice-Hall, 1965).
9. "Museo nacional de Antropología," *Artes de Mexico,* 8 edicíon, numero 66/67, Año 12 (1965), p. 61.
10. There are a variety of accounts as to why Bonn was selected. In all, Konrad

Adenauer played a major role. Frankfurt, Cologne, and Bonn emerged as major contenders for the new (then considered temporary) capital city. Elmer Plischke, in *Contemporary Governments of Germany*, 2d ed. (Boston: Houghton Mifflin, 1961), states that Adenauer exerted certain pressures, others give any number of political reasons. Political wags insist that Konrad Adenauer wanted the capital in which he would have to spend much of his time as chancellor near his home and his rose garden, and that would have to be Bonn.

11. Despite the fact that Mustafa Kemal rose from among the ranks of the Young Turks, they had to bear the brunt of his retaliation almost a generation later. During the summer of 1926, a plot was uncovered against Mustafa Kemal in Izmir. The trial was followed by the execution of the ringleaders. A month later (in August of 1926), a series of trials and executions of Young Turks leaders followed in Ankara.
12. Robert E. Ward, ed., *Political Development in Modern Japan* (Princeton, N.J.: Princeton University Press, 1968), p. 97. See especially chap. 3, Roger F. Hackett, "Political Modernization and the Meiji Genro."
13. Ibid., chap. 9, Takeshi Ishida, "The Development of Interest Groups," p. 302.
14. James Madison, Alexander Hamilton, and John Jay, *The Federalist*, is a series of essays written in support of the proposed constitution in 1787; originally a piece of partisan propaganda, it has become a classic in American political theory.
15. Karl W. Deutsch, *The Nerves of Government* (New York: Free Press, 1966).
16. Government of India, *India, 1967* (Delhi: Research and Reference Division, Ministry of Information and Broadcasting), p. 22.
17. W. H. Morris-Jones, *The Government and Politics of India* (London: Hutchison, 1964), p. 56.
18. Aristide R. Zolberg, *One Party Government in the Ivory Coast*, rev. ed. (Princeton, N.J.: Princeton University Press, 1964). See chap. 4, "The Party Militant."
19. Herbert J. Spiro, *Politics in Africa* (Englewood Cliffs, N.J.: Prentice-Hall, 1962), p. 99.
20. *Newsweek*, July 14, 1969. From a journalist's account of Tom Mboya's death in a drugstore along Government Road in Nairobi.

FURTHER READING

Deutsch, Karl W., and William J. Foltz, eds. *Nation-Building*. New York: Atherton Press, 1966.

Easton, David. *A Framework for Political Analysis*. Englewood Cliffs, N.J.: Prentice-Hall, 1965.

Lipset, Seymour Martin. *The First New Nation: The United States in Historical and Comparative Perspective*. New York: Basic Books, 1963.

Russett, Bruce, J. David Singer, and Melvin Small. "National Political Units in the Twentieth Century: A Standardized List." *American Political Science Review* 62 (1968): 932–51.

PRESA DE
EL PRESIDENTE DE LOS
GUSTAVO DIAZ ORDAZ
AMISTAD DAM
DEDICATED BY
THE PRESIDENT OF THE
UNITED STATES OF AMERICA
AND
THE PRESIDENT OF THE
RICHARD M. NIXON
SEPTEMBER 8 1969
INTERNATIONAL BOUNDARY AND WATER COMMISSION
UNITED STATES AND MEXICO

chapter 2

WHAT MAKES A STATE?

To study national states in this day and age perhaps is to indulge in an anachronism. The territorially bound sovereign state is obviously outdated by jet planes, space explorations, lunar expeditions, seeing-eye satellites, and worldwide communications. Indeed, the concept of sovereign nation states has been obsolescent since its inception. The commercial revolution that marks the end of the Middle Ages came about because of the material interdependence of the peoples of the world. Natural resources have never been distributed in proportion to national needs and national aspirations. Germs, bacteria, fleas on rats (and the rats, for that matter), epidemics, the people themselves, and the ideas they want to communicate to others have never been contained within nor deterred by political frontiers, however guarded.

Some political scientists anticipated that novel constitutional and legal entities would emerge from the disintegrating empires—and Africa was to be in the forefront of new experiments. But a look at Africa shows that more than thirty states just on that continent have proclaimed their sovereignty and independence since 1951. For some time to come, then, students of international relations and comparative politics must be prepared to examine nation states as continuing, if not viable, political systems.

Since states are the principal actors in international politics, and have been so for at least half a millennium, we would expect to find agreement among scholars and statesmen on a basic definition of the state. Instead, we

Mexico and USA, Presidents Diaz Ordaz and Nixon meet at the border
(Wide World Photos)

find an abundance of controversial literature, with each author designing a definition to suit his own purpose. Two of our favorite quotations are from the classical literature, from Plato and Aristotle, still considered among the greatest contributors to Western political philosophy. In the second book of the *Republic,* Plato attributes to Socrates the notion of the state as arising "out of the needs of mankind; no one is self-sufficing, but all of us have many wants." [1] Aristotle, in the opening of his book *Politics,* observes that every society is established for a good purpose, "for an apparent good is the spring of all human actions"; he judges the political society the most excellent since it has for its object the best possible, and because it comprehends all the rest.[2] But alas, Plato and Aristotle knew the political community only as a city state and not as a nation state.

SOME LEGAL CONCEPTS OF STATEHOOD

The modern concept of the state is primarily a legal one. It may therefore be useful for us to examine briefly what attributes a state—defined as a "sovereign political unit"—claims to possess as of right under international law.

Sovereignty and Equality

Most students of political science shy away from the concept of sovereignty, because it is so clearly a legal fiction. Nevertheless, sovereignty symbolizes a basic assumption in international politics: that each state has complete authority and is the ultimate source of law within its territorial boundaries. Note that the Charter of the United Nations explicitly affirms this assumption: "The organization is based on the principle of the sovereign equality of all its members." One reason why new states immediately seek membership in the United Nations is to establish their recognized right to sovereign equality.

It takes no great insights into the operations of the international political system to discover that sovereign states are not really equal. The legal claim to equality, or even independence, is belied by many factors of real inequality, such as territorial size, geographic location, population size, natural resources, technological development, standards of living, political stability, and cultural values. But every independent state claims a legal right to do its own thing in its own territory. Basically, this is the meaning of sovereignty and equality.

The political map of the world is in effect a system of legal demarcation to show the territorial jurisdiction of each state. Indeed, the doctrine of territorial integrity—the notion that a state has the right to resist and reject any aggression, invasion, or intervention in its affairs from outside its territorial boundaries—is the basic premise of the state system in international law. Corollary to the doctrine of territorial integrity is the doctrine of territorial supremacy—the notion that a state has the legal authority and power to do what it wants inside its territory. In summary, then, these are the fundamental attributes of a state within the legal environment of international relations: sovereignty, territorial supremacy, territorial integrity, and equal rights to existence and independence. But if these legal principles are to be turned into politically operational concepts, states must seek the ingredients of power which will reinforce their legal competence with real capabilities in the world arena.

Territorial Jurisdiction

Territory is of course the absolute necessity for every state. The return of the Jews to their homeland in Palestine (now Israel) illustrates the point. International Jewry has many of the aspects of a nation—it is a cultural community from ancient times—but without a territorial base it could not become a nation state. Israel symbolizes the realization of Jewish aspirations: As a sovereign state it was admitted to membership in the United Nations in 1949, and today it maintains diplomatic and consular relations with over a hundred other nation states on all five continents.

An immediate step toward recognition and existence as a state is defining the territorial boundaries. The early nation states struggled to reach natural frontiers: the sea, rivers, mountains, lakes. Thus, the United Kingdom could count on the English Channel to deter invasion from the Continent, even until World War II, as demonstrated dramatically at Dunkirk. Much of modern European history can be written around territorial disputes over natural boundaries—the Alps, the Pyrenees, the Caucasus, the Rhine, the Elbe, the Oder-Neisse. The nineteenth-century drive of the United States to span the continent from sea to shining sea was regarded officially and popularly as Manifest Destiny.

The concept of territorial contiguity (jurisdiction over lands in close contact) was once considered as important as having natural boundaries. India's broad-wedged position between East and West Pakistan was undoubtedly Pakistan's number one problem. Yet the citizens of Alaska and Hawaii, though far removed from the people in the other forty-eight states, still consider themselves within the territorial boundaries of the United States and identify themselves with the political community as a whole.

Boundaries need not be natural physical phenomena; they may be mathematical projections; many of them are, for example, the forty-ninth parallel between the United States and Canada. Whether the boundaries are natural or merely mathematical, they become symbols of territorial supremacy and the people therein will fight for the symbol. In the 1840s American frontiersmen in Oregon were ready to go to war with the British: "fifty-four forty or fight."

Because the will to survive and remain independent is the salient characteristic of all states, every political system is bound to give the highest priority to national security policy in allocation of national values. One might suppose that the sophisticated weapons of modern warfare—nuclear submarines, intercontinental ballistic missiles, spy ships, and communications satellites in outer space—would make the concept of land boundaries obsolete in the framework of military defense. But, despite the fact that man has walked on the moon, earthly boundaries remain a psychological must in meeting the claims of nationalism as well as a practical imperative for defining the legal jurisdiction of each state.

Ironically, there is no rational justification for most of the political boundaries. The newest states in the international arena, the Asian and African states, are involved in numerous border disputes, all the more complicated because the boundaries for which they now fight are the result of arbitrary colonial divisions of continents; many times those boundaries cross ethnic lines and cut across tribal lands. Many of the boundaries have been established by force, as was the boundary between the United States and Mexico. Some boundaries have been imposed by third parties. One of the most famous examples was the effort of the Congress of Vienna to freeze the boundaries of Europe within the eighteenth-century framework of the balance of power. More recent examples are the boundaries laid down by the post-World-War-II conferences. In the case of Austria and Japan the boundary settlements now appear to be permanent; the German boundaries are still contested, at least verbally; the Korean and Vietnam boundaries have led to international wars. Some boundaries are still in bitter dispute; for example, between the USSR and the People's Republic of China, between India and Nepal, and between Israel and her Arab neighbors. In 1971, Israel was claiming that until the cease-fire agreements of June, 1967, were replaced by peace treaties with the Arab states establishing secure boundaries for Israel, Israel would consider herself responsible for law, order, and administration in the area enclosed within the cease-fire lines. And neither the Arab states nor the United Nations were acceding to this claim.

TABLE 2–1
Territorial Size of Nation States

Country	*Area in Thousand Square Miles*	*World Rank in Area* *
USSR	8,649	1
USA	3,615	4
India	1,262	7
Mexico	762	13
Colombia	440	25
Turkey	302	35
Kenya	225	44
Japan	143	54
Ivory Coast	125	58
Germany, FR	96	68
UK	44	70
Israel	8	133

* *Statistical Abstract of the United States 1970* lists 138 sovereign countries with populations of 100,000 or more. World rank is within these 138 countries.

SOURCE: US Bureau of the Census, *Statistical Abstract of the United States, 1970,* 91st ed. (Washington, D.C.: Government Printing Office, 1970), No. 1251, p. 807.

The territorial areas of nation states vary tremendously. The larger the area, the more possibility a state has to become a great power. A large area can sustain large populations and is more likely to possess varied natural resources. A large area has always had strategic advantages; it is more difficult for invaders to conquer in entirety; and today, in the era of nuclear strategy, a vast area makes it more improbable that a first strike could wipe out an entire population. Table 2–1 shows the territorial size of our twelve nation states and their ranking in world order.

Of the twelve states in our sample, only three are included in the world's largest territorial states: the USSR, the USA, and India. Our initial comment that territorial size is an indicator of power among nations is borne out by the high world rank of the USSR and the USA. On the other hand, India, despite her vast territory, is not yet a great power in international politics, nor for that matter are Canada (world rank, second), Brazil (fifth), or Australia (sixth). The People's Republic of China (third), however, is a great power.

DEMOGRAPHIC BASES OF STATEHOOD

Man-Land Ratios

The most important ingredient in the composition of a state is, of course, the people who inhabit its territory. The ratio of territorial size and population size may be more significant in estimating the power potential of states. Demographic Map 1 shows the area and population density of the countries of the world as of 1968. The size of a population roughly determines manpower available for military service and also for the labor force. Moreover, the larger the population the more possible are diversification in production and the development of special skills in the labor force. Table 2–2 gives us the population size of our twelve states, their world rank in population size, population density per square mile, and the annual rate of population growth. Demographic Map 2 shows population and birth rate by country as of 1970. Table 2–2 suggests a more significant correlation between population size and world power. Six of our twelve states fall within the top eleven nation states ranked according to population: of these the USSR, the USA, Japan, the Federal Republic of Germany, and the United Kingdom must be rated as powerful nation states in contemporary international politics. On the other hand, India (second in world rank) is far from being a world power, and if we look at the other nation states that top the list in population size—the People's Republic of China (first), Indonesia (fifth), Brazil (eighth), and Nigeria (ninth)—all of them safely categorized as less-developed countries, we conclude that neither great territory, nor large populations, nor both of these, are firm indicators of state power in international relations.

Only seven states in the world have a population of 100 million or more: These are great powers, or potential great powers. More than half the people of the world live in these seven states: the People's Republic of China, India, the USSR, the USA, Indonesia, Pakistan, Brazil, and Japan. The *World Bank*

Atlas (1968) points out that only one-fourth of the states in the world have a population exceeding 10 million; and half the states in the world have a population of less than 3 million.[3] Note in Table 2–2 that the Ivory Coast with 4.1 million ranks eighty-third on the world list and Israel with less than 3 million ranks ninety-ninth. Even so the international political system is organized on the principle of sovereign equal states. In the United Nations Assembly the Ivory Coast and Israel each have one vote; the USSR and the USA each have one vote.

Data for quantitative analysis in comparative politics are readily available. Most states publish a wide variety of statistical information: area, size of population, density of population, growth of population, gross national production, national income, indexes of employment, composition of the labor force, natural resources, transportation, communications, and so on. Because of different population sizes, the statistics are frequently given in per-capita form so as to provide something like a standard unit of measurement. Per-capita figures, however, are mathematical abstractions that may not represent at all accurately the actual conditions of individuals within the state. Similarly *population per square mile* is a mathematical expression which is derived simply by dividing the total area of the country by the total population.

The figures in Table 2–2 do not really tell us much about the man-land ratio in the areas where the people actually live, nor about the quality of the land which is inhabited. For example, the statistics show that Colombia has forty-four persons per square mile. What the statistics do not show is that about 98 percent of the population is concentrated in the western third of the country and that the eastern plains which make up about 60 percent of the country are almost uninhabited. Colombia has more than twenty cities with populations exceeding one hundred thousand. Bogotá, the capital, has a

TABLE 2–2
Population Size of Nation States

	Estimated 1968 Population in Millions	*World Rank*	*Population Per Square Mile*	*Annual Rate of Population Growth 1963–68*
India	523.9	2	416	2.5
USSR	237.8	3	29	1.1
USA	201.1	4	55	1.2
Japan	101.0	7	710	1.1
Germany, FR	60.1	10	617	0.9
UK	55.3	11	590	0.6
Mexico	47.3	14	62	3.5
Turkey	33.5	17	112	2.5
Colombia	19.8	29	44	3.2
Kenya	10.2	49	47	2.9
Ivory Coast	4.1	83	34	2.3
Israel	2.8	99	346	2.9

SOURCE: *Statistical Abstract of the United States, 1970,* no. 1251, p. 807.

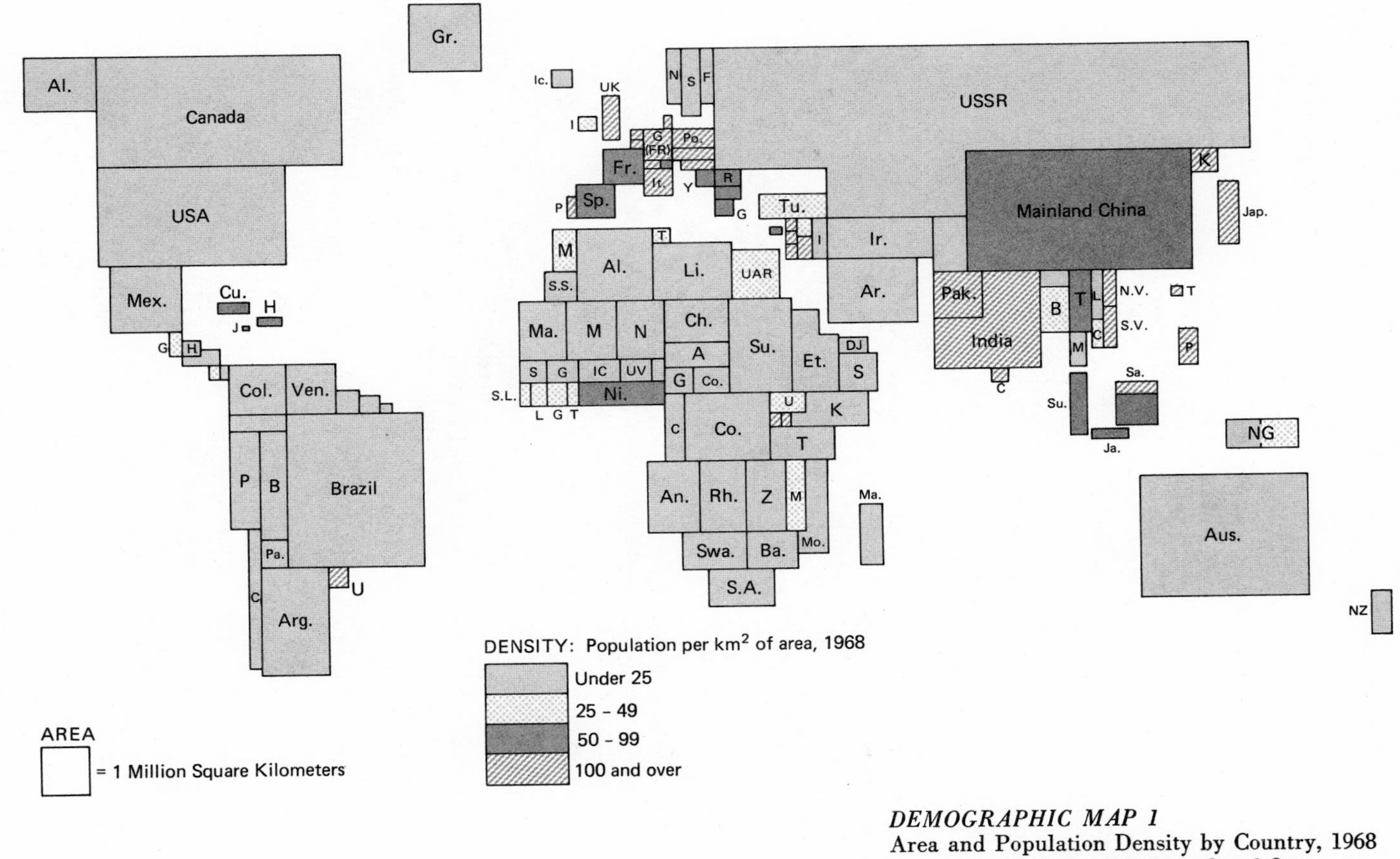

DEMOGRAPHIC MAP 1
Area and Population Density by Country, 1968
Countries with Areas of 9,000 km^2 and Over
SOURCE: *Trends in Developing Countries*, 3rd edition (World Bank, August 1970).

population of about two million, but much of the country is uninhabitable. The high Andes cut three ways across the terrain and, until air traffic was feasible, problems of transportation and communications were in some sections of Colombia virtually insurmountable.

Comparative data on inhabitants per square mile are not particularly useful, although demographers (population specialists) tend to view with alarm the figures in the fourth column of Table 2–2. Note that the most developed states—the United Kingdom, the USSR, the USA, and Japan—show the smallest annual growth rate; the less developed countries have the highest annual growth rate. A country like India, growing at the rate of almost a million persons a month, poses tremendous problems in terms of providing bare subsistence for such a rapidly increasing population. It is estimated that the People's Republic of China is growing at an annual rate of 1.4 percent, a rate only slightly higher than that of the USSR or the United States. But keep in mind that the population size of the Chinese People's Republic is already about three times the size of the Soviet Union and nearly four times the size of the United States. Overall the current rate of growth for the so-called developed countries of Europe and the United States is 1.1 percent; the current rate for the less developed countries is 2.5 percent.

Economic Growth and Modernization

In our introductory frame of reference we have already indicated that our twelve states achieved sovereignty and independence at very different times in history and under very different circumstances. When we compare these states in the contemporary context and introduce such categories as most developed and less developed, we are not referring to historical origins but rather to the degree of modernization. *Modernization* is admittedly a biased term, a term laden with Western values—industrialization, urbanization, and economic growth. The most frequently used measurement of degree of development is gross national product (GNP). The GNP refers to the total worth of goods and services produced by a nation's economy, the total market value of all consumer and capital goods and services produced in one year. It may be used to compare the rate of economic growth in the nation's economy from year to year or to compare the rate of modernization within different countries. Because of differences in population size and also different rates of population growth, GNP statistics are more meaningful if given in per-capita units from year to year. Table 2–3 shows the GNP per capita, the GNP growth rate, 1961–67, and the world rank in GNP per capita. Demographic Map 3 shows GNP by country as of 1968.

When we look at Table 2–3 quickly we find some startling—and some dismaying—comparisons. The United States leads the world in GNP per capita, $3,670, more than twice that of the Federal Republic of Germany or the United Kingdom, approximately four times that of the USSR or Japan, more than thirty-five times that of Kenya and India. Without question the United States is the richest country in the world. The gap beween the richest and the poorest countries in our sample is appalling. Moreover, our sample gives us only an inkling of the overall disparity between rich and poor nations in

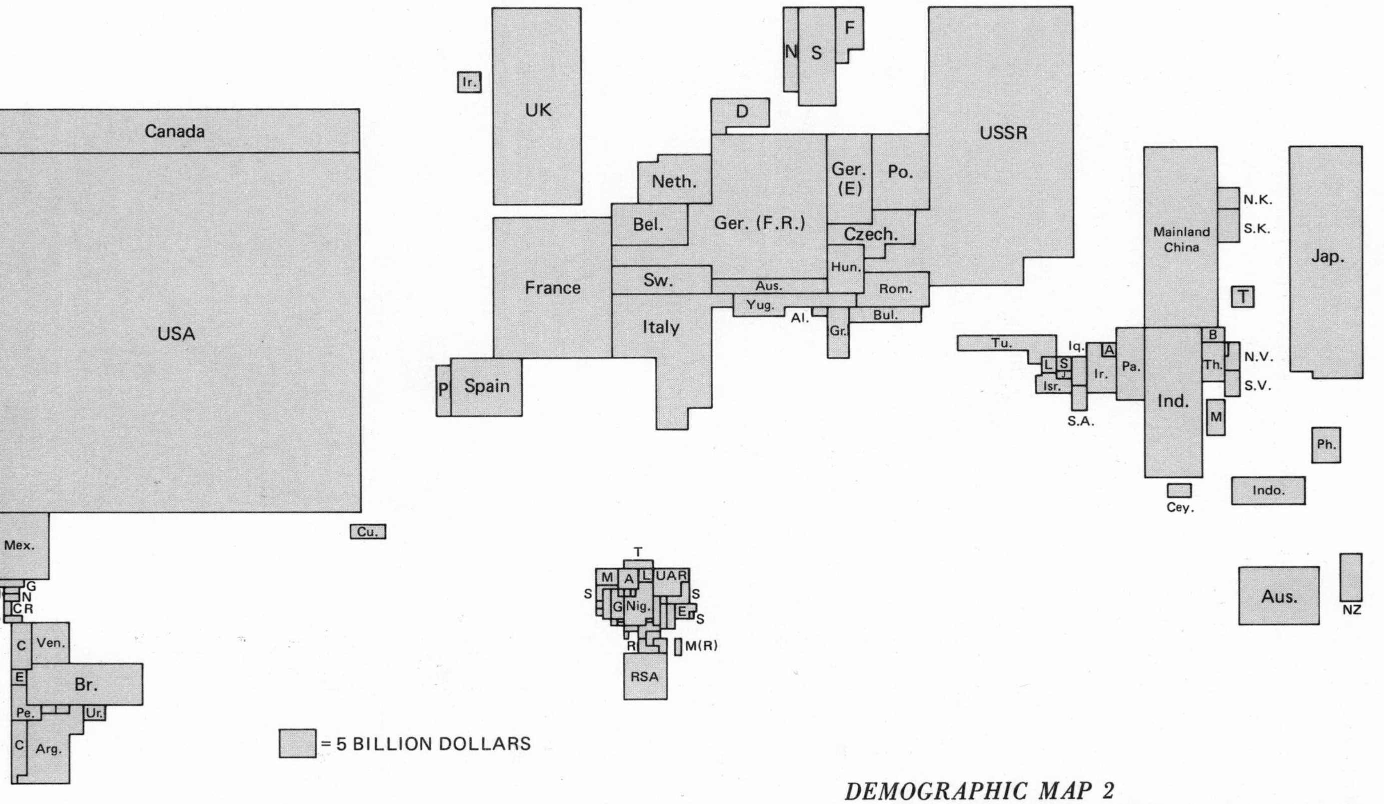

DEMOGRAPHIC MAP 2

Gross National Product (GNP) by Country, 1968

Billions of U.S. Dollars of 1964

SOURCE: *Trends in Developing Countries*, 3rd edition (World Bank, August 1970).

the world. The *World Bank Atlas* (1968) tells us that about two-thirds of the world's population lives in countries with a gross national product of less than $300 a year per capita. Of the big six states with a population of more than one hundred million, only the United States and the USSR have a GNP per capita of more than $100. In the 1968 list of states with high GNP per capita ($1,500 and over) there is only one superpower, the United States; only three great powers, France, the Federal Republic of Germany, and the United Kingdom; all the rest are small states with populations under twenty million. Moreover, nearly all of the states with high GNP per capita are Western European or have used Western technology in building their economies, e.g., Australia, Canada, the United States, and New Zealand.

A few words of caution may be advisable at this point. The GNP statistics in Table 2–3 give us only rough indicators of economic performance and may not be too reliable for comparative studies. The GNP per capita is given in US dollars so as to provide a standard measuring unit but this involves conversion of currencies. In countries where the economy is highly centralized and controlled, exchange rates may represent overvaluation of the domestic currency. The times and bases of estimating, the methods of data collection, the scope of definitions, and the margin of error may differ considerably from one country to another. For example, the USSR reports material net product rather than gross national product; in accord with its political ideology the Soviet government (and other Communist countries also) does not include

TABLE 2–3
Gross National Product

	GNP Per Capita—1966 US $	*World Rank in GNP Per Capita*	*GNP Growth Rate 1961–67 Percent*
USA	3,670	1	3.3
Germany, FR	1,750	10	2.8
UK	1,700	12	2.2
Israel	1,200	18	4.2
Japan	1,000	21	9.3
USSR	970	22	5.2
Mexico	490	41	2.8
Colombia	300	53	1.5
Turkey	290	55	3.1
Ivory Coast	230	65	5.4
Kenya	120	92	1.1
India	90	102	0.9

SOURCES: *World Bank Atlas,* International Bank for Reconstruction and Development (Washington, D.C., 1969); and AID, Statistics and Reports Division, Office of Program and Policy Coordination.

The *World Bank Atlas* lists 115 countries with populations of one million or more; rank is within these 115 countries.

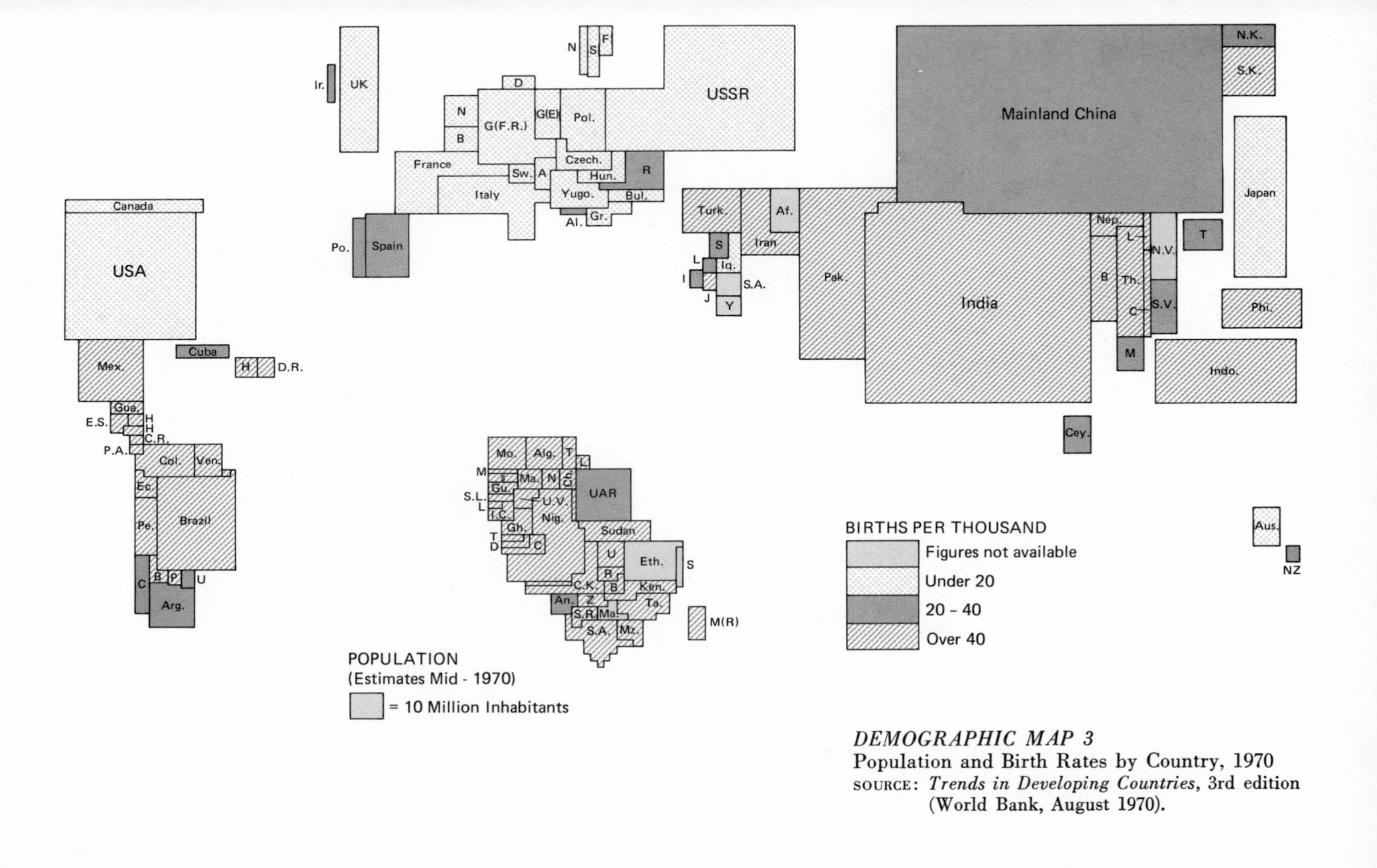

DEMOGRAPHIC MAP 3

Population and Birth Rates by Country, 1970

SOURCE: *Trends in Developing Countries*, 3rd edition (World Bank, August 1970).

most of the personal and professional services that the United States (or other capitalist countries) report as part of the gross national product. Because the GNP refers to market value, it does not include unpaid family labor; thus the disparity is exaggerated between industrial systems where unpaid labor is a small component (as in the United States) and rural family-oriented systems (as in India) where there is a great deal of unpaid labor. Furthermore, reports from some of the newest and least developed countries must be viewed rather skeptically; they may be doctored for political purposes or deficient for lack of technically trained accountants.

What then does Table 2–3 tell a student of comparative politics about states in the modern world? It simply tells us that the per-capita GNP puts six of our states in the category of economically well-to-do states and six in the category of rather poor, or undeveloped states. In subsequent discussion we will want to consider why some states with vast territories and huge populations (like India) seem to have more difficulty in modernizing their economies and stabilizing their political systems than do some small states with small populations (like Israel). Most states are not, never have been, and are not likely to become superpowers or great powers. We note, however, that some small states, such as Sweden, the Netherlands, and Switzerland, which do not aim at world leadership, nor make the pursuit of power a primary foreign policy, may survive as independent sovereign states with relatively prosperous economies and relatively stable political systems. On the other hand, other small states, such as Albania, Ceylon, and Haiti, which are also inner-directed nations, remain among the poorest and least developed countries in the world. Hence we are concerned with what kind of an economic base seems necessary, or desirable, to support a viable political system in any size country.

Resources and Resource Development

When we consider the economic base of any nation state, we begin with the natural endowment of its territory and its people. In the 1930s, political geographers were inclined to equate the potential power of a state with the availability of natural resources within its own territory. States were thus categorized as haves or have-nots depending on their holdings in, or ready access to, strategic and essential raw materials—strategic for modern military technology and essential for an industrial economy. Japan, for example, was regarded as a have-not nation because she had to import practically all of the essential raw materials for her industry, oil, iron ore, coking coal, rubber, cotton, wool, etc. A US Army Service Forces manual, analyzing the economic potential of Japan as it was organized before World War II, reported "only four important elements: fish, raw silk, electric power, and human labor."[4] Knowledgeable scholars warned that a nation lacking in resources but determined to develop a modern economy would try to secure access to what it needed in other states, if necessary by force and aggression. Thus Japan's seizure of Manchuria in 1931 (a region containing valuable raw materials, notably iron and coal) and Japanese aggression in the 1940s in

Southeast Asia (a region producing, before World War II, 95 percent of the world's natural rubber, 90 percent of the quinine, 80 percent of the copper, 70 percent of the tin) seemed to demonstrate the calculated belligerent strategy of an ambitious have-not nation.[5]

No doubt a state possessing within its own territory all the natural resources that it needs would have a great advantage over other less well-endowed states. But the distribution of the world's resources is not in accordance with the political maps. No nation, not even the superpowers, the United States and the Soviet Union, is wholly self-sufficient; all must seek strategic and essential raw materials beyond their own borders.

Natural resources are only what people can and do make of them. The North American Indians had plenty of coal available to them, but they did not know how to use it. Coal had no great economic significance until after the invention of the steam engine in England; then and there it was lucky that coal was available to furnish power for the opening of the industrial revolution. Waterfalls were once viewed as scenic attractions—or impediments to river navigation—until the development of hydroelectricity; the development of the Tennessee Valley as part of the New Deal in the United States in the 1930s is a good example. In all the detailed listings of critical raw materials in the 1930s, uranium does not appear; but after World War II suddenly it became one of the world's most sought-after materials when it was learned that fission of uranium produces nuclear energy.

Abundant raw materials are available in many of the less-developed countries of the world, Mexico and Colombia, for example. Mexico has vast mineral resources and great oil reserves. Colombia also possesses extensive and varied mineral resources; its coal reserves alone make it potentially one of the richest countries in Latin America. But it is not so much the availability of resources as it is resource development that marks a modern economy. And resource development we now envisage much more broadly than in the 1930s; we see it as a process that encompasses technology, productive skills, planning and management for consumption, public service, capital investment, and exportation. Note that the emphasis has shifted from inventory of material resources to analysis of human resources.

There are many different indicators of material resources, resource use, and resource development. Table 2–4 shows the net supply of food per person and the daily caloric intake per person.

In rank order of calories consumed per person, Table 2–4 shows the United States at the top of the list, with the United Kingdom second, and Colombia and India at the bottom, close to subsistence. The listing does not really tell us much about the nutrition of the people, which is, of course, much more than a matter of caloric intake per person. A Senate committee investigating hunger in the United States in 1969 startled us with the discovery that possibly half the American people are suffering from malnutrition and dietary deficiency. The differentials in net supplies of selected foods per person give us some clues as to national diets. If one were to symbolize the diet of the United States, which shows the highest meat supply per person, we would probably select the hamburger, the hot dog, and the barbecued steak; if we were to symbolize the diet of India or Japan, we would offer up a bowl of rice; in Germany, potatoes; and in Colombia, bananas and plantains.[6]

Table 2–5 indicates a correlation between national resources and industrialization. Using steel consumption per capita as a prime indicator of industrialization, we find the United States in the lead followed by the Federal Republic of Germany, Japan, Soviet Union, and the United Kingdom in that order. These are still the great powers in world politics. We also perceive a correlation between industrialization and national production of key raw materials. The United States which leads the world in industrial production is also first in coal production, first in oil production, first in steel production, and second in iron ore production; the USSR, its closest competitor in world politics, is second in coal production, second in oil production, second in steel production, and first in iron ore production.

If we use steel production as an indicator of industrialization we get some very interesting insights into resource development. Note that the United States in 1968 still ranked first, the Federal Republic of Germany second, and Japan third. Note also that Japan is near the bottom of the list on production of iron ore which means that Japan must import nearly all of its raw materials for steel production. The Japanese steel industry was totally destroyed by the end of World War II; nevertheless, by 1956 it had recovered to its prewar level, and twelve years later its production surpassed that of the Soviet Union and the United Kingdom. Similarly the German steel industry was completely collapsed at the end of World War II, but it too has largely recovered and now surpasses steel production in the Soviet Union and the United Kingdom as well as Japan. This is what we meant when we remarked that abundant material resources may be less significant than resource develop-

TABLE 2–4
Selected Foods—Net Supply per Person 1966–68

	Daily Calories Per Person	*Pounds Per Year*		
		CEREALS	POTATOES ETC.	MEAT
USA	3,200	142	107	237
UK	3,160	161	228	164
USSR	n.d.	n.d.	n.d.	n.d.
Turkey	3,110	492	89	30
Germany, FR	2,960	154	244	155
Israel	2,920	230	79	116
Mexico	2,570	286	19	43
Japan	2,460	306	151	30
Ivory Coast	n.d.	n.d.	n.d.	n.d.
Colombia	2,200	142	154	66
Kenya	n.d.	n.d.	n.d.	n.d.
India	1,810	278	31	n.d.

n.d. = no data.
SOURCE: *Statistical Abstract of the United States, 1970,* no. 1255, p. 811.

ment as an indicator of a state's capacity to build a viable economy. Resource development, let us emphasize the point once more, is dependent on the character as well as the skills of the people. It takes a lot of character, a special kind of character, to accumulate the capital savings out of net income that are necessary to establish and operate a modern industrial system.

Probably the most revealing indicator of industrialization is the degree to which manpower and horsepower have been replaced by the energy revolution. Table 2–6 shows country by country the total production of energy in million metric tons of coal equivalent and consumption of energy in kilograms per capita. Those countries highest on the list, either in production or consumption, are most highly industrialized; those at the bottom of the list are obviously still in the very early stages of industrial development. Total energy production in the United States is approximately double that of the USSR and more than a thousand times that of the Ivory Coast. Per-capita consumption figures offer a more realistic measurement since they are geared to population size. But again the United States is way at the top of the list. Its per-capita consumption is more than double that of the United Kingdom, the USSR, the Federal Republic of Germany, and almost four times that of Japan.

Energy consumption statistics point up the problem that confounds states with large populations: An enormous increase in overall production is required for even a small increase in per-capita consumption. In 1968 India ranked fifth in energy production but was still tenth in per-capita consumption. Similarly the USSR, which ranked second in total energy production, ranked fourth in per-capita consumption. On the other hand, Israel, demon-

TABLE 2–5
Industrial Resources
Production and Consumption, 1968

	Consumption	*Production*			
	STEEL PER-CAPITA POUNDS	COAL, 1,000 SHORT TONS	OIL, 1,000 BARRELS	IRON ORE 1,000 SHORT TONS	STEEL, 1,000 SHORT TONS
USA	1,510	551,883	3,329,040	55,305	131,460
Germany, FR	1,276	123,639	56,413	2,275	45,370
Japan	1,089	51,332	5,466	1,377	73,736
USSR	944	458,804	2,314,873	101,412	117,431
UK	930	183,768	616	4,301	28,965
Israel	595	n.d.	15,485	n.d.	93
Mexico	165	1,570	142,187	2,188	3,621
Turkey	57	5,257	21,939	1,377	1,222
Kenya	n.d.	n.d.	n.d.	n.d.	n.d.
Colombia	62	3,307	63,839	593	219
India	24	78,058	43,230	18,783	7,107
Ivory Coast	n.d.	n.d.	n.d.	n.d.	n.d.

n.d. = no data.
SOURCE: *Statistical Abstract of the United States, 1970,* no. 1269, p. 823.

strating an advantage of being a small state, ranked tenth in total production in 1968 but sixth in per-capita consumption, illustrating one of the effects of population pressure. Colombia markedly increased its total energy production between 1962 and 1968 but its per-capita consumption in the same period actually showed a decrease. The years 1962 and 1968 are too close together to draw any conclusions about energy production or consumption; generally we observe an increase, both in production and in consumption. But if we were to hazard projections into the next decade or into the next century, when the sources of energy for industrialization may be very different from those in the 1960s, our country-by-country analyses might show radical differences. If, for example, fossil fuels have been consumed—coal, gas, oil—and if the world turns to nuclear energy or solar energy, another phase of the industrial revolution may overturn all of the present neatly tabulated comparisons.[7]

We could, of course, consider many more indicators of economic capabilities; percentage of labor force in manufacturing or percentage of gross national product in capital investments, for example. But all of these tables make the same point: some states are more industrialized than others. The economic disparities between the industrialized and the nonindustrialized states are generally stated in the current cliché, "the growing gap between rich and poor nations."

In the framework of comparative politics, and also international relations, economic differentials among states are officially recognized in the assessment of members of the United Nations and members of its agencies. The regular budget of the United Nations is financed by contributions from the member states on a scale determined periodically with capacity to pay

TABLE 2–6
Energy

	Total Production in Million Metric Tons of Coal Equivalent		*Consumption Per Capita in Kilograms*	
	1962	1968	1962	1968
USA	1,431.70	1,876.06	8,263	10,331
USSR	741.64	1,087.44	3,029	4,059
UK	201.88	173.70	4,929	5,004
Germany, FR	185.55	165.30	3,889	4,484
Japan	65.59	59.87	1,391	2,515
India	64.27	82.67	161	184
Mexico	35.99	50.78	892	1,064
Colombia	13.44	n.d.	535	532
Turkey	5.46	n.d.	280	n.d.
Israel	0.19	2.94	1,409	2,014
Kenya	0.02	0.03	132	144
Ivory Coast	0.01	0.03	83	167

n.d. = no data.
SOURCE: *UN Statistical Yearbook* (1969), no. 136.

as the major factor, subject to principles of maximum and minimum percentages. In principle the maximum percentage is not expected to exceed 30 percent of the total budget,[8] and the lowest assessment is established at 0.04 percent. Similarly, capacity to pay determines the percentage of contributions to the UN agencies, again within predetermined maximum and minimum percentages.

Table 2–7 shows the percentages of the total budgets contributed by each of our twelve states to the United Nations and to related agencies: Food and Agriculture Organization (FAO), United Nations Educational, Scientific, and Cultural Organization (UNESCO), and the World Health Organization (WHO).

What is a state? The question to which we have addressed our discussion is one of mounting concern, specifically with reference to membership in the United Nations. By 1969 membership in the United Nations had increased from 51 to 126. Despite vast differences in area, population, resources, and economic development, under the legal doctrine of sovereign equality, which the United Nations regards as an operational concept, each member has only one vote in the General Assembly. The United States and the Ivory Coast in this framework are equal. The Maldive Islands (population a little over one hundred thousand) has the same voting power as India, whose population is now close to half a billion. Recently, the United States formally requested the Security Council to consider the admission of microstates on the basis of a checklist—area, population, economic resources—by which suit-

TABLE 2-7
United Nations and Certain Specialized Agencies—Member Assessments

	Percentage of Total Budget			
	UN	FAO	UNESCO	WHO
USA	31.57	31.57	29.73	30.87
USSR	14.61	nonmember	13.75	13.13
UK	6.62	8.49	6.23	5.95
Germany, FR	nonmember	8.99	6.60	6.30
Japan	3.78	4.85	3.56	3.40
India	1.74	2.23	1.64	1.56
Mexico	0.87	1.12	0.82	0.78
Turkey	0.35	0.45	0.33	0.31
Colombia	0.20	0.26	0.19	0.18
Israel	0.20	0.26	0.19	0.18
Ivory Coast	0.04	0.04	0.04	0.04
Kenya	0.04	0.04	0.04	0.04

SOURCE: *Statistical Abstract of the United States, 1970,* no. 1277, p. 838.
(Note that because the German Federal Republic is not a member of the United Nations it does not contribute to the UN proper, but it does have membership in related UN agencies and in those it pays its share. Note also that the USSR is not a member of the Food and Agricultural Organization and therefore makes no contribution to that organization.)

ability of potential applicants could be judged more realistically. Other members of the Security Council, however, have been reluctant to act upon the United States' request lest delegations from small states already in the United Nations be offended.

If, at this point, we had to answer the question What constitutes statehood? we should have to stress the legal definition—a sovereign political unit with full power to allocate resources and values, if the government so chooses, and to govern the people within its territorial boundaries. But the answer to such questions as What constitutes a viable state? and What makes some states more powerful, or more advanced, than others? requires us to compare the demographic bases of many different states. Obviously all states do not enjoy equal status in the world community, and to explain why this is so we have briefly looked at some of the differentials in size of territory; topography; distribution of natural resources, especially the man-land ratios; the size and composition of the population; and the stage of economic development. In the chapter that follows, in an effort to understand what makes a nation state, we attempt a more in-depth analysis of the human element, the sense of community that underpins a national political system.

NOTES

1. Plato, *The Republic,* book 2, in *The Dialogues of Plato,* Jowett Translation (New York: Random House, 1937), 1: 632.
2. Aristotle, *Politics,* trans., William Ellis, the first lines of book 1, chap. 1, in William Y. Elliott and Neil A. McDonald, *Western Political Heritage* (New York: Prentice-Hall, 1949), p. 197.
3. International Bank for Reconstruction and Development, *World Bank Atlas* (Washington, D.C.: 1968).
4. Philip Dunaway, *Geographical Foundations of National Power,* US Army Service Forces Manual M-103-2 (Washington, D.C.: Government Printing Office, 1944), chap. 8, reprinted in Harold and Margaret Sprout, *Foundations of National Power* (Princeton, N.J.: Princeton University Press, 1945), p. 514.
5. Similarly, Mussolini's imperialism in the 1930s, including his war against Ethiopia, was rationalized in the framework of a have-not nation on the make.
6. Dr. Jean Mayer, professor of nutrition and member of the Center for Population Studies, admonishes us not to take too seriously the factor of food scarcity in population problems. He is more concerned about the population problem in rich countries than in poor countries. In rich countries, people use up the natural resources at a more rapid rate, disturb the ecology more, and create more land, air, water, chemical, thermal, and radioactive pollution than people in poor countries. See "It's the Rich That Do the Crowding," in *Washington Post,* "The Outlook," July 20, 1969, excerpted from *Columbia University Forum.*
7. For an extremely interesting discussion of resources and population problems and projections into the future, "prepared for leaders of American industries," see Harrison Brown, James Bonner, and John Weir, *The Next Hundred Years* (New York: Viking, 1957), and *The Next Ninety Years,* the proceedings of a conference held at California Institute of Technology (March, 1967) focusing on the Brown et al. book.
8. The United States is still paying a little over this maximum.

FURTHER READING

SPIRO, HERBERT J. *Politics in Africa.* Englewood Cliffs, N.J.: Prentice-Hall, 1962.
COPLIN, WILLIAM D. *The Functions of International Law.* Chicago: Rand McNally, 1966.
FRIEDRICH, CARL J. *Man and His Government.* New York: McGraw-Hill, 1963.
BRIERLY, J. L. *The Law of Nations.* 6th ed., HUMPHREY WALDOCK, ed. Oxford: Clarendon, 1963.

AZIR

chapter 3

WHAT MAKES A NATION?

This discussion of nation states began with an analysis of the legal concept of the state. Since we found that not to be a very satisfying key to unlocking a complex phenomenon, we centered on the sources and resources a state needs to be a viable political entity. The ingredients are many and varied, and as Tables 2–1 through 2–8 in the previous chapter demonstrate, are unevenly distributed among the states of the world. The USSR ranks first in world area but it does not even stand among the top dozen states in gross national productivity. India, which ranks second in population size, places ninety-second in productivity. The United Kingdom, small both in area and in population size but high in skills and productivity, seems to feed her citizens almost as well as the United States, at least in measures of caloric intake per person. Yet all these tables, ranking states according to size, population, natural resources, productivity, etc., do not really tell us much about the relative power position of the states and certainly they do not offer us much illuminating data on what is required for a people to emerge and survive as a nation. Territorial boundaries, population statistics, tabulations of raw materials, productivity figures, these may be regarded as building blocks in the making of a state, but they do not create a nation nor do they provide the interested student with a blueprint on how a nation state is built.

Turkey, political rally—a girl holds a picture of Atatürk
(Wide World Photos)

NATIONALISM: SOME MYTHS AND THEORIES

Although far younger than the concept of the state, the concept of the nation is no more clearly defined than the concept of the state. Hans Kohn, the great chronicler of nationalism, insists that "nationalism is unthinkable before the emergence of the modern state in the period from the sixteenth to the eighteenth century. Nationalism accepted this form, but changed it by animating it with a new feeling of life and with a new religious fervor."[1] Kohn links nationalism and religion and endows both with an almost identical mystique. His definition of nationalism approaches the style of the catechism, that ancient form of question and defined answer, used in many religions as a form of instruction:

> *What is nationalism? Nationalism is a state of mind, in which the supreme loyalty of the individual is felt to be due the nation state. A deep attachment to one's native soil, to local traditions and to established territorial authority has existed in varying strength throughout history. . . . Nationalities are the products of the living forces of history, and therefore fluctuations and never rigid. They are groups of the utmost complexity and defy exact definition. Most of them possess certain objective factors distinguishing them from other nationalities like common descent, language, territory, political entity, customs and traditions, or religion. But it is clear that none of these factors is essential to the existence or definition of nationality.*[2]

In a searching essay, Lester B. Pearson, former Canadian prime minister who earned the Nobel Peace Prize in 1957, tackles the concept of nationalism. He suggests that "the most frequently occurring factor is what I will call a common culture . . . common habits, common traditions, common customs, and, above all, a common desire to live together as a separate group, a communal society with certain well-defined loyalties and objectives."[3]

Certainly, the latter part of Pearson's comment is an apt description of contemporary Israel. Despite her internal factions which derive from a multitude of origins, her overriding concern is the maintenance of Israel. Israelis may have an orthodox or a liberal interpretation of religious rules; they may stem from Jewish families who grew up in the confines of the ghettos of Eastern Europe or in North African settlements or in the midst of the cultures of Spain and Portugal; they may be the descendants of early settlers of Palestine, among the first waves of immigrants into Israel, or they may have entered with the tidal waves of immigration from the Arab countries in the 1950s; they may be sophisticated inhabitants of the urban centers or dedicated to the communal living in the *kibbutz.* They all, however, share one overriding concern. National morale in Israel is high, and it centers around the determination to survive as a nation state, to maintain the homeland for the Jews. Israeli nationalism is accentuated by the real presence of an enemy equally conscious of having a mission, of preserving a homeland for people from a variety of backgrounds. The fact that both Arab and Israeli nationalisms are deeply rooted in a religion-oriented culture exacerbates the Middle East conflict.

Among our twelve selected nation states, Japan probably would be at the opposite end from Israel on any scale of the origins of nationalism. The Jews streamed into Israel from all over the world, sustained by the belief in a common heritage, a communally shared way of life. The Japanese for centuries lived a self-contained way of life on a group of islands, surrounded by vast oceans; and, unlike the English whose island situation made them world travelers and conquerors at an early time in their history, the Japanese developed an inner-directed way of life, self-conscious to the point of being stylized. When the Japanese islands finally did open up to Western influences in the nineteenth century, they did so with great curiosity and great enthusiasm for learning about the new Western ways. The Meiji Restoration was largely an attempt to adopt Western European economic and political practices—once they had been tempered by Japanese political and social mores, especially by the roles of the emperor and other members of the ruling elite.

In the aftermath of their disastrous defeat in World War II, the Japanese, who initially were given very little choice by the Allies in the reconstruction of their political life, came to accept the so-called MacArthur Constitution; they made it their own symbol, just as they had earlier adapted many Western ideas to Japanese ways. Their consciousness of being a cultural entity, of shaping centuries of a highly uniform heritage, enabled them to select from the vast range of outside influences which converged upon Japan in the fifties and sixties those they found useful and productive. Their insistence on having the newest and the best in technology is tied to a tremendous awareness of their shared past and to being Japanese.

Japan developed her national consciousness because for centuries the Japanese lived almost undisturbed by the external world; they had virtually no contact with influences totally alien to their own culture.

By contrast, Colombia was one of the provinces in South America to which the conquistadores came in the fifteenth century in their search for gold for Spain and Portugal, for souls for the Roman Catholic Church, and the fountain of youth for themselves. Despite the fact that the area that later became Colombia did not have flourishing Indian civilizations comparable to those of the Aztecs, Toltecs, and Mayans, the native Indians must have experienced the most jolting culture shocks. No doubt, the conquistadores needed all their sense of mission to make their own experience bearable in the New World. Enough of them did adjust (or perhaps we should say were able to force a mutual adjustment on the natives) and remained to form the core of a political elite centuries later when the Latin American colonies fought for their independence from Spain. Among the descendants of the Spanish settlers as well as among the descendants of the English settlers in North America, a sense of national identity with their new country emerged which made them proud of their cultural heritage and yet added another dimension to the heritage they felt was theirs, that of the pioneer who adapted the culture of his own nation selectively, in order that he, and it, would survive in originally alien surroundings.

Colombia ultimately became part of Simón Bolívar's dream of a union of American republics. Like the founding fathers of the United States, the early Colombians were sharply divided between proponents of a strong central government and those who wanted a more loosely organized federal system. Simón Bolívar himself preferred a centralist government, which he felt would unite a "Gran Colombia," embracing those vast areas that later became the states of Colombia, Venezuela, Peru, and Panama.

W. O. Galbraith, a British Latin American scholar, points out that although Bolívar achieved his plan, before his death in 1830 Gran Colombia disintegrated.

> *In those days of primitive transport and communications, the area was too vast and too geographically split up to be governed from one centre. It had never formed one administrative unit, and while it could find a community of interests and therefore an identity in its struggle for independence, once this was achieved, its constituent parts had little or nothing in common to hold them together.*[4]

This might well be an analysis of similar problems faced by some of the new nation states arising out of the collapsing British, French, and Dutch empires after World War II, whose initial political boundaries have been adjusted since, as the disappearance of the common enemy—the colonial power—brought to the forefront the many cleavages that existed before independence. Galbraith perceives one source as having played an important role over the past century in the development of Colombia as a nation state:

> *The Colombian Press is flourishing; its standards are high. Its influence as an organ of public opinion is second to none; it is a well-known saying that "the history of Colombia smells of printer's ink." One of its leading journalists, Dr. Fabio Lanzo Simonelli, claims that "journalism is to a large extent responsible for the formation of our national being." In the light of the history and the political evolution of the country, this claim has considerable substance.*[5]

These two quotations from a study of the Colombian experience point to two different elements of nationalism which occur over and over in the histories of nations. The common culture must be a truly shared one, and the means of sharing must somehow be related to the particular needs and resources of the political community.

COMMUNICATIONS AND NATIONAL INTEGRATION

We have spoken of Hans Kohn before, as the great chronicler of nationalism as a force in history. But despite the abundance of examples he cites and classifies, Kohn does not really penetrate what he calls the "myth of nationalism." A contemporary political scientist, Karl W. Deutsch, attacks the theory that nationalism is a myth. Both Deutsch and Kohn agree that the growth and development of mass publics, the ever-increasing demands on the state, and the consequently deeper involvement of large numbers of people in political processes are major factors in the development of nationalism. Deutsch insists that "the stakes of politics all over the world have tended to increase, and so have the levels of literacy, of popular education, of mass communications and of potential participation in politics—and often actual participation in politics as well."[6]

Language is man's basic means of sharing common experience, developing common values and traditions, and transmitting them. No community can exist without the ability to communicate. As man has devised more and more sophisticated means to communicate, many of which implement and clarify, but some of which also tend to supersede the written and the spoken word, our communications have undergone far-reaching changes.

To state categorically that better communications technology automatically results in closer communications and better understanding in human communities is to state the absurd. "Getting to know you," unlike the statement of Anna, schoolmistress to the extensive offspring of the King of Siam in the musical *The King and I*, does not necessarily mean "is getting to like you." Nor does more communication mean higher quality and more significant communication. The telephone probably transmits more useless drivel between neighboring housewives in suburbia anywhere in the world where we find suburbia equipped with phones than do the drums in a jungle village which serve that village as official means of communication.

To measure an increase in mail flow certainly is an indicator of increased quantities of community interaction, but it tells us nothing about the quality of the messages being transmitted. After all, there is a difference between junk mail soliciting "Occupant" to subscribe to a magazine, the government's annual reminder that income tax is due, the campaign brochure of a candidate for public office, a love letter, or that long-expected confirmation of a verbal job offer. On a less frivolous note, we should mention, however, that the hot line was installed between Washington and Moscow to facilitate direct access of communication between top decision-makers in two countries on whose shoulders, jointly and individually, rests the fate of much of the rest of mankind.

The Impediment of Illiteracy

Where written communications are limited by a high percentage of illiteracy, where only a privileged few have access to books, periodicals, or newspapers of general interest, the building of a community is impeded. Wherever long distances and poor transportation facilities curtail direct contacts between the government and the governors, where telecommunications are still underdeveloped or even nonexistent, there the development of a community which is prerequisite to nation-building is bound to be slow.

Table 3–1 shows the great disparities that exist between modern nations and less-developed countries in basic communication by written word. Illiteracy is minimal, less than 3 percent, in the United States, the Federal Republic of Germany, the USSR, and Japan; but in Turkey and India more than half the adult population still cannot read and write. If communications are the nerves of government, then the ruling elites have a tough job setting up and maintaining a nerve center when the general citizenry in any large number is illiterate. Moreover, if we pursue the problem of illiteracy in greater depth, using the latest data in UNESCO analyses, we find that within our twelve countries there is even more discrepancy in certain categories than appear in the overall percentages shown in Table 3–1.

In traditional societies women are less likely to be educated than men. Thus, in India, although the overall percentage of illiteracy as of 1960 was 72.2, male illiteracy, 58.5 percent, was contrasted with female illiteracy, 86.8 percent. Similarly in Turkey, male illiteracy is now 45.2 percent, but female illiteracy is 78.9 percent. Illiteracy is also generally higher among people who live in the country than among those who live in the cities. Thus in Mexico, although the overall percentage of illiteracy is 34.6, it is down to 21.3 percent in the cities, in contrast to 48.9 percent in the rural areas. We also note apparent discrimination against Mexican women; in the cities, where illiteracy is lowest, the percentage for men is 16.7, for women 25.5. Evidence of discrimination with respect to minority groups is equally striking. In Israel the overall percentage of illiteracy is 15.8; for the Jewish population only it is 12.2, but for the non-Jewish population it is 51.7; for Jewish women it is 17.1 and for non-Jewish women 71.5. Another example of basic inequality is the United States. According to the 1960 United States census the overall percentage of illiteracy was 2.2; for whites the percentage was 1.7, but for nonwhites 9.81; the overall percentage for people in the cities was 1.8; in the rural farm areas, 5.6; the highest percentage of illiteracy was among the nonwhite farmers, 18.9 percent.

TABLE 3–1
Communications: The Written Word

	Percentage of Illiteracy		*Number of Daily Newspapers 1966–67*
	AROUND 1950	AROUND 1960	
UK	n.d.	n.d.	106
Germany, FR	n.d.	1.0	423
USSR	n.d.	1.5	616
USA	3.2	2.2	1,749
Japan	n.d.	2.2	172
Israel	6.3	15.8	24
Ivory Coast	n.d.	80.0*	1
Kenya	n.d.	80.0*	3
Mexico	43.2	34.6	228
Colombia	37.7	27.1	n.d.
Turkey	68.1	61.9	371
India	80.7	72.2	588

n.d. = no data.

* Estimates given in US AID, *Economic Data Book: Africa* (Washington, D.C.: Government Printing Office, 1968).

SOURCE: *UNESCO Statistical Yearbook, 1965*, No. 4, pp. 36–46; and *UNESCO Statistical Yearbook, 1968*, No. 6·1, pp. 478–82 (New York: UNESCO Publications, 1966 and 1968).

Modernization of a people begins with reducing illiteracy. This calls for mass education in the public schools, which is always an expensive proposition and a relatively slow process. Meanwhile the political leadership in a developing nation can hasten political socialization by providing and utilizing the new tools of communication made possible by electronics. The *Un'ted Nations Statistical Yearbook* provides a number of indicators for measuring the development of instant communication. Although the data are somewhat incomplete, Tables 3–2 and 3–3 give us a comparative picture of the growing potential of communication media in the process of political socialization.

The Function of the Mass Media in Political Socialization

Quantitative data do not tell us much about the character of communication, but they do indicate the potential of the media in bringing people together. Table 3–2 suggests that the telegraphic service has a declining function in some countries—Kenya, the United States, Japan, Germany, and the United Kingdom. But between 1953 and 1968 the number of telephones in use dramatically increased in every country, and especially in the developing countries: threefold in Kenya and Mexico, fivefold in India, sixfold in Colombia, eightfold in Japan. The numbers game, of course, can be played in different ways. The number of phones in use in the United Kingdom and the United States in the same period merely doubled. Even so, in 1968 there were more phones in use in the United Kingdom than in the USSR, and more phones in use in the United States than in the other eleven countries together.

Tables 3–3, 3–4, and 3–5 give us some data for comparing the develop-

TABLE 3–2
Telegraph and Telephone Service

	Number of Telegrams Sent or Received (in Thousands)		*Number of Telephones in Use*	
	1953	1968	1953	1968
Ivory Coast	190 (1962)	203	15,612 (1962)	24,390
Kenya	2,064	1,022	20,407	65,445
USA	153,889	71,135	50,373,000	109,255,000
Colombia	11,375 (1966)	12,915	128,970	817,423
Mexico	37,828	42,433	330,221	1,174,885
India	24,678	43,200 (1967)	183,575	1,057,193
Israel	615	826		
Japan	93,793	72,463	2,594,506	17,330,791
Turkey	7,297	10,183	97,176	450,485
Germany, FR	19,336	13,139	3,300,909	11,248,979
UK	34,195	7,833	6,093,872	12,799,000
USSR	252,000 (1962)	339,000	7,100,000	10,800,000

(Dates in parentheses are closest dates available.)
SOURCE: *United Nations Statistical Yearbook* (1969), from nos. 156 and 157.

ment of radio and television as means of mass communications. Table 3–3 indicates the modes of organization for radio communications, whether government owned and operated or privately owned and operated. Seven of the twelve states have a government monopoly of radio communications, five have mixed systems with both government and private sponsorship. As might be expected, the United States is way at the top, and again the disparity between the top and the bottom of the list is appalling: in the United States 6,337 transmitters and 285,000,000 receivers; in the Ivory Coast 8 transmitters and 60,000 receivers. Nevertheless, between 1950 and 1967 the trend appears as a rapid rise in radio communications in every nation, including the less-developed countries. In the United States, the number of receivers tripled, they multiplied by seven in the USSR, and they increased fivefold in Mexico, eightfold in Turkey, and fourteenfold in India.

Table 3–4 indicates the modes of organization for television communications, again a government monopoly in seven states, mixed sponsorship in five states. As in radio communications the differential between the modernized and the developing states is almost incredible: 2,703 transmitters in the United States, 1 in India; 78,000,000 receivers in the United States and 4,000 in India. But the progress of television communication is practically phenomenal in every country, and especially in the more advanced states.

Table 3–5, which shows the number of daily newspapers, radio receivers, and television receivers for each 1,000 inhabitants, demonstrates the changing patterns of communication in both the advanced and less-developed states. The trend is away from written communications with a great expansion in telecommunications. The number of people reading newspapers actually

TABLE 3–3
Telecommunications: Radio

	Mode of Organization	*Number of Transmitters* 1967	*Number of Receivers (Thousands)* 1950	1967
USA	*D*	6,337	85,200	285,000
USSR	*G*	407	11,452	80,700
Germany, FR	*G*	298	9,018	27,800
Japan	*D*	652	9,139	25,466
UK	*G*	(1966) 286	12,356	17,493
Mexico	*D*	528	1,892	10,932
India	*G*	125	546	7,579
Turkey	*D*	52	362	2,789
Colombia	*D*	225	500	2,200
Israel	*G*	41	153	774
Kenya	*G*	(1963) 14	(1960) 57	(1968) 350
Ivory Coast	*G*	(1965) 8	(1960) 55	60

(Dates in parentheses are closest dates available.)
G = government; *D* = both government and private.
SOURCE: *UNESCO Statistical Yearbook* (1968) (New York: UNESCO Publications, 1969), tables 9.1 and 9.2.

declined in both the United Kingdom and the United States, and in both countries the number of radio receivers and television receivers for each 1,000 inhabitants increased markedly. In the less-developed countries, as illiteracy declined, newspaper circulation rose for each 1,000 inhabitants; in Mexico from 79 to 109, in India from 7 to 13, in Kenya from 3 to 9. But the use of telecommunications as means of expression in the public forum and for mobilizing support in the political arena has dramatically increased. The increase in television communications from 1953 to 1967, measured in number of receivers per 1,000 inhabitants, is most apparent in the advanced countries: in the United States from 169 to 392; in the USSR from 1 to 96; in the United Kingdom from 58 to 263. The potential of telecommunications as instruments of political socialization in the less-developed countries is also most promising: From 1953 to 1967 the number of radio receivers per 1,000 inhabitants jumped in Israel from 122 to 290, in Colombia from 44 to 115, in Kenya from 2 to 37. The number of television receivers per 1,000 inhabitants increased in Mexico from 2 in 1953 to 40 in 1967, in Colombia from 11 in 1960 to 21 in 1966. On the other hand, the chance of watching world events on a television screen anyplace in India is still virtually nil. As late as 1967 there was only 1 TV transmitter for the whole vast territory and the total number of TV receivers for the entire population was about 4,000.

"The medium is the message" [7] The message to be read into the media of telecommunications is that underprivileged, oppressed groups have become less willing to put up with their status because they have heard and they have seen that others live differently. There is a coincidence between the rising ex-

TABLE 3–4
Telecommunications: Television

	Mode of Organization	*Number of Transmitters* 1966–67	*Number of Receivers (Thousands)* 1953	1966–67
USA	*D*	2,703	27,300	78,000
USSR	*G*	890	225	22,700
Japan	*D*	1,687	8	20,016
UK	*D*	207	2,957	14,463
Germany, FR	*G*	660	12	13,806
Mexico	*D*	49	70	1,792
Colombia	*D*	15	(1960) 150	400
Israel	*G*	1	(1965) 15	26
Kenya	*G*	2	(1965) 10	14
India	*G*	1	(1965) 0.8	4
Turkey	*G*	1	(1960) 1	2.5
Ivory Coast	*G*	4	—	(1965) 6

(Dates in parentheses are closest dates available.)
G = government; *D* = both government and private.
SOURCE: *UNESCO Statistical Yearbook, 1968* (New York: UNESCO Publications, 1969), tables 10.1 and 10.2.

pectations of people the world over and the extension of instantaneous global communications. Other messages are inherent in the technological advance of communications. The political leader, or the ruling elite, who can be seen on television, whose voice can be heard over the radio, is no longer the remote source of law and authority that he might have been before those he governs saw or heard him. Visibility may in some ways destroy the mystique that envelops traditional government. On the other hand, it may enhance the image, as radio did for President Franklin D. Roosevelt who introduced the technique of fireside chats from the White House to "my fellow Americans," or as television did for John F. Kennedy who indeed might never have been president were it not for his brilliant performance on television during the 1960 campaign, especially in the debates with his Republican opponent. In the electronic age a new environment has been created for all who are reached by the new media. TV is the extension of man into space—instantaneous, worldwide extension.

On April 13, 1970, a faint voice from Apollo 13, outbound from earth to moon, told the ground controllers at the Houston Manned Spacecraft Center, "We've got a problem." What a problem! An oxygen tank had inexplicably exploded, disabling their command and service module. The whole world —people in Nairobi, Liverpool, Bogotá, and Washington—anxiously listened to their radios, watched their television screens, while three American astronauts, using their small lunar excursion module as a lifeboat, made their way 205 thousand miles through space, back to earth alive.

TABLE 3–5
Daily Newspapers, Radio Receivers, and Television Receivers per 1,000 Inhabitants

	Newspapers		*Radio Receivers*		*Television Receivers*	
	1952	1966–67	1950	1967	1953	1967
UK	573	477	244	318	58	263
Japan	374	476	111	255	0.1	200
Germany, FR	242	328	180	464	0.2	231
USA	342	309	560	1,431	169	392
USSR		305	205	342	1	96
Israel	167	188	122	290	(1965) 6	10
Mexico	79	109	73	239	2	40
Colombia	55	53	44	115	(1960) 11	(1966) 21
Turkey	31	(1960) 51	17	85	(1960) 0.04	(1966) 0.08
India	7	13	1	15	n.d.	n.d.
Kenya	3	9	2	37	(1965) 1.1	1.4
Ivory Coast	2	3	(1960) 17	(1965) 16	1.6	n.d.

n.d. = no data.
(Dates in parentheses are closest dates available.)
SOURCE: *UNESCO Yearbook, 1968* (New York: UNESCO Publications, 1969), tables 6.1, 9.2, and 10.2.

No matter where we lived in 1970, if we had access to a TV receiver, at home, in the local pub, or a coffee shop, we could observe the spectrum of events taking place in the international setting: President Nixon in Washington and Premier Kosygin in Moscow celebrating the ratification of a treaty to halt the proliferation of nuclear weapons; Chancellor Willy Brandt and Premier Willi Stoph in the first meeting of the heads of the two Germanies in twenty-five years; Chancellor Brandt and Premier Kosygin signing a treaty which pledged their two nation states to observe the inviolability of the current borders; the Emperor Hirohito commemorating the twenty-fifth anniversary of Japan's surrender to the United States in World War II, praying for national prosperity and peace in the world; war in Vietnam and its extension into Cambodia; war in the Middle East, Arabs against Israelis, Arabs against Arabs; fighting and riotous activities in Northern Ireland, Roman Catholics in Belfast standing up to British troops; Labourite Prime Minister Harold Wilson moving out of Number 10 Downing Street, following British elections to the House of Commons; Conservative Edward Heath moving into the locus of power; the pomp and circumstance of state funerals, of Charles De Gaulle, last survivor of the Allied leaders of World War II, of Gamal Abdel Nasser, the Egyptian president and beloved leader of the Arabs; the awarding of the Nobel Peace Prize to Dr. Norman Borlaug, a US scientist, working in cooperation with the Mexican government to improve strains of wheat, a prime mover of the green revolution that might make it possible for developing countries to break away from hunger and poverty.

Mass communications are understood to be the keys to modern nation-building. The same television set, however, which may draw a nation closer as it watches its festivals, its leaders, the best (or worst) its entertainers have to offer, which enables the illiterate to see and hear what he cannot read, also brings events, practices, and people from across the boundary lines drawn by politics and culture. In many nation states today the flow of communications is fairly open. A Japanese tea ceremony can be seen by an English housewife, to whom tea is a highlight of an equally important and yet vastly different afternoon procedure in her own home. Americans can view the annual May Day parade on Moscow's Red Square from the camera angle on top of Lenin's Tomb. And Russians get to see campus unrest in the United States.

Communications can bring about integration (a cohesive relationship between the political structure and other social organizations) both on a national and international level. Integration, however, is not an automatic process, as any political leader knows. Communication may be associative—it may strengthen the cultural experiences and an awareness of sharing by transmitting joint values. Communication may also be disassociative—it may break up communal ties by introducing competitive goals and policies which may promote division rather than unity on basic values. Activities and processes designed to utilize communications as an integrative force are, of course, extremely important ingredients in the process of political socialization in new nations. Some ruling groups, however, recognize the potential dangers to their own positions and regulate the communications flow through a variety of censorship measures, as we shall point out more specifically in Chapter 11.

On an individual basis the extent of socialization can be measured in quite simple terms. With whom do we choose to spend most of our time? With whom do we share the most meaningful events in our life? To whom do we turn in time of need? On whom do we rely to back up our views of what is right and the acceptable way of doing things? This extensive interaction is considered a salient feature of nationalism and political socialization.

THE GROWTH OF NATIONHOOD

Two of our twelve states with a tradition of nationhood evolving over centuries illustrate the classical model of indigenous nationalism. Both are island communities, but that is where the similarities in their national evolution end. The British and Japanese patterns of political socialization and interactions among the people developed quite differently.

Two Classical Models of National Growth

For centuries the Japanese as a society were self-contained. Their contacts were essentially among themselves, and until the nineteenth century, any outside contacts were generally restricted to their own part of the world—Korea and China—and even those were kept at a minimum. A distinguished student of the Japanese political system points out that until about a hundred years ago, "Japan was a little-known kingdom, just emerging from a period of self-imposed isolation that lasted for almost two and a half centuries." [8] Salience, to the Japanese for several hundred years, meant interaction first and foremost among themselves, and it led to a highly complex set of sociopolitical structures, tightly interwoven with, and often derived from, religious beliefs.

The British, too, were an island community, whose contacts with each other evolved and were reinforced over the centuries. However, the British Isles were not the only center of interaction for their inhabitants. Unlike the Japanese, the British did not use the sea as a shield to keep their contacts with the outside world to a minimum. It served them the dual purpose of protection and highway to the world. To the British, salience meant contact with every faraway place which the British fleet could reach and which British trade companies and garrisons could help maintain.

Interaction, however, took on various patterns. The British among themselves evolved a highly stratified, class-conscious society, and it went with them into all parts of the British Empire. The Empire, "on which the sun never set," became a perfect example that only the globe could be the limit for social, political, and commercial interaction. Yet it did not lead to assimilation between the British and the people over whom they ruled, although the British probably left more of a legacy in the parts of their Empire than any other Western power.

No doubt the ability of the British to reach out and utilize all possible contacts with peoples all over the world, coupled with their awareness of "doing their own thing" which has been caricatured and grudgingly admired throughout the world, has given British nationalism its unique flavor. If the extent of political socialization is measured in terms of the ability to develop a distinct identity and to communicate a joint sense of superiority, the British are an example par excellence. They have the oldest functioning political institutions, which have been modified and adjusted to fit the changing needs of society. Transformation of an empire into a commonwealth, imitated without much success by other imperial powers, most notably the French, has been achieved with a minimum of internal disruption.

In the age of written constitutions the British concept of the constitution as a way of life survives as the most perfect example of political socialization. In stark contrast we have the ill-fated Weimar Constitution which was meticulously designed to cover every exigency and became the instrument with which Hitler legitimized the Third Reich.

Religion: Functional and Dysfunctional in National Development

Salience was determined by religion in the case of the Israelis, a people often referred to as the oldest nation in Western history. No matter how scattered the Jews were—whether their political, social, and economic roles in the societies in which they lived were restricted to very narrow confines which often reached the level of persecution or whether they could have opted for assimilation and submersion into the nations among whom they lived—their consciousness of themselves as a people with a separate identity based on religious particularism remained.

Two recent events, one the publication of a highly successfuly work of fiction, the other an archaeological expedition, serve to illustrate that Israeli nationalism is rooted deep in religion. No matter how much the young generation of Israeli citizens chafes under the rules of the orthodox rabbinate, no matter how the state of Israel reflects a variety of immigration waves and all the problems that go with absorbing all the newcomers, Israel as a nation survives. The nation is older than the state because the rabbis, since Moses, have insisted that the children of Israel are special, are set apart, and that they must look to each other for strength and support.

James Michener in his novel *The Source* [9] traces the history of the Jews through the reactions of an assortment of modern archaeologists to their finds at a fictitious dig in Israel. At about the time Michener was at work on his book, an archaeological expedition in Israel under the direction of Yigael Yadin uncovered the fortress of Masada. Here, in 73 AD, 960 Zealots refused to surrender to the Roman legions commanded by Flavius Silva and killed themselves rather than become slaves to the Romans. Eleazar, their leader, exhorted them to kill their families and each other rather than fall into the hands of the soldiers of the Tenth Legion:

> *Since we, long ago, my generous friends, resolved never to be servants to the Romans, nor to any other than to God himself, who alone is the true and*

> *just Lord of mankind, the time is now come that obliges us to make that resolution true in practice . . . put the case that we had been brought up under another persuasion, and taught that life is the greatest good which men are capable of, and that death is a calamity: however, the circumstances we are now in, ought to be an inducement to us to bear such calamity courageously, since it is by the will of God, and by necessity, that we are to die: for it now appears that God hath made such a decree against the whole Jewish nation, that we are to be deprived of this life which (he knew) we would not make a due use of . . . let us die before we become slaves under our enemies, and let us go out of the world, together with our children and our wives, in a state of freedom.*[10]

What becomes clear to any reader of Jewish history is the fact that the children of Israel never wavered in their certainty that they were separate and chosen and that they were a community. Wherever secular rules intruded upon, or clashed with, their sense of community, those rules had to be subordinated, no matter what the price might be in human sacrifice.

Thus it was possible for the Jews to return to Israel from all over the world after millennia of separation and retain a sense of nationhood that is stronger than the generation gap in Israel and surmounts the very real social, political, and economic problems of integration in a state made up of a multitude of immigrants.

What is a Jew? is a question that has plagued Jew and Gentile alike since early biblical days. Here we have emphasized the religious connotation. The question was recently posed as a legal issue before the Supreme Court of Israel by a young native Israeli officer in the Israel navy on behalf of his two children whose mother is Scottish and atheist. The registration card which every Israeli citizen must carry includes one item of identification, *le'om*, meaning "peoplehood." The options to check on le'om were Muslim, Druze, Jewish, foreign, or a blank. Since under rabbinical law Judaism is inherited through the mother, the two children were not permitted to check Jewish. The father took his objections to the highest court, pointing out that his children went to Israeli schools, spoke Hebrew, considered themselves Jews in culture (but not in religion). The judges of the high court decided, five to four, that for such purposes of national identification a Jew is anyone who considers himself a Jew. The decision, however, provoked an uproar among the 15 to 25 percent of the Israelis who are Orthodox Jews. And the Israeli cabinet immediately responded to the popular din by reversing the judges and ruling that only persons who meet the rabbinical definition of a Jew can register as a Jew. Premier Golda Meir personally opposed more liberal members of the cabinet who suggested that the le'om be removed from the identity cards. As she explained it, there can be no differentiation between Jewish religion and Jewish nationality. Note, however, that while rabbinical law still dominates Israeli nationalism, it does not control Israeli citizenship. In the celebrated case, the Israeli citizenship of the two children or their Scottish atheist mother was not in question.[11]

Israel became a nation state by strengthening its ancient communal ties, by letting the ancient prophecies of joint rewards based on religious observance and the joint penalties which came from breaking the Mosaic laws shape the initial years of the young republic. Once statehood was achieved and the political system became a functioning entity, some members of the younger generation were inclined to believe that Israel now could survive as a secular nation state without so much advice from the bearded elders in black fur hats and silk caftans. Modern Israel was founded by Zionists-socialists, most of them atheists. The ruling elite, however, has accepted a religious base for the community as the political price for bringing the various small religious parties into the government coalition.

The Turkish nation is traditionally identified with the faith of Islam. More than 98 percent of the people are Muslims, and while non-Muslims (Christians and Jews) may hold legal citizenship, they are not regarded as true Turks. Nevertheless, Mustafa Kemal Atatürk, the father of modern Turkey, did not build a nation on the basis of religious, communal experiences. To the contrary, he used every device possible to remove the Turks from Islam. He used his role as a political leader to induce a series of religious, social, and political reforms which separated the Turks, who had once been the core of the Ottoman Empire, from other Muslim peoples. By discrediting Islam, secularizing society, and through a series of social and political reforms designed to shock the firm believers in Islam, Atatürk separated the Turks from their surrounding Arab neighbors. He forced the Turks to look toward themselves, or to the West, for salient relationships.

After he became president of the Republic of Turkey (October 29, 1923), Mustafa Kemal made it clear to his countrymen that in the future as a community they would no longer be rooted in Islam. His three major reform programs were aimed at a thorough alienation from the Muslim world by complete secularization (forcing the Turks to seek their joint, or communal, rewards in an inner- or Western-directed society); at the development of an educated elite that could take the lead in achieving political socialization; [12] and at establishing a civil code that would link the Turks with modern, Western nation states and would result in joint (or communal) punishments if adherents to the old Islamic traditions persisted in their ways.

Atatürk did not attempt to eradicate the Muslim faith of the Turks, but he did deliberately cut the ties between Islam and the Turkish state. In 1924 he abolished religious schools and courts. In 1925 he closed religious tombs as places of worship and prohibited his countrymen and women from wearing garments in their daily lives that had been of religious origin. Secularization was completed by the adoption of a new Civil Code, based on the Swiss Code, on February 17, 1926, which relegated the Koran to religious use only, instead of being also the fundamental source of Turkish law (as it still is today in most Islamic countries). In 1928 Atatürk substituted the Latin alphabet for Arabic characters in Turkey, thereby depriving the Turks of the most fundamental tools of communication with their Arabic neighbors, and in 1934 he passed what must have been the most shocking law to the Muslim neighbors of Turkey: Women became eligible to vote in national elections and could run for elective office in the National Assembly.[13]

These bold reforms had their desired results. Kemalism did become a basis of Turkish nationalism. Turkey found an identity as a nation state apart from the Islamic world. Despite many criticisms levied against the autocracy of Atatürk, Turkey has survived counterrevolutions and military coups as well as a variety of internal purges of opposition movements (many of which were rooted in the Islamic religious groups). We do not mean to imply, of course, that Turkish nationalism was imposed solely through the efforts of Atatürk. We doubt that any powerful leader, however able and ambitious, can single-handedly create national consciousness by rejecting popular tradition. Atatürk, like most successful politicians, saw his opportunities and seized them. The timing was opportune between World Wars I and II.

Religion, however, remains an integral element of Turkish nationality—and is still an important issue in Turkish politics. It was, in fact, the single most important issue which ousted the Republican Peoples party founded by Atatürk and brought the Democratic party to power in 1950. The Democratic party made no attempt to restore the institutional role of Islam in the Turkish government, but it was inclined to relax the restraints on religious activities which Atatürk had imposed in the early period of nation-building.

The religious reformation of the 1950s—it was never intended to be a restoration—continued through the 1960s. It is marked by increasing public worship, with the building of many new mosques, with more and more pilgrimages to Mecca. The reformation is symbolized by the call to prayers in Arabic and by the tolerance of Arabic in the religious meetings. More concretely, religious education has been reintroduced in the school system under the supervision of the Ministry of Education. (Parents who do not want their children to be instructed in the tenets of Islam may ask for exemption, but few parents choose to exercise this option.) The Ministry of Religion administers the publicly supported Iman-Hatip schools—schools for Islam prayer leaders or preachers. It appears then that Atatürk's policy of secularization served its purpose—to put the Turkish people on the road to modernity—but now that the Turkish nation is modernizing, the Islamic faith becomes once again a functional, rather than dysfunctional, force in Turkish nationalism.

FOUR CATEGORIES OF NATIONALISM

Bruce Russett and his associates, to whose work we referred earlier, set up a list of "National Political Units in the Twentieth Century" [14] and categorized them according to their status of dependence, independence, or belonging to a larger entity, among other variables. We mentioned that this listing aroused quite a bit of controversy when it was published, and we raised a few questions ourselves.

As we look at our twelve examples and try to analyze them as nations, the problem we face is to find some concept or devise some index by which we can distinguish them as nations. Even to the casual student of nationalism it is not very satisfactory to find out that India became independent in 1947, that Japan was dependent from 1945 to 1952 and independent thereafter, or that the Ivory Coast preceded Kenya by three years in achieving independence in 1960.

Dates of independence, as we stated earlier, tell us little about the status of nationhood or the existence or viability of a community. Kohn looks at nationalism as a mystique; Deutsch perceives it in terms of the ability to communicate and thereby establishes spheres of salience; Lester Pearson suggests common culture. We offer our own attempt at categorizing the elusive phenomenon of nationalism.

Among our twelve examples, we have found at least four different types of nationhood, separated on the basis of their origins. They are by no means neat little pigeonhole classifications into which a specific set of nation states can be filed to stay for purposes of definitive identication. To the contrary, several of our twelve nations are difficult to classify, because they have gone through several types or phases of nationalism, as Table 3–6 indicates.

Indigenous Nationalism

We have pointed to the United Kingdom and Japan as two nation states whose sense of national identity evolved over centuries. Both would represent the prototype of indigenous nationalism (some students of the concept would refer to it as the nineteenth-century, or classical, type of nationalism), which grew quite gradually and is based on a homogeneous culture.

The British and the Japanese developed their sense of national identity around a set of cultural practices. Their social stratification and their way of doing things became so ingrained in all the members of their community that they needed few written rules and regulations to prescribe their behavior. A community which looks back on centuries of a common past needs no detailed script on how to act. No matter where the British moved, the rights of an Englishman moved with them. No matter how interested the Japanese became in new outside influences after the Meiji Restoration, their own symbols and behavior patterns remained strongest.

We have singled out the Israelis as one of the oldest nations. Their indigenous nationalism grew around their religion—and Zionism. Religion played a considerable role in the Russia of pre-Soviet days. Czar Peter the Great realized that the church could be used as a potent arm of the state to maintain conformity to the rules set up by the state. He was confronted

TABLE 3–6
A Conspectus of Four Different Types of Nationalism

Indigenous Nationalism	*Self-conscious Nationalism*	*Anticolonial Nationalism*	*Reconstructed Nationalism*
Germany	Israel	Colombia	Germany
Israel	Turkey	India	Japan
Japan	USSR	Ivory Coast	
United Kingdom		Kenya	
USSR		Mexico	
		USA	

(not unlike the rulers of the USSR today) by the task of holding together a multinational empire and used the church to enforce compliance. Over centuries Russian society became stratified around four major elements: the czar (the autocrat, by God's grace, according to his formal title), the Holy Synod (the government of the Russian Orthodox Church, headed by the patriarch, who was appointed by the czar), the aristocracy (some of whom were the descendants of the *boyars*, the old noble families whose rule antedated that of the czars, some of whom had been given their titles and land for military services rendered, and still others who owed their status to their role as administrators for the crown), and the serfs (most of them artisans who had lived in slavery for centuries and whose lives did not change much with the Emancipation Proclamation of Alexander II in the spring of 1861). Those four pillars held up a community of multiethnic roots. It was an uneasy community, to be sure, disrupted by many rebellions,[15] but it persisted over centuries. Russian nationalism was restructured during the Stalin era, under the slogan of "socialism in one country," and during World War II even the symbol of Mother Russia came to life again to sustain the struggling Red Army.[16]

Language and its use by poets and philosophers was the main element in German nationalism. Until the nineteenth century, German politics were characterized by particularism. Any political map of Europe, from the disintegration of the Holy Roman Empire until 1871, depicts the German states as a patchwork quilt. Yet the roots of German nationalism go back into the Middle Ages.

Despite the bloody battles of the Thirty Years' War which resulted in a multitude of German political entities born out of religious strife,[17] German nationalism, too, has close religious ties. Martin Luther's translation of the Bible into German provided hundreds of thousands of faithful readers with a written form of communication in the vernacular; that is to say, it provided a uniform written German language.

The clergy instructed peasants and shopkeepers who otherwise would not have learned to read and who would not have had any access to the prevalent elite languages (Latin and French) in Europe during that period and thus provided the subjects of many different political rulers with a communications medium which did not remain restricted to and reserved for Holy Scripture. Among the more well-to-do, written German became the link in business and literature; commerce, poetry, and drama, in addition to the Bible, provided forceful roots for the growth of a community despite political particularism.[18]

Self-conscious Nationalism

Many of the preceding pages have been taken up with the activities of Atatürk and his role in establishing Turkey as a modern nation state out of the remains of the Ottoman Empire. We have pointed out the deliberateness of Atatürk's undertaking. Among our twelve nation states we would classify Turkey as the prime example of self-conscious nationalism.

World War I had cataclysmic implications on the international scene, just as World War II did. Probably the most crucial international consequence of World War I was the dissolution of three empires which had dominated much of world politics during the nineteenth century—the Ottoman Empire,[19] the czarist Russian Empire, and the Austro-Hungarian Empire.

Woodrow Wilson's statement of national self-determination provided the trigger for many of the activities we have classified here as self-conscious nation-building. No doubt, President Wilson intended to provide guidelines for reconstruction of nation states within the two empires famous for their multinational composition—the Ottoman and the Austro-Hungarian.

A biographer of Atatürk suggests that he, more than anything, resented the foreign influence which had increased during the decline of the Ottoman Empire. He had a deep and genuine love of country and determined to do something about its future:

> *In Kemal this derived from a pride in its destiny, nourished in boyhood; from a sense of shame at its visible decline at the hands of the foreigner and of its own decadent rulers. This feeling was rooted in a certain earthiness of spirit and love of the soil—the mountains and valleys of Rumeli, the wide-open spaces of Anatolia—for which he had fought and was about to fight again. It was animated above all by a knowledge of the men who had fought with him. Kemal saw the Turkish people without illusion. He knew that they were dour, conservative, fatalistic, slow in mind and initiative. But he knew also that they were stubborn, patient, capable of endurance; a race of fighters ruthless in battle, responsive to leadership and ready to die on order.*[20]

We have described Atatürk's methods of carving out a new, independent nation from the ruins of the old Ottoman Empire. The term *self-conscious nationalism* emerged from our study of Turkish nationalism. Nations which grow over centuries gradually evolve a way of doing things. Societal and cultural patterns develop slowly, imperceptibly, and, much to the chagrin of latter-day scholars, are hard to trace. Who could prove today, in the days when men walk on the moon, just how the Japanese emperor descended from the sun—especially when the Aztec aristocracy made an almost identical claim? Who could even trace the origin of such legends.

By the same token, how frustrated must be the lawyer practicing his craft under the *Code Napoléon*, with its highly detailed instructions, when he is confronted with a case arising under common law—one of the major contributions the English made to Western adjudication. Just who, exactly, decided that a man's home is his castle? Whoever said it went far beyond a simple statement of real-estate rights. He created a symbol of privacy, of a whole legion of statements about unreasonable search and seizure, and he, whoever he was, initiated a whole series of precedents that have left their mark in much of Western legal history. No legal scholar today can attribute the history of protection of privacy of the person to any particular source. It just "grew" that way. It evolved over generations.

By contrast, we see Atatürk deliberately overturning centuries of religious practices and introducing a set of rules and regulations for political, social, and economic behavior that must have seemed unthinkable to the elder generation of Turks. He had a kind of charisma that appealed to the Young Turks who were eager for the joint rewards of modernization.

Israel—or rather her predecessor as a legal state, Palestine—is linked to Turkey in self-conscious nationalism not at all by the way her intellectual elite felt about nationhood (note that we have cited Judaism as one of the oldest forms of evolutionary nationalism), but instead by the way Palestine emerged from the decline of the Ottoman Empire. Certainly, there is no clear-cut assessment of how carefully it was thought out, how far it was backed up by political and diplomatic (not to mention military) guarantees, and how much it represented the beliefs of an individual as opposed to a government, but the declaration of Lord Balfour on November 2, 1917, that Britain favored the establishment of a national home for the Jewish people gave Zionism a renewed impetus to strive for the establishment of a Jewish nation state.[21] The children of Israel were conscious of their nationhood for millennia, and yet they reassessed that national identity in a self-conscious way as an aftermath of political developments following World War I.

Russia presents an equally ambiguous example of the origin of its nationalism. It evolved as a nation state over the centuries, despite the fact that the czars headed an empire of a broad variety of peoples. The church, the autocratic rulers, and the institutions of a strict military regime and serfdom had molded a national consciousness of being children of Mother Russia and Father Czar.[22]

In 1917 Russia became the battleground of the Bolshevik Revolution which was based, for a time, on the internationalism of Karl Marx's ideology. How deep the internationalism of V. I. Lenin really went is hard to say. The facts remind us that Lenin's successor, Joseph Stalin, used the old symbol of Mother Russia to build up the morale of his troops in World War II, and that the slogan of "socialism in one country" became one of the most effective forces in Stalin's determined drive to show the rest of the world (Communist as well as capitalist) that Russia, an agricultural state, could be transformed into one of the most powerful industrial countries in the world. (Elsewhere in these pages we discuss the meaning of industrialization, the various ways of measuring industrial development.)

Stalin, a native-born Georgian who resented the superiority of the Rus,[23] became the originator of a self-conscious form of nationalism which often substituted the concept of Russia for the name of the legal entity—the Union of Soviet Socialist Republics.

Anticolonial Nationalism

Six of our twelve nation states emerged from three enormous colonial empires —Colombia and Mexico were Spanish colonies, the Ivory Coast was part of the French overseas territories, and the United States, India, and Kenya belonged to the British Empire.

The history of their independence spans centuries, beginning with the declaration of 1776 "in the Name, and by the Authority of the good People of these Colonies . . . that these United Colonies are, and of Right ought to be Free and Independent States."[24] In the early nineteenth century Spain lost several of her American colonies, among them Mexico and Colombia. We have mentioned already Father Hidalgo's proclamation of September 16, 1810, as well as the declaration of independence of Bogotá in 1810 and the establishment of the Republic of Colombia in 1819.

India won her independence after a long and protracted struggle in 1947.[25] The Ivory Coast dates her complete independence from 1960, and Kenya became a state in 1963.

The three oldest nation states to emerge out of a rejection of their colonial past kept many of the social and cultural patterns of their former mother countries, including the most important tool for human communication, language. Spanish remains the language of Mexico and Colombia, English that of the United States. The nationalism of these three also took on evolutionary forms after the initial period of violent rejection of the colonial status. In the United States, the English influence of colonial times merged gradually with and provided much of the absorptive base for the many different culture patterns the various immigrant groups brought with them. Spanish culture, first and foremost shaped by the Roman Catholic Church, gradually merged with a broad spectrum of native Indian cultures in Mexico and Colombia.

It is much too soon to tell whether the nations which have emerged from colonialism more recently will have similar experiences. Both India and Kenya look back on a recent period of violent struggle against the British. The bloodshed in the Indian nationalist movement was great until Mahatma Gandhi's nonviolent tactics somewhat curbed it. Kenya's Mau Mau were legendary for their violence, and they were suppressed with equal vengeance. In each case, native leaders were available who could overcome the dissident elements of tribalism and fragmented indigenous societies long enough to provide the nationalist movement with a cohesive force based on the hatred of the colonial power. In the case of India and Kenya, a reaction of tribalism set in after the first euphoria of independence had disappeared.

The internal fragmentations in each society posed the greatest obstacle to political socialization. Kenya and India both relied at first on the language, skills, and behavior patterns of a British trained elite. Thus, they, too, kept a legacy of their former colonial power. But the English language and the reliance upon British training of an administrative elite are only temporary solutions. In India we find a systematic drive aimed at elimination of English as the major language and the substitution of Hindi. Both, so far, in their written and spoken form, are essentially the language of an elite. In Kenya, in the person of Tom Mboya there was a symbol of a new, indigenous elite—men who could reach national prominence without the help of exclusive British schooling. But Mboya was murdered in the summer of 1969.

The Ivory Coast presents quite a different case among our sample of twelve. To use the language of detective stories, anticolonial nationalism in the Ivory Coast might be titled "The Case of the Reluctant Nationalist." Felix Houphouet-Boigny is not the prototype of the native leader who wants to build a nationalist movement around the elimination of the colonial power. In five out of the six nation states of our sample that emerged as nations by rejecting their colonial status, indigenous leaders were the driving force behind anticolonialist nationalist movements. In the case of the Ivory Coast, it took pressures from various groups among the population to persuade their most distinguished national leader to strike out for independence.

Reconstructed Nationalism

We have referred to Japan as one of the oldest, most homogeneous nation states in the world. German nationalism, too, we have cited as an example of culture-bound evolutionary nationalism.

Yet both Germany and Japan constitute the fourth category of nationalism among our twelve nation states. Both are examples of nationalism which was carried to its extreme and therefore became thoroughly discredited and had to be reconstructed.

Much of the literature of international relations is devoted to the question of whether there is such a thing as a world community, a conscience of mankind. The claims that a world community exists would be difficult to substantiate with empirical evidence. Yet there seems to be an underlying code of human behavior that presupposes the existence of a primitive form of community among mankind. If a community is to survive, any attempt on the part of any of its members to get out of line, to develop extremely different patterns of behavior, is punished.

German and Japanese nationalism became implied threats to this primitive concept of a communal human base. Each of the two nations carried the concept of an elite to an extreme. At the same time, neither one could support its claim of elitism by the necessary force to emerge victorious in a war which tested its claims. Certainly, the history of mankind abounds in struggles between elites. Charles Darwin's assessment of the origin of man is based on an elitist theory: the survival of the fittest. His theory was adopted by some philosophers who used social Darwinism as the underpinning for their theories of the inferiority and superiority of certain peoples.

German and Japanese nationalism took on the forms of social Darwinism in the twentieth century. Both nations, claiming a long history of national consciousness based on cultural homogeneity, stressed that very homogeneity to the point of excluding any other cultural patterns. Anyone who refused to acknowledge the superiority of either of the two cultures was considered inferior, and National Socialist Germany even refused him the right to existence.

Using nationalism as their main source of appeal, the ruling elites during the 1930s in both Germany and Japan were able to build a totalitarian society. German and Japanese nationalism became synonymous with highly oppressive authoritarian political systems, and both became identified with a new form of imperialism.[26] Both countries were allied in World War II, and both fought the war to the limit. Both were opposed by a group of allied powers who also fought for total stakes (demands for total surrender extended the fighting toward the end). Germany and Japan were completely defeated and the initial reaction of the victors was one of absolute animosity toward the forms German and Japanese nationalism had taken on between the two world wars.

Compared to some of the plans for utter annihilation, the settlements ultimately pursued by the Allies were quite moderate. Hiroshima and Nagasaki have entered the history books as the first cities which became the targets of atomic bombs. Yet the MacArthur Constitution has become a symbol of popular government for the postwar generation of Japanese.

Henry Morgenthau's plan to turn Germany into a scorched field[27] ultimately became transformed into a series of conventions which enabled those German leaders who had not fallen prey to the perversion of German nationalism in the Third Reich to play the role of founding fathers for the new German nation state.

The Federal Republic of Germany and Japan are both strong hybrids. They combine the histories of indigenous nationalism with the rules laid down by tutelary military governments. Both are examples of a gamble—that outside forces could utilize a strong nationalistic movement, prune it and tailor it to suit their own ideals of a nation state, and retain enough of its own force to assure it not only of survival but to transform it into a strong, new form of nationalism.

Nationalism is probably the most important single ingredient in making and moving the modern state. It is to the body politic what the spirit is to man himself. Nationalism in the political system is man and his ideas writ large, the alter ego of a people who have known a common history, who anticipate a common destiny. When nationalism becomes identified with political community, it gives rise to the nation state. In this chapter we have seen that nationalism can gradually evolve out of the common culture; it can be hastened by various devices of political socialization, including public schooling and mass communications; it can emerge out of common causes such as the recent revolutionary movements against colonialism and imperialism; and it can be remodeled and reconstructed by outside assistance. Because nationalism is a collective state of mind, a pattern of public values and public attitudes, it is bound to be a driving force in the modern state. In the chapter that follows we shall examine more specifically how national goals and national interests actually motivate political systems.

NOTES

1. Hans Kohn, *The Idea of Nationalism* (New York: Macmillan, Collier Books, 1967), p. 4.
2. Hans Kohn, *Nationalism: Its Meaning and History*, rev. ed. (New York: Van Nostrand, Anvil Books, 1965), pp. 9–10.
3. Lester B. Pearson, "Beyond the Nation State," *Saturday Review*, February 15, 1969, pp. 25–26.
4. W. O. Galbraith, *Colombia*, 2d ed. (London: Oxford University Press, 1966), p. 16.
5. Ibid.
6. Karl W. Deutsch, *Nationalism and Social Communication*, 2d ed. (Cambridge, Mass.: MIT Press, 1966), p. 2. For a highly technical exposition of Deutsch's theory of communications and its role in the political system see Karl W. Deutsch, *The Nerves of Government, Models of Political Communication and Control* (New York: Free Press, 1966).
7. The catchy phrasing is that of Marshall McLuhan. His controversial book *Understanding Media: The Extensions of Man* (New York: McGraw-Hill,

1964), p. 7, is a good analysis of the new environment created by telecommunications.

8. Robert E. Ward, ed., *Japan's Political System* (Englewood Cliffs, N.J.: Prentice-Hall, 1967), p. 1.
9. James Michener, *The Source* (New York: Random House, 1965).
10. Yigael Yadin, *Masada* (New York: Random House, 1966), pp. 232–36.
11. The case was widely discussed in the United States press. See the *New York Times*, January 31, 1970, for story on the cabinet decision. Outside Israel, however, a Jew is still likely to be anyone Gentiles take as a Jew, as Felix Frankfurter once observed. Jews recognize themselves as Jews, but Jewish self-hood has frequently been imposed from without. A Jew is a Jew, whether he likes it or not, in the eyes of non-Jews, and this external discrimination has, no doubt, also played an important role in giving Jews a sense of community.
12. Although highly critical of the tutelary nature of Atatürk's regime, Frederick W. Frey in his study, *The Turkish Political Elite* (Cambridge, Mass.: MIT Press, 1965), p. 409, comments on the role of the political elite: "in Turkey this national consciousness initially arose among those who represented the state in its dealings, diplomatic or militarily, with other states."
13. For a chronological table of Atatürk's reforms, see Lord Kinross, *Atatürk* (New York: William Morrow, 1965), pp. 573–78. For a commentary on post-Atatürk reformations, see *Area Handbook for the Republic of Turkey*, prepared by the Foreign Area Studies Division, SORO, American University (Washington, D.C.: Government Printing Office, 1970), especially chap. 1.
14. Bruce Russett, J. David Singer, and Melvin Small, "National Political Units in the Twentieth Century: A Standardized List," *American Political Science Review* 62 (1968): 932–51.
15. For an excellent historical account of the many rebellions and an engrossing study of the various rebellious and revolutionary motivations, read Avrahm Yarmolinsky, *The Road to Revolution* (New York: Macmillan, 1959).
16. Merle Fainsod comments on the fact that "patriotic sentiments so assiduously revived in the prewar years were cultivated with redoubled vigor during World War II." Merle Fainsod, *How Russia Is Ruled*, 2d ed. (Cambridge, Mass.: Harvard University Press, 1963), pp. 112–16. See also Richard Pipes, *The Formation of the Soviet Union: Communism and Nationalism, 1917–1923* (Cambridge, Mass.: Harvard University Press, 1954), pp. 21 ff., for the resolution of the problem of nationalism within an essentially internationally oriented ideology.
17. Among the outcomes of the Treaty of Westphalia was that territorial rulers continued to determine the religion of their subjects, but this was coupled with some modification—the decree that a subject could worship as he had in 1624. On the other hand, the treaty provided for territorial exchanges among rulers to make up for territories lost to a neighbor who might have had a different faith and that faith attracted many subjects. For example, the elector of Brandenburg received compensation for the loss of Pomerania.
18. One of the most insightful accounts of the growth of German nationalism which contrasts the political developments with the cultural ones is Golo Mann, *The History of Germany, since 1789* (New York: Praeger, 1968), especially chaps. 1, 2, 3, and 12; the latter ends on the note that the French probably captured the schizophrenia in German nationalism all along, when they named Germany "Les Allemagnes," i.e., the plural concept rather than a singular.
19. *Balkanization*, the synonym for unviable political entities, has been an entry in the vocabulary of international politics ever since.

20. Kinross, op. cit., p. 191.
21. As early as 1897 Theodor Herzl had called the first Zionist Congress in Basle, Switzerland, and proclaimed the right of the Jewish people to a state based on the territory from which their ancestors came. After the Balfour Declaration was followed up by the League of Nations mandate affirming the validity of the historic claims made by the Zionists, Jewish settlements in Palestine increased. To this period dates the generation of the Yishuv, whose role as the generation of elder statesmen in Israel we discussed above.
22. Note the language of the scathing indictment which Father Gapon sent to Nicholas II after the massacre of Bloody Sunday on January 9, 1905 (old-style calendar): "With naive belief in thee as father of thy people, I was going peacefully to thee with the children of these very people" as cited in Merle Fainsod, op. cit., p. 10.
23. See Bertram D. Wolfe, *Three Who Made a Revolution* (Boston: Beacon Press, 1955); T. H. Rigby, ed., *Stalin* (Englewood Cliffs, N.J.: Prentice-Hall, 1966); and Leonard Schapiro, *The Communist Party of the Soviet Union* (New York: Random House, 1960).
24. For the formative years of the United States, see Marian D. Irish and James W. Prothro, *The Politics of American Democracy*, 5th ed. (Englewood Cliffs, N.J.: Prentice-Hall, 1971), and Seymour Martin Lipset, *The First New Nation: The United States in Historical and Comparative Perspective* (New York: Basic Books, 1963).
25. Mohandas K. Gandhi emerged as leader of an already existing Indian nationalist movement right after World War I, and from then on agitation for independence continued systematically under the very diverse leadership tactics of the Mahatma, of Jawaharlal Nehru and Subhas Chandra Bose, and within the framework of a very uneasy on-again-off-again alliance with the Muslim League. For a detailed account see Norman Palmer's chapter "The Political Heritage of Modern India," in George McT. Kahin, *Major Governments of Asia*, 2d ed. (Ithaca, N.Y.: Cornell University Press, 1963).
26. Hans Kohn, *The Mind of Germany* (New York: Scribner, 1960), especially chaps. 1, 11, 12; Golo Mann, op. cit., chap. 11; Richard Storry, *The Double Patriots: A Study of Japanese Nationalism* (Boston: Houghton Mifflin, 1957); Hugh Borton, *Japan's Modern Century* (New York: Ronald Press, 1955).
27. President Harry S. Truman refers to "what was then loosely called the Morgenthau Plan—that is, the reduction of Germany to a wholly agrarian economy. . . . I had never been for that plan even when I was in the Senate, and since reaching the White House I had come to feel even more strongly about it." Harry S. Truman, *Memoirs by Harry S. Truman* (Garden City, N.Y.: Doubleday, 1955), 1: 235–37.

FURTHER READING

DEUTSCH, KARL W., and WILLIAM J. FOLTZ, eds. *Nation-Building*. New York: Atherton, 1966.

JACOB, PHILIP E., and JAMES V. TOSCANO, eds. *The Integration of Political Communities*. Philadelphia: Lippincott, 1964.

PYE, LUCIAN W., ed. *Communications and Political Development*. Studies in Political Development, vol. 1. Princeton, N.J.: Princeton University Press, 1963.

WARD, BARBARA. *Nationalism and Ideology*. New York: Norton, 1966.

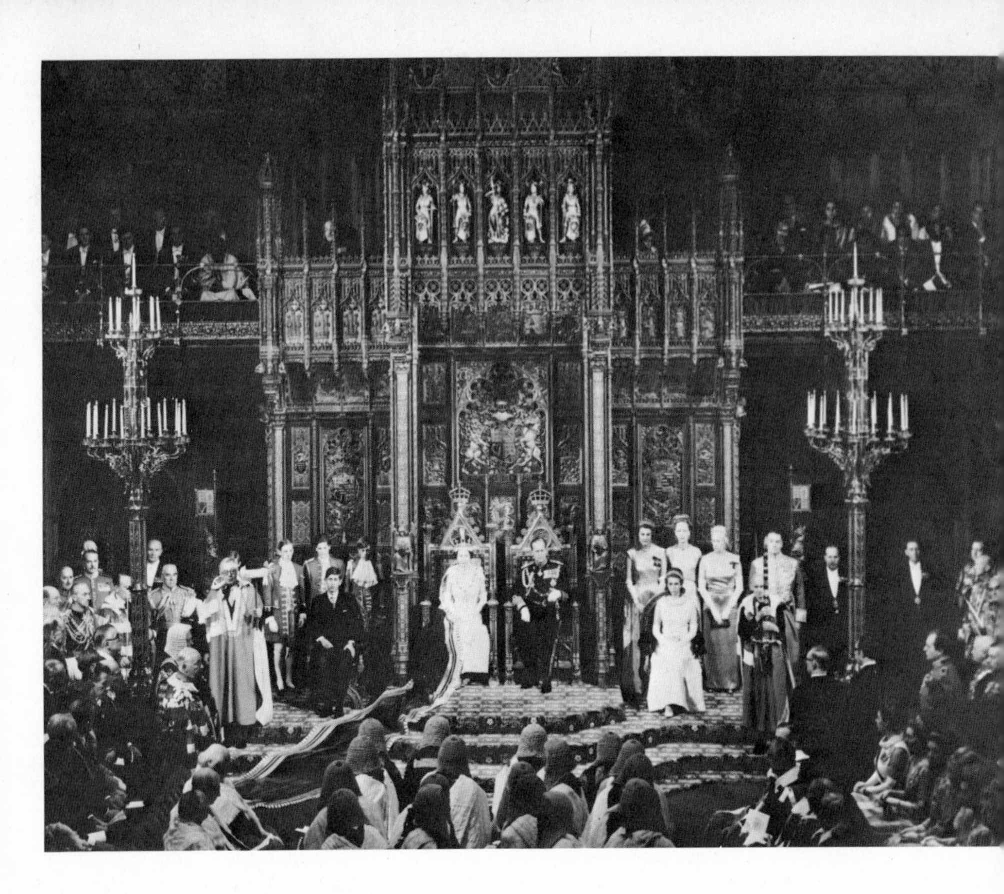

chapter 4

WHAT MOTIVATES A NATIONAL POLITICAL SYSTEM?

NATIONAL GOALS

On July 4, 1776, the Representatives of the United States of America boldly proclaimed:

> . . . *in the Name and by the authority of the good People of these Colonies . . . these United Colonies are, and of right ought to be Free and Independent States . . . as Free and Independent States, they have full Power to levy War, conclude Peace, contract Alliances, establish Commerce, and to do all other Acts and Things which Independent States may of right do.*

In those memorable words, the American revolutionary leaders have expressed the primary motivation of every nation state; to be "Free and Independent . . . and to do all other Acts and Things which Independent States may of right do." For revolutionary leaders in eighteenth-century North America, in nineteenth-century Latin America, in twentieth-century Asia and Africa, the overriding goal has been the achievement of independent statehood—the recognition of sovereignty and equality of status among all other sovereign states in the world. But once independence was gained, the founding fathers of the new nation, and even more so their posterity, found the definition of national goals much more complex and much more pragmatic.[1]

United Kingdom, the opening of Parliament (above)
(United Press International)

USSR, Lenin's tomb (below)
(Marian D. Irish)

Fundamental Goals

The Preamble to the Constitution of the United States succinctly states the fundamental goals of the first new nation:

> to form a more perfect union
> establish justice
> insure domestic tranquility
> provide for the common defense
> promote the general welfare
> secure the blessings of liberty.

These goals established in the eighteenth century remain the paramount goals of the United States. If we regard goals as operational concepts, then we are more concerned with policies, that is, with commitments and courses of action directed toward specific objectives. The current goals of the United States may still be verbalized exactly as they were in 1787. But the specific objectives which the United States government pursues in the world today—the nature of its commitments and the courses of action which it takes both in domestic politics and in international politics—bear little resemblance to its policies and activities in the early years of the republic.

The United States Constitution, now the oldest written constitution in the world, has served as a prototype for many constitutions. In more recent constitutions, however, we perceive some significant differences in statements of fundamental goals. The Japanese Constitution illustrates a major shift in emphasis and perspective with its references to the outside world. Its Preamble firmly establishes the national goals of the Japanese people within the framework of "an international society striving for the preservation of peace" and it recognizes that "all peoples of the world have the right to live in peace, free from fear and want." The American revolutionary leaders expected that the new United States would assume a separate and equal station among the powers of the earth. The Japanese people who survived the holocaust of Hiroshima and Nagasaki were determined to seek for themselves and their posterity "the fruits of peaceful cooperation with all nations" as well as "the blessings of liberty throughout this land."

We have already noted the eagerness with which the new nations of the post-World-War-II period have sought membership in the United Nations. Membership in the United Nations is partly a matter of prestige and protocol, a symbol of sovereign equality. Most importantly, however, membership in the United Nations signifies that the new state is accepted as an integral component in the international system which recognizes the interdependence of peoples in the modern world.

Similarly a written constitution has come to be a symbol of respectability among modern states. It may not be the most reliable indicator of how the political system actually operates and functions (achieves its goals), and yet it does give us some insight into the ultimate goals of the people. Even in governments which are totalitarian and/or dictatorial, the constitution is expected to depict the popular ideal of government. Among modern governments the Stalinist regime in the USSR must rank among the most repressive and least democratic, and yet the Stalin Constitution of 1936, the basic law under which the USSR still professes to operate, expresses the principles of democratic government.

The Constitution of the USSR, especially Article 10, the Fundamental Rights and Duties of Citizens, also has served as a model for many recent constitutions. In scope and content it goes well beyond the legalistic provisions of the United States Bill of Rights. Citizens of the USSR have the right to guaranteed employment and payment for their work in accordance with the amount of work done and its quality; the right to rest and leisure; the right to maintenance in old age and in case of sickness or disability; the right to education. All citizens of the USSR, irrespective of nationality, race, or sex, have legal equality in all spheres of economics, government, and other public activity. In conformity with the interests of the working people, and in order to strengthen the socialist system, citizens of the USSR are also guaranteed the traditional liberties, freedom of speech, press, and assembly. Further, they are guaranteed inviolability of their persons, their homes, and their correspondence. To anyone familiar with the brutal record of the Stalinist dictatorship—acknowledged to be so by the Communist leadership after Stalin's death [2]—these constitutional guarantees appear utterly meaningless. Yet the fact remains that even Stalin thought it politic at least to express the aspirations of the Russian people to live in a democratic society. Breaches in the constitutional law could always be justified as action taken by the government in conformity with the interests of the working people and to strengthen the socialist system.

The Constitution of the United States mentions the general welfare in the Preamble statement of goals and once again in connection with the taxing power of Congress, but nowhere does it spell out what general welfare really means. People embarking upon statehood in the twentieth century, understandably, find the United States model inadequate with respect to the social and economic aspects of the modern state. Because the Russian Constitution seems more attuned to rising expectations, the provisions of Article 10, with various modifications, have been incorporated into the fundamental law of many recent constitutions. For example, Chapter 3 of the Japanese Constitution contains forty articles on "the rights and duties of the people." Among these are:

> *Article 14: All of the people are equal under the law and there shall be no discrimination in political, economic, or social relations because of race, creed, sex, social status, or family origin.*
>
> *Article 25: All people shall have the right to maintain the minimum standards of wholesome and cultured living. In all spheres of life, the State shall use its endeavors for the promotion and extension of social welfare and security, and of public health.*
>
> *Article 27: All people shall have the right and the obligation to work. Standards for wages, hours, rent, and other working conditions shall be fixed by law. Children shall not be exploited.*

The Basic Law for the Federal Republic of Germany, like the Japanese Constitution, reflects the Allied influence following unconditional surrender in 1945; but in both instances it is influence by persuasion as well as by coercion. The Preamble to the German Constitution, like the Japanese, states the determination of the people "to serve the peace of the world." In the case of Germany, the goal is to act as "an equal partner in a united Europe." Article 1 of the German Constitution defines the basic rights of the people; and again, as in the Japanese Constitution, in addition to enumerating the legal and political rights of individuals the German Basic Law details a variety of social and economic rights intended to insure the well-being of the people, including special protection for marriage and the family, and state supervision of the entire educational system. The German Constitution also places special emphasis on the right to membership (citizenship) in the state. No doubt, Article 16, according to which no one may be deprived of his German citizenship, is a direct reaction against the Hitler era, when hundreds of thousands of persons were stripped of their citizenship and then became open prey for destruction by the state. Moreover, Article 15 of the German Constitution explicitly provides that "for the purpose of socialization" the land, natural resources, and means of production may be transferred into public ownership or other forms of a publicly controlled economy, with compensation to the private owners.

A much broader perspective toward the world outside and the much more extensive demands for government planning and programming the general welfare which characterize today's new nations add new dimensions and different emphases to the goals proclaimed by the first new nation. But still people everywhere seek the blessings of liberty which so strongly motivated the Americans in the eighteenth century, and modern constitutions embody libertarian ideal—if not reality. Today's nation-builders realize that democracy—in the Western sense—may not be appropriate to the initial stages of development. Nevertheless, political modernization carries with it the expectation of representative government and individual freedom. Hence, constitutions which embody the highest goals of the people are bound to express democratic principles and libertarian ideology. Whether these ideals are activated is beside the point; they do set forth the nation's goals.

The Turkish Constitution of 1961 is a case in point. In 1960 a military coup overthrew the tutelary regime which Atatürk had established in the early 1920s to modernize the country. A Committee of National Unity headed by General Cemal Gürsel ruthlessly liquidated the Democratic party founded by Atatürk and which had been governing Turkey by increasingly authoritarian methods. Leaders of the Democratic party were publicly tried for disgraceful offenses; ex-Premier Adnan Menderes and ex-Foreign Minister Fatin Rüstu Zorlu were hanged. The former president and eleven others in top positions were condemned to life imprisonment, and hundreds more who had been prominent in the old regime were jailed. Having thus cleaned up Turkish political life, the Committee of National Unity proceeded to write a new constitution and to establish a new political system.

The Turkish Constitution of 1961 describes the Turkish Republic as "a nationalist, democratic, secular and social state based on human rights and law." Part 2 of the Constitution which elaborately delineates fundamental rights and duties provides that "a law can not violate the substance of a right or freedom even if it is for the benefit of public welfare, public morale, public order, social justice and national security." A lengthy statement of individual rights and liberties guarantees protection of private life, security of domicile, secrecy of the postal service, freedom of travel, rights of opinion and creed, freedom of conscience and religion, liberty of science and art, freedom of the press, rights of meeting and demonstrating, and also includes many specific provisions for fair judicial and penal procedures. The statement of social and economic rights and duties requires the state "to realize economic, social and cultural developments under democratic methods and to augment national saving, to direct the investments to the priorities necessitated by the public welfare, to make development plans for this purpose." A chapter on political rights and duties grants the franchise to all citizens; "elections are free and equal and are held by public vote by means of secret balloting"; and "political parties, either in power or in opposition, are the inalienable elements of democratic political life."

The Turkish Constitution of 1961 was submitted to popular referendum. The new version of Turkish democratic government opened with parliamentary elections in which the dissolved Democratic party was not permitted to participate. The people seem to have experienced some difficulty in transferring their old political loyalties and attitudes to the new dispensation. Since none of the authorized political parties obtained a majority vote, General Gürsel was inaugurated as president of a four-party coalition government. Later in this book, when we discuss how governments operate and what functions they perform, we shall return to the Turkish situation today and reexamine it in the light of the constitutional goals set in 1961.

Operational Goals

For every nation state the fundamental goals are much the same: independence and survival as a state; recognition of independence and sovereignty by other states; territorial integrity and national security; economic and social well-being for the people, meaning a modern standard of living; political stability, domestic tranquility, and individual liberties. All of these are perceived as ultimate goals—more or less—by every nation state in the modern world. More or less implies a variety of qualifying factors which transform ultimate goals into operational goals—goals with more immediate objectives that can reasonably be reached by specific policies—and these operational goals vary according to particular circumstances from state to state.

In every political system the government in power is expected to ascertain the national goals, rank them in accordance with national values and national interests, and then pursue those policies which appear most appropriate and feasible in reaching the goals. (Such expectations, of course, may be frustrated by irrational political behavior, but we shall discuss this point later.) National security is the prime goal of every state, but the perception of national security, and thus the policies geared to achieve it, differ widely among the states of the world, as our sample of twelve states attests. Paradoxically, the superpowers and the great powers in the world, the richest nations, the most modernized nations, appear to view the problem largely in military terms.

Table 4–1, with data compiled by the United States Arms Control and Disarmament Agency, provides us with some comparisons of military expenditures related to gross national product and also the number of persons and percentage of the population serving in the armed forces.

Four of our twelve states in 1966 allocated more than a billion dollars for military expenditures: the United States, the Soviet Union, the Federal Republic of Germany, and the United Kingdom, in that order. Note that three of them are nuclear powers. The United States expended approximately twice as much as its nearest competitor, the Soviet Union (Soviet expenditures are estimated by Western analysis and may be understated, however). The USSR has more persons in military service, but the USA runs a close second; on the other hand, the percentage of population in the armed forces is slightly higher in the USA than in the USSR. In total military expenditures, Israel is eighth among our twelve states, but it expends a higher percentage of its population in the armed forces than either of the superpowers. The ACDA lists the percentage of GNP which some 120 states expended for military purposes in 1966. The top 6 in rank order are: North Vietnam 20.1 percent; Laos 18.5 percent; South Vietnam 14.5 percent; Saudi Arabia 12.1 percent; the Republic of China 11.2 percent; and Israel 10.5 percent.[3] That Israel allocates more than 10 percent of its GNP for military expenditures and keeps a relatively high percentage of its population in uniform is not surprising.

TABLE 4–1
GNP, Military Expenditures, and Related Data 1966

	GNP Million $	*GNP Per Capita*	*% of GNP Military Expenditures*	*Armed Forces Thousands*	*% of Population in Armed Service*
USA*	747,600	3,696	8.5	3,094	1.6
USSR*	357,000	1,531	n.d.	3,165	1.4
Germany, FR	119,580	1,990	4.1	450	0.7
UK*	105,310	1,924	5.8	424	0.8
Mexico	21,770	493	0.8	62	0.1
Turkey	9,420	295	4.7	440	1.4
India	36.895	74	3.8	1,000	0.2
Israel	3,822	1,454	10.5	71	2.7
Japan	97,480	986	1.0	246	0.2
Colombia	5,457	293	1.7	220	0.3
Ivory Coast	1,020	260	1.3	4	0.1
Kenya	1,114	116	1.1	3	0.1

n.d. = no data.
* nuclear powers
SOURCE: USACDA, *World Military Expenditures, 1966–67* (Washington, D.C.: Government Printing Office, 1968), table 1.

Israel is fighting for its very existence as a homeland for the Jews, surrounded by hostile and belligerent Arab countries whose land area, population size, and natural resources are overwhelmingly greater than the Israeli Republic. What Israel counts on is her own fighting spirit—and a great deal of outside diplomatic, economic, and, of course, military assistance.

Tabulations do not always tell us about the qualifying factors that enter into specific allocations. Table 4–1 indicates that India with the lowest GNP per capita among our twelve states keeps a million men under arms (only 0.2 percent of its population) and expends 3.8 percent of its GNP for military purposes. Like many new states in the world India still feels relatively insecure in the world and makes survival its prime concern. The government is determined to maintain India's territorial supremacy and territorial integrity (as evidenced in 1971). But territorial supremacy is challenged from within by numerous subnational loyalties and linguistic groups; and it is also confounded outside by Pakistan which covets Kashmir, and by that huge and potentially rapacious neighbor to the north, the People's Republic of China. The ACDA estimates that Mainland China expends 8.1 percent of its GNP on military purposes, has 2.5 million men under arms (0.3 percent of its population), and is the only non-Western state to have nuclear military power. Similarly, Turkey, with a relatively low GNP, allocates a relatively high percentage to the military and keeps nearly half a million men in the armed services. Like India, Turkey has an overpowering neighbor to the north, and historically the USSR has maintained a predatory attitude toward the Bosporus. India, fearful of getting caught up in the politics of the superpowers, has posited her national security policies upon nonalignment, whereas Turkey has found it both militarily strategic and economically profitable to join the NATO powers in opposition to the USSR and its Warsaw Pact partners.

For Japan national security presents a special problem. Unlike any other major power, Japan has no normal security arrangements. Under the MacArthur Constitution, the Japanese may not rearm nor make war an instrument of national policy. Hence, among our twelve states, the Japanese, with a relatively high GNP, allocate proportionately less of it to military expenditures than even Kenya or the Ivory Coast. The Japanese, however, have managed to turn a negative policy toward war into a positive policy toward peace. In terms of survival and economic development they consider favorable trade relations of paramount national importance. The man-on-the-street in Tokyo is more likely to be knowledgeable about the monthly balance of payments than any other aspect of national policy.

The United States Arms Control and Disarmament Agency reports that the relative rise in military expenditures from 1964 was more rapid than the growth of world GNP. Military expenditures per capita for the world at large rose 16 percent while the GNP per capita increased only 9 percent. These figures present an ominous prognosis for peaceful international relations. But more significant to our study of comparative politics is the striking differential between industrialized and less-developed countries. The ratio of military expenditures to GNP in the developed countries averaged about 8 percent compared to 4 percent in the less developed countries. The ACDA sums up the overall picture:

By 1966 the 27 developed countries in this survey, representing 29 per cent of the world's population, had 83 per cent of its product and spent 89 per cent of world military expenditures. . . . The 93 less developed countries with 72 per cent of the population had only 17 per cent of the world GNP, and spent 11 per cent of world military expenditures.[4]

Public expenditures give us some idea of the dominant values within the various political systems. Unfortunately, the statistics on nonmilitary expenditures on a country-by-country basis are not as current as the military figures. If, however, we take the ACDA statistics, we can roughly estimate the public allocations of the GNP for military, education, and health expenditures. In the case of military expenditures, of course, the public allocations are the only allocations. In countries like the United States, however, we must keep in mind that private allocations out of the GNP may considerably augment the public allocations for both education and health expenditures. Table 4–2 shows us no more than the public priorities with respect to military, education, and health expenditures.

When we look at the figures in Table 4–2 we are awestruck by the enormous differential in productivity between the United States at the top of the list and the Ivory Coast at the bottom, or for that matter, between the United States and any other country on the list. The GNP determines the ultimate limits of public expenditures; it is the political system, however, that determines the priorities within the public sector. And, of course, it is the political system that determines what part of the GNP is produced and consumed in

TABLE 4–2
*GNP and Ratio of Public Expenditures 1965–66 **

	GNP Million $	*$ Per Capita*	*Military Expenditures Million $*	*% of GNP*	*Public Education Million $*	*% of GNP*	*Public Health Million $*	*% of GNP*
USA	747,600	3,696	63,283	8.5	34,308	4.5	12,188	1.6
USSR	357,000	1,531	47,000	n.d.	30,600	8.6	21,000	5.9
Germany, FR	119,580	1,990	4,950	4.1	3,832	3.2	1,547	1.3
UK	105,310	1,924	6,150	5.8	5,094	4.8	2,820	2.7
Japan	97,480	986	933	1.0	4,111	4.2	138	1.4
India	36,895	74	1,400	3.8	1,002	2.7	161	0.4
Mexico	21,770	493	166	0.8	365	1.7	240	1.1
Turkey	9,420	295	445	4.7	331	3.5	108	1.1
Colombia	5,457	293	92	1.7	120	2.2	39	0.7
Israel	3,822	1,454	400	10.5	169	4.4	36	0.9
Kenya	1,114	116	12	1.1	35	3.1	19	1.7
Ivory Coast	1,020	260	13	1.3	14	1.4	7	0.7

n.d. = no data.

* The data are based on latest available statistics, some 1965, some 1966. See *Source* for complete reference.

SOURCE: USACDA, *World Military Expenditures, 1966–67* (Washington, D.C.: Government Printing Office, 1968), table 1.

the public sector, what part is allocated for private production and consumption. We shall have more to say later about this overall allocation. But note at this point that in our twelve countries, eight of them choose to spend more on public health and education than on the military sector: the USSR, Germany, the United Kingdom, Japan, Mexico, Colombia, Kenya, and the Ivory Coast.

Table 4–3 shows how the ranking of the states changes when we employ different physical, strategic, economic, and social indicators. In Table 4–3 we begin to see distinct country-by-country profiles emerging from the comparative data. India, the most populous state, ranks sixth in productivity, twelfth in GNP per capita, seventh in ratio of military expenditures, eighth in percentage of population in the armed forces, and ninth in ratio of expenditures for public health and education. Israel, the least populous state, ranks tenth in productivity, fifth in GNP per capita, but first in ratio of military expenditures and first in percentage of population in the armed forces. The United States comes out first in productivity, first in GNP per capita, second in percentage of GNP for military expenditures, second in percentage of the population in the armed forces (and this before maximum involvement in Vietnam), but third in percentage of expenditures for public health and education.

NATIONAL INTERESTS

In a broad sense, the national interests are whatever the government considers essential, desirable, and feasible to meet the expectations and demands of the people. Presumably the operational goals of the state are geared to the funda-

TABLE 4–3
Comparative Ranking of Twelve States, 1966

Rank	Population Size	GNP	GNP Per Capita	% of GNP Military Expend.	% of GNP Population Armed Forces	% of GNP Public Health Education
1	India	USA	USA	Israel	Israel	USSR
2	USSR	USSR	Ger., FR	USA	USA	UK
3	USA	Ger., FR	UK	USSR	USSR	USA
4	Japan	UK	USSR	UK	Turkey	Israel
5	Ger., FR	Japan	Israel	Turkey	UK	Kenya
6	UK	India	Japan	Ger., FR	Ger., FR	Ger., FR
7	Mexico	Mexico	Mexico	India	Colombia	Japan
8	Turkey	Turkey	Turkey	Colombia	India	Turkey
9	Colombia	Colombia	Colombia	Ivory Coast	Japan	India
10	Kenya	Israel	Ivory Coast	Japan	Mexico	Colombia
11	Ivory Coast	Kenya	Kenya	Kenya	Ivory Coast	Mexico
12	Israel	Ivory Coast	India	Mexico	Kenya	Ivory Coast

SOURCE: USACDA *World Military Expenditures, 1966–67* (Washington, D.C.: Government Printing Office, 1968), table 1.

mental goals and basic values of the nation as a whole. But when we look at political systems in action we perceive that in the making of policy only some of the people are in authority and these assume sole responsibility for determining which goals take precedence and how the nation's resources will be mobilized and allocated to reach specific objectives. The distribution of power and influence between the governors (those who govern) and the governed may vary greatly according to the patterns of political organization and the nature of the policy process. But in every political system it is the current ruling elite in the society which defines the national interests and decides who gets what in the form of rewards or penalties attached to particular policies. (The ruling elite refers to the relatively few people in any society who because of family, class, economic status, profession, and ability, are influential and powerful in the politics and/or government of their country. We shall expand on the concept of ruling elites in the chapter that follows.)

In an ideal political system the people communicate to their official policy-makers what they expect the government to do for them. The demands of the people may be channeled to the government through influential individuals, by special interest groups, or by political parties. The political decision-makers consider the many different demands, calculate the various degrees of support for themselves and their policies, and respond with what they decide are appropriate public policies. To the extent that these policies please the people or are accepted at least by a majority of them, the government can expect allegiance, obedience, and compliance from the general citizenry.

In the operating political system, however, the people appear to the decision-makers in a kaleidoscope of ever-changing patterns. For example, in the United States, whether we the people are active, attentive, aggressive, apathetic, or alienated depends on the issue at stake. Each issue has its own public: air pollution, the fat content of hot dogs, provisions for medicare, oil depletion allowances, defense contracts, selective service policies—each has a different set of concerned advocates and opponents. Perhaps the most widely touted national policy of the United States in the past decade was to land a man and plant an American flag on the moon. Those in power deemed this an important ploy in international relations, warranting the expenditure of billions of dollars from the national treasury. The ploy paid off in a dramatic upsurge in American prestige in the world, and it also brought substantial rewards to the military, scientific, and industrial elites within the country. On the other hand, many Americans with less influence felt that the national interest would have been served more effectively had the budgets of the 1960s given higher priorities and greater allocations of resources to modernizing the inner cities, developing rapid mass transit in the metropolitan areas, and helping poor people reach a decent standard of living. Governmental decision-makers, however, respond to public demands according to their own perceptions of the national interest, their own special interests, their professional assessment of the intensity of public opinions, their party preferences, and, of course, the wishes of influential constituents.

Dominant Interests versus the National Interest

In the twelve countries which we are examining we find everywhere that the ruling elites tend to equate the continuance of their own power and authority in the political system with the advancement of the national interest. What is good for the governors is good for the governed! We could use many examples, but for the sake of brevity two will suffice on the point: Israel and the USSR.

In Israel the settlers of the Yishuv still dominate the political system. The Yishuv is the period of settlement between the 1880s and 1948. The first wave of immigrants came mostly from Eastern Europe, young idealists from Russia and Poland. The second wave brought more intellectuals, many of them trade union socialists, from the United States and Western Europe. These early settlers whose ultimate goal was the establishment of an autonomous Jewish homeland were for the most part committed to an ideology of collective enterprise and equal distribution. The prime virtues of the Yishuv were self-sacrifice and communal effort; its heroes were those who fought the Arabs and the British in defense of the settlers and those who worked most zealously in the agricultural communes, the kibbutzim. Today the *Knesset* (the national parliament) is an assembly of notables, veterans of the Yishuv; once young pioneers, they now hold political power on the basis of seniority and long service in the parties.[5]

But great changes have been taking place within Israel since it achieved independence. It is one thing to aspire to utopia and quite another thing to meet pressing issues with specific policies. The Israeli government has had to make decisions regarding immigration, resource allocation, welfare programs, and defense activities. Since 1948 a new wave of immigrants, most of them fleeing from increased harassment of Jews in the Arab countries, is much less motivated by ideology than the Yishuv settlers. Moreover, the *sabras* (an Arabic word for a tough cactus native to the area), a generation of Jews born in Palestine and Israel, are much more nationalistic and much less Zionistic than their parents. Now that the Jewish homeland is established, these indigenous Israelis have different ideas about how to develop a modern nation. And there is increasing tension between those who cherish the socialist ideology and religious motivations of the past and those who prefer more opportunistic and secular approaches to the present.

The Yishuv had put its trust in collective agriculture; today's modernists are demanding more urbanization and industrialization, with encouragement of free enterprise. The old notion of equalitarianism is challenged on practical grounds: teachers, doctors, engineers, and skilled workers expect higher income and higher status. New economic groups are forming which value skills, productivity, efficiency, and profits. It is only a matter of time before the politics of bargaining replace the politics of ideology in the political parties and then in the Knesset. Veterans of the Yishuv who moved into positions of power when the new state was established are now on the way out. This is the fate of all founding fathers. The politics of a dynamic political system are inexorable; aging and obsolescent elites are replaced; new and more progressive elites are recruited to steer the policy machinery.

In the USSR the main problem of the Communist leadership today is how to stay at the center of control. At a time when the USSR has become a modern industrial state, indeed a superpower, the leadership of the Communist party is aging, and its governing mechanism appears to be even counterproductive. So far, however, the ruling elite has solved the problem of succession to authority in a Mafia style. The Politburo, the secret police, and the army still retain overriding power. The collective leadership in the government and in the party which aims at a balance of interests within the country is perceptibly tipping to the right of center. Nobody represents the farmers and workers per se; these are recognized as claimants for national resources, but the Kremlin still gives its top priorities to the military and heavy industry.

For more than fifty years, the men with full authority in the Kremlin have held that industrialization, along with military power, is the prime national interest of the socialist state. In the early years when most Russians were peasants, the policy of industrialization had to be imposed by force, with extreme cruelty, and against the general will. The forced industrialization of the economy was largely at the expense of the farmers. The Soviet government ruthlessly depleted the agricultural assets; negative incentives—punishments rather than rewards—were meted out to the peasants especially during the Stalin regime. Following Stalin's death the new Soviet leadership attempted to reorganize the agricultural system, to modernize production methods, train more skilled agronomists, and raise the level of living in the rural areas. Even so, as one authority notes, "in many respects agriculture represents the least developed sector of the Soviet economy." [6] Recent efforts to unionize farm workers may well constitute the first successful stratagem to confront the establishment in the Ministry of Agriculture.

The time bomb in the present Soviet system, however, is more likely to be the multiethnic composition of the peoples of the USSR. The Communist elite who have been in power since the 1917 Revolution are mostly Slavs (one of the most notable exceptions was Stalin, a Georgian), and, as might be expected, most of the modernization and development has taken place in the Slavic sector of the nation. For some time, however, people in the rural areas of central Asia, non-Slavs most of them, have, as one observer crudely puts it, "been breeding like rabbits." The Slavs still hold nearly all the key positions in the political system but, if and when the population becomes predominantly non-Slavic, the democratic centralism which has served to keep the Slavic elite in power may well be fragmented by this population explosion among the now peripheral non-Slavic elements in the system.

A ruling elite is generally in a position to impose and perpetuate its ideology upon the political system. Obviously it is in the interest of the Communist party leadership in the USSR to maintain the Marxist doctrines of class struggle and world revolution. Ironically, the entrenchment of Communist leaders in the upper rungs of the hierarchy has tended to bring about new class struggles within the Soviet system. In the USSR today class depends largely upon position and status within the political structure. Thus government and party officials enjoy many advantages because of their positions: better housing, cars, chauffeurs, access to vacation resorts and rest homes, the right to travel abroad, air transport, etc. Moreover, the offspring of this new privileged class begin to inherit certain advantages, e.g., entrance into the better schools and more cultural opportunities. Despite the official ideology of egalitarianism, the emerging class system in the USSR is producing sharp economic and social differences between the ruling elite and the general citizenry, differences which are bound to nourish envy and discontent among the lesser privileged.

Plural Interests versus the Dominant Interests

In all developing countries wherein the ruling elite makes it a policy to educate the people and to employ education as a technique of social control, tutelary democracy tends to be hoist by its own petard. Tutelary democracy refers to a dictatorship which holds out the promise of representative government as soon as the general citizenry have learned how to participate in the political life of the community—the process which political scientists call "political socialization." But as a people become literate and educated, they become increasingly aware of the world outside. They learn to communicate more effectively among themselves and to project their demands more forcefully upon the government. It is not merely coincidental that the politics of alienation and rejection flourish among student groups and in intellectual circles the world over. When people are educated to the advantages of participatory democracy, they are also prepared to throw out their professors of tutelary democracy.

We have already noted the role of education in the political socialization of a people. In the USSR the Communist regime transformed an overwhelmingly illiterate population into an almost universally literate one. The Soviet educational system turned a tradition-oriented, peasant-minded people into a highly industrialized and urbanized society. It educated scientists and technologists as well as a dynamic managerial class and "in the process won admiration and prestige for the regime abroad and support for the regime at home."[7] It was also instrumental in training ideologically committed and politically active young people who were prepared to regenerate the political system. But it never wholly succeeded in producing a monolithic or totally homogeneous culture.

The output of a political system is always conditioned by the economic and social environment, perhaps even more than by the political process itself. In the USSR the multiethnic character of the population made virtually impossible the mass production of a model new Soviet man. Moreover, the social engineers in the Soviet system discovered that the more authoritative and rigid the instruction for the purposes of influencing political attitudes, the more indifferent the students became. In the Stalinist era, terrorism and education were linked together as complementary techniques of coercion and persuasion to insure both negative and positive support for the Communist regime. When terrorism was deemphasized by Stalin's successors, educational reforms were introduced to secure more activist and imaginative responses from the students. But the dilemma is inescapable; when education is designed for more creative thinking, the resulting intellectual independence becomes a political boomerang. Participatory democracy is a familiar slogan among university students everywhere—Tokyo, Paris, Berlin, Abidjan, Mexico City, and Washington, D.C.

That the ruling elite identifies the national interests generally with its own ideology and its own special interests appears to be a common phenomenon in all political systems. No nation is homogeneous, however, because in every country we find people with competing and/or conflicting interests; the prevailing definitions of national interest may be the source of dissatisfaction ranging from malaise to rejection. In Turkey, for example, the ruling elite—whether in the Justice party which succeeded Menderes's Democratic party after the military coup of 1960 or in the Republican People's party founded by Atatürk and in power from 1923 to 1950—regards modernization as the primary national interest of Turkey today. The Justice party won a full majority in the parliamentary elections of 1969 under the leadership of Suleyman Demirel, described as "a husky, balding engineer-administrator . . . a modern, pragmatic executive and organizer." [8] The description is particularly apt for it depicts a modern politician with technical know-how in contradistinction to the father image of Atatürk and the autocratic pasha, Ismet Inonu. The Justice party claims to be broadly based, attracting small landholder peasants and wealthy farmers as well as businessmen, labor groups, and commercial interests in the cities. The Republican party, now the major opposition party, comprises the military officers, bureaucrats, city intellectuals, and large landowners who played the dominant role in Atatürk's tutelary democracy. Despite the fact that both parties together scored about 89 percent in the 1969 parliamentary election, there are still many Turks, especially in the rural areas, who feel strongly that the national interest would be much better served if the state were to liquidate its European veneer and return to the pristine purity of Islam.

Similarly in Mexico, politics operate through a single official political party, the Revolutionary party (PRI) that dates back to 1929. The PRI embraces a wide spectrum of interests, but it focuses on development as the national interest. Most Mexicans are caught up in the development process and believe that they are all working together for a more prosperous and democratic future. The dominant elite within the PRI has determined that it is in the national interest for the country to move as quickly as possible from a primary-production economy based on agriculture and mining to a more balanced economy. It has promoted public investment in roads, irrigation projects, electrification, railroads, and communications, thus building an infrastructure (economic, social, and political base) capable of supporting a broad range of industrial activities.[9] More than half of the working population is engaged in agriculture and lives in rural communities with an annual per-capita income of about $125 compared to approximately $650 for the average urban dweller. It is understandable that Mexican peasants may not be so enthusiastic about industrial development, which seems to be largely at the expense of rural development; peasant leaders play only a minor role in the politics of the PRI.

The Ivory Coast also operates through a one-party system, with one man at the controls—the old man, Felix Houphouet-Boigny. At a time when most African leaders were enthusiastically promoting immediate political independence, Houphouet-Boigny was still plugging for a Franco-African community and urging his countrymen to reject the narrow concept of nationalism.[10] To his way of thinking, a people ought not to seek statehood until they have developed an economic base that will insure them a decent standard of living. When it became clear to him, however, that the Ivory Coast people more than anything wanted their independence like all other Africans, he reversed his position. Retaining the dominant role in the new state, Houphouet-Boigny nevertheless returned to his original hypothesis of nation-building, that economic development is the most important prerequisite. Thus he skillfully practices the politics of reconciliation using the party machinery as a modernizing device to bring about what he considers the national interest. The task has been complicated by many diverse elements: some sixty differing tribal groups, a few wealthy planters, many small farmers, native workers, cheap migratory labor, businessmen, restive labor unions, missionaries and priests, government bureaucrats leftover from French colonialism, newly imported technicians, rebellious students, Africans and non-Africans. Whether the overall response to all the different demands and varying supports among the citizenry constitute the national interest is, of course, a matter of perspective. From the point of view of the commercial and business interests Houphouet-Boigny's regime has been most rewarding. Abidjan, the capital, is an impressive modern city with high buildings and the usual urban amenities, including hospitals, primary and secondary schools, and a university. Urban workers in the Abidjan area are among the most highly paid in the African states. The per-capita level of income in 1965 was $1,100, although if one subtracted the non-African income from the total, then the African level of income even around Abidjan dropped to $850. But 85 percent of the population live in the rural areas where incomes are mainly measured by levels of subsistence rather than in currency.

Theoretically the national interest is a composite or aggregate interest which those in authority and official position are expected to project into national policies. We have observed, however, that the ruling elite is rarely a disinterested party in policy-making, that it tends to identify the national interests with its own interests, and to hold onto its position of power in order to perpetuate this identification. We have also observed that every nation is more or less pluralistic with various groups making claims for special consideration or demanding specific rewards in the policy process. Moreover, the distribution of influence among the people at large, even in the most democratic or the most dictatorial system, is continuously shifting and always uneven. Thus those who attain—and then want to retain—positions of power in the political system, and all the privileges and perquisites that go with such positions, must be constantly alert and responsive to changes in the social environment. The ruling elite get to decide who gets what only so long as its decisions are accepted as legitimate. In the chapter that immediately follows we shall observe how political elites rise and fall as the bases of influence shift within the nation and also in international relations.

NOTES

1. Of course, not all states are of revolutionary origin and therefore do not have preset goals formulated by founding fathers. Among our twelve states, the United Kingdom, Germany, and Japan developed national goals through the centuries of their existence as states.
2. The de-Stalinization campaign was launched at the Twentieth Party Congress in 1956. At the close of the congress Nikita Khrushchev delivered a sensational indictment of Stalinism. The disclosures included massive details—the murder of thousands of innocent citizens during the great purge, the liquidation of high-ranking officers in the Red Army on the basis of slanderous and unproved charges, Stalin's failure to protect the USSR against the Nazi invasion, the mass deportation of nationality groups whose loyalties he questioned, etc. The attack was designed to destroy the cult of personality which had developed under Stalin's dictatorship; it may also have been offered as a promise of more respect for human dignity and individual rights under Khrushchev's leadership. Certainly it did enhance Khrushchev's image at home and abroad—and, as a matter of fact, although Khrushchev's government continued to be authoritarian, it was not based on terrorism and was much more aware of basic human rights. See Merle Fainsod, *How Russia Is Ruled,* rev. ed. (Cambridge, Mass.: Harvard University Press, 1963), especially chap. 11, "Constitutional Myths and Political Realities."
3. US Arms Control and Disarmament Agency, *World Military Expenditures, 1966–67* (Washington, D.C.: Government Printing Office, 1968), research report 68–52.
4. Ibid., p. 4.
5. For amplification of this discussion and for additional insights into the interaction of the ruling elite with the old and the new pluralism of Israel see Lester A. Seligman, *Leadership in a New Nation: Political Development in Israel* (New York: Atherton Press, 1964).
6. Merle Fainsod, op. cit., chap. 16, "Controls and Tensions in Soviet Agriculture," p. 575.
7. James S. Coleman, ed., *Education and Political Development* (Princeton, N.J.: Princeton University Press, 1965); see Jeremy R. Azrael, "Soviet Union," on p. 247. The entire essay is relevant to our discussion of the educational system as an agency of political socialization within the USSR. See also in the same volume Herbert Passin's essay on Japan and the introductions to each section by the editor.
8. W. B. Sherwood, "The Rise of the Justice Party in Turkey," *World Politics* 30 (October, 1967): 54–64. See also Frederick W. Frey, *The Turkish Political Elite* (Cambridge, Mass.: MIT Press, 1965), an empirical and quantitative study of the Turkish elite in the tutelary stage of its political development. The study was completed before the military coup of 1960 and the subsequent installation of parliamentary democracy.
9. United States Department of Commerce, Bureau of International Commerce, Overseas Business Reports, *Basic Data on the Economy of Mexico* (August, 1967). See also Robert E. Scott, *Mexican Government in Transition* (Urbana, Ill.: University of Illinois Press, 1959).
10. Aristide R. Zolberg provides useful background material in *One Party Government in the Ivory Coast,* rev. ed. (Princeton, N.J.: Princeton University Press, 1969).

FURTHER READING

APTER, DAVID E. *The Politics of Modernization.* Chicago: University of Chicago Press, 1965.

DIETZE, GOTTFRIED, ed. *Essays on the American Constitution.* Englewood Cliffs, N.J.: Prentice-Hall, 1964.

GOVERNMENT OF INDIA. *India: A Reference Annual, 1969.* New Delhi: Publications Division, Ministry of Information and Broadcasting, 1969.

REPUBLIC OF TURKEY, PRIME MINISTRY STATE PLANNING ORGANIZATION. *Second Five-Year Development Plan, 1968–1972.* Ankara: Central Bank of the Republic of Turkey, 1969.

chapter 5

WHO ARE THE RULING ELITES IN THE POLITICAL SYSTEM?

The first step in understanding how any government actually works is to identify its ruling elite. The ruling elite in any country may be said to comprise 1) those persons in the political system who have significant decision-making authority; 2) leading persons in the opposition who may be expected to gain legitimate power in the future or who are currently able to influence policy-making in a negative way; and 3) persons who have held positions of authority in the system, who retain an active interest in politics, and who remain influential in any current policy-making. In the broadest sense the ruling elite includes the social strata from which most persons are recruited for political leadership.

TRADITIONAL ELITES

Traditionally, the ruling elite comes from certain functional classes in the society: the military—the warriors on whom the people count for national security; the church—the priests to whom the people look for moral guidelines, rules of ethical conduct, and spiritual comfort; and the landlords—men who possess the arable lands which constitute the basic means of subsistence for the community. When a traditional society modernizes, we can expect new ruling elites to emerge representing new economic classes in the political

Colombia, religious procession
(Sergio Larrain : Magnum)

system: industrial entrepreneurs, financiers, managerial bureaucrats, scientists and technologists.

The Military

In our discussion of operational goals, we provided some data comparing allocations of national resources for national security. Understandably, civilian rulers depend to a very considerable degree upon the professional expertise of the military in determining what is necessary to maintain territorial integrity against external aggression and to make the nation strong enough to win any prospective war with any potential enemy. In the era of total war and nuclear weaponry, when decision-making in matters of national security may be absolutely crucial, not only to the survival of the nation but also to all mankind, civilian leaders, confounded and frustrated by their own ignorance, are inclined to pass the buck finally to the military. Warriors—from medieval knights in armor and yeomen with crossbows to strategic bombers and experts in biochemical warfare—are expected to have special training, insight, and technical know-how, and to advise accordingly.

In the modern state the military can never really be apolitical since their profession—i.e., their means of livelihood as well as their status in society—depends on their role (how they are expected to perform) and functions (how they meet expectations of performance) within the political

USA, Joint Chiefs of Staff
(United Press International)

system. The military comprise the armed services of the state and as such they must maintain continuous working relationships with the political decision-makers. In all states, but especially among the great powers, the principal activities of the military are related to external defense, providing for and directing combatant forces against all enemies. Such activities include determining what weapons systems are suitable, producible, and most likely to be reliable in deterring the enemy or in retaliation against enemy attacks. The armed forces may also be employed to maintain internal security, to quell riots and insurrections, to maintain law and order, and in general to give support to the regime in power. Paradoxically, the armed forces are also not infrequently employed in the politics of alienation and revolution; revolutionary coups are familiar and recurrent phenomena in the rejection of one system and the installation of another. The armed forces may be mobilized for civil actions, infrastructure development, improving rivers, harbors, and waterways for navigation, making maps, building highways, ditches, drains, and dams.

The military perform these several functions within all twelve states that we are studying; but the roles they play within the respective ruling elites vary greatly. The allocation of economic resources for military expenditures is a strong indicator of the influence of the military in the political system. Looking back at Table 4–1, we find, for example, that the military slice of the public financial pie is negligible in the Ivory Coast or Kenya.

Israel, at a business convention in Jerusalem
(Leonard Freed : Magnum)

But at the other end of the scale in the two superpowers, the United States and the USSR, the military have persuaded the political decision-makers to jack up the public expenditures for national security and sophisticated weaponry literally to astronomical levels. On the other hand, the United Kingdom, also in the nuclear club, whose political leaders pride themselves on being educated generalists rather than trained specialists, have not been nearly as susceptible to the demands of the military technologists.

The military have always played an important, and sometimes dominant role, in the United States. General George Washington, commander in chief of the revolutionary armed forces, presided over the Constitutional Convention of 1787 and was unanimously elected first president of the new republic. Indeed, the United States appears to have been conceived as a fighting organization, with nearly half the powers granted to the national government relating directly to problems of defense and the conduct of war. The president is named commander in chief, and in that role he has five times requested the Congress to declare war—in 1812, 1848, 1898, 1917, and 1941; he has twice recognized a state of war—in 1861 and in 1950; and he has on his own entered into and carried on a major war in Vietnam since 1965. All in all quite a belligerent record for a peace-loving nation. The constitutional office of president is civilian in concept, but surely it is more than happenstance that ten of the thirty-seven American presidents have been army generals, and that still others have had military experience at lesser rank. Harry Tru-

USSR, professor at Moscow University
(Marc Riboud : Magnum)

man, for example, was a field artillery captain in World War I, an experience which certainly colored his presidency. "My whole political career," he was later to claim, "is based on my war service and war associates." [1] The reorganization of the whole national security policy machinery in the Truman administration and its enormous impact upon subsequent policy-making in the American political system heavily underscores Mr. Truman's own perception.

The epic debate in Congress over the controversial Safeguard Antiballistic System during the summer of 1969—the longest debate on any military authorization since World War II—attests to the power of the Pentagon, not only over national security policy, but also over the entire economy. President Nixon, acting on the advice of the military establishment—and also no doubt influenced by those industrial concerns which stood to gain rich rewards in the form of ABM contracts [2]—determined that the ABM System was necessary to provide a credible deterrent to any enemy considering a nuclear attack on the United States. Following the constitutional process, the president requested congressional authorization and appropriations for the ABM policy. Despite a great ground swell of protest in the public arena, skepticism widely expressed in the mass media, and strong opposition by congressional leaders of both major parties, when the chips were down, a majority of congressmen yielded to the request of the commander in chief. Whatever the order of priorities expressed in public policies within the con-

Ivory Coast, a judge at Abidjan Courthouse
(Marc & Evelyne Bernheim : Rapho Guillumette)

text of the Cold War, the advice of the military is regarded as crucial to the ultimate priority—survival.

The USSR is caught in the same Cold War squeeze. As long as the United States maintains a strongly belligerent posture toward the Communist world, and continues to develop its nuclear weaponry as to both strike and deterrent power, the USSR can be expected to demonstrate a similarly militaristic posture, all the way to Armageddon. But even were the two superpowers to reach a political détente ("relaxation of strained relations") and even if they came to agreement on arms control and disarmament, the military in the USSR still have extraordinary functions to perform. The USSR has the longest land boundary in the world, and along most of the length of that boundary lies the People's Republic of China, also a nuclear power with a clearly hostile attitude toward its rival in the Communist world (the hostility, however, antedates the present political systems, going back to imperial China and czarist Russia).

The role of the military in external defense varies according to time and circumstances and from state to state. Prior to their unconditional surrender in 1945, the military in imperial Japan and in the German Third Reich reached the zenith of power; but in both countries the military was so discredited in defeat that today its influence in Japan is negligible, and it is relatively minor in the Bonn Republic, although in the latter instance Germany's participation in NATO gives the military a wedge for reentry into the ruling elite. In India the military's role is strictly a professional assignment, defending the borders against sporadic Chinese or Pakistani incursions. Gandhi's policy of nonviolence and Nehru's policy of nonalignment, carried forward today, offer little encouragement to a military elite. The case of Israel is quite different. Since external security is Israel's most critical problem, the influence of the military is bound to be considerable. But the Israeli army is really a citizen army under citizen control, a small professional army backed up by a large reserve in which all adults are expected to serve. Table 4–1 shows that of all twelve states, Israel keeps the highest percentage of her population in the armed services and allocates the highest percentage of her GNP for military expenditures. But, for the most part, civilians rather than the military determine defensive (and offensive) policies.

In all twelve states the military is expected to support the regime and maintain domestic security. This function is particularly onerous in totalitarian systems where the ruling elite stay in power by frequent resort to force. The most obvious example is the USSR. As soon as the Bolsheviks entrenched themselves in the Kremlin in November, 1917, they began recruiting a volunteer Red Army. The sorry performance of this volunteer operation soon led Leon Trotsky, people's commissar for war, to remobilize a professional army. Despite protests on practical as well as doctrinal grounds, Trotsky recruited thousands of former czarist officers to act as skilled and trained commanders. To insure the loyalty of these old army officers, Trotsky decreed that if an officer betrayed the Red Army, his whole family would be punished.[3] This new Red Army, disciplined and loyal perforce, was used during the Civil War to beat back the Allied interventionists and to consolidate the Communist monopoly of power within the Soviet system.

In the tandem relationship between the military elite and a party dictatorship, the question is bound to arise: Who's steering whom? In the Soviet Union the Communist *apparatchik* ("the men of the party machine") have managed to keep the controls through periodic purges of the military command. In 1937, at the height of Stalin's government by terror, the execution of eight high-ranking Soviet generals for espionage and treason to the fatherland was followed by massive liquidation within the lower ranks. During World War II, as might be expected, the military played a dominant role in the government. After Stalin's death in 1953 when Beria, the head of the secret police, made use of his power to advance his position in the party, his rivals in the Presidium courted the military as a counteracting force. Whereupon, as Merle Fainsod observes, "the elimination of Beria and the downgrading of the security police inevitably increased the importance of the military on the Soviet political scene." [4] It is virtually impossible for an outsider to assess the current influence of the military elite within the Soviet Union. We indicated earlier that the now-aging leadership of the Communist party counts heavily on military support. Rumor has it that both the military and scientific establishments within the USSR (as in the United States) can get just about whatever they want from the political system.

Among our twelve states, Turkey most clearly illustrates the role of the military elite in the politics of alienation and rejection. The Young Turks associations which united in common cause against the despotic rule of Abdulhamid in 1908 recruited their membership from among young army officers and government officials. Their chief purpose was to force the sultan to abide by the Constitution of 1876; their main concern was the modernization of Turkey.[5] We have already noted that the establishment of the Turkish Republic in 1923 was in its beginning a military coup. Kemal Pasha, once a Young Turk, had acquired great prestige as the commander in chief in 1922 who forced the Greeks to evacuate Turkey. A grateful National Assembly conferred on him the title of *gazi* ("hero"). In 1935, as president of the Republic, Kemal chose to renounce his titles of *pasha* and *gazi*, and to designate himself Atatürk, "father Turk." [6] Certainly it is as Atatürk that we regard him as the founding father of modern Turkey, but it was in the role of gazi that he made the most of his opportunities to seize political power from the sultan. Ironically, again it was the reformist element in the Turkish army that brought to a close the autocratic regime established by Atatürk in the 1920s. A new military elite cleared out the old political elite, sponsored another attempt at constitutionalism, and proctored the subsequent parliamentary elections in 1961. Thereafter, the army remained ready to remove any political actors whose performance did not follow the new script. In 1971 Premier Demirel and his Justice party were ousted and replaced by an "above-party" government under military auspices.

The military elite acquire their influence in the political system, not only because they comprise the legitimate armed force of the regime but also because they usually come from the better-educated class in the society. This is especially true in nations still in transition from traditional to modern society. We noted above that the armed forces are frequently used for infrastructure development. The assignment has been especially effective in developing countries like Colombia, Mexico, Kenya, or Israel. It is generally a congenial assignment for young officers whose military education has infused their thinking with idealistic nationalism, whose training in the modern techniques of warfare has also, no doubt, brought them into contact with other aspects of modernization, and who being young are still likely to show an enthusiasm for progress. At any rate, when the rich and modern nations offer assistance to the poor and less-developed nations of the world, it is frequently the military elite who act as brokers in the transaction.

The Priests

Initially we planned to use "The Church" as the title for this section. Then we realized that the concept of the church stands for a clearly defined, institutionalized elite only in Western society, a concept nurtured in the Middle Ages by the Catholic Church. In non-Western and traditional societies, priests function as a religious elite, but not necessarily in a formal association comparable to the Western notion of a church. Thus, in Kenya or the Ivory Coast, the church would refer only to the Christian churches brought in by the missionaries or settlers during the colonial period. On the other hand, in the history of Mexico or Colombia, the church definitely has reference to the Roman Catholic Church whose priests accompanied the conquistadores, as much in search of saving the souls of the Indians as the conquistadores were in search of the treasures of the New World. The role of Judaism in Jewish history or Islam in Arabic history is more nearly comparable to that of Christianity in medieval Western Europe, a pervasive way of life conditioning the values of the whole society, transcending the institutional forms. In India, although Hinduism plays the role of a major religion, its organization and functions are so different from the church as a social institution in the West that any analogy is apt to be misleading.

The church as a ruling elite played a crucial role in the history of France, where until the Revolution the princes of the church represented one of the three estates that made up the ruling elite. In German history the church provided most of the cohesion of the Holy Roman Empire for centuries, when the Empire, according to the interpretations of St. Augustine and St. Thomas Aquinas, was the City of God on this earth. Later on, however, the tremendous influence of the clergy prevented the emergence of a unified German nation state. German particularism (political fragmentation) was as much the result of the influence of the religious elites as the political ones.

With the advent of the Reformation the church split into the Roman Catholic Church and many Protestant churches—some of the latter more oriented toward a formal and hierarchical organization (the Lutherans) than others (the Hussites, the Puritans). In England, during the reign of Henry VIII, the church became the Church of England, and the political and the religious elites merged when the monarch became the titular head of the church, just as the Holy Synod was used by Czar Peter the Great of Russia to forge unity among the temporal and spiritual elites in imperial Russia.

Japan was ruled for centuries by an elite that combined politics and institutionalized religion. Robert E. Ward refers to the "political militancy of national Shintoism before the war, with its systematic emphasis on the divine descent of the Emperor." [7] In tracing the origins of Shintoism, Robert

Karl Reischauer describes it as a theocracy going back into ancient Japanese history—although at a very early time competition was introduced by Buddhism and Confucianism. Reischauer's account of how the chieftain of one of the many clans reinforced his demand for absolute rule with his claim of the Great Sun Goddess as one of his ancestors [8] reminds us of the way in which the aspirants to the throne of the Holy Roman Empire linked their claims to the divine right to rule. Shintoism also is an example of how the ruling elites of traditional societies traced their origins to gods and goddesses. Despite the competition with Shintoism in Japan of Buddhism and Confucianism, the ruling elite, based on descent, i.e., blood relation, to the Sun Goddess, prevailed for thousands of years in Japan. The Allies utilized the prestige of the position of the emperor to legitimize the new constitution after World War II. Emperor Hirohito proclaimed the new constitution and renounced his divine role at the same time.

The divine sanction of earthly rulership had been part of the traditional investiture of ruling elites in the Western world for centuries. Coronation ceremonies usually included leading roles for the princes of the church—especially the coronation of emperors. Since Christianity made it impossible for the Western political elites to claim descendance from God, Western monarchs claimed legitimacy from the New Testament exhortation to "render therefore unto Caesar the things which are Caesar's." The unity of the spiritual and the temporal worlds which were the bequests of the medieval philosophers maintained a unity (at least to all outward appearances) between political and religious elites for centuries in the Western world. Coronation by the pope provided for European monarchs the same spiritual sanction and linkage with the religious elite as did the claim of a divine ancestor for the Japanese emperor or the princes of the ancient Incan, Mayan, or Aztec empires.

Napoleon Bonaparte shocked his contemporaries when he not only placed the French imperial crown on his own head, but also proceeded to crown his wife. When William of Prussia became emperor of Germany in 1871, the "*Good Housekeeping* seal of approval" by the princes of the church was no longer deemed necessary.

Much of the history of the United States of America is bound very closely to religion. However, in the United States, despite the European origins of most of the people, we cannot speak of "the church." The history of the New England colonies abounds with references to the Puritans; the Puritan ethic is often referred to in explaining many American traditions and habits. But Maryland was founded as a Roman Catholic colony, Pennsylvania as a refuge for Quakers and all dissenters, and the Anglican Church was established in New York and Virginia. Today the United States has more religious denominations and groups than any other of our twelve examples. These range all the way from the Roman Catholic Church to Zen Buddhism, the Baha'i faith, and the Vedanta Societies. There are more Protestant sects than any other type of religious groups, and all the Protestant churches put together have much the largest membership.[9]

Since many of the early settlers came to the British colonies in North America in order to escape a system in which the political and religious elites were closely joined and because many of these had suffered persecution in their native lands because of their religion, the establishment of a national church found little favor in the new republic. The Constitution of 1787 as it was presented to the state conventions for ratification did not provide for, but neither did it prohibit, the establishment of an official religion. This was considered a weakness in the document, and in a number of states ratification was made contingent upon the addition of a Bill of Rights that would specifically guarantee freedom of religion and specifically forbid a religious establishment. The original proposal leading to the First Amendment, introduced by James Madison in the first Congress read: "The civil rights of none shall be abridged on account of religious belief or worship, nor shall any religion be established, nor shall the full and equal rights of conscience be in any manner, or on any pretence, infringed." In the federal union, however, this turned out to be a more sweeping restriction than some states were prepared to accept. At that time some states did have established religions, notably in New England where the Congregationalists were predominant. Hence the First Amendment now states, "Congress shall make no law respecting an establishment of religion, or prohibiting the free exercise thereof." In a letter written to a group of Baptists in New England (1802), President Jefferson declared that it was the purpose of the new amendment to build "a wall of separation between Church and State," and this explanation has become firmly fixed in American constitutional law.[10]

During much of Western history the church was an establishment, an institution reaching back into the early Middle Ages, and the clergy constituted an intricate ruling elite. The hierarchy of the Roman Catholic Church, headed by its princes and resting solidly on the activities of hundreds of thousands of parish priests has its modern institutional counterpart in the administrative hierarchy of a twentieth-century corporation—headed by the board of directors and based on hundreds of thousands of clerks and maintenance personnel. Some of the Protestant churches, most notable among them the Lutheran and the Anglican (or the Episcopalian), followed the institutional arrangements of the Roman Catholic Church, and they too developed a pyramidal hierarchy whose top echelon exercised tremendous authority. The elite of the institutionalized churches not only are a spiritual ruling elite but sometimes and in some places they have also made their influences strongly felt in the political sphere. Take for example the role of the church in Colombia.

In 1962 the *Instituto Colombiano de Opinión Pública* estimated that 90 percent of Colombians belonged to the Roman Catholic Church. Ever since the colonial period the Church has played a major role in the country. It is one of the largest landowners, and its influence especially in the areas of education and welfare has been crucial. Politically, the Church in Colombia has lent strong support to conservative politicians, and during the initial phase of Rojas Pinilla's military dictatorship, the Church was closely aligned with the governing elite. During the 1950s the Church was totally opposed to religious freedom, and the persecution of Protestants included techniques and tactics that harked back to the Middle Ages and the days of the Inquisition in Spain.[11]

The Colombian Constitution permits the state to enter into concordats with the pope, and so far it seems that the main outcome of this provision has been a merger of political and Church ruling elites. According to the Concordat of April 22, 1942, archbishops and bishops in Colombia, even though they are elected by the Holy See in Rome, must be Colombian citizens and must swear their allegiance to the state.

The Colombian Church is one of the most conservative and tradition-oriented in Latin America. In outward observances, at least, Colombians appear highly devout—most Colombians regularly attend mass, receive the sacraments, and participate in the numerous holy days. The Church, which is authoritarian and paternalistic, has extensive controls over education. Nearly all political leaders are practicing Catholics, and both major parties accept the present role of the Church in national politics. But the present role is one of support for change in the social system. The Colombian Church has given its endorsement to government-sponsored land reforms and has also become involved in urban problems. Within the ranks of the clergy, the traditionalists and the progressives have engaged in a running battle, with the progressives actively on the side of social change and social reforms. The result of this running battle has been more awareness within the Church of the need for change and deinstitutionalization.

In an article called "Dichotomies in the Church," John J. Kennedy talks about the authority claimed by the Church:

> *This is an authority which, by definition cannot be determined by the state. Yet the state is asked to recognize it. The recognition originally demanded was an official endorsement of the necessity of the Church in society in accordance with its own credal concepts. . . . The Church has, however, undoubtedly learned from experience that, in practice, official recognition is not quite the* sine qua non *that it is theory.*[12]

No doubt, the last sentence best describes the role of the Church in Mexico. Here we have a country in which the Catholic priests exert a tremendous influence in education and social welfare, but where the Church as an institution plays virtually no role at all. Although most Mexicans are Catholics, the Church as an institution owns no property even though the clergy are responsible for the care and upkeep of the church buildings. Many priests and nuns are involved in teaching and nursing, but they are salaried employees of the state. The Center of Intercultural Documentation in Cuernavaca, Mexico, publishes a

> *selection of the most remarkable variety of fact and opinion . . .* [*on*] *such emotion-laden topics as agrarian reform, birth control, capitalism, foreign investment, workers' wages, and nationalization of industry . . . drawn mostly from Latin-American sources, on the present agonizing reappraisal of these problems by both clergy and laity.*[13]

In referring to Hinduism, we stated that it cannot be called "the church" in India, even though it does assume the role of an institutionalized religion. It is no more possible to comprehend India's history without examining the role of Hinduism in that history than to understand the development of the Western world without analyzing the role of the church. "Religious belief is the most characteristic social organizing principle in India."[14] Struggles between the Hindu majority and the Muslim minority have dominated the politics of the Indian subcontinent since colonial times. Hinduism is the dominant religion of India (83.51 percent of the population), yet it is not a church, i.e., it is neither confined to a strict dogma, nor does it have a highly institutionalized structure:

> *the term "Hinduism" encompasses a wide theological range; from abstract intellectual speculation through mysticism and idolatry, to atheism. In a practical sense, anyone born to Hindu parents who recognizes (but does not necessarily accept) the hierarchy of castes, as well as the sacred standing of the Vedic literature may be considered a Hindu.*[15]

Although Hinduism is not a church, the interpretation of Hinduism by the priests has had a profound impact on India's social structure. The concept of caste [16] with its manifold social, economic, and political implications is essentially rooted in religion and interpreted over and over by a religious elite—the priests who have assigned themselves to the highest order, that of the *Brahman.* In India the priests who are the interpreters of social mores are crucial building blocks in the development of a community. It does not take an institutionalized form of religion such as the church in the Western sense for a religious elite to play a major role in any community.

The government policies of secularism, modernization, economic development, and national integration have gradually had their impact upon the practices of Hinduism. The intelligentsia and upper castes, as well as the untouchables, have begun to question and even attack the prescriptions of custom and social stratification hitherto sanctified by orthodox Hinduism. The Constitution rejects the notion that religion should form the basis of social and economic endeavors; it provides for freedom of religion, prohibits discrimination in education on the basis of religion, bans religious instruction in the public schools, and provides for political representation on the basis of territory rather than religion. Even so, because the Hindus comprise the great majority of the population, their leaders tend to dominate the local political scenes. Conflicts between Hindus and Muslims are still common in the local communities, and Hindu beliefs still get written into the law of the land, as for example, bans on the slaughter of cows or special protection for monkeys (both cows and monkeys are sacred to Hindus).

The majority of Kenyans are pagan.[17] African priests have contributed considerably to the survival of intense tribal loyalties and, no doubt, priests in many of the newly emerging states comprise as obstructionist a group in the process of nation-building in their respective states as did the various leaders of Protestant elites in Europe who contributed to the breakup of the Holy Roman Empire. A certain religious grouping in Israel, for example, "the Neturei Karta, . . . regard the State of Israel as an impious and presumptuous attempt to forestall the coming of the Messiah." [18]

No matter whether a religious elite has been transformed into an institution (the church) or not, the priests generally play a significant role in the life of any community. They are the transmitters of the values and the ultimate arbiters of the mores of that community. In that dual role they influence the setting of the goals and the formulation of laws in their respective communities, as illustrated in our twelve nation states.

The Landlords

One need not be a Marxist to perceive that ruling elites in the political system generally represent the dominant economic classes. Thus in an agricultural society where the livelihood of most people in the state is derived from the land, the landlords comprise a natural aristocracy. Certainly the development of the European nation states prior to the industrial revolution reflects the upper-class role of the landlords.

European nation states in the eighteenth century were still based on a primitive agrarian economy, not very different from the medieval manor system. Although serfdom had largely disappeared in Western Europe (some serfdom still existed in France on the eve of the French Revolution and as an institution it was not abolished in Russia until 1861), the lot of the English plowman or the French peasant was fairly similar to that of the Russian or Hungarian serf. A serf was attached to the soil and not free to leave the lord's estate; he was expected to labor for the lord of the manor, usually three days a week, and, in exchange for a plot of land to cultivate for his own family, he owed the lord stipulated shares of his produce. A freeman, on the other hand, could pay quitrent for the use of a bit of land, although he still had to pay the landlord all manner of fees, for use of the mill, the oven, the winepress, as well as for military protection. In addition to all these various dues to the landlord, the peasant was expected to pay his tithes to the church and taxes to the king. Throughout all Europe, economic and political conditions were much the same: The peasantry labored to support the privileged classes—the clergy and the landlords—paid the major share of state taxes, but had no voice in the making of laws or the allocation of resources.

The French Revolution signaled the end of feudalism not only in France, but eventually over all of Western Europe. Serfdom was abolished and peasants were relieved of personal servitude to the manorial lords. In France the great landowners were dispossessed and deprived of their special privileges. Large estates were broken up and put on the market as small farms to be bought on the installment plan. The landholdings of the fleeing landlords were confiscated by the state and resold in small lots to the peasants. Peasants, subsidized by the state, were encouraged to become proprietors rather than tenants. Titles of nobility, along with silk stockings, knee breeches, and powdered wigs, were suddenly out of fashion. It became more than hazardous to claim the status of nobleman, or even gentleman. The popular enthusiasm for equality and fraternity was symbolized by the dropping of all titles except that of *citizen.* The official record of expenses for the funeral of Marie Antoinette reads, "five francs for a coffin for the widow of Citizen Capet." [19]

The French Revolution was a basic revolution that overturned the whole social order, not only in France but in most of Western Europe. Wherever the armies of Napoleon marched, they carried with them the revolutionary principles of liberty, equality, fraternity. Later the forces of reaction set in, but all the king's horses and all the king's men could not put Humpty-Dumpty together again. With the abolition of serfdom and feudalism, the manorial lords ceased to be the ruling elite. Peasants in the countryside and workers in the towns emerged as freemen, prepared to fight at the barricades for their rights in the political system. And wherever the Code Napoléon was incorporated into the law of the land—in France, the various German states, the Netherlands, the Iberian Peninsula, and a large part of Italy—the legal prescription of social equality made an enduring impression upon the people.

Ironically the United Kingdom, first to industrialize its economy and to modernize its government, did not experience a basic revolution comparable to that which toppled the social hierarchy on the Continent. Well into the nineteenth century the parliamentary government of England represented the common people of the realm in name only. The House of Lords comprised the lords spiritual (the rich and powerful bishops of the Anglican Church) and the lords temporal (the hereditary peerage, most of them great landlords). The House of Commons was a euphemism; most of the common people, peasants and artisans, could not vote. The landed aristocracy generally controlled the elections and sat in the seats of political power. Such populous new industrial towns as Leeds, Manchester, and Sheffield were not even represented. The property qualification for membership in Parliament was not abolished until 1858.

Ernest Barker gives us a word picture of the social environment of British statesmen during the three centuries from the dissolution of the monasteries in 1536 to the Reform Bill of 1832 (and even after the Reform Bill):

> *it was a society of which the tone was set and the affairs were largely guided by a landed aristocracy and gentry. The landed interest ruled the countries through the Justices of the Peace: the landed interest filled the Parliament at Westminster, and entrenched itself on the steps of the throne. "As is the proportion or balance of dominion or property in land," Harrington wrote in the introduction to* Oceana, *in 1656 "such is the nature of the empire." Government smelled of the honest soil; statesmen moved in a landed society where the talk was of bullocks and turnips, mixed with the classics, Italian architecture, the music of Gluck, and the general culture of the country house. . . . It was essentially English and it was essentially an aristocracy—in living touch with the soil and all who lived on the soil. It was an elite; but it was an elite which recruited itself freely and struck its roots deep in the country.*[20]

The Reform Bill of 1832 is a landmark in the modernization of the English political system. It did not end the elitist influence of the country gentry, which survives even to this day, but it did provide the first building blocks for a more democratic political structure. By wiping out the rotten boroughs and providing for representation of the growing industrial cities, it effected a redistribution of seats in the House of Commons and gave the urban industrial middle class more direct channels of communication within the political system. Although it extended the franchise both in the countryside and in the boroughs, its electoral reforms were far from radical. The proportion of voters to the population after the great reform of 1832 was still one to twenty-two, with workmen in the cities and laborers in the country still disfranchised. We shall not go into the long drawn-out battles to enlarge the suffrage; urban workers got the vote in 1867, rural workers in 1884, women thirty years of age or over in 1918, women on the basis of equality with men in 1928. As the law now stands, British citizens enjoy universal suffrage and exercise their voting rights in periodic elections.

The point we make here, however, is that the great expansion of the British electorate has not brought about a comparable broadening in the governmental structure. In some ways, especially in the area of civil rights, the United Kingdom is perhaps the most democratic of our twelve states. But when we look at who governs we find a traditional aristocracy. As Professor Barker perceives and admires it, "Political form has corresponded to social structure; and political form, like social structure, and along with social structure, has affected the nature of statesmanship."[21] Certainly among the modern states in our sample, the English government more than any other seems to operate within a class-conscious environment, not in the Marxian sense where a dominant economic class controls the political system, but in an almost medieval sense, of *noblesse oblige* on the part of the upper class and a habitual pattern of deference on the part of the lower classes.

A long-time student—and also admirer—of the British government observes: "The upper classes are still today, despite democratization and economic leveling, ascendant: in the Cabinet, in Parliament, and in the Civil Service; and what is more important, their ascendance is almost beyond dispute."[22] We could dwell at length on what distinguishes this upper class: the right education, the right public schools, Oxford and Cambridge; the right religion, Anglican High Church; the right sports, polo, shooting, and rowing; the right food and drink, roast beef, port, and Stilton; the right clothes, mostly tweeds; the right accent; and, of course, a sense of sportsmanship—all of which adds up to the very model of a country gentleman who makes a successful career for himself as an amateur in politics or as a generalist in public administration.

At the time of the French Revolution the United States was just embarking on its own political course. But a short time before most Americans had been transplanted Englishmen, colonists by choice, who kept their cultural ties with the mother country. (This is an important point to remember when we try to compare the colonial experiences of the United States with those of the new nations more recently emerging from colonialism. Most of the people of India, for example, are not transplanted Englishmen; their own civilization is based on very different values and very different behavioral patterns than those of their former colonial administrators, which it antecedes by several millennia.) The American war for independence was not a basic revolution. Unlike the French Revolution, it made no fundamental changes in the existing social structure.

When we look at the social environment of the United States at the end of the eighteenth century we realize that it was not really a modern nation, judged even in its own times. Certainly its economy was underdeveloped compared to England or, for that matter, compared to any Western European state. The industrial revolution was just beginning to take effect. Towns were few, far between, and none compared to the great cities of Europe. One historian informs us that the new republic was in some ways "actually old-fashioned, having shared less than Europe in the scientific, literary, capitalistic, governmental, and bureaucratic development of the preceding two hundred years."[23] Most Americans, according to the first census in 1790, lived in the country, tilling their own small farms, virtually the only available means of subsistence for themselves and their families. Land ownership was widespread, and since the frontier was open—and would remain open until the last decade of the nineteenth century—those who wanted more land could get it by moving west.

Much has been written about the coonskin democracy of the American frontier; there was a great deal of liberty, equality, and fraternity in the pioneer communities. But if we look at the older and more settled communities along the Eastern Seaboard, we find considerable class consciousness and social stratification. There were no peasants or serfs on the American scene, but the census of 1790 indicates that 20 percent of the population were nonwhite, most of them slaves on the Southern plantations. There was no feudalism as such, but the nature of the colonial land grants produced a manorial system not too different from the English country gentry rule described by Ernest Barker. The distinguished American historian, Samuel Eliot Morison, tells us that no fewer than ninety-two manors were granted to individuals in the colony of Maryland during the first fifty years of its existence; these were genuine manors, not merely big houses, and the lords of the manors exercised their prerogatives in much the same style as their counterparts in England.[24] New York, especially along the Hudson River originally settled by the Dutch *patroons* in the seventeenth century, came closer to pure feudalism than any of the American colonies. A patroon was a landlord who brought his own retinue from the Netherlands, who held feudal domain over his land grant with exclusive fishing and hunting privileges and with civil and criminal jurisdiction over his tenants. When the English took New Netherlands from the Dutch and renamed the colony after the Duke of York, King James I reconfirmed the patroonships and made a number of enormous grants to English and Scottish landlords. The Van Rensselaers, the Roosevelts, the Livingstons, the Pells, the Gardiners, these and other wealthy families were landed aristocracy in colonial New York, and many of their descendants were influential in the politics of the new republic.

The great houses of America, Mount Vernon and Monticello, for example, were cottagelike compared to some of the castles of the great landlords of England or on the Continent. Nevertheless there was a country gentry, gentlemen farmers, who comprised a ruling elite in the latter years of colonial America and in the early years of the republic. With the industrialization and urbanization of America in the nineteenth century most of them would lose their special status in the political system, but in the formative years of the first new nation they were definitely on top.

The political influence of the landed aristocracy, especially that of the Southern planters, is manifest in the debates and decisions at the Constitutional Convention of 1787. Two examples will have to suffice (if you read the document in the context of the social environment of the times you will discover some others): 1) The heated arguments over the question of suffrage, Who should have the right to vote, all freemen or just freeholders, i.e., landowners? The final agreement was not to establish any national suffrage but simply to authorize each state legislature to define its own electorate. Most states at the time limited the vote to property, i.e., landowners. 2) The protracted debates over the matter of representation, What or who should be represented, property or persons? And in either case, How should slaves be counted? The final decision—to provide for representation of the people in the states proportionate to their members, and to include three-fifths of the slaves as part of the count—is inexplicable in terms of logic or political philosophy, but it does illustrate the ruling role of the Southern planters at the convention.

As we see it, the country gentry still have a pervasive influence in English politics, an influence that stems from social status rather than any position of legal privilege. Obviously the landed aristocracy alone is no longer running the show in the United States and has not been since the Civil War deposed King Cotton. On the other hand, even a casual study of who gets what in the annual appropriations for agriculture suggests that the big farm operators, cotton, tobacco, corn, and cattle, are still treated as a very special class in United States politics. Among their members are families who made their money in the natural resources (oil, coal, iron) that provide the bases of industrialization, but the family fortune enables them to play the role of landed gentry.

When we look at the rule of the landlords in the Latin American countries, we do not have to go back to history long-past. Despite current elaborate plans for progress—meaning industrialization—the power and tenure of the landlords, usually supported both by the military and the clergy, remains the most explosive single issue in Latin American politics.

To make our point, we will sketch out an oversimplified version of the complex land-tenure system that exists in Latin American countries. There are three principal forms: 1) the traditional *communidades*, which are the village collectives, basically the same system which existed among the Incas, Mayans, and Aztecs when the conquistadores arrived; 2) the *latifundios*, which are the extremely large estates, similar to the Spanish feudal fiefs of the late Middle Ages, in which the landowner is literally lord of all he surveys, including the workers on the estate, who are paid in usufruct, some produce from a parcel of land in return for their manual work in the landlord's fields or service in the big house; and 3) the *minifundios*, which are very small, submarginal farms owned by individual peasants, many receiving the land as the result of recent so-called land reforms.[25]

Latin American latifundios are of two main types, plantations and haciendas. The plantations are frequently foreign-owned, with absentee landlords and commercial managers; the workers are usually paid in cash, and the lowest possible wages. The haciendas go back to the early years of the Spanish conquest. The landlord (*haciendado*) maintains his peons on a feudal basis; they reside on his property, do all of his work for him; he provides their living facilities, the store, and the church; he regards them more or less as his chattels and cares for them accordingly. Obviously the haciendas (or the plantations) pose problems for nation-building. Since each hacienda is an autonomous social and economic unit, frequently remote from any town or city, the peon is almost totally dependent on his own haciendado and is likely to be only vaguely aware of the world outside; hence he has very little sense of identity with the national government. Moreover, despite the fact that the latifundios usually occupy the richest lands in the country, they are for the most part worked by primitive methods, with extremely low yield. Given the fact of population explosion, the rural poor who cannot make even a submarginal living on the haciendas keep crowding into the cities where they find even more poverty and misery in the burgeoning barrios.

A seminar on elites and development in Latin America held at the University of Montevideo in 1965 dealt with the current patterns of specific elite groups. Seymour Lipset, present at the conference, reports that "The period of the predominance of *latifundio* social structure is far from over." [26]

Latifundios of one thousand or more hectares comprise about 1.5 percent of all the farms in Latin America, but they possess 65 percent of the total agricultural lands. Although the much-heralded Alliance for Progress in the 1960s made land reform the sine qua non for United States economic assistance, actually little has been done to reduce the economic source of the influence of latifundio families. The persistence of preindustrial values in most Latin American countries can be attributed largely to the continuance of the rural social structure in which these values were originally fostered.

This traditional linkage between the latifundio families and the political elite still holds generally true for Colombia, although a Colombian law of 1960 declares the intent of the government to reform the agrarian social structure through procedures designed to eliminate and to prevent the concentration of rural property.

The Agrarian Reform Institute (INCORA) began to implement the government's land reform policies in 1962, but the rate of progress was hardly perceptible throughout the 1960s. Land ownership remained concentrated in the hands of a few powerful families; 1.7 percent of the producers held 55.1 percent of the land; 50.2 percent of the producers worked and lived on very small farms, less than three hectares (a hectare is 2.47 acres) in size. Colombian society remained highly stratified, a small elite class which enjoyed weath, education, culture, leisure, and political power; the masses lived in poverty, uneducated, disease-ridden, politically apathetic. In the cities, what appeared to be an emerging middle class, could be, for the most part, identified as the sons and daughters, grandsons and granddaughters of the landed aristocracy. Few of the lawyers, merchants, industrialists, and officeholders in Bogotá, Cali, or Barranquilla could really be described as self-made or risen from the ranks; much more likely they were relatives of the ruling elite, the landlords.

Mexico, however, is a striking exception. The initial thrust of the Mexican Revolution in 1910 was to unseat a dictatorial regime and to weaken the influence of the military and the church which had supported it. But over the next several decades the Revolution brought about an agrarian upheaval: Traditional land tenure was abolished; the state laid claim not only to the land but to the subsoil resources; and the great haciendas and foreign-owned plantations were broken up. Land redistribution proceeded rather slowly and reached its peak in the 1930s under President Lazaro Cardená (1934–40). For the most part the nationalized lands have been granted to rural communities, *ejidas*, rather than to individual farmers, who gained only the right to use the land, not to sell it or mortgage it. It is estimated that the ejidas now possess about half the farmlands of Mexico. Even so, about two-fifths of the farm workers still do not own land.[27]

The Mexican Revolution was a basic revolution, though less far-reaching than the French Revolution of the eighteenth century. Nevertheless the Mexican Revolution has to a large extent eliminated the power base of the traditional oligarchy, particularly the priests and the landlords. Thus it has radically changed the character of the political process. In Mexican politics today, not only do we perceive a new configuration of special interests beginning to develop around an industrializing economy, but also a very different concept of national interests is reaching even into the rural areas. Mexico is well on the way to becoming a modern nation state.

MODERNIZATION AND NEW POWER BASES

Without attempting to impose a theory of history, asserting that agrarian societies eventually develop into industrial states (as we see it, some do, some do not, some may yet, and some probably will not), we observe that the modernization of a nation state is bound to bring about radical changes in the social structure; and in the process of transformation, new power bases and new ruling elites are bound to emerge within the political system. Social changes and power shifts do not take place, however, without a good deal of infighting. The extent and the intensity of the struggles and the amount of violence involved depends somewhat on the time allowed for accommodation. In the cases of the United States and the United Kingdom, the industrial revolution picked up momentum gradually through decades that stretched over more than a century. In the case of Mexico, it took a bloody revolution to shake up the social structure before the industrial revolution could even get under way.

The Case of the Soviet Union

The most spectacular transformation of an agricultural people into a modern industrial state is the case of the Soviet Union. Because it was done on a grand scale and with remarkable speed, the process was marked by unprecedented social engineering and also by extreme violence and systematic terrorism.

When the Bolsheviks seized the Kremlin in November, 1917, in accord with Marxian doctrine which calls for the abolition of private ownership of the land, the revolutionary regime immediately decreed confiscation of the great landed estates. The peasants, not yet imbued with the spirit of Communism and having been misled by war slogans of land and peace, forthwith took possession of the land and the livestock for themselves, and in the process (the Black Partition) liquidated virtually the whole landlord class of the old regime. Throughout the 1920s the Communist leadership, itself urban, proletariat-oriented, struggled to enlist and keep the support of the peasants who then comprised the mass of the Russian population. The first major move of the revolutionary government was certainly non-Marxian, all land to the peasants; but until the Communist leadership felt itself securely entrenched in power it recognized the need for massive peasant support. Under Lenin's New Economic Policy (NEP) peasants were required to surrender part of their produce to the state but were permitted to sell the remainder in the market. By 1928 there were twenty-six million peasant-owned farms and a new class of well-to-do farmers, *kulaks*, were prospering in what was basically a nonsocialist economy. Whereupon the Communist leaders decided to eliminate the kulaks as a class—perhaps five million of them were uprooted from their farms and forced into Siberian exile. The decision was to collectivize the agricultural lands at a tempo much more rapid than had been envisaged in the first Five-Year Plan. By 1936 almost 90 percent of the peasants had been absorbed by the collective farms. Harry Schwartz concludes, "with this victory over the independent peasantry, the Soviet State won complete control of the economy of the U.S.S.R., a control that has not been seriously challenged since." [28]

There is no denying that the new rulers of the USSR achieved the modernization of Russia in record time. They restructured the whole society, created a totalitarian political system, and engineered a new and viable socialist economy. Before World War I, despite her vast territory, great natural resources, and large population, Russian agriculture and industry lagged far behind the United States and Western Europe in productivity and technology. Today the USSR ranks with the United States, a superpower among all the nation states of the world. Some critics of the Communist system are quick to point out that the modernization of Russia was already well under way and that had a liberal democratic government succeeded the czarist regime the Russian people might have achieved the same status without such terrible costs. But, as a matter of fact, a liberal democratic government did succeed the czarist government in March, 1917, and it muffed its big chance, essentially because the autocratic regime which preceded it had left a social structure in which neither liberalism nor democracy could take root immediately.

The costs of the Soviet success have been incalculable, both materially and in intangibles: the liquidation of the traditional elite, the elimination of the independent peasants, the use of slave labor, the regimentation of the people, the subordination of the individual to the state, the restrictions upon personal freedom, the loss of privacy, and always the uncertainties of arbitrary rule. Even so, the achievements are remarkable, and to many of the new states of the post-World-War-II period, eager to modernize in the present or the immediate future, the Soviet way appears an attractive model for economic development.

Modern Elites: Entrepreneurs, Financiers, Managers, Engineers

It is relatively easy to discuss ruling elites in a traditional society based on an agrarian economy. The concept of elites becomes much more complicated in an urban industrial society which in itself is a highly complex system with many of its components in competition and conflict with each other. There is no single dominating interest, hence no natural elite comparable to the landed aristocracy in an agrarian society. Resources, capital accumulation, technology, labor specialization, and exchange are the foundations of a modern economy. And just as the traditional elites bear a functional relationship to society, so do the new elites develop out of their respective functions in the modern state.

We refer frequently to the industrial revolution which transformed the United States and Western Europe from a rural agrarian to an urban industrial society. More accurately the process was one of industrial evolution, slow-paced in the beginning, gradually accelerating to its present tempo. In the early stages, in England and in the United States, the entrepreneurs emerged as a new elite; they were the innovators, the organizers, the risk-takers who applied new technology to resources, both human and nonhuman, and developed the new patterns in production of goods and services that characterize our modern civilization. The entrepreneurs began as capitalists; they had accumulated the wherewithal to build factories, to buy machinery, to hire workers, and they invested their capital in the new means of production in anticipation of profits from their enterprise. The nineteenth century was the heyday of private enterprise in a free economy, especially in England and the United States.

Toward the end of the nineteenth century, as the populations increased, as demands mounted for more and more goods and services, as the profits piled up, industrial enterprise turned to mass production, large-scale operations calling for enormous accumulations of capital. A new class of financiers emerged whose function was to amass collective capital; the individual entrepreneurs, the great captains of industry, were gradually but generally replaced by corporate enterprise. Capital in the corporate economy came from multiple investments in stocks and bonds sold by the financiers in the money markets to people whose interest was not in goods and services but in profits. Look at the financial pages in your daily newspaper for the reports of the New York Stock Exchange or the American Stock Exchange. There you will find listed the great corporate-capitalist enterprises that dominate the American economy today: giants like American Telephone and Telegraph, Bethlehem Steel, Campbell's Soup, Coca-Cola, General Electric, General Motors, International Business Machines, Standard Oil of New Jersey, Sears Roebuck, and TransWorld Airlines. Thousands of listings, representing the greatest part of the GNP of the United States, cover the whole gamut of our modern industry, transportation, and communications. (AT&T—American Telephone and Telegraph—largest corporation in the world, employs nearly one million workers, and pays dividends to more than three million stockholders.)[29]

The size and complexity of these great corporate enterprises—and conglomerations of them—as well as the divorce of ownership and capital investment from the actual operations have given rise to what is now the most important elite in the modern state, the managerial class. Members of the managerial class, unlike the warriors, the priests, or the landlords, have manifold, diverse, and specialized responsibilities: fiscal management, production management, labor management, market management, etc. Fiscal managers have to keep accumulating and investing more capital to insure growth of the business. Production managers have to keep alert to more advanced technologies, to promote research in science and engineering, to meet ever-increasing demands for more and better products and services. Labor managers have to supply the requisite skilled workers and to keep them satisfied in their jobs. (Organized labor has its own managers whose job it is to bargain with the company managers for increasingly favorable terms of employment.) Market managers have to see that the goods or services are attractively packaged, widely advertised, and always reaching a bigger and increasingly competitive market. (They depend more and more on the advertising and public-relations men to the point that some economists feel that the real elite in the free market economy is more likely to be found on Madison Avenue than on Wall Street or in the factories.)

The modern industrial system evolved in Western Europe and in the United States in a so-called free economy, with a great deal of latitude for private enterprise. From the outset, however, even in the United States, in whose economic history the private entrepreneur has been given top billing, the government has played an important role in the development of the economy. Although private enterprise contributed most of the capital for the industrial establishment in the United States, the government made great grants-in-aid in the areas of transportation and communications. From the time of the first secretary of the treasury, Alexander Hamilton, the government has been concerned with the protection and promotion of industry. Hamilton's "Report on Manufactures" advocated a protective tariff in order "to increase the number of ligaments between the government and the interest of individuals." The first Congress was not receptive to Hamilton's proposals, but a quarter of a century later, when the manufacturing interests had built up a considerable political base, a protective tariff became part of the public policy. In the early stages of industrialism the official policy toward the business community was one of laissez faire, hands off, but the very forces that promoted the industrial economy also promoted the regulatory state. A modern economy requires an urban concentration of population; urban living calls for a great many public services as well as governmental controls. A modern economy calls for advances in science, technology, engineering, and mechanical skills; and all of these are posited on the general education of the citizenry. An educated people demand higher standards of living and are more likely to channel their demands both as producers and consumers through political processes. At any rate, even in the United States the modern economy is a mixed economy, private enterprise and government regulation, less of the first and more of the second as time moves on.

Among our twelve states, the USSR is the prime example of a modern economy achieved by political planners rather than private entrepreneurs. We note, if only in passing, that it is far from true to say that the Communist regime turned a primitive agrarian economy into a powerful industrial state within one generation. On the eve of World War I the industrial evolution was obviously accelerating in czarist Russia, which then ranked fifth in industrial production, outranked by the United States, the United Kingdom, France, and Germany. It is fair to say, however, that a determined Communist leadership, by taking over the whole of the economy, setting grand new goals, and implementing the plans systematically, ruthlessly, and extravagantly in terms of human values and lives, did in fact move the USSR into the second position among the great industrial nations of the world.

When we start looking for the ruling elites within the USSR, we discover much the same stratification that we observed in the American economy. Again, the most important elite (aside from the veteran party leadership) appears to be the new managerial class, with manifold, diverse, and specialized responsibilities: fiscal managers, production managers, labor managers, market managers, with an impressive retinue of economic planners, scientists, engineers, technicians, and public-relations experts. The fact that these are all in the employ of the state, and hence in the category of government bureaucrats, should not obscure our recognition of them as members of the ruling elites within the society.

The government of the USSR is so concerned with controlling and channeling the talent of its youth into the various managerial elites that it actively recruits youngsters into and promotes them for higher education—both technological and managerial. From time to time it finds itself with a glut on the market and arbitrarily cuts back on the number of admissions to universities and technical schools, thereby dealing a terrible blow to the aspirations of thousands of young people.

A student may have found himself preparing during all his primary and secondary schooling for the entrance examination to a university or technical college—passed with flying colors—only to find out that he will have to resign himself to do "honorable labor for the people's economy," i.e., be a workman. According to current reports, the USSR is experiencing such an overflow of technologists, managers, and academically trained elites as she enters the 1970s. (Perhaps the technological race between the industrial powers that began with Sputnik has had similar effects on all involved.)

Rulership by Bureaucrats and Technocrats

We can talk about an agrarian society wherein a minimum of governmental regulation is needed. But we have to equate a modern economy with an industrial state. It is virtually impossible for a modern economy to develop without a considerable degree of political intervention, both positive (promotion) and negative (regulation). This observation becomes particularly relevant when we try to understand the problems of today's developing new nations.

The case of Japan is instructive on this forced linkage between politics and economics. Japan was able to skip from medieval feudalism to modern capitalism without going through a long drawn-out industrial evolution via private enterprise (as in England and the United States) because the Meiji oligarchs used the political system effectively to engineer major changes in the Japanese social structure. Determined to meet, if not outreach, Western competition, the Japanese government in the last quarter of the nineteenth century sponsored and promoted economic development of the country. It built, or encouraged the building of, the whole infrastructure of transportation and communication in addition to providing modern public utilities and an extensive system of public education. It established numerous industrial plants to serve as models for private enterprise: cotton mills, cement and brick plants, food factories, iron and steel plants, etc. It subsidized shipping, mining, and the textile industries. Private entrepreneurs, some of them in family combines, others organized in associational units (the Bankers' Club, the Cotton Spinners Federation, etc.) joined in the political process, lobbied for legislation favorable to the business community. Government bureaucrats provided a great deal of technical assistance, including applied and developmental research intended to upgrade technology in the private economy.

Most important, the Meiji Restoration included a complete rebuilding of the Japanese educational system under a new national Ministry of Education. Primary education was made compulsory in 1872, but the public school system was made available to all with low-cost tuition, through the secondary levels to the imperial universities. Many high schools, as well as institutions of higher education, offered special training in mechanics, commerce, navigation, and education. And the products of this modernized educational system formed the new elite, whether they entered the government bureaucracy or took managerial positions, or professional posts, in private business. On the eve of World War II Japan was counted among the great industrial states of the world. The political system and the economy were both reduced to shambles by the end of the war, and yet in less than a decade a reconstructed Japan was again rivaling the top industrial states in the world. Its ruling elite includes scientists, engineers, technologists, highly skilled mechanics, managers in finance, production, labor relations, and public relations, and, of course, a vast array of bureaucrats with special competencies—nearly all of them recruited from the public educational system, which is geared to economic and governmental demands.

All of the less developed countdies in our sample of twelve are officially embarked on economic development: Colombia, Mexico, Israel, Turkey, Kenya, the Ivory Coast, and India. What can they learn from the experience of those industrial states which have already effected the transformation from a traditional agrarian society to a modern nation state? The experience of the United States (or the United Kingdom or Western Germany) is based on industrial evolution, a slow process at the outset, accelerating rapidly as new elites emerge with new interests and new competencies. Beginning in the context of laissez faire and free enterprise, the interaction of politics and economics results in a great deal of governmental intervention in the economy and a great many economic considerations in the political arena. The experience of the Soviet Union under Communist leadership demonstrates that the process of modernization can be hastened by government ownership and control of nearly all the means of production, transportation, and communication. But modernization by violence is a grim means to an end that might be achieved just as effectively by some other social strategy, and totalitarian government is not the happiest political system for human beings who seek individual freedom. For peoples with rising expectations who do not want to wait another hundred years or so for industrial evolution or for peoples who do not have the ideological fervor to press for social upheaval whatever the costs to the current generation, the modernization of Japan may appear the most attractive model to emulate, a combination of private enterprise and government promotion, with social reorientation achieved through public education.

The immediate problem for every developing country is the accumulation and investment of capital. In countries that are poor, whose people live generally at a subsistence level, there are few native capitalists or private entrepreneurs. The ready solution is to invite foreign capitalists to make the initial investments. But in states just beginning to inculcate a sense of national identity and independence this solution can be hazardous, particularly if the foreign capitalists are more interested in exploiting than developing the natural resources. In Mexico the public policy now opposes foreign investments and has expropriated major foreign investments in land, oil, and railroads. This is the reaction to a long, unhappy experience with foreign exploitation. In the Ivory Coast the government of Houphouet-Boigny solicits foreign investments as well as foreign loans, and indeed the business community is largely dominated by European, especially French, investors. A more difficult approach, but probably more successful in the long run, is for the government to engage in long-range planning and to implement its plans gradually with capital saved out of public taxes or from grants and loans from foreign governments or international agencies.

The Indian government was advocating planning even before its independence was proclaimed. Economic planning has been viewed broadly and not merely as the development of resources in a narrow technical sense. The first Five-Year Plan (1951–56) emphasized government projects in agriculture, irrigation, power, and transport. The second plan (1956–61) shifted emphasis to the development of basic and heavy industries and laid down guidelines for a democratic socialist state. The third plan (1961–66) aimed to increase the national income, to step up the rate of capital investment in steel, chemicals, fuel, and power, and to achieve self-sufficiency in agriculture. The establishment of new industries involved enormous capital investments and also called for large-scale imports of equipment and technicians. The fourth plan (1967–71) gives highest priority to increasing agricultural production, land reforms, and rural electrification: a frustrating effort to cope with population explosion. Although India ranks at the bottom in almost every one of the cross-national economic statistics in the preceding chapter, if we compare India in 1970 with India in 1950, the planned advance toward a modern state appears to be more than a euphemism.[30]

The importation of capital, machines, and know-how from outside the country is not going to modernize a nation state, however elaborate the official prospectus. The industrialization of an agrarian society, whether by evolution or revolution, demands a basic restructuring of society and a marked transformation of the ruling elites within the political system. In all the less developed countries in our sample of twelve, traditional elites are still unyielding: the priests and landlords in Colombia; the wealthy planters, the European businessmen, and imported French bureaucrats in the Ivory Coast; rival tribal leaders in Kenya; Islam, the rural landlords, and the military in Turkey; the most orthodox rabbis and the early Zionists in Israel; the whole caste system in India as well as rival religious leaders. Only in Mexico do we perceive really basic changes in the social structure reflected in the economy and represented in the political system. What all of these countries lack are the human resources requisite to development, native enterpreneurs, skilled workers, engineers, and trained mechanics. A modern state requires more than political leadership, however charismatic or visionary. It needs an educated citizenry as a solid foundation, and above all, an indigenous ruling elite that includes a managerial class capable of running a diverse and specialized economy and carrying out manifold and technical governmental operations.

NOTES

1. Quoted in Cabell Phillips, *The Truman Presidency* (New York: Macmillan, 1966), p. 14.
2. *Congressional Quarterly Weekly Report,* May 30, 1969, pp. 845–50 offers a lobby report on conflicting antimissile pressures, listing the largest ABM contractors for research and development and production, the pro-ABM lobbyists, and the anti-ABM lobbyists.
3. Merle Fainsod, *How Russia is Ruled,* 2d ed. (Cambridge, Mass.: Harvard University Press, 1963), p. 468. See his chap. 14, "The Party and the Armed Services."
4. Ibid., p. 482.
5. See Kemal H. Karpat, *Turkey's Politics* (Princeton, N.J.: Princeton University Press, 1959), especially part 1, chap. 1, "The Ottoman Empire and the Beginning of the Reform Movement."
6. Lord Kinross, *Atatürk* (New York: William Morrow, 1965), pp. 537–38.
7. Robert E. Ward, *Japan's Political System* (Englewood Cliffs, N.J.: Prentice-Hall, 1967), p. 39.
8. Robert Karl Reischauer, *Japan: Government-Politics* (New York: Thomas Nelson, 1939). See chap. 2, pp. 40–56.
9. The *1969 World Almanac* gives a census of religious bodies in the United States. A rough summary of figures given in the *Almanac* results in about seventy-four million Protestants as compared to forty-seven million Catholics. Many religious groupings in the United States do not make membership data available, for example, the Baha'i, the Muslims, or the Christian Scientists. The *1969 World Almanac* (New York: Newspaper Enterprise Association, 1968), pp. 219–20.
10. For a brief authoritative discussion on the constitutional law relating to established religion in the United States, see *The Constitution of the United States of America,* prepared by the Legislative Reference Service, Library of Congress (Washington, D.C.: Government Printing Office, 1964), pp. 845 ff. Although the First Amendment was intended to restrict only the national government, the Fourteenth Amendment incorporates the provisions of the First in the overall concept of liberty. Hence, today under the Fourteenth Amendment, no state may establish a religion.
11. W. O. Galbraith, *Colombia,* 2d ed. (London: Oxford University Press, 1966), pp. 46–50.
12. John D. Martz, ed., *The Dynamics of Change in Latin American Politics* (Englewood Cliffs, N.J.: Prentice-Hall, 1965), p. 282.
13. As cited in Lewis Hanke, *Modern Latin America, Continent in Ferment: Mexico and the Caribbean* (Princeton, N.J.: Van Nostrand, 1967), 1: 128.
14. Richard L. Park, *India's Political System* (Englewood Cliffs, N.J.: Prentice-Hall, 1967), p. 41.

15. Ibid., pp. 41–42.
16. For detailed discussions of the caste system see ibid., pp. 42–43, and W. H. Morris-Jones, *The Government and Politics of India* (London: Hutchinson, 1964), pp. 54–59.
17. Violaine I. Junod, ed., *The Handbook of Africa* (New York: New York University Press, 1963), pp. 175–78, gives the following figures: Out of 6,586,700 (1960 census estimate) persons, 963,000 are Christian missionary society adherents, coastal inhabitants included Muslims, "the rest are pagan." Figures for the Ivory Coast included 11 percent Christian, 22 percent Muslim, and 67 percent Animist (p. 168).
18. Misha Louvish, *The Challenge of Israel* (Jerusalem: Israel University Press, 1968), p. 163. The book includes a discussion of the various established branches of the Jewish religious elites and their various concerns, such as Sabbath and dietary observances and the political impact of each religious group.
19. Reported in Carlton S. Hayes, *A Political and Social History of Modern Europe* (New York: Macmillan, 1925), 1: 510.
20. Ernest Barker, *Essays on Government* (Oxford: Clarendon, 1945), pp. 25–26.
21. Ibid., p. 27.
22. Samuel H. Beer and Adam B. Ulam, eds., *Patterns of Government: The Major Political Systems of Europe*, rev. ed. (New York: Random House, 1962), p. 96.
23. R. R. Palmer, *The Age of Democratic Revolution* (Princeton, N.J.: Princeton University Press, 1964), p. 519.
24. Samuel Eliot Morison, *The Oxford History of the American People* (New York: Oxford University Press, 1965), p. 81. For example, the Brooke manors, 4,100 acres on opposite sides of the Patuxent River, granted to an Anglican clergyman who arrived at Baltimore in his own ship in 1650 with wife, two daughters, eight sons, seven maidservants, and twenty-one manservants.
25. The discussion of Latin American land tenure is drawn chiefly from John D. Martz, ed., op. cit., chap. 3, "The Hacienda," by Frank Tannenbaum, and chap. 17, "The Land Reform Issue in Latin America," by Thomas F. Carroll.
26. Seymour Martin Lipset and Aldo Solari, eds., *Elites in Latin America* (New York: Oxford University Press, 1967), p. 9.
27. Robert S. Alexander, *Today's Latin America* (Garden City, N.Y.: Doubleday, rev. Anchor Book, 1968), p. 61.
28. Harry Schwartz, *Russia's Soviet Economy*, 2d ed. (Englewood Cliffs, N.J.: Prentice-Hall, 1963), p. 115.
29. *Fortune*, May, 1970, pp. 182–221.
30. For India's own evaluation, see *India, 1969*, compiled by the Research and Reference Division, Ministry of Information and Broadcasting, Faridabad: Government of India Press.

FURTHER READING

FREY, FREDERICK W. *The Turkish Political Elite*. Cambridge, Mass.: MIT Press, 1965.

KELLER, SUZANNE. *Beyond the Ruling Class: Strategic Elites in Modern Society*. New York: Random House, 1963.

LA PALOMBARA, JOSEPH G., ed. *Bureaucracy and Political Development*. Princeton University Press, 1963.

LIPSET, SEYMOUR MARTIN, and ALDO SOLARI, eds. *Elites in Latin America*. New York: Oxford University Press, 1967.

ELEPHANT BOOK-ENDS
EAST AFRICA JOURNAL
NYOTA Afrika
NYANZA TIMES
SAUTI YA MWAFRIKA
Animals
AFRICA and the WORLD
Reporter
TIME
TAIFA
East African Standard
DAILY NATION
THE PEACE-MAKERS
Tshombe flies in today

chapter 6

HOW DO POLITICAL OPINIONS AFFECT GOVERNMENT?

In this chapter we cross the line between the social environment and the political system. Using the conceptual model of David Easton, we identify the political system as "a set of interactions abstracted from the totality of social behavior through which values are authoritatively allocated for society."[1] This is a behavioral concept which helps us to analyze the relationship between politics and the whole of society. In reality, of course, there are no visible or tangible boundaries between the totality of social behavior and the system of political behavior. We find the model useful, however, in explaining how members of the political system are influenced by conditions and activities and transactions outside of the political system and also in considering how the political system, viewed as a pattern of behavior, affects the members of other social systems, e.g., the church, the family, economic organizations, and cultural groups.

INTERACTIONS BETWEEN THE GOVERNORS AND THE GOVERNED

We use the term *member* in a broad sense. We are all members of the political system: Citizens and subjects, we are the governed, we are the public, we are the electorate, we are the taxpayers, we get drafted. Some members participate

Kenya, newsstand in Nairobi
(Bruno Barbey : Magnum)

in the political system more actively than others, as individuals or in group associations; some engage in unofficial activities which may influence official decisions; some have more authority than others because they belong to one of the ruling elites. Later we shall be discussing at some length the various roles members play, the different levels of participation, the different degrees of influence and power within the political system. But at this point we are focusing on the interactions that occur between members of the political system and members of social systems that have their own patterns of behavior, their own functions, which are separate from, and external to, the political system.

Note that any member of the political system is bound to hold a variety of memberships in other social systems. He is a family member, perhaps head of a household, a father, a husband, a son, a brother, with multiple ties of kinship. He belongs to an economic order: He may be a soldier, a landlord, a wage earner, a farmer, a salesman. He may be a church member: a Roman Catholic, a Mormon, a Hindu, a Muslim, a Baptist, or a Seventh-Day Adventist. He may play in a neighborhood bowling league; he may play the flute in a chamber-music group; he may belong to a fraternity, to a stamp club, or a soccer team. How do multiple memberships in these various social systems affect the political life of the community?

Joseph Zilch is a United States citizen; he is a family man with five children ages six to sixteen; an ex-G.I., he is a skilled mechanic and belongs

Japan, shipbuilders reading and conversing
(Henri Cartier-Bresson : Magnum)

to a labor union; he lives in the suburb of a large industrial city in the Eastern United States; he is buying a house with Veterans Administration financing. What special interests do you think he might have as a member of the United States political system? Abraham Jefferson is also a United States citizen; he too is a family man with five children ages six to sixteen; he is a day laborer and is frequently unemployed; he rents a three-room apartment in the inner city of the nation's capital; the United States census counts him as nonwhite. What special interests do you think he might have as a member in the United States political system?

Pedro Cervantes is a citizen of Colombia, a large landholder, owning one of the big coffee plantations, a graduate of the National University of Bogotá, living with his family in Bogotá. Hans Mueller is a citizen of the Federal Republic of Germany, a small shopkeeper (shoes and leather goods), now living with his family in Hamburg; his parents, however, live in Dresden, in the GDR. B. R. Jog is a citizen of India; he has a large family and a very small farm; he is a Hindu, speaks no English, and can neither read nor write in any language. Ivan Skivitsky is a citizen of the USSR, a professor of economics at the University of Moscow, he wants very much to make an extended tour of the United States and to bring his family with him. Ukai Taki is a citizen of Japan, a student at the University of Tokyo, studying law; his father manufactures small cars for export. Moses Gold, an immigrant from the United States, has become a citizen of Israel; he is a chemical engineer. Making allowances for individual idiosyncrasies, can you imagine what special interests each of the above persons might have in the political life of his own nation state?

There are, of course, no ready-made answers to the questions above. But if you have read this far in the text, you already have some "pictures in the head" [2] about the differing status of special interests and the differing patterns of national interests in our twelve nation states. Now we shall try to observe more closely the process of interaction between the special interests and the national interests.

THE MODEL OF COMMUNICATIONS AND CONTROL

In our discussion of nationalism in Chapter 3 we have already referred to models of political communication and control. If we think of the political system as a network of communication channels, receiving and transmitting information in a continuous two-way flow of messages, then we can picture the essential process of politics and government. For example, How does Joe Zilch communicate with his government? We note that he belongs to a labor union, thus we surmise that he uses his labor union as a transmitter, communicating to government his special interests as a member of organized labor. We note also that he has VA financing on his home. Whether or not he himself is a member of the American Legion or the Veterans of Foreign Wars, as a veteran he can count on these articulate interest groups claiming special privileges for veterans. He may write letters to the school board, to his congressman, and to the president of the United States; he may join the political party of his choice; he may wear a campaign button, affix political stickers to his car bumper, or join a demonstration parade down Main Street. He may even decide to run for office himself—"Vote for Zilch, the people's candidate!" But what about B. R. Jog? What lines of communication are open to a poor farmer in India who can neither read nor write in any language? Obviously the instruments of communications between the governed and the governors are set up differently in a developing country where the great masses of people are illiterate.

Not only do Joe Zilch and B. R. Jog need different kinds of transmitters to get their messages across to their respective governors, the governments of the United States and India must be equipped with different kinds of receivers attuned to different environments. Because of great contrasts in the external settings—differences in size of territory or size of population, quantity or quality of economic productivity, standards or levels of living, in social structure—the demands from outside the political system and the response from within the system are bound to vary greatly among our twelve nation states. Moreover, variations in the political systems—limited government or totalitarian government, federal or unitary government, presidential or parliamentary government, democracy or dictatorship—also account for different kinds of interaction between the governed and the governors. Nevertheless, however different the instruments of communication or the systems in which they are used, the processes of government are basically similar. Who among the governed makes special demands? With what show of strength? How did the governors get to fill their roles? Who among the governors interprets the demands, evaluates their source, and decides who gets what responses? This is the very essence of politics and the nub of policy-making.

If we think of the political system as a hierarchy, then we perceive the importance of keeping open the lines of communication between the governors and the governed. As Karl Deutsch observes in the *Nerves of Government,* information precedes both compulsion and compliance.[3] In the final analysis, every political system rests on the consent of the governed. Hence the governors must be continuously informed as to who wants what; more specifically, policy-makers need to know which policies will hold or gain popular support; which policies will provoke little public reaction; and which policies, if enforced, are liable to provoke protests, rejection, even revolution.

The model of communication is also the model of control for any political system. The power and influence of the governors depends primarily on the way in which commands are transmitted and received. Obviously, the governed cannot be expected to comply with a command which has not been transmitted to them. If the authority of the governors is accepted as legitimate and if the governors use the communications networks to explain their policies to the governed, then the transmission of commands normally sets up habits of willing compliance on the part of the governed. Only when the techniques of persuasion fail is it necessary for the governors to resort to coercion. Every political system must sometimes turn to the machinery of enforcement—the military, the police, and/or secret agents—but no political system can long survive the stress of continuous use of force as a technique of government. Even the most brutal dictatorships recognize the need for positive communication (keeping the citizens reasonably happy so they will remain loyal and do the government's bidding), as attested by the elaborate propaganda apparatus of Stalin's government in the USSR.

Concepts, models, and generalizations are helpful insofar as they provide a theoretical underpinning for empirical studies. In any approach to comparative politics, however, one needs to question "whether a concept with very specific empirical referents and definable meaning when applied in one kind of political system, can be applied in another kind of system . . . without creating utter miscomprehension or becoming meaningless."[4] In this chapter we make use of our analytical tools to observe distinctive as well as similar patterns of behavior in the interactions of the governors and the governed among our twelve nation states.

PUBLIC OPINIONS AND THE MASS MEDIA

It is part of the conventional wisdom to assert that every political system rests on the consent of the governed. It is a much more difficult exercise in political science, however, to produce the empirical evidence that substantiates such conventional wisdom. The conversion of public opinion into public policy is a very complicated process in any political system. Obviously we cannot begin to provide a definitive discussion within a frame of reference that includes twelve very different nation states.

Nor can we begin to cover all lines of communication between the governors and the governed. In this chapter we confine our attention to three kinds of instruments which appear to be variously useful in the public-opinion process: the mass media of communication, interest groups, and the academic community. These are familiar patterns of political behavior in Western governments. We realize that the mass media of communications serve different functions in the United States and in India, that interest groups play quite different roles in Mexico and in Japan, and that the academic community has different kinds as well as different degrees of influence in the United Kingdom and the Soviet Union. The task we have set for ourselves is to discover similarities as well as dissimilarities in motivation, structure, and function.

In Representative Government

In Table 3–1 we reported that the United States leads the world in quantity of newsprint. Most Americans read a daily newspaper; many subscribe to both morning and evening papers. We count on the newspaper to tell us about the principal news events of the day, in our local community, on the national scene, in the world at large. We expect the reporting to be reasonably objective and fairly accurate—who, what, when, where, and why. We call this the function of surveillance. We also expect our newspapers, particularly the great metropolitan dailies, to perform the function of interpreting and evaluating the news for us. This is the specific assignment of the editorial page, but is also taken on by the special correspondents, such opinion-makers as Max Frankel and Tom Wicker of the *New York Times*, Chalmers Roberts of the *Washington Post,* and Mary McGrory of Washington's *Evening Star,* as well as by numerous syndicated and widely read columnists such as Marquis Childs, William S. White, James Reston, Joseph Alsop, Art Buchwald, and William F. Buckley.[5]

Two other important functions which the daily papers provide for us are cultural transmission and a guide to daily activities. As this page was written in manuscript, a brief strike deprived us of both our morning and evening Washington papers. We missed the critics' reviews of current plays and concerts, the movie, radio, and TV guides, as well as the illuminating accounts of who entertained whom in the official merry-go-round in the Capital. We missed our daily perusal of "The President's Schedule" (we like to keep track of who has access to the White House) and "Activities in Congress" (which tells us times and places for congressional committee meetings and who is testifying on what issues). We also missed the closing prices on the New York Stock Exchange, and last but not least, we missed some crucial frames in "Li'l Abner," "Mary Worth," and "Orphan Annie."

No doubt a contributing factor to the importance of newspapers in the public-opinion process within the United States is the constitutional guarantee of a free press. The First Amendment prohibits Congress from passing any law abridging the freedom of the press; and the Fourteenth Amendment, by judicial construction, imposes a similar restriction upon state or local government censorship. The tradition of a free press in the United States is interpreted to mean freedom from governmental control but not necessarily freedom from political control. A newspaper may serve as a party organ; its selection of news stories, its editorials, its choice of syndicated columnists may all reflect a strongly partisan bias. A newspaper may act as advocate or defender of the special interests of its private owner, or managing editor. Nevertheless any law requiring newspapers to print all the news fit to print, or to report all news fairly and objectively, or to give more than one side in a controversial public issue would be interpreted as an abridgment of a free press. The fact that most communities are served by only one paper still does not put the paper in the category of a public utility subject to regulation in the public interest.

How influential are the newspapers as national political opinion-makers in the United States? We really do not know. The press corps in Washington (nearly a thousand correspondents for wire services, newspapers, magazines, radio, and television) report and analyze the news of the day in many different versions. But whose versions are regarded as most reliable appears to depend more on the political leanings and intellectual orientation of the readers than upon the veracity of the reporters or acumen of the analysts. The authors of this textbook subscribe to the *New York Times* and the *Washington Post,* but these are the very papers that Vice-President Agnew has attacked for inadequate and biased (liberal) reporting on the activities of the Nixon administration. The vice-president made it clear, however, that the Nixon administration was not proposing censorship of any kind. And as long as the constitutional guarantees of a free press still hold, then citizens in the United States may pick and choose from a remarkable galaxy of opinion-makers: *Newsweek, Time,* or the *New Republic;* the *Nation* or *US News and World*

Report; the *Washington Post* or the *St. Louis Post-Dispatch;* the *New York Times* or the *Daily News.*

No country in the world has such an extensive network of telecommunications as the United States—more television sets than bathtubs (see Table 3–2). In 1959 a Roper survey of news media in the United States indicated that more people obtained their political information from newspapers than from radio or TV. Within the decade of the 1960s, however, TV had become the basic news medium for national and international events, with newspapers second and radio third. In 1959 respondents to the Roper survey said they found the newspapers the most believable medium, but within a few years this opinion was reversed. By 1969 TV was leading the newspapers two-to-one in credibility.[6] Thus TV becomes a tool of a new kind of participatory democracy in the United States.

TV, like the newspapers, performs multiple functions: surveillance of events (more on the international and national scenes, less on the state and local level), with interpretation and evaluation of the news largely through a selection of visual images rather than verbal editorializing. TV also provides extensive facilities for transmission of the culture, with emphasis on popular entertainment. Since the major networks are all commercial enterprises, with nearly all shows sponsored by advertisers, the level of culture and entertainment is geared to mass viewing; the rating of shows is determined by the size of audiences rather than quality of the program. The commercials advertising consumer goods add to transmission of the American way of life. Each radio and television station selects its own programs; most television time is given to entertainment rather than information or education.

Unlike the newspapers, TV and radio in the United States are subject to government controls. The technology of American telecasting does not permit free enterprise or free competition; radio and TV transmitters must operate on assigned wave lengths and therefore are required to operate under government licenses. The Federal Communications Commission was created for the purpose of regulating interstate and foreign commerce in communications "to make available so far as possible to all the people of the United States a rapid, efficient, nationwide and worldwide wire and radio communication service with adequate facilities at reasonable charges."[7] Most radio and television stations, independent and/or in the major networks, are privately owned and operated, but all are licensed by the FCC. Although the primary justification for governmental licensing is technical, the FCC treats telecommunications somewhat like public utilities and to some extent regulates the content of communications in the public interest. For example, the FCC applies a fairness doctrine to political broadcasts. If a radio or TV station gives time to one side of a public issue or allows one candidate to present his views, then in all fairness the station must allow equal time for other sides of the controversy or equal time to opposing candidates. A recent United States Supreme Court opinion upholding the fairness doctrine pointed up the overriding function of telecommunications: to keep the electorate informed through fair presentation of public issues and to make possible more intelligent resolution of vital controversies.[8]

The First Amendment does not permit the government to tell any newspaper, magazine, radio, or TV station what or what not to publish or broadcast. Nevertheless engineering consent through the mass media is a regular activity of governmental agencies in the United States. Although the media may resent and resist outright manipulation of the news, they are generally cooperative in giving time and space for messages the government believes to be important. If the president of the United States calls a press conference, the entire Washington press corps as well as journalists from all over the world are eagerly present. If the president wants to speak directly to the people of the United States, the combined networks of radio and TV give him whatever time he requests; and by Intelsat, his message is heard instantly by peoples all around the world. His annual State of the Union message before the joint session of Congress is carried by all television stations. If the secretary of defense or the secretary of health, education, and welfare, or any other high-ranking administrative official wants to test out public opinion on a new policy or to shore up existing policy, his public-relations staff can get out all kinds of persuasive materials in reasonable expectation that the media will use them as intended. Direct broadcasting of cabinet meetings or congressional debates is not yet in order, but many congressional committees not only permit but even encourage televised coverage of public hearings. If the chairman of the Senate Committee on Foreign Relations decides it is time to reeducate public opinion on foreign policy, he can stage public hearings and be assured of headlines, front-page stories, and a frame or two in the nightly kaleidoscope of TV news. And, of course, many members of the administration and of Congress, as well as party leaders, find a nationwide forum in such regularly featured telecasts as "Face the Nation" and "Meet the Press."

Even so, the fact that the mass media are regarded as private enterprise raises some troublesome questions about their power and influence (especially of the networks) upon the formation of political opinions in the United States. Approximately forty million Americans watch the TV newscasts every night: about seven million of these turn to ABC; the rest divide their attention between NBC and CBS. Who determines what news and comments the TV audience will see and hear? For millions of Americans nearly all they know about the events and issues of the day are what they view on television. Vice-President Spiro Agnew angrily charges that a handful of executive producers, commentators, and anchormen not only select but also create the news. Through documentaries and specials they also select and focus on many public issues: pollution in the Great Lakes, conservation of wildlife in the Everglades, black lung diseases in the mining communities, violence in Chicago during the Democratic Convention of 1968, protest rallies against the war in Vietnam, etc. The immediate occasion for Vice-President Agnew's anger was the "instant analysis and querulous criticism"[9] of TV commentators of a speech by President Nixon on the subject of Vietnam. Whatever one's reactions to the subject of Vietnam, the vice-president's charges need to be considered seriously. Who does control the selection of news and political coverage on TV in the United States? Who should have control? The first question calls for some empirical investigation; it is not easy to pinpoint responsibility in corporate management. The second question is even more difficult to answer for it involves us in value judgments which challenge much of the conventional wisdom of our free society.

In the United Kingdom, as in the United States, the press operates as a private industry deriving its profits from circulation and advertising. It is a free press; that is, free from government censorship (except in wartime). National newspapers are available daily throughout the United Kingdom, and since the introduction in the latter part of the nineteenth century of free compulsory education, the readership is extensive. Five morning papers enjoy a circulation of well over a million; the Sunday newspapers boast even higher circulation figures. The *News of the World*, for example, has over six million readers. The largest-selling United States newspaper, the New York *Daily News*, has just under three million.[10]

The political views expressed by the British newspapers generally reflect the views of the owners (or the advertisers). For the most part the owners are major corporations with diversified interests in publication and communications. On the whole, the British press, like the American, adheres to the principle of straight reporting of the news. In editorial views the quality newspapers tend to be independent (the [London] *Times*) or independent-conservative (the *Daily Telegraph*), while the popular newspapers tend to be left of center (*Daily Mirror*) or independent (*Daily Express* and *News of the World*).

Like the American press, the British press takes a dim view of news management by the government. Nevertheless most government departments employ press secretaries or public-relations officers whose job it is to get into the newspapers what the government wants the people to know about official activities and governmental policies. British journalists attend press conferences or collect handouts of their own volition. Again as in the United States, although government officials cannot command publication of their handouts, they can anticipate considerable cooperation from newsmen who consider it part of their function to help keep the public politically alert and informed. Reprinting information from a government handout is, of course, not necessarily synonymous with keeping the public either alert or informed about politics.

The stunning upset victory of the Conservative party over the Labour party in the 1970 elections is partially attributed to the news media. The newspapers and radio and television gave extensive coverage to the prediction of a solid Labour victory by the public opinion polls. The low vote turnout—70 percent of the electorate—is credited with the victory for the Conservatives. The Labour vote, it is said, was so sure of victory that many Labour voters simply did not bother to go to the polls.

With respect to telecommunications, as early as the 1920s the British government rejected the idea of a free-enterprise broadcasting system with private companies operating on a profit basis and also the idea of a communications system owned and operated directly by the government as a political instrument. From 1927 to 1970 the British Broadcasting Corporation (BBC), a public corporation with a royal charter, possessed a monopoly over radio broadcasting, free from commercial as well as political pressures. Governmental policies prohibited the BBC from broadcasting its own views on any public issues, from broadcasting any sponsored program, or from taking payment for any broadcast. When the Conservative government went into office in 1970, one of its first proposals for policy changes was the introduction of commercial radio.

Since the 1930s the BBC has provided news services and a wide variety of entertainment and informational programs, not only for the domestic audience but also for an extensive foreign network. The government has assumed financial responsibility for the foreign broadcasts—"a link of information, culture, and entertainment between the peoples of the United Kingdom and those in other parts of the world." Although the government specifies which countries are to be served and how many hours of service are desired, the BBC maintains the same independence for content of programming abroad as at home. During World War II the external services of the BBC were extremely important in keeping the lines of communication open to friends and foes in Western Europe, the Arab countries, Latin America, and, of course, to all parts of the Empire. The wartime domestic programs were also designed to raise the morale of the British people, to give them a stronger sense of national direction and unity, as well as to provide them with entertainment even during the grimmest hours of the Battle of Britain. Today, despite the increasing audience for television, radio continues to be an important medium of mass communication, partly because portable transistor radios are inexpensive, but also because the BBC tries to serve simultaneously different levels of taste and interest.

The BBC, which was initially given a monopoly over television along with radio broadcasting, may not broadcast any commercial advertisement nor any commercially sponsored programs. Since 1955, however, the Independent Television Authority (ITA), a nonprofit holding company comprising a number of independent commercial television companies, has provided alternate programs. The ITA is forbidden to present any sponsored programs, but it may sell time to advertisers provided the advertising is clearly recognizable as such and does not detract from the quality of the programs. Both the BBC and the ITA are regarded as engaged in public service, "a purveyor of information, education and entertainment to a public of widely varying outlook, intellectual standards and tastes." [11] Today BBC and ITA programs are accessible to virtually the entire population in Britain.

Both the BBC and the ITA operate as political instruments, but under conditions very different from those in the United States. The government has a right to radio and television time for ministerial broadcasts to inform the public on specific issues, to explain new statutes, and to enlist public support. The opposition in Parliament also has a right to radio and television time approximately in proportion to its showing at the polls. For example, when the chancellor of the exchequer appears on radio and television during the week in which he presents the annual budget to Parliament he is immediately followed by a spokesman for the opposition. The BBC is required to carry the main series of party political broadcasts during the year; the ITA may carry the whole, but not part of the series. The allocation of time for and the number of broadcasts is a matter of negotiations between the broadcasting authorities and the party leaders, again roughly in proportion to the show of party strength in the last election. No party is obligated to broadcast if it prefers not to do so; each party, of course, designates its own speakers and makes its own choice of topics. In the general elections the BBC and the ITA carry an agreed number of party broadcasts, not only by the major parties but also by the minority parties, including the Communist party. In addition to the ministerial and party broadcasts, both the BBC and the ITA provide a wide range of programs on policies and issues of the day. They have the duty to give equal opportunity for expression of differing and opposing opinions. The BBC and ITA may not broadcast their own views on policy matters or political subjects but in effect are expected to function as "a trustee for the national interest." [12] When the Conservatives returned to power in 1970 and included a proposal for commercial broadcasting in their initial legislative program, the Laborites responded with the outcry that the Tories had sold out to the commercial broadcasting lobby.

In Totalitarian Government

In a representative government, the mass media are regarded as indispensable instruments of communication and control. The mass media are no less essential to the operations of a totalitarian government. The role of the mass media in the Soviet Union, however, must be examined within the context of the Communist system. Agitation and propaganda (AGITPROP) are among the most important instruments of Communist dictatorships. Propaganda explains to the masses the theoretical foundations of Marxism-Leninism and shows how the theory of Communism can be turned into public policy. Agitation, more emotional than intellectual in its approach, is intended to arouse a feeling for Communism, through catchy ideas and slogans.

The task of propaganda and agitation in the USSR is the political education and socialization of the masses so that they willingly support the Communist regime. Thus the salient characteristics of the Communist press are: its ideological content, its partisan bias, and its mass orientation. Surveillance through objective reporting is not regarded as a function of the press unless it promotes the aims and policies of the Communist party. Information about foreign countries is considered dysfunctional if it presents conditions of living under non-Communist systems in a favorable light. An important aspect of press control is to filter outside news so that the people will have a negative impression of achievements in other systems. Accordingly, the Russian people may know very little about American exploits in outer space, but they are fully informed on ghetto problems and racial tensions in the United States.

The Communist press is expected not only to educate the masses in party ideology but also to help organize them for constructive roles in the socialist state. Hence considerable space in the news is given to exchange of experiences and comparisons of productivity and progress among individual workers, factories, and farm collectives within the various territorial units of the USSR and also with other socialist countries. Moreover, the press is utilized as a steam valve; it is used for a great deal of criticism, criticism both from the top and from the bottom: party or government officials complaining that certain factories, or farms, or writers, or artists, or regions, are not adequately performing their economic or political assignments; individual workers, trade union organizations, farm collectives complaining about specific inefficiencies or shortcomings in the bureaucracies.[13] The mass character of the press is reflected not only by circulation figures but also by participation of the masses in shaping the content of the newspapers. A considerable portion of the daily press (perhaps as much as half in a typical edition) consists of readers' letters and contributions by nonprofessional writers.

No individuals or groups are free to publish their own newspapers or periodicals within the USSR. The right to publish is limited to three groups: government agencies, party organizations, and public associations serving the party. The Constitution guarantees "freedom of the press in conformity with the interests of the workers and in order to strengthen the socialist system." So that newspapers will be available to the people in all parts of the country, the structure of the press parallels the territorial units of the Soviet political system. More than twenty all-Union newspapers serve as channels of communication from the central government or the central party organization to the entire Soviet people. Most prestigious and authoritative are *Pravda,* the chief organ of the Communist party, and *Izvestia,* the official organ of the central government. All activities of the press at every level are planned, controlled, and reviewed ultimately by the Department of Agitation and Propaganda (AGITPROP) of the Central Committee of the Communist party.

Much of what we have said about the press in the Soviet Union is also applicable to radio and television. Like the newspapers, radio and television transmitters serve as mass media for purposes of Communist propaganda and agitation. Partly as an economic solution to the problem of covering a vast territory and reaching a very large population, but also as a psychological approach to building a socialist state in conformity with the interests of the workers, telecommunications are planned especially for group experience rather than entertainment in the home. Thus all the people in an apartment house, or workers in a factory, or farmers in a kolkhoz will gather together not only to receive but also to react collectively to the various programs, which are always in a political context even when the content is cultural entertainment. Indeed it is part of the Communist strategy to use the mass media as agents for raising the cultural level of the people, according to criteria set by the government and party hierarchy.

In Developing Countries

Without attempting to explore communications theory in depth, we need to note some significant correlations between the status of mass media and the various stages of economic and political development. Perhaps the most obvious correlation is the extent and technical sophistication of the mass media and the industrial development of the state. Whether or not a state can produce, or make use of, an extensive system of mass communications depends on its material resources and technology as well as on a variety of sociocultural factors. For example, newspapers with a national circulation require a rapid national transportation system; facilities for rapid communications such as post and telegraph; a considerable capital outlay for buildings and equipment, Linotypes, rotary presses, and newsprint; skilled personnel, printers, reporters, copyreaders, editors, business managers—and, of course, a literate population.[14] Telecommunications make even greater demands: electric power not only for transmitters, but also for receiving sets in the villages and countryside as well as in the cities; and more skilled personnel, engineers and mechanics, technicians, programmers, performers, managers. Hence we find that among our twelve countries, the most highly industrialized states (the United States, the United Kingdom, the USSR, the Federal Republic of Germany, and Japan) possess the most extensive mass media, while the least industrialized countries (India, the Ivory Coast, Kenya, and Turkey) have the least extensive mass media.

Because the costs of building and operating modern mass media run high, less developed countries, where capital is in short supply, are prone to give higher priorities to roads, railroads, power plants, and steel mills. India could develop a stronger sense of national unity much more quickly with more extensive help from the mass media. But the development of mass media in India must wait until basic social and economic improvements have been accomplished. It is not practical, for example, to establish a massive circulation for newspapers until India has first overcome the problem of massive illiteracy; hence the overall cost of developing a national press in India must include vast expenditures for modern schools where all the people are taught to read a common language. Radio and television might circumvent the problem of illiteracy, but the sheer size of India—in land and people—raises almost insurmountable problems in technology as well as financing. The Ministry of Information and Broadcasting reported in 1969 that radio programs were reaching 56 percent of the country and 73 percent of the people, but television was available only within a twenty-five-mile range of Delhi.[15]

The size of the mass media is generally correlated with economic development. Ownership and control of the media and the content of the communications are largely determined by the stage of political development and by the political philosophy of the people. Among the developing countries we find varying patterns of ownership, regulation, and programming. In Turkey, for example, the government owns and controls all communications media except the newspapers. The metropolitan papers are widely read; but in the countryside where illiteracy is still a serious problem, the government counts especially on radio to politicize the people and to help develop a sense of national identity. As in most traditional societies, oral communications are most persuasive; hence the Turkish coffeehouses, both in the cities and in the villages, are natural centers for group-shared communications, whether a government-sponsored radio program or a newspaper read aloud. In countries like Kenya and the Ivory Coast, where most of the people are illiterate, the newspapers reach a relatively small readership. Nevertheless the government keeps a tight control over content. In both Kenya and the Ivory Coast the government owns and operates the broadcasting systems, but these have very limited use. Government officials and party leaders find it more effective to do a good deal of traveling into the back country, meeting and talking with people directly, receiving their petitions and complaints, and in turn explaining and boosting government policies and party plans.

Generally, there is a high correlation between democratic governments and open channels of communication and a high correlation between totalitarian governments and controlled media. In Turkey, for example, when the one-party system came to an end, there was an immediate jump in the number of newspapers as well as in circulation figures.[16] In Japan, where there is no dominant political ideology, where the government is expected to represent all the people, where literacy is high, the mass media are used as instruments for an open society. Thus the newspapers, which are privately owned, enjoy a large national circulation and provide national news coverage including extensive facilities for external communications. They constantly monitor government activities and are traditionally critical of government policies. As in the United States, Japanese broadcasting networks are owned and operated by private corporations and government controlled as to conduct but not as to content of communications.

The roles and functions of the mass media may be perceived quite differently in developing countries and in industrialized states. Journalism, for example, is traditionally a Western profession that only recently has become influential in non-Western societies.[17] In most non-Western societies the national press is not really indigenous. Colonial governments in Asia and Africa found it expedient to encourage the publication of newspapers or journals to carry official announcements or in other ways to function as a public information service. Resident foreigners frequently established their own press for the purpose of circulating news of the outside world. In the transitional period between colonialism and independence, the newspapers performed numerous services, bringing news of the outside world into the country, providing vehicles for the political views of intellectuals, serving as instruments of propaganda for and against government policies, encouraging agitation and promoting organization of the agitators. This is approximately how the Indian press became an agent and provocateur first for independence and then for modernization of the country.

In Mexico where illiteracy has been substantially reduced through compulsory education, the circulation of newspapers has increased correspondingly. The government relationship to the press appears to be pretty flexible. The government depends on the newspapers to carry essential public information and generally to support government policies. On the other hand, the press is relatively free from government censorship; criticism of minor officials and minor policies is tolerated or overlooked, but it is unlikely that the government would long brook any serious criticism.

Mexican telecommunications are regulated by the Secretariat of Communications and Transport, but both radio and television broadcasting are products of commercial enterprise, featuring popular entertainment rather than political communications. In fact, in many ways the pattern of political communication in Mexico and Colombia, as well as other Latin American countries, is more traditional than modern, relying less on the mass media than upon pervasive personal contacts. Certainly the Mexican government appears to have done a remarkable job of interchanging communications with the governed: on the one hand mobilizing public opinion and giving the people at large a sense of national direction, and on the other hand ascertaining what individuals and groups in the society want and what they will support. Much of this interchange is person to person, government officials and party leaders exchanging views with peasant leaders, labor leaders, business leaders, not only in the capital but throughout the country.

INTEREST GROUPS

In a general way we can define politics as the process of interaction between the governors and the governed. The key word in this bit of jargon is *interaction:* Both the governors and the governed are actors in the political system, each vying to influence the actions of the other. Who influences whom is the most fascinating, yet most elusive, facet of political behavior. In the preceding section we discussed the uses of the mass media in keeping open the lines of communication between the governors and the governed. In this section we will observe how individuals with common interests join together in order to maximize their political pressure upon official decision-makers. Note that both communications and interest-group theories are based on the hypothesis that interaction between the governors and the governed on the one hand induces the governors to formulate and implement popular policies and on the other hand induces the governed to comply with official decisions and to accept them as public policies.

Now let us test out group theory with reference to our twelve nation states. How do the governors react to the politics of pluralism? How do they manage to translate the competing, even conflicting, special interests of diverse groups into public policies which appear to embrace the national interest?

In Representative Government

The politics of pluralism probably reaches its zenith in the United States where Americans generally are inclined to establish their individual identity with reference to their group membership. Who am I? Remember Joe Zilch? He tells us he is a Roman Catholic, a member of the Steam Fitters' Union, a Veteran of Foreign Wars, a member of the National Rifle Association, and a Republican. In the United States even congressmen are prone to identify themselves and to impress their constituents by referring to their own group membership. A random look at the *Congressional Directory* provides any number of illustrations.[18]

We would be going way out on a limb if we claimed that an individual citizen or decision-maker establishes his political stance according to the political views of the groups with which he identifies himself. An individual with multiple group memberships may find himself at odds with his various associates on any number of significant issues. In the United States, university professors cover the spectrum of political opinions about the war in

Vietnam, government-sponsored research on campus, or socialized medicine. Members of a labor union are more likely to be Democrats than Republicans, though both parties bid for their votes; church affiliations appear to be totally irrelevant to union membership; as to hobbies, union men may collect first-day stamp covers, hike mountain trails, shoot pool (or rabbits). Nevertheless, group membership may be considered at least as an indicator of personal values and special interests which an individual shares with other members. Hence a practical politician, as well as an observant political scientist, finds it worthwhile to study the roles and functions of interest groups in the political process.

The principal purpose of any interest group is to influence governors with respect to specific policies. Ordinarily a pressure group does not enter an election contest; it does not put up candidates of its own; rather, it seeks party candidates favorable to its interests. Thus it will try to impress its strength upon the power structure of the political parties in order to gain recognition of its special interest in the parties' platforms. It will try to influence Congress through lobbying; that is, by persuading congressmen by various means to protect and promote the group interests. It will try to influence bureaucrats whose activities may impinge on the special interest of the group. Indeed, membership of the group may extend into the bureaucracy itself; e.g., interlocking personnel in the American Farm Bureau and the United States Department of Agriculture or in the National Education Association and the United States Office of Education. The group may even enter the judicial arena to gain what it wants through group-sponsored litigation, as the NAACP did so successfully in the 1950s. Finally, it may try to influence the political environment generally through informational programs and public propaganda in the mass media.

Pressure groups in the United States perform a variety of functions important in democratic politics: 1) They stimulate an atmosphere of social awareness and single out crucial issues to which the governors are expected to respond. The NAACP, CORE, and similar groups were very influential in advancing racial integration as a public policy in the 1950s. The National Rifle Association, on the other hand, was remarkably successful in the 1960s in blocking any national control over private firearms. 2) Pressure groups not only indoctrinate their own members, but through the mass media they also mobilize the political opinions of the general public to the point that political parties are impelled to include a composite of special interests in their respective national platforms. 3) They join in the process of electioneering, help get out the vote, and thus help provide popular support for the governors elected to office. 4) The major pressure groups, representing organized labor, organized farmers, organized capital, organized professions, and organized veterans furnish the governors with needed counsel both in the formulation and implementation of specific policies. AFL-CIO groups, for example, furnish basic intelligence for drafting labor legislation and also for activating labor policies. When, as it often happens, spokesmen for the National Association of Manufacturers or the Chamber of Commerce provide different information and different advice on labor-management issues, then it behooves the practical politician to consider the relative merits of the special interest within the framework of the general interest and also to weigh the relative influence of the competing groups measured in such terms as size of membership, financial backing, and intensity of group feelings vis-à-vis public opinions generally. Hence, 5) The very pluralism of American politics, many different groups openly and fiercely competing for their own special interests, forces official decision-makers to work out patterns of consensus. 6) Because the national interests, as perceived by the decision-makers, reflect generally a coalition of group interests, the continuous jockeying for power positions within the several interest groups as well as the ever-changing status of the groups within the societal structure promotes an on-going appraisal of public policies by practical politicians attuned to the changing tides of public opinion.[19]

Political pressure groups may be most numerous and most highly organized in the United States, but the politics of pluralism appear in various configurations in all twelve of our nation states. Pressure groups have been operating in the United Kingdom since the earliest days of representative government. In the nineteenth century they were major agents of political reform, demanding and obtaining much of the landmark social legislation of that age. British pressure groups of today are far different "in social base, structure, purpose, political tactics, relations with government, and the foundations of their political power" than the transient reformist groups of the Victorian era.[20] The major sectors of the British economy—business, labor, agriculture, and the professions—are organized to do continuous business with the government; they derive their power and influence from their respective roles as producers in a modern industrial state. In essence, Britain has gradually worked out a system of functional representation to complement its traditional parliamentary representation. An elaborate and complicated network of communications and consultation brings together government officials and spokesmen from the diverse interest groups. Thus, each government agency has access to the particular information and expertise it needs to perform its regulatory and control functions over the economy and, by the same arrangement, each economic group gets an opportunity to make its demands and to give its advice and consent upon the matters which concern its members most directly.

Organized labor has long been a potent factor in British politics.[21] British trade unions date back to the eighteenth century as voluntary associations of workers, joined together for mutual protection, to secure decent conditions of employment and fair wages. Today nearly half of all employees in the United Kingdom are members of trade unions. The trade-union movement became politically active at the turn of the twentieth century when the Trade Union Congress proposed that the socialist societies, trade unions, and other workers' groups form a political party to secure the direct representation of labor in Parliament. In the 1906 general election this newly formed Labour party won twenty seats in Parliament.

During most of its existence as a major political party, the Labour party has been the opposition party, but twice in coalition with the Liberal party it has been the Government party (in 1924 and again in 1929–35) and twice it has been the Government party (1945–51 and 1966–70).

Although the British trade unions are directly linked to the Labor party, they also retain a quite separate identity. British trade unions are still organized to get what they want by direct economic action. Trade unions are forbidden by law to use their ordinary funds collected as dues from the members for political purposes. Union members, however, may choose to establish a special political fund, and also as a matter of fact, these special union funds constitute the principal source of finances for the Labor party with which the Trade Union Congress shares one building, Transport House, as headquarters.

The British concept of parliamentary representation does not lend itself easily to pressure-group politics. An MP is expected to represent the national interest rather than to serve his local or economic constituents. This is in contrast to the American views of representation which tend to emphasize the ties of congressmen to the particular constituencies wherein they reside. Moreover, the functional organization of the British Parliament makes it less susceptible to pressure politics than the American Congress. The congressional committee system is based on special policy concerns; e.g., the committees on agriculture, labor, commerce, etc. British committees, on the other hand, have been organized to expedite the legislative process rather than to develop a special expertise; thus, committees A, B, C, etc., handle all kinds of legislation simply in chronological order. In the United States interest groups given access to congressional committees considering special policies frequently engage in lobbying to obtain, or block, legislation relating to their respective interests. Pressure politics in the British system, however, appear to be more effective in the form of continuous contacts between government officials and interest-group representatives concerned with the same special issues. These are not so much ad hoc opportunistic contacts as they are for the most part in the United States, but rather part of a carefully designed overall pattern of economic representation.

Both major parties, Labour and Conservative, accept the idea of functional representation throughout the structure and process of British government. For example, the National Economic Development Council includes at the highest level representatives of government, the management of private and public industry, the Trade Union Congress, and independent experts in economic development. The Economic Development Committee for Agriculture comprises representatives of landlords, farmers, agricultural workers and also representatives from the government agricultural agencies, the Department of Economic Affairs, and the National Economic Development Office. And, in fact, most of the country's important industries now operate under EDCs. The overall pattern is complicated, the process is bugged by bureaucrats, but the underlying concept is more than reminiscent of old-fashioned British syndicalism, a managed economy with continuous interaction among representatives of 1) the government; 2) associations of owners, employers, and managers; and 3) the organized workers.

A considerable part of the British economy is now run by public corporations in the public interest (the nationalized industries): the fuel and power industry (coal, gas, electricity, and steel), surface transport (railways, buses, docks), civil aviation (airways and airports), and communications (post, telegraph, radio, and television). Each nationalized industry is expected to establish its own machinery, under ministerial control, to negotiate with the representatives of labor and management to determine working conditions and wage schedules. Moreover, the public corporations as producers, traders, and employers share the experiences and interests of the business community, as evidenced by the admission of their representatives to the Confederation of British Industry.

Even in a collectivist economy (public ownership of utilities, transport system, and some industry), the trade associations representing the British business community have an influential role. Trade associations cover virtually all the major industries: the Society of British Aircraft Contractors, the British Man-Made Fibers Federation, the Federation of Master Cotton Spinners Association, the Cake and Biscuit Alliance, the Society of Motor Manufacturers and Traders, etc. Just as the trade unions are joined in the Trade Union Congress, so the trade associations have set up supergroupings such as the Confederation of British Industries, the National Union of Manufacturers, and the British Employers Confederation (the latter negotiates with 70 percent of the employed population). Following the collectivist model, multiple advisory committees are attached to all of the government's economic control agencies, with representation on all of these committees drawn from related trade associations and trade unions, as well as from the reservoir of independent experts.

We get quite a different perspective on the role of interest groups when we turn our attention from producer groups to consumer groups in the collectivist economy.[22] Political parties bidding for electoral support appeal to the whole gamut of consumers and multiple beneficiaries of public welfare programs. Electioneering styles of the major parties attest to the influence of pressure groups in the general electorate. Labor and Conservative candidates alike must take cognizance of diverse demands and supports, and campaign accordingly for the votes of families who want better housing, motorists who want better roads, parents who want better schools for their children, old people who want higher pensions, people generally who want better medical care, etc. Thus the process of elections conditioned by the politics of pluralism in turn affects the political obligations of members of Parliament in the translation of public opinion into public policies.

In Totalitarian Government

In any modern state the politics of pluralism must take cognizance of diverse economic groups all expecting to get what they want out of the political system. The more modern the state, that is, the more industrialized and urbanized, the more imperative it is for official decision-makers to draw from the whole spectrum of expertise and technological skills in the society. Planning and implementing public policies in such areas as national security, mobilization of resources, large-scale economic planning, mass communications, social security, and education call for highly sophisticated social engineering, as well as political leadership. Among our twelve states the government of the USSR appears most dictatorial, but when we examine the process of policy-making we perceive that numerous interest groups are actually quite articulate and influential within the bureaucracy and the party apparatchik. True, all of the groups must subscribe to the overriding concept of state socialism; all policies promoted must conform to the interests of the proletariat, i.e., the public, and no group is so brash as to challenge the legitimate monopoly of the Communist party in the final allocation of values. Nevertheless, up to the point of decision, controversy is not only permitted, it flourishes. As we noted in the preceding section on communications, special points of view as well as new ideas are encouraged in the mass media. Thus occupational groups may create public interest and mobilize party support through public debates, provided, of course, that all the debaters remember to include frequent professions of loyalty to the regime and cease opposition once a policy decision has been made.

American political scientists trying to apply group theory to the Soviet system observe that Russian officials do consciously take into account the needs and demands of diverse factions in the society. They point out that expertise is recognized as a desirable component of decision-making. Hence persons with special competencies or knowledge related to the issues in debate may become quite influential as resource authorities in determining the outcome. The modernization of Russia under the virtually monolithic direction of the Communist party leadership has, rather ironically, brought about a complex economic and social pluralism which more and more impels the politics of accommodation within the system. The old Bolsheviks and Stalinists could impose their will—by force and/or persuasion—upon a largely agrarian society in which the masses of peasants were unorganized and unaccustomed to an active role in the political system. But continuous political agitation to popularize Communism has made the Russian people generally much more aware of and alert to public issues.

The newly prestigious groups in Russia—the scientists, technologists, economic specialists, managerial specialists, and even teachers and writers—have gained access to the political decision-makers in the government and in the party for the very obvious reason that their counsel is functional, almost indispensable, in the policy process. But even the peasants have become conscious of their political power—measured in sheer numbers and developed in active association—so that they voice their demands with increasing temerity and insistence in the public forum as well as in government and party circles.[23] This does not mean that communications between the social environment and the political system are as effective as in the United States nor that the consultative arrangements between the social strata and the official hierarchy are as elaborate as in the United Kingdom, but it does suggest that the pressures of pluralism are pushing even the Soviet Union toward participatory democracy.[24]

National priorities set by official decision-makers reflect their own perceptions of national interests within the framework of the dominant ideology, and in turn these priorities determine at least in part the role and status of interest groups in the political system. Thus we are not surprised to find that interest groups play a relatively minor role and occupy a definitely subordinate status in the politics of the USSR. The ruling elite within the Communist party is still in position to impose totalitarian government upon the Russian people. (The means of imposition we shall discuss more fully in Chapter 7.) Hence, despite evidence of increasing demands from middle-class professionals, farmers, and consumers, Soviet official policies still award the highest priorities to the military and heavy-industry sectors of the economy. This stress on strategic considerations is in accord with hard-line policies that were developed in the years of Russian alienation from the West. But as the new Soviet man emerges, and the aging Communist party leadership goes the way of all flesh, and if détente progresses between the East and West, then we may expect the Soviet political system to accommodate itself to various internal demands as well as to different external pressures.

We find the politics of pluralism—diverse groups making competing and conflicting demands upon the political system—in all twelve of our nation states. Group theory thus serves as an analytical construct for pointing out who gets what in different kinds of political systems. We must beware, however, of any simplistic equations between inputs and outputs in the policy process. Note, for example, the similarity of strategic policies of the United States and the Soviet Union which favor the military-industrial complex in both countries. In the United States we are inclined to stress the role of the defense industries and to point accusingly to big business and to big labor. But in the USSR, where there are no big business or big labor groups in the private sector, we ascribe the heavy emphasis on defense policies to the ideological concerns of the Communist party leadership! In Japan, where professional militarists have been almost entirely removed from the political system, business and labor groups, highly organized and effectively articulated with official policy-makers, find their rewards in a broadly diversified peacetime economy.

In Developing Countries

We are wary of generalizations, especially when we try to apply them in developing nations. In would-be socialist India, the Congress party gets massive support from private business. The linkage between the Congress and the Indian Chambers of Commerce antedates independence. Today the Federation of Indian Chambers of Commerce and Industry has its own spokesmen in Parliament and has ready access to the various ministries of government. On the other hand, Gandhi's interest in organized labor was minimal, and since independence the trade union movement has gotten under way very slowly. In the cities, as late as 1963, membership in the four national labor federations totaled less than 10 percent of the labor force.[25]

Social and economic factors account in part for the weakness of organized labor in India. Most of the workers, illiterate and caste-conscious, are not inclined to engage on their own in collective bargaining with their employers. Union leadership is usually assumed by middle-class politicians, lawyers, and social reformers; it is rarely recruited from the rank and file, who do not feel comfortable or competent in bargaining with representatives of a higher social and economic class. Actually, the strongest support, even impetus, for India's planned economy with its expanding public sectors comes from business rather than labor (or agricultural) interests.

In Colombia freedom of association for representation of occupational and professional interests is guaranteed in the 1936 Constitution. The Labor Code of 1950 deals elaborately with the respective rights of employers and employees, collective labor contracts, management-labor relations, and the internal government of labor unions. The Ministry of Labor is responsible for administration of the code and labor law generally. Because the Labor Code is so comprehensive and the social security legislation so paternalistic, labor unions have not had much opportunity to develop as independent political groups. The unions draw most of their membership from the urban centers. The petroleum processing industry is the most extensively organized. More than 90 percent of the petroleum workers belong to the militant Confederation of Unions of Colombian Workers (CONSICol). The two major federations of unions are the Confederation of Colombian Workers (CTC) and the Union of Colombian Workers (UTC). As in the United States, the unions are forbidden by law from engaging directly in partisan political activities. Nevertheless, members of the CTC (founded in 1936 by leftist liberals and Communists), most of them in the textile, steel, and shipping industries, tend to line up with the Liberal party. Members of the UTC (organized in 1946 by rightist conservatives with support from the Catholic Church) tend to line up with the Conservative party.

Management and business associations, however, appear to have much more influence than the labor unions in the shaping of national economic policies. The National Association of Industrialists (ANDI) with headquarters in Medellín, the industrial capital of Colombia, is most effective in representing its views within the government, cooperating with the government in planning national economic development and providing technical services to the bureaucracy in connection with regulation of industry. The National Federation of Merchants (FENALCO) in a similar fashion represents the commercial interests, the merchants in the cities. As in India, the influence of the management and business associations is tied into the social structure of the country. The industrialists, the managers, and the merchants not only belong to the same class as the legislators and the bureaucrats, more than likely they belong to the same ruling families. The workers, on the other hand, are separated, as a class, both from their employers and their governors —they are still, for the most part, the uneducated, the unwashed, the *obrerismo* (not too different from the Indian untouchables).

The patterns of economic organization for political purposes vary but little among developing nations. Whether the economy leans toward free enterprise or state socialism, the business community is generally most influential in government planning, though the activities of its members are more likely to be confidential and personal rather than openly political. This comment may well be applied to Colombia, Kenya, the Ivory Coast, and even to Turkey. For the most part agricultural and labor interests in developing countries are still expressed in amorphous associations rather than in effective political organizations. When a traditional society suddenly adopts Western political institutions—universal suffrage, general elections, and representative legislatures—its politicians who need the support of broad segments of the population frequently resort to personalistic appeals and extraneous issues.

The one-party socialist system of Mexico makes elaborate provisions for the representation of plural interests, formally organized and explicitly presented. The Revolutionary party (PRI) which has enjoyed a commanding position in Mexican politics since 1929 is functionally organized on a group base: labor, agricultural, and popular. The labor sector comprises a number of different groups, including the Mexican Workers Federation (CTM), the largest and most important single labor organization. The farm sector also represents various groups, including the National Confederation of Farmers (CNC), the principal spokesman of agricultural interests. The popular sector is the most complex, acting as a kind of holding company for numerous and diverse groups of small-farm proprietors, small-business men, artisans, government employees, and intellectuals.

Individual and group membership in the sectors of the PRI appear in varying proportions and strength, reflecting continuous changes in Mexican society. Most Mexicans who expect their demands to be met in the political arena are impelled to join one of the groups incorporated in the PRI structure which has a virtual monopoly in recruiting bureaucratic specialists as well as official decision-makers. This is not to suggest, however, that the PRI exercises the kind of totalitarian rule that the Communist party maintains in the USSR. First, although Mexico is characterized as a one-party state, actually the PRI is not the only party in Mexican politics; a number of minor parties appear and disappear, most of them reflecting the personal ambitions of would-be leaders, rather than ideological or functional aspirations, although some of them draw their followings from interest groups, usually interests too specialized or too extreme for the official party to embrace. Secondly, we must note that some of the most important and influential groups remain outside the party apparatus, notably such organizations among the business community as chambers of commerce, associations of employers, and industrial associations. Obviously, such associations do not conform to the revolutionary image of the PRI. Nevertheless, in order to advance its plans for a modern economy, the PRI in government is quite pragmatic in taking advice and counsel from the business community, despite protests from organized farmers or workers to the contrary.

Noneconomic Interest Groups

So far our discussion has centered on economic and mainly occupational interest groups. Perhaps this reflects our Western value system! We know that in the politics of the United States many noneconomic groups make special demands, such as religious groups, veterans, patriotic societies, and ethnic groups. In some political systems, noneconomic associations may be more significant than occupational groups—tribalism in Kenya, religious association in Israel, the caste system in India, for example.

In Kenya the one-party system, the Kenya African National Union (KANU) dominated by Jomo Kenyatta is in fact a volatile balance of traditional tribal interests. Thus, political analysts are inclined to attribute the massive rejection of parliamentary incumbents in the 1969 KANU primary to hostile reactions of Luo tribesmen to the assassination of their leader Tom Mboya by a Kikuyu in the summer of 1969. At any rate, recent political turmoil in Kenya clearly attests to tribal rivalries and antagonisms which can scarcely be contained by Western political processes.

In Israel, the pillar of pluralism, the *Histadrut* antedates the state. Originally founded as a socialist-labor organization in the Yishuv, financed largely by Jewish unionists in the United States, it has become an economic colossus in modern Israel. Its operations include not only trade union activities but also sports, newspapers, films, magazines, medical services, savings funds, marketing cooperatives, etc. Though outside the official structure of the state, the Histadrut exerts enormous political influence through interlocking leadership with the Mapai party dominant in the government. Members of the Knesset are generally responsive to Histadrut demands. Nevertheless the Histadrut, which has its roots in the Yishuv and world Zionism, is being challenged today by a newer pluralism, by new occupational, geographic, and ethnic groups, new nationalists who are more likely to identify themselves with Israel as a developing state than with the ancient promised land of world Jewry.

A study of voting behavior in the 1962 elections in India dwells on the traditional ties of caste, religion, kinship, and language.[26] The caste system based on color, kinship, social status, and occupational group goes back to ancient times. More than three thousand years ago, Aryan people invaded and conquered the indigenous people of India. The Aryans were generally more light-skinned than the natives; hence, *Varna*, which refers to caste groups, means "color." The light-skinned conquerors, who assumed the dominant roles in society, developed a social structure based on color, but gradually the four major castes of India came to be based on occupation: the Brahmans (priests), *Kshatriyas* (warriors and rulers), *Vaisyas* (merchants), and *Sudras* (native workers). After centuries of intermingling and integrating, these primitive castes evolved into a complex social system comprising thousands of subcaste groupings with varying bases of membership from village to village, region to region.

The Indian Constitution was intended to restructure this traditional social system so that every Indian might have an opportunity to develop himself according to his own capacity. Thus Article 17 of the Constitution abolishes the concept of untouchability (referring to the *Pariahs*, lowest level of the Sudras) and forbids discrimination in all public places on account of caste, race, religion, sex, or place of birth. The caste system survives, however. Subcastes (*jati*) may vary in size from a handful to thousands of members; each jati is a closed group with distinctive rituals, rules, social customs, cultural patterns, and economic functions. To what extent India's modern political structure embraces the traditional caste system is still debatable. Universal adult suffrage and parliamentary representation on a geographical basis certainly cut across caste and sectional lines. Apparently middle- and low-status groups have capitalized on their political situation to upgrade their social status and economic condition. Even so, the selection of candidates and the results of elections as late as 1963 suggest strong correlation between caste-consciousness and political cohesion, especially in rural areas.

Remember B. R. Jog, the illiterate Hindu farmer whom you met early in this chapter? He still has not grasped Western notions of political participation. He has never read a newspaper; he cannot read. He has rarely heard radio broadcasts, though there are a few transistor radios in his village; he has never seen television and neither has anyone else in his village. Interparty and intraparty struggles for power in the national arena are remote from the politics of his small village. There are, however, several factions in his village, most of them antedating party organizations, but he is too poor and low in caste to count himself a member of any faction. Nevertheless faction leaders vie for his support in Western-type, one-man-one-vote elections. B. R. Jog will most likely vote for the faction leader who promises to improve life in the village, to build new water wells or dig irrigation ditches, or bring in better seed and more fertilizer. When faction leaders make similar promises, personal associations and the ties of caste and kinship are more persuasive than party platforms and political ideologies.

THE SPECIAL ROLE OF THE ACADEMIC COMMUNITY

Remember Pedro Cervantes, citizen of Colombia, a graduate of the National University of Bogotá; Ivan Skivitsky, citizen of the USSR, professor of economics at the Moscow University; and Ukai Taki, citizen of Japan, a student in the University of Tokyo? Note that each of these individuals is singled out for his connections with the academic community. Stretch your imagination a bit and let us speculate about the political implications of membership in the academic community.

In Colombia Pedro Cervantes with his degree from the National University of Bogotá (one of the oldest universities in the Western hemisphere, founded in 1572) belongs to the oligarchy—a member of one of the well-to-do families with European background who still comprise the upper class in the country. The Colombians prize education; their Constitution guarantees freedom of education, but education is not compulsory and even today fewer than half the children of school age are in schools. According to official estimates (1951–60) less than 10 percent of the adult population had any secondary education and less than 1 percent held university degrees. In Latin American politics the two most prestigious titles are said to be *general* and *doctor;* in Colombia *doctor* usually outranks *general.* Doctor Cervantes's university degree may be considered an admission card to the oligarchy, but the fact that he was able to attend a university in the first place suggests that he was also born into the oligarchy. As a university student Pedro may have participated in various protest movements and strikes; Colombian students have a long record of political activism. But as Doctor Cervantes he may be expected to claim the rights and privileges of the intelligentsia, sit in Congress, accept a cabinet post, head his own business, or run his own hacienda. The University ties are tightly woven around the oligarchy in all its activities.

As a professor of economics at the University of Moscow, Ivan Skivitsky occupies an important position in the intellectual setting of the Soviet Union. The setting, however, is very different from that which we have sketched for Colombia. The University of Moscow, founded in 1755, the largest educational and research center in the country, has a staff of nearly three thousand professors, instructors, and research workers; an enrollment of more than twenty-two thousand students. There are nearly eight hundred institutions of higher learning in the country with a total student population of more than four million.[27] The USSR has had universal compulsory education since 1934. In the 1960s the New Party Program called for compulsory eleven-year secondary, general, and polytechnical education for all children of school age in urban and rural communities, with higher education made available to all able and willing to pursue it.

Since the official ideology of the Soviet Union is based on Marxian economics, Professor Skivitsky is expected to expound and defend Marxian economics against all other economic philosophies—in the classroom, in publications, in the public forum. As a recognized specialist in economics he will be drawn into the bureaucracy where his advice will be sought on how to make the most rational allocation of the nation's resources in line with the nation's goals and the party ideology, how to improve the governmental methods of planning and organizing industrial and agricultural production, specifically and technically, how to build and promote a viable Communist society. He will also be expected to advise the party organization and to provide party workers, leaders, and the rank and file with theoretical grounding for propaganda and agitation. Academic freedom as it is touted in the United States, including notions of neutrality and objectivity in scholarship, is rejected outright in the Soviet system. Thus Professor Skivitsky's request for permission to take his family on an extended visit to the United States is likely to be judged not so much on the merits of his scholarship as upon the firmness of his commitment to the official ideology and upon his demonstrated loyalty to the Communist regime. The institutions of higher learning in the Soviet Union are under the jurisdiction of the All-Union Council, fairly rigidly supervised by the Union-Republic Ministry of Higher and Specialized Secondary Education.

Ukai Taki, a student at the University of Tokyo, belongs to one of the most violent and dissident groups in Japan—the student protest group: antimilitary, antiwar, antiauthoritarian, antibureaucratic. Student unrest in Japan, as in France, Mexico, or the United States, tends to be anarchistic, intensely ideological, and generally antiestablishment. The University of Tokyo where Taki is studying law is the oldest state university in modern Japan, founded in 1877. Members of its prestigious faculty have long been noted for their influence in government and business circles. Its graduates are systematically recruited for the upper echelons of the government bureaucracy and for the managerial elite who now control the big business organizations of Japan. The University of Tokyo symbolizes the establishment. But in the summer of 1970 Taki joined thousands of his fellow students in street demonstrations against continuation of the Japan-United States Security Treaty. This was part of a new-left movement that comprises militant students, labor factions, leading intellectuals, and housewives.

The present educational system of Japan dates from 1947, but education has always ranked high on the scale of social values in modern Japan. Compulsory education through the elementary school was established in 1907. Today the Japanese public school system extends through four years of university training. Japan has six main state universities; but, counting public and private schools, there are some three hundred institutions of university or collegiate level, with approximately a million students enrolled. Admission to the universities is highly competitive and student fees are rising. It is still true, however, that a poor man with ability can rise to influence and affluence through education; the universities especially may be regarded as social and economic escalators. The chances are good that Taki who now belongs to the student protest movement will join the establishment when he graduates; he may enter one of the government offices or he may be drawn into the family business. In either case he will probably keep in touch with his professors and consult with them from time to time; in this way the academic community is tied to the political system and the economic order.

Pedro Cervantes, Ivan Skivitsky, and Ukai Taki are stereotypes used to illustrate various relationships between members of the academic community and the political system in different national environments. Pursuing these relationships in a more analytical discussion we perceive that the academic community, particularly at the collegiate and university level, performs a number of important functions for the political system: 1) teaching—transmitting the culture from one generation to the next; 2) professional training —preparing the youth of the nation for positions of leadership in an increasingly complex and technological society; 3) research—advancing the frontiers of knowledge and technology; and 4) public service—keeping open "the channels of communication between the world of thought and the seat of power." [28] How well the academic community performs these functions is a matter of debate in every country today. Let us briefly examine some facets of the debate.

Teaching and Political Socialization

Transmitting the culture from one generation to the next is in itself a highly important activity, basic to the political socialization of the nation. Without question, the values and ideals of a nation are largely fashioned in ivory towers. But what shall the faculties teach? Obviously the university's philosophers, economists, sociologists, historians, and political scientists have a special responsibility to provide the taught tradition of the people. We noted that Professor Skivitsky lauded Marxian economics at Moscow University, just as Professor John Doe expounds the economics of free enterprise at the University of Chicago. A professor at the National University of Bogotá may take sharp exception to a textbook in political science entitled *The Politics of American Democracy* on the grounds that the authors are so parochial that they seem to equate American government with United States government, without regard to differing patterns of democracy in the republics of Latin America. Two eminent and dispassionate scholars, one a professor of history at Oxford, the other at Yale, view the American Revolution in quite different contexts. Middle East history as it is taught at the

University of Ankara is at considerable variance with Middle East history as it is taught at the Hebrew University in Jerusalem. Teachers in the Federal Republic of Germany, in accordance with official cultural policy, are trained to handle the period 1933 to 1945 "with great forcefulness . . . in order to ingrain the values of freedom and democracy at an early age." [29] In new and developing countries where the imperative of nation-building calls for systematic political socialization, the educational system is expected to inculcate attitudes and dispositions that will support state authority over and against the traditional demands of the family, tribe, or caste, and promote acceptance of technology over traditional methods of production.

The community of scholars may be dedicated to the search for universal truth, but the truth seems to be "that national universities are, in most ways and in large degree, national in their outlook and parochial in the range of their knowledge and interests." [30] The distinguished American anthropologist Margaret Mead reminds us "today, nowhere in the world are there elders who know what the children know, no matter how remote and simple the societies are in which the children live." [31] This, she observes, is at the root of student rebellion in the universities all over the world. Students born into the world since the explosion of the first atom bomb at Hiroshima "are like the first generation born into a new country." More at home in the modern world than their parents or their professors, they are eager to do their own thing in a world of their own choosing. Living in a time when the whole human race is immediately threatened by nuclear annihilation, population explosion, mass starvation, environment pollution, racial conflicts, and ideological warfare, youth may well construe the transmission of the culture in the academic manner as a delaying action, an irrelevant function.

Universities, we observe, are in turmoil everywhere. An academic revolution is underway; it appears to be a genuine revolution, not merely a reaction or a reform. It is happening at Berkeley, Berlin, Bogotá, London, Mexico City, Tokyo, and on your own campus. It is transforming the historical function of the academic community—the preservation of the humane values of a civilized society—into a future-oriented, highly politicized function, calling for active engagement in the reshaping of our culture. How all of this will affect the political system in specific countries we leave you to discuss.

Recruiting and Training for the Establishment

Recruiting and furnishing the establishment with a continuing supply of intellectuals and professional people is also a primary function of a university. In the United States public and private universities share the responsibility for training the country's leadership. Prior to World War II, the Ivy League schools prided themselves on preparing the children of America's upper class for positions of influence and power in the nation's polity. But the pattern has changed—population pressures, the GI bill, government contracts supplying much of the funds for private universities, increasing federal support for the state universities, national defense scholarships for bright but needy students, all of these factors, as well as rising expectations with respect to the material rewards of higher education, have brought millions of young people to public and private campuses all over the country. In 1969 in the age bracket eighteen through twenty-four, 35.2 percent of the men and 20.9 percent of the women were enrolled in college. What do all these college students expect from their membership in the academic community? Most of them anticipate moving into higher-income jobs, and most of them will not be disappointed. The lifetime mean income of males twenty-five and over (computed for 1968) who will have completed four or more years of college will be nearly $13,000 as compared with about $8,000 for those completing four years of high school.[32]

Most college students in the United States following graduation start climbing the career ladders of the establishment: scientists, engineers, corporation managers, public-relations counselors, advertising executives, bond salesmen, doctors, lawyers, bureaucrats, and professional politicians. Why then are some students so unruly on campus, hell-bent on disrupting the academic routine? Possibly, probably, because they recognize the university for what it is: the principal feeding ground of the industrial and political establishment.[33] Some students do not want to be trained, or adjusted, or integrated into a world they never made, into a culture which, as a way of life, they reject.

In every country the academic community is expected to educate young people for positions of leadership in the society. Inevitably this is an elitist activity. We noted earlier that the British political system is still dominated by a social upper class. Members of this social upper class today are rarely rich, only sometimes wellborn, but they are generally well-educated. They are still predominant in the political leadership. Of the twenty-two Labor and Conservative party leadership who held the key posts of prime minister, chancellor of the exchequer, or foreign minister between 1945 and 1967, fifteen were graduates of Oxford or Cambridge (jointly referred to as Oxbridge), one from Sandhurst, one from London, and one from Woolwich.[34] Moreover, the administrative class of the British civil service is traditionally recruited from Oxbridge. Although the Civil Service Commission tries to guard against class discrimination and as a matter of policy endeavors to attract young people who have not attended the famous public schools or the right universities, Oxbridge, be it noted, symbolizes not merely a university education but a particular kind of general education which inculcates a class pattern of values, norms, attitudes, and dispositions that go beyond mere manners and sportsmanship.

In a totalitarian system institutions of higher education are designed to serve as instruments of the state. In the Soviet Union there is no doubt as to who controls the universities. The Union-Republic Ministry of Higher Education supervises all institutions of higher education and semiprofessional schools. "It controls teaching staff, curriculums, textbooks, enrollment quotas, and the assignment of graduates."[35] Admissions are highly competitive, based on examinations. Only the top 5 percent of graduates from secondary schools are eligible to apply. Higher education means professional training; the Ministry of Higher Education determines enrollment quotas in the various professional curricula according to shifting state needs: A single standard curriculum is devised for each basic field. Whatever the student's professional field, his instruction will include considerable political indoctrination, the foundations of Marxism-Leninism, political economy, and at least one course in dialectical and historical materialism. Initial assignment of graduates to posts in the government bureaucracy or in economic enterprises is according to government-determined priorities. Traditionally, Russian students have played revolutionary roles, but not since the Revolution of 1917. Today the academic community is part and parcel of the Communist regime.

The educational system in every country is geared to the whole productive enterprise of the people. Quite clearly the requisites of a modern political system include educational planning at the national level. The academic community in most industrial Western countries, however, is inclined to look askance at government-controlled higher education. Universities which cater to consumers' choice are most likely to flourish in democratic states where there is a permissive social climate, where public opinion is influential in the policy process, and where traditional cultural values have already been widely adapted to modern life. On the other hand, educational planning based on such concepts as state investment in human resources development or allocation of manpower and relevant technical training appear more attractive, i.e., more practical, in newly developing states such as Turkey or Israel.[36]

The Jewish academic community, which antedates the establishment of the political system in Israel, has performed yeoman service in nation-building. The official fact book of Israel expresses the situation frankly:

> *What Israel lacks in quantity, she must make up in quality, and one of the most important factors in her progress is the extent to which she can train scholars, professional men, scientists and technicians of high calibre. . . . The Hebrew University of Jerusalem, the finest of its kind in the Middle East, . . . plays a cardinal role in training the country's intellectual and academic leaders. . . . The Technion-Israel Institute of Technology, Haifa, the oldest institute of higher learning in Israel, trains engineers, technologists, scientists, and architects. Over 70% of the engineers and applied scientists practicing in Israel today are its graduates.*[37]

The Turkish government is similarly pragmatic in its approach: "higher level education as a whole is developed to meet manpower needs." [38] Recognizing that the lack of faculty members for higher education limits the opening of new universities and colleges, it plans to provide new faculty members through state-sponsored special programs. In 1969 there were 126 thousand students in the institutions of higher education; 5.3 percent of the college-age (nineteen through twenty-two) population. The second Five-Year Plan calls for 183 thousand in 1972, 6.3 percent of the college-age population. The plan also calls for selective and incremental increases in professional training where manpower shortages indicate the public need is most critical. Highest priority is given to teacher training, from 1,750 graduates in 1968 to 8,950 in 1972. Other professionals singled out for planned promotion include architects and civil engineers, electrical engineers, industrial engineers, agricultural engineers, physicists and geophysicists, medical doctors, dentists, and pharmacists.

Educational systems in the new nations come under frequent criticism for failing to justify the public expenditures and to meet the needs of national development. Thus the International Development Commission in its 1969 report to the World Bank charges that African students are generally subjected to irrelevant curricula and taught in poor imitations of European universities inherited from colonial days. "Growing numbers of school leavers and even university graduates are remaining unemployed, a sign of an educational system ill-adapted to the economic, social, and cultural requirements it is supposed to fulfill." [39] The Ivory Coast is a case in point. Its educational system, modeled after the French, is staffed mainly by foreigners in the second and third levels; in the secondary schools 946 out of 1,075 teaching posts are held by foreigners, in the technical and vocational schools 229 out of 313, and in higher education 109 out of 130.[40] At the college level 64 percent of the students are majoring in the humanities, 10 percent in the social sciences, 21 percent in the natural sciences, 6 percent in engineering, medicine, and agriculture.[41] And in line with these figures, nearly all of the professional and technical positions in the country are filled by foreigners while recent African graduates with their degrees in humanities or social sciences are out looking for suitable employment.

Research and Science Policy

Advancing the frontiers of knowledge is the most exciting and innovating function of the academic community. In the United States, however, academic research has become a battleground for opposing political forces. Whether academic research should be directed toward military, political, or industrial payoff has become a subject of violent debate on many American campuses. So far as official policy is concerned, however, the issue is moot. Although the lion's share of federal funds for the conduct of research and development go to private industry, the federal government provides about three-fourths of all sponsored research funds now spent by colleges and universities in the United States. The 1969 budget proposed the overall figure of $1.4 billion for campus research, this in recognition of "the predominant role which researchers in institutions of higher education play in the performance of basic research that provides the foundation for the general advancement of the nation's science and technology." [42] Federal funds for research are avowedly mission-oriented, and it is the nature of the mission which has lately produced up-tight reactions among many students and faculty. Nevertheless the 1971 budget increased the academic research obligations to more than $1.5 billion without any substantial modification in the missions.

The principal mission agencies of the federal government sponsoring academic research are the Department of Defense, the National Aeronautics and Space Administration, the Atomic Energy Commission, and the Department of Health, Education, and Welfare. (Table 6–1 shows the trend of total federal spending for research and development by major agencies, 1954–69. The statistics speak for themselves on national priorities as our top decision-makers perceive them.)

The Department of Defense alone spends hundreds of millions of dollars every year to fund research in the academic community. The operating budgets of some of our most prestigious universities have become largely dependent upon continuing research contracts with the military establishment. On the other hand, mounting student strikes and a great deal of unrest in the faculty ranks have forced many university administrators to reappraise their government-sponsored research programs. The 1971 United States Budget makes plain that the federal government has allocated the largest proportion of its research funds for problems relating to military defense and a relatively small percentage of its funds for problems relating to environmental pollution, racial conflicts, or protection for consumers in the free market, all political rhetoric to the contrary. Keeping in mind that research, especially in the sciences, including the sciences of medicine and agriculture, requires costly equipment that cannot be financed out of student fees and private donations, how should the academic community react to mission-oriented public funds for research? Your answer, of course, involves a value judgment, not only your own, but judgments about the nature of society, what it is, what it could be.

TABLE 6–1
Expenditures for Research and Development,[1] *1954–71*
(in Millions of Dollars)

Fiscal year	*Department of Defense* [2]	*NASA* [3]	*AEC*	*D/HEW*	*NSF*	*Other*	*Total*
1954	2,487	90	383	63	4	121	3,148
1955	2,630	74	385	70	9	140	3,308
1956	2,639	71	474	86	15	161	3,446
1957	3,371	76	657	144	31	183	4,462
1958	3,664	89	804	180	34	220	4,991
1959	4,183	145	877	253	54	294	5,806
1960	5,654	401	986	324	64	315	7,744
1961	6,618	742	1,111	374	83	356	9,284
1962	6,812	1,251	1,284	512	113	409	10,381
1963	6,849	2,539	1,336	632	153	490	11,999
1964	7,517	4,171	1,505	793	203	518	14,707
1965	6,728	5,093	1,520	738	206	604	14,889
1966	6,735	5,933	1,462	879	241	768	16,018
1967	7,680	5,426	1,467	1,075	277	917	16,842
1968	8,164	4,724	1,594	1,283	315	950	17,030
1969	7,858	4,252	1,654	1,221	342	882	16,208
1970 estimate	7,714	3,889	1,623	1,323	342	998	15,889
1971 estimate	7,782	3,403	1,640	1,377	347	1,147	15,696

[1] Including research and development facilities.
[2] Includes civil functions.
[3] National Advisory Committee for Aeronautics prior to 1958.
SOURCE: *Special Analyses, Budget of the United States, Fiscal Year 1971* (Washington, D.C.: Government Printing Office, 1970), p. 266.

Advances in science and technology are generally regarded as crucial to national security and economic well-being; hence every modern state has been persuaded to adopt a science policy that includes government-sponsored research and development especially in the natural sciences. Germany is a prime example. The institutes of German higher education are based on the unity of teaching and research. The Federal Ministry of Scientific Research, created in 1962, assists in the extension and equipping of the university and college research facilities for long-term research and development projects deemed in the national interest, such as nuclear research, the development of nuclear technology, extraterrestrial research, and space-flight research and technology.

A Council of Arts, Science, and Research (the *Wissenschaftsrat*[43]) coordinates the *Bund* (federal) and the *Länder* (states) programs for encouragement of science. Following the recommendations of the Wissenschaftsrat, the Bund and the Länder have undertaken joint financing for extension and improvement not only of the universities and colleges but also of such outside academic communities as the German Research Association and the Max Planck Society. The German Research Association (an independent central organization for the promotion of scientific research in the Federal Republic), which advises the political authorities on scientific matters and cultivates the links between the state, industry, and science, is largely responsible for the allocation of public and private funds for scientific research. It is jointly supported by the Bund, the Länder, and also by the Donors' Association for German Science (a private organization representing German industry, trade, and the independent professions). The Max Planck Society for the Advancement of Science comprises over fifty institutes where scientists are given financial assistance for basic research and encouraged to pursue their studies freely without teaching assignments. Other outside agencies assisting science development include the Fritz Thyssen Foundation in the private sphere, the Volksworks Foundation in the public sphere, and the Working Party of Industrial Research Associations which underwrites many joint research facilities owned by trade and industry.

There is little or no controversy about research as a function of the academic community in the Soviet Union. Members of the faculty in all the institutions of higher education are required by law to engage in research which the government considers essential to industry, agriculture, medicine, or whatever sector of the society in which the government perceives a need to modernize. Professors are expected to act as consultants to the government, or the party bureaucracy, or some branch of the economy and to take on outside contract work connected with their particular specialities. Advanced students are also expected to carry on academic investigations which will give them training for continuing research in their chosen fields. The official view is that on-going research is necessary to keep the professions up to date in knowledge and advancing in technology. That this government-imposed policy has paid off is manifest in the spectacular advances which the Russians have made in military technology, space exploration, medical science; not so evident is the payoff in standards of everyday living.

The Commission on International Development observes that "the developing countries are well aware of the importance of scientific and applied research" but for various reasons expenditures for research and development have been extremely limited in the new nations. In Asia such expenditures fall between 0.1 percent and 0.5 percent of GNP; in Africa public and private expenditures for scientific research are negligible, except for some programs sponsored by assisting industrial countries. Even in Latin America in the decade of development, the 1960s, the percentage of GNP for research and development hovered around 0.2. "Comparable figures for the Soviet Union and the United States are 4.2 and 3.2 of GNP respectively, and for most European countries between 1 and 2 percent." [44]

India illustrates the problem. Its stated policy is categorical: The Indian government proposes to promote and sustain scientific research in all its aspects, to insure within the country an adequate supply of research scientists of the highest quality, to recognize their work as an important component of the strength of the nation, to encourage with all possible speed the training of scientific and technical personnel on a scale adequate to fulfill the country's needs in science, education, agriculture, industry, and defense.[45] Under charge to implement this policy the federal Council of Scientific and Industrial Research has set up numerous laboratories, institutes, and community development projects throughout the country and "through a liberal system of grants-in-aid" individual scientists have been encouraged to pursue fundamental and applied research.

The reference annual published by the Indian Ministry of Information and Broadcasting gives us an impressive account of research projects under way: research on ceramic processes, food engineering and fruit technology, metallurgical research, new techniques in road construction, leather technology, research in biochemistry and bacteriology, public health engineering, development of atomic energy as a source of inexpensive electricity, hydraulic research, etc. Official presentations are not always objective, however. The Commission on International Development offers us a very different perspective on the stage of development in India.[46] Actually, all the research and development projects under way add up to a few drops in an enormous bucket of educational plans. Because the primary problem of the Indian government, as in most new nations, is how to achieve literacy, the bulk of expenditures for public education is allocated to the primary schools. The Indian problem is all the more acute because of the magnitude of the country, the tremendous backlog of illiteracy, the regional diversity in language, the federal pattern of government which fragments responsibility for the educational system between the national government and the sixteen states. Add to these the population explosion, with enormous annual increases in the numbers of school-age children. And so it is that despite rising expenditures for education and tripling of primary school enrollments, the overall picture remains grim. Functional literacy has hardly changed, the curriculum content is largely unrelated to modern manpower requirements, vocational education is still very much a stepchild, and improvements in science education are but at the starting stage.[47]

The research activities of the academic community may have a direct bearing upon national development. But governmental policies generally respond to public demands and supports. It is understandable that in countries where the first level of education is still a major concern, official decision-makers are assured of more popular support when they accord higher priorities to quantitative enrollments than to scientific investigations. On the other hand, in the modern states, where the third level of education is widely established and the academic community has itself become an active and articulate pressure group, the scientific estate has come to play an important role in the policy process. When we reach the final chapter in this text, in which we discuss some salient functions of the political system, we shall have more to say about the role of the scientific estate in comparative politics. Suffice it at this point to note this admonition:

> *Only with the help of scientists can we deal with the great issues of war and peace, of the population explosion and its effects in the underdeveloped countries, or of the dangers to our environment from our technological advances not only in weaponry but also in civilian industry and agriculture.*[48]

Public Service

Whether bureaucrats should be generalists or specialists is a continuing argument in academic and administrative estates. Note, however, that in the modern industrial states—like the United States, the United Kingdom, and Japan—the entire population is literate, public support of the educational system extends through the third level, the majority of children enter the secondary schools and many go on to the third level, a high proportion of the labor force is skilled in crafts and industry. The third level provides professional training—engineering, medicine, law, public administration, business administration, etc.—as well as a liberal education in arts and sciences. Even so, faculty and students who seek more relevant or action-oriented instruction protest that the academic community fails to meet its public-service obligations: they judge it to be too disinterested, too dispassionate, too little involved in the real world, or too ready to aid and abet the establishment, too meek to advocate any radical changes in the social and economic system.

In totalitarian systems there is no debate about the service role of the academic community. Its members are expected to undertake many activities outside the classroom on behalf of the party and the government. In the new nations the kind of public service provided by the academic community is crucial to economic and political development. The political estate is pressured to meet the rising expectations of the people; to bring about massive changes in the mores; to raise the standards and levels of living both in the cities and in the countryside; to provide modern media of communications and transportation; to build adequate facilities for education, health, and welfare—and withal to preserve human dignity. All of this takes highly sophisticated planning, a wide range of specialized knowledge, and a great deal of professional expertise. Hence the political estate is almost wholly dependent upon the bureaucracy to provide the necessary intelligence and advanced technology; and in turn the functions of the bureaucracy are almost wholly dependent upon the academic estate from which it derives its education, training, and continuing advice.

We surmise that the widening gap between the modern states and the developing states may be attributed in part to differing degrees of articulation between the world of thought and the seat of power. Academic communities in the new nations tend to emulate rather than innovate. Kenya, for example, has tried to pattern its higher education after Oxbridge; the Ivory Coast imports both its curriculum and its instructors from France, with emphasis on arts and letters rather than science and technology. Higher education is regarded as prestigious rather than functional, reserved for the elite rather than open to the qualified or tailored to the needs of the nation. And yet every political system needs an indigenous bureaucracy, one educated and trained within the national culture, rather than technical advisers on loan from foreign academic communities.

Students who resent irrelevant or sterile education on the American campus should have no difficulty understanding student revolts in the developing nations. The strikes and demonstrations at the National Autonomous University in Mexico 1966–68 illustrate the point, for the demands and issues raised there by the faculty and students touch upon the governance of a nation as well as the governance of a university.

The National Autonomous University of Mexico, oldest university in the Americas, founded in 1553, has become the symbol of modern Mexico, showplace of the nation's capital, a huge complex of strikingly modern edifices, with more than eighty thousand students, about half of them at the third level. Apparently only a minority of faculty and students with leftist views were actually engaged in the organized and violent demonstrations of 1966–68. Nevertheless the manifesto of the Strike Committees of the Schools of Economics and Political and Social Sciences bespeaks widespread causes of discontent and frustration: "Class privilege and educational discrimination are prevalent from primary instruction and become more sharp as one ascends the educational levels."[49] The National Polytechnical Institute, the second largest institution of higher education in Mexico, established in 1937, offers second-level technical courses and general preparation for college as well as professional training and graduate programs. As a dependency of the Secretariat of Education it is expected to respond to the government plans for economic development and to meet the educational needs of a rapidly modernizing nation. In return for government assistance, students at the National University and the National Polytechnical Institute are required to give some of their time before graduation to public service.[50]

Actually neither the federal government nor the states control higher education in Mexico, although between them they foot most of the bills. The universities operate largely as recruiting and training agencies for the private sector of the economy, with the heaviest enrollments in engineering, accounting and business administration, medicine, and law, in that order. Large-scale business and industrial enterprises have not been persuaded, however, to make any substantial contributions to the educational system; nothing comparable, for example, to the private endowments and foundations which underwrite private education in the United States. In 1966, 183 thousand students were enrolled in institutions of higher education, 15 percent in private schools, 85 percent in public institutions.[51] In order to spread the national culture, and also to equalize opportunities for higher education on a regional basis, the federal government provides considerable support to the state universities. Even so, more than 60 percent of the students in higher education are enrolled in colleges and universities in the Federal District. The imbalance between educational facilities in the urban and rural districts is a matter of some concern to the PRI government hierarchy, but as the student protesters put it, "The authorities of the country accept the fact that higher education is a privilege."

The kind of public service the academic community renders—or should render—depends on a set of values. Faculty, students, parents, professional associations, private business, bureaucrats in the civil service, policy-makers in the political system—all of these are likely to make different demands. The resolution of such competing and conflicting values in the public arena becomes a significant function of the political process in every country. In the chapters that follow we shall deal more directly with the conduct of policy through official channels and examine more intensively the manner in which the political system determines value-priorities for the state as a national entity.

Overarching Functions

Don K. Price delineates four estates: the scientific, the professional, the administrative, and the political.[52] Note that he places the four estates along a continuum of interrelated interests and activities. The model is quite useful in explaining the overarching functions which the academic community performs for the political system. Thus the scientific estate—which Price views as "merely a subdivision though perhaps the most influential one" of the broader academic community—is concerned with knowledge and truth per se, regardless of social utility or moral aspects. To this estate belong the physicists, chemists, botanists, economists, political scientists, etc. The professional estate puts scientific knowledge to practical use; its members transmute physics and chemistry into engineering, biology into medicine, botany into agronomy, economics into banking, etc. The administrative estate (the bureaucrats) draws upon the academic disciplines and professions to organize the structures and systems that are necessary to the formulation and implementation of policy. The political estate is responsible for policy decisions that reflect the public demands and supports. Both in the process of decision-making and in directing specific courses of action, policy-makers are in large measure dependent upon the specialized knowledge and professional expertise of the bureaucracy.

Policy-making in the modern states is perforce a highly complex and sophisticated operation. Take, for example, the public policies relating to national defense: Most, if not all of the decisions in this strategic area today are directly related to scientific and technological developments. When the United States Congress was debating whether the national security depended on deployment of antiballistic missiles, the House Foreign Affairs Committee called on the assistance of some of America's most knowledgeable experts so that the committee members might gain some understanding of the dynamics of weapons technology and space exploration. Among those summoned to give their expert testimony were: Jerome B. Wiesner and Herman Kahn. The biographical memoranda of these two gentlemen as submitted to the committee point up the continuous interlocking relationships of the academic community, the governmental bureaucracy, and the policy-makers.[53]

Members of the academic community no longer live (if they ever did) strictly in ivory towers. Like Jerome B. Wiesner and Herman Kahn, many natural scientists, as well as social scientists, regard public service as part of their professional obligation. Hence they frequently appear as witnesses before congressional committees, act as consultants to governmental agencies, and serve on numerous advisory commissions and task forces. Many of them also appear in the public forum as writers and lecturers on current policy issues [54] and not always in the areas of their specific professional competence.

When President Nixon sent his 1970 environmental message [55] to Congress, it was acknowledged to be a team effort of research scientists, technologists, bureaucrats, public-relations men, and high-level policy-makers. Air pollution has become America's number one environmental problem; it is serious and rapidly becoming critical. Hence it has to be tackled simultaneously by all four estates. Although the problem is basically technological, the political estate is now impelled to spur technological advances. Scholars on the campuses have been recruited to investigate the permissible level of pollutants in the air and to determine the standards of clean air required for normal breathing, i.e., living, in industrial communities. Behavioral scientists are examining the psychological and sociological consequences of mounting environmental hazards. Public health workers are studying the injurious effects of smog in the cities. Engineers are testing alternatives to internal combustion engines and alternative devices to control the emissions of deadly carbon monoxide gases. Economists and fiscal managers are figuring the costs of alternatives. Statisticians are determining trends and calculating the prospects for keeping technological advances ahead of population growth, accelerating urbanism, and industrialization. And given all this data, the bureaucrats are working out national standards for pollution abatement and regulations for pollution controls at all levels of government. Public-relations men are enlisted to bring about a popular consensus on the need for governmental action. And, finally, the political estate will make the decisions, determining what policies, what courses of action will be enforced with respect to air pollution.

We have perhaps allowed our own predilection for the academic community to overemphasize the influence of professors in the political process in the United States. Actually, we have very little hard data on who influences whom in the decision-making process. We can report, for example, that presidents Kennedy, Johnson, and Nixon, each in succession, chose as his special assistant for national security affairs an eminent academic figure. We know that McGeorge Bundy (Harvard), Walt Rostow (MIT), and Henry Kissinger (Harvard) all had immediate access to and close working relations with the presidents. What we do not know, however, is how influential they really were: Did the presidents heed their academic advisors? Usually? Sometimes? Rarely? When other voices were offering different or countering advice? We can, of course, raise the same kinds of questions about the professors who give their testimony to the congressional committees, who serve on task forces and advisory commissions, who act as consultants to governmental agencies, or who sometimes take their turns as bureaucrats. What kinds of advice are they asked to give? Do policy-makers respect and accept the advice of academic experts when the advice does not support prevailing policies or fall in line with popular opinions? Frankly, we do not know.

What we have said about the various roles of the academic community in the United States is more or less applicable to all twelve of our countries. Certainly the political system in every modern, or would-be modern, state depends upon the academic community for public services.

Although the problems of modern states may be different in magnitude, they are similar in kind. In the summer of 1970 New York City and Tokyo almost simultaneously had to cut down on automobile traffic in the main shopping areas for several days because of oppressive smog. Air pollution may not be Mexico's number one environmental problem, nevertheless, it is a menacing problem in Mexico City and one viewed with grave concern by the Mexican national government. Mexico City, now the second largest city in the Western Hemisphere, may be bigger than New York City by the end of this decade if present growth projections are sustained. "The Federal District now forbids construction of industries that produce smoke. But 40,000 establishments got in under the deadline contributing to the city the world's most contaminated air. Two million cars and buses on 72 lines add din and smoke." [56]

National defense in the age of nuclear missiles, technological development of conventional weapons; economic problems, GNP targets, investment calculations, production indexes, trade patterns, consumer demands, consumer protection, price policies, monetary policies, tax policies; problems of the cities, housing, sanitation, drinking water, crime in the streets, traffic snarls; population problems, public health, family planning, social welfare services, aid for the aging, relief and rehabilitation for the depressed and backward peoples; problems of the countryside, land utilization, soil and water resources, rural slums, communications and transportation and so forth —these are the complex problems of the 1970s that plague the policy-makers not only in Washington but also in London, Bonn, Moscow, Ankara, Delhi, Bogotá, Tokyo. And these are problems that cannot be solved by politicians responding simply to demands and supports in their constituencies. Not one of these problems can be tackled without broad and basic knowledge as well as technical expertise.

Policy-makers the world over depend on bureaucrats to provide a rational base for political decisions that must keep pace with developments in science and technology. Hence the education and training of bureaucrats may be viewed as a major public service of the academic community. We have already called attention to old-school ties and interpersonal relationships that join significant segments of the scientific and administrative estates. Graduates of the Ivy League schools still enjoy distinct advantages in the recruitment and career patterns of the United States Foreign Service (less so in the civil service generally).[57] Similarly (as we have already noted), the administrative class in the British civil service is largely composed of Oxbridge men. In Japan, Tokyo University holds almost a monopoly in higher civil-service positions.[58] The point we would stress here is not so much the elitist character of the educational institutions from which so many of the top bureaucrats are drawn nor the ingroup favoritism which tends to develop with respect to assignments to posts, promotions, as well as consultantships and grants for outside services. More important in the framework of public service is the kind of education which these elitist institutions are transmitting into the civil service in the form of common traditions, common values, shared experiences, enduring personal associations, and general education based on arts and sciences.[59]

NOTES

1. David Easton, *A Framework for Political Analysis* (Englewood Cliffs, N.J.: Prentice-Hall, 1965), p. 57.
2. Walter Lippman, *Public Opinion* (New York: Macmillan, 1922), chap. 1, "The World Outside and the Pictures in Our Heads."
3. Karl W. Deutsch, *The Nerves of Government* (New York: Free Press, 1966), p. 151.
4. The question posed by Giovanni Sartori, as quoted by Tang Tsou in "Western Concepts and China's Historical Experience," *World Politics* 21 (July, 1969): 659.
5. As opinion-makers some metropolitan newspapers are much more influential than others. William L. Rivers in *The Opinion Makers* (Boston: Beacon Press, 1965) reports that in response to a recent survey question put to news correspondents, "Which newspapers do you use in your work?" the ranking top ten are: *New York Times, Washington Post, Washington Star, Wall Street Journal, Baltimore Sun, New York Herald Tribune, Washington News, Christian Science Monitor, Journal of Commerce, The Guardian.*
6. "Our Basic News Medium," *Saturday Review*, August 9, 1969.
7. *United States Government Organization Manual, 1968–69* (Washington, D.C.: Government Printing Office, 1968), p. 443. (The 1971–72 edition of the *Manual* states it a bit differently: "The commission was created to regulate interstate and foreign communications by wire and radio in the public interest.")
8. Red Lion Broadcasting Company vs. FCC. See Robert Lewis Shayon's interpretation of the opinion in *Saturday Review*, June 12, 1969, p. 55.
9. The Vice-President's speech was delivered at Des Moines, Iowa, November

13, 1969. The full text appears in the *Washington Post,* November 14, 1969. Excerpts from the vice-president's speeches were carried on the major networks!

10. Morning papers:

Daily Mirror	5,282,137
Daily Express	3,947,543
Daily Mail	2,144,856
Daily Telegraph	1,400,581
Sun	1,130,560
Daily Sketch	966,192
Times (London)	405,513

Sunday papers:

News of the World	6,274,169
People	5,607,670
Sunday Mirror	5,349,636
Sunday Express	4,268,477
Sunday Times (London)	1,501,108

These are 1968 circulation figures; they keep changing, of course. See *The British Press,* prepared for British Information Services, RFP 5572/68.

11. *Sound and Television Broadcasting in Britain,* British Information Services, RFP 5531/69, p. 1.
12. *In the period preceding the 1966 general election the Conservative and Labour parties each had 12 broadcasts totalling 130 minutes and the Liberal party had seven broadcasts totalling 75 minutes. The Scottish and Welsh Nationalist parties each had one broadcast of five minutes on the radio and one of five minutes on television in Scotland and Wales respectively. The Communist party had two national broadcasts of five minutes each on radio and television.* (*Sound and Television Broadcasting in Britain,* p. 19.)
13. "Criticism and self criticism are a constant feature of the newspapers. Practically every issue, from the central organ, *Pravda,* to the lowest city or factory contains some type of criticism." Antony Buzek. *How the Communist Press Works* (New York: Praeger, 1964), p. 52.
14. On the large-scale supporting developments required for widespread mass media developments, see Wilbur Schramm, "Communication and the Development Process," in Lucian W. Pye, ed., *Communications and Political Development, Studies in Political Development,* vol. 1 (Princeton, N.J.: Princeton University Press, 1963), pp. 43–45.
15. Government of India, *India, 1969,* comp., Research and Reference Division, Ministry of Information and Broadcasting (Faridabad: Government of India Press, 1969) pp. 131, 135.
16. "The number of daily newspapers published has increased from 75 in 1945 to 380 in 1966. The total number of periodicals published in Turkey has increased from 150 in 1945 to 950 in 1966." Republic of Turkey, Prime Ministry, State Planning Organization, *Second Five-Year Development Plan, 1968–1972* (Ankara: Central Bank of the Republic of Turkey, 1969), p. 67.
17. See Herbert Passin, "Writer and Journalist in the Transitional Society," in Pye, op. cit., pp. 82–123.

18. See *Congressional Directory*, 91st Cong., 1st sess., March, 1969. Shirley Chisholm, Democratic congresswoman from New York, indicates that she is a Brooklyn College Alumna, a member of the League of Women Voters, a member of the Brooklyn Branch of the National Association for the Advancement of Colored People, and a member of Jane's Methodist Church. Otto Passman, Democratic congressman from Louisiana, tells us that he is a member of the First Baptist Church, the American Veterans of World War II, the American Legion, and that he's a Scottish Rite Mason. John Sherman Cooper, Republican senator from Kentucky, is a member of the American Bar and Kentucky Bar associations, American Legion, Veterans of Foreign Wars, Rotary International, Beta Theta Pi, and a Baptist. Theodore Stevens, Republican senator from Alaska, lists among his group memberships: Rotary, American Legion, Veterans of Foreign Wars, Elks, Petroleum Club, Anchorage Press Club, and Alaska Press Club.
19. *The Congressional Quarterly Weekly Report* keeps tabs on the activities of interest groups lobbying in Washington. For an annual summary of how the lobbies fared in 1969 in getting what they wanted out of Congress, see *CQWR*, January 9, 1970, pp. 1–14.
20. Samuel H. Beer, "The British Legislative and the Problem of Mobilizing Consent," in Elke Frank, ed., *Lawmakers in a Changing World* (Englewood Cliffs, N.J.: Prentice-Hall, 1966), p. 35.
21. For a brief official survey, see *Trade Unions in Britain*, Reference Division, Central Office of Information (London: June, 1966).
22. See Samuel H. Beer, *British Politics in the Collectivist Age* (New York: Knopf, 1965).
23. See Jeremy R. Azrael, "The Legislative Process in the USSR," in Frank, op. cit., p. 83.
24. The *Washington Post* (November 25, 1969) reports that Party Leader Brezhnev and First Deputy Premier Dmitri Polyansky (the Politburo agricultural specialist) presented a model kolkhoz charter for approval by a collective farm congress. The congress, 4,521 delegates, represented 32 million collective farmers from 36 thousand kolkhozys. The charter proposed a new hierarchy of representative councils at national, republic, regional, and district levels. Although the councils would not have decision-making authority, they would be consultative and recommendatory. Western Sovietologists anticipate that the councils would give the farmers more direct channels of communication to the powers-that-be in the party hierarchy and the official agencies, counterbalancing voices from the military and industrial sectors of the economy who still claim the largest resource allocations in the economy.
25. *India, 1969*, p. 419. See also *Area Handbook for India*, Foreign Area Studies Division, American University (Washington, D.C.: Government Printing Office, 1970), pp. 585–90.
26. Myron Weiner and Rajni Kothari, eds., *Indian Voting Behavior: Studies of the 1962 General Elections* (Calcutta: Firma K. L. Mukhopsfsysy, 1965).
27. In prerevolutionary Russia there were 105 higher schools in 21 cities, attended by 127,000 students—80 out of 10,000 persons. Today there are over 785 higher schools in 250 cities, with 4,300,000 students—176 out of 10,000 persons. *International Yearbook of Education, 1968* 30 (Geneva: UNESCO Publications, 1969), p. 494.
28. The felicitous phrasing is from John F. Kennedy's formal announcement that he intended to run for the presidential office. *Congressional Record*, 84th Cong., 2d sess., January 18, 1960, pp. A353–54.

29. Press and Information Office of the Federal Government, *Facts about Germany,* Public Document 914, 30 g2/2-2, 7th ed., 1968, p. 55.
30. Norman Cousins, "Toward a World University," *Saturday Review,* October 11, 1969, p. 24.
31. "Youth Revolt: The Future Is Now," *Saturday Review,* January 10, 1970, p. 23.
32. US Bureau of the Census, *Statistical Abstract of the United States, 1970,* 91st ed. (Washington, D.C.: Government Printing Office, 1970), No. 61, p. 111.
33. John Kenneth Galbraith in *The New Industrial State* (Boston: Houghton Mifflin, 1967), p. 382, makes the point that colleges and universities in the United States "serve the needs of the technostructure and reinforce the goals of the industrial system." He also argues that "the educational and scientific estate has the power to exercise its option"—it can commit itself to the industrial establishment, or it can promote the intellectual and artistic development of the nation. An academic community can determine its purpose, or mission, in the society.
34. David Butler and Jennie Freeman, *British Political Facts 1900–1967,* 2d ed. (London: Macmillan, 1968), from the biographical notes, pp. 59–65.
35. United States Department of Health, Education and Welfare, *Education in the USSR* (Washington, D.C.: Government Printing Office, 1960), p. 35.
36. See George Z. F. Bereday and Joseph A. Lauwerys, eds., *World Year Book of Education, 1967* (New York: Harcourt, Brace, and World, 1967). The entire volume, devoted to "Educational Planning," includes a number of case studies of modern and developing states.
37. *Facts about Israel, 1969,* Ministry for Foreign Affairs, p. 157.
38. Republic of Turkey, Prime Ministry State Planning Organization, *Second Five-Year Development Plan: 1968–1972* (Ankara: Central Bank of the Republic of Turkey, 1969), p. 190.
39. *Partners in Development,* report of the Commission on International Development (New York: Praeger, 1969), p. 270. The report is sometimes referred to as the Pearson Report since Lester B. Pearson was chairman of the commission.
40. *International Yearbook of Education, 1968,* p. 265.
41. From *UNESCO Statistical Yearbook, 1966* (New York: UNESCO Publications, 1967), "Education at Third Level: Percentage Distribution by Fields."
42. *Special Analyses, Budget of the United States, Fiscal Year 1969* (Washington, D.C.: Government Printing Office, 1968), table 1, p. 154.
43. For a brief survey of the complete German organization, public and private subsumed under the term *Wissenschaft,* see *Facts about Germany,* pp. 298–315.
44. *Partners in Development,* p. 66.
45. Paraphrased from *India, 1969,* p. 83. The statement was formulated by the Indian government as a resolution and laid on the table of both houses of Parliament in 1958.
46. Ibid., pp. 83–92.
47. *Partners in Development,* p. 294.
48. Don K. Price, *The Scientific Estate* (Cambridge, Mass.: Harvard University Press, Belknap Press, 1965), p. 19. The student will find it a highly instructive exercise to observe the politics of science in the United States and to discover for himself how the scientific estate became a potent political force after World War II.
49. The Strike Committees of the Schools of Economics and Political and Social Sciences, "The Need for Educational Reform and an End to Privilege," 1966,

reprinted in translation from the Spanish in Richard R. Fagen and Wayne A. Cornelius, Jr., eds., *Political Power in Latin America* (Englewood Cliffs, N.J.: Prentice-Hall, 1970), p. 323.

50. Clark G. Gill, *Education in a Changing Mexico* (Washington, D.C.: Government Printing Office, 1969), pp. 70–73.
51. Ibid.
52. See Don K. Price, op. cit., chap. 5.
53. US, Congress, House, Subcommittee on National Security Policy and Scientific Developments of the Committee on Foreign Affairs, *Hearings*, 91st Cong., 1st sess., 1969, H. Rept. 91–185, pp. 9, 95.

    During World War II, as a member of the Massachusetts Institute of Technology staff, Dr. Wiesner was engaged in developmental research on radar. In 1945 he was assigned to the Los Alamos Scientific Laboratory to work on the atomic devices for tests at Bikini. Following World War II, Dr. Wiesner held many important consultantships and memberships in governmental, business, and scientific organizations, including the position of staff director of the 1957 Gaither Committee's study of American military posture. From 1961 to 1964 Dr. Wiesner served as special assistant to the president for science and technology and as director of the Office of Science and Technology in the Executive Office of the president. In the latter post he acted as principal adviser to the president on major policy matters to assure that science and technology would be effectively utilized in the interests of national security, foreign policy, and general welfare. In 1964, he returned to MIT as dean of the School of Engineering and in 1966 he became provost of MIT.

    Herman Kahn was senior physicist and military analyst from the Rand Corporation (an autonomous think tank which does a great deal of research for the national government) from 1948 to 1961. Since 1961 he has headed his own think tank, the Hudson Institute at Harmon-on-Hudson, New York. He has served as a consultant to numerous public and private groups, including the Oak Ridge National Laboratory, the Gaither Committee, the US Air Force Scientific Advisory Board, the Atomic Energy Commission, the Office of Economic Planning, the Office of the Secretary of Defense, and the Department of State.
54. Dr. Wiesner's writings include *Where Science and Politics Meet* (New York: McGraw-Hill, 1965). Mr. Kahn's books include *On Thermonuclear War* (Princeton, N.J.: Princeton Uuiversity Press, 1961), *Thinking About the Unthinkable* (New York: Avon, 1969), *The Year 2,000* (New York: Macmillan, 1967).
55. February 10, 1970.
56. Lewis H. Dulguid (staff writer), *Washington Post,* February 9, 1970.
57. John Ensor Harr, *The Professional Diplomat* (Princeton, N.J.: Princeton University Press, 1969). See table 26, "Top Universities for the Foreign Service and the Civil Service," p. 181.
58. About 70 percent of the key posts in the Japanese bureaucracy are held by graduates of the Faculty of Law of Tokyo University. Japanese legal studies, however, are neither specialized nor highly professional in content, but come closer to the American concept of general education with a core curriculum in political science. Hence graduates of the prestigious Law Faculty are sought by all of the Japanese ministries, foreign affairs, finance, economic planning, international trade, etc., as well as by the Ministry of Justice.
59. See Akira Kubota, *Higher Civil Servants in Post-War Japan* (Princeton, N.J.: Princeton University Press, 1969), chap. 4, "Educational Backgrounds."

FURTHER READING

BEER, SAMUEL H. *British Politics in the Collectivist Age*. New York: Knopf, 1965.

GOLDWIN, ROBERT A., ed. *On Civil Disobedience*. Chicago: Rand McNally, 1970.

KELMAN, HERBERT C., ed. *International Behavior*. New York: Holt, Rinehart & Winston, 1965.

PYE, LUCIAN W., ed. *Communications and Political Development*. Princeton, N.J.: Princeton University Press, 1963.

chapter 7

HOW DO POLITICAL PARTIES AFFECT GOVERNMENT?

One of the most familiar means of modern electronic communications is the walkie-talkie. This is a sophisticated version of a children's toy—two cans connected by a string that serves as a communication link between two small boys, enabling them to pass their secret messages to each other across several backyards. The walkie-talkie fulfills the same function, allowing people to engage in simultaneous communications from different vantage points: on the battlefront, on construction sites, in city traffic jams, in street demonstrations. In the political system a political party may be likened to the walkie-talkie, providing a simultaneous communications link not only between the members of the political system and those who hold leadership roles, but also between factions of members and factions of leaders. Whether we look at competitive or noncompetitive party systems, the political party acts as a major link of communication between the governed and the government and between the political system and its environment.

VARIOUS THEORIES OF PARTY ROLE AND FUNCTION

A contemporary student of American political parties observes that "classical theorists ignored the need for a link between government and the people," hence their treatises in political theory tended to ignore or obscure the role

India, Indira Gandhi campaigning
(Marilyn Silverstone : Magnum)

of political parties in the governing process.[1] When we move into a study of comparative politics, however, we realize that the political party serves in many ways to link the leaders and the members in every political system. The primary function of every political party is to create an electoral organization whereby leaders are recruited for official positions in the government and the members are organized as an electorate that endorses the party's choice of leaders. In many political systems there would be no political leaders but for the fact that the new party functions as the catalyst to sift out the winners in a competition for office and to perform a legitimizing function in the struggle for "who gets what, when, how." [2]

Rare is the political leader in a modern government who can negate his ties with his party and still remain in power. President Dwight D. Eisenhower found it difficult to think of himself as a party leader; he viewed his election as a mandate from the people. He was, nevertheless, the candidate of the Republican party in 1952 and 1956, and without the party activities he could not have been nominated, much less elected. Prime Minister Indira Gandhi of India is a notable exception. When she was expelled from the ruling Congress party in November, 1969, she not only managed to maintain her position as prime minister but also to persuade the Parliament that she was the real leader of the Congress party in Parliament, notwithstanding the protests of those who had tried to oust her.

In the history of Western governments the concept of party has commonly stood for "division, conflict, opposition within a body politic." [3] Hence Western political scientists discussing the role and function of political parties are apt to focus on competitive party systems as representing the norm and noncompetitive systems as illustrating the aberration. Certainly among our twelve states we will find that such representative governments as the United States, the United Kingdom, Japan, and the Federal Republic of Germany are served by two-party or multiparty systems which are organized to present the electorate with a choice between competing candidates for office and competing political programs.

Competitive political parties provide indispensable links in the operation of representative and responsible government, reflecting the plural interests of the people and at the same time channeling unifying directions from those vested with authority. Political parties not only enable political leaders to obtain the support of the electorate and so to legitimize authoritative roles, they also enable the members individually and through groups to communicate to the leaders their various interests and values and so to make their demands felt upon the political system. Political parties, as instruments of communication, may be used routinely and regularly or for special occasions, ceremonies, and emergency situations. Congress or parliament is organized and controlled by whichever party (or coalition of parties) has won most support in the electorate; but competing or opposition parties which have also won seats in the representative body are accorded active roles in the policy-making process. Political parties serve as walkie-talkies among the various components in representative government, among executives, bureaucrats, legislators, and judges, as well as among nonofficial members of the political system. Political parties may play somewhat different roles in presidential or parliamentary, federal or unitary systems (see Chapter 9), but their primary function turns out to be substantially the same—providing simultaneous communications from various vantage points in the political system. We shall shortly take a look at several of these countries to illustrate our points with more detail.

The single-party system in Western governments is usually associated with authoritarian or totalitarian political structures, such as the National Socialist party which dominated Adolf Hitler's Third Reich or the Fascist party of Benito Mussolini in Italy between the two world wars. Among our twelve states the Communist party in the USSR is currently our leading example. As in the competitive party systems, the single party is a kind of walkie-talkie among the pluralistic interests of the people, between the governors and the governed, and among the various components of the policy machinery. The party seeks to legitimize its positions of leadership within the government by submitting to the electorate its single slate of candidates for office; it also uses the election campaign period to publicize its ideology, to expound prevailing policies, and to justify new programs. In general it keeps open the lines of communication between the leaders and the members to inform and to indoctrinate as well as to generate loyalty and compliance. Some students of development theory are inclined to regard the single party as an effective communications control system, useful for promoting uniformity of purpose, building consensus on priorities, furnishing firm guidance, and providing long-term continuity unbroken by party defeats at the polls and consequent government turnover.[4]

Mexico and the Ivory Coast have been one-party states during most of their modern political existence. Kenya has tried both two-party and one-party systems. Since 1969 it has been in the category of a one-party state. Although Turkey was a one-party state during its most crucial stages of modernization, it appeared to be headed toward a two-party system as evidenced by the election returns of 1969 (out of 450 seats in the National Assembly the Justice party won 256 and the Republican People's party 143).

In the early spring of 1971, however, the military ousted Premier Suleyman Demirel and his Justice party. After days of uncertainty an outright military government was avoided. President Cevdet Sunay asked a former law professor and distinguished member of the Republic party (PRR) to head an "above-party, togetherness" government. Nihat Erim, a deputy in the parliament, immediately resigned his PRR membership to head what amounted to a united front government. The government was formed under military auspices, yet it is headed by a Kemalist. Perhaps this points to a significant lesson in Turkish party politics—a two-party or multiparty system does not work in a time of change.

India's struggle for independence was dominated by a one-party system —the Congress. As long as independence was the main issue, the Congress, dominated by such strong personalities as Gandhi and Nehru, was without a doubt the leading party. The independence movement, a thing of the past, confronted by the overwhelming problems of a multilingual, multiracial society, facing the transition from a traditional agricultural way of life to a modern industrialized system, the Congress party no longer could assume an automatic position of leadership. What is more, the Congress party no longer was united. Indira Gandhi's first government was a coalition government, led by the Congress party. As dissident voices arose in the party, she defied the party's old ruling elite, headed a splinter group, and led the New Congress party to a two-thirds majority victory in the 1971 elections.

SOME TYPOLOGIES OF POLITICAL PARTIES

A number of political scientists have developed indexes or typologies of political parties.[5] A German scholar, Manfred Haettich,[6] who assesses parties first of all on their status in the social order, raises such questions as: Is the party an ingroup or an outgroup? Is it the government party or a member of the government coalition? Has it been a government party for very long—so long in fact that its ingroup position colors its whole outlook and activities? Has the party recently entered the government? What are its chances of staying in? With respect to the outgroup, is the perennial opposition too small or too way out from the general consensus of society ever to get into the government? What are the long-term goals of the party? Does it want to conserve or to reform the existing order? Does it want to innovate, to radicalize, or even destroy the present system? Does it want to create a totally new order?

In developing a typology of political parties it is instructive to examine the origins and to trace the institutionalization of parties in different political systems. Parties, like other groups, are likely to originate as more or less loose associations with private status. A clandestine band of rebels may turn into a governing party, and their initial freewheeling association may become as burdened with rules and regulations, membership books and dues, and closely circumscribed behavior as the ingroup they overthrew. Similarly, a group of reformers, motivated by common goals but with no formal structure, starting out perhaps in a storefront office with a small working capital from voluntary contributions, may wind up as an establishment institution.

The initial goals of the party are related to its status in the society, and in turn its status in society affects its own structure as well as its place in the overall political structure. Does the party speak only for a particular sector of the population, an economic group (the business community or trade unions), or a religious group (Buddhists or Catholics), or a group with a particular ideological persuasion (pacifists or communists)? Does it represent a particular region (the South, the North)? A party that aims eventually to become the government at the national level must widen its appeal to many sectors of the society, to all parts of the country.

Human associations over a period of time tend to become rigidified and formalized. In the life of a political party the ultimate formalization is the party's identification with the structure of the state; the most extreme case of institutionalization, of course, is the single party in a dictatorship or totalitarian system. Depending on the extent of institutionalization, a party fulfills differing functions. In its early, loosely knit stage, it may be merely an influencer or expediter of public opinion; in short, little more than an interest group. But as it widens the areas of its interest and tries to attract a larger membership (crucial to winning national elections), it must develop more complex patterns of communication which in turn call for more formal organization and coordination. The party becomes institutionalized as it ties in with the political structure, either as the governing party or as a recognized party in opposition, and at this point the members can use it most effectively to help shape or enforce the public will.

At the peak of its success, the party becomes the government, an instrument of rule. In representative government, the party (or coalition of parties) that wins a majority of seats in the legislature is charged with organizing and dominating the rule-making process. In the United Kingdom the majority party leadership joins the executive and legislature into a single policy machine. Thus in Britain the prime minister is the leader of the majority party in the Parliament. He and the members of his cabinet not only head the entire executive establishment but also control the whole legislative process. In a dictatorship or totalitarian government where there is but one party, as in the USSR, party and state are practically indistinguishable.

We find it helpful to our understanding of the role and function of political parties to raise our questions first in the framework of theory and typologies. For possible answers we turn now to the real world, to our twelve examples to illustrate how parties originate, how they are structured, how they operate, and how they perform within different political systems.

COMPETITIVE PARTY SYSTEMS

Traditional Two-Party Systems

The United Kingdom The British party system is usually regarded as the very model of the traditional two-party system. Since World War I two major parties have alternated as the ingroup and the outgroup—the government party and the loyal opposition: the Conservative party and the Labour party, with the latter more often in opposition than in government. Actually, however, Britain is a three-party system; the third party, the Liberal party, is much courted by the governing party when the margins between government and opposition are narrow. After the 1964 parliamentary elections, which brought the Labour party to power for the second time since the end of World War II, the government margin over the opposition consisted of fourteen members of parliament (Labour had 317 MP's, the Conservatives had 303 MP's) which meant that the Labour party sought support from the nine Liberal MP's on crucial pieces of legislation whenever maverick party members or sickness threatened to reduce the narrow margin to nerve-rackingly close proportions. In the 1966 elections the governing party's margin rose from 14 to 110, so that the new block of 12 Liberals was no longer so important to the Labourites; whereupon the Liberals were promptly courted by the Conservatives.

Although Britain generally operates under one of the classic two-party systems, the opponents have not always been Conservatives and Laborites. In a study of *British Politics in the Collectivist Age*,[7] Samuel H. Beer touches on three phases of British party struggles: old Tory versus old Whig; Liberals versus Radicals; and Socialists versus Tory Democrats, with salient social and economic issues in every phase. The current political parties are outgrowths of the nineteenth-century struggles of the industrial revolution. This was the period when England changed from an essentially rural agricultural into a highly urbanized centralized society. In the nineteenth century the political battle lines were drawn principally between the proponents of free enterprise and the advocates of an economic system attuned to the needs and demands of the masses. But even the once highly individualistic Conservatives and Liberals have come a long way from their earlier positions. Today all three parties, Conservative, Liberal, and Labour, are working within a framework of collectivist political action.

The United States The British and the American political systems have this in common: In both countries the major political parties may be in- or outgroups, competing peacefully within constitutional bounds for the privilege of filling the official leadership positions and translating the demands of their respective constituencies into governmental policies.[8] There are, however, notable differences. In the United States both the Democratic and the Republican party organizations are loose federations of individual members; not even the party activists are card-carrying, that is, dues-paying members. At the national level the Democrats and the Republicans each call a quadrennial convention for the purpose of nominating the party's candidates for president and vice-president and for constructing the party platform for the ensuing election. Neither party, however, espouses any closely woven doctrine or ideology. Congressional candidates who run for office on the same party ticket as candidates for president and vice-president need not run on the national party platform, and when elected to Congress they are not obligated, or even expected, to vote regularly along party lines. In comparison to the American parties the British Labour party is a tightly organized, rigidly controlled party, and even the less structured Conservative and Liberal parties are much more disciplined in parliamentary behavior.

The concept of coalition government, quite common in European politics, is nonexistent in American government and is a deviation from the normal political processes in the United Kingdom. Separation of the executive and legislative branches in the American government, with independent elections and tenure for each component, is reflected in what James MacGregor Burns calls "four-party politics."[9] The Democratic and Republican presidential parties compete with each other to put their official leader in the White House and to man the policy-making positions in the executive departments. The Democratic and Republican congressional parties compete with each other to capture a majority of seats in both houses of Congress.

American four-party politics sometimes results in really offbeat governmental patterns. The Democratic (or Republican) presidential and congressional parties may simultaneously capture both the White House and the Congress (this is the way it happened for Dwight Eisenhower in 1952 and for Lyndon Johnson in 1964). But the presidential and the congressional parties have such different kinds of linkages with their respective constituents that the executive and legislative branches may still be in continuous conflict over policies and programs even when the same party is in nominal control of both components in the system. (Such was the experience of President Eisenhower in the first two years of his term in office as he tried to work through the Republican congressional party leadership. Such also was the experience of President Johnson in the last two years of his term as he faced mounting criticism from the Democratic congressional party leadership.) The Republicans (or Democrats) may win the presidential election and lose the congressional elections by failing to gain a majority of seats in one or both houses of Congress. (This is what happened to Richard Nixon on his way to the White House in 1968; he is the first president in this century to face a Congress controlled by the opposition in the first two years of his time in office. It is a difficult role to play.)

British political battles are usually an either-or proposition; the winning party goes it alone as the government, while the losing party assumes the role of the loyal opposition. The opposition party, working within the constitutional framework, continues to act as walkie-talkie for the many different sectors in the electorate, keeping open the channels of communication with special interest groups, in anticipation of the next election, when it may in turn profit by the principle of winner take all. If it emerges victorious from the polls, it becomes the sole source of power on the basis of a majority in Parliament. There have been only four exceptions to that rule in recent British history, two of which occurred during World Wars I and II. Since 1900, out of eighteen governments fourteen were one-party governments.[10]

A Multiparty Coalition: The Federal Republic of Germany

In the Federal Republic of Germany, where the multiparty system still prevails, coalition government is common. In the absence of an absolute majority of popular votes, the leaders of the major parties confer with their colleagues in the smaller parties, and whoever can work out a compromise that will unite the majority of the parliamentary deputies behind them, will head the government in a coalition. For example, following the 1969 elections to the Bundestag (Parliament) Willy Brandt, leader of the Social Democratic party (SPD) and former foreign minister in the so-called Grand Coalition of Christian Democrats (CDU) and Social Democrats (SPD), was able to work out a compromise with Walter Scheel, leader of the Free Democrats (FDP). The FDP had been a coalition partner with the CDU, but had played the role of loyal opposition in Parliament, 1966–69, after splitting away from their coalition with the CDU. The result of Willy Brandt's maneuvering was a new coalition between Socialists and Free Democrats. Together the SPD and the FDP now hold the majority in the Bundestag and the CDU has been consigned to the role of loyal opposition.

The 1969 changeover in the politics of Bonn was especially hard for the Christian Democrats, who had played the role of ingroup, or ruling party, ever since the birth of the Federal Republic of Germany. Governing over twenty years, from 1949 to 1969, either alone or in coalition, they had all but turned the party into a permanent ingroup and apparently relegated the Social Democrats to the role of the permanent outgroup. The Bundestag election in September, 1969, and the outcome of the negotiations between party leaders in October, 1969, therefore, have assured the Federal Republic of Germany of a party system in which the in- and outgroups now vie with each other within the constitutional framework for the roles of political leadership and the opportunity to transform party goals into public policy.

Currently, party structure in the Federal Republic much resembles that of Britain, two major parties with a third, the smallest party, playing the role of balancer. Note, however, that the third party is elevated formally to the role of balancer as a coalition partner in the German system. Over the past twenty years the German multiparty system has been transformed into a modified two-party system, partially through government action.

When German parties were allowed to function again after 1945 in the western zones of Allied occupation, it first appeared that the multiparty pattern of the Weimar Republic would be repeated. Some of the traditional German parties applied for licenses from the Allies and, having obtained them, immediately set up shop. The Communists and the Social Democrats capitalized on their strong anti-Nazi stands during Hitler's "Thousand-Year" Reich. The nationalistic German party (*Deutsche Partei*, DP) tried to appeal to nationalism at a time when Germany was an occupied territory. The Free Democrats, whose roots were in the liberal free-enterprise movement prior to the Weimar Republic, made a strong comeback and ultimately produced the first president of the Federal Republic of Germany, Theodor Heuss, a distinguished scholar. President Heuss, fully aware that he would be setting trends and traditions for his office, filled it with distinction, but he also resigned his party membership in order to show that the office of the president is above partisan politics.

Newcomers on the political scene were the Christian Democratic Union, and its state-based counterpart in Bavaria, the Christian Social Union (CSU), which emerged largely from the remnants of the former Catholic Center party under the leadership of Konrad Adenauer, whose highest political office had been the mayoralty of Cologne during the Weimar Republic. Konrad Adenauer attracted especially those democratic elements in postwar Germany which were not tied to the economic persuasion of the socialists and Communists but who felt the need for a more doctrinal framework than that offered by the Free Democrats. His program combined the notions of free enterprise, democratic persuasion, and Christian (not only Catholic) doctrine. The CDU/CSU, which held considerable appeal among the rural areas of northern and southern Germany, made great inroads among the well-to-do electorate (professional groups, top businessmen, senior civil servants), as well as among unskilled and unorganized workers. Its largest constituency came from women.

From 1949 to 1969, the CDU/CSU was the ingroup party. It won a popular plurality in the first parliamentary election in 1949 and an absolute parliamentary majority in 1953 (the first time in a free election in German history), and it was senior partner in every coalition. During those twenty years, the number of political parties in the Federal Republic of Germany declined from more than ten to three: the CDU/CSU, the SPD, and the FDP. The other parties lost out, either because they could not gain 5 percent of the votes cast in a national election (a rule of German electoral law) or because their appeal was limited to very special groups who, on becoming integrated into West German society, deprived the parties of their appeal (for example, the BHE, the Federation of the Expellees and Refugees). In 1966 when the CDU/CSU and the SPD entered into the so-called Grand Coalition and the FDP with barely 10 percent of the electoral votes became the parliamentary opposition, students of German politics assumed that the end for the German multiparty system was near.[11]

With the 1969 parliamentary elections the party system of the Federal Republic of Germany entered into a new phase. As soon as the election results were known (CDU/CSU 46.1 percent, SPD 42.7 percent, FDP 5.8 percent), President Nixon wired former Chancellor Kiesinger congratulations on his reelection. The president erroneously interpreted the elections results from his perception of American politics. First, he assumed that the leader of the party with the highest electoral count would head the executive branch. Second, he assumed that the party with the largest popular vote would be the ruling party in the legislative branch.

Not so in Germany, however. In the Federal Republic, as in the United Kingdom, the outcome of the parliamentary elections determines the makeup of the government. In the Federal Republic's twenty-year history, the CDU/CSU led coalitions in four out of five governments. In the 1969 elections, however, the vote was split so closely that either of the two major parties could rule if it could recruit the third party, the FDP, as a coalition partner. Ultimately the SPD leadership proved itself more persuasive with the FDP leadership than that of the CDU/CSU. The FDP, whose extinction like that of the proverbial dodo bird had been forecast in the 1960s, found itself the junior partner in a new SPD/FDP coalition government that provided a more realistic split between the government and opposition parties. The 1970 division—48.5 percent for the government and 46.1 percent for the opposition—is a far cry from the situation during the Grand Coalition when the opposition barely represented 10 percent of the electorate. The 1969 elections also, for the first time in the history of the Federal Republic of Germany, paved the way for an outgroup party to become an ingroup party and removed the threat that the CDU/CSU and the SPD leadership each would be frozen in respective roles of government and opposition.

For much of their histories both the British Labour party and the German Social Democratic party found themselves cast in the role of opposition

—a role which stifled positive leadership and constructive programs. The prospect of permanent opposition tends to make a party destructively critical. Realizing it has only a very slim chance to be the party in power it can press unreasonable demands on the system without fear of being assailed in the same way when the tables are turned and it has become the in-party. Much of the domestic nationalization program of the British Labour party and the foreign policy program of the German Social Democratic party proved to be unrealistic until the parties were faced with coming up with all the modifications of a government program. Nationalization of the coal and steel industry was not a wholly successful experiment in the United Kingdom (the Conservatives returned the steel industry to private hands, but the Labour party under Prime Minister Wilson put it back under public ownership). Kurt Schumacher's foreign policy proposals (anti-European, anti-Western, anti-integrative) forced the German SPD into one disastrous election defeat after another and cast a lingering shadow over the party's voter appeal for ten years after Schumacher's death. Only after the SPD became a partner in the Grand Coalition and the party's most cosmopolitan leader, Willy Brandt, became foreign minister was the SPD able to reverse its politically disastrous stand in foreign policy. As governing mayor of West Berlin, Brandt found very little usefulness in hard-line party doctrines and so had concentrated on what was politically feasible. The major difference in the approach to government between the ingroup and the outgroup, at least in representative government, is the matter of feasibility.

The National Front in Colombia

Colombia is a unique example of party government, for its two-party system is not truly competitive as in the United States or the United Kingdom, nor is it a coalition system comparable to the Brandt government in the Federal Republic where the opposition party is a force to be constantly reckoned with.

The traditional two-party system of Colombia has been operating as a National Front since 1957. The National Front is a bipartisan, noncompetitive arrangement agreed upon by the leadership of the Conservative and Liberal parties. The arrangement was endorsed by plebiscite, incorporated into the Constitution in 1957, and is scheduled to remain in force until 1974. As we have earlier recounted, the intensely partisan character of Colombian politics had led to violent civil disorders in the 1940s and 1950s, the period shudderingly remembered as "the Violence." To secure the internal order requisite to economic development, representatives of Colombia's most powerful and prestigious families drafted the 1957 Sitges Agreement which provided for equal distribution of all elective and appointive offices between the two major parties with alternative occupation of the presidency determined before the elections. Although the agreement proscribed outright competition between the two parties, considerable factionalism and jockeying for position in both parties have been increasingly manifest in successive elections.

The National Front is, in fact, a facade for oligarchical rule in Colombia. The rank-and-file members of the parties, the industrial and agricultural workers, have had little influence upon party deliberations or government policies. The Sitges Agreement was engineered by the oligarchs not only to restore the country to normalcy following "the Violence" but also to prevent the masses from rallying around such demagogues as deposed President-General Rojas Pinilla. With army support, General Rojas had been installed in the presidential office in 1953 by a coalition of Liberal and Moderate Conservative leaders. The general's assignment was to stop the violence and to restore order but in this endeavor he was only partially successful. Though his regime was highly authoritarian and in many ways oppressive, he attempted to win popular support by increasing national expenditures for public works. He was frankly proud of his populist methods and frequently made the boast, "There's not a town in Colombia without some public works projects of mine." But when he began to make disquieting promises involving land reforms and other programs to help the dispossessed, he was suddenly ousted from office by the army with the support of a coalition of Liberal and Conservative party leaders.

The overthrow of Rojas and the subsequent establishment of the National Front brought twelve years of relative political stability and economic growth to Colombia. Especially under Liberal President Carlos Lleras Restrepo (1966–70) the country made notable gains in crop diversification (away from sole dependency on coffee), foreign trade, and domestic reforms. But, in the same period, the population skyrocketed by 2.5 million and the number of unemployed rose to an estimated 1 million in a total work force of 7 million. Under these conditions many Colombians, especially in the lower class (to which most Colombians belong) were unappreciative and apathetic toward what the elitist National Front was achieving for the country. Normally less than 40 percent of those eligible to vote bothered to participate in what they considered to be rigged elections between the ins and the outs.

The Colombian oligarchy experienced a rude awakening, however, when many of these people did go to the polls on April 19, 1970. Egged on by energetic young workers in the Popular National Alliance, they delivered a solid 1.5 million votes for that enterprising ex-dictator, General Rojas, who made no bones about his intention to stage a social revolution if he were returned to office. The immediate returns looked as if Rojas had won the election, but the Lleras government warned against any premature predictions until after the official count a week later. By that time Rojas's lead had somehow evaporated. The National Front was sustained and the ruling elite was given a green light to govern the country until 1974. In the spirit of the Sitges Agreement, Misrael Pastrana Borrero, the Conservative candidate who had served as secretary of government under Liberal President Carlos Lleras became the new president. A lawyer, economist, former ambassador to Washington, with impressive governmental experience in national planning and economic development, an able representative of the ruling elite, President Pastrana promises political stability and economic progress. The mass following of the charismatic populist General Rojas is not likely, however, to disappear from the political picture. The National Front is facing widespread disaffection.

NONCOMPETITIVE PARTY SYSTEMS

Among our twelve nation states we find several two-party or multiparty systems in which only one party has been the in-party for so long that for all practical purposes the party-government relationship is similar to that in a one-party state.

The Turkish Experience

For much of Turkey's history, and especially during most of its crucial period of modernization, the Republican People's party, founded in 1923 by Atatürk, was the ruling party—from 1923 to 1950—and it was the major governing party from 1961 until 1965. It was the only political party from 1923 to 1946. During this time the major reforms which transformed the Ottoman Empire into the modern Turkish state were engineered under the leadership of Atatürk: the introduction of the Latin alphabet in place of Arabic characters, the adoption of compulsory universal education at the elementary level, the separation of civil law from the Islamic law (the Koran), the introduction of a civil code patterned after the Swiss Code, the emancipation of women, and the adoption of Western dress (no more veils for women, no more fezzes for men). Atatürk's commitment to the Westernization of Turkey extended to lip service at least for concepts of democratic government, and toward the end of his regime he did try to open the way for a multiparty system.

Turkish politics are embedded in party politics. Certainly during the Atatürk era the overwhelming influence on the Turkish political system was the dominance of the Republican People's party and the charismatic leadership of Atatürk. He made full use of the party to obtain the support of the electorate and through elections to legitimize his own power and authority. He also used the party most effectively to maintain operational links between the component parts of his government.

Sometimes in a democratic, or would-be democratic, system the majority party serves not only to integrate demands from the people and to secure popular support for the government, but it may also be used first to develop dissension and then to encourage opposition. Thus dissenters from the Republican People's party of Turkey were permitted to organize the Democratic party in 1946 and to enter its candidates in opposition to the dominant regime. The 1946 elections, however, were not free elections; apparently Atatürk's old party had second thoughts about allowing organized dissent. But the mere entry of opposition candidates in the general elections was a significant step toward representative government in Turkey.

The 1950 elections, which ousted the Republican People's party and put the Democratic party in the seats of authority, were an extraordinary phenomenon. A one-party system sponsored and sanctioned free elections, took the chance of being reversed at the polls, was in fact ousted by popular vote, and then accepted the electoral decision.

Various explanations are offered for the changeover from one-party to multiparty politics in the 1950 Turkish elections. In its latter years Atatürk's government was in effect the victim of its own reforms. Its innovating programs had given rise to a new elite: well-to-do businessmen, a professional class, and intellectuals. It had also aroused the political instincts of the masses and nurtured conflict between the rural and urban sectors of the population. In trying to achieve its goals, nationalism and modernism, the Republican People's party became more doctrinaire and more forceful in its exercise of authority. The Democratic party was able to capitalize upon the government excesses as well as upon pent-up resentments to wartime austerities throughout Turkey. In 1950, by free elections, the Democratic party became the government party.

Between 1950 and 1960 the Democratic party and the Republican People's party vied with each other for in-party control of the Turkish government. Actually this was a period of multiparty politics in Turkey in which a number of protesting groups broke away from the Republican People's party. The protests seemed to center more around personalities than to represent any strong doctrinal disagreements on economic and/or social issues. Caught in the same bind as its predecessor, the Democratic party tried to stifle dissent by restricting personal liberties, curbing the press, attacking the universities; and as happens to so many parties in power, it probably yielded too much to opportunism and the possibilities of personal payoff and did not live up to its doctrine and promises made to the electorate. At any rate, in 1960 by a coup d'etat, the Democratic party suddenly lost its in-power status and shortly thereafter many of its leaders were brought to trial for their political offenses: some were jailed, some were executed.

After a short period of purely military dictatorship, a new constitutional government was designed to facilitate a multiparty system. The old Constitution, built originally around one-party rule, had simply not provided adequate machinery to handle and conciliate opposing demands. For a while, it appeared that Turkey had a multiparty system with half a dozen or more parties represented in the National Assembly. As an outcome of the 1969 elections, the Justice party (in effect a reconstruction of the Democratic party of the 1950s) was the government party and the Republican party its principal opposition party. Then, in early 1971, when the military threatened a coup d'etat, the outcome was a United Front government. Turkey, in a very short time span, has gone from a one-party system to a two-party system and to a no-party system (or an all-party system) via the road of an artificially constructed multiparty system and a military coup d'etat.

The Indian Experience

The struggle for independence in India, followed by reform and modernization, are linked to one party, the Congress party. Successor to the Indian National Congress which took the lead against British colonial rule under Mahatma Gandhi, the Congress party became the governing party after independence was achieved in August, 1947. Mahatma Gandhi's personality had dominated the Indian National Congress prior to independence. Gandhi's martyrdom and the personality of his successor, Jawaharlal Nehru, India's first prime minister, dominated the politics of the Congress party after 1947.

Even though India was nominally a multiparty state after independence, none of the other parties has yet reached the position of the ruling party in the national government. The Congress party until recently had been held together by a series of strong leaders, all of whom were closely linked with the independence movement. Mahatma Gandhi, now elevated virtually to the role of a saint, was the leader of the Congress during the crucial years in the fight for independence. His teachings of nonviolent resistance have been emulated by political action groups in other countries, most notably by the Southern Christian Leadership Conference under Martin Luther King in the struggle for equal rights for black people in the United States.

Gandhi's heir, Jawaharlal Nehru, became the first head of government in an independent India. He led the Congress party and the government until his death in 1964. At that time party and government were so closely fused that the question of his succession became one of the survival of the state as well as the party. Not until the sudden death in 1966 of Nehru's successor, Lal Bahadur Shastri, who had been elected prime minister and leader of the Congress party in 1964, did succession to party leadership and government leadership become two separate issues. Again a personality emerged as leader of both party and state. Indira Gandhi, the widowed daughter of Prime Minister Nehru, was elected prime minister to succeed Prime Minister Shastri; she won reelection in 1967. She gained a two-thirds majority for her New Congress party in the election of 1971 when she single-handedly challenged the Congress party leadership to give her the mandate she asked for.

In 1957 Myron Weiner, an American political scientist, made this comment on Indian party politics:

> *For the moment, at least, India could be described as having a one-party democratic system, based not on the coercion found in one-party dictatorships, but on consent. The opposition parties in India, although small in comparison with Congress, have the right to organize, agitate and express their views freely.*[12]

Professor Weiner's observations had to be modified considerably in light of the elections ten years later. After the 1967 general elections the Congress party no longer held a monopoly of power in the national Parliament. Its number of seats in the key lower house of Parliament dropped from about 75 percent to 55 percent. As a result of the 1967 elections, the Congress party also lost its control in nine out of the seventeen state governments. When all the 1971 election returns were in, Indira Gandhi's New Congress party had won at least 350 of the 518 seats at stake in the lower house of Parliament.

We referred earlier in this chapter to Indira Gandhi's ability to weather the internal frictions in the Congress party. The attempts of the older party leadership to expel her in November, 1969, and her retaliation, asserting her role as leader of the Congress party in Parliament, focused the spotlight on the deep frictions within the Congress party. The growing strength of other parties among the electorate seemed to indicate that India was entering a new phase in her political history. She no longer felt tied to the one-party system and its individual leaders who led the struggle for independence. India has emerged as a highly complex, independent political system, utilizing parties to express her many and diverse demands, views, and interests. As India continues to develop a pluralistic society, the one-party system may prove no longer sufficient to carry the many messages between government and the governed. As one communication device between government and electorate becomes overloaded, others may have to be added. No doubt, Indira Gandhi and her New Congress party read the handwriting on the wall. The split in the Congress party and Mrs. Gandhi's willingness to take on the other parties on her own merits, not on the independence history of the Congress, shows that the days of the one-party system, which was tied to the issue of independence only, are over in India.

One-Party Governments in Africa

The KANU in Kenya In the years just prior to independence, Kenya seemed to be favoring a two-party system. Parties were organized along tribal lines: Jomo Kenyatta's Kenya African National Union (KANU) was supported mostly by members of the two largest tribes, the Kikuyu (about 20 percent of the population) and the Luo (about 14 percent of the population). The Kenya African Democratic Union (KADU) was composed of members of the smaller tribes (the Kalenjin, Masai, and Baluhya). Neither one of the parties could claim a long history or tradition, since both were formed in 1960. Both reflected the tribal jealousies and conflicts within Kenya which had erupted most violently during the years of the Mau Mau rebellion (1952–59). KANU and KADU leaders had very little basis for compromise over issues, and each set of leaders was deeply caught up in tribal fears and rivalries. During the constitutional debates of 1963, the KANU leaders opted for a unitary state; the KADU leadership wanted a federation with much control vested in the regions, based on tribal divisions.

Neither the KANU or KADU could be compared to institutionalized party structures. They had no governing experience and many of their party issues were more closely related to tribal infighting than any concrete political programs. During the constitutional debates, at the time of transition from colonialism to independence, the KADU tribal leaders threatened to use spears and poisoned arrows as well as to secede if their demands for autonomy were not granted.[13]

During 1963 the KANU emerged as the strongest party, and Jomo Kenyatta became the head of government. The KADU membership dwindled and, within a year of Kenyan independence, the Kenya African Democratic Union was dissolved and its remnants joined with Kenyatta's KANU. After constitutional revision, Jomo Kenyatta, a member of the Kikuyu tribe, became Kenya's president, and Oginga Odinga, a Luo, served as vice-president.

Although Kenya had been restructured as a one-party state following the dissolution of the KADU, the KANU was not a united party. Tribal frictions persisted within the party. Two strong Luo leaders, Oginga Odinga and Tom Mboya, took off on sharply differing courses within the party. Mboya built a strong base of support within the party and also served as an innovative minister of economic planning and development in Kenyatta's government. A rift developed between Odinga and Kenyatta, with the president accusing his vice-president of being overly ambitious. Odinga and Mboya feuded, too, as they disagreed more and more over economic policies. In 1966 Kenyatta stripped Odinga of party leadership in the KANU. Odinga resigned as vice-president and, taking with him a dissident faction of the KANU, established the Kenya People's Union (KPU). It appeared that this was the end of the one-party state in Kenya.

The KPU was largely a Luo-based party, and the initial Kenyan party politics based on tribal splits began to reappear. The KPU remained small on the national level, however, and held less than 10 seats in the 170-seat Parliament. In by-elections in March, 1969, the KPU won a victory in Western Province. By-elections provide a sounding board for a party's standing in a representative system, and indications were that the Kenya People's Union would try to enlarge its base in the electoral process.

Although party loyalties of the Luos were split between Tom Mboya (who continued his membership in the KANU and his cabinet post) and Oginga Odinga (who became the opposition leader), the rift was closed after the murder of Tom Mboya in July, 1969. The Luos closed ranks behind Odinga and his KPU. Rumors circulated throughout the country that the Kikuyus were taking secret oaths to kill the Luos. These rumors were especially terrifying to Kenyans who remembered that secret oaths and initiation rites had played a major role in the organization ritual of the Mau Mau during the 1950s. President Kenyatta appealed for national unity and traveled to areas of strong KPU support. His appearance, especially in Western Province in the fall of 1969, promptly resulted in bloody clashes with several deaths and many injured.

On October 30, 1969, Kenya became once more a one-party state. President Kenyatta, in an emotion-charged speech, banned the KPU, charged it with trying to overthrow the government, and then he proceeded to jail his former vice-president Odinga on the grounds that Odinga was the tool of outside forces. The return to one-party rule was made more significant because it took place shortly before the first general elections since Kenyan independence.

The PDCI in the Ivory Coast Many African leaders believe that one-party systems are best suited to their countries, since tribalism is in itself such a divisive force. Parties, tending to grow around tribal affiliation, make national consensus and political compromise very difficult. To a leadership group or a leader concerned primarily with economic development, mobilization of national resources, and political socialization, the party that can count on being the only ingroup seems to be more effective than one facing continuous opposition and the ever-present possibility of ouster.

These considerations no doubt played a major role in the development of the Ivory Coast as a one-party system. The Ivory Coast is the confluence of four African civilizations, none of which emerges as the major or dominant one. Various scholars as well as politicians put the number of languages spoken and the number of tribes living in the Ivory Coast between sixty and sixty-two.[14] In a speech before the Constituent Assembly in 1959, President Felix Houphouet-Boigny stated that "For the time being—and I am sure you know why I hope that this will last—the Ivory Coast is fortunate enough to have a movement that has gained a large majority throughout the country." [15] In the same speech he outlined that "*within the framework* of the Community which we have freely chosen, there is room for a policy of opposition, *but not outside it*." [16] Ever since he assumed the office of president, Houphouet-Boigny has made sure that the community which he leads will not provide an opportunity for a concerted policy of opposition in the form of an opposition party. His concern is to bridge the gap between a tribal-oriented traditional society and a modern, industrialized nation state. To him, political parties, other than the Parti Démocratique de la Côte d'Ivoire (PDCI) which he leads and which he uses to link his government with the peoples in his state, would be destructive instruments of tribalism in the nation state he is trying to build.

The PRI in Mexico

Building a nation state, or to use another concept familiar to political scientists, national integration, was one of the major problems confronting Mexican political leaders throughout the late nineteenth and early twentieth centuries. In Mexico the main obstacle to political and economic development was not the issue of tribalism (as it applies to our African examples) but rather the problems of regionalism and particularism (which we mentioned in our example of the Federal Republic of Germany). Unlike Germany, however, particularism and regionalism were not based on religion (since the days of the conquistadores all of Mexico had been under the influence of the Roman Catholic Church), but rather on the vastness of the country.

Mexico is the third largest country in Latin America. Although one-fourth the size of the United States, its topography has presented far greater barriers to internal communication than that of the United States. Much of the history of the United States is linked to the development of roads, railroads, and cross-continental communications. Much of the tradition of particularism and regionalism in Mexico may be attributed to lack of communication. Local and regional leaders were able to keep close reign over their territories because their territories were not joined to others—not even by the simplest roads. Mountains, jungles, deserts, and plateaus prevented the inhabitants of the various areas from making contacts with their neighbors and kept each region pretty much self-contained.

During the Revolution of 1910 a number of leaders emerged from various parts of the country. Among them, and therefore rivals for power, were Francisco Madero, Venustino Carranza, Emilio Zapata, and the one who has probably been most romanticized as hero and as villain, Pancho Villa. They came from different parts of Mexico, and their squabbles resulted in a prolonging of the aftereffects of the revolution—poverty, chaos, and the continued infighting of regional leaders who ruled for their own profit.

Since 1928 one political party has dominated Mexican politics. After a few name changes, the Institutional Revolutionary party (PRI) emerged. The PRI has stressed the building of a communications network incorporating such vastly different forms of communication as roads and schools. Overcoming the problems of regionalism and the parochial hold of political leaders have been among the principal aims of the PRI. Party leaders have faced up to the fact that political socialization—the installation of a feeling of national consciousness and identity in all Mexicans—is the main force in modernization.

The PRI has mobilized workers, peasants, and concerned citizens in its three main organizational branches: labor, agrarian, and popular, thereby absorbing into the party apparatus the three main pressure groups arising from a developing society. Mexico faces a multitude of problems before it completes the transition into a fully integrated nation state, however.

> *Probably it is fair to say that . . . given the multiplicity of problems and the speed with which change took place, the PRI has done more than any other party in Latin America to assist government in providing the physical means and the social-economic environment to encourage national integration and resolution of the crisis of development. . . .*
>
> *. . . it (the PRI) has imposed a sense of legitimacy for the modernizing goals of the government, until few politically aware Mexicans fail to accept these norms.*[17]

The CPSU

At the outset of this chapter we quoted an American student of political parties on the point that classical political theorists tended to ignore the need for a link between government and people. Nowhere in contemporary political practice, and certainly in no one example among our twelve, does the party perform more of a linkage function between people and government than does the Communist party of the Soviet Union (CPSU). In the preface to what is considered the definitive history of the CPSU in the West, Leonard Shapiro points out:

> *The method of government which Lenin evolved after 1917 is, so far as I am aware, unique in the history of political systems—or was so until imitated in other countries. There have, of course, been autocracies, dictatorships, despotisms, autocratic democracies, or whatever one likes to call the Soviet system of government, throughout history. But Lenin's government had in addition the unique quality that it brought into being what were ostensibly independent political institutions—Soviets, courts, trade unions and the like —but ensured from the first that each and everyone of the institutions should*

> *function only under the control of a single political party, of which the members were linked by an ideology and by strict discipline.*[18]

To read the history of the USSR as it is published by the government of the Soviet Union is,[19] at the same time, to read the history of the CPSU. Stalin rewrote Marx's concept of the dictatorship of the proletariat into a new set of roles for proletariat and party in the USSR.

> *The highest expression of the leading role of the Party, here, in the Soviet Union . . . is the fact that not a single important political or organizational question is decided by our Soviet and other mass organizations without guiding directions from the Party.*[20]

The Communist party of the Soviet Union has been totally transformed from its revolutionary origin into a completely institutionalized structure. It permeates every aspect of Russian life. The party's main function is to link every individual and every group within Soviet society with the state. The CPSU controls every leadership position in society, be it the role of membership in the Supreme Soviet, head of a ministry, manager of a kolkhoz, or the post of prima ballerina in the Bolshoi Ballet. This does not mean that party membership automatically assures the aspirant his role. Party membership is essential, however, in addition to talent, ability, and training, in order to succeed, and more often than not, it is the party membership which weighs most strongly.

Since the Communist party in the USSR links society and state, it would follow that membership in the party is highly desirable and that there would be as many party members as citizens in the USSR. Actually, the current number of party members is about 13.5 million out of a total population of about 241 million. Although the party is the controlling element in society and even though the official ideology of the USSR emphasizes the role of the people, the CPSU has never been a mass party. Stalin referred to the dictatorship of the party as the dictatorship of the proletariat's vanguard.

Party members are carefully selected and must spend at least a year of candidacy for membership, during which time they are closely scrutinized at work, at home, in their activities in the many party auxiliary organizations which influence Russian life (labor unions, youth groups, housewife organizations). Admittance to candidacy and approval by party members and officials does not mean automatic admission to party membership. The party leadership rewards certain groups in society with larger membership quotas periodically, whenever it wants (and needs) to involve those segments of society more actively in the building of the USSR.

Our friend Ivan Skivitsky, the economist, for example, grew up in party auxiliaries and was much involved in all the right organizations. You might call him an activist since childhood. He was in the Little Octobrists, the organization for primary-school children. As soon as he reached the eligible age of ten he joined the Young Pioneers. At that stage he was not so different from most of his schoolmates because membership in the Young Pioneers is virtually universal in the ten-to-fifteen-year age group.

As a university student, Ivan Skivitsky applied for and was accepted into the Young Communist League (*Komsomol*). He was very active and became a leader of the Komsomol among the economics students at his university. When he finished the university, he applied for party membership at a time when it was in the interest of the state to involve factory workers in the political process. Intellectuals, students, and professors had a relatively small quota for party membership. So Ivan Skivitsky became a candidate for membership in the CPSU in 1955, but when he thought he could get full membership in 1956 he was disappointed, despite the fact that he was a highly qualified candidate.

In 1957 the first man-made satellite orbited the earth. Sputnik represented a triumphant achievement of the engineers and intellectuals in the USSR. The status of university-trained scientists and social scientists changed in the USSR (as it did in the USA). The party rearranged its membership quota in favor of engineers and scientists and the social scientists rode into party membership on the coattails of the engineers and natural scientists. Ivan Skivitsky became admitted to full membership in the Communist party of the Soviet Union.

Although he had been a member of all the auxiliary organizations in his country during his childhood and his young adulthood, by the time Ivan Skivitsky became a full-fledged party member he really was no longer interested in spending most of his time on behalf of the party. He had studied, married, graduated, become professionally ambitious, and wanted full-fledged party membership because he knew that he could not advance as an economist who wanted to teach unless he was a member of the CPSU. He is one of the members of the party who carry a membership card, pay their dues, contribute to party drives—but he is not an activist in the party. The CPSU, even though it represents less than 10 percent of the population in the USSR and is intended to be an elite organization of those members of society who are politically active, is not a very active party. Within the party only about 10 percent are politically active, i.e., involved in causes; the rest are in the party for the advantages it offers them. So, in fact, an elite runs a party which the ideological leaders of the USSR have labeled as the vanguard of the proletariat.

Still, the party is the link between the society and the state in the USSR, and it has been since the 1917 Revolution. The CPSU is facing many problems as the only in-party. It has never yet found a way to recruit successors to its leaders and has pretty much handled the succession problem through cooperation within a small, self-perpetuating ingroup, punctuated by purges. In a society that has become more and more dynamic, the party is too institutionalized and too calcified to satisfy the demands of the younger generations. In many ways, the party has outlived its reason for existence, since its goals in transforming Russia have been largely achieved. Yet the CPSU hangs on and manages to remain the major link between society and the state. The USSR is a one-party state, and no doubt it has influenced the party-political structure and the ideology of many a developing country. The roles of the party as the unifier in propelling development have been two aspects of party politics that the leaders of the USSR have expounded in the newly emerging countries. It is understandable why the single-party system appears to be most attractive to the developing countries among our sample.

We have chosen to categorize political parties as competitive and noncompetitive. In the competitive system, two or more parties offer the electorate a choice between candidates for public office and an opportunity to express a preference as to alternative public policies. In the one-party system, the voters, faced with a single slate of candidates and an officially endorsed platform, have little option at the polls except to approve the party candidates and the party platform. Some students of political science think it logically absurd even to talk about one-party systems, which do not permit open competition among opposing groups in the society. Our brief survey of political parties in twelve very different political systems indicates, however, that political parties generally—two-party, multiparty, or one-party—perform similar functions.

In any state the most important function of the political party is that of linkage—organized and ongoing communications—between the government and the people. The strategies and tactics of two-party, multiparty, and one-party systems appear to be at great variance. But in every state it is a major function of the party system to articulate the plural interests of the people within the overall framework of national interest and general welfare. In two-party systems, where a majority vote is needed to put a party in power, the major parties bid for the maximum popular vote each by selecting a balanced ticket and constructing a platform that appeals to many different groups within the electorate (witness any presidential election in the United States). In multiparty systems, each party tends to be identified with a particular constituency, but if no one party represents a majority constituency then interparty bargaining regroups the various constituencies under a national front (as in Colombia) or in a coalition government (as in Germany). Even under totalitarian government, where one party dominates the entire political system, the party process operates so as to filter various public demands to those in authority as well as to secure public support for party policies. (We observe that the Communist party in the USSR, increasingly sensitive to consumer demands, in its current five-year plan has recommended a massive switch of the whole national economy toward improving the people's welfare, their working and living conditions.)

In the next chapter on elections we shall focus on what are probably the most salient activities of every party system, alerting the electorate to pending public issues, rounding up the voters for a mass march to the polls, and, in so doing, giving to the government its most valuable political asset, the outward visible sign of legitimate authority—consent of the governed.

NOTES

1. Judson L. James, *American Political Parties* (New York: Pegasus, 1969), p. 22.
2. Harold Lasswell, *Politics: Who Gets What, When, How* (Cleveland and New York: World Publishing, Meridian Books, 1958).

3. Seymour Martin Lipset and Stein Rokkan, eds., *Party Systems and Voter Alignments* (New York: Free Press, 1967), p. 3.
4. Aristide Zolberg, *One Party Government in the Ivory Coast*, rev. ed. (Princeton, N.J.: Princeton University Press, 1969). See also Ruth Schachter Morgenthau, *Political Parties in French-Speaking Africa* (Oxford: Clarendon, 1964).
5. Sigmund Neumann, ed., *Modern Political Parties* (Chicago: University of Chicago Press, 1955), p. 400 ff; Joseph La Polombara and Myron Weiner, eds., *Political Parties and Political Development* (Princeton, N.J.: Princeton University Press, 1966), especially chaps. 1 and 2.
6. Manfred Haettich, "Zur Typologie der Politischen Parteien," in Gilbert Ziebura, ed., *Beiträge zur Allgemeinen Parteienlehre* (Darmstadt: Wissenschaftliche Buchgesellschaft, 1969), pp. 375–410. Unfortunately, this work has not been translated into English.
7. Samuel H. Beer, *British Politics in the Collectivist Age* (New York: Knopf, 1965).
8. In the United States, as in Britain, the two-party system is a misnomer because there are other parties in the United States running candidates at election times. In the 1968 presidential elections 86.1 percent of the American electorate that went to the polls voted for the Democratic and Republican candidates, but 13.9 percent voted for the candidates put up by the Socialist and Socialist Labor parties, the Communist party, the Prohibition party, and a category called "Miscellaneous Independent," of which George Wallace's American Independent party got the biggest chunk—9,906,000 votes. (United States Bureau of the Census, *Statistical Abstract of the United States, 1970*, 91st ed. Washington, D.C.: Government Printing Office, 1970), p. 354.
9. James MacGregor Burns, *The Deadlock of Democracy: Four-Party Politics in America* (Englewood Cliffs, N.J.: Prentice-Hall, 1963).
10. See the table on p. 106 in Douglas Verney, *British Government and Politics* (New York: Harper & Row, 1966).
11. "Of the seven smaller parties represented in the first Bundestag only one, the Free Democratic Party, has thus far managed to survive the trend toward a two-party system. However, the future of the FDP as a competitive, national party appears most uncertain," wrote Lewis Edinger in 1968 in his *Politics in Germany* (Boston: Little, Brown, 1968), pp. 237–38.
12. Myron Weiner, *Party Politics in India* (Princeton, N.J.: Princeton University Press, 1957), p. 287.
13. Rupert Emerson, "Parties and National Integration in Africa," in La Palombara and Weiner, eds., op. cit., p. 291.
14. Aristide Zolberg, op. cit., p. 11. For a chart of the various ethnic groups in the Ivory Coast, see p. 13.
15. Ivory Coast, Constituent Assembly, *Debates*, March 1959; quoted in Zolberg, op. cit., p. 261.
16. Ibid.; italics supplied by the authors.
17. Robert E. Scott, "Political Parties and Policy-Making in Latin America," in La Palombara and Weiner, op. cit., p. 352.
18. Leonard Schapiro, *The Communist Party of the Soviet Union* (New York: Random House, 1960), p. viii.
19. *Outline History of the USSR*, trans., George H. Hanna (Moscow: Foreign Languages Publishing House, 1960).
20. As quoted in Merle Fainsod, *How Russia is Ruled*, 2d ed. (Cambridge, Mass.: Harvard University Press, 1963), p. 137.

FURTHER READING

EPSTEIN, LEON D. *Political Parties in Western Democracies.* New York: Praeger, 1967.

LAPALOMBARA, JOSEPH, and MYRON WEINER, eds. *Political Parties and Political Development.* Princeton, N.J.: Princeton University Press, 1966.

LIPSET, SEYMOUR M., and STEIN ROKKAN, eds. *Party Systems and Voter Alignments.* New York: Free Press, 1967.

SCALAPINO, ROBERT A., and JUNNOSUKE MASUMI. *Parties and Politics in Contemporary Japan.* Berkeley, Calif.: University of California Press, 1962.

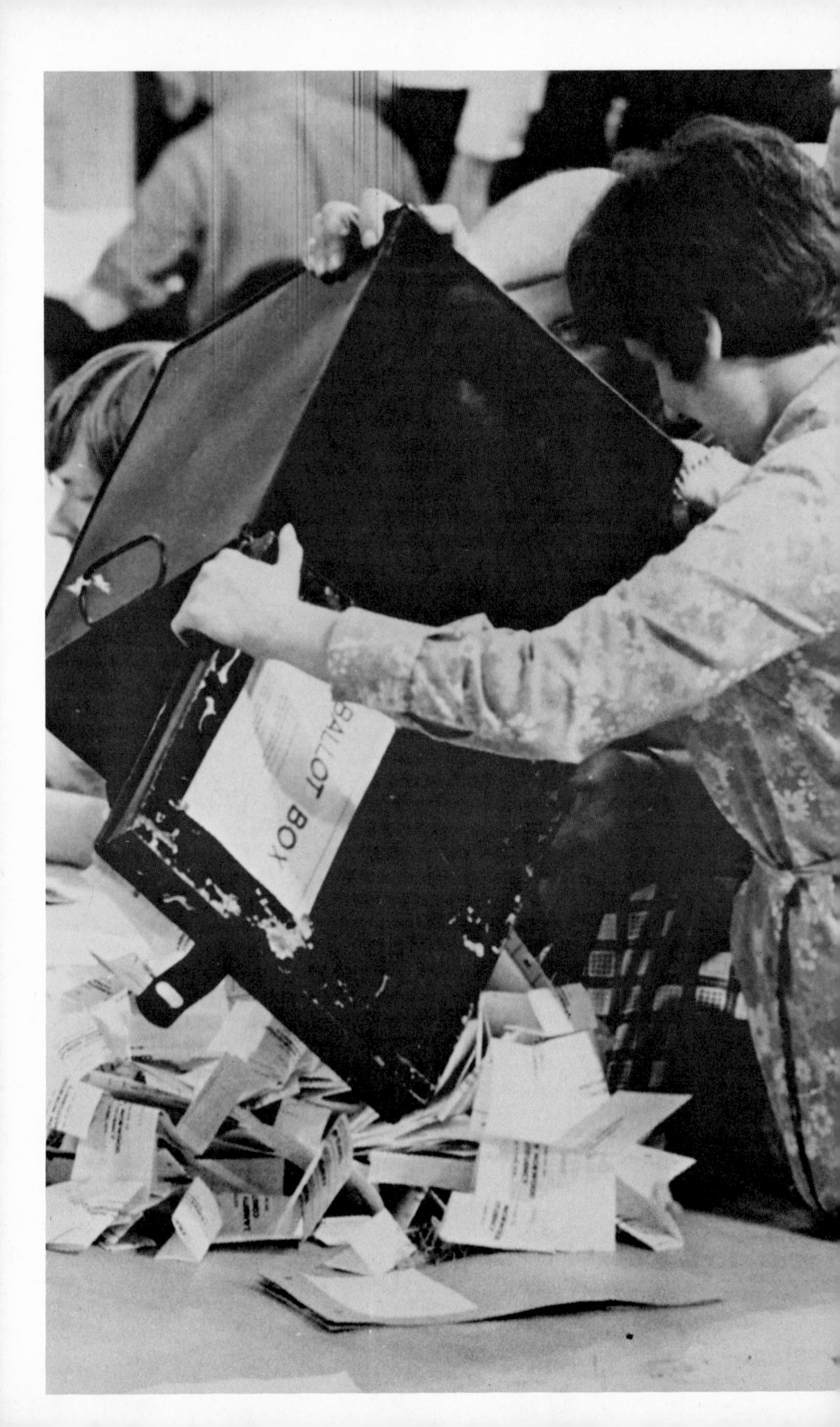
BALLOT BOX

chapter 8

HOW DO ELECTIONS AFFECT GOVERNMENT?

Mass elections, the one political act that involves most adult citizens, are a phenomenon of modern government. In even the most democratic countries after the middle of the nineteenth century the franchise was considered a privilege reserved only for certain classes of citizens, such as property holders, rather than the prerogative of the people as a whole. Today universal suffrage, periodic elections, and secret balloting are regularities in political behavior that appear to characterize every modern state, and certainly all twelve states in our sample.

THEORIES OF ELECTIONS

In everyone of our twelve states the direct election of a national legislature is a major political procedure. Here is another regularity that we observe in modern political systems; the people not only demand representation in their government but also expect to choose their own representatives. We pointed out in the preceding chapter that political parties are organized and function to: 1) get out a mass vote; 2) persuade the electorate for whom (candidates) and for what (issues) to vote; and, most important, 3) provide simultaneous communications among the components of government and between the government and the people. Now let us take a look at some recent

United Kingdom, counting votes
(United Press International)

elections to see how the electorate has variously responded to party communications.

The most striking correlation between party activity and voting behavior is, of course, to be found in one-party governments. In the Soviet Union more than 99 percent of the eligible electorate participated in the 1970 elections for the Soviet of the Union and the Soviet of Nationalities; endorsement of the 1,517 candidates nominated by the Communist party was also more than 99 percent. The Ivory Coast showed a similarly singular voting pattern in its 1970 elections: The Parti Démocratique de la Côte d'Ivoire (the only party permitted to operate) retained all the seats in the National Assembly; President Felix Houphouet-Boigny was reelected for a five-year term, receiving more than 99 percent of all the votes cast.

From the most recent elections in our twelve states it is clear that the greatest turnout at the polls and the highest degree of support for the party in power occurs in one-party states where the voters have no opportunity to register a choice as to party or issues.

One wonders how people in the USSR or the Ivory Coast would respond if questioned about their private assessment of their importance during election campaigns or on going to the polls to cast their ballots. Such questions were put to citizens in the United States, the United Kingdom, Germany, and Mexico in the 1950s as part of a broad study of civic culture by a team of American social scientists. Table 8–1 summarizes the responses.

Presumably the degree of satisfaction, enjoyment, irritation, or anger that a voter feels on going to the polls depends at least partly on how he perceives the role and functions of elections in his own political system. When we refer to role and functions we have in mind the operative rationale: Why do all modern states expend such effort at bringing masses of citizens to the polls and what is supposed to be accomplished through such regular nationwide elections?

Quite obviously elections play different roles and serve different functions in different kinds of political systems. First let us look at our Western

TABLE 8–1
Attitudes and Feelings about Voting and Election Campaigns

Percentage Who Report They:	USA	UK	GER., FR	MEXICO
Feel satisfaction when going to polls	71	43	35	34
Sometimes find election campaigns pleasant and enjoyable	66	52	28	34
Sometimes find campaign silly or ridiculous	58	37	46	32
Never enjoy, never get angry, and never feel contempt during campaigns	12	26	35	41

SOURCE: Gabriel A. Almond and Sidney Verba, *The Civic Culture* (Boston: Little, Brown, 1965), p. 109. Originally published in Almond and Verba, *The Civic Culture: Political Attitudes and Democracy in Five Nations* (Princeton, N.J.: Princeton University Press, 1963), p. 146. Copyright 1963 by Princeton University Press.

representative governments where consent of the governed is regarded as a fundamental principle. In terms of the electoral process this means the right (or even obligation?) of the citizen to: 1) participate in the choice of policy-makers, 2) register preference among alternative public policies, and 3) turn out of office policy-makers whose performance has failed to satisfy the electorate. When, however, we try to compare the application of these electoral principles among the democratic states in our sample, we find some significant variations.

PARTICIPATION IN ELECTIONS

The right to vote is regarded as a prime prerequisite of citizenship; hence universal adult suffrage is a characteristic feature of all democratic political systems. Election returns, however, show wide discrepancies between the number who vote and the number who can vote. In the United States, for example, in the 1968 presidential elections about 60 percent of the 120 million Americans of voting age went to the polls. Richard M. Nixon, the Republican candidate, received 43.4 percent of the popular vote, the lowest proportion for any winning candidate since 1912 when Woodrow Wilson emerged as the winner of a three-way race. (As a matter of record, sixteen American presidents, including President Nixon, were elected by less than a majority of the popular vote.) Moreover, the highest proportion of voters participate in presidential elections; less than a third of the adult population are inclined to vote regularly in national, state, and local elections.

Among the twelve states in our sample, with one exception, the American voter has the poorest attendance rate at the polls; the exception is Colombia. Less than a fourth of the eligible Colombian voters participated in the 1968 congressional elections. In contrast, 86.7 percent of the German electorate exercised their franchise in the 1969 elections for the Bundestag. In 1969 the Israeli electorate turned out about 80 percent to elect the members of the Knesset. In the same year 65 percent of the Turkish electorate voted for members of the National Assembly.

It is difficult to find a common denominator in explaining discrepancies in voting behavior in democratic political systems where participation at the polls is voluntary. Studies of political participation in the United States indicate that many aspects of a citizen's background may influence his voting behavior: social class, ethnic group, family pattern, educational level, occupation, income level, age, sex, etc. We surmise how Joe Zilch voted in the presidential election of 1968: an ex-GI, a family man, living in a middle-income suburb of a big Eastern industrial city, making good union wages with overtime, mowing the lawn on Saturday, passing the collection plate on Sunday, and concerned about crime in the streets and violence on TV. His candidate won. We also have a pretty good guess as to why Abraham Jefferson, an ex-GI living with his family in a three-room flat ten blocks from the White House, a day laborer frequently unemployed, passed up his constitutional right under the Twenty-third Amendment to vote for three presidential electors from the District of Columbia in 1968.

We are wary of establishing definite causal relationships; the unpredictable personal dimension is often the decisive factor in political behavior. Moreover, the kind of systematic data that political scientists have collected on the American voter is not yet available on the electorates of other countries. Suffice it for us here to mention some of the institutional aspects of the political system that help explain the differing roles and functions of elections in presidential and parliamentary governments.

ELECTION OF THE NATIONAL EXECUTIVE

In presidential governments—as in the United States, Mexico, and Colombia—the president is both titular head of state and chief executive. Directly elected by the people, his term in office is independent of the congress. In parliamentary governments—the United Kingdom, Germany, Israel, Turkey, Japan, and India—the party (or coalition of parties) that wins control of the legislature determines the selection of executive actors, and the tenure of both is interdependent.

In Presidential Systems

The separation of powers that characterizes presidential government in the United States makes it virtually impossible for the voters to exercise any decisive influence on the selection of policies even when alternatives with respect to specific issues are presented in competing national party platforms. When the president is elected to office, presumably he has at least an initial commitment to the party platform on which he campaigned. But, as we have pointed out earlier, the congressional candidates are not required, nor even expected, to stand on the national party platforms constructed for presidential elections. Only the president (and vice-president) can claim a national constituency (to have been elected by the nation as a whole). Elected at the same time as the president, each member of the House of Representatives represents a district within his state; one-third of the senators are elected at the same time as the president and each represents the people of his entire state. Thus Congress is only incidentally the national legislature.

If as a result of elections in the United States both the president and a majority of the members of Congress are of the same party, the national electorate might reasonably expect the Congress to accept presidential leadership in pursuit of the national party platform, but such expectations are usually frustrated.

Dwight D. Eisenhower received an overwhelming mandate for change at the polls in 1952,[1] but the mandate was difficult to implement not only because the Republicans had won a bare majority of seats in Congress but also because the Republican leadership was more inclined to obstruct the president than the Democratic leadership. Similarly, after the 1960 elections when the Democrats captured both the White House and a majority of seats in both houses of Congress, President John F. Kennedy found it hard going to get through Congress the very policies for which he had successfully campaigned, and his stiffest opposition came from old-timers of his own party in Congress. Even more confusing, however, in appraising the role of American elections in the policy-making process is the situation when the electorate at large chooses the president from one party and voters in the states and districts choose a majority of congressmen from the opposing party.

In the United States, where voting even in national elections depends on state and local residence requirements, the mobility of the American population is bound to cut down the percentage of eligible voters in any given election, possibly as much as 5 percent. Moreover, as voter apathy is more likely to exist in free elections where party opposition is minimal, the numerous one-party constituencies that still exist in the United States, particularly in the New England and some Southern states, but also in other sections of the country, undoubtedly contribute to the low level of electoral participation in those constituencies.

The frequency of American elections may also have something to do with the truancy of the American electorate. It is difficult to whip up partisan zeal and popular interest to its highest on the first Tuesday after the first Monday in November in even years. Members of Congress are elected every two years and the president every four. All too often the great controversies that stir the nation occur between elections. For example, three American presidents won their election to office on specific campaign promises to keep the country out of war: Woodrow Wilson in 1916, Franklin D. Roosevelt in 1940, and Lyndon B. Johnson in 1964. The events and the policies that led the United States into three major wars under these same presidents did not take place until after the elections were decided. What do American elections decide?

Both Colombia and Mexico elected new presidents in 1970. Both elections were held on schedule, but the outcome in Colombia was something of a cliff-hanger. General Rojas presented himself in opposition to Misrael Pastrano Borrero, the National Front candidate. An ultranationalist and right-wing extremist, Rojas conducted a flamboyant campaign, promising to abolish Congress and to provide the poor with cars, promises that appealed particularly in the rural areas. Voting was heavy and there were no reports of violence during the elections, partly because the government had ordered the military out in force to the polling places. Following his defeat at the polls Rojas cried "fraud," and thousands of his supporters took to rioting in the streets. Claiming that he had actually won by three hundred thousand votes, Rojas declared, "God has chosen me to be President of the Colombians. I consider myself elected President of the Republic." [2] But after allowing a week for cooling off, incumbent President Lleras announced the official results: The electorate had chosen Misrael Pastrano Borrero as their next president.

What did the Colombia election mean? In the first place, it showed that the class struggle is alive and well in this Latin American republic. The Rojas vote was clearly a protest vote, an attempt on the part of the lower class, the poor, and the dispossessed to change the system, to overthrow the oligarchy. And the attempt was within a hair's breadth of succeeding—the absentee votes of Colombians overseas made the crucial difference. The political science faculty at the National University researched the voting behavior according to class structure in the barrios of Bogotá. Their survey clearly showed the lower-class base of the Rojas vote—64 percent of the lower-class and 50 percent of the lower-middle-class vote went to the old general. On the other hand, 76 percent of the upper class and 67 percent of the upper-middle class voted for Pastrano.

The Colombian election reforms also show, however, that the lower classes do not automatically vote for leftist or liberal candidates and upper classes do not always support the ruling elite. The Bogotá survey discloses a 27-percent vote for Pastrano from the poorest people in the city. At the top of the social pyramid, Rojas pulled 12 percent of the vote. The fact remains, however, an ex-dictator, a flamboyant demagogue who promised quick fixes —cars for the poor and pesos strong as dollars—whatever the long-range costs in economic development and civil liberties, was almost elected by mass vote.

In Parliamentary Systems

In parliamentary government the head of state has a symbolic position: He represents the unity of the state and the people; his activities are largely ceremonial. The Turkish Constitution puts it most bluntly, "The President of the Republic is irresponsible for his proceedings relating to his function."[3] The same description, more or less diplomatically worded, fits most heads of state. Since the titular head of state plays a separate role in parliamentary government, he is chosen on a different basis from the head of government. In all parliamentary governments the head of government—variously called "premier," "prime minister," or "chancellor"—plays the leading role in the political process. In two of our states the hereditary monarch is still the titular head: the British queen and the Japanese emperor. The president of the Federal Republic is elected by the Federal Convention comprising members of the Bundestag and an equal number of representatives from the German states. The president of India is selected by an electoral college following a complicated formula for proportional representation including the elected members of both houses of the national parliament and the members of the legislative assemblies in the states. The president of Israel is elected by the Knesset, the president of Turkey by the National Assembly. In each instance the president is elected for a specified term in office with the possibility of reelection, except in Israel where the president's tenure is constitutionally limited to a single period of seven years. Whether the head of state ascends to the office in an elaborate coronation ceremony or in a formal process involving the representative bodies, the method of selection is intended to enhance the symbolic status of the position and to endow it with more dignity than authority.

Traditionally the head of state designates the head of government. In practice, however, the head of government is determined by the majority or coalition party leadership in the parliament. The German Basic Law, for example, provides that the federal chancellor shall be elected, "without debate," by the Bundestag on the proposal of the federal president and that the person who obtains a majority of the votes in the Bundestag election "must be appointed by the Federal President." [4] The constitutional script is not only dull reading, it is almost irrelevant to the actual performance, unless you keep in mind the political setting. The selection of Willy Brandt as federal chancellor in the fall of 1969 was in fact one of the most dramatic events in the politics of the world as well as of Germany. It took a lot of fast talking and shrewd political maneuvering behind the scenes to join members of the Social Democratic party (SPD) and the Free Democratic party (FDP) in a new coalition that would overturn the ruling Grand Coalition of Christian Democratic party (CDU) and Social Democratic party (SPD) (with the FDP in opposition) under Chancellor Kurt Kiesinger (CDU). But that's what happened and Willy Brandt, leader of the SDP, was elected "without debate" by a majority of votes in the Bundestag, the first leader of the Social Democratic Party to become federal chancellor in forty years.

ELECTION OF NATIONAL LEGISLATORS

In Competitive Party Systems

Germany, India, Israel, Japan, Turkey, and the United Kingdom all exemplify competitive party systems with parliamentary government. In all of these states the members of parliament are directly elected by the people. The prime minister and the members of the cabinet, usually called "the government," are selected by the parliament, or more accurately, by the party (or coalition) that holds a majority of seats. The prime minister and the cabinet are collectively responsible to the parliament in the formulation of policy and individually responsible in the implementation of policy. The fact that the parliament has selected the government pretty well assures that the government-sponsored legislation will be enacted as policy. If, however, the government loses the confidence of parliament or faces mounting criticism in the public arena, the government may be forced to resign or alternatively to call for dissolution of the parliament.

In contrast to fixed election dates and prescribed terms in office as in presidential government, parliamentary elections occur at the discretion of the prime minister but within the constitutional or statutory limits of a parliamentary term. In the United Kingdom, for example, the statutory term for Parliament is five years. The prime minister may determine when within the five-year period an election may most advantageously be called, but he, his government, and Parliament must face the electorate at least once every five years. A statutory limit may always be waived, as it was in the United Kingdom during World War II. A constitutional limit sets the maximum term, but again the actual term depends on the discretion of the party in power. Thus in Japan the government dissolved the House of Representatives ten times between 1947 and 1969, each time calling for general elections that cut short the constitutional four-year term of the representatives.

Variations in procedures for electing members of parliament may be significant in appraising the role and functions of elections within particular political systems.[5] In the United Kingdom all members of the House of Commons are selected from single-member constituencies. The voters in the constituency, however, have no voice in the nominations. Party candidates for particular constituencies are chosen by local committees, usually from the national party pools of prospective MP's. It is not necessary, or even usual, for the candidate to be a resident of the constituency in which he runs for office. Moreover, the contest is strictly partisan with the focus on issues rather than personalities. With two or three candidates in the running (Conservative, Labor, and possibly Liberal), whoever gets the highest number of votes (plurality) wins the election. The British voter who wants to make the most of his one chance to participate directly in the political process will consider the candidate's party affiliation more important than any other qualification for the reason that an individual MP owes his political allegiance and all his votes in Parliament to the party under whose auspices he was nominated and elected. In the American Congress crossing party lines is a common occurrence; in the British Parliament all MP's are expected to vote according to instructions from their respective party whips, and because party discipline is so tight in Parliament, party responsibility is highly credible at the polls.

The single-member constituency with a plurality of votes determining the winner is the simplest form of elections. It is favored by states in which two parties generally predominate;[6] the United States and the United Kingdom are conspicuous examples. States in which the multiparty system prevails are inclined toward proportional representation.[7] In Israel, for example, the Knesset is elected by universal suffrage with the entire country comprising a single constituency. The statutory term of the Knesset is four years, subject to the government's determination to call new elections at an earlier date. Israeli voters choose between national party lists, and seats in the Knesset are allocated in proportion to the number of votes obtained by each list. Our friend, Moses Gold, the Israeli voter, has no chance to select individual candidates; he must choose the party slates; the winners are drawn from the party lists in the order of rank assigned by each party. The number of winners on each party list reflects the percentage of total votes cast in the general elections for that party.

The German electoral system combines the single-member-district system with proportional representation of the parties. The Bundestag comprises 248 district seats and an equal number of list seats. Under the present electoral law the individual voter casts his ballot for both a district representative and a party deputy; he may vote for the district candidate of one party and the list of another party, but knowing that party discipline in the Bundestag is very strict, he is unlikely to split his vote. Seat distribution from the party lists reflects the proportion of party votes cast, except that a party may not be seated unless it wins at least 5 percent of the total vote as well as three representatives from the districts. In the 1969 election (the sixth since 1949), in accordance with this formula, only three parties won seats: the Christian Democrats, the Social Democrats, and the Free Democrats. The National Democratic party (NPD), the extreme rightist, neo-Nazi party, polled only 4.3 percent of the total votes cast and hence could not be seated. The Communist party (DKP), on the extreme left, is likewise not seated, since it failed also to gain 5 percent of the votes cast.

Remember Hans Mueller, the small shopkeeper in Hamburg? Herr Mueller regularly votes for the Christian Democratic party, political behavior that sets him apart from most of his customers, since Hamburg traditionally gives the Social Democratic candidates and slate a thumping majority. In 1969, however, he faced up to a personal dilemma: He was somewhat persuaded by the promise of Willy Brandt's party to open the lines of communication with East Germany, a promise that delivered a personal message to him since Herr Mueller's parents still live in Dresden. He decided to act in a most unorthodox manner, i.e., to split his vote. Thus he voted for the district candidate of the Christian Democratic party as a matter of party allegiance, and he voted for the Social Democratic party slate as a matter of policy preference. Frau Mueller, however, disapproved of her husband's irregular behavior. She voted as usual both for the CDU candidate and the CDU party slate. A very strong Lutheran, she was not about to give aid or comfort to the SPD or to take a chance on her mother-in-law from Dresden coming to visit them frequently (the personal dimension!).

The National Assembly of Turkey is elected with universal suffrage in sixty-seven multimember constituencies under a system of proportional party representation. The individual voter casts his ballot for the party list that he prefers and not for individual candidates. Unlike the German electoral laws, the Turkish electoral system puts no restriction upon small parties. In the 1969 elections, however, the Justice party won 57 percent of the 450 seats, the Republican People's party 32 percent, and the remaining 11 percent was split among three small parties. In contrast to the high percentage of voting in Germany and Israel under similar provisions for proportional representation, less than two-thirds of the Turkish electorate went to the polls in 1969.

Increasing absentation on the part of the Turkish electorate is probably to be attributed to apathy rather than deliberate disengagement from the political process. When elections are free and voting voluntary a massive turnout at the polls is to be expected only if the voters believe that the issues involve their vital interests and/or that their choice of parties is in effect a significant decision. A party slate has little charismatic appeal unless the party leadership manages to dominate the scene and to inject some drama into the elections. In the spring of 1971, however, drama entered Turkish politics through an ultimatum from the armed forces demanding a strong and active government which resulted in the enforced resignation of Premier Suleyman Demirel and his government (the Justice party). His successor Nihat Erim, a Kemalist (follower of Atatürk's ideas) took over an "above-party, togetherness" government under military auspices. Still, despite unrest especially among students and younger people in the urban areas, the government in Ankara remains outside the normal concerns of many Turks (especially in the villages and rural regions) who could not care less about modernization as a national goal.

The Japanese electoral system offers still another variation. The House of Representatives, the lower house of the National Diet, with 486 seats is elected from 118 constituencies, the number from each constituency depending on the population of the district. Although each district gets to elect multiple representatives, three to five, the individual voter has a single vote. Each party—or faction—will try to capture as many seats as possible in each district; but obviously the rules for winning are quite different than in a multiple-member constituency with proportional representation, as in Turkey, or a single-member constituency with plurality election, as in the United States.

Political engineering by Japanese multiple parties and factions is technically as sophisticated as one finds in any of our twelve states. The constitutional term of members of the House is four years, but invariably the cabinet dissolves the House and calls for general elections before the end of the term. The ensuing election period is limited to thirty days; the parties maximize their efforts through extensive use of the mass media—newspapers, radios, television, face-to-face public forum. Japanese elections are "tense and gala"; [8] and, if one measures effectiveness in terms of popular participation, then the Japanese system rates high. In 1969 under universal suffrage, seventy million citizens possessed the right to vote in the general election; of these approximately 69 percent went to the polls, a considerably higher proportion of the eligible electorate than turned out for the 1968 elections in the United States.

The Liberal Democratic party, under the leadership of Prime Minister Eisaku Sato, won a solid victory in the December, 1969, elections—288 out of 486 seats in the House of Representatives, plus 12 seats held by Independents who chose to join the governing party immediately following the election. The Japan Socialist party experienced a severe setback. Its previous total of 134 seats was reduced to 90. On the other hand, the Communist party more than tripled its seats from 4 to 14, and the Democratic Socialists maintained its 31 seats and gained 1 Independent seat after the elections.

What did the elections mean to the Japanese electorate? To our friend Ukai Taki, a student in the University of Tokyo, it was a frustrating experience. He and many of his fellow students had planned massive demonstrations against the government's foreign policy and especially against renewal of the Security Treaty with the United States. Student protests against the Security Treaty in 1960 had brought about the downfall of the government. In 1970, however, the police were alerted and prepared to make short shrift of student demonstrations. In one brief foray, Ukai Taki got a whiff of tear gas and beat a hasty retreat into the law library. Ukai Taki's father, in the business of exporting cars, supported the governing party. He had confidence in Sato's ability to make a good deal for Japanese business in the United States and a double deal for more business with the Chinese mainland. Liberal Democrats in their 1970 convention expressed their trust in Sato by electing him to an unprecedented fourth term as president of the party. Since the president of the governing party has always been elected to the post of prime minister, this action by the convention presumably insured Sato's top position in the government for another two years, a tenure longer than any prime minister in Japanese history. Ukai Taki is not happy with the situation: Like many students he is antiestablishment. By the time he gets to vote in the next elections, however, he will probably have finished his law course and himself become part of the industrial-bureaucratic establishment.

In our comparative analysis of elections in competitive party states we have no difficulty in gathering the data on election returns: who voted, what percentage of the eligible electorate participated, who won the elections, what the relative strength of the competing candidates and/or competing parties was on election day. We have noted numerous variations in electoral procedures for choosing official policy-makers and for counting up or aggregating policy preferences of the electorate: independent candidates, party lists, single-member districts, multiple-member districts, plurality elections, proportional representation. Presumably the function of these various procedures is to legitimize the government, to obtain the consent of the governed, and to secure representative government.

Elections and Representation

Representative government is a hoary notion in political science, but like much of our time-honored conventional wisdom it lacks an empirical base. As we see it, the modern state has not yet come to grips with the fundamental question regarding representation: Who and/or what is/are to be represented by the duly elected representatives? How does an American congressman determine what is for the general good of his district, a metropolitan district with some rural fringes? How can he represent the plural and diverse interests of his constituents—bankers, plumbers, preachers, teachers, hotelkeepers, refrigeration mechanics, engineers, shoe salesmen, beauty-parlor operators, taxi drivers, gentlemen farmers, tenant farmers, the rich, the poor, the very old, the very young, and all those in between? And it is easier to answer that question than to explain how elections are supposed to achieve representative government in Kenya or India.

Under the 1919 Government of India Act about 3 percent of the Indian population were permitted to vote; in 1935 the franchise was broadened to include nearly 10 percent of the adult population. But when India became an independent state, the principle of "one man, one vote, one value" became a constitutional principle. Thus the first general election in India, 1951–52, was a gigantic enterprise, and one almost wholly alien to Indian society. We are told, however, that "the elections were free and fair and were held in a truly democratic atmosphere. . . . Not less than 75 parties, big and small, national and regional, moderate and extremist, participated." [9] The electoral procedure was modeled after the British, with single-member constituencies and plurality elections; and the turnout at the polls was impressive. More than a hundred million citizens (about 45 percent of the total electorate) cast their ballots for members of the state assemblies and the House of the People. The Congress party was given an overwhelming mandate to organize the first Indian government, having won 364 out of the 489 seats in the national parliament.

B. R. Jog, a poor and illiterate farmer living in a village remote from Delhi, cast his first vote in 1951. What did this event mean to him? He went to the polls on election day having been told that it was a very special ceremony. There had been much discussion in the village before the elections. Many strangers, called "candidates," had visited the village and explained what they could do for B. R. Jog and his family if elected to office in the new government. B. R. Jog was persuaded to vote for the candidate of the Congress party because that was the party of Mahatma Gandhi and Nehru. B. R. Jog could not read, but election procedures were designed to assist illiterate voters; most voters in India were (and still are) illiterate. All he had to do was deposit his ballot in the box that bore the familiar symbol of the Congress party.

Since the first election in 1951 B. R. Jog has dutifully gone to the polls in the general elections of 1957, 1962, 1967, and 1971. Each time he has voted for the candidates of the Congress party, though by now he is well aware that quite a few of his friends and neighbors are voting for different candidates. A funny thing happened to B. R. Jog on his way to the polls in 1967; his wife joined him. This was unusual behavior for a woman in his village (about 40 percent of the Indian women eligible to vote now participate in the elections). In the election for the House of the People in March, 1971, not only B. R. Jog and his wife, but their oldest son, who had learned to read and write in the new village school, went to the polls. The parents cast their ballots in the box marked by the symbol of a cow nursing her calf, which their son explained to them was the box of the New Congress party of Indira Gandhi. To B. R. Jog the politics of democracy and the idea that he has any choice between alternative governmental policies are still incredible, incomprehensible notions. (No doubt this attitude discouraged the growth of splinter parties in the various Indian states, especially during the years when the Congress party ruled firmly in New Delhi.) Nevertheless he has become part of the political process; his vote has been courted by various important persons in his village (even by Indira Gandhi during her 1971 personal campaign tour through the countryside). And he himself senses that a new kind of life is opening up for his children because the government in New Delhi is changing the ancient ways of the people, even though change may still be slow.

It is difficult to generalize about the functions of elections in the modern state. Our difficulty, in part, stems from the different notions of representative government to which the various electoral systems cater. Is the consent of the governed obtained when the governors are elected in free elections? Is the degree of consent to be measured by the extent of participation at the polls, or by the extent of opposition? In representative government is it more important that the representatives be made responsible and accountable to the electorate at stipulated intervals, or that they be made continuously responsive to changing public opinion? Should electoral procedures be devised to maximize the authority of the representatives so that they have a mandate to govern by enlarging their constituencies, or should electoral procedures be designed to elect a representative body that mirrors the wishes of the electorate, corporate representation, for example? There are, however, no ready-made answers in political science for such value-laden questions.

There is no sure way of telling how electoral procedures affect the party system, or vice versa. We noted that two-party governments seem to favor the single-member constituencies, as in the United States and in the United Kingdom. We could as easily remark that single-member constituencies tend to favor the two-party system, although the case of India confuses the hypothesis. India, borrowing its electoral system from the British—the single-member constituency with plurality elections—emerges with a single dominant party and multiple minor parties. Multiple-party systems tend to favor multiple-member constituencies, or vice versa, as in Germany and Israel. Nevertheless multiple-member constituencies with proportional representation seem to have produced a two-party system in Turkey. It may be logical to suppose that electoral procedures have a bearing on the number, size, influence, and activities of political parties, as well as more fundamental repercussions upon the role and function of the electorate in representative government; but our observations and data, our empirical base, are weak. So far our examination of elections in competitive party states reinforces our hypothesis that comparative political analysis must proceed with understanding of the unique social context that distinguishes every nation state. Thus in India we find it is more important to look at the overall organization of the party, to observe how it subsumes the roles of family, caste, class, and village associations, than it is to study the electoral rules borrowed from a foreign culture.

In Noncompetitive-Party Systems

We need to reorder our thinking and to change our perspective as we shift our study of elections from competitive to noncompetitive party systems. In one-party states—the Soviet Union, the Ivory Coast, Kenya, and Mexico currently fall into this category—elections may be held with the same regularity, frequency, and fanfare as in competitive party states. What is the point of staging elections in which the electorate is offered no choice as to candidates or policies? To understand why noncompetitive party states periodically go through the whole elaborate ritual of campaigning and electioneering to bring masses of voters to the polls, we have to examine the purposes and functions in context within each state.

Elections in the Soviet Union are a momentous occasion every four years. Both houses of the Supreme Soviet (as well as state and local soviets) are directly elected, the Soviet of the Union with 767 members elected on the basis of population and the Soviet of Nationalities with 750 members elected from territorial units. In both cases the elections proceed in single-member districts with one candidate for each office, sponsored by the Communist party. Since 1936 suffrage has been universal—for all adult citizens, elections are secret—each voter marks a printed ballot in the privacy of the polling booth. Attendance at the polls is nearly 100 percent. The voter has no difficulty in marking the ballot since only one name appears as candidate for each office. Technically the voter may cross out this name or write in another name, but except in a few local elections where the personal dimension is apparent, no candidate whose name appeared on the ballot has been defeated. Nominations may come from a variety of sources—trade unions, factory groups, sports clubs, and cooperative associations—but the Communist party, as the only party permitted under law, scrutinizes and finally decides upon all nominations.

Why does the Soviet Union hold these quadrennial elections? Partly, it is a matter of emulation. Modern democratic states hold such elections, ergo, the USSR must hold elections. The elections serve a shared purpose and function with those in the competitive party states—they legitimize those who are taking office. Elections to the Supreme Soviet are in the nature of a vast national rally or patriotic celebration. Everybody turns out to register support for the government and the Communist party. The campaigns are also educational and doctrinal: The party workers enlist the mass media to elucidate the Communist ideology, to explain the pending policies, and to step up the popularity of the current leadership. In elections for competitive offices in two-party or multiparty states the candidates chosen reflect the will of the electorate. One-party systems also utilize elections to make sure that the will of the electorate is reflected.

How does our friend Professor Skivitsky regard elections? As a member of the Communist party and as a member of the academic community, he is regarded as an important resource person in the staging of elections. His services are sought by the party for lectures to local groups and for the preparation of campaign literature in which he manages to popularize the economic policies of the government and relate them to the fundamental principles of Marxism. Ivan Skivitsky, age forty-three, was born after the Revolution of March, 1917; he has been brought up under the soviet system, and he is a true believer. He has been taught and he believes that "another major principle of Soviet state law is electiveness and sovereignty of the representative organs, the Soviets of Working People's Deputies. . . . The fact that the Soviets are elective and that their deputies can be replaced when the people so desire, that they are responsible to the people and have to report to them, is a salient feature of Soviet democracy." [10]

Professor Skivitsky is not disturbed by the fact that the Communist party is the only party in the country and that it plays the leading role in Soviet society. He believes that the party is the vanguard of the people "because of the great trust it commands among the masses, whose interests it expresses and defends with consistency." [11] He observes that the Supreme Soviet is a responsible and accountable body; "fresh forces are brought into the Soviets at each election when at least one-third of the total number of deputies is elected anew." [12] He also points out that non-Communists as well as members of the CPSU may be elected to the soviets. He does not feel that the Communist party is dictatorial. As he tells it, "The Party's guidance of the Soviet state . . . is truly democratic, for the Party itself is organized on genuinely democratic lines." He believes that "broad and direct participation of the masses in government is a basic principle of the Soviet system." He does not expect the electoral system to offer the people a one-shot chance to vote on alternative policy platforms. He prefers the continuous operation of "democratic centralism" in which nationwide discussion of proposed policies occurs in local and concerned groups under the sponsorship of the Communist party. In other words, from his perspective the Russian people appear to enjoy a very different kind of relationship with their government than exists in the Western democratic states, and obviously he perceives the role and function of the party in a very different context than do his academic counterparts at Oxford University, the University of Hamburg, or the University of Tokyo.

The Communist party in the USSR operates from a highly sophisticated ideological base. Moreover, elections in the soviet system, under exclusive sponsorship of the party for more than half a century, have served to promote a stable and effective government that now appears to rest firmly on the consent of the governed. The rationale for one-party elections in the soviet system, however, is hardly applicable to the Ivory Coast or Kenya.

ELECTIONS IN NEW AND DEVELOPING STATES

In the Ivory Coast

According to their present constitution, the people of the Ivory Coast exercise sovereignty through representative government. They directly elect their head of state, a president, for a five-year term, and he in turn selects his cabinet, the government, from outside the National Assembly. The National Assembly, a single chamber with eighty-five members, is elected by direct universal suffrage for a five-year term.

Actually the government and politics of the Ivory Coast revolve around the person of Felix Houphouet-Boigny, the elected president and the party chief. To put it bluntly, "the old man is the national boss." The development of the Ivory Coast is largely the personal success story of Felix Houphouet. The story begins in the mid-1940s when Houphouet, a wealthy planter and minor chief in the Baoule tribe, became involved in the *Rassemblement Démocratique Africain* (RDA). The RDA started out as a militant West African mass movement protesting French colonialism, especially forced labor of the natives and the double-college electoral system which divided the European and the native electorate. In 1945 the African block of the RDA succeeded in electing Houphouet as the African representative from the Ivory Coast to the French Constituent Assembly called to draft a constitution for the Fourth French Republic. (It was at this time that Houphouet added Boigny to his name, a Baoule name meaning "irresistable force.") The subsequent success of Houphouet-Boigny in French and African politics is the personal dimension to which we largely attribute the shape and substance of current government and politics in the Ivory Coast.

In the early years, when the Parti Démocratique de la Côte d'Ivoire (PDCI) played the role of a classical revolutionary party, organizing mass demonstrations and violently opposing the French administration, Houphouet-Boigny was its first successful candidate as Ivory Coast deputy to the French National Asembly. Initially, along with other African deputies, Houphouet frequently aligned himself with the French Communists, but at least as far as Houphouet was concerned, the alliance seems to have been one of political expediency rather than ideological commitment. Continuously reelected to the National Assembly in the 1950s, Houphouet came to enjoy French culture in Paris and to realize the rewards of cooperation with the French government; he became the first African to hold a ministerial post in the French cabinet. Meantime his position in PDCI was enhanced by the prestige he gained as a *parlementaire* who could even tell the French governor where to get off; and his position in French politics was enhanced by the influence he was known to wield in the African community. Understandably, he became less and less inclined to press for national independence and at the same time more and more preoccupied with turning the PDCI into a highly disciplined political machine. Under his leadership and dictatorship the PDCI was transformed from a nationalist revolutionary party into an authoritarian and repressive institution prepared for the transfer of power when the Ivory Coast became a self-governing republic in the French Community under the Gaullist Constitution of 1958. Officially, the people of the Ivory Coast made the decision in a nationwide referendum. They could choose between membership in the Community (*oui*) or independence (*non*). Under PDCI guidance 98 percent of the electorate participated in the decision, and 99 percent of those voted "oui." [13]

In accordance with their first constitution, adopted in March, 1959, the people of the Ivory Coast elected, with universal suffrage, their first national legislature. Not by any coincidence, the PDCI won all the seats in the parliament, which promptly elected Felix Houphouet-Boigny the first prime minister, who then resigned his post in the French government. This was what he planned and this is how he achieved it: one-party government, "self-government" with close ties to the French Community. This, it turned out, however, was not the way many people in the Ivory Coast wanted it. Militant students, trade unionists, RDA "martyrs," and disaffected intellectuals stirred opposition. In 1960, when Mali declared its independence from the Community, Houphouet-Boigny used his discretion and finally proclaimed the independence of the Ivory Coast.

Party politics and electoral procedures in the Ivory Coast are much the same under the second constitution as under the first. Felix Houphouet-Boigny was elected president in the first election, 1960, reelected in 1965 and 1970. Similarly in 1960, 1965, and 1970, the PDCI presented a Union List of candidates for the parliament, and without opposition the entire slate was elected. One point needs to be mentioned, however: Although Houphouet-Boigny, as leader of the PDCI, personally approves all candidates on the PDCI Union List, he does not necessarily agree with their views. In order to maintain the semblance of unity, he may deliberately bring into his cabinet or into the parliament nonparty members, even potential leaders of opposition, acting on the proposition that rewards are more likely to be persuasive than deprivations in politics.

We are told that Ivory Coast campaigns are "conducted with verve: symbols and slogans proliferate and drumming and dancing accompany campaign rallies, which are opened with prayers and the pouring of libation." [14] The turnout at the polls is almost universal, and the PDCI candidates are swept into office without opposition.

Unlike the Communist party in the Soviet Union, however, the PDCI in the Ivory Coast offers the electorate no ideological base. Rather it acts as an agency of accommodation that keeps its principal, Houphouet-Boigny, at the apex of power. Elections in the Ivory Coast do not reflect political opinions so much as personal commitments. The ruling elite, comprising a very small percentage of well-to-do planters, businessmen, educators, and senior bureaucrats, have real stakes in the politics of the country. They understand what Houphouet-Boigny is trying to do, and they go along with him, and he pleases them. Houphouet's approach to politics, as we have said, has been opportunistic and pragmatic. His orientation is more European than African; his plans to develop the Ivory Coast are based almost wholly on Western ideas of modernization.

But the long lines of people who wait at the polling booths to cast the ballots they cannot read—laborers on the cocoa and coffee plantations, sharecroppers, small farmers, fishermen, artisans in the villages, ivory carvers and basket weavers, people in the bush country, "the forest people"—what does it mean to them to line up three times in ten years to elect a president and the PDCI Union List for a government in Abidjan? The political party, free elections, a representative parliament, and president—these are the Western facade. But behind the facade what are the governing patterns? Family ties? The lineage structure? The chief of the land? The village elders? The plantation owners? It is the function of the PDCI leadership, especially those elected to the National Assembly, to link the people with the government, a function which individual members of the assembly are inclined to take seriously. Since most of the population is still illiterate, the party keeps in touch with the electorate through frequent face-to-face encounters and much exchange of spoken communications.

In Kenya

Although the constitutional pattern of government in Kenya appears to be quite similar to that of the Ivory Coast, the political dynamics are actually quite different. The Independence Constitution (1963) provided for retention of the British monarch as head of state, to be represented in Kenya by a governor general. The parliamentary government was also modeled after that in the United Kingdom with the prime minister and his cabinet responsible to the parliament. We will not labor over this lengthy document, however. It lasted exactly one year, from Independence Day, December 12, 1963, to Republic Day, December 12, 1964.[15]

The Republican Constitution (1964), an amended version of the first constitution, makes the president head of state, head of government, and commander-in-chief. It specifies that the prime minister who was in office on December 12, 1964 should become the first president but succeeding presidents should be elected. Presidential candidates are to be nominated by petition of voters eligible to vote for members of the House of Representatives. A presidential candidate must run for a seat in the House since the Constitution requires that the president be an elected member of the House. In the general elections all candidates for membership in the House must declare which of the presidential candidates he supports. If a presidential candidate is elected to the House and if a majority of the House membership supports him, then he is declared elected. If no presidential candidate wins a seat in the House then the House must elect a president under a complicated set of rules. Jomo Kenyatta was the first and only prime minister under the Independence Constitution; he is the first and only president under the Republic Constitution. How his successor will be chosen, we surmise as we follow the news about political developments in Kenya, will more likely be determined by circumstances than by constitutional law.

The National Assembly of the Republic was bicameral until 1969. Members of both House and Senate were elected from single-member constituencies by plurality vote. Suffrage for the House was universal; for the Senate it was restricted by property and residence requirements. Voting for members of the first National Assembly took place in 1963, before Kenya was officially self-governing. More than 7.5 million paper ballots were prepared, with instructions on posters in leaflets printed in English, Swahili, and six vernacular languages. Since some 70 percent of the voters were illiterate, however, party workers gave careful oral instructions. In this election the Kenya African National Union (KANU) won 54 percent of the popular vote and 70 of the 112 seats in the House; the Kenya African Democratic Union (KADU) won 26 percent of the popular vote and 32 seats in the House.

The semblance of party competition in the 1963 election is, however, somewhat misleading. At the time of the election both the KANU and the KADU were actually in a coalition government pressing for independence from the British. The immensely popular leaders in KANU, Jomo Kenyatta and Tom Mboya, personified the combined support of the two largest tribal groups in Kenya, the Kikuyu and Luo respectively. Their platform stressed Africanism, nationalism, centralism, and socialism. The KADU, representing a coalition of smaller tribes with scattered territorial bases, was more sectional in its political views and wary of central control over the economy. It was also more cautious in this approach to independence, favoring retention of ties with the British government. We have no hard data on voting behavior in Kenya; we don't know whether political, economic, or ethnic factors were most important in the minds of the electorate. Certainly the KANU emerged as the dominant national party; the KADU did not put up enough candidates to win a majority of seats even if all their candidates had won in their respective districts. The KANU's appeal to African nationalism was more exciting than the KADU's plea to stay a little longer with the British. However, the tribal associations were most significant in getting out the vote and in casting the ballots.

Kenya became a one-party state in November, 1964, when the KADU was voluntarily dissolved and its leaders asked to work within the ruling party. President Kenyatta promptly enlarged his cabinet to include former leaders of the KADU as well as representatives of various tribal groups. Personal rivalries, doctrinal dissensions, and tribal disaffections now wracked the KANU from within. In the spring of 1966, thirty representatives and senators in the left-wing contingent of the party, including Vice-President Oginga Odinga, resigned to form a new party, the Kenyan People's party (KPU). Their seats were immediately declared vacant and a little general election was held in June, 1966, to fill the vacancies. As a result of that election the KPU returned seven representatives and two senators; the KANU won the rest of the contested seats. In January, 1967, the Senate, which had never played a significant role in Kenyan politics, was abolished and the senators were absorbed into the enlarged House of Representatives, now called the National Assembly. Technically, from June, 1966, to October, 1969, Kenya was a two-party state; the KPU, with 9 seats in the Assembly out of 158 elected seats, formed the opposition. As we have already recounted, however, on the eve of the first general elections to be held since independence, Kenyatta ran scared and outlawed the KPU. Hence the 1969 elections were held in a noncompetitive party setting. Even so, the results of the elections indicated considerable opposition within the KANU. Some 600 candidates competed for the 158 elected seats; and although all candidates were endorsed by the KANU, they represented a wide spectrum of views within the party.

Moreover, the electorate rejected 77 of the incumbent representatives and 5 of Kenyatta's cabinet members and returned 108 new members.

The Ivory Coast and Kenya Compared

Similarities between the Ivory Coast and Kenya are immediately apparent: two African states emerging from European colonialism in the early 1960s, each impelled to develop modern, i.e., Western, political and economic systems. In both states the leadership has used representative government and general elections to legitimize the exercise of authority and reallocation of national resources. In both states one-party government under strong personal leadership has imposed the appearance of political unity upon a traditionally fragmented society. If we compare the electoral process in both states, however, we realize that there are significant differences. We have already observed that Houphouet-Boigny controls the PDIC in the manner of a political boss; in the 1960, 1965, and 1970 elections he picked the Union List of candidates for parliament; the entire list was elected without opposition in a big turnout at the polls. Once elected, the members of parliament give their complete support and allegiance to their head of state, head of government, and party chief, Houphouet-Boigny.

Contrast the political situation in Kenya: The KPU was able to win nine out of thirty seats in the "little general election" of 1966, and in the general elections of 1969 the electorate was free to unseat approximately two-thirds of the incumbents in the National Assembly. Quite obviously, the KANU is not a rubber stamp for Kenyatta, either at the polls or in the Assembly. The back-benchers in the Assembly, the elected members who do not hold posts in Kenyatta's government, feel quite free to criticize and oppose government proposals and keep up a continuous interchange of views with their local constituents. Kenyatta has to keep switching his strategy to accommodate dissidence within his own party. Thus immediately following the 1969 election returns, Kenyatta announced that he intended to broaden his government base and to secure more balance in its composition.

We commented above on Houphouet-Boigny's European orientation and his predilection for private capital in the development of a modern economy for the Ivory Coast; he pursues his plans in a purely pragmatic fashion, with little regard for public opinion, except perhaps for the views of the ruling elite and agents of foreign aid. In contrast, Kenyatta is deeply committed both to African nationalism and to a planned socialist economy for Kenya. Herein is the dilemma that confronts many African leaders: A planned socialist economy calls for central direction and a way of life that runs counter to the indigenous culture of Africa. As an Africanist, Kenyatta is tolerant of tribal and regional particularism as is evidenced in free elections with genuine competition among candidates, freedom of debate among back-benchers in the Assembly, as well as continuous efforts on his part to keep the government in balance. On the other hand, as a nationalist and socialist he keeps trying to develop consensus and impose centralism, as is evidenced by recurrence of one-party government, specifically by the way in which he forced the dissolution of the KADU and eliminated the KPU.

In Modernizing Mexico

We debated whether to include the Mexican government under the competitive or noncompetitive party system for elections. On the basis of election returns, however, we decided that when one party commands nearly 90 percent of the popular vote and the other 10 percent is splintered among several parties, we could realistically call this a one-party government.

According to the Mexican Constitution of 1917 the president and both houses of Congress are elected by direct popular vote, the president for six years, the senators for six years, and the deputies for three years. The president may not hold office for a second term and members of Congress cannot be reelected for consecutive terms. The Constitution proclaims that "all public power originates in the people and is instituted for their benefit," and specifies that it is the prerogative of citizens to vote in the popular elections and to be voted for, for all offices subject to popular election.

Actually, the Institutional Revolutionary Party (PRI) has a virtual monopoly on political power. Since 1929 all of its presidential candidates and nearly all of its congressional candidates have been elected. In the 1964 elections the PRI presidential candidate, Gustavo Diaz Ordaz, won 8.4 million votes as against 1 million for his only opponent, Gonzales Torrens, candidate of the National Action Party (PAN). In the same election all 60 PRI candidates for the Senate were elected; and 175 out of 210 of its candidates for the Chamber of Deputies were elected. A 1962 electoral law provides that minority parties which poll at least 2.5 percent of the total vote receive, in addition to seats won in single-member districts, 5 seats in the Chamber of Deputies, with an additional seat for each additional 5 percent polled, up to 20 seats.

In Mexico, PRI endorsement of a presidential candidate is tantamount to election; but nevertheless the Mexican people go through the whole throes of a nation at election. In October, 1969, after innumerable conversations and dickering among party leaders, the three sectors of the PRI—farmers, labor, and middle class—named Luis Echeverria Alvarez as their presidential candidate. For the next seventeen months, Echeverria was on campaign tour, bringing with him his party's slogan "upward and onward with the revolution" to remote villages as well as into every state capital. He won, as expected, a stunning victory in July, 1970, polling more than 80 percent of the vote. (Official tabulation of the 1970 returns, however, show that only 34 percent of the registered voters went to the polls.) The new president was party-groomed for his present position. In 1946 as a graduate of the Law School of the National University he was hand picked by General Rudolfo Sanchez Taboada, president of the PRI, to be the general's assistant and the party's director of press and propaganda. In 1948, Echeverria began the climb upward through the official bureaucracy. In 1964 he entered the cabinet as secretary of the interior and from there moved into the presidency.

How do Mexicans regard their political system and how do they respond to the notion of citizen participation in the political process? The cross-national survey of political attitudes in five nation states—the United States, the United Kingdom, Germany, Italy, and Mexico—gives us more empirical data about Mexican politics than are available to us on other one-party states.[16] The survey was made more than a decade ago, however, and in a rapidly developing country such as Mexico the tempo of political dynamics can make substantial changes in the empirical base in a relatively short period. Nevertheless we find some of the data quite useful in explaining partisan activities and voting behavior in Mexico even today.

The following are excerpts from some Mexican and German responses to the same questions.[17] To begin with, Mexicans point with pride to their government and political institutions. When asked, "What are the things about this country that you are most proud of?" Mexicans replied in this order and percentage: 1) government and political institutions (30 percent); 2) the economic system (24 percent); 3) the physical attributes of the country (22 percent); and 4) characteristics of the people (15 percent). In contrast, the Germans responded: 1) characteristics of the people (36 percent); 2) the economic system (33 percent); 3) the physical attributes of the country (17 percent); and 4) government and political institutions (7 percent). When asked how free they felt to discuss politics, 21 percent of the Mexicans answered that they did not feel free to discuss politics with anyone, and 19 percent said they felt free to discuss politics with anyone; 32 percent of the Germans said they did not feel free to discuss politics with anyone, and 23 percent felt free to discuss politics with anyone. As to feelings on going to the polls, 34 percent of the Mexicans and 35 percent of the Germans thought election campaigns were necessary. With respect to partisan feelings in elections, 25 percent of both Mexicans and Germans claimed to be intensely partisan; 42 percent of the Mexicans and 44 percent of the Germans thought of themselves as open partisans. But when asked to name four or more party leaders, only 5 percent of the Mexicans could do so in contrast with 69 percent of the Germans.

Questioned as to what impact the national government had upon conditions in the country, 58 percent of the Mexicans and 61 percent of the Germans thought that the government did improve conditions. Asked whether they thought they could do something personally about a national regulation they felt was unjust, 38 percent of the Mexicans and 38 percent of the Germans responded affirmatively. As to their informational background, 15 percent of the Mexicans and 34 percent of the Germans said that they regularly read accounts of political and governmental affairs; 31 percent of the Mexicans and 53 percent of the Germans said they read about politics in the newspapers at least weekly; 28 percent of the Mexicans and 52 percent of the Germans listened to radio or television accounts of public affairs.

What kind of insights do we gain from these data? Certainly Mexicans are proud of their country and its political institutions. The Mexican Revolution antedates the Russian Revolution; the PRI as the Revolutionary party has done a pretty good job of politicizing the revolution. It presents its candidates for all elective offices every three years and all candidates stand on the party platform, which still carries the rhetoric of revolution. The Almond and Verba survey emphasizes the aspirational aspects of Mexican politics, a general feeling that Mexico is rapidly developing a democratic government and a prosperous economy. The survey findings highlight the self-esteem of the Mexican citizen and his feeling of individual competence in the political system; this also may be attributed to the rhetoric of the PRI which frequently refers to the sovereignty of the people and the constitutional prerogatives of the citizens. The data also point up the difference between commitment and involvement, between aspiration and performance.

Juan Ortiz, who carves little onyx donkeys in Puebla, is perhaps a typical Mexican citizen. He belongs to the labor sector of the PRI, votes regularly for the PRI slate, and feels a glow of satisfaction in having personally participated in the cause of revolution and development. So far as he is concerned the PRI is the government and the PRI knows best. Juan Ortiz, now in his sixties, is getting ready to collect his old-age pension from the government. Juan himself is illiterate, never had a day of schooling, but his children, who were required by law to attend the elementary school in Puebla, can all read and write. His youngest son, Antonio, the scholar in the family, was able to use the educational escalator to the civil service. PRI officials in Puebla were very helpful in arranging scholarship assistance for him at the National University in Mexico City. The whole Ortiz family, and a large family it is, vote the PRI slate.

The PRI has all kinds of patronage to dispense, and it thrives on the loyalty of the grateful. It provides the government with a broad base of public consent through its three sections, labor, agriculture, and popular. It does a good job in communications, telling the government what the people want and telling the people what the government expects. The government expects to step up the pace of industrialization; modernizing the economy is its main goal. And the PRI is able to convey the message in aspirational terms even to the rural proletariat who are generally shortchanged by the development programs. Elections become gala affairs, and on national holidays there is much dancing in the streets, courtesy of the PRI.

Elections have a recognized symbolic value in legitimizing political authority, and universal suffrage enhances the credibility of governmental claims to the consent of the governed. We observe that all of our twelve states hold regular elections and generally extend the franchise to all adult citizens. These are obvious generalizations. But when we try to answer the more empirically oriented question, How do elections affect the government? we run into many difficulties.

Consider, for example, some of the practical questions relating to voter turnout and competition in free elections. In 1970, both the United States and the Soviet Union held national elections. About half the eligible electorate in the United States participated in the congressional elections; Democrats, Republicans, Conservatives, and Independents vied for the 35 seats in the Senate and the 435 seats in the House.[18] When the results were tallied, the Democrats had a majority of 54 seats out of 100 in the Senate; the Republicans a total of 44 seats; the Conservatives 1 seat; and the Independents 1 seat. In the House, the Democrats captured 255 seats, a clear majority; the Republicans retained 180 seats. In the Russian elections, the Communist party presented the Soviet electorate with 1,517 candidates for the 1,517 seats in the two houses of the Supreme Soviet; no other party or group offered competing or opposing candidates. When the Russian returns were announced, it was no surprise to hear that over 99 percent of the electorate had gone to the polls and endorsed the Communist party slate. But, given very different values in the two political systems, how do we appraise their electoral performances in the framework of public interest and popular support?

Theoretically, universal suffrage is an important criterion in establishing consent of the governed. Nevertheless, the extension of the franchise to all adult citizens came about gradually and grudgingly in the older democratic states. Only in this century has universal suffrage been granted (or imposed) as a natural right of citizens. Ironically, if a high percentage of participation in elections is viewed as an indicator of popular support for the political system, then the function of elections has a relatively low rating in some of the older democratic states (as in the United States) and a very high rating in some of the newer political systems (as in the Soviet Union). Yet, even the older democratic states look for a more broadly based electorate, as shown by the passage in 1971 of the vote for the eighteen-year-old citizens in the USA. We are, however, reluctant to conclude that a 99-percent turnout at the polls is in itself an overwhelming demonstration of public interest or approval. A mass march to the polls may be prompted by official duress, by such legal devices as compulsory registration, Sunday voting, or compulsory voting, and of course, by high-powered partisan propaganda. On the other hand, we must be skeptical of the degree of democratic government in any state where more than half the eligible electorate, for whatever reasons, fail to exercise their franchise. Indeed, widespread voter apathy and absenteeism from the polls may signal a general feeling that the government is indifferent to the people's welfare (as in Colombia and to a lesser extent in Mexico.)

All of our twelve states hold regular elections. Whether we judge these as free elections depends largely on how important we consider the existence —or tolerance—of competition and opposition in the political system and which offices are elective. In a traditional democratic state (as in the United Kingdom or the Federal Republic of Germany), a two-party or multiparty system is assumed to be crucial for the representation of the plural interests in the society. In a totalitarian state (as in the Soviet Union) where a single party, committed to a basic ideology, operates as vanguard of the people, competition is regarded as confusing and opposition as treasonable. In new and developing states, where tutelary democracy has been adopted as the most practical approach to political socialization and long-range planning (as in Turkey), opposition or even competition may be viewed as threatening to stability and as a hindrance to progress.

The voice of the voter is heard in all twelve states, but the extent to which it is heeded and therefore influential in the shaping of public policy is difficult to determine, in part because it is almost impossible for those in power to ascertain the real substance of an electoral mandate. How does an American president read his charge from the electorate which, in the same year, puts his party into power in the executive branch and gives control of the legislative branch to the opposing party? What kind of mandate does a German chancellor claim to have when his party fails to win even a plurality of votes and can exercise the power of government only by bargaining with other minority parties to form a coalition? And what kind of popular support could the Russian Communist party expect to muster if other parties were permitted to enter the political arena?

In the final analysis, the answer to the question, How do elections affect the government? depends on the nature of articulation between the electorate and their elected representatives. In competitive party systems, the electorate does have a decisive role in the selection of their official representatives and in subsequent elections may hold these same officials accountable for their actions in office. In the noncompetitive system the voters have little option but to accept the candidates that the party in power has nominated or chooses to keep in office. We are not prepared, however, on the basis of the evidence collected in our brief study of twelve states to hold that once elected representatives have been placed in policy positions those selected competitively are more truly representative than those selected in noncompetitive systems.

Whom does (should) an elected official represent? Should (is) he free to use his own judgment or should (does) he take his mandate from the electorate? Such questions reach to the roots of policy in every country, but they cannot be answered with broad generalizations. They have to be considered within the unique context of each political system. In our discussion of various electoral devices, we have been wary of suggesting cause and effect relationships, though we have indicated that such devices as the single-member, or the multimember, constituency, as well as majority, plurality, and preferential voting may have some bearing on the kind of representation. We are not at all sure, however, that the German or Japanese multiparty election systems with their elaborate provisions for proportional representation assure a legislature that is more truly representative of the popular will or the national interests than does the British two-party election system with single-member constituencies. And, as we have indicated in the text of this chapter, new states which have imported party apparatus and electoral machinery from Western democratic states are still in the process of learning how to manipulate the unfamiliar models. We are not convinced that a largely illiterate population that has to choose its officials on the basis of pictorial party symbols (as in India) is ready for popular representation. In the next two chapters, however, we shall explore further some of the problems of territorial and popular representation in long-established as well as new and developing political systems.

NOTES

1. Significantly, former President Dwight D. Eisenhower titled the first volume of his memoirs *Mandate for Change: The White House Years, 1953–56* (Garden City, N.Y.: Doubleday, 1963).
2. *Washington Post,* April 21, 1970. See also Universidad de los Andos faculty, "El Voto Prosidencial en Bogotá," *Boletin Mensual de Estadistica,* no. 229 (August, 1970).
3. Section IV, Article 98.
4. Section VI, Article 62.

5. In nine out of our twelve states the national legislature (congress or parliament) is bicameral; Israel, Kenya, and the Ivory Coast are the exceptions. In parliamentary government the prime minister and his cabinet are responsible to the lower chamber. We have, therefore, focused here on elections to the lower chamber. Students who want to do extra homework can pursue the subject with respect to the upper chamber. In some instances the suffrage requirements as well as the territorial constituency may be different than for the lower chamber.
6. It may also be argued that the single-member constituency tends to support a two-party system.
7. Similarly, it may be argued that proportional representation tends to encourage multiple parties.
8. Robert Ward, ed., *Japan's Political System* (Englewood Cliffs, N.J.: Prentice-Hall, 1967), p. 53.
9. M. V. Pylee, *India's Constitution*, 2d rev. ed. (New York: Asia Publishing House, 1967), p. 384.
10. P. S. Romashkin, ed., chap. 2, "Constitutional Law," *Fundamentals of Soviet Law* (Moscow: Foreign Language Publishing House, n.d.), p. 36.
11. Ibid., p. 39.
12. Ibid., p. 37.
13. *US Army Area Handbook for the Ivory Coast*, prepared by the Foreign Area Studies Division, SORO, American University (Washington, D.C.: Government Printing Office, 1962), p. 259.
14. Ibid., p. 258
15. See *US Army Area Handbook for Kenya*, prepared by the Foreign Area Studies Division, SORO, American University (Washington, D.C.: Government Printing Office, 1967), especially section 2, "Political."
16. Gabriel Almond and Sidney Verba, *The Civic Culture* (Boston: Little, Brown, 1965). See also in Robert E. Scott, "Mexico: The Established Revolution," Lucian W. Pye and Sidney Verba, eds., *Political Culture and Political Development* (Princeton, N.J.: Princeton University Press, 1965).
17. The interested student may extend the comparisons to the United States and the United Kingdom by culling the data from Almond and Verba, op. cit.
18. One-third of the Senate's 100 seats are up for election every two years; a senator's term is six years. All 435 seats in the House are in contest every two years; a representative's term is two years.

FURTHER READING

Lasswell, Harold. *Politics: Who Gets What, When, How.* Cleveland and New York: World Publishing, Meridian Books, 1958.

Lipset, Seymour Martin. "The Changing Class Structure and Contemporary European Politics." *Daedalus* 93, *Proceedings of the American Academy of Arts and Sciences* (Winter, 1964): 280, 281.

Lester W. Milbrath. *Political Participation: How and Why Do People Get Involved in Politics.* Chicago: Rand McNally, 1965.

Pitkin, H. F. *The Concept of Representation.* Berkeley, Calif.: University of California Press, 1967.

Smith, T. E. *Elections in Developing Countries: A Study of Electoral Procedures Used in Tropical Africa, Southeast Asia, and in the British Caribbean.* London: Macmillan, 1960.

VIRGINIA
VIRGINIA
VIRGINIA
CALIFORNIA
CALIFORNIA
CALIFORNIA
CALIFORNIA
CALIFORNIA
CALIFORNIA
CALIFORNIA
CALIFORNIA
CALIFORNIA
CALIFORNIA
CALIFORNIA
CALIFORNIA
CALIFORNIA
CALIFORNIA
CALIFORNIA
CALIFORNIA
CALIFORNIA
LOUISIANA
LOUISIANA
LOUISIANA
LOUISIANA
LOUISIANA
LOUISIANA
LOUISIANA
MASSACHUSETTS
MASSACHUSETTS
MASSACHUSETTS

chapter 9

HOW ARE NATION STATES ORGANIZED TERRITORIALLY?

Every state has its own particular place in the world atlas. One student of modern comparative politics claims that "dividing and subdividing the world according to the territorial principle is probably as old as humanity." [1] It is difficult to exaggerate the significance of territorial awareness in politics. "My country 'tis of thee" is the tap root of patriotism. Economic associations, political ideologies, and religious creeds may cross national boundaries but most peoples in the world, rationally and/or emotionally, identify their values, interests, and goals with the country in which they live and with its government, to which they give allegiance.

The nationality of a person is determined first of all by the country in which he was born. The laws of citizenship vary greatly from one state to another, but jus soli (law of soil) is universally recognized as the primary basis of nationality. It is well understood in international relations that a state may forbid the entrance of aliens into its territory or admit them on grounds of its own choosing. US immigration quotas based on national origins, or more recent restrictions based on manpower needs, illustrate the point. People within a nation state are expected to give their allegiance to the territorial authority regardless of their personal feelings, and they are not always free to "love it or leave it," as Russian Jews who want to emigrate to Israel bitterly attest today.

USA, at the national political convention each state is represented
(United Press International)

The government of every state expects compliance, can compel obedience to its commands, whether or not there is popular consensus. But, wherever people live together in a political order and under a common law, they tend to develop a sense of territorial solidarity. Moreover, all nation states engage in systematic indoctrination to enhance the feeling of territorial togetherness. Symbols are frequently used to promote and emphasize the unity and distinctive character of the people within the territorial boundaries. The "Star Spangled Banner," the liberty penny with its picture of Lincoln and its double motto "In God we trust" and "E pluribus unum," Washington's birthday, the Fourth of July, and Thanksgiving—these have a special meaning for the people who live in the United States. But every nation state has its own flag, its own anthem, emblems, slogans, national holidays, and commemorative stamps. Indeed the whole process of civic education, or political socialization, is designed to build a territorial community.

In international law the recognized government of a state has complete authority over all persons and things within its established boundaries. But, in every state, the interests of the people are plural and conditions within the country are diversified; uniform rules and regulations for the many different activities of modern government are practically impossible. Hence all states find it necessary and proper to divide and delegate political authority between the national or central government and the local communities. In this chapter we shall look at different patterns of geographical distribution of political powers as exemplified by unitary and federal types of government.

UNITARY GOVERNMENTS

Most nation states in the world today are organized under unitary government. In this kind of political system the powers of government generally emanate from the national government as the central authority. The subnational units of administration are created by the national government and derive their authority from delegation of powers, with direct lines of communication between the national government and the local communities. Seven of our twelve nation states are organized under unitary government: Colombia, Turkey, Kenya, Japan, the Ivory Coast, the United Kingdom, and Israel. Note that our definition of unitary government is keyed to the process by which the powers of government are geographically distributed. In effect, the process is one of decentralization, from national uniformity and central authority to local diversity and plural units of self-rule. *Unitary government* is a flexible term; it covers democratic and authoritarian types of rule, it includes modern and traditional governments. The important point to remember is that the national government has plenary power and that it decides, as a matter of administrative expediency, or in response to subnational political pressures, which of its powers to share with the local communities, how much or how little.

The United Kingdom has a unitary government. Legally, and theoretically, the crown possesses all powers of government in the United Kingdom, but for hundreds of years crown power has been delegated to the

Parliament, the cabinet, and the courts, until in fact Her Majesty has very little real power in the governance of her realm. Nevertheless she is the symbol of unity, "the magnetic center of the State." [2] According to the constitutional convention, Her Majesty enacts the laws, by and with the assent of Parliament. All royal proclamations, executive orders, appointments to office, diplomatic agreements are in the name of Her Majesty; she must lend her signature to legitimize the acts of her ministers. The cabinet is politically responsible to the Parliament but acts in the name of the queen; the ministers are her ministers and "they would not be what they are unless they had that dignity and style." [3] The courts of law, the civil service, these too act in the name of the queen. And all of this is more than form or ceremony; the emotions and loyalties that attach to the monarchy "are themselves an actual fact and an operative reality." [4] The government of the United Kingdom is a unitary government in which all the powers of government emanate from the crown. The fact that the queen as a person has become a mere figurehead in the modern political system has not altered the original source of authority, the central locus.

In Britain today the Parliament is apparently omnipotent. Conceivably the Parliament could abolish the monarchy and establish a democratic republic. It is unlikely to do so, however, not because it would be unconstitutional to act in this way, but because tradition and public opinion would not countenance it. Legally, Westminster rules the whole of the United Kingdom. Actually, over centuries, a process of decentralization has brought about a considerable degree of home rule for the component units. Wales has its special representative in the cabinet, the secretary of state for Wales, assisted by a minister of state who resides in Wales. At the local level, the Welsh are permitted to maintain their own schools, where Welsh is the first language, and English the second. Scotland also has its own secretary of state in the cabinet; its elected representatives in Parliament form a special committee for the consideration of all Scottish bills; and within its geographical boundaries it maintains its own system of law (Roman-Dutch), its own educational system, and its own national church (the disestablished Presbyterian Church of Scotland). Northern Ireland is virtually self-ruling, with its own Parliament and prime minister as well as representatives in the British House of Commons. Conceivably Parliament could reverse the long-time process of decentralization and tighten the controls from London. But, even in this small island kingdom, geographical boundaries delineate ethnic and cultural divisions which call for a prudent devolution of authority from the national government to local units of administration. Indeed, the mounting force of nationalist movements in Northern Ireland, Scotland, and Wales suggests that decentralization may have to be accelerated if the United Kingdom is to survive as a unitary state.

Another major power, Japan, also exemplifies the unitary organization. In the imperial era all power was legally vested in the person of the emperor and through him was concentrated in the national government. In imperial Japan the local governments enjoyed no autonomy. But after World War II the American Occupation authorities, determined to democratize the Japanese system, and apparently equating grass-roots politics with democracy, insisted upon drastic decentralization in the Japanese government. Hence the Japanese Constitution designates the Diet (the national parliament) as the highest organ of state power and the sole lawmaking body of the government. It requires that regulations for the organization and administration of local governments be "in accordance with the principle of local autonomy." The forty-six prefectures operate as subnational units; they are not sovereign in the sense that states in the United States are (or claim to be). The governors of the prefects and the prefectural assembly are, however, elected within their respective geographical units; and within the prefectures, each city, town, and village elects its own mayor and assembly.

No doubt the Japanese Constitution, as it was designed under American tutelage, has effected some decentralization of authority, but the autonomy of the local governments still appears to be more in form than in operation. None of the local governments is financially self-sufficient. All must look to the national government for subsidies and grants-in-aid. Moreover, as one observer notes, the long-ingrained bureaucratic habit of looking to Tokyo and to the national government for guidance still persists in practice.[5] The Japanese government is a unitary government.

FEDERAL GOVERNMENTS

Federalism, as we define it, refers to a political system in which the national government and autonomous territorial communities (states as in the United States or Mexico, republics in the Soviet Union, länder in Germany) share the powers of government, with both sets of government operating directly upon the people. Federalism is a pragmatic political organization reflecting both the unity of the nation as a whole and the diversity of its component parts. The United Kingdom and Japan are both relatively small island states wherein the people over centuries have developed a fairly homogeneous culture and a strong sense of nationalism. In both instances unitary government is quite feasible, given certain concessions to the local communities in policies touching upon distinctive local values. But where the territory to be governed is vast, or the political system new, or the people have not yet developed strong feelings of allegiance or behavioral patterns of respect toward the central government, the political system is likely to develop as a federal organization. Some political scientists are inclined to regard a federal nation as an unfinished nation in which sovereignty is still divided and intergovernmental relations are likely to be in flux between conflict and cooperation.[6] In unitary governments, the territorial distribution of powers generally appears as a process of decentralization or devolution. In federal governments the process is usually in reverse, a movement toward centralization, a joining together of territorial communities to form a more perfect union.

Out of some one hundred forty nation states in the world only twenty-one claim to be federal unions; but these include five of the largest states, and altogether they cover more than half the land surface of the globe. In our sample of twelve states, five have developed the federal organization: the United States, Germany, the Soviet Union, Mexico, and India.

The First "More Perfect Union"

Historically the United States is the first new nation to have become a federal union. At the time of the American Revolution there was no model of central self-government for the thirteen colonies. The main lines of communication and control were with the mother country rather than between colonies. Then, in the process of fighting for their independence from Britain, they entered into a "perpetual union" and "a firm league of friendship" under the Articles of Confederation. Each state, however, retained its sovereignty, freedom, and independence within the union. Though they established a central government —in order to promote the common defense, the security of liberties, and mutual and general welfare—this government had no authority over the people as individuals. Operating entirely through the states, the central government could not even raise revenues, but rather had to count on financial contributions from the several states. Congress, its principal organ, was not really a representative lawmaking body since its members acted merely as delegates and voted as state units. Any important measures required the assent of at least nine states; and no change could be made in the Articles except with the consent of every state.

In 1787 Congress invited the states to send delegates to a convention in Philadelphia "for the sole and express purpose of revising the Articles of Confederation . . . to render the federal constitution adequate to the exigencies of government, and the preservation of the Union." The overriding exigency was the deteriorating condition of the national economy and the obvious necessity of protecting interstate commerce from too many onerous local regulations. From the outset, the convention leaders were determined to strengthen the central government. Some indeed would have abolished the states and set up a unitary government. But the fact that the thirteen states had long been separate entities, developing distinct cultural and economic patterns during the colonial period and continuing to enjoy independent status under the Articles, militated against such a drastic move. Despite common background and shared experiences as British colonists and American revolutionaries, the people in the states were not prepared as yet to merge their diverse identities into a single nationality. Moreover, the magnitude of territorial jurisdiction dismayed even the proponents of a unitary system. Given the transportation and communications facilities of the time, it appeared practically impossible for a national government to exercise its authority effectively the whole length of the Atlantic seaboard and into the western wilderness.

The more perfect union envisaged at the Philadephia convention grants to the central government enumerated powers relating to specific objectives: 1) national security (declaring war, providing for armed forces, levying taxes, and borrowing money), 2) regulation of foreign affairs (diplomatic exchanges, treaty-making, foreign commerce), and 3) regulation of the national economy (interstate commerce, the monetary system, weights and measures, patents and copyrights). Certain prohibitions are placed upon the states to strengthen the central government in pursuit of these objectives (no state shall enter into any treaty, alliance, or federation, no state shall coin money). To provide flexibility in the application of federalism—the distribution of powers between the central government and the states—Congress is given the power to make all laws "necessary and proper" for carrying out its specified powers. The residual powers of government (all those not specifically enumerated) remain with the states, subject to certain limitations with respect to individual rights.

Members of the Philadelphia convention regarded the change relating to taxation as the most important since it brought the central government into direct contact with the people as taxpayers. The only significant new power concerned the regulation of interstate commerce, but given the local character of most of the economy, this was not viewed as any major extension of the central authority by most people. Hamilton, Madison, and Jay, authors of *The Federalist,* anticipated that the operations of the central government would be "most extensive and important in times of war and danger; those of the state governments in times of peace and security." [7]

Applying this eighteenth-century federal design to the major problems of government in the United States today boggles the imagination. Even so, policy-makers in Washington, Atlanta, Boston, Boise, Austin, Springfield, and Honolulu are constrained to act within the constitutional framework for intergovernmental relations. If we tick off some of the most pressing issues of the day (not including national security and foreign policy)—public education, environmental pollution, urban renewal and model cities, mass transportation, public health, drug traffic, care for the aged, adulteration of foods and drugs, misleading advertising, rural slums and rural development, highway safety, crime in the streets—how do we apply the doctrine of strict construction of the Constitution? None of these problems was discussed in the summer of 1787 in the secret deliberations of the Constitutional Convention. Few of them can be solved under the direct authority of the central government without violating the constitutional principles of federalism.

Whatever the intent of the founding fathers, the original distribution of powers between the central government and the states has, over the course of almost two centuries, been radically altered and turned into a jerry-built system of shared finances, shared activities, and shared powers. President Lyndon Johnson euphemistically called it "creative federalism." [8]

Contemporary federalism in the United States has, in fact, become a maze of intergovernmental relations in which the states are no longer key components in the political system. If we look beyond the constitutional and legal concepts of federalism, we discover perhaps six or seven levels of government interposed between the national government and the states; a multiplicity of new bodies diverse in origin

> *created at different times, by different authorities, in response to different sets of concrete problems. . . . Their purpose is to make the federal system itself work better. They are planners, coordinators, expediters, facilitators, communicators. They bridge the vertical and horizontal gaps in the federal structure; they narrow the span of communication; they act, so to speak, as the intermediate pumping stations along the federal-state-local-citizen pipelines through which demands flow upward and funds flow downward.*[9]

Both the national government and the local communities tend to bypass the states in official and unofficial consultative patterns and planning processes. Complicated coordinating structures and fiscal arrangements are employed to carry on such national-local programs as environmental control, economic opportunity, manpower training, and crime control.

The United States has been legally defined as "an indestructible union of indestructible states." The Constitution of 1787 provided for the admission of new states to the union but was silent on the possibility of secession. The terms of admission are left entirely to the discretion of Congress but, without exception, the practice has been to admit each new state on equal footing with the original members of the union. Each state—Rhode Island to Texas, Alaska to New York, regardless of its size, population, resources, or stage of economic development—has two senators in Congress, and this provision for equal representation cannot be abridged even by constitutional amendment. The issue of secession, which plunged this country into its most bloody war, its only civil war, has been moot since Appomattox. When eleven Southern states, resisting the industrialization of the nation and trying to protect the peculiar institution of slavery, attempted to secede in 1861, the national government moved with full force against what it regarded as rebellion. Since the force of the national government proved at length to be superior to that of the rebellious Southern states, the secession was prevented. The union is indissoluble.

The Federal Republic of Germany

German federalism is a compromise between a long history of nationalism and an equally long tradition of particularism. German nationalism, based on common language and history, goes back to the Middle Ages; German particularism dates back to the seventeenth century. Martin Luther, who was most instrumental in giving the Germans a common written language (when he translated the Bible into the vernacular) also introduced one of the most divisive forces in German history—the Protestant Reformation.

The Thirty Years' War (1630–48), which was an outgrowth of the Reformation, broke up the Holy Roman Empire of the German nation. When the Treaty of Westphalia was signed in 1648, the various subjects of the many German ruling houses were tied to the religious beliefs of their princes in some 300 sovereign states. In all of these states the people spoke German and shared a common cultural history, but in each state the people owed allegiance to the ruling house and were required to practice the religion of its prince. Thus each state remained identified with one or the other of the two main religious factions of the Thirty Years' War.

During the next century and a half religion continued to be a divisive force among the German people, but foreign politics intervened. In the first decade of the nineteenth century Napoleon and his French armies of occupation did a great deal to forge political unity among the Protestant states. After the Congress of Vienna the more than 300 German principalities were consolidated into a loose confederation of thirty-nine states, under the "perpetual" presidency of Austria.

The German Confederation was, from the outset, torn by the rivalry of Prussia (Protestant) and Austria (Catholic). Like the Congress of the United States under the Articles, the German Diet (consisting of representatives appointed by the princes) did not operate directly upon the people of the states and had no real powers of government. The Confederation was financially dependent upon the states for revenues since the Diet could not levy taxes. A customs union (a *Zollverein*) among the states gradually developed a common economic base, but this was controlled, not by Austria but by Prussia, another divisive factor.

An abortive attempt on the part of German liberals to establish a real union during the revolutionary movement of 1848 almost succeeded when panic-stricken princes in state after state yielded to demands for manhood suffrage and parliamentary government. But the impetus of the movement was braked as the liberals fell to arguing among themselves whether they wanted a unitary or a federal government and whether they would retain the monarchies or opt all the way for republicanism. Meantime, the rival ruling houses of Austria and Prussia, the Hapsburgs and the Hohenzollerns, scorned the movement; the lesser princes gradually plucked up courage; the revolution failed and for another twenty years the Confederation survived, albeit weaker than ever.

The federal structure of the German Empire was achieved by blood and iron. When Otto von Bismarck became prime minister of Prussia in 1862, he determined to bring about German unity under the hegemony of Prussia, not by "speeches and resolutions of majorities," but by marching soldiers. He deliberately dragged Austria into a disastrous war with Denmark (1864–66) and then when Austria was in no shape to resist he declared the Confederation dissolved and marched the well-trained Prussian army against the already beaten Austrian troops. With the defeat of Austria, Bismarck was in position to engineer a new German union, the North German Confederation in which Prussia supplanted Austria. This new Confederation comprised some twenty-two states, all of them German in language, customs, and traditions, but each looking back, as an aftermath of the Reformation, to a long and independent dynastic rule and political experience.

When Prussia emerged victorious from the Franco-Prussian War in 1871, Bismarck saw his dream of a united Germany under Prussian hegemony finally realized. The king of Prussia was crowned emperor of Germany, but the Reich was a federal union rather than a unitary state. The *Bundesrat*, the upper house of the national legislature, represented the states; the *Reichstag*, the lower house, represented the people. During the Prussian war with France, the southern states (largely Catholic) cast their lot with Prussia and after the war became part of the Reich. Unlike the United States, however, the principle of equality did not prevail. In the Bundesrat the Prussian government rated seventeen votes, Bavaria had six, and seventeen of the smaller states had only one vote apiece. A contemporary political scientist aptly described the German union as "a compact between a lion, a half dozen foxes, and a score of mice." Prussia, of course, was the lion, Bavaria was one of the foxes, and among the mice were the free cities of Bremen and Hamburg.

The constitution of the Reich (personally prepared by Bismarck) followed the now century-old model of the United States in many respects. The powers of the imperial government were enumerated and delegated by the states; the residual powers remained with the states. Powers delegated to the Reich included control over citizenship, the navy, the merchant marine, posts and telegraph, patents and coinage, and tariffs. Vestiges of particularism were still evident, however; whereas in the United States the national government guarantees a republican government to all the states, the forms of government and the laws of succession were left up to the individual German states. Specifically, the relations of church and state and matters of public instruction were vested in the separate states. Administration of imperial laws, except in case of the foreign service, the postal service, and the navy were largely left in the hands of state officials. In many ways, the German federal government of 1871 was much less finished than the more perfect union of the United States of 1787.

The German Reich went down to defeat in World War I. The Weimar Republic which succeeded it retained the federal form and particularism continued to thrive despite a constitutional prescription that appeared to give much greater powers to the central government. The central government had exclusive jurisdiction in foreign affairs, national defense, currency, customs, communications, and citizenship. It shared with the states power to legislate over civil rights, civil and criminal law, public health, trade and industry, and transportation, but in the event of conflict the national legislature overrode the states. Finally, but not least, it was empowered to establish fundamental principles to guide the states in matters of taxation, education, religious and other social subjects. The states were represented in the *Reichsrat* in proportion to population, except that each state had at least one representative, and no state, however large, could have more than two-fifths of the representation. This was a move to reduce Prussian influence.

Federalism as a constitutional pattern was obliterated in the totalitarian government of Hitler's Third Reich, but the indigenous particularism which had so long characterized German nationalism could not be eradicated. The Third Reich ended in holocaust, and between 1945 and 1948 the Allied powers argued among themselves whether and/or how to reconstruct the German nation. When the Western powers broke with the Soviet Union over the German question in 1947, the three Western powers, in company with the Benelux countries, decided that an independent democratic West German state was the answer to an intransigent Soviet policy. In June, 1948, in the face of Russian protests, a six-power conference agreed upon the establishment of a West German federal union which would protect the rights of the respective states and at the same time provide for adequate central authority to develop a strong national economy. And not incidentally the federal form was considered a suitable device for eventual reunification of West and East Germany.[10]

The real basis for German federalism today, however, is not a fortuitous decision on the part of the six-power conference to support a Federal Republic instead of another Reich. Rather it is the outcome of German history from the Middle Ages. Despite a common language and a shared culture, most of the German states in the contemporary system exemplify a long history of political particularism. Some of the states are new creations brought about by territorial shifts during the Allied Occupation: Prussia, which had been the dominating center of the Reich, no longer exists. Even so, most German people though proud of their German nationality were accustomed to identifying their citizenship and political allegiance with particular states. The city-states of Hamburg and Bremen had been republican in tradition since the time of the Hanseatic League. Bavaria long ruled by a Catholic monarchy still retains its Catholic culture. Schleswig-Holstein, a merger of Protestant duchies, remains just as strongly committed to the Luthern tradition. Thus, federalism which recognizes the national interests and uniformities in the culture and yet accommodates to the territorial diversities among the people was the only viable possibility for renewing a German nation state.

The Soviet Pattern: Federal or Unitary?

The Constitution of the USSR provides for a federal union. To understand why the founding fathers of the Soviet Union adopted a federal rather than a unitary political system we must again turn to history.

Unlike the United States in the eighteenth century, the Soviet Union was not a new state; it succeeded czarist Russia in which the central government had possessed extensive powers and had exercised them autocratically. The decision to opt for the Russian Soviet Federal Socialist Republic (RSFSR) in 1918 was a diplomatic ploy on the part of the Bolshevik leadership, intended to reunite the various territorial units that had broken away from the former jurisdiction of the Russian Empire during the Civil War. The ploy was successful; a Treaty of Union, drafted in 1922, ratified in 1924, established the Union of Soviet Socialist Republics comprising the RSFSR, the Ukraine, Byelorussia, and Transcaucasia. Subsequently the Uzbek, Turkmen, and Tadzhikistan autonomous socialist soviet republics also entered the USSR. In 1936, the Eighth Congress of Soviets adopted a new constitution (the present one) retaining the federal form.

The federal structure of the USSR is much more complicated than that of the United States. Today there are fifteen Union Republics, each representing a major ethnic group territorially based: the RSFSR, the Ukraine, Byelorussia, Azerbaijan, Georgia, and so forth.[11] All of the Union Republics are accorded equal representation in the Soviet of Nationalities, thirty-two delegates each, although the Republics vary greatly in size, both of land and of population. The RSFSR is by far the largest, occupying more than three-fourths of the total area of the Soviet Union. Four-fifths of the people in the RSFSR are Russians, but there are about two score other nationality groups within the Republic, including Tartars, Jews, Poles, Bashkirs, Germans, and others. Because of its vast size and diverse ethnic groups, the RSFSR is itself organized as a federal republic, with multiple autonomous republics, regions, autonomous regions, and other lesser territorial political units. The Soviet of Nationalities of the USSR provides for representation not only of the major constituent republics but also of the many lesser ethnic groups. The autonomous republics are each entitled to eleven delegates, the autonomous regions have five deputies, and the smallest ethnic-territorial units (national districts) have one each.

The geopolitical lines of the USSR coincide roughly with the principal nationality and linguistic subdivisions of the population. The Supreme Soviet, like the American Congress and the German Parliament, is bicameral, with the upper house, the Soviet of Nationalities, representing the territorial units according to the federal principle. As a matter of record, however, the behavior of the Soviet Nationalities appears to be identical with that of the lower house, the Soviet of the Union, which purports to represent the population generally. Both houses meet together to endorse policy decisions already made by the Communist party leadership, and there is no public evidence of disagreement in the reactions of the two soviets. (In the next chapter we shall have more to say about legislative roles in the USSR and the overwhelming influence of the Communist party leadership upon the official legislators.)

Initially, the Bolshevik leaders, bent on liquidating the Russian Empire, pledged self-determination for all the nations of Russia. In accordance with this view, the Constitution of the USSR provides for secession as well as accession to the polyethnic union. When the communist movement still appeared headed for world revolution, a highly flexible form of federalism was considered a good recruiting device. The annexation by force of such territorial ethnic communities as the Baltic states of Estonia, Latvia, and Lithuania early in World War II belie the constitutional provisions. Certainly Soviet armed intervention in Hungary (1956) and Czechoslovakia (1968) offer grim proof that the Soviet leaders in fact will not permit self-determination or the right of secession in associated states, much less within the Soviet Union.

Ivo D. Duchacek in his list of "measuring rods" for federalism asks first of all, "Has the central authority exclusive control over diplomacy and defense as befits a nation-state in its relations *with other nation states?*" [12] The United States and the Federal Republic of Germany meet the test in the affirmative. So, in fact, does the Soviet Union, but not according to its Constitution. In 1944, while Stalin was still undisputed dictator, the Soviet Constitution of 1936 was amended to permit each Union Republic to enter into foreign relations, to conclude agreements with foreign states, and to exchange representatives with them. Provision was also made for each Union Republic to maintain its own armed forces. On paper, this made the USSR a very loose league of states, much more so than the United States under the Articles of Confederation which at least retained British crown power over foreign affairs for the new national government.

The purpose of the 1944 amendments to the Soviet Constitution became clear when a few months later at Yalta Stalin demanded separate representation for each of the (then) sixteen republics in the USSR. As a result of Stalin's move, the USSR, the Soviet Ukraine, and Soviet Byelorussia all hold individual membership in the United Nations, and each has a vote in the General Assembly. Curiously, the USSR has never pressed the argument to its logical conclusion to secure membership for all of its Union Republics. (Nor has the United States been prompted to amend its Constitution to insure like membership in the United Nations for all fifty of its states.) Actually, the effect has been simply to give the USSR three votes, rather than one, in the General Assembly since there is in fact no separate foreign policy between the Union and its constituent republics.

The distribution of powers between the central government and the constituent republics of the Soviet Union is a far cry from the eighteenth-century pattern under which the United States still operates. The central government in the USSR possesses a monopoly of authority on all matters relating to national security, foreign trade, economic planning, and economic development. This central authority is buttressed by complete fiscal control over the entire system. Unlike the states in the United States, which retain their independent powers of purse, the territorial units in the USSR cannot raise revenues or determine expenditures on their own. The central government exercises total budget authority; this in line with Marxian ideology that whoever controls the economy controls the society. The central government makes the authoritative allocations, of both revenues and expenditures for all of the republics, albeit conceding some flexibility in internal administration. Keep in mind also that the central government controls the banking system and that the only source of credit is the state-owned and state-managed bank.

The planned socialist economy is the basic tenet of Marxism and as such is the key determinant in application of governmental power to the economy. Hence the central government in the USSR has unquestioned authority in all matters relating to economic planning, production priorities, investments, and development. All industrial and commercial enterprises are state-owned, and two-fifths of the agricultural lands are now also state-owned and operated. The problem of government is not complicated as it is in the United States by the issues of limited government, states' rights, individual rights, and private enterprise. The Communist party guarantees an overriding uniformity when that appears to be the most effective resolution to local or ethnic differences.

As a matter of practicality, however, in a country as vast in territory, with as much ethnic and cultural diversity as exists within the various territorial units of the USSR, there is considerable decentralization in economic operations and public administration. The structural-functional arrangement is manifest in the two types of ministries recognized in the present Constitution: the All-Union ministries which give exclusive direction from Moscow and the Union-Republic ministries in which the central government shares power with corresponding ministries in the several republics.[13]

Whether a particular governmental function is most effectively obtained through an All-Union ministry or through a Union-Republic ministry has been a subject of on-going debate within the Communist leadership over many years. The policy pendulum, which swung from extreme centralism under Stalin toward substantial decentralization under Khrushchev, seems now to be swinging back toward center.

In the early years policy-makers in the Kremlin felt that a rapid expansion and forced industrialization of the economy required highly centralized management as well as planning, with concentration on the heavy industries that contributed to national security. After Stalin's death, Khrushchev pushed for decentralization in operations and more emphasis on development of consumer goods industries. As he viewed it, centralized management which had been effective in immediate modernization of the economy was hardly feasible for the more than two hundred thousand state industrial enterprises and one hundred thousand construction projects scattered across the entire country. In 1957, he introduced the system of *sovnarkhozy*, councils of national economy established in economic regions as defined by the republics. Each sovnarkhoz ("economic council") was expected to maintain direct contact with all industrial plants within its territorial jurisdiction and to insure cooperation between related industries. The All-Union ministries, except for a few with functions that transcended the republican boundaries, were abolished. The State Planning Committee of the USSR, in conjunction with State Planning commissions in each of the republics, was given responsibility for overall planning and for coordinating implementation of plans. Very shortly, however, it appeared that the very detailed instructions from the central planning authorities to the local bodies were in effect a move toward recentralization. In 1962 and 1963 the sovnarkhozy were subjected to sweeping reforms; the territorial jurisdiction of each sovnarkhoz was enlarged and the number of sovnarkhozy was reduced. In 1965 the whole sovnarkhoz system was liquidated, its principal proponent, Khrushchev, having been ousted from power by the Communist leadership in 1964.

As it now stands, the reconstituted All-Union ministries are in central command of those industries where standardization in production is important, for instance, the tool industries, manufacturers of heavy equipment, road-building, the aviation industry, and the automobile industry. The Union-Republic ministries, with their counterpart ministries in the republics, share authority over industries that use, rather than manufacture, equipment such as fishing, trading, water resources, public health, and culture. Quite clearly, central controls have been reasserted over planning and operations in the defense industries and over the entire economy with respect to capital investment, construction priorities, manpower allocation, and national growth plans. In 1966 the Communist Party Congress approved a Five-Year Plan to step up agricultural production as well as to increase industrial efficiency. Even so, what appears to be a regression to the Stalinist concept of centralism has been officially disclaimed. The explanation given is that a balance has now been struck between demands for national security and consumer needs, between centralized planning and local operations.

We are informed that "today the U.S.S.R. has a largely self-sufficient economy with a broad industrial base and a largely self-developed technology." The same statement as aptly describes the United States. In recent years both states have constructed a huge and pervasive military-industrial base. The United States is now the first-ranking industrial power in the world; the Soviet Union ranks second. Both of these great powers are federal unions, but it would be fallacious logic for us to argue that the economic progress of these industrial nations can be attributed to the federal form of government. In our concluding chapter when we examine how different political systems function, we have to consider more definitively the patterns of economic distribution, who gets what because of how the system is motivated, organized, and operated. Here we pass over the question of motivation—

Communist or capitalist—to dip a bit deeper into problems of territorial organization.

The basic rationale for federalism is that it provides central government where uniformity in policy is desired and permits subnational governments to rule where diversity in policy is more feasible. Certainly this was, and still is, the principal rationale for federalism in the Soviet Union. The USSR is a vast territory with a very large population. That in itself poses all the problems of big government, problems which are magnified and all the more complicated because a great many different kinds of people—more than 170 distinct nationality and cultural groups—live in the Soviet Union. About 70 percent of the population is Slavic—Russians, Ukrainians, and Byelorussians—living mostly in the European southern and western regions, but scattered across the two continents are peoples of such diverse backgrounds as Turkic, Finno-Ugric, Japhetic, and Iranian. Despite the fact that Russian has been taught in all the schools of the Soviet Union since the 1920s, it is still a second language to many Soviet citizens. It is said that more than two hundred different languages and dialects are used daily within the territorial boundaries of the USSR.

The function of education in the USSR is to create the new Soviet man who serves the needs of the state, whether he teaches economics in the University of Leningrad, dances in the Bolshoi Ballet, runs a tractor on a state farm, or works in a steel mill. The Constitution of the USSR proclaims the right of all Soviet citizens to education. Seven years of schooling has been compulsory since 1949, and since 1955 all fees for education have been abolished through the tenth grade. The communist ideology is taught in every school and the same basic curriculum is prescribed in elementary and secondary schools throughout the Union. Even so, there is a great deal of parochialism, and necessarily so. Communities widely separated and some of them isolated for months every year, from Murmansk to Vladivostok; communities with very different environments and very different values, the marshy tundras in the north, the banks of the Volga and the steppes of Eurasia, the deserts in Central Asia and the semitropical shores of the Black Sea; communities with different cultural traditions, different religious backgrounds, different languages. Uniform educational practices imposed upon all these different communities would have been impossible and attempts to impose them would have been politically dangerous.

Federalism is the fortuitous device which makes allowances for diversity under central direction. Russian is taught in all the schools, along with Russian literature, but in the non-Russian republics the primary language of instruction is the language of the republic, and the children are also taught the literature of their own nationality. Vocational training is geared to the manpower needs of the Union but it is also suited to the needs of the local community. Children in the Arctic region are not taught to be refrigeration engineers, and children in Moscow are not trained to operate diesel tractors, combines, and other farm machinery as are many of the children in the Ukrainian SSR.

Another important area of decentralization in the Soviet Union has been that of law and justice. Law, in the communist ideology, is "the will of the working class and all the working people. . . . a system of rules established by the state to promote consolidation of the social order which helps society advance toward communism."[14] In pursuance of this basic concept—"the grand program of communist construction"—the second session of the Supreme Soviet of the USSR in 1958 adopted Fundamental Principles of Law relating to judicial system, criminal legislation, and military jurisdiction. Within the federal union the central government develops the Fundamental Principles, but the several republics each establish their own operational codes.

Even in the most repressive years of the Stalinist regime all civil suits (legal controversies between individuals) were heard in the republican courts, thus permitting continuation of local mores. The Union courts were (and still are) courts of criminal jurisdiction only; but the totalitarian character of the Soviet government permits extraordinary latitude in defining crimes against the state. Theft, for example, in a socialist system that vests property rights in the state, becomes a crime against the state. And in the planned economy, failure to meet deadlines on engineering or construction projects or to reach production quotas in an industrial plant or on a state farm may quite logically be regarded as economic sabotage and, so, counterrevolutionary. Thus, in the Stalinist era, especially in the 1930s, due process of law turned into political terrorism.

The death of Stalin in 1953 was a turning point in the Soviet system of justice. The Special Board of the Ministry of Internal Affairs—the most dreaded instrument of terror under Stalin—was immediately abolished. Within a few years all of the special courts of the Union, as well as special procedures for dealing with antistate crimes, were abolished. Thousands of reforms in the codes were introduced which appear to liberalize both the content and process of Soviet laws. And most important, decentralization of decision-making was effected through the republican courts, with separate law codes in each of the republics replacing the All-Union codes authorized in the 1936 Constitution. "Hundreds, indeed thousands, of organizations" and "Tens of thousands of expert consultants" were recruited for advisory roles in the process of recodification.[15] The courts, from the people's courts in the local communities to the Supreme Court in each republic, are staffed by lay and professional judges in proportion two to one.

From the outside, looking at the post-Stalinist reforms on paper, Soviet law and justice appeared to be both decentralized and democratized. All the courts, however, are functional components of the Communist system, and the fundamentals of Soviet law have not really changed; the main outlines of criminal law and procedure, labor law, family law, land law, and administrative law were retained much the same as they were under Stalin.

Federalism in the Soviet Union is a useful device for meeting local situations and placating diverse local opinions, but the overriding factors that make federalism feasible are the unifying ideology of Communism and the central dictatorship of the Communist party. Note that the justice pendulum has begun to swing back toward the center as part of the current strategy of the Communist leadership to strengthen the fight against economic crime. News reports in recent years increasingly call attention to such economic crimes as black marketeering, embezzlement, use of state property for personal gain, illicit private enterprise, and common theft. In 1968 the Union Ministry of Public Order, renamed the Ministry of Internal Affairs (MVD), among other responsibilities was given central control over the ordinary police and prisons. Moreover, the Union Ministry of Justice, established by Stalin in 1936, abolished by Khrushchev in 1956, was reconstituted in 1970 for the express purpose of reinforcing socialist legality and state discipline and preventing and eradicating crime throughout the Union.

UNITARY VERSUS FEDERAL GOVERNMENTS IN DEVELOPING STATES

The crucial problem of government for any developing nation is how to encompass the national economy and how to develop unified policies for the rapid building of a modern economy. It is easy to say that the structural organization should fit the functions, from which it follows that centralized command is probably best suited to the economic functions that confront the political system in any developing or, for that matter, advanced country. Given the primacy of the economic function in the modern state, a unitary government like the British or the Japanese appears to be the most practical solution. This is the way taken by Colombia, Turkey, and Israel.[16]

Unitary Examples

Colombia In Colombia and Turkey the authority of the national government is comprehensive, reaches into the largest cities and most remote villages, and is coterminous with the nation's political boundaries. Note that in each of these countries the population is fairly homogeneous, with no sharp religious, linguistic, or cultural differences. Colombia is predominantly Catholic and Spanish-speaking, and for more than four centuries the native Indian culture has been thoroughly permeated with Spanish traditions.

Colombia has tried ten different constitutions between 1811 and 1886. The key issue in each of these constitutional documents has been the relationship between the national government and the local communities. Political and intellectual leaders have alternately swung from the federal example of the United States (which seemed more practical given the rugged and separatist character of the Colombian terrain) and the unitary experience of Europe, especially the mother country (which had more appeal to Colombian nationalists).

The present Constitution of the Republic of Colombia, which established a unitary system, was ratified in 1886, not by the former states, but by the municipal councils. Colombia is sometimes described quite reverentially as a federation of cities. Numerous amendments to the 1886 Constitution have strengthened the authority of the national government, especially in economic and social functions—the progressive moves toward centralization are regarded as necessary for effective national economic planning and development.

Turkey The unitary government of Turkey represents a conscious choice of Turkey's modern nation-builders. The Turkish political system was deliberately constructed on the foundations of nationalism and secularism in contradistinction to Ottomanism and Islamism. Much as the Western European nations emerged centuries earlier out of the crumbling Holy Roman Empire, so the Turkish Republic has its beginnings in the disintegration of the Ottoman Empire. Every major political party today espouses a strong national government; one that did not is not likely to draw much of a following. Political organizations or propaganda based on cultural differences are officially forbidden. And, although Turkish nationalism today tends to identify itself with Islam, it is generally liberal in attitude. Members of minority groups, such as Christians, Jews, Kurds, and Freemasons, once treated as second-class citizens, have come to be accepted under national law as Turks regardless of race or religion.[17]

Israel Israel also has a unitary government, but this we cannot attribute, as we have in the case of Colombia and Turkey, to a homogeneous nationality. The linguistic and cultural differences within this very small state are almost monumental. Before World War I Jewish immigrants to Palestine came principally from Russia and Eastern Europe most of them atheistic, social revolutionaries, infused with the messianic mission of Zionism. They furnished the first ruling elite of Israel, and they (and their descendants) are still dominant in the government. Between the world wars, and especially in the 1930s, a great many Jews emigrated to Palestine from Austria and Germany (fewer from the United States); most of these were religious Jews, nonsocialist, anti-Zionist, business and professional people. After World War II the composition of Israel's population was drastically changed by the arrival of the remnants of European Jewry, but even more by the influx in large numbers of Jews forced to leave their homes in Arab countries after the Israel War of Independence. The new immigrants, orientals from the Middle East, now comprise over 50 percent of the population. They are mostly dark-skinned, culturally backward people who speak Arabic or French but little or no Hebrew or Yiddish. But however heterogeneous the population of modern Israel, there is one great centralizing force: Israel is the promised land for all. The territorial motif has played a significant role among the dispersed Jewish community for millennia—"If I forget thee, O Jerusalem, let my right hand forget her cunning" (Psalm 137). A unitary government for Israel may be difficult and yet it is achieved by the course of Jewish history.[18]

Federal Examples

Mexico Two of our less-developed countries have adopted the federal form: Mexico and India. Mexico's first constitution in 1824, modeled after that of the United States, provided for a federal union of nineteen states. The geographical rationale was obvious. At that time Mexico's territory, stretching from the Isthmus to Colorado and Oregon, was approximately the size of its neighbor to the north. The facilities for transportation and communication among the Mexican states were even more primitive than among the United States. Unitary government over such vast territory was virtually impossible, and given the spirit of separatism from one remote community to another, federalism was the most opportune political approach. Following the war with the United States, 1845–48, Mexico was considerably reduced in size, but even so, the terrain of Mexico was hardly conducive to internal integration and centralization of political controls. Two-thirds of the country is covered by high mountain ranges in which there are deep valleys and isolated basins. Most of the people were living on the *mesa central*, a plateau seven to eight thousand feet above sea level, once the heartland of the Aztec Empire. Isolated villages and remote regions had little contact with the federal capital. Indeed, not until 1958 was a connecting road completed between the Yucatan and the mesa central. It was, therefore, practical in the 1857 Constitution to continue the federal form already in existence.

The present Mexican Constitution retains the federal arrangements of 1857, although the geographical rationale is no longer so compelling. Modern facilities of communication and transportation now tie the country together, at least physically, into a manageable unit. The 1917 Constitution, written in the same year as the Russian Bolshevik Revolution, bears the imprint of that Revolution as well as the older influence of American constitutionalism. "It is the will of the Mexican people to organize themselves into a federal, democratic, representative Republic composed of free and sovereign states in all that concerns their national government, but united in a Federation established according to the principles of this fundamental law." [19]

Whether Mexico today has a truly federal union is a matter of debate. Certainly there is much more centralism inherent and explicit in the Mexican Constitution than in the Constitution of the United States. Since the central government in Mexico is granted the preeminent powers of taxation, the Mexican states are largely dependent upon it for handouts—and the handouts are pretty miserly. Moreover, the central government is authorized to intervene in the state governments to settle contested elections of governor and legislators, a frequent occurrence in some states. Actually, as we noted in the preceding chapter, the Institutional Revolutionary Party (PRI), as the dominant party in control of the central government, also keeps a tight rein on who gets to sit in the state offices. The PRI itself is highly centralized. Its Central Executive Committee, which "represents the party throughout the country," exercises its authority over state and local as well as national party activities, including broad control over selection of party officers and party candidates at all election levels.

As in the USSR, however, the real power of the central government is that which it possesses by virtue of its control of the economy. Under Title 6 of the Constitution, the central government has extensive jurisdiction over labor and social security laws, and as a concomitant of this legal authorization it has a big bureaucracy in personal contact with the people, playing the role of benefactor not only in the national capital but also in local offices throughout the country. This cash nexus between the central government and the people—millions of checks for workmen's compensation, medical care, old-age pensions, etc., paid out regularly to individuals in the most remote villages as well as in the big cities—has built massive support for the national government and for the PRI, which dictates the government policies.

Mexico has not gone Communist, nor even socialist: Private enterprise flourishes, but the determination of the PRI to modernize the Mexican economy gives to the central government what in effect amounts to command powers over economic planning and development for the nation as a whole. Ostensibly the government does not intervene in the private sector if the private sector responds satisfactorily to the government policies for economic growth, but government policies cover a widening range of economic activities: land redistribution, expansion of agricultural production, industrial development, promotion of tourism, etc. Implementation of these policies gives to the central government a pervasive presence in the economy. For example, through the national development bank (*Nacional Financiera*), the government participates in a lengthening list of manufacturing industries, e.g., iron and steel, industrial chemicals, fertilizers, foodstuffs, paper, automobiles, textile machinery, etc. The government also maintains a monopoly on such industries as oil, forestry, fishing, railways, telegraphs, and electric power plants. It keeps a watchful control over foreign investments and requires majority Mexican interest in mining, transportation, soft drink bottling, publishing, commercial broadcasting, advertising, etc.[20] Obviously, federalism is obsolete, i.e., nonfunctioning, in the operation of government controls over the economy.

India The Indian decision to form a federal union can be explained in terms of geography and cultural diversity. It is no coincidence that the four largest states in our sample of twelve—the USSR, the USA, India, and Mexico —are all federal in form. The rationale for Indian federalism, however, is closer to that of the USSR than to that of the USA or Mexico: The compelling pattern is linguistic. At the time of independence the Indian people had no real national base except a common aversion to British colonialism. As late as June, 1948, the British viceroy to Delhi was under instructions from the home government to transfer British colonial power to a single Indian government; but assessing realistically the disagreements between the Muslim League and the Indian Congress as imminently explosive, Lord Mountbatten recommended the creation of two self-governing states, India and Pakistan, with Bengal and the Punjab partitioned between the two new states. This partition was accomplished with widespread violence during which Mahatma Gandhi, father of independence and a foe of partition, was assassinated.

In the transition from colonial government to independence, the several hundred princely states hitherto under British rule but not as part of British India were permitted to choose whether to remain independent or to join one of the two new states. By 1949, individual agreements had been worked out with the princely states for accession on a limited basis. Each would be bound to the Centre[21]—India or Pakistan—in three areas only: defense, foreign affairs, and communications. The notable exception was Kashmir, contiguous both to India and Pakistan, with a predominantly Muslim population and a Hindu maharaja. Bloody fighting between Indian and Pakistani troops and among the Kashmir tribesmen ensued. On solicitation of the Indian government the United Nations obtained a cease-fire, but to this day the conflicting claims have not been settled and fighting goes on intermittently.

The most difficult problem to surmount in India's progress toward nationhood has been the barrier of language. The governing elite all speak English and English is still the principal means of communication between peoples in different parts of India. India needs an official language which can reach more than the 2 percent of the population who now have some fluency in English. Although Hindi is the language spoken by the largest number of Indians, it is a language of the marketplace rather than a literary language, and it is a regional language, of the North, understood by less than a third of the Indian citizens. Although the 1949 Indian Constitutional Assembly proclaimed that Hindi would be the only official language of the Union after 1965, the proclamation was not popular and opposition to Hindi mounted to hysteria in some regions. In 1963, with the reluctant acquiescence of Nehru, the Indian Parliament authorized the continued use of English as a second language after 1965. Even so, there were widespread disorders, and especially in the south when some ministries attempted a changeover from English to Hindi. Prime Minister Shastri had to follow Nehru's example and again make promises that the Centre would continue to communicate to all regions in English as well as Hindi. And, further, a three-language formula was worked out so that instruction in the mother tongue would be offered in the elementary schools, with English and Hindi taught as second and third languages in the upper grades.

Meanwhile this fierce battle over languages resulted in a breakup of the original federal Union. As early as 1920 the Indian National Congress had organized itself according to the territorial boundaries of the major language groups. In 1955 a States Reorganization Commission recommended that the state boundaries of the Indian Union be similarly redrawn along linguistic lines. Accordingly, in 1956 the Indian federal Union was reconstituted with fourteen instead of twenty-seven states, all but two of which were fairly homogeneous as to language. In the two states language minorities continued to stir strife. In 1960 one of these, Bombay, was subdivided along more satisfactory language lines, and in 1966 the second one, the Punjab, was subdivided, separating Sikhs, who speak Punjabi, from the Hindi-speaking people. As of today the Indian Union comprises seventeen language states.

The Indian Constitution is much more elaborate and detailed than the American Constitution in its distribution of powers between the central government and the states. The United States Constitution enumerates specific powers for the central government and leaves the reservoir of powers to the states. The Indian Constitution sets forth three lengthy lists of powers to cover all the subjects of modern government that the Constituent Assembly could envisage as it pursued its monumental task over a period of nearly three years, 1946–49. Many of the items in the Indian Constitution could not have been even imagined by the Philadelphia Convention of 1787, much less incorporated into their document. The Union List contains ninety-seven items over which the Union is given exclusive power: defense, armed forces, atomic energy, foreign affairs, transportation, communications, banking, currency, insurance, control of industries, mining, income taxes, customs duties, estate taxes, etc. The State List includes sixty-six items which are basically of local interest and/or for which diverse treatment seems desirable: administration of justice, public health and sanitation, education, agriculture, forests, fisheries, burials, duties on alcohol, land taxes, taxes on professions, etc. The Concurrent List includes forty-seven items on which uniformity of legislation throughout the country is considered desirable though not essential: marriage and divorce, contracts, bankruptcy, civil suits, trade unions, social security, labor welfare, price controls, etc. Both the Union Parliament and the state legislatures may enact legislation on subjects included in the Concurrent List, but in the event of conflict the law of Parliament prevails.

There is some doubt whether the Indian Union is a true federal union. The marked imbalance of power—tilted toward the Centre and away from the states—is, for example, accentuated by explicit provisions for the transfer of items from the states to the Centre to meet emergency or temporary situations in the national interest. As Indian constitutional scholars view it, a country like India, struggling for political and economic stability, cannot afford to take "the long winding way along which federal power had advanced slowly and painfully in the older federations." [22] In explaining its new federal scheme in 1955, the States Reorganization Commission reported that it had taken into consideration "four major principles": 1) the unity and security of India; 2) linguistic and cultural homogeneity; 3) financial, economic, and administrative considerations; and 4) successful working of the national development plans.[23]

Since independence, the overriding concern of the Indian leadership has been the fourth principle, national development. Leaders of the Constituent Assembly were for the most part Western-oriented, many of them British-educated and recent participants in the nationalist movement for independence. Hence they rejected the traditional pattern of rule by caste and class in local autonomous communities, opted for a Western form of government—a parliamentary democracy—and charted a course of national development based on Western values. Since independence the Indian leadership has staged a series of plans designed to transform India into a modern industrial state. The first Five-Year Plan (1951–56), which concentrated on agriculture, irrigation, power, and transportation, was intended to lay the groundwork for the new economy. The second plan (1956–61) was aimed at expanding the basic industries, such as steel, chemicals, fuel, and power, to increase the national income and to secure a more even distribution of the national wealth through equalization of opportunities. The fourth plan (1967–72) gives highest priority to agricultural production, including production of agricultural machinery, rural electrification, land reforms, etc.[24]

> *The central objective of planning was defined as initiating an integral part of a wider process aiming not merely at the development of resources in a narrow technical sense, but at the development of human faculties and the building up of an institutional framework adequate to the needs and aspirations of the people.*[25]

The imposition of a Western political structure upon a highly diverse culture could have resulted in a mere facade and all the grandiose plans might have dissolved into rhetoric had not the Indian leadership in a very practical way tried to link national development with community development. In 1958 the National Development Council, endorsing the principle of democratic decentralization, promoted the system known as *Panchayati Raj* in the several states.[26] The Panchayati Raj comprises a three-tier structure of local governing bodies at the village, block, and district levels for cooperative planning, financing, and programming of local development projects. At the village level (keep in mind that four-fifths of the people in India still live in villages) the *panchayat* (the "elected council") has charge of all developmental programs in the area and the village school serves as a community center, filling a variety of educational, cultural, and recreational needs. The central and state governments share in helping to finance such local projects as irrigation, animal husbandry, cottage industries, adult literacy, sanitation facilities, water wells, paved lanes, and rural electrification.

We conclude that all of our twelve states meet the pressures of centralization and decentralization pretty pragmatically. Whatever the constitutional design or the political structure, unitary or federal, the political system tends to adjust to the current demands: central command where uniform action seems necessary or most desirable and decentralized programs when these appear more feasible or appropriate given the local diversities.[27] "Support your local police," the familiar message on American automobile bumpers, is a voice heard around in the world, in Russian, Mexican, Hindi, Cockney, and Swahili!

NOTES

1. Ivo D. Duchacek, *Comparative Federalism: The Territorial Dimension of Politics* (New York: Holt, Rinehart & Winston, 1970), p. 3.
2. Ernest Barker, *Essays on Government* (Oxford: Clarendon: 1945), pp. 8–9.
3. Ibid.
4. Ibid.
5. Robert E. Ward, *Japan's Political System* (Englewood Cliffs, N.J.: Prentice-Hall, 1967), p. 101.
6. Duchacek, op. cit., p. 192.
7. The student is urged to look at *The Federalist* for a contemporary explanation and justification of the new federal union, especially numbers 41 to 46. The quotation is from number 45 by Madison.
8. For an overall view of the changing character of federalism in the United

States see the study submitted to the Intergovernmental Relations Subcommittee of the Senate Committee on Government Operations, *Metropolitan America: Challenges to Federalism,* prepared by the Advisory Commission on Intergovernmental Relations (Washington, D.C.: Government Printing Office, 1966).

9. James L. Sundquist and David W. Davis, *Making Federalism Work* (Washington, D.C.: Brookings Institution, 1969), p. 242. An excellent albeit rather technical study of concrete problems involved in program coordination at the community level.
10. For a perceptive discussion of "federalism, subsidiarity, and solidarity" in the Federal Republic, see Peter H. Merkl, *The Origin of the West German Republic* (New York: Oxford University Press, 1963), pp. 28–34. For a study of continuing conflict between the Germanies, see Elke Frank, "East and West Germany" in Steven L. Spiegel and Kenneth N. Waltz, eds., *Conflict in World Politics* (Cambridge, Mass.: Winthrop, 1971).
11. The fifteen constituent republics are: Armenia, Azerbaijan, Byelorussia, Georgia, Kazakhstan, Kirgiz, Moldavia, Russian Soviet Federated Socialist Republic, Tadzhikistan, Turkmen, Ukraine, Uzbek, Estonia, Latvia, Lithuania.
12. Duchacek, op. cit., p. 207.
13. Article 72 of the Constitution of 1936 as amended to 1967:

The Ministers of the U.S.S.R. direct the branches of state administration which come within the jurisdiction of the U.S.S.R.

Article 74: The Ministries of the U.S.S.R. are either All-Union or Union-Republican Ministries.

Article 75: Each all-Union Ministry directs the branch of state administration entrusted to it throughout the territory of the U.S.S.R. either directly or through bodies appointed by it.

Article 76: The Union-Republican Ministries, as a rule direct the branches of state administration entrusted to them through corresponding Ministries of the Union republics; . . .

Article 77: The following Ministries are all-Union Ministries:
Aviation Industry
Automobile Industry
Foreign Trade

Article 78: The following Ministries are Union-Republican Ministries:
Higher and Specialized Secondary Education
Geology
Public Health
Foreign Affairs
Culture

See John N. Hazard, *The Soviet System of Government,* 4th ed. (Chicago: University of Chicago Press, 1968), Appendix, for charts showing "The Structure of the Soviet Governmental Apparatus" and "The Federal Pattern," and also a text of the Constitution as amended to November 7, 1967.

14. P. S. Romashkin, ed., *Fundamentals of Soviet Law* (Moscow: Foreign Languages Publishing House, n.d.), p. 20. Romashkin is corresponding member of the Academy of Sciences of the USSR.
15. We take our quantitative and qualitative impressions of the post-Stalin changes from Harold J. Berman, *Justice in the USSR,* rev. ed. (Cambridge, Mass.:

Harvard University Press, 1963), chap. 2, "Soviet Law Reform after Stalin 1953–62." We also found useful Hazard, op. cit., chap. 11, "Enforcement of the Law."

16. Kenya and the Ivory Coast also have unitary governments, each emulating its erstwhile colonial power. Kenya's government follows the British model, the Ivory Coast is patterned after the French.

    For historical settings of developing patterns of unitary government in Colombia and Turkey see *Foreign Area Handbooks, Colombia and Turkey*, Foreign Area Studies Division, American University (Washington, D.C.: Government Printing Office, both 1970).
17. See Kemal H. Karpat, *Turkey's Politics* (Princeton, N.J.: Princeton University Press, 1959), especially chap. 9, "Nationalism," and chap. 10, "Secularism."
18. See Rafael Rosenzweig and Georges Tamarin, "Israel's Power Elite," *Transaction* 7 (July–August, 1970): 26–42.
19. Political Constitution of the Mexican United States, Title 2, Chapter 1, Article 40.
20. United States Department of Commerce, Bureau of International Commerce, *Basic Data on the Economy of Mexico* (August, 1967).
21. The Indian term for the central government.
22. M. V. Pylee, *India's Constitution*, 2d rev. ed. (New York: Asia Publishing House, 1967), p. 302. See also *Area Handbook for India*, Foreign Area Studies Division, American University (Washington, D.C.: Government Printing Office, 1970), esp. chap. 13.
23. Pylee, op. cit., p. 61.
24. For more comprehensive information on the succession of Five-Year Plans see Government of India, *India 1969* (New Delhi: Publications Division, Ministry of Information and Broadcasting), chap. 14, "Planning."
25. Ibid., p. 189.
26. Ibid., p. 235. A block generally comprises one hundred villages with an area of 390–520 square kilometers and a population sixty to seventy thousand. A district is an administrative unit of the state, varying in size and population. By 1967 the Panchayati Raj had been established in all but four of the Indian states.
27. See William Riker's review of "Six Books in Search of a Subject or Does Federalism Exist and Does It Matter?" *Comparative Politics* 2 (November, 1969), 135–46. Riker takes a dim view of "the rather trivial constitutional structure" of federalism. As he views it, what counts is the political and economic culture and, however useful the fictions that federal unions solve the problems of diversity, "we should not overlook the fact that it is fiction." He concludes that federalism makes hardly any difference to the way that people are governed. Do you think that the people of the United States would be willing to give up the fiction of federalism for a more effective unitary government?

FURTHER READING

CARTER, GWENDOLEN M., ed. *National Unity and Regionalism in Eight African States.* Ithaca: Cornell University Press, 1966.

DUCHACEK, IVO D. *Comparative Federalism: The Territorial Dimension of Politics.* New York: Holt, Rinehart & Winston, 1970.

EARLE, VALERIE, ed. *Federalism: Infinite Variety in Theory and Practice.* Itasca, Ill.: Peacock Publishers, 1968.

EASTON, DAVID. *A Framework for Political Analysis.* Englewood Cliffs, N.J.: Prentice-Hall, 1965.

LIVINGSTON, W. *Federalism and Constitutional Change.* New York: Clarendon, 1956.

chapter 10

HOW ARE NATION STATES ORGANIZED INSTITUTIONALLY?

Explaining how a political system works is a bit like trying to explain what makes an automobile go. The dictionary definition of an automobile mentions only the internal combustion engine. But many different and intricate parts are required to make a car move—the key, the battery, the gear shift, the transmission, the drive shaft, the four wheels, the steering wheel, and, of course, the driver. The operator's manual says, "Before moving off, check the fuel, the brakes, the lights, the oil level in the engine, and the tire inflation pressures." It is a complicated business trying to explain what makes a car go, but not nearly so difficult as trying to explain how a political system really works. An automobile will not move until each part performs its particular function and unless the various parts are synchronized and intermeshing. Similarly, the political process (the system at work) is a complex of organized and interacting patterns of behavior that we call "institutions."

National governments are organized in many different ways (just as there are many different automobile models—big cars, small cars, family sedans, station wagons, sports cars, trucks, and jeeps). Nevertheless every modern state possesses a definite political structure (every car has its chassis), and certain governmental institutions, namely, an executive, a legislature, courts, and a bureaucracy. Such institutions are not discrete units; their activities are interlocked in the whole political process, but each has developed specific functions. We turn to our twelve states for specific examples of how

USA, the State of the Union message
(United Press International)

the executive, the legislature, the courts, and the bureaucracy act—and interact—in modern government.

THE EXECUTIVE

The executive is the oldest and most universal political institution. The authority of the state is symbolically vested in the executive. In the protocol of international relations the head of state is the only official spokesman for his countrymen, the only government figure who has the legal authority to make binding commitments for the nation. In the typology of governments we still make our primary distinctions on the basis of how the head of state is recruited. If the head of state occupies his position by virtue of hereditary right, we call that a "monarchy." If he (she) is co-opted (chosen by peers), or popularly elected, we call that a "republic."

In 1787, when the United States was established as a federal republic, it was almost unique among the nations of the world, which everywhere were ruled by emperors, kings, or princes. But today there are few monarchs in the world. Among our twelve states, we have two constitutional monarchies, the United Kingdom and Japan. Time was when most monarchs claimed to rule by divine right, but constitutional monarchies are now secularized and legitimized by the law of the land. Though Queen Elizabeth and Emperor Hirohito are heads of state by hereditary right, they both have constitutional status, implicit in the case of Queen Elizabeth since the United Kingdom has no written constitution and explicit in the case of Emperor Hirohito since his position is carefully defined in the Constitution of 1947. Both act as head of state in ceremonial occasions; each symbolizes the unity of the people; neither exercises any real authority in the political system.

Ten of our states are republics, that is, the head of state is chosen by direct or indirect election by the people. The head of state in a republic may be a titular executive; he may also be a working executive. The president of the United States, who is both head of state and head of government, exercises considerable leadership, influence, and authority in the making of policy. In India the president is the titular head of the state, but the prime minister is the working executive.

The head of government stands at the apex of authority in most political systems. In all twelve of our states the head of government holds an elective position in the government, which means that he (she) is responsible to the people for the major decisions taken and policies pursued by his (her) government. The head of government performs many important functions in the political system: he represents all the people, even though he may have reached office by partisan activity; he is the recognized leader of the government and is expected to participate in the formulation as well as the implementation of policy; he is the chief administrator and as such has responsibility for controlling and supervising the bureaucracy; he is the principal spokesman for the government and the people, and in that dual role he is continuously engaged in directing the traffic of communications between the governors and the governed.

Working executives reach their positions by various routes. In the United States the president seeks the office through party channels. He is nominated by his party, meeting in national convention and stands for election on a party platform. He is not, however, popularly elected. Under the Constitution the president is elected by a cumbersome constitutional device called an Electoral College. Each state is entitled to as many votes in the Electoral College as it has representatives and senators in the United States Congress. Under constitutional prescription, the voters in each state select their delegates to the Electoral College on the basis of party preference. If the majority of the voters in New York State prefer the Democratic candidate then New York delegates to the Electoral College will cast all of New York's votes for the Democratic candidate. If a majority of the voters in Iowa register their preference for the Republican candidate, then all of Iowa's votes in the Electoral College go to the Republican candidate. The Constitution requires that the winning candidate obtain a majority of votes in the Electoral College, and if no candidate gets a majority, then the selection of a president is left to the House of Representatives, which chooses from the top two candidates. The representatives then vote by states, and each state has but one vote. If the New York contingent of representatives in Congress is split, then the vote of New York is determined by the majority of representatives from New York. The Electoral College was invented by the Constitutional Convention of 1787 as a substitute for popular election, which many members of the Constitutional Convention deemed the worst of all possible ways of choosing a head of government. As a matter of fact, the Electoral College has come up with the requisite majority vote in every presidential election since 1824. But nearly half the presidents of the United States have failed to obtain a majority popular vote preceding the Electoral College decision.

In the United Kingdom the prime minister is the working executive, but unlike the president of the United States he himself is not chosen by a national electorate. He becomes prime minister because he is the designated leader of the majority party in Parliament. On June 18, 1970, the British electorate returned a majority of Conservative party members to the House of Commons. The 1970 elections turned out to be a surprise decision on the part of the electorate. Nevertheless the decision was quickly translated into a turnover in the government. On the day following the election, Prime Minister Harold Wilson, whose party (Labor) had suffered unexpected defeat at the polls, tendered his resignation as prime minister to the Queen. Twenty minutes later the Queen invited Edward Heath, leader of the Conservative party in the newly elected Parliament, to head the latest government. That same evening Prime Minister Heath moved into Number Ten Downing Street, the official residence for Britain's head of government.

In a parliamentary system an election which results in the defeat of the prime minister's party ushers in a new government under the party—or coalition of parties—which won the election. We have earlier pointed out that in the German elections of 1969, even though Chancellor Kurt Kiesinger's party, the CDU, won the largest number of seats in the Bundestag, Willy Brandt became the new chancellor because his party, the SPD, in coalition with the FDP, controlled a majority of votes in the Bundestag.

In a parliamentary government, a prime minister may be forced to resign if he loses the confidence of a working majority in parliament. For example, Turkish Prime Minister Suleyman Demirel had to resign when a substantial bloc of members from his own party, the Justice party, joined the opposition to defeat his 1970 Budget. In that instance, however, President Cevdet Sunay, cognizant that the Justice party possessed a working majority in the National Assembly, asked Demirel to reform his government. The new government then obtained a vote of confidence from a majority of the National Assembly, with some dissident members of the Justice party boycotting the vote. In presidential government, as in the United States, Mexico, and Colombia, if the president fails to obtain or retain support of a majority of members in congress, he does not resign. Conversely, if the congress resists presidential direction, it cannot be dissolved by presidential action and forced to stand elections as in parliamentary governments.

In one-party states, which profess to operate through representative institutions, it is sometimes difficult to identify the real head of government and the actual bearer of authority. In the Soviet Union, presumably the chairman of the Council of Ministers is the official head of government. The first secretary of the Communist party of the Soviet Union, however, wields the largest amount of power, but the chairman of the Presidium of the Supreme Soviet (president) is the head of state—or the representative figurehead.

As party secretary under Lenin, Stalin built the political machine which enabled him to consolidate his role as head of party and head of government after Lenin's death. Nikita Khrushchev followed a somewhat similar road to success. Ultimately, however, it was the Presidium of the Communist party (a group of influential men) that ousted Khrushchev from his official position as chairman of the Council of Ministers and his office as secretary of the party. What is more, Leonid Brezhnev, who had served as chairman of the Presidium of the Supreme Soviet (head of state)—a position considered purely a figurehead—emerged as first secretary of the party, with Alexei Kosygin as chairman of the Council of Ministers (head of government). This may well mark a trend in the role of the head of state in the USSR, which may mean that this is no longer a position filled by people who have been kicked upstairs.

In the Ivory Coast, Felix Houphouet-Boigny is president of the Republic and minister of economy, finance, defense, and agriculture. Unquestionably he is both head of state and head of government. He is the elected and re-elected president by overwhelming popular vote; he is also the unchallenged leader of his party, the only party in the country, the PDCI. Similarly, Jomo Kenyatta, president of Kenya, is head of state, head of government, and head of his party, the only party now in Kenya, the KADU. In both of these African states, however, despite the institutionalized executive modeled on the European parliamentary form, the charisma of the leader, the personal (and probably the tribal) relationships are more significant in mobilizing support for the head of government than the constitutional structure or the party activity.

The prime minister of India likewise depends more upon personal following than on institutional arrangements or party support. Despite the fact that Prime Minister Indira Gandhi was read out of the Congress party in the Indian Parliament, she has more than managed to hold her own. As prime minister, minister for atomic energy, minister for planning, and minister for external affairs, there is no doubt that she is the real head of the Indian government.

Table 10–1 gives us some general background information on the heads of governments of our twelve states in the decade of the 1960s. Note that two of the current heads of government are women—Indira Gandhi of India and Golda Meir of Israel; this is happenstance. If we had included 140 states in our study, we could have added only one more woman to the roster of heads of government, Mrs. Sirimavo Bandaranaike of Ceylon, who succeeded her late husband as prime minister. Of the thirty-five heads of governments in the 12 states of our study between 1960 and 1971 all but two attained their positions by regular constitutional elections. The two exceptions were in Turkey, both the results of army coups.

Among our thirty-five heads of government the median age was on the elderly side, sixty-seven years old. The span was from Chancellor Konrad Adenauer of the Federal Republic of Germany (born in 1876) to Prime Minister Suleyman Demirel of Turkey (born in 1924). All were uncommon persons, twenty-three were college and university graduates, two were products of military schools, two were products of industrial schools; only Ben Gurion of Israel had less than a high school education. Most of them were politicians or bureaucrats by profession.

THE LEGISLATURE

Compared to the executive, the legislature is a relative newcomer among political institutions. The British Parliament, prototype of the modern legislature, dates back to the thirteenth century when English kings began to summon with increasing frequency not only the great lords of the realm but also the knights from the counties and the burgesses from the towns to meet in representative assembly—to give the king counsel on such matters as he chose to present to them and to approve taxes for such enterprises as he had in mind. Only gradually did the Parliament at Westminster emerge as a great law-making institution. It is, in fact, difficult to pinpoint a date for the transition from advise and consent to authorize and appropriate; it began in the sixteenth century under the Tudors; it was well-advanced under the Stuarts, especially after Charles I was convicted of treason and beheaded for levying war against Parliament (1649). Parliamentary supremacy was already achieved at the end of the eighteenth century when the American colonists broke away from the mother country, partly on the grounds that they had been denied their fundamental rights as Englishmen—to be represented in the Parliament and to be taxed only by the consent of their representatives.

The Congress of the United States was patterned after the British Parliament as it existed in the third quarter of the eighteenth century. The British Parliament was bicameral because of the traditional separation of lords and commoners. The American Congress, however, was made bicameral in

TABLE 10–1
Heads of Government 1960–71

Country	*Type*	*Name*	*Term*	*Born*	*Sex*	*Schooling*	*Profession*	*Party*	*% of Vote † Elected*	*Year*
Colombia	president	Lleras Camarago	1958–62	1906	M	high school	journalist	Liberal	67	1958
		Valencia	1962–66	1909	M	university	diplomat	Cons.	64 ‡	1962
		Lleras Restrepo	1966–70	1908*	M	university	economist	Liberal	71 ‡	1966
		Pastrana Borrero	1970–74	1923	M	university	gov. official	Cons.	40 ‡	1970 §
Germany, F.R.	chancellor	Adenauer	1949–63	1876	M	university	politician	CDU	45	1961
		Erhard	1963–66	1897	M	university	gov. official	CDU	48	1965
		Kiesinger	1966–69	1904	M	university	lawyer	CDU	¶	¶
		Brandt	1969–	1913	M	some university	journalist	SPD	43	1969
India	prime minister	Nehru	1947–64	1889	M	university	lawyer	Congress	45	1957 1962
		Shastri	1964–67	1904	M	college	politician	Congress	¶	¶
		Gandhi	1967–	1917	F	university	social worker	Congress	48	1967
Israel	prime minister	Ben Gurion	1955–63	1896	M	grade school	independence ldr.	Mapai	45 ‡	1961
		Eshkol	1963–69	1895	M	high school	union leader	Mapai	55 ‡	1965
		Meir	1969–	1898	F	college	union & gov. official	Mapai	46 ‡	1969
Ivory Coast	president	Houphouet-Boigny	1960–	1905	M	med. schl.	gov. official	Démocratique	100 † 100 †	1965 1970
Japan	prime minister	Ikeda	1960–64	1899	M	university	gov. official	Lib.-Dem.	57	1960
		Sato	1964–	1901	M	university	gov. official	Lib.-Dem.	49	1967
Kenya	president	Kenyatta	1963–	1891	M	university	independence ldr.	KANU	100 †	1969

Mexico	president	Lopez Mateos	1958–64	1910	M	university	professor	PRI	90	1958
		Diaz Ordaz	1964–70	1911	M	college	gov. official	PRI	83	1964
		Escheverria	1970–76	1922	M	university	gov. official	PRI	85	1970 *
Turkey	prime minister	Gürsel	1960–61	1895	M	mil. college	army officer	none (military coup)		1960
		Inonu	1961–65	1884	M	mil. college	army officer	Rep. Peoples	42	1961
		Demirel	1965–	1924	M	university	engineer	Justice	53	1965
		Erim	1971–	1912	M	university	lawyer	Rep. Peoples appointed	47	1969
United Kingdom	prime minister	Macmillan	1957–63	1894	M	university	politician	Cons.	50	1959
		Douglas-Home	1963–64	1903	M	university	politician	Cons.	¶	¶
		Wilson	1964–70	1916	M	university	economist	Labor	44	1964
									48	1966
		Heath	1970–	1916	M	university	politician	Cons.	47	1970 *
United States	president	Eisenhower	1953–61	1890	M	mil. acad.	army officer	Rep.	55	1952
									57	1956
		Kennedy	1961–63	1917	M	university	politician	Dem.	50	1960
		Johnson	1963–69	1908	M	college	politician	Dem.	61	1964
		Nixon	1969–	1913	M	university	lawyer	Rep.	43	1968
USSR	premier	Khrushchev	1958–64	1894	M	indus. col.	party official	Comm.	100 †	1962
		Kosygin	1964–	1904	M	indus. col.	textile exec.	Comm.	100 †	1966
									100 †	1970

* Rounded off.
† Voting age lowered to eighteen.
‡ No opposition, a few blank ballots.
§ More than one party on a combined list (Labor Alignment in Israel, National Front in Colombia).
¶ No election during his tenure.

order to serve the federal system, the Senate providing equal representation of the states, the House representing the people of the states according to their numbers.

In addition to serving a class function as in the British Parliament or a federal function as in the United States, the bicameral legislature has a practical rationale. One house acts as a check upon the other, slowing up the policy process, giving people an opportunity to react to pending proposals for legislation, permitting the second house to receive feedback from public opinion on what transpired in the first house. On the other hand, as critics of the bicameral form point out, since the legislature as a representative institution is expected to act according to the will of the people, if one house is in conflict with the other, then one house must be out of tune with prevailing opinion; its check upon the other house becomes a deflection of public opinion. Among our twelve states, nine have adopted the bicameral legislature; three of the newest states, however, have established unicameral legislatures: the Knesset in Israel, the Assembly in the Ivory Coast, and the National Assembly in Kenya. (See Table 10–2).

In the British Parliament the lower chamber is the House of Commons; in the American Congress it is the House of Representatives; in India it is the House of the People. By whatever name it is known, the functions of the lower chamber are much the same in every state: to represent all the people, to legitimize government policy, to authorize the public expenditures, and to

TABLE 10–2
The Legislatures

	Exec.–Leg.	*Structure*	*Upper House*	*Lower House*
Colombia	presidential	bicameral	Senate	House of Representatives
Germany, FR	parliamentary	bicameral	Bundesrat	Bundestag
India	parliamentary	bicameral	Council of States	House of the People
Israel	parliamentary	unicameral	Knesset	
Ivory Coast	presidential	unicameral	National Assembly	
Japan	parliamentary	bicameral	House of Councillors	House of Representatives
Kenya	parliamentary	unicameral	National Assembly	
Mexico	presidential	bicameral	Senate	House of Representatives
Turkey	parliamentary	bicameral	Republican Senate	National Assembly
United Kingdom	parliamentary	bicameral	House of Lords	House of Commons
USA	presidential	bicameral	Senate	House of Representatives
USSR	parliamentary	bicameral	Soviet of Nationalities	Soviet of the Union

approve the levy of taxes. In all twelve states the members of the lower house (or the unicameral legislature) are directly elected by the people. As an institution it is rooted in the local communities and affords the most direct linkage between the people and the official policy-makers.

In most states, the upper chamber certainly does not imply the upper hand in power. The British House of Lords is still a highly aristocratic body; over eight hundred of its nine hundred members are hereditary peers (or peeresses). Not since 1911, however, has it been able to claim even formal legislative parity with the House of Commons. In 1909 the Lords had their last big fling when they rejected the Liberal (Lloyd George's) Budget. Out of that crisis came the Parliament Act of 1911 which gave the Lords one month to debate money bills and two years to consider other bills already passed by Commons. The Parliament Act of 1949 further reduced the Lords' power to delay legislation to one year.

In contrast, the Senate of the United States has become the most powerful second chamber in the world. It has equal power with the House of Representatives over all legislation and, although all money bills (revenue bills) must originate in the House, no bills can be enacted into law without the approval of the Senate down to the most minute detail, even to commas. The Senate, which sets its own rules of debate, acts as a forum for all the great issues of the day. (The House, which sets its own rules also, is too large in membership to indulge in unlimited debate.) In addition, by constitutional prescription, the Senate shares with the president powers of appointment for the principal offices in the national government (the president nominates but cannot make a major appointment without Senate approval). Also by constitutional prescription the Senate shares with the president the treaty-making power which the Senators broadly construe to cover the whole range of foreign policy. The term of the president is four years. He may be reelected for a second term, but his maximum time in office is eight years. The term of the Senator is six years, and he may be reelected indefinitely. Thus the Senators tend to serve the function of elder statesmen in the system. Chairmen of the standing Senate committees, who reach their positions by the rule of seniority (years of service in the Senate and on particular committees), often consider their judgments more experienced than those of the president—and accordingly are inclined to act independently of executive directions.

The Japanese Diet more nearly resembles the British Parliament than the American Congress, despite American influence in drafting the Constitution of 1947. The Diet is bicameral; the prime minister and most of the members of his cabinet are chosen from the House of Representatives (the lower house). The prime minister is always the designated leader of the majority party in the Diet. The Japanese upper house, the House of Councillors, was intended to be a living hall of fame. Two-fifths of the members are elected from the country at large; three-fifths are elected from broad constituencies, much larger than the electoral districts for the representatives. Many of the councillors represent nationwide interest groups such as farmers and businessmen; others are elected simply because they are well-known personalities, familiar names on the ballot; most of the councillors, however, like the representatives, are party politicians. Constitutionally, the two houses of the Diet have equal powers except for money bills and treaties, in which matters the representatives have the final decision if there is disagreement between the two houses.

EXECUTIVE–LEGISLATIVE RELATIONS

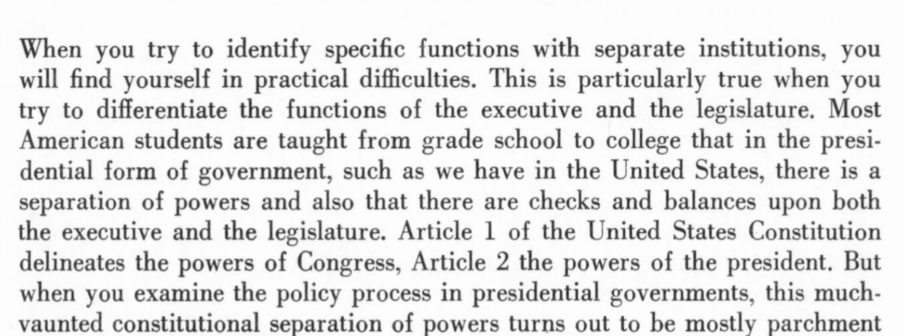

When you try to identify specific functions with separate institutions, you will find yourself in practical difficulties. This is particularly true when you try to differentiate the functions of the executive and the legislature. Most American students are taught from grade school to college that in the presidential form of government, such as we have in the United States, there is a separation of powers and also that there are checks and balances upon both the executive and the legislature. Article 1 of the United States Constitution delineates the powers of Congress, Article 2 the powers of the president. But when you examine the policy process in presidential governments, this much-vaunted constitutional separation of powers turns out to be mostly parchment barriers.

Article 1, Section 1 of the United States Constitution specifies that all legislative powers are granted to the Congress. Nowadays, however, most legislation does not originate in Congress. Congress rarely exercises initiative but rather sees its legislative function as one of reacting to executive proposals. Administration bills are usually given priority both in committees and in floor debates where congressmen feel quite free to criticize, amend, and even to reject presidential policies. If the Congress gives the president what he asks for, whether legislation authorizing certain policies or appropriations for particular programs, then we say that the Congress has legitimized executive policy. If the Congress fails to act upon presidential requests or refuses to make the necessary appropriations for implementation of his policies, then we say that the Congress is checking executive power. Political scientists, as well as professional politicians, frequently measure presidential leadership by keeping a box score on congressional reactions to administrative requests for legislation or appropriations.

When Congress enacts legislation, it is making law, but statutory law is only part of the great mass of laws that govern the behavior of American citizens. Executive orders, administrative rules and regulations, judicial decrees and court orders all have the force of law. Certainly law-making is one of the major activities of Congress, but it is not a distinctive activity. The executive, the bureaucrats, and the judges all make laws, or in the jargon of political science, "exercise rule-making authority." [1]

In parliamentary government the executive and the legislature are so interlocked that it is virtually impossible to differentiate their activities. In the United Kingdom, the Government refers to the members of Parliament who comprise the cabinet; the cabinet is the working executive; members of the cabinet are individually and collectively responsible to the Parliament for their official acts. As in the United States and in every modern government, the executive is expected to formulate as well as to implement policy. Parliament spends much of its time in consideration of legislative business, but it rarely has time for any bills introduced by private members. Nearly all bills are introduced by the prime minister or a member of his cabinet. Parliament may engage in spirited debate both on the principles and the details of a bill; the loyal opposition may be highly critical, but party discipline within the ranks of the majority party insures passing of the bill substantially as it was initially submitted by the government. The legislative function of the Parliament is certainly not its most significant activity, if we include in our concept of legislative function the initiation of policy and deliberation in decision-making.

We noted earlier that an original function of Parliament was to provide representation of the people in the financial policies of the realm. But today, as one noted authority on British politics observes, "the Government's control over finance is, if anything, even greater than its control over the parliamentary agenda."[2] Sometime in April every year, the chancellor of the Exchequer addresses the House of Commons on what is called "budget night." The budget is not only the government's statement of fiscal policies—of expenditures projected and revenues needed—but also a statement of the government's plans, policies, and program for the year to come. The House immediately passes all tax measures except one which it selects out just to keep open the channels for later debate. The House debates the proposed expenditures over a period of twenty-six days spaced out in the legislative calendar from April into the middle of the summer. The debates do not center on the budget itself but rather upon a wide range of peripheral matters. Unlike in the American Congress, the private members may not alter the government plans, change the government policies, or in any way amend the government's financial figures. It is clearly understood that a planned economy (and Britain is that whether under a Labour or Conservative government) cannot be subjected to the vagaries and uncertainties of decision-making in a large legislative body. The government can be so sure of the outcome of the parliamentary debate on the public finances, given the party discipline that is characteristic of both major parties, that it can go ahead with its programs even while members of Parliament are still venting the grievances of their various constituents and ostensibly debating the government's budget.

What then are the important functions, if any, of the British Parliament? It serves as a representative institution; its members are directly elected by the people and while the individual members are not tied as closely to their respective constituencies as are American congressmen who must be residents of the districts they represent, the British MP's do provide links of communication between the government and the various constituencies. The Parliament may not act as a deliberative and decision-making body, but it does offer a forum for debate on all the public issues. After public debate it enacts the legislation which the government requests and in doing so legitimates the government's activities. Individual members keep the government continuously on the alert by exercising their right to question members of the government on specific policies or programs, and Parliament itself may undertake more extensive investigations of administration. And finally, Parliament reserves its latent power to turn the government out of office if it fails to respond to persistent criticisms or mounting opposition, both in Parliament and in the public arena.

One function of the legislature is basically the same in democratic and in totalitarian governments, in modern states and in developing nations: The legislature is a representative institution calling to the attention of the government the spectrum of interests and changing demands of the people. The Soviet Union held its general elections in 1970 the same week as the British elections. The turnout was considerably more impressive. More than 150 million citizens, virtually all citizens over eighteen, went to the polls to choose the members of the Supreme Soviet, the bicameral legislature of the USSR. The vote was 99.74 percent in favor of the slate prepared by the Communist party, the only slate presented to the voters. Despite the absence of any real choice in the elections, the Supreme Soviet is a fairly representative body; 50.3 percent of the deputies are workers and collective farmers; 30.5 percent are women; 18.5 percent are under thirty years of age; 72.3 percent are members of the Communist party. By comparison, how representative is the competitively elected United States Congress, with respect to blue-collar workers, dirt farmers, women, and youth?

The Supreme Soviet, however, has no legislative function. It does not originate or control its own agenda. It does not deliberate or make any political decisions on its own. It simply listens to (and applauds) the government's statements of plans, policies, and programs and thus offers a forum for government propaganda. Finally, and swiftly, it legitimates the government's activities with rubber-stamp approval. The important thing about the Supreme Soviet is that it does exist, it is elected, and in order to give the impression of massive popular consensus the Communist party makes up its slate with patent attention to the diversity of local and community interests to be subsumed in the national interest, through the institution of representation.

How the national legislature is actually used in the less-developed states depends largely on the degree of political socialization. Tutelary democracy under Atatürk seems to have served its purpose in Turkey. The Turkish National Assembly is by no means a rubber stamp for the government, not even for the government's budget, as its rejection of Prime Minister Demirel's 1970 Budget demonstrates. In the Ivory Coast where President Houphouet-Boigny's party (PDCI) has a monopoly on all seats in the Assembly, the government encounters no overt criticism or opposition. President Houphouet-Boigny is a shrewd politician who handpicks the members of his cabinet in consultation with various strata in the country outside the Assembly. In 1970, for example, he reorganized his cabinet to accommodate more representatives of youth and labor. Despite his hard-line policy toward left-wing student agitation (the government closed down the University of Abidjan and broke off diplomatic relations with the Soviet Union for its alleged part in 1969 student demonstrations), Houphouet-Boigny has tried to bring more young people into the government. The average age of his cabinet officers is about forty, considerably younger than the average age of President Nixon's cabinet.

An American political scientist points out the ambivalent status of members of Kenya's National Assembly. President Jomo Kenyatta, addressing the legislators in 1964, asserted, "Members of Parliament must serve as a bridge between Government and the people." [3] In Kenyatta's opinion the legislators have an obligation so to interpret government policies to their constituents as to mobilize popular support for government activities. Even though Kenya is a one-party state, members of the National Assembly do not consider it part of their legislative function to drum up support for the government; to the contrary, legislative debates are often highly critical of government policies.

Kenyatta's party, the KANU, is not well-disciplined (as in Houphouet-Boigny's PDCI). It has few rewards to offer the party faithful, few penalties to impose on the government's critics. Individual legislators regard representation of their constituents as their most important legislative function, representation not so much in the making of general policy as in presenting concrete and specific demands or in venting particular grievances from local communities and/or tribal groups. The government in its turn is not bound by legislative motions and is inclined to ignore many of them which are either obstructive or irrelevant to the plans and policies pursued by the government. Kenya then is still in an early stage of tutelary democracy: the government is dominated by the strong personality of the president; all important decisions are made by the government, which tolerates but scarcely responds to critics in the legislature; the legislators themselves have no focal interest in policy-making except to protect and advance the local and communal interests which they represent.

THE COURTS

General Functions of the Judiciary

Judicial institutions—the courts—perform the same basic functions in every modern state. They hear and decide disputes: between private persons, between society and individuals, between government agencies, between public officials and private citizens. Whereas the executive and the legislature make decisions that affect people generally, the courts make decisions that affect particular persons. When the executive or the legislature exercises rule-making authority, the norm of political behavior is presumably the public interest, what the people need, or demand, or will support. But when the courts engage in adjudication, the rule of law which they apply is presumably based on concepts of justice, what is right according to the conscience of the community, rather than what is politically popular or expedient.

The institutional arrangements for the performance of judicial functions are much the same in every modern state. Most court systems are established in a three-level hierarchy: the trial courts in the local community, a tier of regional appeals courts, and a national Supreme Court to render final judgment. The United States has the most complicated territorial arrangements for the administration of justice of any of our twelve states—a national hierarchy with three levels and fifty different and separate state hierarchies, again each with three levels. The national hierarchy is established under the national Constitution; the state courts are organized and operate quite independently under their respective state constitutions. The Supreme Court of the United States takes cases on appeal from the state courts, but only after the highest court in the state has rendered judgment and only if there is a question of constitutional law involved.

Other federal states in our sample—India and the USSR—have not followed the American precedent. Each has preferred an integrated system of national and state courts. The drafters of the Indian Constitution considered a supreme court an essential part of a federal system, "at once the highest interpreter of the Constitution and a tribunal for the final determination of disputes between the Union and its constituent units." [4] The Indian Supreme Court not only decides cases and controversies, but unlike the Supreme Court of the United States, it is also authorized to advise the president of India on any questions of public importance which he (or she) may choose to submit for a judicial opinion. The judges of the Supreme Court are appointed by the president in consultation with the chief justice of the Supreme Court and also with the judges of the high courts of the states. Every state in India has a high court; but, unlike the United States, the high courts are organized and the judges appointed according to specifications in the Union Constitution. The judges of the high courts are appointed by the president of India after consultation with the chief justice of India, the governor of the state, and the chief justice of the High Court concerned. For purposes of judicial administration each state is divided into districts with a hierarchy of courts under a district judge who is appointed by the governor of the state in consultation with the judges of the High Court. All judges in the district courts, except the district judge, are recruited by competitive examinations, as for the civil service. We are told that, "except for minor local variations, the structure and functions of the subordinate courts are uniform through the country." [5]

Judges are recruited in various ways, but everywhere judges are expected to have a professional competence—to be learned in the law. In the United Kingdom, judges are appointed by the crown, which in practice means by the prime minister and the lord chancellor. British judges are generally recruited from the category of lawyers called "barristers." (There is a sharp distinction, social as well as professional, between the barrister who is qualified to appear as an advocate in court and the solicitor who does the paperwork in the law office. Barristers are most likely to be products of private schools and Oxbridge and to come from one of the ancient Inns of Court in London which prepare candidates for the bar.) The British make almost a fetish of the majesty of the law, as symbolized by wigs and gowns still worn by barristers and judges in court to distinguish them from ordinary citizens.

In India, which has modeled its judiciary after the British, judges of the Union Supreme Court are customarily appointed from the judges of the high courts, and judges of the high courts are usually drawn from the district judges. All of these judges, as in the United Kingdom, must be qualified to practice before the bar and in addition must have had years of experience as advocates. In the Federal Republic of Germany, judges are initially recruited for judicial careers much like other civil servants. They are specially trained in the law, they must pass rigorous qualifying examinations, and they must submit to a lengthy period of probation before they can be appointed to serve on one of the trial courts. Appointment to the appellate courts, even to the Federal High Court, is by promotion only from the lower levels of the judiciary.

In both the United States and the Soviet Union, although judges are expected to be professionally qualified, their appointments are usually well-seasoned with politics. All of the federal judges in the United States are appointed by the president with the consent of the Senate, and as might be expected party politics has much to do both with the president's nomination and the Senate's confirmation. In the Soviet Union, factory groups or apartment residents may organize comradely courts and choose judges from their own membership to settle their local disputes. Judges of the people's courts (local trial courts) are popularly elected, but all appellate court judges are appointed by legislative bodies. The Supreme Soviet of the USSR chooses the judges of the Supreme Court of the USSR, and each Union Republic Soviet chooses the judges for its Union Republic Court.

According to the Anglo-American rule of law, all persons are subject to the law and none is exempt. Hence, both in the United States and in the United Kingdom, public officials are sued or prosecuted in the ordinary courts. Some countries, however, have established special courts, administrative courts, to settle disputes between public officials and private citizens. In Germany, citizens with claims against state and local government or with complaints about the activities of public agencies bring their suits into state administrative courts. Judges for these administrative courts are usually recruited from administrative positions rather than the professional judiciary. The Federal Administrative Court, established under the Basic Law, hears disputes arising out of actions by federal agencies and also hears cases on appeal from state administrative courts if a federal question is involved. There are also a number of special federal administrative courts such as the Federal Labor Court and the Federal Social Court which consider problems in connection with labor administration or administration of social security or public welfare laws.

The Ivory Coast follows the French practice of separate courts for administrative law. The Administrative Section of the Supreme Court handles cases of alleged abuse of administrative power. Whether bureaucrats should be treated differently than ordinary citizens can be argued either way. The Anglo-American concept of due process of law requires public officials to take their chances like ordinary citizens in the regular courts. Advocates of the German or French practice point out that separate administrative courts are more easily accessible to private citizens and are intended not so much to give special consideration to the public officials as to protect the citizens against an overzealous or arbitrary bureaucracy.

In the Soviet Union, the Procuracy performs an important dual function in the judicial and administrative institutions. Headed by a procurator general appointed by the Supreme Soviet, the Procuracy is a special unit in the Union bureaucracy whose job is to check the legality of all judicial actions and to investigate complaints of administrative abuses of power. It is an agent of the central government, a kind of watchdog over the local authorities to see that the judges are actually administering justice and that officials are abiding by the rules of law. Harold Berman, recognized authority on Soviet justice, gives a high rating to the Procuracy for its activity in checking abuses of human rights in a totalitarian society.[6]

Judicial Review: A Special Function of the Courts

Judges in the United States have a very special function, that of judicial review. Since all laws in the United States must be in pursuance of the Constitution (which defines itself as "the supreme law of the land"), all judges have the duty of adjudicating disputes involving constitutional law. The exercise of judicial review is a very sensitive political assignment, for the words and phrases of the Constitution—most of them written in the eighteenth century—cannot be strictly construed in contemporary situations. Does a urinalysis for narcotic addiction violate the constitutional prohibition against self-incrimination? Does the guarantee of equal protection of the laws cover the exclusion of Jewish students from some fraternities, or Blacks from some labor unions, or women from quota systems in professional schools? Does congressional legislation regulating radio and television come under the power to regulate commerce among the states or does it abridge freedom of the press? These and a multitude of other complicated controversies are brought into courts for the judges to decide. Most of the great public issues in American history have at one time or another been framed as questions in constitutional law and have been brought to the Supreme Court for authoritative decisions: national-state relationships, government-business conflicts, labor-management disputes, majority-versus-minority rights, national security versus individual liberties. Once the Supreme Court has made its decision the question is finally answered—until the court reverses its own judgment or the Constitution itself is amended.

When the Supreme Court exercises judicial review it not only settles the case before it, it functions as a political instrument. If it finds that the act in question (be it a statute, an executive order, or an administrative regulation) was constitutional, then it legitimates the policy. If the court decides that the act was unconstitutional, then it declares the act null and void and in so doing checks the power of the Congress, or the president, or the administrative agency. In exercising their judgment, the judges are expected to examine the text of the Constitution, refer to previous interpretations, and reason from analogy, but even so, they enjoy considerable latitude in reaching their decision. Over the years, the people of the United States (and the political branches of the government) have come to accept judicial review as necessary and proper for constitutional government.

Among our twelve states, several have followed the American precedent in giving the courts the final decision on questions of constitutionality, notably the Latin American countries, Germany and Japan, whose postwar constitutions were written under American influence. In Colombia, the Supreme Court of Justice "is entrusted with the guardianship of the integrity of the Constitution." In Germany, the ordinary judges do not have the power of judicial review, but a special constitutional court rules on questions arising out of the basic law. In Turkey a special constitutional court "checks whether the laws and House-keeping regulations of the Turkish Grand National Assembly are reconcilable with the Constitution." But in none of these states do the ordinary judges, or the judges of the constitutional courts, have anything like the political power of the Supreme Court of the United States. In most countries judges occupy prestigious positions because they are politically independent and at the same time discreet about jumping into what Justice Felix Frankfurter used to call "the political thicket." Judges can usually avoid getting tangled in political issues simply by deciding that the controversy is not justiciable, that is, not amenable to an established rule of law.

In the United Kingdom the judges are highly regarded and enjoy a great deal of political independence. They also exercise considerable political power by virtue of the latitude they possess in statutes or administrative regulations in specific cases. But British judges cannot declare an act of Parliament unconstitutional. Similarly, in the Soviet Union the courts have an important job to do in the political system—they adjudicate disputes—but they do not presume to legitimate or to check the political branches of the government.

Political Justice

In every country the laws which the judges interpret in the settlement of private disputes or public controversies reflect the norms of political justice as well as the social and cultural values of the ruling elite. In the USSR, for example, Russian courts, like all other agencies in the Soviet system, serve as instruments of the Communist party. In the Stalinist era special federal courts were used as highly effective instruments to purge the government and the party apparatus of persons whose behavior or attitudes did not conform to the standards of those in power. Turkish judges performed a similar service for the National Unity Committee, the military junta which overthrew the government in 1960. After a mass trial lasting nearly a year, the judges found the president, the prime minister, and hundreds of lesser officials of the preceding regime guilty of all kinds of offenses against the state. Three were hanged, including former Prime Minister Menderes, and many were sentenced to long terms in prison.

In the United States the courts are not expected to serve quite so firmly as instruments of the party in power. It is only fair to observe, however, that the president normally regards judicial appointments as rewards or patronage for his party. A new administration is always eager to make its own appointments to the Supreme Court. The fact that President Franklin D. Roosevelt was unable to make a single appointment to the Supreme Court in his first administration is one reason why his New Deal foundered in the courts. The extraordinary difficulty that President Nixon had in trying to fill a vacancy on the Supreme Court in the first two years of his administration was largely due to the fact that the other party, which controlled the Senate, was determined to delay the appointments as long as possible. To the extent that the United States has an official ideology, judges are expected to expound it from the bench—the American way of life, private enterprise, and the principles of constitutional democracy. Similarly, Russian judges illuminate Soviet norms and reflect the Communist ideology—the socialist economy, public ownership of the means of production, and the collective obligations of the private citizen. In every country, the body of laws is the product of the political system—albeit the political system itself is conditioned by the culture and norms of the people.

Judges are expected to interpret the laws of the land according to traditional and acceptable concepts of justice. It is equally important that judges not only do justice but that the people recognize that justice is done. As early as the twelfth century in England, several centuries before Parliament began to function as a legislature, the King's Court was institutionalized as the fountain of justice. The king designated members of his court not only to hear disputes at Westminster but also to ride on circuit and to dispense justice in the local communities in the name of the king. Lacking any body of statutory law, these early judges simply made their decisions as a reasonable man would think just, drawing from custom, canon (church) law, and Roman law. Gradually the judges developed the great common law of England, building it slowly upon precedents. When we examine the origins of British nationalism, we discover that common law is one of the principal ingredients, for the very reason that the rule of law embodied the people's own sense of justice.

Long years later, when English colonists settled in North America, they brought their common law with them. And again, when we look for the roots of early American nationalism, we find the common law in Massachusetts and Virginia, New York and Georgia—judge-made law accommodating to different and changing conditions overseas but still keeping continuity with customs and traditions of the mother country. In British India and Kenya, the British colonial administration imposed the English rule of law upon people with very different customs and values than those understood and accepted by Englishmen. Nevertheless the notion of a common law with justice for all was instrumental in helping to integrate caste-ridden India and tribal-torn Kenya. As each of the British colonies became independent the courts provided a ready-made stabilizing institution. Judge-made law could (and would) be adjusted to the native customs and values and gradually become an indigenous common law. Meanwhile, however, the new national legislatures could take their time in adding whatever statutory law appeared necessary to move the new nation more quickly toward its own goals.

In each of our twelve states we discover that the courts are universally regarded as instruments of justice where citizens may claim their rights and seek redress from wrongs according to the traditional norms of the people. Even in Russia, when the Bolsheviks established their revolutionary government, they continued to utilize a court system rather than martial rule. The procedural guarantees as well as the substance of the laws were drastically altered by soviet government and socialist values. And certainly the introduction of elected lay judges to sit with the professional judges in every court was an innovation that created a revolutionary atmosphere in the old courtrooms. Nevertheless the courts provided a reassuring continuity in government even while the system itself was undergoing radical change.

At the outset the Bolsheviks found it expedient to retain a regular set of courts for routine cases in civil and criminal law and to establish a new set of revolutionary tribunals to administer political justice, that is, to liquidate the enemies of the proletariat. In the Stalinist era special federal courts still handled cases concerned with internal security. The mass trials of the late 1930s fulfilled their function—to punish and to deter political deviation—with much publicity. But all civil disputes and most cases in criminal law were reserved to the regular courts in the republics and disposed of in routine fashion. Following Stalin's death all of the special courts were abolished except the military tribunals, which still have jurisdiction over cases involving the armed services or charges of espionage brought against civilians. It is noteworthy that the coup of 1966 in which Nikita Khrushchev was ousted from office was not accompanied by any mass political trials. Khrushchev himself was treated to a comfortable rest cure in the country. The Communist party leadership was sufficiently sure of its position in the soviet system that it could afford to retire rather than execute its former chairman.

The law of the land stems from the mores of the people, their social customs, and in some countries from their religious beliefs even more than from political prescription. Israel has institutionalized the dichotomy between secular and religious law. Separate religious courts rule on matters of personal status such as marriage, divorce, and alimony—rabbinical courts for Jews, *Shau'a* for the Muslims, and other special courts for the Druzes and Christians.

The regular courts in Israel include magistrates' courts in the major towns that deal with small money claims, misdemeanors (less serious criminal charges), and other minor local controversies. District courts hear all cases in civil law (cases between private litigants) and in criminal law (where the state is prosecuting for offenses against the state). A Supreme Court hears appeals from the district courts and also sits as a high court of justice for citizens who seek redress against the government. Earlier in this book we discussed a recent case before the High Court of Justice—the case of a father seeking redress for his children who could not be classified as Jews under administrative rules. The High Court upheld the father's contention that the children, native-born citizens of Israel, should be considered Jews, whatever their religion (in this instance, lack of religion). The reaction of Orthodox Jews to the High Court's decision was so vociferous and disapproving that the government quickly responded to the judicial decision and reaffirmed its support for rabbinical law by reviewing and tightening up its legal perquisites for Jewishness in line with rabbinical law.

In the very large states, like India, the Soviet Union, and the United States, where the population is heterogeneous and dispersed over vast territory, the law of the land is bound to have diverse connotations reflecting the pluralist character of the nation. The trial courts at the local level dispense justice with an eye to the norms of attitude and behavior in the community. The fifty-state court system in the United States, each with its own rule of law, is designed to take into account the diverse values of the people, in Alaska, Texas, Hawaii, Mississippi, Massachusetts, and Iowa. Even in the Soviet Union where the courts are subject to detailed supervision and control from above and where the law itself is completely subservient to Communist ideology, judges at the local level enjoy considerable independence. The people's courts, which adjudicate everyday disputes, are manned by an elected judge who has some professional training and two elected lay assessors. Proceedings are informal, sometimes turning into shouting matches; the decisions are by majority vote, following public argument among the judges. In such courts one expects the custom of the community to prevail, tempered, of course, by the thought that the central Procuracy might question a judgment not up to party standards.

In all twelve of our countries, courts are (more or less) deliberately disconnected from the political institutions in order to stress the impartiality and independence of judicial function. On the other hand, the courts cannot function at all except in connection with the legislature and the executive. Courts must count on the legislature to appropriate whatever funds are necessary for judicial expenditures and depend upon the executive to enforce judicial decisions. Moreover, the courts cannot initiate any business on their own; they can only adjudicate the cases which the government or private litigants choose to bring into court.

THE BUREAUCRACY

The modern state is what political scientist Frederick C. Mosher calls "the professional state."[7] The professional state functions mainly through the bureaucracy, institutionalized specialization. The governmental bureaucracy is responsible for implementing decisions made by the political and judicial branches of the government for carrying on all the manifold activities of the modern state.

Theory and Practical Variations

When we look at governmental bureaucracies in a comparative framework, we find it useful to refer to the Weberian model. Max Weber, a German sociologist in the early part of the twentieth century, constructed an abstract model of bureaucracy, which Weber himself admitted could not be replicated in reality. Nevertheless, the mental construct helps us to analyze and understand similarities—and dissimilarities—in the bureaucracies of our twelve states.

We define bureaucracy as that part of the political system which is organized to carry out the public policies. Bureaucratic structure usually includes four characteristic features:

1 *a hierarchial organization:* The offices in the government are arranged in a pyramidal form, with the lines of authority running from apex to base, each lower office responsible to and supervised by the next higher office.
2 *a functional organization:* The organization of each agency, ministry, and office is based on specific assignment of tasks. Every position is classified

according to the tasks it performs, and recruitment to the position is based on the qualifications and competencies requisite for that particular position.

3 *professional management:* An administrative staff with requisite qualifications and skills provides professional management for the big organizations performing specialized functions.

4 *institutionalized procedures:* Rules and regulations are formulated to prevent capricious or arbitrary decision; records are made and filed so that the ongoing activities maintain continuity with past experience and plans projected.

In the Weberian model, the bureaucracy is politically neutral, carrying out the public policies regardless of which party is currently in power. In highly developed states the model is fairly descriptive. Germany, Weber's own state, is a particularly good example of how the bureaucracy managed to carry on governmental activities despite great tensions and upheavals in the system as a whole. Thousands of German bureaucrats conducted the public business with remarkable continuity in the transitions from the German Empire to the Weimar Republic, from the Weimar Republic to the Third Reich, through the period of postwar military occupation, and into today's Federal Republic.

The contacts of the private citizen with the bureaucracy ordinarily come at the base of the organization with subprofessional and unskilled personnel: social security clerks, tax collectors, mailmen, nurses in the public health centers, food inspectors in the canneries and packing houses, customs inspectors searching baggage for extra fifths and Paris postcards, secretaries and receptionists. On the other hand, the executive officers and the legislators meet with the top administrators and the professional elite. The *Executive Inventory* for the national government of the United States comprises around thirty thousand managerial and professional positions in a bureaucracy that includes some three million government workers.[8] When we discuss the functions of the bureaucracy in the policy process, we refer principally to that 1 percent of government personnel who have an influential, even decisive, part in the making of public policy.

Public policies in the modern state—national security, pollution control, public health, industrial development, agricultural planning, social security, public education—all call for a great deal of expertise both in formulation and in implementation. Bureaucrats at the top of the administrative hierarchy are expected to provide the executive and the legislature with their counsel and assistance at every stage in the policy process from planning to programming.

In modern governments a professionally disciplined bureaucracy is expected to carry on the day-to-day activities of the government regardless of which party happens to be in power. In the United States, Japan, or the United Kingdom, where a change in party government is not likely to provoke any radical change in the government, bureaucrats are regarded as public servants, the civil service, providing continuous direction and oversight for on-going governmental programs. But in countries which experience drastic or violent changes in constitutional authority, bureaucrats may enjoy a higher political status, comparable to public officials. This is particularly evident in the new nations emerging from colonialism to independence in the 1950s and 1960s where the bureaucrats provided the experience and expertise in public administration which the political leaders themselves lacked.

Carl J. Friedrich notes that bureaucrats in any government tend to cultivate certain behavioral traits, "among these the most important are objectivity, discretion, precision, and consistence." [9] The professional discipline and behavioral traits of the bureaucrats must, however, be viewed in the cultural and political context of each state. In the Soviet Union, for example, because the Communist party completely controls the governmental operations, Russian bureaucrats can hardly demonstrate much objectivity or discretion; consistency, yes, consistency with Communist directives. Similarly, civil servants in the United States cannot be hired, and they may be fired, if they hold disloyal views, that is, views not consistent with the American creed. In the United States there is much ado over conflict of interests; the American bureaucrat is forbidden to use his official position to enhance his private interests. But in some cultures the compounding of private and public interest may be regarded with much more tolerance.

When we were establishing our overall frame of reference for this book, we asked information officers and country specialists to give us their impression of the status of bureaucrats in each state. Admittedly the capsules in each nstance reflect one man's view—another information officer or country specialist might have given us a different view. Here are a few quotes:

> *In Colombia, education is reserved for children of the oligarchy who go to the Colombian universities, travel and study in Europe, especially France and Spain, and more recently in the Soviet Union and East Europe, and finally go home to claim a top job in the bureaucracy, a status symbol as well as a job. There are more bureaucrats than children of the oligarchy, of course, but the oligarchy has a monopoly at the top.*

> *An essential feature of the German civil service that has existed for donkey's years is the absence of all kinds of patronage in the appointment of officials. The German civil service is recruited today from all classes of the population, the selection made according to suitability, talent, and expert knowledge. No consideration is paid to sex, origin, race, religion, political convictions, or political connections.*

> *Political mobility in Mexico depends largely on ability. Party leaders and top bureaucrats are recruited generally from the universities; PRI scouts are always on the watch for active and talented students. The law requires competitive exams for the civil service but the powers that be (the PRI) decide who gets the top jobs.*

> *Turkish bureaucrats run the show. The universities of Ankara and Istanbul furnish the bureaucrats for the government; they are prone to be legalistic, class-conscious, very proud of being bureaucrats. They have an important role in formulating decisions as well as in implementation.*

Prime Minister Wilson was touted as an economist, a bureaucrat who had know-how; expectations ran too high. Bureaucrats rose to political position in the Labour government but the government returned policy initiatives to the bureaucrats.

Israel is egalitarian in outlook. Salary levels in the civil service are based on the number of dependents, and there is no great spread in civil service pay schedules from bottom to top. The civil service is still recruited largely from "the old group" (mostly East Europeans born abroad). Children of the recent immigrants (from North Africa and Asia) will have to go through the Israeli schools before they are prepared for participation in government.

The bureaucracy of the Ivory Coast is French style, centralized administration with the French much in evidence. The civil service has a merit system in principle but the top administrators are mostly French or products of French universities.

In Japan, the cabinet, chosen from the majority in the Diet, is theoretically the highest decision-making body but in practice this is qualified by the power of the bureaucrats. The top bureaucrats are products of the Japanese universities and maintain close ties with their former professors. The bureaucracy is closely interlocked with the universities.

Kenya has a regular civil service on the British model, now largely native. Training bureaucrats is still a major problem; the United States has given some technical assistance.

Soviet bureaucrats are not so important in terms of influence. Policy changes are made at the top with not much initiative left to the governmental machinery. Absolute trivia may go to the Politburo for decision; it issues many directives on small matters. Scientists and technologists are extremely favored in the system but they are cynical about party rule; most of them do not support the party ideology but support the system that favors them. Hard scientists are not required to show ideological conformity so long as they do not agitate. What they produce in the lab determines their importance. Unimportant scientists or technicians have less leeway.

The United States has a classified civil service open to all persons regardless of sex, race, color, religion, or political affiliations. Two-thirds of the top bureaucrats who appear in the Executive Inventory *have spent more than twenty years in the federal service but more than half have been in and out of government employment at least once. More than four-fifths of them have at least one college degree and more than half hold degrees at the master's level or higher.*

When we take an overall view of these separate impressions, several themes recur throughout: The stage of political development is important; the degree of egalitarianism, or class-consciousness, is reflected in recruitment to the civil service; the kind of party system, competitive or totalitarian, affects the behavioral patterns of the bureaucrats. But the single factor which appears to predominate in every state is the interlocking relationship between the bureaucracy and the academic community. The universities provide the specialized knowledge and the professional training which, in effect, determines the qualifications and standards of performance for position classification in the professional state. Continuing contacts and consultative arrangements between the bureaucrats and their academic mentors furthers the influence of the academic community upon the policy process, especially in the planning stage.

In the more advanced states the government bureaucracy can draw from a large and continuously replenishing reservoir of administrative talent, technical skills, and specialized competencies. Recruitment is mainly a matter of articulation between the government personnel offices, the professional associations, and the academic community. (Attracting and retaining high-grade personnel also, of course, calls for compensation and fringe benefits in the public service competitive with those prevailing in private employment.) Among the less-developed states, however, the bureaucracy is perhaps the most vulnerable institution in the political system simply because the available academic resources—facilities and instruction—are not adequate to meet the urgent needs of a modernizing government.

Because the bureaucracy subsumes the entire policy process, recruitment of highly qualified personnel in the public service is crucial to government operations in every state. Among our twelve states, the Western European states—the United Kingdom and the Federal Republic of Germany—have a long tradition of professional career service with appointments based on educational qualifications, a strict testing system, and promotions determined by experience and merit within the service. In both countries career service in the government is regarded as a prestigious occupation. Those who rise to the top of the service comprise a solid core of influence and power within the system. Their advice and consent are virtually prerequisite to any important policy decisions in the government.

Bureaucracy and Nation-Building

Enlisting a well-qualified bureaucracy for new and developing political systems is a different story.[10] In the USSR when the Bolsheviks first came to power, Lenin indicated that the whole administrative apparatus of the czarist regime would have to be liquidated and replaced by an organization of the proletariat. But it was soon apparent that even a revolutionary government needs to operate in a routine way, public administration has to be regularized, and public policies on a large scale cannot be planned or put into operation without managerial, technical, and specialized assistance. Hence Lenin's government fell back on the old bureaucracy to carry on government activities, while taking measures to insure if not the political loyalty, at least the traditional neutrality of the civil service.

Perhaps the greatest single problem which the Communists faced in trying to establish the new soviet system was that of recruiting trained and experienced workers capable of undertaking managerial and technical tasks required for the planned industrialization of the country.[11] As early as the 1930s the Soviet leadership determined to create a new technical intelligentsia —scientists, engineers, skilled workers, and professional managers. As we have indicated earlier in this book, the central government set up the requisite technical institutes and provided for appropriate training in the universities. Massive reforms throughout the entire educational system combining positive socialist indoctrination with training for an industrial culture made it possible for the government to build a modern bureaucracy prepared to assist the Soviet leadership in achieving a super-industrial state.

A bureaucracy needs to be educated and trained within the culture of the country. The political architects of the Soviet Union realized this and made a supreme effort to restructure the whole educational system of Russia in order to produce a new bureaucracy which could carry out the governmental activities according to Communist blueprints.

The leadership of India has reacted differently. The British Indian civil service was regarded as a model bureaucracy. For the most part recruited from the graduates of Oxbridge, the Indian service was a career service in which one moved up the ladder by merit with assignments both in the central government and the states. The newly independent Indian government tried to follow the model. The Indian Constitution calls for a Union Public Service Commission to act in an advisory role to the government. Its major task is to conduct competitive entrance exams and to establish suitable criteria for advancement in the national service. A State Public Service Commission performs a similar assignment in each of the states. The problem in India, however, is not how to but where to recruit qualified government workers.

The planned development and modernization of India calls not only for scientists, technicians, and engineers but also for clerks, key-punch operators, and accountants. India, however, has featured a crash program in higher education rather than all-out educational programs for the masses, like those implemented in the Soviet Union. After twenty years of independence, the great bulk of the Indian people are still illiterate. Setting up a pilot project for teaching physics and chemistry by television in New Delhi apparently was easier than training primary school teachers for remote villages. In India, as in many developing countries, more qualified applicants compete for the top positions in the public service than for the middle and lower grades. Consequently the quality of service at the point where private citizens come into contact with the bureaucracy is likely to be very poor.

Among our newest states, the Ivory Coast and Kenya have tackled the problem of nation-building via the bureaucracy from very different perspectives. Personally enamored of French culture, President Houphouet-Boigny retained the French colonial administration virtually intact after the proclamation of independence. Since then he has continued to recruit most of the professional and managerial class for the government service from France. Only recently has he been persuaded to make concessions to the youth of his own country and to educate more of them for the public service.

On the other hand, President Kenyatta has from the outset been committed to the Africanization of Kenya's civil service. As in India, Kenya inherited a generally excellent civil service from the British colonial administration. Since independence, however, most of the high and middle ranks which had hitherto been staffed by European settlers, Asians, and South Africans were vacated in favor of Kenyan blacks. Within five years after independence more than 80 percent of the Kenyan civil service had been Africanized. Recent reports indicate, however, that Kenya, in its zeal to attract young Africans into the government, overextended its recruiting program. Kenya's civil service, now about one hundred thousand, cannot continue to absorb a great number of annual recruits.[12] Hence students receiving state aid are no longer required to offer to work for the government for three years after they have completed their educational program; in fact, many recent graduates are finding difficulty getting any jobs. Higher education in Kenya, patterned after the liberal arts of Oxbridge, simply does not prepare students for the middle range of jobs in a modernizing state—architects, engineers, accountants, plumbers, refrigeration mechanics, and primary school teachers. Hence in Kenya, as in other developing countries (even the older ones like Colombia and Mexico), there is much unemployment and at the same time many jobs unfilled.

Bureaucracy and Administrative Management

Administrative organization and managerial controls tie in most directly with how governments operate and how governors govern. First of all, the governors must devise means of governing the government to keep the political leadership in firm command of the bureaucracy. Hence, when new political leaders move into positions of power—whether by elections or coups—their first step is usually toward sweeping reorganization. In practical politics such reorganization conveys a double message to the governed. The first is intended to discredit the outgoing regime—the organization we inherited is a hopeless confusion of form and function. The second is calculated to build support for new policies—the time has come to match structure and purpose, to meet the new needs of a new era.

Shortly after the Conservative party won in Britain's parliamentary elections in 1970, the new administration pledged itself to "a new style of government." [13] Declaring that the Labour government had been attempting to do too much and had therefore overloaded the governmental machinery, the Conservatives proposed to improve the quality of policy formulation and decision-making with "less government, and better government, carried out by fewer people." Reorganization would follow a more "functional approach"; the government departments would be organized according to the main tasks to be done, with related tasks grouped together in unified departments. A unified Department of Trade and Industry, for example, was made responsible for general industrial policy covering both the public and private sectors. The secretary of state for trade and industry, with a seat in the cabinet, was charged with identifying strategic issues of policy and priorities and with establishing an overall framework of requirements, incentives, and restraints within which British industry and trade might prosper at home and abroad.

A new Department of Environment was given jurisdiction over the whole range of governmental activities which affect the environment of the people: land use; housing; transport; protection of the coast and countryside; preservation of historic towns and monuments; and control of air, water, and noise pollution. A third major reorganization provided central and unified direction for personal social services: welfare, child care, and some aspects of health.

How to organize the activities of government for maximum effectiveness is always a controversial subject in public administration. The simplest solution is a unifunctional department, a department based on a single product (education, transportation), a special clientele (veterans, indigents), a particular process (finance, personnel, supplies). But as modern government undertakes more and more functions and its operations extend more deeply into the economy and culture of the country, the number of departments tends to proliferate beyond the governors' span of control. A prime minister (or president) may bring a dozen, or more than a score, of ministers into his cabinet, but if the membership of the cabinet reaches say fifty or sixty, then the cabinet becomes too unwieldy to serve as a policy-making body. Thus the usual reform is to reduce the number of departments by consolidating the existing departments into multifunctional units. It is more than coincidence that both the British and American governments have moved in this direction.

Reorganization is a perennial technique of government in the United States. Since World War II, the president has proposed and Congress has approved approximately a hundred major reorganizations in the executive establishment. President Nixon in his first term of office urged "a complete reform of the Federal government . . . to keep up with the times and with the needs of the people." [14] Specifically, he advocated reducing the twelve cabinet departments to eight: the old-line departments—state, treasury, defense, and justice—were to be unchanged, but the remaining eight departments were to be consolidated into four new departments—human resources, community development, natural resources, and economic development. Like the reorganization of the British administration, the Nixon reorganization was an attempt to get away from departments organized to serve particular clientele (labor, agriculture, commerce) and so to put a greater stress on the great purposes of government. Unlike the British prime minister, however, whose position as leader of the majority party in Parliament assures the enactment of his proposals, President Nixon is not in a position to determine the organization of the executive establishment for whose activities he is constitutionally responsible. The Congress whose approval President Nixon needs to effect reorganization is controlled by the opposition party. Moreover Congress itself is organized in a committee system that also serves special clientele (labor, agriculture, commerce). In the British Parliament, the committees acquire no vested interests in designated policy areas, presumably all committees are equally involved in the grand strategy of government.

In every government the policy process requires organization of activities according to some rational division of labor. The basic problem of organization—and reorganization—is how to group the government workers in effective units that correlate purpose, structure, and operations. Table 10–3

TABLE 10–3
Major Departmental Organization in the Industrial States

United States *	*Japan* †	*Germany* ‡
Agriculture	Agriculture and Forestry	Agriculture Forests
Commerce	Construction	All-German Affairs
Defense	Finance, Justice, and Education	Bundesrat and Länder
Health, Education, and Welfare	Foreign Affairs	Defense
Housing and Urban Development	Health and Welfare	Economics
Interior	Home Affairs	Economic Cooperation
Justice	International Trade and Industry	Families and Youth
Labor	Labor	Finance
State	Posts and Telecommunications	Foreign Affairs
Transportation	Transportation	Health
Treasury		Housing and Reconstruction
		Justice
		Labor and Social Order
		Nutrition
		Posts and Telephones
		Refugees and Expellees
		Scientific Research
		Transport

SOURCES:
* *US Government Organization Manual, 1970–71* (Washington, D.C.: Government Printing Office, 1970).
† *Statistical Handbook of Japan*, 1970. (Bureau of Statistics, Office of the Prime Minister).
‡ Press and Information Office of the Federal Government, *Facts about Germany*, Public Document 914, 30 §2/2–2, 7th ed., 1968.
§ *British Information Services*, November, 1970. (I.D. 702, rev. Mimeographed).
¶ *Constitution of the Soviet Union as amended to 1967*, in John N. Hazard, *The Soviet System of Government*, 4th ed. (Chicago: University of Chicago Press, 1968).

TABLE 10–3
(Continued)

United Kingdom §	*Soviet Union* ¶	
	ALL-UNION MINISTRIES	UNION-REPUBLICAN MINISTRIES
Agriculture, Fisheries, and Food	Automobile Industry	Agriculture
Defense	Aviation Industry	Assembly and Special Construction
Education and Science	Chemical and Petroleum Industry	Building Materials
Employment	Civil Aviation	Coal Industry
Environment	Construction Machinery	Chemical Industry
Exchequer	Construction and Transportation	Communications
Foreign and Commonwealth Affairs	Defense Industry	Construction
Home	Electronic Industry	Construction of Heavy Industrial Enterprise
Justice	Electrotechnical	Culture
Posts and Telecommunications	Foreign Trade	Defense
Scotland	Gas Industry	Education
Social Services	General Machine-building	Ferrous Metallurgy
Trade and Industry	Heavy Machine Industry	Finance
Wales	Household Machines	Fisheries
	Instrument-making	Food Industry
	Machine Tools	Foreign Affairs
	Medical Industry	Geology
	Medium Machine Industry	Higher and Specialized Secondary Education
	Merchant Marine	Industrial Construction
	Radio Industry	Irrigation
	Shipbuilding	Light Industry
	Tractor and Agriculture Machine Manufacturing	Lumber, Pulp, and Paper Industry
	Transportation	Meat and Dairy Industry
		Nonferrous Metallury
		Petroleum Extracting
		Power and Electrification
		Protection of Public Order
		Public Health
		Trade

lists the major departmental units in the national governments of our five industrial states. The titles indicate generally the principal assignments of each department. Note that the traditional departments—foreign affairs, defense, finance, and justice—appear in all the listings.[15] For other functions, however, the organizational patterns vary considerably. Japan, for example, groups agriculture with forestry, and the United Kingdom puts agriculture with fisheries; the United States groups education with health and welfare, the United Kingdom puts education with science. Table 10–3, of course, does no more than tell us how the governments have chosen to organize their activities at a given time. Every incoming administration has its own ideas of how to reorganize for more effective outputs. In parliamentary governments especially, the hallmark of a new government is its reconstituted cabinet, suggesting a new style of government and different priorities in the public policies.

The organization of every bureaucracy rests on a number of principles, among these, rational division of labor, social utility, and managerial controls. When President Nixon speaks of "the great purposes of government," he has in mind the kind of governmental activities which he perceives to be necessary and proper. Social utility, as a criterion of organization—how the government is best organized to satisfy the needs of the governed—is a value-laden term, reflecting the official ideology. In the British frame of reference, electricity, gas, coal, atomic energy, steel, airlines, and airports are nationalized industries, and the newly reorganized Department of Trade and Industry is organized to carry on these governmental operations as a matter of social utility. Although President Nixon professed to be recommending reforms "for the next hundred years" when he advocated "a department concerned with our prosperity—with our jobs, our businesses, and those many activities that keep our economy running smoothly and well," it is very unlikely that he had in mind the eventual nationalization of any of these activities.

The departmental titles in Table 10–3 suggest the range of activities which now fall within the jurisdiction of national governments. (The range may be even greater since three out of five of the states are federal in form and some activities now carried on by the states, Länder, or republics may not appear in the national lists.) Apparently the national government of the Soviet Union is most pervasive, that of the United States least so, in the economic and social life of the nation. Note, however, that the chart does not tell us much about the nature of the activities—protective, promotional, regulatory? Nor does it tell us anything about the priorities in public policy or the degrees of public support given to various programs.

Setting the national goals, determining the public priorities, allocating the nation's resources for specific programs, these are the great tasks of modern statesmanship. But as the activities of the government become more extensive and the operations more complex and technical, political leaders experience increasing difficulty in managing their own government. Since most political leaders are not recruited on the basis of managerial skills, their offices have to be outfitted with managerial agencies which help to keep them on top of the bureaucracies and in control of the total policy process.

The traditional agency for coordinating and giving central direction to the multiple and various activities of the government is the cabinet in which each major department is normally represented. The prime minister (chancellor or president) meets with the cabinet, hears the views of its members, views supported by the differing interests and expertise of their separate departments, and then charts with them collectively the strategy of the government as a whole. Cabinet officers, like their chief executive, however, are usually selected for personal and political attributes rather than managerial expertise. Because policy formulation—and even more so policy implementation—calls for highly specialized knowledge and sophisticated administration, the political leadership cannot govern without a great deal of technical and managerial assistance.

ROLE STRUCTURE

Throughout this book we have often used the metaphor of the theater or the stage. We have looked at the cultural and social environment of nation states as if it were a stage set, and we have talked about the various members of the political system as if they were all members of a cast each assigned a different role. The metaphor can be misleading because the world of the theater is purely illusory, whereas the world of politics is very real. Nevertheless we pursue the metaphor as a way to criticize the performance of the political system as a whole (the cast) and of the various members of the system (the individual actors).

If you have seen *Hello Dolly* on stage and in the movies you know that the stage production and the screen version of the same script was very different. Carol Channing, Pearl Bailey, and Barbra Streisand each played the role of Dolly according to her own (and her director's) perception of Dolly, not only as the lead, but also in relation to the rest of the cast. Similarly, on the political stage, different players may read the same script and play it quite differently.

When we talk about political actors and the roles they play, we are shifting our attention to people in the system and observing how individual persons, or groups of persons, act out their assignments in the institutions. The Congress of the United States is an institution; Congressman Jefferson Blow is an individual actor in the institution. If we want to understand why Congress operates as it does, we have to look at the institutional arrangements, for example, the committee system and the rules of parliamentary procedure. But we also have to know how Jeff Blow, and his colleagues, perceive and, accordingly, play their roles as members of Congress. How did Jeff Blow get elected? What did he promise the voters he would do if elected? How sensitive is Blow to constituent pressures? How does he balance in his own mind national interests versus constituent interests if these appear to be in conflict? Where does Blow fit into the party organization in Congress? What are his committee assignments? What is his party rank? How does he react to White

House requests for congressional action? How does he respond to the many various lobbies in Washington? What is his voting record on specific issues? What does he think a Congressman ought to do on the job? What are his priorities? Casework for his constituents back home? Committee work? Participation in floor debates? Party work? The cocktail circuit? Where does he spend most of his time? In Washington, or back home?

A title on the door may entitle the occupant of the office to a carpet on the floor (and an autographed picture of the Big Boss, "To Horace Doe, with highest esteem"), but it does not tell us how the man in the office performs his particular assignment or what status he really has among the policy-makers.

When we discuss presidential power in the United States we need to make clear at the outset which president we are talking about. Dwight D. Eisenhower viewed the presidency in a very different light from his successor, John F. Kennedy. The Eisenhower administration put a high premium on communication through official channels, interdepartmental coordination, and hierarchical staff relationships, as seen in regular and frequent cabinet meetings, the Planning Board and Operations Coordinating Board in the National Security Establishment, and a disciplined White House staff. The Kennedy administration, which went in for a more personalized approach and ad hoc consultative arrangements, scrapped much of the elaborate machinery and formal procedures favored by the Eisenhower administration. Similarly in the USSR, when Nikita Khrushchev succeeded Joseph Stalin, the organization and the operations of the soviet system immediately felt the repercussions of new concepts of executive power and a very different personal style of influence and persuasion.

The policy process itself depends not only on institutional arrangements but also upon personal relationships. According to the official script in the United States, the secretary of state is the president's principal adviser in foreign policy, but the role of Dean Rusk was very different under President Kennedy than that of John Foster Dulles under President Eisenhower. Moreover, the role of Dean Rusk was very different under President Johnson than under President Kennedy. Different persons in office affect interoffice working relations.

In the older and more advanced states the institutional arrangements seem to carry greater weight than in the newest nations. The influence of Golda Meier in Israel stems primarily from her official position as prime minister, but it was the force of personality that put her into that position. Similarly in India, Prime Minister Indira Gandhi's charismatic and dominating personality proved stronger than the Congress party in Parliament. In both of our African states, Kenya and the Ivory Coast, examining the constitutional structure and legal prescriptions is not nearly so fruitful as getting to understand Jomo Kenyatta and Felix Houphouet-Boigny as persons who play the leads on center stage, as it were.

We cannot systematically analyze who's who and why in the government and politics of each of our twelve states. For understanding the policy process, however, role analysis is likely to be more revealing than institutional descriptions. Consider, for example, the role of the British prime minister. First, of course, there is his official position, an elected member and the leader of his party in the Parliament. The title on the door of Number Ten Downing Street equally describes the position of Harold Wilson and Edward Heath. But when we open the door, who sits behind the desk makes a very real difference in policy formulation and in policy outcomes.

Individuals act in accordance with their own perceptions of reality, which may or may not agree with others' perceptions. Individuals, moreover, behave according to their own operational code, how they think they ought to behave. The individual has his own set of values, his own beliefs, his own prejudices and predilections, his own perspective—and all of these enter into the way he sees a situation and the way he acts. The basic assumption of role theory in politics is that the individual in the office (whether it is an executive, legislative, judicial, or bureaucratic office) does have opportunity to make choices and that the choices he makes are both personal and institutional.

The prime minister, whether Harold Wilson or Edward Heath, is a person who acts according to what he perceives to be the situation. His perception begins with his own background—his family, his schooling, his work experiences, his personal friends, his social status. It just happens that Heath and Wilson are the same age, both born in 1916; it is also a coincidence that Heath and Wilson both entered Parliament in the same year, 1950; and they also both went to Oxford, Heath to Balliol College and Wilson to Jesus College. But here the similarities end and the dissimilarities begin. Heath moved up the Conservative party ladder, Wilson up the Labour party ladder, each serving in various ministries, depending on whose party was in power. The British prime minister is primarily a party man; he has worked his way to the top because he is thoroughly indoctrinated in party principles and long experienced in government-party relationships. A member of a Conservative party views the state of the nation and the state of the world differently from a Labour party man. The prime minister's conception of national interest, his ties to special interests in the electorate depend both on his personal predilections and his perception of partisan advantage.

The role of the German chancellor, like that of the British prime minister, depends on who is in the office. When Willy Brandt replaced Kurt Kiesinger, it was immediately apparent that Brandt perceived the external environment of Germany quite differently than had his predecessor in office. Willy Brandt looked at the outside world through party glasses and his SPD glasses offered a quite different perspective from the CDU glasses of Kurt Kiesinger. Personal idiosyncrasies also help to explain their very different political behavior. When Adolf Hitler and his National Socialist party ushered in the Third Reich in 1933, Brandt, then a twenty-year-old activist in the Social Democratic party fled to Scandinavia where he became a political journalist serving the anti-Nazi underground. Kurt Kiesinger was thirty years old in 1933, a university graduate, already well launched on a legal career. He found it professionally advantageous, and personally not too difficult, to enter the bureaucracy of the new regime. When the war was over, both Brandt and Kiesinger entered the politics of the Federal Republic, but their very different experiences between 1933 and 1945 put them poles apart, Brandt in the SPD and Kiesinger in the CDU. No doubt their very different personal and political reactions to the Third Reich have conditioned their outlooks on European and world politics. Certainly it came easier for the long-time Socialist Willy Brandt (who fought in an exile underground group out of Scandinavia) than for Kurt Kiesinger (a former member of the National Socialist party) to tackle the conflict between East and West Germany and to work for a detente between Bonn and Moscow.

How a member of the political system plays his role depends on many things: his official position, his own operational code, how others expect him to act, how he acts, and how others interact. We have here turned the spotlight on a few stellar roles but the play's the thing. The political system comprises the entire cast in the wings and on stage, all the members playing out their roles in various ways, as citizens, voters, party activists, party leaders, lobbyists, members of the ruling elite, elected representatives, top executives, judges, major and minor bureaucrats.

We can use the concept of role-playing for making comparisons within a single system or between counterparts in different systems. Thus we can criticize the performance of Richard M. Nixon and Lyndon B. Johnson in the presidential role, Harold Wilson and Edward Heath as prime ministers, or Willy Brandt and Kurt Kiesinger as chancellors. We can compare the influence and power of two newly elected presidents in Latin America whose constitutional status is almost identical: Luis Echeverria Alvarez of Mexico (elected by an overwhelming majority of the electorate, candidate of the PRI) and Misrael Pastrana Borrero of Colombia (who barely made it despite support of the two dominant parties and the popular press) or two African leaders like Jomo Kenyatta and Felix Houphouet-Boigny whose personal values and goals have certainly entered into their different versions of nation-building.

The concept of role-playing is very important in comparative politics, for it emphasizes our basic assumption in political science that the root is man. We agree with Heinz Eulau that it is not possible to say anything about how man behaves without considering his "acts, goals, drives, feelings, beliefs, commitments, and values." [16] Role-playing highlights the personal idiosyncrasies, not of abstract man, but of man as an individual acting in a particular time and in a specific setting.

We do not, however, underestimate the conditioning of every man by the institutions in which he works. Justice Felix Frankfurter, then on the United States Supreme Court, was once asked, "Does a man cease to be himself when he becomes a justice?" He replied:

> *No, he does not change his character. He brings his whole experience, his training, his outlook, his social, intellectual, and moral environment with him when he takes a seat on the supreme bench. . . . [But] the outlook of a lawyer fit to be a Justice regarding the role of a judge cuts across all his personal preference for this or that social arrangement.*[17]

Willy Brandt does not act solely, or even mainly, according to personal inclinations. His political behavior is conditioned by the way the people in the Federal Republic expect a chancellor to act. Senator J. William Fulbright acts as a representative for all the American people in foreign policy matters which do not interest most of his constituents in Arkansas, but he acts as a senator from Arkansas should when it comes to questions of civil rights or protecting the chicken industry of Arkansas. Even Felix Houphouet-Boigny, who personally takes a dim view of student activism, as president of the Ivory Coast charged with maintaining a stable government is impelled to bring more and more youthful intellectuals into his policy councils. In the chapters that follow on "How Governments Operate," and "How Governors Govern," we shall observe that the whole policy process is institutionalized in every country in order to curb too much free-lancing in the public service.

NOTES

1. Gabriel A. Almond and G. Bingham Powell, Jr., in *Comparative Politics* (Boston: Little, Brown, 1966), refer to "rule making" rather than "legislation," "for the simple reason that the term legislation seems to connote some specialized structure and explicit process, whereas in many political systems the rule-making function is a different process, difficult to untangle and specify" (p. 132).
2. Samuel H. Beer and Adam B. Ulam, eds., *Patterns of Government: The Major Political Systems of Europe*, rev. ed. (New York: Random House, 1962), p. 241.
3. Quoted in Newell M. Stultz, "Parliament in a Tutelary Democracy: A Recent Case in Kenya," *Journal of Politics* 31 (February, 1969): 95–118.
4. M. V. Pylee, *India's Constitution*, 2d rev. ed. (New York: Asia Publishing House, 1967), p. 240.
5. Ibid., p. 288.
6. Harold J. Berman, *Justice in the USSR*, rev. ed. (Cambridge, Mass.: Harvard University Press, 1963).
7. Frederick C. Mosher, *Democracy and the Public Service* (New York: Oxford University Press, 1968), chap. 4, "The Professional State."
8. The *Executive Inventory*, established in 1967, is maintained by the United States Civil Service Commission as a continuously updated, computerized talent bank for use in assigning and reassigning career personnel to professional and managerial positions in the executive branch of the national government.
9. Carl J. Friedrich, *Man and His Government* (New York: McGraw-Hill, 1963), p. 471.
10. See Joseph La Palombara, ed., *Bureaucracy and Political Development* (Princeton, N.J.: Princeton University Press, 1963), for a variety of studies on bureaucracy and development.
11. Ibid., p. 254.
12. See *Washington Post*, September 1, 1970. The article appeared under the by-line of Jim Hoagland from Nairobi in Kenya.
13. *The Reorganization of Central Government*, Message presented to Parliament

by the Prime Minister and the Minister for the Civil Service by Command of Her Majesty, October, 1970. (London: Her Majesty's Stationery Office, CMND 4506).

14. State of the Union Address to Congress, January 29, 1971.
15. Although Table 10–3 does not include a Department of Defense for Japan, a Defense Agency is attached to the office of the prime minister. The director general of the Defense Agency has the rank of cabinet minister without portfolio. He advises the prime minister on defense, plans, mobilization of the self-defense forces, and on all matters involving the national defense. The euphemisms, Defense Agency instead of Ministry of Defense, and self-defense forces instead of army, navy, and air force, refer back to the constitutional demilitarization under Occupation prohibition on war as an instrument of national policy.
16. Heinz Eulau, *The Behavioral Persuasion in Politics* (New York: Random House, 1963), p. 1.
17. "The Judicial Process and the Supreme Court," a paper read at the annual meeting of the American Philosophical Society, Philadelphia, 1954. Reprinted in Philip Elman, ed., *Of Law and Men* (New York: Harcourt, Brace & World, 1956).

FURTHER READING

ECKSTEIN, HARRY. "Political Science and Public Policy." In *Contemporary Political Science,* edited by Ithiel de Sola Pool. New York: McGraw-Hill, 1967, Chap. 5.

ECKSTEIN, HARRY, and DAVID E. APTER, eds. *Comparative Politics.* New York: Free Press, 1963.

EISENSTADT, S. N. "Political Struggle in Bureaucratic Societies." *World Politics* 9 (October, 1956).

GEERTZ, CLIFFORD, ed. *Old Societies and New States.* New York: Free Press, 1963.

GERTH, H. H., and C. WRIGHT MILLS, trans. *From Max Weber: Essays in Sociology.* Fair Lawn, N.J.: Oxford University Press, 1946, esp. "Politics as a Vocation" and "Science as a Vocation."

SPIRO, HERBERT J. *Responsibility in Government: Theory and Practice.* New York: Van Nostrand Reinhold, 1969.

chapter 11

HOW DO GOVERNMENTS OPERATE?

Now we have reached the center of the political system, the crucial point in policy formulation and policy implementation; we are trying to get inside the government and to find out how the governors govern. To explain and exemplify the official operations of nation states it is helpful to expand David Easton's behavioral construct, "the authoritative allocation of values." [1] How is official authority obtained and how is it maintained? How do those in authority perceive and determine the hierarchy of values in a nation state? What processes do they follow in the allocation and mobilization of resources in support of these values? How are policies fashioned and implemented in accordance with the allocation and mobilization of resources?

In policy science, that is, the study of how and why governments make certain policies, the principal subjects are attitudes, values, interests, perceptions, and judgments; in short, government as it exists largely in the minds of men. Obviously, in two brief chapters we cannot cover all the ways by which men govern in one country, much less in twelve. We can do little more than point to some major concepts and significant data, leaving the reader to explore further the subjects that particularly engage his attention.

Israel, census taker with Arab family
(Leonard Freed : Magnum)

CONCEPTS OF LEGITIMACY

Robert Dahl defines authority as "legitimate power or influence." [2] A leader in the political system is said to possess authority if he has a right to request or command members of the system to act—or not to act—in a specific way. His authority is recognized as legitimate if other members of the system acknowledge the right and accordingly feel obliged to acquiesce or obey. Following this line of analysis, Dahl notes that leaders in a political system generally try to convert their influence into authority. Legitimate authority provides the system with a reliable, durable, and economical base for governing.

External Recognition

External recognition, that is, recognition by other states and governments, is not necessary to legitimatize a regime, but it is viewed as helpful. Newly independent states have been inclined to rush their applications for admission to the United Nations in the belief that membership in that organization will give credence to their claims as sovereign and equal states in the international community. Note that all the states in our sample of twelve, except the Federal Republic of Germany, hold membership in the United Nations.

The conduct of external relations is also regarded as one of the prerogatives of legitimate governments. Here one must be careful to distinguish between the claims of legitimacy and legality. Legitimacy embodies the notion of rightful rule; legality denotes no more than accordance with the laws. A government may be authorized under its own laws to accredit and receive ambassadors, make treaties and agreements with foreign governments, and in other ways to engage in international activities. But if that government is not recognized as a legitimate or rightful government, it may find itself in difficulties both at home and abroad. For example, when General Victoriano Huerta overthrew the Madero government in Mexico in 1913 and established a military dictatorship, the Mexican people were forced to accept his rule. But when the newly inaugurated president of the United States, Woodrow Wilson, refused to have any dealings with the Huerta government, declaring that "we can have no sympathy with those who seek to seize the power of government to advance their own personal interests or ambitions," he thereby helped to undermine the legitimacy of Huerta's military government and no doubt contributed to its downfall.[3] On the other hand, a few years later when President Wilson refused to recognized the Bolshevik government in Russia on the grounds that the Russian revolutionaries had not obtained the consent of the governed, his policy of nonrecognition did not faze the new regime in Russia. Initially and for many years afterward, the Bolshevik leaders forcibly imposed the Communist system upon the Russian people, but they also worked at explaining and justifying what they were doing and what they hoped to do, and eventually they did achieve legitimacy, not only for themselves but also for the system they espoused.

The Notion of Rightful Rule

The equation of legitimacy with rightful rule has its roots in the religion, ideology, and philosophy of the people. The coronation ceremony in Westminster Abbey is a modern reminder that Her Majesty is still defender of the faith in the United Kingdom. A high point in the inauguration of the president of the United States is when the chief justice of the Supreme Court steps forward on the Capitol steps to administer the oath of office, and the new president solemnly swears that he will faithfully execute the office of president and will to the best of his ability preserve, protect, and defend the Constitution of the United States. Similarly, the president of the Republic of Turkey, in an impressive ceremony takes his office before the Grand National Assembly. "I swear upon my honor that I shall always respect and defend the laws of the Republic and the principles of National Sovereignty . . . protect and magnify the honor and glory of Turkey." [4] The oath of office and the swearing into office—from head of state down to local government functionaries—is regarded in many modern secular states as a significant, if not essential, ceremony because it symbolizes the investiture of the official incumbent with all the rights and responsibilities that legitimize his political behavior.

Even the most modern of nation states feel impelled to observe rituals and ceremonies that project the image of continuing legitimacy for the contemporary political system. Thus in the United Kingdom the annual opening of Parliament is presented as a medieval pageant, with Her Majesty arriving in a gilded coach to deliver a speech (written by the cabinet) from the throne. Although the present House of Commons was built after World War II (the old House was destroyed in the air raids of World War II), it is a replica of the old House, even to size, too small to accommodate the whole membership at a sitting. To have altered the architecture or enlarged the chamber might have changed the nature of proceedings.

The Speaker of the House of Commons is the very symbol of parliamentary proceedings, solemn and ceremonious. "There he sits in his chair (his 'throne' one should perhaps say), looking like nothing so much as the frontispiece from a biography of Handel, with his flowing wig, his black satin knee breeches, his buckled shoes and long black gown, a figure straight out of the age of squirearchy." [5] His authority is traditional, his role is ceremonial, but his performance is functional. When members of the House in the heat of partisan debate over nationalization of the steel industry or control of telecommunications forget they are gentlemen and sportsmen, the Speaker has but to rise from his chair and order is restored. More important, of course, is the members' readiness to accept the Speaker's rulings, which in effect direct the debate because they recognize the legitimacy of his role. Elected for life by the whole Parliament, his seat traditionally uncontested for as long as he wishes to stay in Parliament, his behavior is purely parliamentary and politically neutral.

Similarly, the British courts hark back to traditional trappings to emphasize the legitimacy of the roles played by the judges, the barristers, and the solicitors in upholding the law and adjudicating disputes: The wigs, the robes, and the ritual procedures accentuate the respect for the law which has characterized the British political system from time immemorial, *circa* the reign of Henry II. Though the substantive concerns of the law have changed with the times, the ancient forms are deliberately preserved to invoke the aura of legitimacy by inheritance from the past.

Perhaps the English example is the most striking: a modern democratic state with a highly industrialized economy and a largely urban population, still holding out for a monarchy and a peerage as significant components of the political system. In our sample of twelve governments each one uses the devices of pomp and circumstance, architectural settings, traditional proceedings, ancient rituals, and special ceremonies to enhance the images of legitimacy and therefore of itself.

Like most big cities, Moscow is building huge high-rise, glass-walled boxes for modern living and office space. But the political and administrative headquarters of the USSR remain in the center of Moscow within the Kremlin and its ancient walls where the czars and patriarchs of the church were invested with authority for many centuries before November, 1917. It is especially noteworthy that the Soviet rulers chose to have their capital in the ancient city of the Muscovites rather than using St. Petersburg (Leningrad), the capital city established by Peter the Great. On May Day, the most important holiday in the calendar of the Soviet Union, the top leaders of the party and the government assemble at the Red Square on the east side of the Kremlin to view the great parade and demonstrations of the people celebrating the rule of the proletariat. The Kremlin provides a magnificent backdrop; the great wall towers dating back to the fifteenth century; the separate bell tower of Ivan the Great with its gold cupola rises high above the grand cluster of cathedrals, palaces, and museums, also replete with cupolas and crosses. The link between the past and the present is implicit; authority has always resided in the Kremlin; it still does. And then, obviously by design, Lenin's Tomb is in the foreground, providing the explicit ideological link between the present leadership and the revolutionary founder of the USSR.

In countries emerging from colonialism the issue of legitimacy is particularly sensitive. The mere winning of independence does not provide the base on which to establish long-run claims to legitimacy. Here it appears to be a sometimes successful ploy to stress the precolonial influences that enter into the new nationalism. We observe this ploy in modern Mexico, a conscious articulation between the contemporary political system and the pre-Spanish Indian culture. Thus in many of the public buildings the famous mosaic murals of Rivera and Orozco recall with visible pride the indigenous civilization of the Mexican people. Since the Revolution of 1910, educational programs have been inclined to short-circuit the Spanish colonial period or to show it in a poor light. On the other hand, the Mexican government has found it good business to promote tourism to the temples and palaces and pyramids of the Teotihuacans, Toltecs, Aztecs, Huastecs, Zapotecs, and Mayans. Moreover, the Museum of Anthropology in Chapultepec Park has attracted streams of schoolchildren from allover Mexico, thus serving both as a national laboratory for Mexican history and as an effective political device joining awe for the past with respect for the present.

The legitimacy of Israel as an independent nation state is still fiercely contested by the Arab countries in the Middle East. But Israel stakes her claim on four thousand years of history. "The land of Israel, once called Canaan and much later Palestine, is indissolubly bound up with the Jewish people . . . there have always been Jews in the Land; they were never completely severed from it. In exile and dispersion, they cherished it in their hearts; over and over again they sought to return." [6] To our friend Morris Gold, an ardent American Zionist in the 1930s, now an Israeli citizen, Israel is first and foremost the promised homeland of his people since biblical times. But he is quick to point out that modern Israel bases its claims to legitimacy on firm legal grounds: the November, 1947, vote of the United Nations Assembly recommending the partition of Palestine into independent Jewish and Arab states; the formal termination of the British mandate and the official proclamation of Israel's independence in 1948; the immediate recognition of Israeli sovereignty by the United States, the Soviet Union, and most of the states of the world outside the Arab sphere; the subsequent admission of Israel to the United Nations, and the exchange of diplomatic representatives with all the great powers in the world. As for the legitimacy of the Israeli government, it rests on popular sovereignty, expressed through regular elections, processed through representative institutions, notably the Knesset.

The Utility of Constitutions

In a new nation or a new government one of the first steps the political leadership takes to insure its legitimacy is to draft a constitution which institutionalizes and rationalizes the political views of the leadership. A constitution establishes the structure and functions of the new political system, and it also sets forth the principles under which the government is expected to operate. All members of the political system are then required to uphold the constitution. Hence, as long as political leaders appear to act within the constitutional prescription their authority is recognized not only because they act in accord with fundamental law but also because they act in conformity with dominant ideology. States have come to view constitutions as necessary for their survival as governments have come to stress recognition and UN membership.

Take for example the Constitution of the Union of Soviet Socialist Republics. Article 1 proclaims a socialist state of workers and peasants. Article 4 states that the economic foundation of the USSR is socialism, state ownership of the instruments and means of production. Article 126 describes the Communist party as made up of "the most active and politically conscious citizens in the ranks of the working class, working peasants and working intelligentsia." Article 131 puts it plainly: Public ownership of property is the sacred and inviolable foundation of the system and persons committing offenses against publicly owned property are enemies of the people. Our friend Ivan Skivitsky, a member of the working intelligentsia, believes that the constitutional law embodies the public philosophy. As a Marxist he subscribes to the socialist economy and to the idea of dictatorship of the proletariat. When the Communist party, acting in the role of vanguard for the workers, dictates government policies, this in his mind enhances the legitimacy of governmental action. He regards un-Communist activities as subversive, and he understands that the government may have to take strong measures to maintain internal security. He has been taught that an international conspiracy, well organized, highly militarized, threatens his country and his way of life, and he recognizes that the Kremlin must exercise its authority to the hilt in foreign affairs and matters relating to national security.

Similarly, the Constitution of India is designed to buttress the authority of the Indian leadership in its determination to embark upon rapid modernization of the country's political, social, and economic institutions. The Constitution of 1949 clearly reflects the ideology of the framers, many of them Western-educated, most of them active participants in the nationalist independence movement. The Preamble begins, "We the people of India, having solemnly resolved to constitute India into a sovereign democratic republic. . . ." The principle of popular sovereignty is more than a bit of constitutional rhetoric, however. The legitimacy of the Indian government rests on the expressed consent of the governed. Despite the ignorance and illiteracy of the great bulk of the Indian people, the Indian leadership rested their case on universal suffrage with remarkable faith in the common sense of the people. That the faith has not been without substance is indicated by the stability of the Indian government since independence. It has conducted five national elections with extensive participation, and within the federal framework it has gradually moved from a centralist focus to a regional pattern of government with local supports.

A novel feature of the Indian Constitution is the section on Directive Principles (borrowed in part from the Constitution of the Irish Republic) in which the framers try to integrate Western ideas with Indian traditions. The Directive Principles are just that, instructions to the future leadership from the Centre to the Panchayats, authorizing them to deal with such indigenous problems as the caste system, tribalism, the socially and educationally backward classes, cottage industries, prohibition of intoxicating drinks and drugs, protection against cow slaughter, etc., keeping in mind the overriding goal, "a society developing on the basis of democracy and socialism." Under constitutional mandate and in line with the Directive Principles, the Indian leadership has formulated and implemented a succession of Five-Year Plans designed to make India a modern socialist democratic state.

From the perspective of B. R. Jog, a poor and illiterate farmer, the Indian government is exercising legitimate, rightful authority. B. R. Jog knows very little about the outside world; he has never seen a television screen, New Delhi is far away, but the local candidates for Parliament and for the state legislature have sought his vote (and that of his wife); the various party organizations have promised to bring the national plans down to the level of community development; he knows the members of the village council who have grown up with him, they have asked for his help in planning a new program in animal husbandry; his children are attending the village school and learning the magic of written words. B. R. Jog (and his wife) have good reason to recognize the legitimacy of the Indian government.

The concept of legitimacy is a sticky one in the Federal Republic of Germany. The Basic Law of 1949 was designed "to pacify a country which has been racked by ideological divisions, socio-economic struggles and maladjustments, and by an insane urge to conquer the world." [7] Authorization to reconstitute a German state, following the disintegration of the Third Reich, had to come from outside the German environment. Specifically, it came at the behest of the six-power conference in London (February to June, 1948) which decided that a democratic West Germany could be an effective buffer between the Western powers and the Soviet Union. The minister presidents of the eleven states then situated in the western zones were not at all certain that they should sponsor a constitutional convention in which the people of the Russian-occupied zone could not participate. Leaders of the Social Democratic party (SDP) especially and also some Christian Democratic (CDU) leaders were dubious of any move that might serve to perpetuate partition of East and West. Nevertheless they were persuaded that, given the intransigence of the Soviet Union, they ought to take whatever action appeared most practical to advance the social and economic status at least of the western states. Although they would not call a constituent assembly to establish a new German constitution, they agreed to convene a parliamentary council to draft a Basic Law, thus using semantics as a device to avoid the issue of unification.

The minister presidents, following the custom of 1870 and 1918, according to which the executive branch assumed the initiative in preparing a constitutional draft, designated a committee of constitutional experts and representatives from the western states to work out general constitutional principles for a new government. This body, known as the Herrenchiemsee committee because it met at Herrenchiemsee in Bavaria, made plans for a democratic federal union. In September, 1948, a parliamentary council with members chosen by the state legislatures and representing the major political parties in the western zones began debate on the Herrenchiemsee Plan. The Soviet blockade of Berlin and the dramatic Allied airlift occurred during this period; the Allied military governments instituted currency reforms in the western zones; the political atmosphere was tense, stirred by German particularism as well as by the Cold-War contenders; still the parliamentary council proceeded with its assignment. On May 23, 1949, the Basic Law for the Federal Republic of Germany was promulgated under signature of the parliamentary council, the minister presidents, and the *Landtag* presidents (presidents of the state legislatures). On August 14, 1949, the German people went to the polls to elect the first Bundestag; 78.5 percent of the West German electorate participated in that election. On September 4, 1949, the Bundestag convened; Theodor Heuss was elected first president on September 12, and Konrad Adenauer became the first chancellor on September 15. And so the new Federal Republic of Germany was authorized and organized to act as the on-going political system for the German people.

The Preamble to the Basic Law points up the problem of legitimation. "The German people" in the eleven Länder of the western zones enacted the Basic Law "to give a new order to political life for a transitional period."

They claimed that they "acted on behalf of those Germans to whom participation was denied." But now the transitional period has stretched out more than two decades, and the German people in the eastern zone have never participated in the Federal Union.

Today there are in fact two Germanies: the Federal Republic of Germany and the German Democratic Republic. Official publications of the Federal Republic still refer to the DDR as "the other part of Germany." [8] To emphasize its role as the legitimate government for a still-to-be-reunified German people, the Federal Republic as late as 1969 made a big deal out of choosing its president in Berlin. We are told that the members of the federal diet (the Bundestag) represent the whole people. "Our Parliament is the supreme representation of the free part of the German people, and therefore also speaks on behalf of those who have for years been suppressed by a government that has no legitimation." [9] But in 1971, as we write this paragraph, it appears that both the Federal Republic and the Democratic Republic are viable political systems each enjoying the consent of the governed. Without regard to Cold-War issues, we can see that the German people within their separate national entities each recognize their own government as rightful for themselves—hence, legitimate.

In order to obtain and maintain authority, it is essential for a government to establish itself as legitimate, that is, having a right to rule. We have briefly touched on various ways in which governments seek to legitimate their authoritative role in society: 1) admission to international organizations in the company of other legitimate governments; 2) recognition by the governments of other independent states; 3) appeals to the traditional values and observance of rituals and ceremonies that link the contemporary system to the historical environment of the nation; 4) development of an ideology, or set of beliefs, that justifies the political behavior of the leadership; and 5) inculcation of the ideology into constitutional law, as the supreme law of the land, as fundamental principles, or as directive principles.

Legitimacy and Popular Sovereignty

But the most pervasive, as well as convincing, source of governmental authority in modern states rests with the people. The Mexican Constitution illustrates the point: "The National Sovereignty resides essentially and originally in the people. All public power originates in the people and is instituted for their benefit." [10]

It is no mere chance that in all twelve of our states the governmental system is designed to appear—if not always to function—as representative of the people. In all twelve states a national legislature is elected by the people to serve as the principal policy-making organ of the government. In the United States it is the Congress; in Israel it is the Knesset; in India it is the Union Legislature; in Turkey it is the Grand National Assembly; in the USSR it is the Supreme Soviet; in the Ivory Coast it is the National Assembly; and in the United Kingdom it is the House of Commons. (In federal unions it is also important that the people of the separate states be represented in one branch of the national legislature: the American Senate, the

German Bundesrat, the Mexican Senate, the Indian Council of States, the Russian Soviet of Nationalities serve this purpose.) Whatever the form of government, federal or unitary, parliamentary or presidential, limited or totalitarian, if it is to enjoy legitimacy, it is imperative that the people elect a national legislature to represent their interests in the government.

Elections then are the devices by which modern governments obtain and maintain their authority. It is more than a matter of prestige, it is a matter of legitimacy, for a government to go into office with impressive support from the electorate. In all twelve states the right to vote is virtually coincident with citizenship. To maintain the concept of continuing legitimation, elections must be held regularly, the franchise must be universal, the voting must be secret. And generally this is the way it is in all twelve of our states.

When one digs below the surface, the particulars uncovered may explode the myth of popular sovereignty. As we pointed out in Chapter 8, the legal provisions for elections and actual voting behavior may be highly disparate. In the United States, to this day, there is no national suffrage; subject to certain directive principles attached as Amendments to the Constitution, the states still determine the qualifications for voting, even for national officers. In every national election millions of American citizens are denied the franchise for no other reason than they have moved from one state to another or from one precinct to another and thus cannot meet the state or local residence requirements. In the USSR the people turn out at the polls almost 100 percent, but the one-party system gives the voters no real choice except to elect the party slate. In Israel a multiparty system combined with proportional representation produces a very different kind of popular mandate than the two-party system with a single-member constituencies in the United Kingdom.

Participation in elections may be an insignificant measure of a citizen's political involvement, or even understanding of politics. Nevertheless regular elections and massive voting have become the most important means of demonstrating legitimacy in modern governments. One more example: In 1960, in a setting of economic unrest and political repression, a military Committee of National Unity overthrew the existing government of Turkey and proceeded to clean up Turkish political life by suspending all political party activities. In a long drawn-out mass trial, members of the former government and leaders of the deposed Democratic party were found guilty; several were condemned to death, others were sentenced to life imprisonment, and many were given jail sentences. Former Prime Minister Menderes and two of his ministers were actually hanged. But this kind of postcoup activity did not serve to legitimatize the military government either at home or abroad. Hence, General Cemal Gürsel, self-appointed prime minister, moved quickly to establish a constitutional base for the new regime. A constitution written at the general's behest by university professors at Ankara and Istanbul was submitted to popular referendum in 1961; this constitution was ratified by 6,348,191 against 3,934,370 votes, whereupon parliamentary elections were called, and about a dozen parties were authorized to enter their candidates for membership in the new National Assembly. Although the dissolved Democratic party was not allowed to participate in this election, a new party, the Justice party, attracted many adherents of the deposed regime. None of the authorized parties, however, managed to draw a majority vote; a succession of coalition governments (1961, 1962, 1963) led by Ismet Inonu of the Republican People's party uneasily ruled the country until 1965. The Republican People's party, successor to Atatürk's monolithic party (1923–50) won 37 percent of the votes in 1961, but only 29 percent in 1965. The Justice party, which won 35 percent of the votes in 1961, captured 53 percent of the popular votes in 1965. Hence the legitimacy of the Turkish government was restored in three steps: 1) constitutional authorization in 1961, 2) elections with competing parties in 1961, and 3) majority party mandate in 1965. The legitimacy of the government in Turkey was extremely strained in the spring of 1971, when the military forces insisted on an alternative choice of a coup d'etat or a united front, i.e., an above-the-parties, government approved by the military. The latter choice won out, when Nihat Erim was appointed prime minister.

MOBILIZATION AND ALLOCATION OF RESOURCES

The basic assignments for every national government—and the awesome responsibility of its official leadership—are to 1) determine the hierarchy of national values; 2) establish the nation's goals in accord with the hierarchy of values; 3) prescribe the courses of action (policies) which are designed to move the nation toward its goals; and 4) see to it that the policies are implemented, administered, enforced.

Since the governors in every nation must—at least in the long run—obtain the consent of the governed, the official leadership is bound to determine the hierarchy of values generally in accord with the national interest(s). Further, the national interest(s) must be set within a value system acceptable to the general citizenry. As we have pointed out in earlier discussion, political leaders are not left in the dark as to the views of the citizenry. The mass media, special interest groups, concerned and articulate individuals, political parties, and popular elections—all of these serve as channels of communication between the governors and the governed. As members of the political system, the leaders are sure to share some, if not all, of the common values. Since, however, the common values may be weighed very differently by the various and many members of the system, those vested with authority may be expected to establish the official rank order of values according to their own predilections as well as in the interest of the ruling elite to which they may belong.

Law and order, justice for all, the blessings of liberty, basic rights, personal freedom, social security, general welfare, common defense, peace in our time, the dignity of man, integrity of the family, private property, public property, the right to work, the right to education, freedom of conscience, the interests of the working people, due process of law, equal protection under the laws, duties of citizens, freedom from want, freedom from fear: these are some significant values which carry different connotations and are held with varying degrees of acceptability, both in terms of extent and intensity in different systems of government. We withhold our judgment as to which values are preferable to our own way of thinking and constrain our discussion to a comparative accounting of allocation and mobilization of national resources in our twelve states. Stripped of rhetoric and ideological trimmings, the national fiscal accounts give us an empirical record of value priorities authorized in each political system—who gives and who gets.

The National Accounts

Examining the national accounts [11] of a given political system may seem like a tedious approach to politics, but we believe that the way a government sets up its system of social accounting provides us with the most telling clues of what it wants and plans to do with the nation's resources, and certainly it gives us an idea of who gets what. In the framework of comparative politics, however, the national accounts fail to give us a true picture, not only because there is no uniform practice or fiscal reporting for all countries, but also because overall classification is apt to be confusing when the political, economic, and social bases are too dissimilar.

The best source of comparative data on national accounts for our twelve states comes from their annual reports to the United Nations. Table 11–1 offers us some illuminating insights into how each of our twelve countries allocates its gross national product (GNP). Using the USA as our first example, let us see what Table 11–1 tells us about the allocation of United States resources in 1967. Column 1 indicates that 61 percent of our GNP was allocated to private consumption, expenditures for goods and services by all households and nonprofit institutions. (Consumer goods include all durable goods except land and buildings. If you bought a transistor radio in 1967

TABLE 11–1
Expenditure of GNP at Market Prices: Percentages

State	Year	*1* *Private Consumption*	*2* *General Government*	*3* *Fixed Capital Formation*	*4* *Increase in Stocks*	*5* *Exports*	*6* *Imports*
Colombia	1965	75	7	16	2	12	11
Ger., FR	1950						
	1967	58	17	23	−1	22	19
Israel	1966	73	20	29	2	3	26
Ivory Coast	1966	66	14	19	2	33	30
Japan	1966	55	10	31	3	11	10
Mexico	1967	79	6	18		9	10
Turkey	1966	74	13	15		−2	
USSR	1966	64	8	14	12	2	
UK	1967	64	18	18	0	18	19
USA	1967	61	21	17	1	5	5

SOURCE: *UN Statistical Yearbook, 1968,* no. 199.

that transaction figures in column 1. If your family bought a house that expenditure shows up in column 3.) Column 2 indicates that general government expenditures took 21 percent of the GNP: civil service payrolls, compensation for members of the armed services, social security disbursements, all government purchases of goods and services from enterprises, and all government disbursements for goods including defense expenditures. Column 3 shows that 17 percent of the GNP went for fixed capital formation, construction work on railroads, harbor facilities, airports, roads, streets, dwellings, etc., purchase of land, dwellings, machinery, and equipment. Column 4 tells us that 1 percent of the GNP was used to increase resource stocks, including strategic stockpiling. And finally, columns 5 and 6 covering international transactions indicate that 5 percent of the United States GNP went into exports and, fortuitously, a balancing 5 percent into imports.

When we use Table 11–1 for comparisons of GNP allocations we must heed the UN classifications. Among our twelve states the UN classifies the United States, the United Kingdom, Germany, and Japan as states with "developed market economies," and the USSR as "a centrally planned economy." The classification has significant implications. Internal transactions in the Soviet economy are centrally planned by the government in accord with Marxian tenets. There is no exact equivalent of GNP in the accounts of the Soviet Union, which are based on the concept of social production. The social product is defined as the aggregate of consumable material goods produced in the branches of national production.[12] The main difference between gross national product in the United States and gross social product in the USSR is that the USSR aggregate does not include such services as passenger transportation, a large sector of communications, administration and defense, banking and insurance, recreation and entertainment, as well as services of individuals like teachers, doctors, nurses, barbers, and scientists. It is a major difference.

Table 11–1 gives us some useful data for comparing allocations of the GNP between the public and private sectors. Keep in mind that these allocations are determined by political authority. We find it interesting that in the USSR, our outstanding exponent of state socialism, 64 percent of the GNP is now allocated to private consumption, as compared with 61 percent in the United States, our prime example of the capitalist economy. When we rank our states from highest to lowest percentage GNP given to private consumption, at the top are Mexico, Colombia, and Turkey, and at the bottom Japan, Germany, and the United States. When we rank the states according to percentage of GNP allocated to general government expenditures, the United States, Israel, and the United Kingdom top the list, and Mexico, Colombia, and the USSR are at the bottom of the list. How would you explain these differing allocations? In the framework of ideology? In the realities of power in the political process?

Japanese allocations of GNP are easiest to explain since Japan is a unitary state with the central government clearly in a command position vis-à-vis the national accounts. The National Plan of the Japanese government in the 1960s was to double its GNP in the decade. To achieve this goal it determined to tighten up on private consumption, keep the expenditures for the general government at a modest level, to set aside as much as possible for fixed capital formation, and to maintain a favorable balance of trade. If you look at Table 11–1 you will see that the national accounts for 1966 demonstrate the plan in action: 55 percent for private consumption (the lowest figure in this column for all our states); 10 percent for general government expenditures (less than half the United States allocation); 31 percent for fixed capital formation (the highest figure in this column for all our states); and an excess of exports over imports providing a comfortable balance of trade in the international market.

Table 11–1 purports to give percentage distribution of the GNP at market prices. But market prices in a centrally planned economy like that of the USSR have a very different base than in the market economy of the United States or Japan. In the USSR producers' prices on goods traded in the productive sector are fixed by the government to defray the costs of labor, materials, and depreciation, plus a small average profit; no allowance is made, as in the market economies, for such factors as land, capital, and entrepreneurship. In the consumers' market of the Soviet Union, in the state stores and cooperative retail, trade prices are likewise fixed by the government to cover production costs but also include turnover taxes on sales. Because of the multiplicity of prices and because prices are fixed through central government planning, it is almost impossible to compare the value of goods and services produced in the market economies. Similarly, it is difficult to compute the individual [13] consumption expenditures because of the Marxian distinction between purchases of goods from socially productive enterprises and purchases of services from service enterprises.

According to UN classification, Colombia, India, Israel, the Ivory Coast, Kenya, and Mexico are "developing countries." Since the national accounts refer only to aggregates, comparisons may be quite misleading; for example, when applied to the quality of private consumption. In the more advanced countries a considerable percentage of consumer durable goods, as well as services, may be merely stylish: color TV's, chrome trim on overpowered automobiles, patio furnishings, and baby-blue, wall-to-wall carpeting. In the developing countries, where people are trying to raise their levels of living to minimum modern, the preponderance of private consumption is more likely to be functional: the basics in food, clothing, and shelter, with a few amenities such as indoor plumbing, window screens, and electricity. Probably most significant in the national accounts of the developing countries is the percentage of GNP that goes into fixed capital formation, for every one of the developing countries desperately needs capital.

One can hardly classify Germany or Japan as "developing countries," but because the impact of war upon their respective economies was so devastating we put them in a special category, "reconstructed economies." Since World War II both Germany and Japan have staged remarkable comebacks among the great industrial powers of the world. At the end of 1968 Japan replaced Germany as the country with the third largest gross national product.[14] (The United States is first, the USSR second, the United Kingdom fifth.) Note in Table 11–1 that both Japan and Germany show a high proportion of GNP given to fixed capital formation: 31 percent in the case of Japan, 23 percent in Germany. Both Germany and Japan enjoy prosperous market economies, but in each country the government exercises considerable control over private enterprise.

The modernization of Japan, following the restoration of the Meiji in the second half of the nineteenth century, was largely motivated and fostered by alliances between enterprising bureaucrats in the government and opportunistic members of the business community. This alliance persisted and flourished down to World War II. The government guided private enterprise in the national interest, giving a head start to some industries and then placing them in private hands. Business leaders in turn consulted with and advised the government on economic development policies especially with respect to industry, trade, and banking. On the eve of World War II Japan was in effect run by an oligarchy comprising interacting military, economic, and political elites. Immediately after the war American Occupation authorities were bent on breaking up the powerful companies and family combines that had designed and operated Japan's war machine, but an enforced policy of free enterprise and economic deconcentration proved to be utterly foreign to the training and habits of the Japanese. An American economist, examining the occupational revolution and the ensuing counterrevolution explains, "An advisory Commission of American businessmen, appointed to investigate the problem, recommended that economic recovery take precedence over deconcentration. The revolution on the anti-monopoly front was accordingly slowed down. Thus the economic counterrevolution was initiated by the Occupation itself." [15]

By the mid-1950s, postwar reconstruction in Japan had proceeded at such a pace that the output of the economy was surpassing prewar levels. In the decade 1956–65 the GNP was growing at an average rate of nearly 10 percent a year, a rate exceeding that of any other industrial nation in the world. In 1960 the Japanese government prepared a National Plan with the declared goal of doubling the national income by 1970. The plan provided investment guidelines for the private sector of the economy and outlined the government's monetary and fiscal policy. Achievement of the goal was predicated on a projected 7.8 percent annual growth rate in the GNP. Since the actual growth rate was considerably higher, the 1960 plan was revised in 1964 to a projected 9.1 percent annual growth rate.[16] Quite clearly, even though we have classified Japan as a "market economy," the Japanese government exercises considerable authority over the economy in order to achieve politically determined goals.

Taxation

Public finances are forceful tools for shaping any society. In large measure the public outlays determine the quality of life in any country. If you can find out what percentage of its governmental expenditures go for rockets or bombers or guns; for land reforms, public parks, or environmental controls; for slum clearance, health centers, and assistance for the aged; for aerospace spectaculars or education; for science, technology, or the fine arts, you are well on your way toward a character analysis of that country.

The sources of governmental revenue (who gives what) as well as the public expenditures (who gets what) tell us a great deal about the dominant values, the ruling interests, and the status of special interests in any country. Taxation is an old and tested technique of government. Taxes are used not only for raising the revenues needed to support the public programs but also for reallocating the national resources. Income taxes are intended to redistribute purchasing power at the household level, estate taxes to pare down inherited wealth. Payroll taxes are used to finance such social security programs as old-age pensions, medicare, unemployment compensation, and disability insurance. Selective sales taxes put heavier burdens or penalties on some industries (production of luxury items like perfumes and mink stoles or goods of questionable value, such as, tobacco or spirits). License taxes are used to regulate some occupations, such as doctors, dentists, beauty parlor operators, gamblers, and restaurant operators. Taxes on imports or exports may be used to protect or promote home industries or to control foreign trade within the framework of national security or national development. Tax collection at the local level, turned in to the national treasury to finance nationwide programs on the basis of need, is a common device to secure more equitable distribution of wealth in all parts of the country. Tax exemptions may also be regulatory or promotional. A country that wants to cut down on population growth may be prompted to reduce special allowances for children in the income tax structure. A state that wants to attract industry may offer various tax inducements.

It is instructive to note that when President Nixon, in mid-1971, undertook to chart a new economic policy for the United States, he relied heavily on taxation tools. To fight unemployment he asked the Congress to enact a Job Development Act to be financed by tax credits for business investments in new equipment in the hope that new equipment would generate new jobs, raise productivity, and improve the competitive position of American industry in world trade. He also proposed repeal of the excise tax on automobiles as a device to stimulate purchase of new cars and hence to increase production in the automobile industry. And he proposed an increase in consumer purchasing power by accelerating planned cuts in personal income taxes. Finally, on the international front, he placed a 10 percent surcharge on all goods imported into the United States, with the intent of protecting American industry from foreign competition and what he considered unfair exchange rates in the world market.

It is also instructive to note how the president's choice in techniques reflected his own (and his party's) public philosophy. In order to fight unemployment he could have opted for more public spending or for an extensive public works program. He chose to stimulate private spending. He could have increased private spending by across-the-board cuts in excise taxes on consumer goods, but he singled out the automobile industry for a preferential cut and recommended tax incentives for business investments in new equipment. He could have increased the purchasing power of the poorest sector in the population by pushing for welfare reform and federal revenue sharing, but he decided to postpone such plans for a year and instead to impose an immediate, if temporary, freeze on wages and prices (but not on profits). On the international front he could have initiated a diplomatic round of trade and currency negotiations, but he chose a unilateral course in order to gain a head-start advantage in the subsequent accommodation of the world market to the new economic policy of the United States. The point we make is that public officials, given the authority, have the power to shape the course of the national economy, to determine the goals, to set the priorities, to reallocate the national wealth, and to choose the means of implementation.

Budgeting

We cannot possibly examine all the ways in which a government (much less twelve very different governments) mobilizes and allocates the resources of the nation. Therefore, we have chosen to focus on the budget process as offering the most revealing overall view of how public finances are designed to achieve national goals and to meet the demands of different interests within the political system.

What is a national budget? Technically, it is a statement of public finances—expenditures, revenues, public debt—for a given period. (The fiscal year varies; in the United States the fiscal year runs from July 1 to June 30 of the next calendar year.) It is a comprehensive statement of governmental policies and programs, indicating the national priorities, allocating the nation's resources between the private and public sectors of the economy, specifying what activities and programs the government plans to undertake in the fiscal year, and spelling out how it proposes to finance all the various operations, with respect to personnel, materials, etc. Although the budget usually is restricted to the fiscal year, it is also a blueprint for the future. Every modern government makes its plans—and commitments—years ahead, not only in accord with the current economic setting but also in anticipation of changing needs and a consequent reordering of priorities.

Preparing the budget is generally regarded as an executive function since it calls for an all-inclusive presentation of government programs: work proposed, work in progress, work completed; detailed estimates of the capital outlays as well as for goods and services required in the various programs; rational justifications for program priorities (who gets more for what—and why); and finally an overall plan for financing the proposed programs. Authorizing the programs, turning the proposals into government policies, and making the necessary appropriations from the public funds to meet the governmental expenditures are generally regarded as legislative functions.

The annual budget of any state tells us a great deal about the economic setting, the relative sizes of the public and private sectors of the economy, the projected goals, the official ordering of priorities, and actual and estimated expenditures and receipts. Let us take a brief look at President Nixon's first budget message, the 1971 Budget, and see what we can learn from it. He informs us at the outset that the 1971 Budget is a balanced budget (expenditures equaling income) which seeks to meet today's needs and to anticipate tomorrow's challenges. "This anti-inflationary budget begins the necessary process of reordering our national priorities. For the first time in two full decades, the Federal government will be able to spend more money on human resource programs than on national defense." [17] This is a cheerful message, and it is accompanied by a pie-shaped diagram of the budget dollar which shows that the human resources piece of pie is bigger than the defense piece of pie. (See Figure 11–1.) The message with respect to the shift in priorities for the 1970s is amplified: "About 41 percent of estimated outlays in the 1971 budget will be devoted to human resources—spending for education and manpower, health, income security, and veterans benefits and services. Spending for national defense, despite continued improvement in our military forces, will claim a smaller percentage of the budget than in any year since 1951." [18]

We get a somewhat different reading, however, when we look at the outlays of the national government grouped according to thirteen "functional categories." (See Figure 11–2.)
Now it appears that national defense has the highest priority; the total bill for defense runs up to $72.3 billion. The major billion-dollar items in the defense bill include, $7.9 for strategic forces ("Our strategic forces are designed to provide a highly reliable and credible ability to inflict unacceptable damage upon those who might attempt a nuclear attack upon the United States or its allies"), $24.7 for general purpose forces ("Versatile general purpose forces are required for a wide range of military contingencies other than general nuclear war. Most of our naval, land, and air forces are designed for such contingencies"), $5.4 for research and development ("Major efforts in 1971 will be made to improve the effectivensss and survivability of our strategic forces and to pursue advanced technology for ballistic missile defense and strategic surveillance"). We mention only in passing that defense hardware, ICBM's, nuclear submarines, bombers, guided-missile frigates, helicopters, tanks, etc., as well as uniforms, food, and barracks for the military personnel are additional major items in the GNP.

Let us take a look at income security which the Nixon Administration selected as a primary target in its 1971 Budget. Income security includes the whole social security system, the railroad retirement and civil service systems, and unemployment compensation programs. These programs are financed by employers' contributions and employee payroll taxes deposited in trust funds. When we read some of the fine print in the budget message, however, we discover that 83 percent of the $56 billion for income security is derived from the trust funds and does not come under appropriations. In other words, the great bulk of expenditures for income security does not come out of appropriations but are payments from the trust funds over which the Nixon administration has no control.

The budget is intended to serve the president as an instrument of coordination and control over all the activities in the national administration of which he is chief executive. No department or agency may go directly to Congress for program authorizations or appropriations. All such requests must first be examined and evaluated in the president's Office of Management and Budget in accordance with presidential directives as to available resources, fiscal limitations, long-range goals, and immediate priorities.

FIGURE 11–1

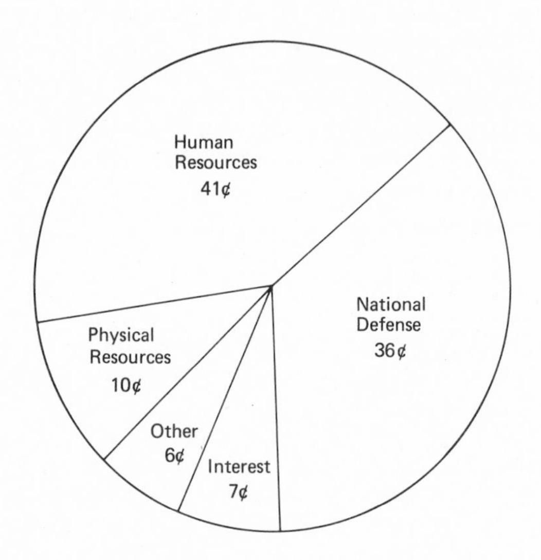

The Budget Dollar, Fiscal Year 1971—Where It Goes . . .
SOURCE: *U.S. Budget, Fiscal 1971,* p. 6.

The budget process, which begins with program planning in each agency, has a way of turning into incremental policy-making: a gradual growth in government operations, a gradual increase in public expenditures. Every agency more or less adopts the same strategy in dealing with the examiners from the Office of Management and Budget. First, as a matter of course, it asks to continue its current programs for which it has already received congressional approval. Then, in order to meet new needs or to reflect shifting emphases, it asks to do a little more and something a bit different, which will, unfortunately, increase this year's estimates over last year's expenditures. Predictably, the budget examiners raise few questions about current operations but concentrate their scrutiny on the new proposals. Predictably also, in their efforts to keep overall expenditures within the limits set by the president, the budget examiners try to pare down the new programs and yet allow the agency leeway for growth. Hence, inevitably, last year's operations and expenditures become the base from which this year's work plans and estimates are expanded. And because the bulk of the budget is used to support continuing obligations, the budget in final form appears to be not so much a plan for the future as a commitment to the past.

President Nixon, attempting to reorder the national priorities for the 1970s, was dismayed to discover that the accumulation of commitments meant that 69 percent of his 1971 Budget was relatively uncontrollable. In this 69 percent he counted expenditures for such continuing obligations as interest on the national debt, pensions for civil service workers, veterans' benefits, medicare, social security, and grants-in-aid to the states for public assistance.

FIGURE 11–2

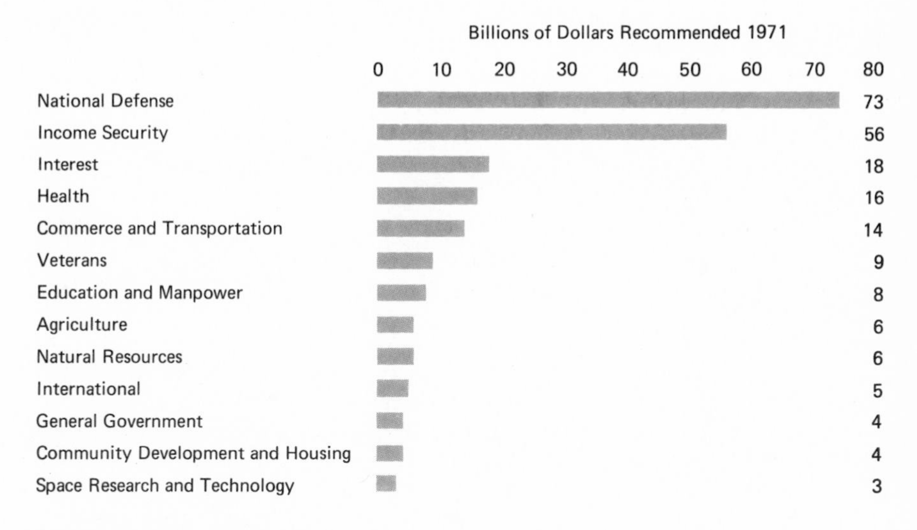

1971 Outlays by Function
SOURCE: *U.S. Budget, Fiscal 1971,* pp. 29 and 75.

If one thinks of government expenditures as controlled by limited governmental resources, then we can better understand the president's dilemma in budget-making. He cannot recommend great outlays of public money for new functions however pressing—for example, environmental control, consumer protection, or remodeling the cities—without reneging on previous commitments and/or raising a great deal of additional revenue through increased taxation. To appreciate the difficulties in reordering the national priorities, try out some alternatives in concrete terms. Imagine the president preempting prime viewing time on television to make several bold policy announcements regarding next year's United States Budget:

> *I am recommending a 50 percent cut in defense expenditures over the next five years, or alternatively a 25 percent increase in personal income taxes so that the national government can make immediate and substantial progress toward modernizing all our cities.*
>
> *I am recommending the elimination of all special benefits for veterans and the reallocation of the $9 billion thus made available to community development and housing.*
>
> *I am recommending the reallocation of all funds used for research and development in the Defense Department, about $8 billion, to research and development projects in Health, Education, and Welfare.*

Who would support, who would oppose, the president's bold policy proposals? When you have answered that question, you will understand why the budget is a blueprint of politics as well as an instrument of national planning in the government of the United States.

The national budget is a blueprint of politics as well as an instrument of planning in every national government. In the United States, however, there appear to be more politics and less planning than in any of our twelve states. This we attribute not only to ideological and behavioral preferences for free enterprise but also to the coordinate relationship between the president and the Congress. Note that in our fictitious examples of bold budget policies, the president recommended reallocations; this is as far as he can go. Only Congress can authorize the programs for which appropriations are required. Congress relies on the president's budget as a guide, but it is not obliged nor expected to accept all of the president's recommendations. Congress may refuse to authorize programs cleared through the president's Office of Management and Budget. Congress may increase, decrease, or even eliminate specific appropriation items recommended by the president. It may stipulate new programs which neither the agency nor the chief executive envisaged or encouraged, and it may hold up appropriations for months while it debates what it wants to do. Neither the president nor the agency can force congressional action.

Congressional changes in the president's budget may result in different emphases than the president planned for his administration. But the same practical and political considerations that entered into the presidential process of budget-making also enter into the congressional processes of authorization and appropriations. Existing programs are usually sustained, rarely terminated. New programs are authorized cautiously and are generally more incremental than innovative. And again, one way of finding out who is most influential in the political process is to ascertain who gets what out of the congressional appropriations.

In the parliamentary system, where the executive works hand in glove with the legislature, it is extremely unlikely that the parliament will do other than support the government budget. In the British system, for example, the Treasury Department decides how the financial resources of the government can best be utilized. The chancellor of the Exchequer, second in party command to the prime minister, is a member of the cabinet. Rarely does another member of the cabinet have the nerve even to question a Treasury decision, and when the chancellor takes the budget to Parliament, he has the collective backing of the cabinet. When the chancellor presents the budget to Parliament, there is no chance that Parliament will make any significant alterations; in any case, Parliament may not increase the estimates of any ministry beyond the Treasury allotment. Parliament does, however, engage in a limited debate on the government proposals and votes annually upon all government expenditures except on certain fixed charges including interest on the national debt, salaries of the judges, and the expenses of the royal family. The fact that the Treasury has such tight control over the budget does not mean that the budget is not part and parcel of British politics. The chancellor uses his Treasury office to carry out the policies of his party in the name of the government.

In a one-party system the national budget is really an instrument of managerial control and central planning. It is, for example inconceivable that the Supreme Soviet of the USSR would freely debate, much less alter the government budget. But even in a totalitarian government, budgeting and planning are essentially political processes that are attuned to expectations, demands, and supports among the general citizenry as well as to the priorities of those at the apex of political power.

Differentials in National Accounting Systems

When we try to compare budgets for our twelve states and to determine the ordering of priorities in allocation of resources we encounter all kinds of frustrations. It is difficult to compare budgets that have different systems of accounting. The United States budget, for example, keeps separate accounts for income security, health, veterans, education and manpower, community development and housing. The British budget has separate categories for education and child care, national health services, housing, and social security benefits. The United States's budget is in dollars, the United Kingdom's in pounds, and the relative purchasing power of dollars and pounds fluctuates even in a year. Even more of a problem in calculation, the United States's budget is for national outlays only and does not cover state and local government expenditures. Since the United Kingdom is a unitary state its budget is much more comprehensive.

Despite their inconsistency, the budget accounts in the *UN Statistical Yearbook* give us a comparative picture of how different national governments report their allocation of resources in three significant areas: defense, education, and health. Table 11–2 gives us an incomplete picture. No account was available on the Ivory Coast; the Indian and the United States accounts were too dissimilar for comparative use.[19]

Table 11–2 tells us that Israel, Turkey, Mexico, and Colombia allocate more of their public funds for national defense than for health and/or education. Since we have classified these four countries as "developing nations," we wonder why they choose to allocate more of the nation's resources to guns and planes than to schoolhouses and health centers. In the case of Israel the answer is obvious. Since the founding of the state, Israel has been in both cold and hot wars with its neighbors; Israel continues to fight for her very existence. The military posture of Turkey is also dictated in part by hostile neighbors. Turkey is a buffer state between East and West, and as a partner in NATO, has assumed active obligations to resist aggression from Communist countries including its gigantic neighbor to the north, the USSR. The military function in Turkey, however, is also related to domestic politics. The present constitutional government of Turkey was established by military coup, and although the military have now left the foreground of the political system, they appear to be standing in the wings ready to move into center position if the government is unable to obtain consent of the governed or to maintain law and order.

Unlike Israel or Turkey, neither Mexico nor Colombia faces any immediate danger of external aggression. In the Latin American countries, the military serves mainly to keep the establishment in power, or to overthrow it. In Colombia, for example, the military is frequently used to control rioting, to check terrorism, and to prevent coups. The 1970 elections illustrate the point: Former military dictator Gustavo Rojas Pinilla, attempting a comeback, was apparently defeated at the polls. Since the election was extremely close, his followers were inclined to resort to violence rather than accept the official results, whereupon President Carlos Lleras Restrepo called upon the military forces to support the official count, and thus from a position of military strength was able to turn over the reins of government to the officially declared winner. Similarly in Mexico, the military now stays in the background but is on call to suppress rioting, to protect the infrastructure, and to safeguard the continued operation of the PRI in the seats of political power.

One of the problems in comparing the current budgetary allocations is that they do not give us a picture of accrued allocations.[20] Obviously a country with a high percentage of illiteracy, if it plans to overcome such a handicap, needs to make greater effort than a country where public education has long been established. Similarly, we would expect that a country planning to move from rural-agrarian to urban-industrial patterns would probably need to make larger allocations for public health than the more advanced states. Now let us see if Table 11–2 gives us any clues as to how national budgets in our selected states take into consideration the social deficiencies of those states. Note that we have used two indicators for social deficiency—the percentage of illiterates in the population and the adequacy of medical care, measured by the proportion of physicians in the population.[21]

Among the nine states listed in Table 11–2, five states allocate more than 10 percent of their national budgets to education: the USSR (17.1 per-

TABLE 11–2
Percentage of 1967 Budget Allocated to Defense, Education, and Health

	Defense	*Education*	*Percentage (around 1960)*	*Health*	*Population Per Physician (1,000)*
Colombia	22.3	13.6	27.1	4.3	2.2
Ger., FR *	9.3	6.9	1.0	12.7	0.7
Israel	25.8	7.5	15.8	2.6	0.4
Japan	6.1	10.2	2.2		0.9
Kenya	6.9	12.5	20.0+	6.2	10
Mexico	10.0	2.5	34.6	6.2	1.8
Turkey	31.5	4.1	61.9		2.8
UK	17.3	15.0	0.1	10.7	0.9
USSR	13.5	17.1	1.5	6.1	0.4
USA			2.2		0.7

* Combined public authority, federal and state.

SOURCE: *UN Statistical Yearbook, 1968.* no. 199, Public Finance, p. 622 ff., and our Table 3–1, and *Statistical Abstract of the United States 1970*, no. 1255, p. 833.

cent), the United Kingdom (15 percent), Japan (10.2 percent), Colombia (13.6 percent), and Kenya (12.5 percent). Since illiteracy is a minimal problem in the first three countries, we assume that the continuing high allocation for education bespeaks its high rank in the official ordering of values. Since illiteracy is a serious problem in both Colombia and in Kenya, the high allocation in these two developing countries may be taken as an indicator of deliberate planning to overcome the national deficiency. On the other hand, four states—Mexico, Turkey, Israel, and Germany—allocate less than 10 percent of their national budgets to education, but spend more than 10 percent for national defense.

Illiteracy is certainly not a major problem in Germany, but there is some suggestion that Germany may be surviving on accrued allocations. Arnold Heidenheimer observes that "The quality of the federal German educational system is rightfully held in world-wide esteem both for its successes in bringing literacy to the masses and for its traditional ability to produce outstanding scholars and scientists." [22] But he also observes that 80 percent of the students leave school at the age of fourteen, and those who do go on to high schools that prepare for university entrance are generally drawn from middle-class families. Perhaps a Social Democratic government will make some reallocations; the latest figures available to us from Germany, however, still support Dr. Heidenheimer's earlier observation.[23]

Correlations between allocation of public funds for health and facilities for medical care are more difficult to draw, especially since medical care has only recently entered the public sector in many countries. Comparing national budget allocations for health, Germany takes the lead with 12.7 percent, the United Kingdom second with 10.7 percent. We attribute these high figures to strong social security programs developed very early in these two urban-industrial countries. Our indicator for medical care available shows one doctor for every 630 persons in Germany, one doctor for every 870 persons in the United Kingdom. On the other hand, Israel and Japan, which make very small allocations for public health programs, also enjoy relatively high rating for medical care available, presumably in the private sector. Israel, which ranks at the bottom of our list for public health expenditures, ranks at the top in medical service available, with one doctor for every 410 persons. The Zionist movement, particularly in the United States and Western Europe, has had a special appeal among Jewish professional people, and many doctors have emigrated to the promised land.[24] Similarly, Japan, which makes an insignificant allocation for public health, nevertheless makes a good showing because of medical aid available in the private sector, one doctor for every 930 persons.

Allocation of the national resources is an important function of budgeting, but translated into standards and levels of living for the people, the total budget may be more important than its various portions. The size of a piece of pie depends partly on who does the cutting, partly on how many pieces are needed to serve all, but always also on how large the pie is to begin with. Kenya and Mexico allocate 6.2 percent of their respective budgets for public health. Although this represents real effort and concern to raise the standards and levels, the payoff is still very low; in Mexico one doctor for every 1,810 persons and in Kenya one for every 10,600 persons. A developing country which has to begin almost from scratch with no longtime enterprise in the private sector and very little cumulative allocation in the public sector has to make much larger allocations in order to show relatively small advances in social services.

Planning and Programming

The national budget is not simply an economic or fiscal accounting system. It is an instrument of government, a tool for management, a device for planning and programming. Basically the budgeting process is a political exercise, deciding at the highest level of government whose values, interests, and preferences will prevail in the public policies. All public policies emerge from competing and conflicting demands among the various sectors of society and also among the several components of the government. In effect, the national budget represents the final outcome of much bargaining, negotiating, and compromising among numerous decisional units within the political system. Whoever directs and controls the budget process is at the very center of policy-making.

Every modern government uses its budget process for the implementation of planning. The USSR is our prime example of the planning state, as the whole Russian economy is organized on the basis of state ownership and management of natural resources, including the land, production, and distribution of goods, transportation, and communications. The State Planning Committee of the USSR (the *Gosplan*) works directly under the Council of Ministers, preparing the annual and long-term plans of economic activity according to goals determined by the Communist party leadership. Thus the annual budget of the USSR is drawn up by the government to shape the public policies and implement the programs in accordance with directions mapped out by the Gosplan: rockets, farm tractors, or refrigerators; diesel engines on the railroads, super passenger planes for foreign travel, or private cars; education for scientists, technologists, economists, agronomists, or poets; more or less foreign trade, what to export, what to import; to trade or not to trade with non-Communist countries. All of these decisions, changing from year to year with the exigencies of the times as well as with changing party perspectives, you can read in the annual budgets of the USSR.

The Five-Year Economic Development Plan of the USSR for 1971–75, endorsed by the Twenty-fourth Congress of the Communist party and subsequently incorporated into the government budgets, attests to the growing sensitivity of the party leadership to popular expectations. Earlier plans had concentrated on strengthening the country's defense capability, building a modern infrastructure, increasing power capacity, and emphasizing heavy industry. At the end of the eighth Five-Year Plan, Alexei Kosygin, chairman of the Council of Ministers, was able to report that the Soviet people had achieved a more than eight-fold increase over 1940 in the output of the national economy. At long last then, the party was prepared to reward the people for their great enterprise and self-discipline. Thus the party directive from the Twenty-fourth Congress (previously discussed in draft form at party congresses in the Union Republics, at territorial, regional, city, and district party conferences, at workers' meetings, and in the press) called for a massive switch of the whole economy toward raising the living standards of the people.

The ninth Five-Year Plan embraces an elaborate mechanism designed to plan, stimulate, manage, and control all key aspects of Soviet life. In the language of Kosygin,

> *In the complicated internal situation with imperialist reaction resorting to military gambles and direct aggression" strengthening the defense might of the state must continue to be a primary concern. Also, "heavy industry has been and remains the foundation of the country's economic might and of the further growth of the peoples' standard of living.*

The ninth Plan, however, manifestly is "a plan for peaceful construction" most attentive to the wants of the people as consumers. The Plan calls for an 80 percent rise in the output of goods for cultural and household needs and provides for a planned redistribution of the national income by budgeting for new wage minimums, higher income for the professions and middle-bracket workers, and for much more extensive and generous welfare provisions.

Chairman Kosygin's 1971 report to the Twenty-fourth Congress (which included representatives from "nearly all the Communist and Workers' Parties of the world") makes clear that the directives for the ninth Five-Year Plan are designed not only for the government of the Soviet Union but also to serve as a working model for the development of world Communism.[25] Certainly, even a cursory study of Soviet budgets which implement the ninth Plan uncovers a remarkable cohesion of Marxist-Leninist ideology, Soviet political organization, and the socialist national economy. Among our twelve states—in sharpest contrast to the United States—the Soviet Union exemplifies the planned political system, operating and managed according to plan. And yet, we note also the play of politics, the fortuitous shift in the plans, the reallocations of resources and redistribution of income effected by budgets, as the planners and managers become aware of changing values and new demands on the part of the people.

Taking many of their lessons in planning from the eminently successful USSR, many new nations, whether or not they espouse a centrally controlled economy or a market economy, have established state planning machinery similar to the Gosplan. For example, since 1960 the State Planning Organization of Turkey has drawn up three Five-Year Plans with the announced goals of increasing the GNP at an annual rate of 7 percent, providing universal primary education, reducing income disparities, and eventually eliminating need for any foreign aid. Although the Turkish economy is a mix of public and private enterprise, the second Five-Year Plan (1968–72) gives the leading role in the projected development to the public sector.[26]

State plans are implemented through various government programs: education, housing, social security, transportation, communications, agriculture, commerce, etc. The main function of the budget process is to offer an annual fiscal formula for underwriting these programs. A corollary function, however, is to give the government managerial control over the entire complex of programs. If all government agencies must clear their projected programs through a centralized budget office, then the government is in position to check for overlapping, competing, and even conflicting activities. Actually the budget is the principal means by which those in authority manage to mobilize and allocate the national resources economically and efficiently.[27]

Getting inside the governmental machinery to find out how policy is formulated or implemented is easier said than done. Governing a modern state is a vastly complicated and highly technical business. This chapter began with an overall view of how official authority is obtained and maintained, discussing such general concepts as legitimacy (the recognized right to rule), the utility of constitutions in establishing the basic principles and institutions of government, and the notion of popular sovereignty manifest in regular elections, universal suffrage, and secret balloting. Among our twelve states we found many variations in practice but more or less universal recognition of the concepts.

Turning our attention to the basic assignments of government in the modern state—the determination of public values and the allocation of the national resources—we attempted some comparative analysis of the national accounts. Despite the obvious difficulties in comparing national accounts for twelve countries with very different political, economic, and social bases (as well as varying practices in fiscal accounting), we think this approach to comparative analysis is most illuminating as to the values, interests, perceptions, and judgments that enter into the public policies in various political systems. The national accounts, for example, tell us how the nation's resources are allocated between the public and private sectors of the society and also how they are mobilized by the government to achieve various politically determined goals.

In our examination of the national accounts, we looked especially at public finance policies to discover who gets what out of the public expenditures and who gives what to the public revenues. The national budgets provide us with blueprints of how a government plans to achieve the national goals and meet the plural interests of society. It also gives us the most precise information on the official ordering of priorities and the actual distribution of the public funds for specific governmental functions.

Budgeting, we have found out in all twelve of our states, is essentially a political process, generally attuned to popular expectations, demands, and supports—as these are perceived and evaluated by those in authority. (As we have reiterated throughout this text, official perceptions and evaluations must be understood within the unique cultural context of each nation state.) Finally, we observed the importance of the budget as a device for planning and programming the public policies. (Some governments make more of a to-do about planning than others, but all modern governments must engage in planning, even those whose rhetoric still stresses free enterprise.) The national budget has become the single most efficient instrument for maintaining central managerial control over the whole range of governmental activities.

In the chapter that follows, we shall look more closely at the policy process, and particularly at the ways in which policies are implemented in various political systems.

NOTES

1. David Easton, *A Framework for Political Analysis* (Englewood Cliffs, N.J.: Prentice-Hall, 1965), p. 50.
2. *Modern Political Analysis*, 2d ed. (Englewood Cliffs, N.J.: Prentice-Hall, 1970), p. 33.
3. See Samuel Flagg Bemis, *A Diplomatic History of the United States*, 5th ed. (New York: Holt, Rinehart & Winston, 1965), pp. 544–51.
4. The *Turkish Constitution*, Chapter 2, Article 96.
5. Samuel H. Beer and Adam B. Ulam, eds., *Patterns of Government: The Major Political Systems of Europe*, rev. ed. (New York: Random House, 1962), p. 125.
6. Ministry for Foreign Affairs, *Facts about Israel, 1969*, p. 11.
7. Peter H. Merkl, *The Origin of the West German Republic* (New York: Oxford University Press, 1963), p. 180.
8. Press and Information Office of the Federal Government, *Facts about Germany*, Public Document 914, 30 §2/2–2, 7th ed., 1968.
9. Hans Trossmann, *The German Bundestag* (Darmstadt: Neue Darmstädter Verlaganstalt, 1965), p. 1. Quoting Dr. Eugen Gerstenmaier, president of the German Bundestag, October 15, 1957, in the Congress Hall, Berlin.
10. Article 39.
11. Quantitative economic and financial data measuring national production, national income, distribution by factors of private and public consumption, etc. International organizations have encouraged the national government to join in developing a comprehensive and uniform statistical tool which could be used for international comparisons. The movement has gained momentum since World War II.
12. All tables in the *UN Statistical Yearbook* include numerous footnotes which explain particulars in national accounts. The footnotes are important in making meaningful comparisons. For an overall understanding of differing national accounts, we recommend M. Yanousky, *Anatomy of Social Accounting Systems* (London: Chapman and Hall, 1965).
13. The USSR accounts refer to individual rather than private consumption; this is a reflection of Marxist ideology.
14. US Department of Commerce, Bureau of International Commerce, *Japan, Foreign Economic Trends* (April 16, 1969).
15. E. Wight Bakke, *Revolutionary Democracy: Challenge and Testing in Japan* (Hamden, Conn.: Archon Books, 1968), p. 208. This study is especially helpful because it looks at the Occupational revolution and the Counterrevolution in the cultural context of Japan and recognizes the need of a people to live and work and interact with each other in the ways which are familiar and customary to them.

16. The economic data on Japan are taken from the *Overseas Business Reports* and *Foreign Economic Trends,* periodicals distributed by the Bureau of International Commerce, US Department of Commerce.
17. See the *Budget of the United States Government, Fiscal Year 1971* (Washington, D.C.: Government Printing Office, 1970), p. 7.
18. Ibid., p. 20.
19. The United States accounts combine health with welfare, and education with manpower. The Indian accounts do not provide a functional breakdown.
20. The student who wants to do an in-depth study of who gets what in any political system will gain significant insights by examining budget trends over a period of a decade or more.
21. Although we do not have the national accounts for India and the United States on public expenditures for education and health, we have supplied indicators for comparative purposes.
22. Arnold Heidenheimer, *The Governments of Germany,* 2d ed. (New York: Thomas Y. Crowell, 1966), p. 42.
23. Statistisches Bundesamt Wiesbaden, *Statistisches Jahrbuch für die Bundesrepublik Deutschland, 1969* (Stuttgart and Mainz: W. Kohlhammer, GMBH, 1969), pp. 74–87.
24. "An extensive system of health insurance benefits, administered both by the government and the Histadrut [General Federation of Trade Unions] is operated with the aim of providing first rate medical care to all citizens." US Department of Commerce, Bureau of International Commerce, *Basic Data on the Economy of Israel,* (December, 1969), p. 2.
25. See *Directives of the 24th Congress of the Communist Party of the Soviet Union for the Five-Year Economic Development Plan of the USSR for 1971–75,* a Report by Alexei Kosygin, chairman of the Council of Ministers of the USSR, April 6, 1971. (Moscow: Novosti Press Agency Publishing House, 1971). "A. N. Kosygin's report was heard with great attention and repeatedly punctuated with prolonged applause."
26. The second Plan, now in operation, has specified investment in the economy between 1968 and 1972 as follows: agriculture 15.2 percent; communications 16.1 percent; housing 17.9 percent; education 6.7 percent; health 1.8 percent; manufacturing 22.4 percent; power 8 percent. Obviously, the heart of the Plan is to step up the process of industrialization. Our information comes from the Republic of Turkey, Prime Ministry State Planning Organization, *Second Five-Year Development Plan 1968–1972* (Ankara: Central Bank of the Republic of Turkey, 1969), table 147, p. 326.
27. See Chapter 12 for further discussion on program implementation.

FURTHER READING

DAHL, ROBERT A. *Modern Political Analysis.* Englewood Cliffs, N.J.: Prentice-Hall, 2nd ed. 1970.

DEUTSCH, KARL W. "Communication Models and Decision Systems." In *Contemporary Political Analysis,* edited by James C. Charlesworth. New York: Free Press, 1967, pp. 273–99.

United Nations. *Statistical Yearbook.* Published annually by the United Nations in New York City.

Yanousky, M. *Anatomy of Social Accounting Systems.* London: Chapman and Hall, 1965.

The budgets, the five-year plans, and various other economic plans of the twelve nation states are the most useful references for this chapter.

chapter 12

HOW DO GOVERNORS GOVERN?

In Chapter 10 we examined the policy process by looking at role structure —the interactions, mutual expectations, and understandings among the official participants. At this point we are more particularly concerned with such questions as: Why are most people in a political system willing to be governed by those in authority? What do those in authority do when they govern? What are the commonly accepted techniques of government?

THE POLICY-MAKING PROCESS

In his discerning analysis of the policy-making process, Charles E. Lindblom remarks that the policy-making task "has to be seized or assigned." [1] As we pointed out in Chapter 11, however, no matter how the policy-making authority is obtained, it must be recognized as legitimate by the general membership in the political system, or it will not be acceptable in the long run. Authority may be seized through revolution or coup d'etat as in the United States in 1776, Mexico in 1910, Russia in 1917, and Turkey in 1960. Authority may be retained through a reign of terror as it was in Hitler's Third Reich, by the Stalinist government in the USSR, or by the violence in Colombia in the 1950s. In every state, authorities do to some degree rely upon the institutions of force (the army and the police) to maintain law and order. But

Japan, demonstrators and riot police
(Wide World Photos)

the most commonly accepted technique for gaining and retaining authority in the modern state is to win popular support for the policy-makers through elections with universal suffrage. This can be seen clearly in all twelve of our countries.

Most people accept and abide by the policies of their government, even those which run counter to their own interests or predilections. Why? No doubt the use of force or even the threat of force is a factor, but political scientists since the time of Aristotle have been pointing out that obedience to the laws is largely a matter of habit and custom. Robert MacIver talked about the "firmament of law" which envelops every government. This firmament of law is derived from cultural tradition, settled modes of procedure, and religious precepts as well as the rules made by political authorities.[2] So long as the public policy-makers do not attempt to prescribe rules of conduct that deviate too far from the normal behavior patterns of the people, the problem of enforcement usually resolves itself into letting people do what comes naturally. Let us take a closer look at how those in authority undertake their various assignments in the policy process.

In any national government—advanced or developing, democratic or dictatorial, representative or totalitarian—only the top leadership in the political system participates in the crucial decisions. The elite group at the apex of authority is charged with determining major policies: the national goals, the order of priorities, the mobilization and allocation of national resources.

Colombia, strike-closed building in Bogotá
(Calogero Cascio : Rapho Guillumette)

But the activities of modern government are so complicated and technical that they cannot be entrusted to politicians alone; they have to be planned and programmed in the bureaucracy by specialists and technocrats.

The policy process in modern government is a continuum of planning, decision-making, and programming by many people with various degrees of authority and different competencies within the political system. Turkey, for example, is embarked on its second Five-Year Development Plan which includes long-term targets for the economic and social structure of the country. The Development Plan is authorized and generally supervised by the top political leadership, the president, the prime minister, and the cabinet ministries. But actual responsibility for the Plan, its general objectives, and the annual implementation of programs, is assigned to the State Planning Organization. The principal objective of the Plan is to show a 40 percent increase in national income by the end of the implementation period 1968–72. The overall strategy is to accelerate development in all sectors of the economy, with priority given to the industrial sector. The Planning Organization sets forth the specific objectives and proposes particular policy measures for sectoral development, but the annual programs have to be worked out by experts in the ministries.

Policy measures designed to advance the Turkish economy range over a wide variety of governmental programs, covering such things as balance of payments in foreign trade, changes in customs and duties, export incentives

United Kingdom, police and ladies outside Buckingham Palace
(Bruce Davidson : Magnum)

and import restrictions, incentive tax policies for new or modernizing industries, investment aids and regulations, state support for technological research and consultative services for particular industries (e.g., chemicals, leather goods, metal products, agricultural machinery), state encouragement of mass production techniques, state controls for standardizing and quality, public projects, reallocation of manpower, on-the-job training, low income housing, and family planning.[3]

Whichever policies and programs a modern government adopts, the policy process is bound to include a great many calculations and agonizing choices. What are the national interests? Does the political system—or should it—respond mainly to majority demands? How does—or should—the system respond to minority demands? Whose demands are most pressing? Whose needs are most acute? Does—or should—the political system capitalize upon apathy among the general citizenry? How close do—or should—policy-makers trim their programs to satisfy public opinions? What are the limits of decision-making, the constitutional and other legal curbs? The inertia of precedents? The previous commitments? Can a representative government promote revolutionary changes? How far can decision-makers hope to go with innovative approaches? Is incrementalism adequate? On what bases do—or should—decision-makers reach their conclusions? Rational analyses? Political expedience? Bureaucratic consensus? Economic feasibility? Social justice?

President Nixon in his 1970 report to the Congress on United States foreign policy provides us with a remarkable description of his view of the foreign policy process in his administration. As he envisages it,

> *If our policy is to embody a coherent vision of the world and a rational conception of America's interests, our specific actions must be the products of rational and deliberate choice. . . . Our policy must be systematic: our actions must be the products of thorough analysis, forward planning, and deliberate decision. . . . We must know the* facts: . . . *Disputes in the government have been caused too often by an incomplete awareness or understanding of the facts. We must know the* alternatives. *We must know what our real options are and not simply what compromise has found bureaucratic acceptance. . . . Finally, we must have effective* implementation. *It does little good to plan intelligently and imaginatively if our decisions are not well carried out.*[4]

President Nixon's description of the foreign policy process in his administration is almost as remarkable for what it does not say as for what it does say. The most conspicuous omission is any reference to the Congress with whom he is constitutionally required to share his powers in foreign affairs. Moreover, the message makes no mention of the influence of political parties, general or special interest groups, or public opinion in all its manifold aspects. The president's accounting of the foreign policy process, somewhat less than candid, tends to perpetuate the myth of rational decision-making rather than to describe the realities of power in the policy process.

Congressmen, senators and representatives, Democrats and Republicans, committee chairmen and influential members of policy committees; bureaucrats with special expertise in the executive establishment including the State Department, the Defense Department, the Central Intelligence Agency, and the Agency for International Development; party leaders at the state and local level as well as in the nation's capital; articulate individuals, editors, preachers, teachers, pediatricians, and TV commentators; organized groups, including those who take to the streets and parks to demonstrate their support—or protest—on particular policies: all of these diverse spokesmen, as well as the silent majority, provide the ingredients for President Nixon's foreign policy process.

President Nixon's explanation of how foreign policy is made in his administration was mostly an exercise in public relations. Telling the people that foreign policy—or any other public policy—is made, or can be made, solely on rational grounds is not telling it like it is. The policy process (even in a totalitarian state) has to react to competing and conflicting values, interests, and attitudes throughout the entire political system. Policy decisions must take into account personal, professional, and institutional preferences and judgments within the hierarchy of official policy-makers. And so, the programs reflect "not simply what compromise has found bureaucratic acceptance" but a great many mutual adjustments that are necessary or desirable to bring the various participants in the policy process into operational agreement.

In our discussion of role structure in the institutional organization of the state (Chapter 10) we viewed policy-makers as actors in an environment. Foreign policy-makers for the most part must work within the international environment, outside the territorial boundaries of their own state. Thus President Nixon's foreign policy machinery may be designed to produce rational decisions, but unilateral decisions, no matter how rationally conceived, even when made by a superpower, may not be able to control the complicated course of international relations. United States foreign policy is affected by decisions being made in Hanoi, Moscow, Peking, London, Paris, Cairo, Tel Aviv, and Bonn. And by the same token, foreign policy formulated in Bonn, Abidjan, or any national capital, is affected by different policy decisions being made in other national capitals.

Policy-makers in every state must operate from home base, from within the domestic environment. The structural and functional organization of the state has a direct bearing on the policy process. Thus Chancellor Willy Brandt trying to steer a new course in foreign policy (the new Eastern policy) for the Federal Republic of Germany may appear to have the leading role, but unlike the president of the United States he is in no position to upstage the rest of his cast. The German chancellor knows that he plays the lead role only so long as he retains his official position and that he retains his official position only so long as he can command a majority coalition in the Bundestag.

We cannot possibly examine the policy process in all twelve of our states, a task horrendous in its dimensions. Analysis of policy-making in a single state might begin with a study of the actors, their individual characteristics, the roles they are expected to play, their official positions and prescribed duties, the institutional arrangements in which they must work, and their own style of acting and interacting within the system. To understand how an Indira Gandhi or a Golda Meier acts as a policy-maker, we would need to find out how she perceives her role as head of government, what kind of political resources she can count on within her own state, and how far she is willing, or able, to go in making use of such resources to achieve what she considers important goals. Clearly this kind of analysis requires more than public information about the individual actor, and it also calls for considerable probing into human behavior.

Moreover, if we are to look for the leverage points in the making of policy, we must go beyond the activities of the official participants, either individual leaders or ruling elites.[5] If we regard policy-making as a function of the political system, then we must concern ourselves with all kinds of political transactions that affect the official decisions. To understand policy-making in India, Israel, or any other state, we need to know what kind of interactions take place continuously between the governors and the governed: What are the lines of communication? What is the nature of the communications? How representative is the government? How responsive is it to public opinions? How does it view its responsibilities to the governed? What role do political parties play? How significant are the elections? What are the ideological goals of the society? We have tried to tackle these questions in a general way throughout this text, but when we come down to the specifics of policy-making we must confess our information is inadequate.

Policy-making is issue-oriented. Hence analysis of the policy process with respect to specific issues calls for relevant data. For example, comparing the policy process concerning public education in the Federal Republic of Germany, the Soviet Union, India, Mexico, and the United Kingdom, we note at the outset that all but the United Kingdom are organized as federal unions. This means we will have to examine the patterns of interaction, official, formal, unofficial, informal, between those in authority in both the central government and the states. Who determines the priorities? Who sets the qualifications for teachers? Who prescribes what shall be taught? What values? What attitudes? What subjects? What skills? Who manages the finances and how? Who gets what? Policy-making is also time-bound. Educational policies in the Soviet Union have gone through many different phases since 1917. Similarly, educational policies in Germany were drastically changed from the Weimar Republic to the Third Reich to the Occupation to the Federal Republic. After the Soviet Union orbited Sputnik in 1957 a commission was appointed to study and evaluate education in the USA. And how does one compare time-bound policies when nations are on such very different time schedules, as India and the United Kindom?

Public education as a policy issue involves a distributive function of the state—who gets what. If, however, we want to examine the policy process with respect to the regulatory functions of the state, e.g., control of banking practices or insurance rates, health and safety codes in factories, licensing of electricians or physicians, inspection of foods and drugs—then we must consider different questions: What is the public interest in regulation? Who determines when regulation is necessary and proper? Who is authorized to make the rules and issue the orders? How are the rules and orders enforced?

Obviously, comparisons between the United States and the Soviet Union must be attuned to the basic differences between a system of private enterprise and a communist system. Similarly, comparisons between the United Kingdom and Kenya must take into consideration very different stages in economic development.

In our concluding chapter we shall make some general observations about the output of policy-making, particularly as it affects the status of the individual members in the political system. We turn now, however, to some of the ways policies are implemented within various nation states.

THE IMPLEMENTATION OF POLICIES

We have moved a long way from the traditional concepts of political science: the state as a lawgiver, the law as command of the sovereign, government as the extension of sovereign power. We now think of the state as the principal policy-maker for society and observe that policy-making takes place in a dynamic milieu: competition, conflict, negotiations, mutual adaptation, bargaining, and, finally, resolution expressed in programs. With this understanding of the policy process, we are not inclined to stress the command-compliance relationships between the governors and the governed. When we try to answer our own question—What do those in authority do when they govern?—various techniques of modern government come to mind: communications, incentives, rewards, penalties, intimidation, command, coercion and force, as well as public administration and managerial controls. We cannot begin to report how each of our twelve states fashions and implements its public policies, but we will try to illustrate how all of them use a variety of governing techniques.

Communications

We earlier discussed the importance of communications in nation-building; communications, of course, have a strategic role in the implementation of all government policies. As Karl W. Deutsch points out, "if politics requires a machinery of enforcement, and a set of habits of compliance, then politics is impossible without a flow of information to those who are expected to comply with the commands." [6]

The United States sets the record for flow of communications among the several components of the government as well as from the governmental agencies to the people. Let us take a look, for example, at the president's communications network. The Constitution requires that the president "from time to time give to the Congress information of the State of the Union and recommend to their consideration such measures as he shall judge necessary and expedient." The modern president, capitalizing upon this requirement, delivers his State of the Union message to Congress in person—with full coverage by the mass media. This is his way of telling not only the Congress but also all the people, what policy measures his administration considers necessary and proper. It is, however, more than an informational message; it is intended to persuade the Congress to take appropriate action; it is also calculated to enlist the support of public opinion for the presidential programs.

Presidential communications may be formal or informal, official or personal. The president may address the nation from the White House over the national television networks at prime viewing time. He may summon the party leaders, the leadership of his own party, or a bipartisan group, for policy strategy sessions, for breakfast, or in a more formal setting. He may invite the leaders, or the entire membership, of congressional policy committees to meet with him for briefing or consultation on pending policies—the war in Indochina, the urban crises, campus unrest. He may appear before the national conventions of such special interest groups as the AFL-CIO, the Veterans of Foreign Wars, the American Society of Newspaper Editors, or the US Chamber of Commerce. And his daily schedule at the White House will include appointments with spokesmen from all sectors of the society—student groups, welfare mothers, Indians, textile manufacturers, West Virginia miners, North Dakota wheat farmers, Wall Street lawyers, and state governors.

The heads of governments in every state follow much the same pattern of communications and use much the same techniques of verbal persuasion. The president's State of the Union address is in fact borrowed from British custom: in Her Majesty's Speech from the Throne, the queen informs Parliament what policy measures her government proposes to take in the coming year. Similarly, the German chancellor, following formation of his government, delivers a major policy statement to the Bundestag, which is carried by the mass media to the general citizenry; and he, too, systematically builds his personal and institutional network of communications—information, explanation, persuasion, orders—that lead to policy implementation. In the USSR the Supreme Soviet is essentially a listening body; it does not deliberate, it does not debate, but its members listen to reports of the government and party leaders.

Communications at the highest level of government are designed to clarify the great goals, to publicize the priorities, to establish new frontiers, to mobilize a consensus, to move a nation. At the operational level of program implementation, communications are more diversified and more specialized. For example, the Development Plan for Turkey provides for research and consultative services by government experts for specific groups in the economy. Compliance, or cooperation, can be anticipated when information is made available, not so much because of the national interest as on the basis of self-interest. If the experts in the Ministry of Agriculture can communicate to the Turkish farmers what use of fertilizers, improved seed, pest control and crop rotation will do for the harvest, then the Development Plan to increase the productivity per unit of land and to develop optimum utilization of land is well on the way toward target. Similarly, if the Industrial Research Institute, which works on technological problems in manufacturing, makes available its findings along with its consultative services to individual manufacturers, one can expect that the Development Plan to upgrade industrial production will be implemented. This indeed is one of the most pervasive elements of governing in every modern state, the network of communications between the service agencies of the government and their respective clienteles.

All of our twelve nations regard communications as exceedingly fruitful techniques in governing. If you have been following our footnotes, you will have observed that much of the information we rely upon for this text has come from such sources as the British Information Service, the Information Division of the Israeli Ministry for Foreign Affairs, the Press and Information Office of the German Federal Government, or the Indian Ministry of Information and Broadcasting. These are mainly public-relations activities for external persuasion. Practically every major agency includes an office of public affairs whose function is to maintain liaison between the agency and the public at home; not only to provide information, but also to engage in the persuasive techniques of public relations that go beyond printed communications. In the developing countries, where illiteracy is still a serious problem and electronic communications are not yet available to the masses of the people, face-to-face, word-of-mouth communications between government leaders and their constituents are likely to be much more effective than formal messages. By the same token, extension services and demonstration projects are much more telling than governmental brochures—in Colombia or the Ivory Coast, for instance.

Incentives and Rewards

Modern government is expected to govern in the public interest, and in practice this is frequently achieved by offering incentives and/or rewards to special interests. We observe a good deal of this today in developing states; and we are reminded that this was the way the United States pursued its manifest destiny: high tariffs on imports to protect and promote industries, government grants of homesteads to pioneering settlers in the West, land grants and subsidies for the transcontinental railroads—these are but a few of the large-scale government programs in aid of private enterprise in the developing United States. Japan, the USSR, and Kenya, three very different political systems, use incentives and rewards in ways that reflect their diverse cultures.

In the latter quarter of the nineteenth century the Japanese government embarked upon a policy of industrialization that would in a relatively short time make Japan a successful competitor among the great powers of the world. At the outset of modernization the Japanese government was significantly involved both in resource allocation and resource management. In one decade (1887–96), the government share in gross domestic fixed capital formation was estimated at 42.5 percent; in later decades the proportion of government investment in the economy was even higher.[7] Almost every important Japanese industry was originally established and operated by the government: railroads, shipyards, postal facilities, steel mills, telephone, telegraph, irrigation, and drainage works.

The rapid industrialization of Japan was achieved through a variety of incentives and rewards including tax exemptions, and grants-in-aid for land, capital, and credit. For example, the textile industry was initially set up by the government and then resold to private interests on installment loans which apparently were never called for payment. Similarly in other industries, the government bought the best machinery abroad, imported Western technicians, and constructed model plants. Then, when these demonstration projects had served their purpose, they were turned over to private enterprise on very favorable terms.

Having given a head start to industry, the Japanese government in the 1920s and 1930s deliberately moved away from its policy of resource management except in key industries related to military programs [8] and in transportation and communication. Since World War II a great deal of government planning and programming has necessarily entered into the restoration of the Japanese economy. We pointed out earlier (see Table 10–1) that Japan currently leads all twelve of our countries in percentage of GNP allocated to fixed capital formation, this in accordance with a series of government development plans. The Japanese government offers incentives and rewards not only to industry, however, but also to other sectors of the economy. For example, the government-established Agriculture, Forestry, and Fisheries Finance Corporation is the chief long-term credit source for persons engaged in these occupations. Moreover, the Ministry of Agriculture and Forestry offers nationwide extension services, subsidizes numerous small-scale irrigation projects, provides fertilizer inspection laboratories, and maintains livestock breeding farms. Like the American way, the Japanese way represents a mixed economy with private enterprise encouraged and subsidized through a great many government programs.

We usually point to the Stalinist regime in the USSR as a prime example of modern government that obtained and retained its authority by the techniques of terrorism and repression. For some twenty years, however, from the early 1930s up to his death in 1953, Stalin also employed an elaborate system of incentives and rewards for individual members in order to modernize the nation with an average annual growth rate of 5 percent per capita. Industries, classified according to priorities established by the regime, were rewarded differentially. A new economic class was created on the basis of incentives: production managers who exceeded their production quotas could expect better housing, a family automobile, travel allowances, college education for their children, perhaps cash bonuses, and certainly social prestige. Workers, paid on a piece system, were rewarded with higher wages for greater output; skilled workers were paid more than unskilled workers, and the most productive workers were treated as an elite group in the proletariat. The system, known as Stakhanovism, after a coal miner who consistently overfulfilled his quota, was a tough one, but it worked in terms of the objectives set for it: to accelerate and increase industrial production. Actually, it generated great resentment after a time, and Stakhanovich had to keep out of the public eye for many years.

Nikita Khrushchev's government was notably less intimidating and coercive than Stalin's. Under Stalin, Khrushchev's special responsibility had been agriculture; hence, when he became the head of government, he moved to correct what he considered an imbalance in the economy favoring industry. Under Khrushchev's direction the government marked up farm prices to give the farmers more purchasing power and thus a higher standard of living. To stimulate agricultural production the government offered cash prizes for farmers who exceeded their quotas, and it also encouraged the cultivation of private plots (which had virtually been prohibited in the Stalin regime). The Khrushchev techniques of government generally reflected a basic change in program implementation, more of the carrot and less of the stick. Thus wage supplements and the assurance of housing were used to induce young workers to resettle in less-developed areas of the country. The workers generally were offered more material rewards for their participation in the managed economy: upgraded wage scales, holiday benefits, and cash awards for extraordinary performance, as well as a shift in resource allocation that allowed a wide variety of consumer goods and so made monetary incentives more meaningful.[9]

Development Planning

All of the developing states in our sample of twelve call for government-sponsored and government-implemented plans for social and economic development. The techniques of public administration in every country include numerous incentives and rewards for individual performance within planned programs: tax exemptions, land subsidies, technical assistance, cash awards, easy credit, and special citations.

Kenya's Development Plan (1964–70) emphasizes agriculture and Africanization. The Ministry of Economic Planning and Development seeks to increase and diversify agricultural production. Kenyan farming is still mainly of the subsistence type, small farms producing for home consumption only. About 20 percent of Kenya's agricultural products currently go to market. But the Development Plan calls for steep increases in commercial production, especially coffee and tea for export; hence, the government now offers special inducements, notably long- and short-term credit to coffee and tea growers.

Kenya is much more bent on Africanization than the Ivory Coast, which prefers to emulate the French way. Kenya's planned Africanization includes numerous programs sponsored by the government to bring Africans into the bureaucracy, commerce, industry, and agriculture. Its educational policies are designed to train Africans for government service. African entrepreneurs are given government assistance in the establishment of light industries. And even before independence, government plans were under way to purchase farmlands from the European settlers. (Although they comprised less than 1 percent of all the farmers, the Europeans owned 20 percent of the land in 1960.) An important aspect of the current Development Plan is to resettle African farmers on good agricultural land. The policy of resettlement is not intended to deprive all Europeans of their land nor to award a farm to all Africans. Nor is it intended that the resettlement program be implemented either by expropriation of the European property or by giveaways to the Africans. The incentive to intensify the development of African agriculture is a homestead for the farmer, no more land than he can till, but enough to give him a fair cash income. In order to raise the net income of farmers, the government offers agricultural extension services and the assistance of experts in improved farm practices.[10]

COMMAND AND COERCION

Finally we come to the traditional techniques of government: the command of the sovereign and enforcement of law and order. Although we have left them last in our discussion, we do not minimize these techniques in the overall operations of government. Indeed the peculiar attribute of the political system which distinguishes it from all other social systems is that it can claim as a right the obedience of its entire membership and it may exercise as a right whatever power is necessary to enforce its rules and orders. Every state implements its rights to command and to coerce through military and police forces.

The Military Establishment

The prime function of the military is, of course, the common defense and the maintenance of national security. While we have been writing this text, three of our twelve states have been engaged in war: the United States in Indochina, Israel in the Middle East, and India against Pakistan—employing military force outside their own borders to obtain their objectives and claiming such military operations necessary to defend their national interests. But we do not know of any country that proclaims its military activities are intentionally offensive rather than defensive.

Virtually every peace-loving state in the world has its record of belligerency in international relations. Lewis F. Richardson in the *Statistics of Deadly Quarrels* tells us that only Sweden and Switzerland fit into the category of "organized states that were never belligerent," [11] but even Switzerland had a civil war in mid-nineteenth century; and if one goes back a bit in history, Gustavus II in eighteenth-century Sweden was far ahead of his times, organizing a national standing army with which he conducted a spectacularly successful campaign in the Thirty Years' War. Quincy Wright, in his massive and systematic study of war, points out that the size of armies in modern times has increased both absolutely and in proportion to population. In the seventeenth century the armies of European states comprised about three persons per thousand of the general population; on the eve of World War I the ratio had increased to five per thousand; and before World War II the ratio had moved up to nine per thousand.[12]

At one point in history, a decade after World War I, some sixty-three nation states (nearly all the states in existence at that time) joined in the Kellogg-Briand Pact to condemn and renounce the threat or use of force as an instrument of national policy. Yet World War II found most of the signers on one side or the other, and since World War II we have seen the greatest buildup of military forces in all human history.

A noted political scientist, examining the nature of cooperation and conflict in international relations, observes that "armed forces are useful, and in a sense used, as instruments of foreign policy whether or not they are actually employed in physical combat. . . . Were they not useful instruments of foreign policy most states would reduce their armaments drastically." [13] A less conventional commentator puts it more cogently:

> *National security is the paramount concern of all nation-states. It is the controlling value, the prime mover in any foreign policy decision. In the contemporary period, where each nation is equally insecure, and none will ever gain total security, the quest for security is surrounded by an aura of make-believe, but is always cloaked in terms of pragmatic realism (e.g. kill ratio, megatonage, survival count).*[14]

Every nation counts on its armed services for the ultimate use of force, to protect the country against invasion, insurrection, or internal disruption. Whether a state conscripts its military force or recruits it on a voluntary basis is a policy decision made by those in authority within each state. Currently seven of our twelve states resort to the draft: the Ivory Coast, the USSR, Germany, Colombia, Turkey, Israel, and the United States. Five prefer to depend on voluntary enlistments: India, Japan, Kenya, the United Kingdom, and Mexico. Such policy decisions change with the times, as they have in Japan and the United States.

Early in the Meiji period Japan imposed universal military service as essential to its goal of becoming a modern world power. Japan was forced to reverse its policy during the American Occupation following World War II. For most of its history the United States as a matter of policy abhorred peacetime conscription and served as a haven for refugees from military draft in other countries. Since 1948, however, the United States has maintained a selective service system which obligates all young men to perform military service but provides numerous exemptions and deferments. Because of United States policy in Southeast Asia, the military draft is highly unpopular with American youth, especially those in the colleges. On the other hand, Israeli youth (both men and women) who are drafted into the Israeli defense forces appear to regard their military service as an enobling experience, a summons to heroism and crucial to the preservation of their homeland.

The call to military service is in effect a command of the sovereign. Most countries, however, try to sweeten the command with incentives and rewards. While in service soldiers enjoy a relatively good standard of living (except of course, in combat), they are usually offered special training and educational opportunities, and when they leave the service they can expect a variety of veterans' benefits. To give the most extreme example, the United States 1971 Budget allocated $8.5 billion for veterans' benefits and services, including medicare, home financing, and career training, as well as financial assistance for disability and old age.

Although we usually associate the armed services with the use of force and the techniques of coercion, actually the military establishment may serve a variety of functions. To varying degrees in our twelve nation states, the military establishment is a status symbol, even when it is not required, nor even expected, to perform its primary function. The men in uniform provide the honor guard for all kinds of political ceremonies: the changing of the guard at Buckingham Palace, the May Day parade before the official viewing stand at the Kremlin, the presidential inaugural parade down Pennsylvania Avenue. Membership in the military is traditionally regarded as the highest form of public service. Even the least-developed nations feel impelled to show off their modern weaponry; the peasants may work in the rice paddies with the most primitive implements, but the air force flies jet fighters.

Military service appears to be most attractive in the developing states when it is associated with the tasks of nation-building and assigned to infrastructure projects such as constructing transportation and communications facilities. Moreover, military service which offers training and educational programs may be viewed as a way up the social and economic ladder in subsequent civilian life. The Mexican army, for example, has been an important instrument in combating illiteracy and in teaching technical skills that meet the nation's civilian manpower needs. The Israeli army has been outstandingly effective in integrating immigrants from all over the world. In Kenya about ninety thousand young men reach the age of eighteen every year; the military establishment recruits around five thousand. Only a few young men can enter the Kenyan armed forces, but many of them vie for the opportunity to wear the uniform, to enjoy a relatively high standard of living, and to take advantage of special training.

The Police Establishment

Domestic tranquility, the maintenance of law and order, the protection of individuals and their property against wrongdoers, the support of public authority, the security of the state: These are basic requirements of any political system. And in the final analysis it is the police who are charged with enforcing these values.

In every state, in any community, the policeman is likely to be the most visible agent of the state. He wears a uniform, displays a badge of authority, and generally acts as the initial point of contact between individual citizens and the social control machinery of the political system. How the policeman sees his duty, what he does, how he does it, how individual citizens react to his presence or view his performance offers us many clues as to the kind of political system in which he is a familiar participant. Recently in Washington, D.C., we saw on TV—in sound and color—a confrontation between the local police and students. What do students have in mind when they toss rocks (and marshmallows) at the policemen and scream, "Pigs"? How do the policemen see their assignment when they don their gas masks and prepare to disperse the demonstrators with tear gas? What does any man think when he hears a jack-booted tread at his door and hears the shouted command, "Open up, the police!"? What about the little old lady to whom the traffic cop gives a ticket for surpassing the speed limit on Interstate 70? What does the same little old lady think when she dials her local police number at the sound of an intruder breaking and entering her back door after midnight? The police image is bound to be kaleidoscopic, depending on the nature of the contact. Let us look first at the police service in the United Kingdom, and then try to make some quick comparisons.

The role of the British policeman is largely determined by tradition and respect for law and order among the general citizenry. From the Anglo-Saxon period until the fourteenth century every freeman was bound by oath to assist in the preservation of peace and in the detection and punishment of crime.

The local constable, the executive agent of the village or township, was the official peace officer, exercising his authority under common law as a person paid to perform, as a matter of duty, acts which if he were so minded he might have done voluntarily. From the fourteenth to the nineteenth century, the constables were made subordinate to the local justices of the peace, who were technically officers of the crown charged with maintaining the king's peace. The shift in authority was intended to enhance the image of crown power and to strengthen the notion of national government. But whether under constables or justices, the responsibility for law and order in effect still rested with the local citizenry.[15] This bit of history is important in explaining how the British police force operates even today.

The rapid industrialization and urbanization of England in the nineteenth century called for a reallocation of values and new machinery of government to implement these values in a changing environment. Broad shifts in population patterns, both occupational and residential, were accompanied by increasing lawlessness. In 1829 Sir Robert Peel secured the establishment of the London Metropolitan Police (the "bobbies," nicknamed after Sir Robert) under the Minister for Home Affairs. In 1835 Parliament required the hiring of permanent constables, thus recognizing that the ancient watch and ward system to guard the town gates was no longer adequate to keep the peace in overcrowded cities. At the same time Parliament empowered the counties to pay a permanent constabulary, although it did not require them to do so until 1856. Even today the local police forces are virtually autonomous, subject to rules of efficiency laid down by the inspector of the constabulary in the Home Office. Only the London Metropolitan Police is under direct control of the Home Office. The national government contributes 50 percent of the financial support for the local police, however, and as every reader of English mystery novels well knows, Scotland Yard provides the country constabulary with professional and technical assistance.

The organization of the police force varies considerably from one state to another. In Israel the organization is highly centralized, controlled by national headquarters, commanded by the inspector general. At the other extreme is the United States with upwards of forty thousand separate police forces in local communities and several hundred separate enforcement units in the national government, units such as the Secret Service, the customs inspectors, the IRS agents in the Treasury Department, and the FBI in the Justice Department. In India each of the sixteen states maintains and directs its own police force, but the national government sets the standards for recruitment, training, and discipline of all police officers. All Indian police officers must meet high educational qualifications, including university degrees, and the police service is regarded as a prestigious career. On the other hand, the rank-and-file constabulary in India, especially those who serve in the villages, come from a low stratum, are likely to be barely literate, and are miserably paid even by Indian standards. And we are told that the Indian police have a reputation for rudeness, brutality, partiality, and dishonesty.[16]

The reputation of the police in any country depends on what they are expected to do, what they actually do, and how they go about doing it. Although there is some variation in police functions from one state to another, there are certain regularities. Policemen are expected to support the authority of those in power and to enforce the policies which those in authority have made into law. They provide protection against those who would evade or break the laws. And they may be assigned numerous administrative duties involving social control, such as licensing and inspection which are designed to reinforce the rules and regulations of the regime.

In every country the military and police establishments are expected to maintain national security and domestic tranquility. When, however, the ruling elite uses military and/or police power to secure its own interests and to perpetuate its own regime, then the military and police may in effect become instruments of external aggression and internal repression. Japan and the USSR illustrate the point, though it is pertinent more or less in all twelve states.

The American Occupation of Japan was designed to eradicate the power of the ruling elite that had led Japan into World War II. One reform was to decentralize the police force, which had been a major instrument in backing up the policy decisions of the imperial government. A National Rural Police, with the help of the Occupation forces, was designed to keep the peace in the countryside and small towns, but each city was required to maintain law and order through its own police force. When the Occupation forces departed, however, the Japanese enacted the Police Revision Law (1954) which restored the central government's broad powers over all police activities. A National Police Agency, once again an elaborate bureaucracy, makes up the police budgets, determines qualifications of police officers, and recruits all senior police officers, although considerable autonomy is retained at the prefectorial and municipal level for basic police functions.

In the USSR the rationale of the Soviet police has always been that it serves primarily as the "Sword of the Revolution." [17] A succession of police agencies, beginning with the Bolshevik *Cheka* organized immediately after the October, 1917, Revolution, have served as instruments of terror and coercion to keep the Communist party in control of the political system. The Cheka, under the People's Commissariat (NKVD) was instituted to combat counterrevolution, sabotage, and speculation. It fulfilled its assignment with efficiency, liquidating the class enemies (aristocracy, bourgeoisie, priests, and White Guard forces) and administering ad hoc justice according to the precepts of the new regime. Under the first Constitution of the USSR, a unified police agency, the OGPU, maintained a monopoly over all police functions until 1934. This was the agency notorious for its forceful collectivization of agriculture, the mass deportation of the kulaks (independent farmers), and the show trials of dissenters and alleged saboteurs.

The Soviet police system has been reorganized many times since its inception, but throughout the years it has effectively carried out its assignment, safeguarding the Communist regime or maintaining internal security. The Soviet police system has not only pursued lawbreakers, it has purged the government, the armed forces, and the party itself of all political deviants. Concerned mainly with crimes threatening state security such as subversion, espionage, sabotage, and destruction of state property, it has exercised widesweeping controls over the whole society, for in a totalitarian government almost any act may be interpreted as threatening state security. One of its most effective control devices is the internal passport which every citizen must carry with him at all times, so that the government can keep continuous track of all political actives. The police also administer various licenses and maintain a continuous check on those licensed to carry weapons, or to buy poison or explosives, or print any kind of materials. For its more routine assignment, to keep peace and order and to protect individual citizens against harm, the police make extensive use of people's squads, self-policing units in the factories, schools, apartments, and on the collective farms.

How the police conduct their activities tells us a great deal about the internal nature of the political system and especially about the relation of the governors to the governed. The United States does not have a national police whose major responsibility is internal security.[18] We usually think of the police as officers of the law whose principal function is to combat crime. Moreover, the primary responsibility for crimes that affect individuals is vested in the state and local governments and not in the national government. True, in the field of organized crime, narcotics, and pornography, national law enforcement agents have assumed special responsibility. And under the Nixon administration, which has expressed strong concern about street crimes, the national budget shows rising figures to cover more assistance to state and local law enforcement agencies.

In recent years, we have heard much about police brutality. In the United States the typical policeman, whether walking the beat, shepherding school children across the street, directing traffic, or in hot pursuit of a rapist or murderer, is fully armed at all times. If he is part of a riot squad dispatched to stop arson, looting, or even peaceful demonstrating, his squad is probably equipped with a full complement of rifles, revolvers, gas masks, tear gas, fire hoses, steel helmets, bullhorns, and walkie-talkies. And no doubt an armed policeman is more likely to be coercive than an unarmed policeman who has to be more persuasive.

The British policeman is usually unarmed. "When on normal patrol duties a police officer carries only a wooden truncheon which he may use only in self-defense or to restore order when all other means have failed." [19] The basic conception of the British police service is that it assists the citizen in keeping law and order. The Indian police service is a kind of compromise between the American and British versions: The policeman on staff duty at the police station, on patrol, or engaged in investigation is unarmed; an armed division, however, is employed for quelling riots, guarding banks, or other hazardous assignments. The Japanese policeman, like the American, is fully armed; his weaponry even on patrol includes a pistol and a short sword! But in every country Gilbert and Sullivan's lyric probably applies, "a policeman's lot is not a happy one."

A professional police force to maintain law and order is a creation of modern government, a necessary concomitant of industrialization and urbanization. We have noted that this was the motivating factor in the creation of the British police force. Before the Meiji Restoration in Japan, each feudal lord was expected to exercise police functions within his own domain. One of the first steps taken in the modernization of Japan was the organization of a national police system under a Central Police Bureau in the Home Ministry and the establishment of a Tokyo Police Force modeled after the London Metropolitan Police Force.

A new nation is confronted at once with problems of internal security. If independence has been obtained by revolution or by any degree of force and violence, then the problems are likely to be aggravated by continuing disrespect for political authority. The role of the police force in effecting an orderly transition from colonial to national status—to buttress the authority of the new regime as well as to protect the life and property of the citizens generally—may be crucial to survival of the new system. In the case of Kenya (as in India), the British colonial police force was retained intact by the new government. Today the Kenya Police, "the largest and best equipped police force in East Africa," [20] is centrally organized, under the policy guidance of the National Security Council. Initially its members were predominately veterans of British colonial training, but gradually, through nationwide recruiting aimed at ethnic balance, the force has been so Africanized that Africans now constitute about 50 percent of the officers and over 90 percent of the total force.

In the Ivory Coast the police force has also been patterned after the colonial model, in this instance following French standards and practices. The Ivory Coast police force comprises two separate agencies, the National Gendarmery and the Sûreté Nationale, both of these developed during the colonial period. The Gendarmery is actually part of the military establishment, but since its special function is to maintain domestic order and internal security it works closely with the police. Compared to Kenya, where racial tension are likely to erupt into violence, the Ivory Coast has a relatively stable government, but President Houphouet-Boigny is taking no chances; he keeps the Gendarmery primed for active duty. The Sûreté Nationale, the regular police force, is directly under the Ministry of the Interior. Its basic assignment is to prevent and detect crime, protect persons and property, and in general preserve law and order. Like most police forces it has ancillary duties such as traffic control and border patrol. As in Kenya (and in India) the police force of the Ivory Coast, which had its beginnings as a colonial force, has been gradually nationalized by selective recruiting and training.

How a government organizes and employs its police force depends on many different factors in the political system. In our concluding chapter we shall try to appraise the functioning of various political systems, focusing on the liberties and welfare of the individual members. We shall, for example, have something to say about civil rights, which are of course closely related to the functions of the police.

PUBLIC ADMINISTRATION AND MANAGERIAL CONTROLS

The more modern the state, the more technical the problems of public administration, the more formidable are the tasks of government strategy and managerial control. It is significant that Prime Minister Heath within the first few months of his time in office established a small multidisciplinary central policy review staff in his cabinet office to help him and his ministers identify areas of policy in which new choices were possible, to recommend relative priorities in programming, and to count the costs of alternative policies. Similarly President Nixon very early concerned himself with restructuring the Executive Office of the president. Among the reforms he effected was the upgrading of the Office of Management and Budget to give him a stronger managerial clout over competing bureaucracies and the creation of a Domestic Council of cabinet-level advisers as a counterpart of the National Security Council, each to be served by a professional White House staff. The intent of the reorganization was to put the president on top of the policy machinery and to give him the benefit of overall assessments of domestic and foreign policies apart from old-line departmental interests.

If we look at our two reconstructed states, Germany and Japan, we perceive quite clearly the role of managerial agencies in linking political decisions with government operations. Neither country could have achieved its miraculous recovery from World War II without a great deal of central planning, budgeting, and programming. The Japanese government, for example, has sponsored ten economic plans, the most recent covering the five-year span from 1967 to 1972. These plans have been prepared by experts in the Economic Council of the Office of the Prime Minister and the Economic Planning Council in coordination with many departmental plans. The present plan, the most ambitious so far, sets long-range objectives for social as well as economic development. Supported by the political leadership, the plan in its totality has been implemented through managerial controls that reach into every department whose activities are relevant to the overall objectives.

Our seven developing states, looking over the five models of political maturity and economic development, are somewhat divided in opinion as to which is the more desirable method of governing the economy: free enterprise with a mix of governmental controls (the United States), free enterprise with governmental controls and considerable nationalization (the United Kingdom, Japan, and Germany), or a socialist state (the Soviet Union). Opinions turn on competing ideologies, but it is obvious that industrialization eventually calls for state intervention in the economy, whether Western or Soviet-style. The industrial revolution, initially left to private enterprise, was a long, slow process in the United States and the United Kingdom, markedly accelerated with government guidance in Germany and Japan, dramatically revved up by state planning and central controls in the Soviet Union. To the emerging nations eager to hasten the process of modernization, to match their political independence with economic development—and to the older low-income countries anxious to raise their levels of living—the Russian model is attractive.

India, more than any other state outside the Soviet orbit, has gone in for planning in a big way, but it has never tried to go the whole way; indeed, agriculture which still dominates the Indian economy remains in the private sector. India has, however, formulated many more plans than it has been able to bring to fruition, leading to the comment that the Indian planners have done little more than promote a functioning anarchy. All seven of our developing states have acclaimed planning as the modern technique of government, and the Russian Gosplan has served as prototype for their state planning agencies. Realities, however, do not measure up to the ideals. It takes more than high aspirations, paper planning, and target dates to cope with the basic problems of underdevelopment—low levels of technology, high rates of illiteracy, low savings ratios, high birthrates and burgeoning populations, and withal political instability and weak public administration.

Developing countries trying to make an immediate transition from traditional to modern ways of governing have little trouble drafting impressive constitutions and designing elaborate political organizations; they can simply copy from the Western models with variations that please them. They are likely to be stymied, however, both by the practical politics of policy planning and the technology of public administration. Planning in the Soviet Union could proceed with a single-minded purpose that is only possible in a totalitarian state. None of the developing states in our sample has been fired by such ideological commitment. Rather, governors in the newly emerging states have been caught in the dilemma of how to make a showing of democratic government with popular participation which the governed have been led to equate with independence from colonial rule, and at the same time impose by central authority an entirely different way of living upon the people. Moreover, if the governors were really to follow the Russian example, planning first to build the infrastructure of an industrial state whatever the immediate costs, it is highly unlikely that the people who had been led to believe that modernization means such consumer conveniences as automobiles, refrigerators and television sets, would be willing to settle—as the Russians did for a whole generation—for superhighways, power plants, and heavy industries.

The formulation of economic development policy requires a small, highly trained elite, a few top-notch administrators who understand the procedural as well as the substantive problems of economic and social planning. Such persons, if not available on the spot, can be sent abroad for training or outside experts can be brought in to give the needed technical assistance; this is frequently done under bilateral or multilateral aid programs. The real crunch in economic development, however, comes at the points of implementation, for the capacity of any government to put its policies into action depends on the responsiveness of the whole administrative structure. For those countries most recently emerging from colonialism the administrative problems are particularly acute. The British government, for example, trained an indigenous civil service in its colonies but mainly in the lower grades. The executive and managerial posts, however, were nearly always filled by Britishers, most of whom left after Independence Day. Thus, when India (and later Kenya), adopted state planning as the most rational and expeditious way to raise the living standards of the people and to offer them new opportunities in a modern environment, the government was seriously handicapped at the outset (it still is but gradually less so) by the lack of trained personnel available for higher-grade positions in the civil service. The Ivory Coast has temporized with the problem; it continues to man the top levels of the bureaucracy with French rather than African administrators, and it gets a great deal of outside aid for development from the World Bank.

The 1960s was touted as the development decade, with the Alliance for Progress its exhibit A. The Alliance was designed to offer external incentives to the low-income Latin American countries to step up their planning for economic development. Economic development in the framework of the Alliance was broadly construed as not only expansion of industry and trade but also as embracing social changes and more equitable income distribution. The Alliance provided for multilateral review of aid estimates submitted by individual countries and multilateral assessment of performance by aid recipients. It was expected that such requirements would accelerate national planning, improve budget procedures, and introduce new managerial techniques in the public administration of Latin American countries.

Both Colombia and Mexico are members of the Alliance for Progress. In the chapter that follows we shall be looking at the relative performance of the developing countries in the 1960s. But we need to note at this point the performance differential between Colombia and Mexico, because we think the differential is partly due (only partly, however) to superior governmental techniques in Mexico.[21] Table 12–1 measures the economic development of both countries using the GNP per capita as the unit of measurement (in 1964 US dollars) between 1950 and 1968. The table clearly indicates an accelerated rate of growth for Mexico while Colombia moves much more slowly, despite the fact that the United States as principal donor in the Alliance had hoped to make Colombia the shining example of what the Alliance could do for recipient members.

One knowledgeable student of Mexican politics attributes the notable success of the Mexican Revolution since the 1940s to the president's power over the national budget.[22] The Mexican president has great flexibility in allocating the federal funds for administrative, social, and economic expenditures. And recent presidents have used their constitutional authority (and the full support of the PRI) to manage the government as a whole, to coordinate all components in the system, and to stress programs designed to achieve social integration as well as economic development. The success of the Mexican Revolution can be measured not only by the rapidly rising GNP per capita, but by an equally impressive decline in the poverty level and by widespread social advances, especially in health and education. Mexico is not run by a totalitarian government; the PRI is not really comparable to the Communist party of Russia, but it does dominate the Mexican political system. It does move with purpose, and Mexican state planning reflects both its ideology and its strategy. We have mentioned earlier how the PRI scouts for political talent, recruits and trains bright young people for the public administration as well as the public offices. To put it bluntly, the PRI has organized the

TABLE 12–1
GNP Per Capita for Selected Years (in 1964 US Dollars)

	1950	*1955*	*1960*	*1965*	*1968*
Colombia	206	233	247	266	281
Mexico	285	330	376	426	476

SOURCE: International Bank for Reconstruction and Development, *Trends in Developing Countries* (Washington, D.C.: Government Printing Office, 1970).

Mexican government so that the political leadership can make authoritative allocations in line with party ideology and has seen to it that the management side of government is trained to implement policy decisions as planned.

As to How do the governors govern? we hazard some generalizations: If those in authority perceive and respect the fundamental values of the people, if they allocate the national resources in accordance with generally recognized national interests, if they are responsive to the needs and demands of the people, if the policies of the government—and the rules and regulations which implement the policies—have the consent of the governed, then the techniques of command and coercion, and the instruments of force, the military and the police, need not play a major role in the maintenance of internal security and domestic tranquility.

NOTES

1. Charles E. Lindblom, *The Policy Making Process* (Englewood Cliffs, N.J.: Prentice-Hall, 1968), p. 116.
2. R. M. MacIver, *The Web of Government* (New York: Macmillan, 1947), see chap. 4, "How and Why Men Obey."
3. It is tiresome to list the hundreds of on-going programs that are prepared annually to implement the Development Plan. The student who wants a deeper insight into the problems and policies—and the philosophy—of development will find the report of the Turkish State Planning Organization most instructive (*Second Five-Year Development Plan 1968–1972* [Ankara: Central Bank of the Republic of Turkey, 1969]). It is not easy reading; it runs to 695 pages, with an enormous amount of detail on plans and programs for sectoral development, but it gives the kind of insight into the values and interests of a people on the make which textbook writers can never quite capture. For example,

   Housing is an important economic and social problem of society. . . . In fact, housing will be the most important aspect of rapid urbanization in Turkey. Therefore, housing cannot be considered merely as a dwelling problem—it is also a yardstick for civilization. The home as the centre of family life has a direct influence over it and the satisfaction of housing requirements accelerates economic and cultural development. (p. 302.)
4. The text in full is available in the *Congressional Record*, 94th Cong., 2d sess., February 18, 1970; in the *New York Times*, February 19, 1970; and in the *Congressional Quarterly Weekly Report*, February 20, 1970.
5. Students interested in the theory, methodology, and practice of policy formation may find interesting reading in Raymond Bauer and Kenneth J. Gergen, eds., *The Study of Policy Formation* (New York: Free Press, 1968).
6. Karl W. Deutsch, *The Nerves of Government* (New York: Free Press, 1966), p. 157.
7. Robert T. Holt and John E. Turner, *The Political Basis of Economic Development* (New York: Van Nostrand, 1966), p. 245.
8. Holt and Turner point out that the central government's involvement in resource allocation vis-à-vis capital formation in the last quarter of the nineteenth century never fell below 30 percent and ranged as high as 83 percent. op. cit., p. 247.
9. We do not have much data on the current government. We understand, how-

ever, that incentives and rewards are still very much a part of the governing technique.

10. For data on Kenya's Development Program we have relied on *Area Handbook for Kenya,* Foreign Area Studies Division, American University (Washington, D.C.: Government Printing Office, 1967).
11. Lewis F. Richardson, *Statistics of Deadly Quarrels* (Chicago: Quadrangle Books, 1960), quoted in Vernon Van Dyke, *International Politics,* 2d ed. (New York: Appleton-Century-Crofts, 1966, p. 358).
12. Quincy Wright, *A Study of War* (Chicago: University of Chicago Press, 1942), quoted in Vernon Van Dyke, op. cit.
13. Charles P. Schleicher, *International Relations: Cooperation and Conflict* (Englewood Cliffs, N.J.: Prentice-Hall, 1962), p. 263.
14. Excerpted from *Foreign Policy Theory: A Comprehensive Study* by Dr. Mirv Strangelove (San Francisco: Yippie Press, 1972, 1984).
15. See *The Police Service in Britain,* British Information Services (London, 1969).
16. David H. Bayley, *The Police and Political Development in India* (Princeton, N.J.: Pinceton University Press, 1969). This is both a study of the Indian police force and a study in comparative politics. The author makes numerous comparisons between the British and American police systems.
17. For our information on the police system in the USSR, we have relied on Robert Conquest, *The Soviet Police System* (New York: Praeger, 1968).
18. The Federal Bureau of Investigation in the US Department of Justice has jurisdiction over some 170 investigative matters. J. Edgar Hoover, the director since its founding, puts espionage, sabotage, treason, and other forms of subversion high on his list of criminal activities. He has assiduously tracked down Communists and other political conspirators. The FBI, however, is not really comparable to a national police system.
19. *The Police Service in Britain,* p. 30.
20. *Area Handbook for Kenya,* p. 627.
21. We surmize that the National Front in Colombia was a facade behind which lay mounting malcontent among the lower classes and uneasy exercise of authority by the government. The postponement of return to bipartisanship from 1970 to 1974 was a move to keep the ruling elite in office. It was obviously not a popular move as evidenced by the 1970 election returns favoring General Rojas and opposing the National Front candidate. Economic development in Colombia has so far effected no great social changes comparable to the Mexican Revolution.
22. James K. Wilkie, *The Mexican Revolution: Federal Expenditure and Social Change since 1910* (Berkeley, Calif.: University of California Press, 1970), see "Conclusion," pp. 276–85.

FURTHER READING

Bauer, Raymond, and Kenneth J. Gergen, eds. *The Study of Policy Formation.* New York: Free Press, 1968.

Lindblom, Charles E. *The Policy Making Process.* Englewood Cliffs, N.J.: Prentice-Hall, 1968.

Tomasek, Robert D., ed. *Latin American Politics.* 2d ed. Garden City, N.Y.: Doubleday, Anchor Books, 1970.

Welch, Claude E., ed. *Political Modernization: A Reader in Comparative Political Change.* Belmont, Calif.: Wadsworth, 1967.

chapter 13

SOME CONCLUSIONS AND JUDGMENTS

In the Introduction to this text we posed a number of basic questions in political science:

What makes a state?
What makes a nation?
What motivates a political system?
Who are the ruling elites in the system?
How do political opinions affect government?
How do political parties affect government?
How do elections affect government?
How are nation states organized territorially?
How are nation states organized institutionally?
How do governments operate?
How do governors govern?

In Chapter 1 we established our frame of reference: twelve nation states selected because they represent certain concepts which are germane to comparative political analysis—concepts such as political sovereignty, territorial integrity, modern government, developing nations, nationalism, national interests, representative government, ruling elites, power, authority, influence,

Ivory Coast, village children walking to school
(Marc & Evelyne Bernheim : Rapho Guillumette)

and the making of public policy. Though we provide a Glossary for this text, throughout the text we have deliberately shied away from capsule definitions and rigid categorization. These are more appropriate in theoretical discussions and in expositions of academic models. We have chosen rather to deal with real nation states in a real world, where each state is unique and the world is infinitely complicated. We have not, however, attempted detailed country-by-country descriptions. Our sample of twelve states is just that: twelve states selected for purposes of illustrating contemporary politics within a comparative framework of analysis. As we moved from chapter to chapter, we raised many more key questions in political science and all too frequently hinted that constructive answers would be forthcoming in the last chapter.

Now that we have reached the last chapter we are acutely uncomfortable because we recognize that any attempt to rate the performance of individual nation states or to engage in comparative analysis must begin with value judgments in a meaningful context. But whose value judgments shall we use? And what context is most meaningful?

The economists have come up with a quantitative formula, the GNP, which measures the market value of goods and services produced by a nation in a given period. To be sure, the GNP measures only the quantity and not the quality of goods and services produced by a nation. When the GNP of the United States surpassed the $1 trillion mark in 1970, public officials in the United States jubilantly observed that no other nation in the world's history

Federal Republic of Germany, park and steelworks in Dortmund
(Leonard Freed : Magnum)

had ever performed so hugely. All kinds of goods and services—for moon missions, strategic bombing, patio entertaining, classroom instruction, wig-making, and street cleaning—enter into the GNP, just so long as someone gets paid for the goods or services. Economists have not yet arrived at any formula, however, for determining how or whether the GNP contributes to the advancement of civilization, the good life, or even a decent standard of living. The GNP is simply a massive statistic.

So far political scientists have not produced any single formula comparable to the GNP for measuring, either qualitatively or quantitatively, the political activity of a nation. Most political scientists, especially those of the behavioral persuasion, tend to focus on the political process: how the system works, rather than on the products (or outputs) of the system. It is almost impossible for a political scientist to demonstrate simply on the basis of empirical evidence means and ends relationships in politics, especially in comparative politics where the context is so kaleidoscopic. To go even further and to specify what political products are most desirable for a given country, or for a number of different countries, calls for value judgments that go beyond the professional skills and knowledge of the academic discipline. On the other hand, political practitioners are continuously faced with the content of public policy and the consequences of its application (the outcome). Those who govern are expected to be responsive and responsible to the governed. Public policy-making is in fact a continuum of appraisal and calculation.

Colombia, outskirts of Bogotá (left)
(Costa Manos : Magnum)

Turkey, Hagia Sophia mosque, Istanbul (right)
(Bruno Barbey : Magnum)

Who wants—who needs—what policies? What policies should be continued, modified, terminated? What are the criteria for deciding? What new policies must be formulated, invoked, implemented? What are the estimated costs? Who will pay the costs? And who benefits?

In this chapter, as we turn our attention from the political process to the outcomes of policy-making, we shall try to restrain our own biases and predilections and to assess the performance of our twelve states according to the expressed values and interests of the various performers. For this purpose, we assume that public policies are generally rational in their inception and oriented toward goal fulfillment. (We are, however, well aware that events and pressures over which policy-makers have no control may provoke gut reactions that turn into public policies!)

The fundamental goals of every nation are much the same: independence and survival as a sovereign state, peace and national security, political stability and domestic tranquility, the well-being of the people and higher standards of living, and withal the guarantees of human rights and fundamental freedoms for individuals. Here we attempt some quantitative and qualitative measurements of the performance of our twelve states in reaching toward these goals. Though the research findings are limited, we shall point out what correlations we can between how a nation is motivated, how a state is organized, how a government operates, and what a political system actually produces.

Mexico, laying water pipes, Chicoutia Mountains (left) (Marc & Evelyne Bernheim : Ralpho Guillumette)

Japan, assembling transistors (right) (Henri Cartier-Bresson : Magnum)

INDEPENDENCE AND SURVIVAL AS A SOVEREIGN STATE

All twelve of our nation states are recognized as sovereign states in the international system. All except the Federal Republic of Germany are members of the United Nations. It is unlikely that the Federal Republic will gain admission to the United Nations, unless the United States and its partners in NATO, agree to recognize the sovereign equality of the German Democratic Republic and to recruit both Germanies simultaneously for membership in the United Nations.

The survival of Germany and Japan as sovereign states now seems assured. Both have risen like the phoenix from the ashes of World War II. In 1949 the three Western zones of occupied Germany, with the consent of the French, British, and American authorities, were merged into the German Federal Republic. An Occupation Statute granted full powers of self-government (with certain exceptions) to the new West German state. Over the next few years, under the leadership of Chancellor Konrad Adenauer, the Federal Republic moved toward partnership on equal terms with the Western Allies. In 1954 the London and Paris agreements acknowledged the full sovereignty of the Federal Republic and provided for its subsequent membership in the North Atlantic Treaty Organization (NATO) and the Western European Union (WEU). The three Allies—France, the United Kingdom, and the

USSR, St. Basil's, Moscow (left)
(Marian D. Irish)

USA, astronauts—their rocket and their objective (right)
(Wide World Photos)

United States—reserved powers relating to the status of their armed forces in Berlin, the issue of reunification, and the final peace settlement. In 1955 the Federal Republic began to establish its own security forces, all under NATO command; Allied forces which still remained in the Federal Republic ceased to be Occupation forces and became part of NATO's joint defense. The long anticipated peace treaty, reunifying the two Germanies, now seems utterly remote. Willy Brandt's *Ostpolitik* of the early 1970s may lead to mutual acceptance by the two Germanies, but we surmize that the outcome of Brandt's negotiations is less dependent on the demands and supports of East and West Germans than upon the interactions of the superpowers—the United States and the Soviet Union. This notion, of course, casts a slight pall over the notion of German sovereignty, if sovereignty implies the power of a state to determine its own destiny, without outside controls.

The Japanese Treaty of Peace was signed by Japan and the representatives of forty-eight countries in 1951 and came into force in 1952, at which time Japanese sovereignty was said to be fully restored. The Japanese Diet ratified the treaty by a vote of 307 to 47 with 112 abstentions. On the same day the Diet also ratified a security treaty with the United States by a vote of 289 to 71 with 106 abstentions. Obviously there was not then, and there still is not, consensus among the Japanese people as to the acceptability of the peace treaty or the security treaty.

Legally there is no question today about Japan's status as a sovereign

India, starving villagers in Kerala
(Marilyn Silverstone : Magnum)

and independent nation state. But politically many Japanese, including our young friend Ukai Taki at the University of Tokyo, are malcontent with a Constitution initially written by enemy Occupation authorities and with national security tied to the right of a former enemy to maintain armed forces and bases in Japan. The Treaty of Mutual Cooperation and Security in 1960 (renewed in 1970) presumably now puts the two countries on equal footing, but there is still considerable rankling from the earlier arrangements. All US ground troops were withdrawn from Japan as early as 1958 and more recently the Japanese air self-defense force has replaced US air forces in Japan. During the 1950s and early 1960s, the United States made sizable contributions to Japanese defense, but all US military assistance to Japan has been terminated since the mid-1960s.

The Japanese Constitution renounces war as a sovereign right of the nation and also denies the threat or use of force as a means of settling disputes with other nations. A direct outcome of military defeat in World War II, imposed by the victors when they drafted the Constitution, this particular provision remains a constant source of irritation in Japanese politics. The Liberal Democratic government (actually conservative) which has retained control of the political system since the Occupation, has gradually increased its allocation of national resources for the self-defense forces. Leftist political parties, labor groups, students, and women's organizations are generally opposed to rearmament, fearful of a resurgence of military influence in the

Kenya, street scene in Mombassa
(Bruno Barbey : Magnum)

nation and resentful of increased appropriations for military purposes which they feel should be better spent on economic and social projects. On the other extreme, the government faces criticism from ultranationalists who not only consider enforced pacifism as an affront to national sovereignty but as a real hazard to national security.[1]

Among our twelve states, only Israel faces a serious problem of survival as an independent state. Conceived in war, Israel has been in turmoil with its Arab neighbors ever since. At this writing there is a de facto cease-fire between Israel and Egypt while United Nations representatives strive to negotiate a peace, and the superpowers—the United States and the Soviet Union—treat both sides as pawns in their continuing Cold War. There is no doubt about Israel's determination to survive as a nation, to fight for her existence as a sovereign state, and to allocate whatever resources are needed to assure victory. But, again, as in the case of Germany, and to a lesser degree Japan, Israel's status is largely dependent upon the outcome of world politics, more so than upon the output of its own political system.

The legal attributes of statehood—sovereignty and equality—do not really tell us much about a nation's chances of survival as an independent unit in the international system. The political history of the world is strewn with the wrecks of former states, some of them once great powers. The Baltic states of Latvia, Lithuania, and Estonia simply ceased to exist as independent nation states when they were incorporated by force into the Union of Socialist Soviet Republics during World War II.

Israel, new homes in the suburbs of Jerusalem overlooking the Judean Hills
(Leonard Freed : Magnum)

Admission into the community of nations is no guarantee of continued existence as a state. Recognition of sovereignty may be important in terms of status and prestige but it is not at all significant in terms of power, authority, or influence. The establishment of legal independence may be the peak of national aspiration for a people determined to live in a state of their own, under a political system of their own choosing, but it gives us no indication whether the people will be able to move on toward the more practical goals of interdependence. No nation state is wholly self-sufficient in this modern world, not even such superpowers as the United States and the Soviet Union. Certainly the legal equality of states is no measure of the very great differences that exist among them—differences in natural resources, differences in motivations and attitudes, differences in economic and political capabilities—differences which are highly germane to the fulfillment of national goals within and beyond the territorial boundaries of sovereign jurisdiction.

PEACE AND NATIONAL SECURITY

All states profess to be peace-loving. Eleven of our twelve states (Germany is the exception), as members of the United Nations, are pledged to refrain in their international relations from the threat or use of force against the territorial integrity or political independence of any state. As members of the United Nations, these states are legally bound to the practice of pacific settle-

United Kingdom, Houses of Parliament
(George Rodger : Magnum)

ment of disputes—"to seek peaceful solution [to any dispute] [2] by negotiation, enquiry, mediation, conciliation, arbitration, judicial settlement, resort to regional agencies or arrangements, or other peaceful means of their own choice." All members of the United Nations are members of the International Court of Justice whose jurisdiction comprises all cases which the parties refer to it. When the Charter of the United Nations was drafted in San Francisco in 1945, the signatories (in the name of the peoples) were determined to save succeeding generations from the scourge of war. What has been the record of performance? Since the creation of the United Nations, the people of the world have known fifty-four wars, and their governments are spending more than $200 billion a year on armaments.

The Record of Peace-Loving States

Since 1945 the United States has fought two major wars in Asia: the Korean War, 1950–53, and the Indo-China War which began with US bombing of North Vietnam in 1965 and, as this chapter is being written, is "winding down" with gradual withdrawal of US troops from Vietnam, accompanied by incursions and bombing in Cambodia and Laos. In 1958 President Eisenhower ordered US troops into Lebanon to help keep the peace in the Middle East. In 1961 President Kennedy sanctioned the Bay of Pigs invasion by US-trained Cuban exiles. In 1965 President Johnson sent US troops into the Dominican Republic. Both of the latter incidents were justified as helping to keep the Western Hemisphere safe from Communist subversion. The official rhetoric which justifies the use of force as an instrument of US policy has been based on the proposition that Communism is an aggressive and subversive force in the world and hence the containment of Communism is perceived as a defense of the American way. On the record, however, we rate the United States least effective among our twelve states in keeping its pledges to settle disputes of any kind by pacific means.

The foreign policy of the United States—along with some forty of its allies, including the United Kingdom, the Federal Republic of Germany, Turkey, Japan, Colombia and Mexico—has been posited on the premise that the Soviet Union—and its allies—and Communist China, are highly motivated to extend their rule and will do so by force unless checked by countervailing military power. What then is the Soviet record of violent behavior in international relations? Its potential power is obvious: The Soviet Union exploded its first hydrogen bomb in 1953, just one year after the United States had successfully tested its first hydrogen bomb. The nuclear race between the two superpowers has been nip and tuck ever since. Unlike the United States, however, the Soviet Union has not directly engaged in a major war since 1945, though certainly it has given support and assistance to other belligerent states, notably in the Middle East and Southeast Asia. In 1956 Soviet troops moved into Hungary to crush an anti-Communist uprising. In 1968 Soviet troops invaded Czechoslovakia as a forceful measure to countercheck the liberal reforms of the Dubcek government which seemed to be leading Czechoslovakia away from the hard-line policy of the Warsaw Pact. In 1969 Soviet forces fought against the Chinese on the Manchurian border. Soviet leaders since the late 1950s have played up the policy of peaceful coexistence, but the rhetoric is not borne out by the record of behavior.

India has made considerable mileage in international relations by an avowed policy of neutrality, or nonalignment. In 1960 V. K. Krishna Menon, Nehru's chief adviser on foreign policy, told the United Nations Assembly, "Our position is that we are an unaligned and uncommitted nation in relation to the Cold War . . . We do not belong to one camp or another." But, for the record, India has not been willing to adjudicate the accession of Kashmir to India. Since 1952 the Indians have claimed that the Kashmir issue is settled in law and fact. The Pakistani vainly point out that a majority of the people in Kashmir are Muslims who feel they are living in a police state. India, however, refuses to hold a plebiscite. Relations between India and Pakistan have been so exacerbated—not only over Kashmir but also over the Bengali revolt in East Pakistan—that they have twice engaged in outright war with each other (in 1965 and again in 1971), both of them using US military equipment. India felt no compunction about annexing Portuguese Goa by force in 1961. She is, however, more cautious in her belligerency toward Communist China (the border forays have been mostly hit-and-run on both sides), but she is firm in her declaration of intention "to defend our borders, and to strengthen them, and thus to protect the integrity of India."

The record of the United Kingdom since 1945 has, for the most part, been one of peaceful withdrawal from dominion over its former colonies in Asia and Africa. Two of our twelve states, India and Kenya, are products of that voluntary withdrawal. Neither India nor Kenya, however, obtained independence without experiencing the trauma of violence preceding the relinquishment of imperial power. The British military posture since World War II has been deliberately low-profile. The government put an end to conscription in 1960, and since then military forces have been maintained at minimum, most of them in NATO or widely dispersed through the remaining bits of the Empire. Although the United Kingdom is a member of the nuclear club in its own right—it produced its first H-bomb in the late 1950s—it has found the cost of building delivery systems too costly, so that its military strategy is primarily conditioned by its defense agreements with the United States and its partnership in NATO. Even so, the British have not hesitated to use force as an instrument of national policy when the occasion seemed to warrant it. In 1956 the British went to war with Egypt over the closing of the Suez Canal; and in 1958 British troops were landed in Jordan to shore up the authority of King Hussein. In 1971 British troops were battling in the religious war in Northern Ireland.

We have already stressed the belligerent behavior of the Israelis beginning with the Arab-Israeli War of 1948–49. Surrounded by hostile Arabs along a six hundred-mile border, the Israelis have continuously fought for their very existence as a nation, but their activities have not been entirely defensive. In 1956 the Israelis joined the British in attacking Egypt during the Suez crisis. In 1967 the Israelis launched a six-day war against Egypt, whom they thoroughly trounced with modern but conventional weaponry. And as this chapter is being written, the Israelis and the Arabs are in an uneasy truce following another outbreak of hostilities in 1970 in which again the Israelis emerged as victors with considerable gains in real estate which they are reluctant to return. Prime Minister Golda Meier has made it clear to whomever it may concern that Israel does not regard an international police force as an adequate substitute for definite and defensible boundaries.

For the record, our two Latin American states and two African states appear to be most peace-loving, or at least most successful in staying out of war. In the nineteenth century it was almost standard operating procedure for Latin American states to settle their boundary disputes by going to war, and since the colonial boundaries had been ill-defined the border wars were frequent occurrences. But no Latin American country has been involved in any major conflict since World War II. From the Latin American viewpoint the most likely source of external aggression or intervention is the United States. In the event of nuclear war between the superpowers, the expectation is that the war would be short and over before either the Latin American or African states could be drawn into the conflict.

National Security Concepts

The foreign policy of every nation is tied to national security as well as to international peace and if, in a given situation, it is not possible to pursue both objectives, then national security normally is given preference. National security is further perceived as dual in kind, guarding the country against external attack and also preserving the national way of life. But again, if a choice has to be made, the highest priority must be given to the first objective.

In the 1950s when international relations was perceived as a Cold War between the free world and the Communist bloc, the national security policies of the United States were based on certain premises: that the Communist bloc was a monolithic conspiracy by the USSR; that the small countries of the world with little military power of their own would soon be crushed by the Soviet military machine as had happened to the Baltic states and countries in East Europe; that the emerging new nations would fall victims to Communist-inspired insurgencies and wars of liberation; that it was the moral obligation of the United States to arrange for the defense of the free world not only with countervailing military power but also with an elaborate network of mutual security agreements.

Early in the 1950s, the national security policies of the USSR were predicated on the obverse premises: that Communism and capitalism were inevitably headed toward confrontation on the world stage; that the United States was engineering a capitalist encirclement of the USSR; that the great buildup in US military power and the network of multilateral military alliances, NATO, the OAS, SEATO, and CENTO were all part of the capitalist strategy to contain the Communist movement.[3] As early as 1952, however, the "great debate" in the Nineteenth Party Congress, convened during the Korean War, questioned the inevitability of war between the two hostile camps. Shortly after Stalin's death, a conference in Moscow drafted the Warsaw Pact, which was signed in 1955, bringing the European Communist states into a military alliance.[4] The Warsaw Pact was psychologically important, for it substituted a multilateral mutual defense arrangement for a unilateral imposition of force by the USSR in the Eastern European countries.

In 1956 the Twentieth Party Congress under the leadership of Khrushchev presented a new Communist image to the world, the image of a nationally secure Soviet Union, surrounded by friendly Communist states in Europe and Asia, embracing one-third of the world's population. Replacing Stalin's grim view of two hostile camps preparing for Armageddon, the new perspective envisaged an extensive zone of peace. Peaceful coexistence was the new ploy in foreign policy, based on the proposition that imperialism and colonialism were already becoming patterns of the past and that the victory of Communism was immiment without a world war.

By the 1960s it was clearly oversimplification, certainly not realism, to regard the world as divided into two power blocs, the one led by the United States, the other by the Soviet Union. NATO had been conceived as a community of nations with common traditions, loyalties, interests, and goals. Given the military posture of the Soviet Union in 1949, it was not too difficult to view Communism on the march across Europe to the shores of the Atlantic. NATO therefore was designed as a mutual defense alliance with coordinated military forces under a unified command. Although all of the members were expected to contribute conventional forces, the crux of the whole arrangement was the nuclear power of the United States. As time passed, however, the European members of NATO recovered their economic strength, the people prospered, unemployment all but disappeared, and American influence which had peaked under the Marshall Plan began to wane. As East-West relations thawed, the danger of Russian aggression appeared less imminent. The NATO allies fell to bickering among themselves over their respective contributions. The nuclear umbrella which the European members had accepted so gratefully in the 1950s became an ominous issue in the 1960s, "heavy, heavy what hangs over." In 1967, the French forces pulled out of NATO and virtually evicted NATO and US forces from France. By the 1970s, NATO was still functioning; the United States continued to regard it as central not only to the defense of Europe but to its own security. Nevertheless the NATO system was obviously in a state of stress and strain.

On the other side, the Communist bloc had also disintegrated. Yugoslavia, under the leadership of Marshall Tito, was the first of the Soviet satellites to defect, as early as 1948. Since then, Poland, Czechoslovakia, Rumania, and Hungary have tried more or less successfully to develop their own brands of Marxism, mixed with nationalism. That the Soviet hold is not entirely relaxed, was attested by the sending of Russian troops into Czechoslovakia as late as 1968 to curb the Dubcek government's efforts to achieve rapprochement with the West, regardless of different social systems. The most critical break in the Communist bloc, however, was that between the Soviet Union and the Peoples Republic of China early in the 1960s. The increasingly inimical relationships between the two erstwhile partners stem from ideological differences, national rivalries, and long-time border disputes. Whether these add up to a clash of vital interests is, of course, a matter of perception. But the fact that the Chinese have developed nuclear weaponry and will probably have an effective delivery system by the mid-1970s no doubt influences the Russian as well as the American strategy for immediate deployment of antimissile defenses and at the same time has spurred both the United States and the Soviet Union to negotiate for international limitation of nuclear armaments.

Military Expenditures as an Indicator of National Security

Both the American and the Russian images of each other in the international environment of the 1950s now seem equally simplistic to us. The recent toning down of the rhetoric, the substitution of negotiations and arms limitations talks for confrontation and the balance of terror seem to us more in accord with reason and reality. Nevertheless both the United States and the Soviet Union have felt impelled to continue the arms race, each side determined to outdo the other in reaching new heights in technological development, in developing more and more sophisticated weapons under the rubric of defense. The *New York Times Encyclopedic Almanac for 1971* provides us with horrendous tables showing the major operational weapons systems of 1970:

TABLE 13–1
Summary Trends in Military Expenditures—1964–69
(Billions of Dollars—Constant 1967 Dollars)

TOTAL	*Military Expenditures*						
	1964	65	66	67	68	69	% INCREASE 64–69
World	155	154	166	181	185	186	20
Developed	137	136	148	161	162	161	18
Developing	18	18	18	20	23	25	38
NATO	81	79	89	100	102	100	23
Warsaw	53	54	56	57	58	58	11
Other	21	21	21	24	25	28	43
	Per-Capita Military Expenditures						
							INCREASE 64–69
World	48	47	49	53	53	52	4
Developed	148	144	156	168	168	165	17
Developing	8	8	8	8	9	10	2
NATO	162	155	173	193	195	189	27
Warsaw	162	163	168	170	171	170	8
Other	9	9	8	9	9	10	1

SOURCE: US Arms Control and Disarmament Agency, *World Military Expenditures, 1969* (Washington, D.C.: Government Printing Office, 1970), p. 10.

ICBM and SLBM launchers, long-range heavy bombers, medium-range bombers, IRBMs and MRBMs, aircraft carriers, helicopter carriers, battleships, attack submarines, missile submarines, surface-to-surface missile ships, destroyers, heavy cruisers. A footnote on the comparative strength of the two superpowers is shrouded in the fantasy of nuclear power. "Although the U.S.S.R. has a sizeable superiority in delivery systems, only 1460 missiles and long range aircraft are capable of reaching the U.S. mainland. The American delivery systems total 2291, all of which are capable of reaching the U.S.S.R." [5] This is the ultimate in national security!

Although the rhetoric of nuclear confrontation so frequently used in the 1950s has been replaced by the rhetoric of rapprochement, the record of mounting military expenditures belies the change in behavioral disposition. From 1964 when the US Arms Control and Disarmament Agency (ACDA) compiled its first estimates on national military expenditures for 120 countries, the rate of worldwide increase was up 20 percent in 1969. Over this six-year period the world's military budgets exceeded all the public money spent on all forms of education and health care.

Table 13–1 summarizes trends in military expenditures and gross national product between 1964 and 1969, with total figures in billions of dollars and per-capita figures in dollars. The trends quite clearly show an accelerating race between the NATO and Warsaw Pact countries.[6] The NATO countries upped their military expenditures 23 percent; during the same period their GNP increased but 22 percent. The Warsaw Pact countries increased their

TABLE 13–1
(Continued)

GNP						
64	65	66	67	68	69	% CHANGE 64–69
2,145	2,259	2,390	2,481	2,610	2,739	27
1,774	1,870	1,982	2,054	2,163	2,272	28
371	389	408	427	447	467	26
1,198	1,250	1,315	1,352	1,411	1,472	22
432	456	492	513	540	563	30
515	553	583	616	659	704	36
Per-Capita GNP						INCREASE 64–69
667	684	711	722	745	767	100
1,915	1,983	2,090	2,151	2,242	2,332	417
162	165	169	172	176	180	18
2,396	2,460	2,558	2,616	2,701	2,789	393
1,323	1,380	1,471	1,529	1,595	1,648	325
216	224	232	239	249	260	44

military expenditures only 11 percent, but their GNP went up 30 percent in the same period. The per-capita comparisons bring the issue closer to the people concerned—every man, woman, and child in the world. The per-capita increase in military expenditures was $27 in the NATO countries, $8 in the Warsaw Pact countries. On the other hand, the per capita increase in the GNP in the NATO countries was $393 and in the Warsaw Pact countries $325. Thus the pinch is felt a little less in the more productive NATO countries.

If we move out of the Cold-War context, the figures in Table 13–1 tell an even more disturbing story about the growing gap between the developed and developing countries.[7] The rate of increase in military expenditures between 1964 and 1969 was 18 percent in the developed countries, 38 percent in the developing countries; the increase in GNP in the developed countries was 28 percent, in the developing countries 26 percent. Given limited resources, the increasing allocation for military expenditures in the developing countries necessarily cuts into the available resources for capital investment or public education and public health, cuts which developing countries cannot afford to make.

Now let us look at the allocation of national resources for military expenditures in our twelve countries and see how they fit into the world patterns. Table 13–2 shows us military expenditures in millions of dollars and indicates the percentage of change for the period 1964–67.[8] We have ranked the states in order of amount of expenditures. In the four-year period, the United States made by far the largest military outlay and Kenya the smallest, but if we were to rank according to degree of change, then Kenya would head

TABLE 13–2
Military Expenditures 1964–67 (in Current Prices)

	(Dollar Amounts in Millions)				
	1964	*65*	*66*	*67*	*% Change 64–67*
World	139,097	143,427	160,345	180,682	29.9
NATO (Eur.)	19,672	20,578	21,335	23,054	17.2
Warsaw Pact	49,480	50,650	53,890	57,070	15.3
USA	51,323	51,844	63,283	75,484	47.1
USSR	45,000	46,000	49,000	52,000	15.6
United Kingdom	5,562	5,855	6,150	6,436	15.7
Ger., FR	4,888	4,979	4,950	5,349	9.4
India	1,800	2,077	1,400	1,486	−17.4
Japan	836	781	933	1,076	28.7
Turkey	385	425	445	511	32.7
Israel	372	413	400	428	15.1
Mexico	128	134	168	168	31.3
Colombia	60	72	85	85	41.7
Ivory Coast	11	13	13	17	54.5
Kenya	8	8	12	15	87.5

SOURCE: ACDA, *World Military Expenditures, 1969.*

the list for increased amounts; only India shows an actual decrease in military expenditures.

Table 13–3 is our most telling table, showing military expenditures as percentages of the GNP for the four-year period 1964–67. Here we get a comparative reading of the official allocation of values in all twelve states. Again, we have ranked the states from highest to lowest percentage of GNP allocated for military expenditures. We note that the two countries that allocate the highest percentage of their GNP to military expenditures have been least successful during this period in achieving their primary goals of peace and national security. Both Israel and the United States have had to resort to war as a means of effecting their respective national policies. On the other hand, the two countries that allocated the lowest percentage of their GNP to military expenditures in 1964–67—Japan and Mexico—have been notably successful in implementing their plans for economic development.

Clearly, vast outlays for the military do not give us a measure for national security. Neither, we hasten to add, do small outlays. Mexico, for example, can allocate less than 1 percent of her GNP to military expenditures because her powerful neighbor to the north has undertaken to safeguard all the states of the Western Hemisphere against aggression or subversion. There have been no major armed conflicts in Latin America since World War II. The resort to war to settle ill-defined colonial boundaries now appears to be past history. As to embroilment in World War III, Latin American countries realistically assume that a nuclear war will be a short war, not likely to reach them before the superpowers will have overkilled each other. Mexico is a member of the OAS, but the OAS is not perceived as a fighting organization.

Similarly, Japan gets by with less than 1 percent of its GNP allocated to military expenditures because of its Security Pact with the United States

TABLE 13–3
Military Expenditures as Percentage of GNP 1964–67

	1964	*65*	*66*	*67*
World	7.3	6.9	7.0	7.3
NATO (Eur.)	4.9	4.8	4.6	4.6
Warsaw Pact	7–8	7–8	7–8	7–8
Israel	12.0	12.2	10.5	10.7
USA	8.2	7.6	8.5	9.5
USSR	8–9	8–9	8–9	8–9
United Kingdom	6.0	5.9	5.8	5.8
Turkey	5.3	5.2	4.7	4.8
Ger., FR	4.7	4.4	4.1	4.4
India	5.8	6.4	3.8	3.4
Ivory Coast	1.4	1.3	1.3	1.6
Colombia	1.6	1.7	1.7	1.5
Kenya	1.0	0.9	1.1	1.3
Japan	1.2	0.9	1.0	0.9
Mexico	0.7	0.7	0.8	0.7

SOURCE: ACDA, *World Military Expenditures, 1969.*

(renewed in 1970 for another ten years). Ardent nationalists in Japan resent this tie-in to US policy in Asia; nevertheless, the continuation of the tie is a guarantee of Japanese national security (though not necessarily peace) at minimum expense to the Japanese people.

The relatively low military expenditures in the African states are explicable, as in the Latin American states, by the fact that Africa is peripheral to the national interests of the superpowers. Both in Latin America and in Africa, the function of the military is more concerned with internal security than with external aggression; the military is generally regarded and used as a second-line police force to combat unrest and to insure stability. The French government still contributes to the defense and security of its former colonies in Africa; it has a bilateral defense agreement with the Ivory Coast pledging its support both against external aggression and internal disturbances. The British offer no such promise to Kenya (nor to any of their former African colonies), but they do furnish some military assistance. Why do Third World countries succumb to pressures for increasing their military expenditures? We surmize it is partly a matter of symbolizing modernity. If the developed countries will give or sell them the latest models in bombers and tanks, these are prestige items in official displays of progress!

We conclude, however, that whether and how a nation state achieves its primary goals of peace and national security depends largely on the international situation, upon external factors which its own government cannot control. We think this generalization with detailed explication can be made with respect to the United States, the Soviet Union, Mexico, India, or any one of our twelve countries.

POLITICAL STABILITY AND DOMESTIC TRANQUILITY

National security in its broadest sense embraces not only defense against external aggression but also political stability at home—what the Philadelphia Convention of 1787 so aptly called "domestic tranquility." The military establishment as well as the police force or constabulary contribute to the maintenance of law and order in every country. But, as we have indicated earlier, many factors enter into the capacity of the governors to govern and the willingness of the governed to accept authoritative decisions: the sharing of common values; perceptions of legitimacy; the flow of communications; the interaction of demands and responses in the formulation of policy; attitudes and skills of the bureaucracy in policy implementation; incentives and rewards for support and compliance; fear of the consequences of disobedience.

But how do we measure the degree of stability or tranquility in a government? A number of indicators have been suggested: the patterns of social change, the frequency and regularity of elections, the degree of popular participation in politics, the statistics on crime, the degree of political violence, the magnitude of civil strife. In Chapters 7 and 8 we have discussed at some length how parties and elections are used to bring about peaceful changes in the political system. Here we focus on sudden and violent changes which adversely affect the stability of government.

A quick recall of such events over the past dozen years highlights political turbulence and acts of political violence in all twelve of our states:

United States: a president, a presidential candidate, the outstanding leader of the civil rights movement, and numerous civil-rights workers assassinated; violent civil-rights demonstrations (pro and con); widespread radical disturbances and rioting in major cities; violent antiwar demonstrations.

Colombia: mounting malcontent with the performance of the National Front, especially in the rural areas, turning to violence in the 1970 elections with the attempted comeback of General Rojas Pinilla; virtually martial rule following the elections.

Germany: student demonstrations at the Free University of Berlin during a visit of state by the Shah of Iran; continuing clashes between students and police in the major university towns leading to the formation of the APO (extra parliamentary opposition) by militant student leaders.

India: recurrent outbreaks of violence between Muslim and Hindu groups; sporadic violence throughout the country during the 1971 elections.

Israel: frequent clashes between Arabs and Jews.

Ivory Coast: in 1963 a mass trial of more than a hundred persons charged with plotting a coup and attempting the assassination of the president; student outbursts squashed with force.

Japan: large-scale antigovernment riots and protests against the ratification of the military pact with the United States in 1960; student antiestablishment demonstrations, usually protesting the American presence, mounting in frequency and intensity as the security treaty with the United States was up for renewal in 1970.

Kenya: tension and clashes between the Kikiyu and Luo tribes; the assassination of Tom Mboya followed in 1969 by antigovernment demonstrations and countered by repressive measures.

Mexico: demonstrations and battles with the police in 1968 and 1969 over alleged violations of constitutional rights; in 1971 mass arrests following discovery of an alleged Communist plot to overthrow the government.

Turkey: the military coup of 1960 followed by mass trials, execution, and/or imprisonment of leaders of the deposed government; anti-American demonstrations against the US military presence accelerating in the late 1960s; a rash of unrest and violent acts, mostly from leftist groups, countered by military pressures, culminating in the overthrow of the Demirel government in 1971.

United Kingdom: bloody riots and armed clashes between Catholics and Protestants (with British troops caught between) in Northern Ireland; street fighting in industrial cities with racial connotations involving recent immigrants from the former colonies.

USSR: an official crackdown on dissenting intellectuals; Jewish protests against repression of individual rights, particularly the right to emigrate.

In 1967 following a summer of racial disorders and urban rioting in the United States, President Johnson appointed a National Advisory Commission to investigate the cause of political violence in America. The commission in turn enlisted a task force of scholars in anthropology, industrial relations, law, psychiatry, psychology, sociology, history, and political science to come up with a comprehensive report dealing not only with the immediate situation in the United States but also with conditions of civil strife and violence in other nations. Some of these academic studies done for the commission provide us with illuminating data on the relative stability and tranquility of our twelve nation states.[9]

The Feierabend study examines the record of eighty-four nation states over the eighteen-year period 1948–65.[10] Political events relevant to political instability were scaled according to intensity on a seven-point scale, from 0 = extreme stability to 6 = extreme instability. Thus using typical examples, 0 = a regular scheduled election; 1 = a cabinet officer resigned or dismissed; 2 = a peaceful demonstration; 3 = assassination or sabotage; 4 = assassination of a chief of state; 5 = a coup d'etat or guerrilla warfare; and 6 = civil war or mass executions. Political instability profiles of the eighty-four nations were obtained by summing up all the violent political events for the entire period. The scoring ranged from 0 (no violent political events) in Finland and Luxembourg to 190 (highest number of violent political acts) in Indonesia. Table 13–4 indicates the scores for the ten of our twelve states which were included in the survey, ranked from least to most turbulent.

The Feierabend hypothesis is that modern and traditional nations tend toward stability while states in transition tend to be more turbulent and unstable. Table 13–5 shows how nine of our twelve states fit into the Feierabend typology of modernity and political stability. We find it difficult, however, to substantiate any generalization as to the relationship of political

TABLE 13–4
Political Violence Profiles 1948–65

Country	*Score*
Israel	8
United Kingdom	17
Ger., FR	20
Japan	32
Mexico	33
Turkey	65
USSR	81
Colombia	96
USA	97
India	124

SOURCE: Hugh Davis Graham and Ted Robert Gurr, *The History of Violence in America,* Ivo K. Feierabend et al., "Social Change and Political Violence: Cross-National Patterns" (New York: Bantam Books, 1969), p. 652

stability to the level of modernization. In our small cross-national sample, the three states scoring lowest for political instability—United Kingdom, the Federal Republic of Germany, and Japan—are modern, highly developed nations.[11] On the other hand, the most highly developed country in our sample, the United States, appears second from bottom on our list, and we surmize that if the duration of the study were extended to the 1970s the violence score of both the United States and the United Kingdom would have moved up.

The Feierabend study, in search of other correlations, also groups the eighty-four countries according to coercive-permissive patterns of government. Using this typology, the study concludes that permissive democratic regimes by and large experience low levels of political unrest. (Table 13–6 shows how ten of our states fit into the Feierabend classification.) Our own much smaller sample does not bear out the generalization. The USSR, characterized as "highly coercive," has a lower score for political violence than the United States, characterized as "highly permissive." We surmise that the attempt to quantify the evidence actually distorts the picture. One can only count the overt acts. We have no doubt that a constant latent threat of violence in a highly coercive state deters violent dissent and so presents at least a facade of stability. Nevertheless, we hesitate to draw the hoped-for observation that as a state modernizes its economic and social structure and democratizes its government it is more likely to achieve political stability and domestic tranquility.

The Feierabend study examines cross-national patterns of political instability in 84 countries between 1948 and 1965. In the same report to the president on the causes and prevention of violence, Ted Robert Gurr submits a comparative study of civil strife in 114 countries for the period 1961–65.[12] Gurr attempted to measure the total magnitude of internal disturbances on the basis of pervasiveness (number of participants per one hundred thousand population), intensity (casualties, dead and injured, per ten million population), and duration (span of time for each strife event). Rank 1, the highest score on total magnitude of civil strife (48.7), went to the Congo-Kinshasa; rank 2, the next highest score (31.7), to Indonesia. Ten countries, six of them at a high level of economic development, and all but one of them democratic, scored less than 0.1 percent. Rank 114, lowest score (0.0), however,

TABLE 13–5
Relationship between Modernity and Political Instability 1948–65

	Traditional	*Transitional*	*Modern*
Unstable	India	Colombia Turkey	
Stable		Japan Mexico	Israel United Kingdom USA Ger., FR

SOURCE: Graham and Gurr, op. cit., p. 655.

went to Volta, an African state with an elitist political system and a low level of economic development. Table 13–7 shows the rank and scoring on total magnitude of civil strife for our twelve states according to the Gurr scores.

Gurr concluded that the magnitude of civil strife is related to a number of factors. "The greater the discrepancy between what men believe they deserve and what they think they are capable of attaining, the greater their discontent." A second level of causation pertains to notions of legitimacy: If people believe that those in power are not exercising their power rightfully, then the greater the likelihood of rebellion. A third level of causation comprises the institutional arrangements for responding to violent manifestations of discontent: Strife tends to be highest in countries with moderate to large military and police establishments, but "the consistency with which coercion is employed is more important in minimizing strife than the size of the forces that employ it." [13]

Throughout this book we have tried to emphasize the dynamic character of politics, the ever-changing faces of power, authority, and influence in government. The relations between the governors and the governed change in every time period, and the dynamics of change differ from state to state within the same time period. We note, for example, discrepancies in rank order between the political violence profiles of the Feierabend study (1948–65) and the total magnitude of civil strife in the Gurr study (1960–65). We surmise, moreover, that if the same methodologies were to be applied to the 1966–71 period that the rank order in both studies might have to be altered.

As this chapter is being written, the Turkish government appears to be the most unstable, most beset by antigovernmental demonstrations, terrorist tactics, and military intervention. In March, 1971, a joint memorandum from the commanders of the army, navy, and air force, addressed to President Cevdet Sunary and the chairmen of both houses of Parliament, charged Prime Minister Demirel's government with having brought Turkey to "the brink of civil strife and social and economic discontent."

TABLE 13–6
Typology of Nation States According to Level of Coerciveness

Type	*Country*	*Scoring*
Highly permissive	United Kingdom	17
	USA	97
Permissive	Israel	8
	Mexico	33
	Ger., FR	20
Mildly coercive	India	124
	Japan	32
	Turkey	65
Moderately coercive	Colombia	96
Highly coercive	USSR	81

SOURCE: Graham and Gurr, op. cit., p. 661.

During the whole of its existence the Demirel government had been subjected to extremist attacks from right and left, especially among the student population. Rightist extremists objected to the government's plans and programs for modernization and economic development and advocated return to the Islamic theocracy. Leftist extremists protested the military influence in the government and particularly opposed the presence of US troops on NATO bases in Turkey. (The capture of four US servicemen by members of the Turkish People's Liberation Army was the final act of terrorism which precipitated military intervention.) Demirel's government also had its difficulties, however, with organized labor which blamed soaring prices and the rising cost of living on the government's fiscal policies. And to top it, the Kurds, some two million people of different ethnic and linguistic roots, living in the remote areas of eastern and southeastern Turkey, were asserting their sense of separate nationalism. The case of Turkish instability is an almost perfect illustration of Gurr's thesis, that consistent military influence in the political affairs of a country is likely to cause instability. Throughout the 1960s the Turkish military stood in the wings of what appeared to be parliamentary democracy, always with the threat implicit, or explicit, that if the government did not act as the military thought best, the military would assert its right to protect the republic as it finally did in March, 1971.

THE WELL-BEING OF THE PEOPLE AND HIGHER STANDARDS OF LIVING

"With a view to the creation of conditions of stability and well-being which are necessary for peaceful and friendly relations among nations . . . the United Nations shall promote higher standards of living, full employment,

TABLE 13–7
Total Magnitude of Civil Strife in Twelve States
1961–65

State	*Score*	*Rank*
Colombia	16.9	13
Kenya	15.0	19
Israel	14.0	21
India	11.0	35
USA	10.2	41
Japan	5.9	68
United Kingdom	5.4	74
Turkey	5.0	79
Mexico	4.7	82
Ger., FR	4.6	83
USSR	3.6	89
Ivory Coast	1.8	100

SOURCE: Graham and Gurr, op. cit., pp. 628–30.

and conditions of economic and social progress and development." This statement from the Charter of the United Nations represents the good intentions and aspirations of every member state, but how do their respective performances measure up to expectations? What are the measures of well-being—or economic and social development? And how can we compare the degrees of well-being, or the rate of social and economic progress, within different political systems?

Measures of Economic Growth

The yardstick of economic growth most frequently used by policy-makers is the gross national product. Table 13–8 indicates how the GNP per capita in market dollars has increased in all twelve of our states during the decade 1958–68. We have ranked the states from high to low in 1958. Note that within the ten-year period several changes occurred in the rank order. Germany moved to second place, and Britain back to third place; Turkey moved up to seventh place and Colombia back to eighth place. Although Japan achieved the most spectacular growth record, she remained in fifth place. (Since data were not available for the USSR in 1958 we have left it out of the ranking exercise.) India remained at the bottom of the list, and, despite her many plans for development, showed the smallest rate of growth. The United States stayed at the top of the list, though her rate of growth was less than that of Germany, Israel, Japan, Mexico, Turkey, and the Ivory Coast.

When President Nixon jubilantly celebrated the $1 trillion GNP for the United States at the end of 1970 (a trillion is one followed by twelve zeroes!) not all Americans joined in the celebration. As one journalist in the nation's capital pointed out, the trillion cited by the president was more of a metaphor

TABLE 13–8
Per-Capita GNP—1958–68

	1958	*Rank*	*1968*	*Rank*	*% of Change 1958–68*
USA	2,602	1	4,379	1	68
United Kingdom	1,254	2	1,861	3	49
Ger., FR	1,066	3	2,206	2	93
Israel	795	4	1,459	4	83
Japan	350	5	1,404	5	301
Mexico	302	6	566	6	87
Colombia	233	7	319	8	37
Turkey	204	8	380	7	86
Ivory Coast	142	9	304	9	81
Kenya	80	10	125	10	56
India	73	11	80	11	9
USSR			890		

SOURCE: US Bureau of the Census, *Statistical Abstract of the United States, 1970,* 91st ed. (Washington, D.C.: Government Printing Office, 1970), p. 810.

than a measure.[14] A Rip Van Winkle, who went to sleep in 1939 and did not wake till the GNP buzzed the trillion mark, would find that the 1970 $1 trillion was but $315 billion in 1939 dollars; a Rip asleep since 1946 would discover that the 1970 $1 trillion had the purchasing power of $486 billion in 1946 dollars. Inflation since World War II has made the GNP a rather unreliable tool for policy-makers who want to calculate the monetary costs of government programs.

In his remarks on the $1 trillion GNP, the president vaguely observed that the GNP "means more" than "material production"; most economists, however, greeted this extraneous observation with raised eyebrows. The GNP includes only market transactions, goods and services produced for a price. If a householder fixes his own power mower that activity does not involve a market transaction and hence does not count in the GNP. But if he takes the mower to the We-Fix-It Shoppe and then plays golf, he has thereby given the GNP clock several extra ticks, the price of labor and parts for the mower, the rental charges on his golf cart, and the price of the three golf balls he played and lost on the course. When an oil well burns for weeks in the Gulf of Mexico, that does not subtract from the GNP; to the contrary all expenditures for the men and equipment used to fight the fire add to the GNP. Only legal transactions enter into GNP calculations (governments anxious to retain the semblance of legitimacy usually take a moral stance). The sale of liquor and cigarettes count in the GNP, the sale of marijuana and heroin do not; medical services and coffins go into the GNP. The pall of smog that lies heavy over American cities most of the time reassures us that the GNP is ticking away (it was programmed to tick $2,000 every second for 1970). Air pollution, noise pollution, water pollution do not slow or stop the clock. The more fragile the bumpers on automobiles the better for the GNP record; garage bills are an increasingly sizable item in the US GNP. All of which is to say that the link between the GNP and the well-being of the people can be quite distorted.

Some Indicators of Levels of Living

The national accounts are not very helpful in depicting different levels of living within a single country and are even less satisfactory for measuring the relative well-being of peoples in different countries. Let us therefore take a look at some of the typical people to whom we have been introduced in the earlier pages of this book. What do they consider a modern standard of living? What are their expectations for higher levels of living?

Abraham Jefferson, who lives in the national capital of the world's richest country, has been unemployed since we first met him. Welfare workers now refer to him as "hard core unemployable" because he has no technical skills, he is practically illiterate, and he is nonwhite. Although he is a family man, Jefferson has had to move out of the apartment so that his wife, Annie Lee, could go on welfare and claim public assistance for their five dependent children.[15] Abraham Jefferson's case is not unique. In 1968 one-third (33.5 percent) of all nonwhite families in the United States were officially counted as living below the poverty level; more than half (55.1 percent) of the blacks living in the metropolitan areas were below the poverty level; and approximately two-thirds (63.7 percent) of those under twenty-five and those over sixty-five (62.5 percent).[16] If, as we believe, political stability is related to equalization of status, opportunities, and incomes, then Abraham Jefferson's level of living—the poverty level—is a clue to the magnitude of civil strife and the profile of increasing violence in the United States.

On the other hand, Joe Zilch's level of living comes much closer to what is usually regarded as the American standard of living—the *Good Housekeeping* standard, replete with a mortaged house, a garage with two cars, a utility room with electric washer and dryer, color television in the family room (all items bought on time) and a Book-of-the-Month on the living room coffee table. The Zilches too are typical Americans: In 1968 nearly a third (31 percent) of American family units belonged in the Zilch income group, $10–15,000. In households of this income group 96.5 percent owned one or more cars, 50.9 percent two or more cars; 78.3 percent have black and white television, 48.2 percent color television; 84.6 percent electric washing machines, etc.[17]

How people live in the United States—their standard and their level of living—depends not only on their income but also upon their occupation, their social class, their personal inclinations. Schoolteachers, garbage collectors, and government clerks may fall in the same income group and yet maintain different levels of living. The same observation holds more or less true in every society.

Pedro Cervantes lives in a relatively poor country but he himself is a rich man; his family lives in elegant style in Bogotá. He belongs to the traditional oligarchy, direct descendant of the Spanish colonial ruling elite. He has fared well under the economic development policies of the National Front. But let us introduce you also to Carlos Uribbe, a *mestizo* (mixed European and Indian) who belongs to the *estrato bajo*, the lower class who comprise about half the population of Bogotá. Carlos Uribbe, like his American counterpart, Abraham Jefferson, has migrated from rural poverty to urban poverty; he has no skills, he is illiterate, and on his own he seems incapable of reaching a modern level of living. He voted for General Rojas in the 1970 elections, as did most of the squatters who lived in the outskirts of Bogotá, because the general promised such things as automobiles for the poor people.

The GNP per capita is a poor indicator of levels of living in Colombia because of extremes in the distribution of income. The select group to which Pedro Cervantes belongs (5 percent of the population) has great wealth, purchasing power, and prestige. The large group to which Carlos Uribbe belongs (45 percent) is at the hovel-level of existence. A middle class is gradually emerging—shopkeepers, schoolteachers, skilled workers, government employees—who do have increasing purchasing power and who are upgrading their levels of living. But, if equalization of social and economic opportunities is the route to stability, as we have earlier suggested, then we foresee instability for some time to come in Colombia.

The GNP per capita is an even more unsatisfactory indicator for levels of living in India where the extremes of riches and poverty are terribly apparent. Immensely rich and powerful princes and rajas still live in traditional oriental splendor—also in a modern manner as symbolized by their Rolls Royces and sports cars. But our friend B. R. Jog who lives with his large family on a very small farm in a remote rural area, has an annual cash income of less than $100. In 1971 he and his wife walked a long stretch down a muddy road to cast their two votes for the New Congress candidate running for a seat in Parliament. What did it matter to the Jogs, or all the other villagers, what party won control of the Parliament in New Delhi? The New Congress candidate, taking his cue from Indira Gandhi, was promising "a dynamic program of agricultural development." Whatever that may mean to the more sophisticated politicians in New Delhi, the majority of the 560 million people who live in the farming villages of India believes it means a higher level of living for them, with government help. To B. R. Jog, government help does not mean socialism or any ism. Government help means free schooling for his children. B. R. Jog and his wife are illiterate, but their children are learning to read and write. The government is the local agent—with the Ugly American—who has taught the villagers how to use fertilizers and higher yield seeds. The Jogs do not have a pink tiled bathroom (like the Zilches), but they have a new outside sanitary pit construction and also a new well with safe drinking water—again thanks to government help.

When we try to compare levels of living in the United States and India, we perceive that the national standards are different. B. R. Jog's cash income is incredibly low; but the produce of his farm gives him a level of living similar to most of the villagers. In Indian village life there is no problem of smog, noise pollution, or traffic jams. Mrs. Jog is not nagging B. R. to buy her a new dishwasher and the oldest boy is not drag racing the family car every night (these are the Zilch problems).

In India, as in the United States, and indeed in all twelve of our states, the lowest level of living is in the ever-growing, overcrowded cities. Modern government everywhere appears to be technologically stymied by the basic problems of urban life—safe drinking water, sewerage and garbage disposal, housing with plumbing, streets with lighting, and mass transportation to and from the shopping and working areas. Moreover, the slums of Calcutta and Bombay, New York and Washington, Bogotá, Mexico City and Abidjan, big cities the world over, filled and overflowing with poor people who have left their rural homes to find a modern way of life, have become centers of anti-establishment movements. As Gurr's study on the causes of violence indicates, people who are frustrated, who feel that they get less than they deserve, or need, or want are liable to turn against the prevailing system. Whether the party of Indira Gandhi with its overwhelming vote of confidence in the 1971 elections can actually step up the war against poverty and achieve its campaign promises is yet to be tested. The challenge is tremendous.

Western interpreters of the 1971 Indian elections believe that Indira Gandhi plans to move her nation to the left. To the left normally means a larger proportion of public expenditures in the GNP. We have observed earlier that the ratio of public-to-private expenditures in the GNP as well as the allocation of expenditures within the public sector are political decisions which reflect the national values—or, more accurately, the national values as these are determined by the ruling elite. In a speech to her party workers shortly after her landslide victory, the Indian prime minister gives her own interpretation of the 1971 mandate of the people:

> *The elections have proved that the path of socialism is the only way which this country can march ahead, by taking all sections of society along. But the object of our socialism is not to take away everything from the rich and give it to the poor. The idea is to reduce economic disparities and bridge the gap between the one and the other.*[18]

Social Security Programs as Indicators of National Well-being

Ideology aside, the most telling indicators of how a state provides for the well-being of the people are those items in the national accounts which are the basic concerns of every man—food and nutrition, clothing, housing, educational opportunities, health facilities, and social security against the universal hazards of income deficiency. In earlier chapters we have discussed many of these items to show differences in national resources as well as differences in political allocations. Here we focus on social security programs designed to protect the individual against the dependency of old age and childhood, invalidity, work injuries, unemployment, and the costs of large families. Such programs reflect some basic differences in public philosophy among our twelve states.

A recent survey indicates that 123 countries now have some kind of government-sponsored social security programs.[19] The great majority of these programs are social insurance programs, financed largely through compulsory contributions by employers, employees, or both, rather than out of the ordinary government revenues. Usually such contributions are placed in special trust funds from which benefits are paid to individuals roughly in proportion to their contributions. In the public service approach to social security the government provides cash benefits directly out of the general revenues for all members of the community who fall within a certain category, e.g., old-age pensions to all residents who have reached a specified age, or survivors' pensions to every widow and orphan, or a family allowance to every family having a given number of children. Such payments are made without regard to a means or needs test. Public assistance constitutes a third approach to social security; the government provides cash payments to individuals with low incomes and limited resources, within certain categories (the aged, dependent children, or handicapped persons) in accordance with means and needs formulas.

All twelve of our states have social security systems which embody one or more of these approaches and in various combinations. The social security system in every country has a statutory base (laws passed by the national legislature) with complicated and technical formulas for application. Table 13–9 categorizes the principal types of social security programs: 1) old-age, invalidity, and survivors; 2) sickness and maternity; 3) work injuries; 4) unemployment; and 5) family allowances. The dates on the table indicate the first law passed in the country relating to the particular program. In most cases subsequent legislation has gradually broadened the original coverage. Note that imperial Germany was the first country to establish a comprehensive social security system, in the 1880s. The United Kingdom was well on the way in the first decade of the twentieth century. The United States lagged behind the European states; it took a major economic depression in the 1930s to bring about a New Deal in government controls over the economy and with it social security legislation.

The earliest social security legislation, to provide workmen's compensation for industrial injuries, was promoted by the pressure politics of organized labor in the industrial states. Note that all twelve of our states have some such legislation. The newest programs in the social security systems—family allowances to insure a decent standard of living for large families—have for the most part developed only since World War II. Only six of our states have so far tried out this kind of social security program.

We cannot begin to detail all the various programs, but let us call attention to salient points that suggest significant differences in public philosophy. All twelve of our states have social security programs which help cushion the decrease in income because of old-age or invalidity. In the United States old-age, survivors, and disability insurance now covers virtually all persons 65 or over (or their dependent survivors). The amount of benefits to individual persons is linked to the amount of contributions made through the working years, jointly by employers and employees. Similar insurance programs for the aged and the invalid have long been in operation in the United Kingdom and Germany.

TABLE 13–9
Social Security Programs throughout the World—1969
(with Date of First Law in Each Category)

	Old-Age Invalidity	*Sickness Maternity*	*Work Injury*	*Unemployment*	*Family Allowance*
WORLD TOTAL OF PROGRAMS	97	68	120	34	62
Colombia	1946	1946	1916		1957
Ger., FR	1889	1883	1884	1927	1954
India	1952	1948	1923		
Israel	1953	1953	1926		1959
Ivory Coast	1960	1952	1932		1955
Japan	1941	1922	1911	1947	
Kenya	1965	1966	1946		
Mexico	1942	1942	1931		
Turkey	1949	1945	1945		
United Kingdom	1908	1911	1897	1911	1945
USSR	1922	1912	1912		1944
USA	1935	1965	1908	1935	

SOURCE: US Department of Health, Education and Welfare, Social Security Administration, Office of Research and Statistics, *Social Security Programs throughout the World, 1969*, Research Report no. 31 (Washington, D.C.: Government Printing Office, 1970).

In the USSR old-age and invalidity programs are regarded as part of the public service. Thus individual contributions are not required. But, as in the United States, the United Kingdom, and Germany, the amount of pension received by the individual in the Soviet Union is directly related to his work record—the longer the work period the higher the pension. The age requirement for retirement in the Soviet Union—60 for men, 55 for women—is comparatively low; however, Soviet policy encourages workers to stay on their jobs beyond the legal retirement age. Survivors benefits in the USSR are comprehensive in principle but limited in application. Recent Soviet family legislation stresses the legal obligation of every citizen to support his needy relatives—parents, children, stepchildren, grandchildren.

Although all twelve countries have some kind of old-age, survivors, and invalidity programs, coverage in the developing countries is usually much less comprehensive than in the industrial states. In Colombia, for example, only employees in industry and commerce are covered; agricultural and domestic workers are specifically excluded, and that in effect excludes the majority of the working population. Similarly, in India the coverage extends only to employees in the large factories; the multitudes who live in the rural villages are not insured. In Mexico, on the other hand, not only industrial workers but also small farmers, members of agricultural cooperatives, sugar cane workers, and some other agricultural laborers are insured; domestic workers are specifically excluded.

All twelve states have made statutory provision for sickness and maternity programs, but there are great differentials among the industrial states as well as among the developing countries. In the United States, hospitalization benefits and other medical services were secured for pensioners under the national social security insurance system in 1965. Thus persons sixty-five and over who have qualified for old-age pensions are also covered by hospitalization insurance and if they pay additional contributions they can also qualify for other medical services. In the United Kingdom, the National Health Service operates as a public service for all residents; this includes medical services provided by doctors and druggists under contract with and paid directly by the National Health Service; it also includes hospitalization, maternity care, dental care, medicines, and home nursing; all of this without regard to individual means.

When comparing wage and salary levels as indicators of well-being, it is important to take into account the social wages that augment the cash incomes of individuals and families. In the United States, for example (as of 1968), the government pays only 37.5 percent of the national health expenditures; this figure embraces the health insurance program for the aged (to which the pensioners have contributed), defense department hospital and medical care, veterans hospital and medical care, military dependents' medical care, and medical research in the National Institutes of Health.[20] In other words, most individuals under sixty-five in the United States must foot their own bills for hospital care, physicians' services, dental services, eyeglasses, hearing aids, and medicines. In the United Kingdom all such expenditures for health services and supplies are covered for all residents through the National Health

Service. In the Soviet Union the social wage statistics include such items as pensions for the aged; support payments to unwed, widowed, and separated mothers; support payments during maternity leave from employment; child-care centers to help working mothers; students' stipends to cover living and miscellaneous expenses (tuition is free); free medical services; passes to sanatoriums and rest homes; and housing subsidies. How to figure per-capita social wages, however, is likely to turn into an exercise in social philosophy rather than econometrics.[21] How, for example, would you compute the per-capita input into the social wages, from the public expenditures for US national parks which offer magnificent recreational facilities to millions of American workers?

Family allowance programs present some tough problems in view of limited national resources and mounting population pressures. Think what universal family allowances would do to the national accounts of India where approximately twenty-one million children are born every year! On the other hand, think what a family allowance plan with cash benefits for each child would do to raise the level of living for B. R. Jog's family (eight children but no more to come—Mrs. Jog has taken advantage of government help in the matter of birth control!). Think what a family allowance system would do for Abraham Jefferson and his family. Under the existing public assistance program in the US District of Columbia Mrs. Jefferson can obtain welfare grants for the dependent children only so long as her husband is out of the picture.

Currently six of our twelve states support family allowance programs. Germany offers family allowances as a public service available to all families with two, three or more children. The government pays the total cost—cash benefits progressing upward for each child, twenty-five marks a month for the second child, fifty marks for the third child, sixty marks for the fourth child, and seventy marks for the fifth and each additional child. The British and Russian family allowance plans are similar to the German: a universal public service, wholly government financed. The Russian approach is more economical, with the government cash supplement to the family income beginning with the fourth child. Three of our developing states have also adopted some form of family allowance programs. Those in Colombia and the Ivory Coast are tied to industrial employment and do not cover most families in either country. The Israeli program is comparable to the European states in extended coverage but is financed through earmarked payroll taxes rather than through general revenues.

The Public-Private Mix

When we try to link the well-being of the people to the scope of activities in the public versus the private sectors of the economy we run into difficulties. Decision-making in the public sector is a political process; public policies not only reflect official perceptions of the general welfare but they also represent conditioned reflexes to the demands of special interest groups. A governmental decision is authoritative and binding. If, for example, the government prescribes a system of social insurance, then the individual taxpayer is not free to decide whether to contribute part of his pay for social insurance or to set up a retirement program of his own design. We do not know how many individuals might be better off if left to the devices of self-help rather than collective assistance. The assumption of social insurance is that more people will benefit from forced savings along with government planning than from voluntary saving along with private charity. In any case, the individual taxpayer is not permitted to decide for what purposes he will or will not contribute to the general revenue; in any tax program some people are sure to be paying taxes to support services they do not want for themselves, or for others (pacifists have to pay taxes that go for military expenditures, urban workers pay taxes that underwrite price supports for farmers, single persons without children help underwrite the costs of burgeoning school systems, and litterbugs pay taxes for trash collection).

Among our twelve states, the USSR is our prime example of a government-controlled economy; but, as we have pointed out earlier, Soviet policy in recent years has tended to give more consideration to consumer interests, to provide more incentives and rewards for individual enterprise, and generally to allow more leeway in the private sector. No state embraces the ideology of pure and unadulterated private enterprise. The United States comes closest to exemplifying the market economy, in which the buying and selling of goods and services are for the most part regulated by the mechanism of supply and demand, and in which the great proportion of productive activities is privately owned and operated. But, as we have also pointed out earlier, the scope of political intervention in the American economy is increasing every year with more government planning, more government regulation, more government operations. Basic ideological differences still set the two political systems poles apart, yet there are striking similarities in the way American and Russian bureaucrats and technocrats tackle similar problems.

What goods and services should belong in the public service is a value judgment that is bound to change with time, place, and circumstance. In the 1930s many Americans, especially Republicans, viewed the introduction of the New Deal social legislation as evidence of galloping socialism. Today both major parties vie with each other, especially in election years, for the chance to sponsor new and increased benefits. President Nixon's proposals for family income security are much more far-reaching than those of his predecessors in office.

In the United Kingdom and in Germany public health services and facilities appear to be more generally accessible to all classes of people than is the case with public education in those countries (the emphasis is reversed in the United States). Is there a notable difference, however, in the performance of the public and private approach—in medical care, for example? If the number of persons per physician is an indicator of medical services available, then among our twelve states the USSR with a public service approach and Israel with trade union insurance programs tie for top spot—four hundred persons per physician. The United States with a predominantly private practice and Germany with a public service system tie for second place—each with seven hundred persons per physician. The United Kingdom and Japan both with national health insurance programs tie for third place with nine hundred persons per physician. India is at the bottom with four thousand eight hundred persons to one physician, Turkey—two thousand eight hundred, Colombia—two thousand two hundred, and Mexico—one thousand eight hundred.[22] Such statistics, of course, tell us nothing about the quality of medical care in any of the countries. They merely suggest that the stage of economic development, rather than the public-private mix, is more significant in performance ratings.

British economist, Barbara Ward, who has given a great deal of thought to the economics and politics of development, observes that "once one leaves behind the ideology of state control," no absolute rule, not even a rule of thumb, can determine the best mix of public and private enterprise.

> *In every country the mix between public and private enterprise is likely to be different, because it will in each case reflect local political pressures, local opportunities, the local scale of developed private enterprise, and the capacity of the country itself to find resources within its own borders. . . .*
>
> *All economics is a matter of choice—of allocating scarce resources to alternative and competing needs. There would be no economics if there were no scarcities. . . . Choice must enter in because there is not enough to go around. And in this field of development it is very easy to make the wrong choices—choices which, in spite of a vast expenditure of money, do not lead to sustained growth, to an upward spiral of interdependent expansion. Getting the "mix" right is the great factual problem of economic development, and it must vary from economy to economy according to local conditions and endowment.*[23]

Take the case of Turkey. The Constitution of 1961 promises that the newly reformed government will provide and protect social and individual peace and prosperity. It recognizes that it is "the duty of the state" to realize economic, social, and cultural development *under democratic methods*,[24] to augment the national saving, and to direct investments according to priorities for the public welfare. Such high intentions embodied in the constitutional law were bound to raise the expectations of the people. Indeed, Article 41 specifically proposes that economic and social life be regulated in a manner aimed to provide everybody [25] with a standard of living suitable for justice and human dignity. So, how did the government go about meeting the popular expectations?

Planning for economic development was the principal aim of the Turkish government in the 1960s. Atatürk's old party, the Republican Peoples' party (RRP), was dominant in a coalition government, 1961–65. It consistently advocated a left-of-center approach with emphasis on promoting the public sector of the economy. The Justice party (JP), a spin-off from the deposed Democratic party of the 1950s, won a majority of seats in the National Assembly in 1965; it also stressed economic development, but tended to favor the private sector. In the 1969 elections the Justice party lost some of its popular following and a schism opened among its members in the National Assembly. Between 1969 and 1971, the JP had increasing difficulty both in maintaining its political power and in controlling the economy, the more so because its leadership was constrained by the constitutional prescription to use only democratic methods. It is not easy, however, to plan and to implement plans by democratic methods, when there is no consensus on basic economic and social issues, if the government party has no working majority in parliament, and especially if the opposition party commands a high degree of support in the bureaucracy and in the military.

How did the Turkish government actually perform in the 1960s? Despite frenetic planning, the Turkish government (whether under RRP or JP leadership) was unable to fulfill its constitutional mandate to provide everybody with a standard of living suitable for justice and human dignity. As of 1968, the average daily wage of industrial workers was estimated at about $3.00, and that was much higher than the cash income of the many more small farmers and agricultural workers whose level of living was simply subsistence.[26] The social security legislation, passed in 1964, provides old age and invalidity insurance for workers in industry and commerce, but specifically excludes agricultural and domestic workers, who comprise the bulk of the labor force. Sickness and maternity benefits and compensation for work injuries have the same limited coverage. Labor legislation covers working conditions, hours of labor, safety and health regulations, and minimum wages, but again such legislation affects only a very small percentage of the total labor force.

Add then to the disquieting function of constant military surveillance, and the increasing difficulty of controlling dissident elements in the nation by democratic means, the widening gap between government promises and performance in the economic and social life of the people, and we have identified the principal causal factors in the increasing instability of the Turkish political system.

The lesson of Turkey is implicit in all new states and developing countries where the political leadership is expected to raise the levels of living for everybody to modern standards, within a short time, and by democratic methods. What mix of public and private enterprise is most suitable to local conditions and endowment? What techniques of government are most likely to move a new nation? Universal suffrage and free elections? Competitive parties or one party systems? Incentives and rewards for private enterprise or the imposition of national sacrifices to accumulate capital for public investment? What are the priorities for investment—education which promises more skilled workers and technicians, in time? Social services which immediately improve the health and morale of the people, but which drain current capital needed to build the infrastructure? Steel mills and power dams or land reforms and modernization of agriculture? As we review in our mind the different routes taken by the developing nations in our sample, we rate Mexico's one-party government most successful at this point. But we surmise that, in the long run, if India sticks to the course which her present leadership is charting, she will gradually move upward on the rating scale to compete with the top industrial states. India has the human and physical resources of a superpower if she learns how to mobilize them and how to use them in pursuance of the national goals.

HUMAN RIGHTS AND FUNDAMENTAL FREEDOMS

It is an ancient adage that man cannot live by bread alone. One of the high purposes of the United Nations, as its founders wrote into the Charter, is to promote respect for human rights and fundamental freedom for all, without distinctions as to race, sex, language, or religion. To fulfill this purpose the Economic and Social Council of the United Nations immediately established a Commission on Human Rights. The commission forthwith prepared a Universal Declaration of Human Rights—some thirty articles—which specifies the basic rights and fundamental freedoms.

The Universal Declaration of Human Rights (1948) epitomizes the development of Western thinking about the obligations of the governors and the rights of the governed in a modern political system. Article 1 reflects the spirit of the eighteenth century, "All human beings are born free and equal in dignity and rights. They are endowed with reason and conscience and should act towards one another in a spirit of brotherhood." The language emulates that of the US Declaration of Independence: "all men are created equal . . . endowed by their Creator with certain unalienable Rights." But, as we read through the thirty articles of the Universal Declaration, we perceive that it is in fact a document of the twentieth century, a comprehensive statement of civil, political, social, and economic rights that goes far beyond the spirit and substance of political thinking in 1776.

TABLE 13-10
Ratifications of Nine UN Human Rights Conventions (as of September, 1970)

	genocide	*freedom of association*	*slavery supplement*	*political rights of women*	*forced labor*	*employment discrimination*	*equal remuneration*	*discrimination in education*	*racial discrimination*	*number ratified*
WORLD TOTAL NUMBER	74	78	75	65	89	72	70	55	39	
Ger., FR	x	x	x		x	x	x	x	x	8
Israel	x	x	x	x	x	x	x	x		8
USSR	x	x	x	x		x	x	x	x	8
United Kingdom	x	x	x	x	x			x	x	7
India	x		x	x		x	x		x	6
Mexico	x	x	x		x	x	x			6
Turkey	x		x	x	x	x	x			6
Colombia	x				x	x	x			4
Ivory Coast		x			x	x	x			4
Japan		x		x			x			3
Kenya					x					1
USA			x							1

SOURCE: UN Association of the United States of America, *Time for Action, Labor Day, 1970* (Washington, D.C.: Government Printing Office, 1970).

"A Common Standard of Achievement for All Peoples and All Nations"

The UN General Assembly proclaimed the Universal Declaration as "a common standard of achievement for all peoples and all nations." But when the Commission on Human Rights got down to brass tacks, to draft specific international conventions for the implementation of this common standard, the ensuing debates in the international forum and within the member states made it painfully clear that different peoples have very different concepts of basic rights and fundamental freedoms. The UN General Assembly designated 1969 as the International Year for Human Rights and called upon the member states to ratify nine human rights conventions in this twentieth anniversary year of the Universal Declaration. Table 13–10 tells us how our twelve states have responded to the international appeal. The Federal Republic of Germany, Israel, and the USSR have ratified eight of the nine conventions; the United Kingdom seven; India, Mexico, and Turkey six; Colombia and the Ivory Coast four; Kenya and the United States one. Let us take a closer look at these nine conventions which become binding only upon states which ratify them.

1 Prevention and Punishment of the Crime of Genocide. This convention, adopted by the UN General Assembly in 1948, declares that the destruction of a national, ethnical, racial, or religious group, in whole or in part, constitutes the crime of genocide. Persons charged with genocide will be tried by a competent tribunal within the territory where the act was committed or by an international tribunal. By the end of 1970, the convention had been ratified by seventy-four states. In our sample of twelve, the Ivory Coast, Kenya, Japan, and the United States were the holdouts.

2 Freedom of Association and Protection of the Right to Organize. This convention, adopted by the International Labor Organization in 1948, largely on the initiative of US delegates, has been ratified by seventy-eight states; in our sample of twelve, India, Turkey, Colombia, Kenya, and the United States have not ratified.

3 Supplementary Convention on Slavery. In 1956 the UN General Assembly approved a supplementary convention to the 1926 International Slavery Convention. The intent of the supplementary convention is to strengthen the international prohibition of slavery, slave trade, and institutions and practices similar to slavery. The convention has been ratified by seventy-five nation states. In our sample Colombia, the Ivory Coast, Japan, and Kenya have not ratified. This is the only convention which the United States has accepted.

4 Political Rights for Women. This convention was adopted by the Assembly in 1952; parties to it agree to accord women the right to vote, to be elected to public office, and to perform public functions on equal terms with men.

It has been ratified by sixty-five states; six of our twelve states have not ratified—Germany, Mexico, Colombia, the Ivory Coast, Kenya, and the United States.

5 Forced Labor. This convention came out of the International Labor Conference in 1957. Parties to it agree not to use any form of compulsory labor as a means of political coercion, as punishment for holding political views opposing the established views, as a method of mobilizing labor for international development, as a means for racial, social, national, or religious discrimination. This convention has had the most universal support of the UN membership with eighty-nine ratifications. It is the one convention, out of the nine, which the USSR has not ratified; India, Japan, and the United States have also withheld ratification.

6 Discrimination in Employment and Occupation. This is another ILO convention, adopted in 1957. It has been ratified by seventy-two states, but not by the United Kingdom, Japan, Kenya, and the United States.

7 Equal Remuneration. Another ILO convention, adopted in 1951, it calls for equal remuneration for work of equal value for men and women workers. It has been ratified by seventy states, but not by the United States, Kenya, and the United Kingdom.

8 Elimination of Discrimination in Education. A covenant from UNESCO in 1960, it has been ratified by only fifty-five states. Among our twelve states, India, Mexico, Turkey, Colombia, the Ivory Coast, Japan, Kenya, and the United States have withheld ratification.

9 Elimination of All Forms of Racial Discrimination. This covenant, adopted by the UN General Assembly in 1965, has been ratified by thirty-nine states. It has not been ratified by Israel, Mexico, Turkey, Colombia, the Ivory Coast, Japan, Kenya, or the United States.

As we read the responses of our twelve states to the international conventions on human rights, the more developed countries have generally evinced greater willingness to accept and enforce universal norms. We are wary, however, of measuring national concern for human rights by verbal posturing in the international arena. Governments are prone to embrace international protection of human rights more in principle than in practice, a matter of ideological sparring or political expediency that has little effect upon behavioral patterns at home.[27] Nevertheless a decent respect for the opinions of mankind should impel democratic nations, and certainly the leader of the free world, to support UN efforts to establish an international bill of rights that could become the supreme law of the land in every country. Accordingly we rate the United States bottom-low for its failure to ratify the covenants on human rights; we do not feel that concern for states' rights should take priority over human rights. We note that other federal states have been willing to ratify.

Civil and Political Rights

In Chapter 4, when we looked at the fundamental laws of our twelve countries, we discovered that all of them incorporate most of the civil rights enumerated in the Universal Declaration. But when we try to extrapolate reality from the rhetoric, we do not find a universal code of conduct, nor do we find that civil-rights behavior in a single state is always in accord with its expressed legal norms.

It is one of the ironies of American history that the author of the Declaration of Independence was himself a Southern slaveholder whose belief in unalienable rights did not extend to Negroes, Indians, or the mobs of great cities. When the founding fathers in 1787 invoked the blessings of liberty for themselves and their posterity they did not have in mind such blessings for one-fifth of the population then held in slavery. Not until 1865, after four years of bloody Civil War, was the peculiar institution of slavery prohibited in the United States. In 1869, by constitutional amendment, the United States forbade any state to deny equal protection of the laws, but as late as the mid-1950s this was construed so as to permit racial segregation in public schools, public transportation, and public accommodations. Not until the mid-1960s did Congress assume responsibility for making equal protection of the laws a positive national policy.

The Universal Declaration holds that all persons are entitled to civil and political rights without distinction of any kind—neither race, color, sex, language, religion, political nor other opinion, national nor social origin, property, birth, nor other status. As a matter of fact, this is a fairly comprehensive description of the discriminations that exist in all states. Discrimination against members of minority groups is pretty universal—Volga Germans and Jews in Russia, Palestinians in Israel, Indians, Chicanos, and blacks in the United States, Roman Catholics in Northern Ireland, Christians in Turkey, Protestants in Colombia, Muslims in the Hindu states and Hindus in the Muslim states of India, the poor and dispossessed in all states.

The removal of legal barriers is not likely to fulfill the expectations of equality in any community. This was the hard lesson learned by the civil-rights movement in the United States in the 1960s. The crisis of the cities, rioting and mob violence, came about when black people migrated in large numbers from rural poverty areas to the cities in anticipation of improving their levels of living. At the same time white people were moving out of the cities and into the suburbs to protect their standards of living. Despite equal protection of the laws and the end of segregation as official policy, more and more Blacks were crowded into the urban ghettos and in fact there was more segregation than ever. The US Commission on Civil Rights, reporting in 1970, observed that equal opportunity was advancing at a pace barely discernible in employment practices and housing.[28] So far as the enforcement efforts of the national government are concerned, the policy of equal opportunity is more on paper than in action. Hence, the civil-rights movement of the 1960s turns toward more militant demonstrations in the 1970s.

The UN General Assembly in its first session in 1946 recommended that all member states grant women political rights equal to those of men. The Commission on the Status of Women has concerned itself with such questions as equal pay for equal work, equal access to posts of responsibility, equal educational opportunities for women, and equal rights in property. Women can vote and hold public office in all twelve of our countries; but we observe that it is still a man's world. Two exceptional women, Golda Meier of Israel and Indira Gandhi of India, appear among the heads of government, but it is unusual for women to reach the policy levels of government in any of our states.

Ratification of the UN Convention on the Political Rights of Women illustrates the point we made earlier that official acceptance of the international norm does not always tell us about the domestic pattern of behavior. Turkey, for example, has ratified the convention and Colombia has not. But in Turkey, as in most Muslim states, the political and economic status of women is generally low; women are still rarely seen in public places except with male escorts and they are traditionally barred from the coffeehouses where the men gather to play backgammon and discuss politics. In Colombia, despite the dominance of the Roman Catholic Church which stresses the family role of the wife and mother, women are quite active politically, more so than in most Latin American countries. Neither of our African states has ratified the convention, and in fact women have virtually no part in the politics of Kenya and the Ivory Coast, although women play an important role in the traditional communities.

Women constitute an important sector of the labor force in every country, both in agriculture and in industry, though women do not usually make it into more highly paid jobs. The economic and professional status of women is highest in the Soviet Union where heavy male losses in the working population during World War II (and from political purges under Stalin) gave the women something of a head start in the 1950s (this rating is moving downward, however, as the proportion of males in the Russian work force increases).[29] The Womens Liberation Movement has recently publicized the inferior status of women in the United States, both in politics and in the economy. The wage-salary median for women workers in the United States comes off a poor second to the median for men in every major occupational grouping. Moreover, a very small percentage of women ever reach top-level managerial and executive positions in either the public or private business. There are no legal barriers to appointment or promotion of women in the US civil service; 75 percent of full-time white collar employees in the first four grades (GS 1–4) are women: less than 2 percent of the total number of employees in the top four grades (GS 16 and above) are women.

In developing countries especially where there are great differentials in the social structure and limited resources to meet all the public needs, minority groups are likely to fare poorly in the official allocations. Discrimination may occur by design or by default. The employer who chooses to hire the more qualified applicant for a job may not intend to discriminate, but if the disparity in qualifications is due to unequal opportunities available in the community, the effect is nevertheless discriminatory. Thus, in India, a low-caste Hindu may not be denied entrance to the public service because he is a low-caste Hindu; it is not unreasonable to require literacy in the public service, but if most low-caste Hindus are illiterate, the requirement appears to discriminate against low-caste Hindus in the public service. Similarly, it may be observed that Colombian mestizos, the pastoral Masai in Kenya, Palestinians in Israel, and inner-city Blacks in the United States are likely to be treated as second-class citizens, ostensibly because they lack the kind of education or skills which are useful in a modern state and not because of their ethnic or social origins. The effect, however, is discrimination.

The UN General Assembly declared in 1946 that "freedom of information is a fundamental human right and is the touchstone of all the freedoms to which the United Nations is consecrated." The principle is one of great concern to all political systems; but which rights, obligations, and practices should be included in the concept of freedom of information is still a matter of debate, especially in the context of the Cold War between the United States and Soviet Union. The crux of the debate is whether citizens have more access to information and whether the information they get is more reliable if left to public or private enterprise.

Newspaper publication of excerpts from the "Pentagon Papers" (forty-seven typescript volumes of the official and confidential *History of the United States Decision-Making Process on Vietnam*) revealed to a shocked American public in June, 1971, how inadequate—and unreliable—government handouts had been on US-Vietnam policy through three administrations, Eisenhower to Johnson.[30] When the *New York Times* (and then the *Washington Post*) began to publish a series of articles based on the "Pentagon Papers," the US Department of Justice attempted to restrain further publication on the grounds that the national defense interests and the nation's security would suffer immediate and irreparable harm. The case moved with remarkable speed into the US Supreme Court. In a memorable decision, by vote of six to three, the justices refused to support "prior restraint" of publication, a decision in line with previous judicial rulings.

The Supreme Court decision on the "Pentagon Papers" was hailed as a great victory for freedom of the press, and in a way it was. Freed from legal restraint, newspapers across the country published reams of hitherto secret information about how various government officials had acted and reacted to US involvement in Indochina. It was, however, a Pyrrhic victory, for the information became public knowledge only after all had been said and done in official places. The fact that the Nixon administration tried to suppress publication suggests that the public cannot expect to know currently how and why decisions are made in the area that the decision-makers themselves prefer to classify as "secret." Moreover, government prosecution of Daniel Ellsberg, the former Pentagon analyst who on his own made the documents available to the *New York Times*, indicates that the US government takes a dim view of any unauthorized purveying of official information to the press or public.[29]

We have a predilection for private enterprise as long as this is understood to include freedom of inquiry, a free press (not subject to government censorship), freedom of opinion, freedom of expression, freedom of assembly, freedom to engage in peaceful demonstration. We find these freedoms explicit in the First Amendment and implicit in the Fourteenth Amendment in the US Constitution.

The right to differ is accepted as public policy in the United States not so much because of the constitutional guarantees, or faith in the democratic credo, but more pragmatically because of the pluralism of American society. The American Medical Association, the Aerospace Industries Association, the Sierra Club, the Chamber of Commerce, the Southern Christian Leadership Conference, the National Cotton Council of America, the Liberty Lobby, the Tobacco Institute, SANE, the American Security Council, the Daughters of the American Revolution—hundreds of citizens groups with special interests feel free, are free, to express their views in the public forum. The *silent majority* is a cliché referring to a heterogeneous public that rarely if ever has a majority viewpoint on any issue, whose spokesmen constantly exercise their right to differ—Carl Oglesby, Carl MacIntyre, Jack Newfield, Jack Anderson, William F. Buckley, I. F. Stone, William M. Kunstler, James Reston, Martha Mitchell, Betty Friedan, Shirley Temple Black, Shirley Chisholm, etc.

On March 22, 1971, the news of the day was that nine hundred persons were arrested in Washington, D.C. for staging a peaceful demonstration in front of the Soviet Embassy. Police reported that the number was the highest total arrest for any demonstration in the nation's capital to date. The process of rounding up the demonstrators who refused to disperse under police orders took three hours, and, as the demonstrators were being bussed to jail, they chanted, "The Jewish People Lives" and "Let My People Go." And what was the demonstration all about? The Jewish Defense League which marshaled the demonstration contends that 3.5 million Jews in the Soviet Union are being repressed and denied exit visas for Israel.[31] (The Universal Declaration states that "every one has the right to leave any country including his own.")

The citizens of the USSR are guaranteed freedom of speech, freedom of the press, freedom of assembly, including the holding of mass meetings, and freedom of street processions and demonstrations. But such guarantees do not mean that the Soviet government tolerates freedom of dissent. A government wholly committed to a single ideology and controlled by a single party system cannot admit the right to differ from the official consensus. The case of Aleksandr Solzhenitsyn, winner of the 1970 Nobel Prize for Literature, illustrates the point. During the cultural thaw under Nikita Khrushchev, Solzhenitsyn published his first novel, *One Day in the Life of Ivan Denisovich*, an account of his own experiences in a Soviet labor camp during the Stalinist regime. Subsequently two more of his novels, widely acclaimed in the West, were banned in the Soviet Union because of their increasingly critical views of the Communist establishment.

In 1966, when two well-known Soviet writers, Andrei Sinyavsky and Yuli Daniel, were packed off to prison camp for having sent anti-Soviet manuscripts abroad for publication, Solzhenitsyn was active in organizing a public outcry of protest from fellow intellectuals. Solzhenitsyn himself became an object of surveillance and, as he became increasingly involved in the human rights movement, the government-controlled press denounced him as a scandalmonger and traitor. In 1969 he was expelled from the Soviet Writers Union with the suggestion that he go into exile, a suggestion which he scorned. His friend, Mstislav Rostropovich, the world-renowned cellist, offered him a cottage on the Rostropovich country estate near Moscow. But when Rostropovich attempted to defend his literary friend in an open letter, the Soviet authorities also cracked down on Rostropovich by making him an unperson in his own country. Any mention of Rostropovich's name was forbidden in Russian publications and his projected tour abroad was canceled.[32]

Literary figures and musicians may be expendable in the Soviet political system; it is, however, much more difficult to treat scientists as unpersons. In 1970 Zhores Medvedev, a biologist, was arrested and put in a mental institution, following his public attack on censorship in the mails; shortly afterwards, Revolt Pimenov, a mathematician, was imprisoned on political charges. These incidents aroused the ire of academician Andrei Sakharov, one of the fathers of the Soviet H-bomb. He and several of his colleagues organized a human rights committee to defend the freedom of science. The chief complaint of Sakharov and his associates is that the Soviet authorities do not permit the freedom of information which is essential to the advancement of science. Specifically they want more contact with scientists outside the country and free access to science publications abroad.[33]

The case of Solzhenitsyn, Rostropovich, and Sakharov are known to us because these are famous names outside Russia. What happens to less well-known dissidents in the Soviet Union is, however, the subject of much hearsay. We are told that the dissenters come from every corner of Soviet life—students, writers, economists, scientists, soldiers, industrial workers, and managers—and that in recent years hundreds of them have been arrested or placed under surveillance because of their political views. And yet most of these dissidents are not anti-Communists, they do not advocate the overthrow of the existing government, they merely want what the Universal Declaration recognizes as a fundamental right—"The right to freedom of opinion and expression . . . to hold opinions without interference and to seek, receive, and impart information and ideas through any media and regardless of frontiers."

The Universal Declaration holds that "everyone has the right to life, liberty and security of person. . . . No one shall be subjected to arbitrary interference with his privacy, family, home or correspondence, nor to attacks upon his honour and reputation." The US Bill of Rights and the subsequent civil-rights amendments make such guarantees to the American people. Nevertheless, today's news media are full of stories about the surveillance of private persons and public officials by the Federal Bureau of Investigation, army intelligence, and other government agents. We are warned that millions of individual dossiers in the government files have been computerized for instant retrieval. (The FBI has name checks on one out of every seventy Americans.) Presumably, the justification is the need to insure internal security, but a government that resorts to the tactics of big brother to spy upon the citizenry, to intercept their mail, to tap their telephones, to bug their private conversations, to listen to the hearsay of faceless informers has moved a long way from those concepts of freedom which the authors of the Bill of Rights had in mind for the American people.

Americans can read in their Constitution about the rights of defendants to a speedy and public trial, due process of law, and equal protection of the laws. And then they can read in the daily newspapers about delays in the administration of justice, persons arrested and held in jail without bail (or with high bail) for months while awaiting trial. And if they want to delve into official reports they can learn about bargaining for justice, pleading guilty for lesser charges to avoid trial by jury on the original charges.

Not long ago Yale University president Kingman Brewster told students on his campus that he was skeptical about the ability of Black revolutionaries to get a fair trial anywhere in the country, given the political atmosphere of these times.[34] Black Panther leader, Bobby Seale, was then on trial for murder of one of his own following in New Haven. Seale, one of the "Chicago Eight" tried for conspiracy to cross state lines with the intent of inciting to violence in Chicago during the 1968 Democratic Convention, attempted to conduct his own defense in the Chicago trial, but his disorderly conduct in the courtroom so infuriated the presiding judge that Seale was actually ordered gagged and manacled to his chair under court order. The New Haven court managed the trial procedures with more judicial decorum, but whether due process of law and equal protection of the laws were achieved is in doubt since the outcome of the case was a mistrial; the jury was unable to agree on a verdict.

How does the US record on defendants' rights stack up with the record in other countries? The USSR makes a point of exposing the US violations of civil rights. When Angela Davis, former professor of philosophy at the University of California in Los Angeles, an avowed Communist, was arrested as a suspected accomplice in a shoot-out in a California court, the Soviet press played up the fact that she was a progressive persecuted for her political views and discriminated against because of her race. Fourteen Russian scientists, leaders in the human rights organization in the USSR, cabled their indignation to President Nixon. With rare political acumen the US government invited the scientists to attend the Davis trial so that they could base their judgments about due process of law in American courts on personal observation. The offer, if accepted, could lead to similar requests from concerned citizens in the United States to observe firsthand the nature of political justice in Soviet courts.[35]

Ideological differences between the Soviet Union and the United States account for different concepts and different priorities in the protection and advancement of human rights—individual freedom versus social security, private property versus public property. No doubt also the condition of civil rights in both countries is affected by the Cold War between them; each believes that its internal security is threatened by subversion and sabotage plotted by the other. We have no hard data, however, to confirm or refute the grounds for their mutual apprehension.

How to draw an optimum line between individual liberties and internal security is a perennial—and universal—problem in government. The United States with a large heterogeneous population and a generally permissive ideology (democracy) experiences considerable political turbulence. If the Soviet Union, also with a large heterogeneous population, appears to be more successful in controlling civil disorder, this is no doubt a function of Communist ideology which is totalitarian in scope and authoritarian in practice. The magnitude of civil strife is less in the Soviet Union than in the United States but the degree of personal freedom is also much less than in the United States.

In each country, however, the government takes what steps the ruling elite deems necessary to secure the survival of the system and that means curbing civil and political rights, more or less, depending on time and situation.

The ultimate test of political rights is freedom to oppose the existing government and publicly to espouse an alternative political system. Competitive parties are overt indicators of such political freedom. In Chapter 7 we observed that the USSR, the Ivory Coast, Kenya, and for all practical purposes, Mexico, operate under one-party governments. Therefore, we rank these countries low on our scaling of political democracy. But before we rate countries with competitive parties high on the scale, we must take note that in some of these states the right to organize opposition to the party in power does not extend to organizations that aim to overthrow the prevailing system of government.

Among our twelve states, the Communist party is in power only in the USSR, which of course does not permit the organization of any anti-Communist party. Turkey has two major political parties and about half a dozen minor parties, but the Communist party is proscribed. The United States has two major parties and several "third parties," but the Communist party is in effect outlawed and underground. The Federal Republic of Germany has three parties currently entitled to representation in the Bundestag, but it too has proscribed the Communist party. Outside the USSR the Communist party is legally recognized in Colombia, Mexico, Israel, the United Kingdom, India, and Japan. Only in India and Japan does the Communist party have any sizable following. Legal existence, moreover, cannot be equated with political freedom. Over the years Indian Communists have frequently been detained under emergency suspension of constitutional guarantees. The Japanese Communist party has entered its candidates in every general election since 1946 with some small success. In our judgment, however, the United Kingdom ranks first in our scaling of political democracy for its toleration not only of loyal opposition but also of disloyal opposition. As Justice Holmes once remarked, the real test of freedom to differ is "not free thought for those who agree with us but freedom for the thought we hate." [36]

Because political stability is a must for economic development, internal security is likely to be the primary goal and individual freedom a secondary consideration in new and developing states. India is a case in point. Part 3 of the Indian Constitution delineates the Fundamental Rights, rights which are justiciable, such as the rights to life, liberty, and property, rights which can be enforced in the courts of law. The novel and most controversial feature of India's Constitution, however, is its provision for emergency suspension of the Fundamental Rights by the Union executive (with subsequent approval of Parliament) if the national security warrants such action. The emergency provision has been invoked on numerous occasions—six times in the first decade—because of internal disturbances and threats of external aggression.

The Prevention Detention Act, passed one month after the Indian Constitution went into effect, and renewed many times since, provides for detention (euphemism for imprisonment) of people whose prospective activities might jeopardize the public order or be injurious to community welfare. Under this act the Indian government detained some ten thousand persons in its first year of operation. The figures on detention for political reasons vary from year to year; as late as 1968 nearly six hundred persons were detained, not because of what they had done but because of what the government surmized they might do if allowed to go free.[37]

How concerned are people about their civil rights? During the 1970 Russian elections a *New York Times* correspondent reported very little excitement. "Probably the quickest way to bore a Russian today is to divert his conversation from World Cup Soccer or his vacation plans to the election." One man "with a sour look on his face" opined that there were rumors that the price of cognac and vodka would go up after election day.[38] We have been told that the Soviet people are not so much alienated as they are apathetic about government. They realize they have very little say in government policy, but they have no great urge to participate in policy-making. All they are concerned about is to improve their personal lot. They have a very negative picture about pre-Communist Russia; anything since Stalinist days is an improvement: Housing is better, wages are higher, and consumer welfare has been upgraded. Most Russians are totally ignorant in comparative politics; the government denies them knowledge of alternative systems. Only the intellectuals who have some contact with the outside world have a basis for dissent.

How different is the situation in the United States? In the mid-1960s when civil rights appeared to be a prime issue in American politics professional pollsters asked a cross-section of the American people about their personal aspirations and personal fears. The concerns most frequently mentioned were improved or decent standard of living (40 percent), adequate opportunities for their children (35 percent), a healthy family (25 percent), no more war or threat of war (17 percent), better housing (12 percent). Only 8 percent mentioned the threat of Communism as a personal fear; only 6 percent feared lack of freedom, including freedom of speech, religion, etc. A cheerful 10 percent claimed they had no fears or worries! Asked to react to the 1964 Civil Rights Act passed by Congress, 60 percent approved, 29 percent disapproved, 11 percent did not know. But to a leading question as to whether most of the organizations "pushing for civil rights have been infiltrated by the Communists and are now dominated by Communist troublemakers," 47 percent agreed, 33 percent disagreed, 20 percent did not know.[39]

Economic, Social, and Cultural Rights

The Universal Declaration of Human Rights goes well beyond the traditional civil and political rights of Western democracy. It includes such economic, social, and cultural rights as the right to marry and found a family without any limitation due to race, nationality, or religion; the right to work, equal pay for equal work; social security; the right to a standard of living adequate for the health and well-being of every family; the right to education, the right to participate freely in the cultural life of the community.

The implementation of such rights, however, calls for much more positive action on the part of government than some nation states (notably the United States) deem necessary and proper. The concept of the welfare state, implicit in governmental promotion of social, economic, and cultural rights, appears at variance with many traditional notions about individual liberties. Some nation states (notably the Soviet Union) feel that the enjoyment of social and economic rights is prerequisite to liberty and security of the person.

The Human Rights Commission finally produced two complementary covenants—one on civil and political rights, the other on economic, social, and cultural rights. Both were offered simultaneously for ratification in 1966, with significant differences, however, with respect to the immediate obligations incurred by the ratifying parties. In the case of civil and political rights, the parties agree to recognize and enforce the rights as specified in the international covenant; the inference is that any state, given a willingness, has an immediate capability for securing these rights. In the case of economic, social, and cultural rights, the parties merely promise to take progressive steps toward realization of such rights within the limits of their available resources.

The distinction as to implementation of the two international covenants is of practical import to all states, but especially so for developing countries that do not have the capability—however well-intentioned the governors, however eager the governed—for the establishment of a modern standard of living for all the people at once. The Indian response to the problem is instructive.

The Indian Constituent Assembly was in session about the time that the Universal Declaration of Human Rights was reaching the final stage of adoption. Part 3 of the Indian Constitution, as we have already pointed out, emulates the British and American tradition of civil and political rights. The Fundamental Rights are enforced in the courts of law (if not suspended for emergency reasons by the executive). Part 4, which reflects the indirect influence of the Soviet viewpoint incorporated in the Universal Declaration of 1948, lists a variety of social and economic rights, such as adequate means of livelihood to all citizens, a decent standard of life, leisure, and social opportunities for people, the right to education, and equal pay for equal work for men and women. Although the government is directed to promote these rights, failure to secure them immediately is not a justiciable issue. The government is expected to take what steps it can toward "a social order which stands for the welfare of the people." Expectation is still the nub of Indian politics. When the New Congress candidate spoke in B. R. Jog's remote village in the 1971 elections, he talked about human rights, but not in abstract terms of rights and obligations; rather he explained how Indira Gandhi's plans for economic development could better their everyday living. B. R. Jog who thought it was a very good talk, now expects the government to do some of the things that the New Congress man was promising before the elections.

For the record, Colombia and Israel have ratified both the Convention on Civil and Political Rights and the Convention on Social, Economic, and Cultural Rights. The United States whose representatives in the UN Commission on Human Rights so vigorously pushed for the Convention on Civil and Political Rights has taken no official action. The Soviet Union which took the lead in championing a separate convention on social, economic, and cultural rights has also taken no official action. In the final analysis, however, how far each of our twelve nation states has been willing and able to move toward the realization of the Universal Declaration of Human Rights is a matter of value judgment. What, for example, is a decent or a modern standard of living? Juan Ortiz, who carves little onyx donkeys to sell to American tourists in

Puebla, now in his sixties and getting ready to collect his old-age pension from the Mexican government, tells us he has had a good life (he never had a day's schooling and he never owned an automobile).

We asked some of the people whom we have met in this text—B. R. Jog of India, Moses Gold of Israel, Pedro Cervantes of Colombia, Joe Zilch of the USA, Hans Mueller of Germany, Ukai Taki of Japan, and Professor Skivitsky of the USSR—"Given a free choice, what political system do you think is the best one in which to live a good life?" We thought it rather touching and illuminating that each in turn replied with a variation of "My country, right or wrong."

And so we conclude, to each his own.

NOTES

1. For a brief treatment of the postwar status of Japan in foreign relations and national security, see *Area Handbook for Japan*, Foreign Area Studies Division, American University (Washington, D.C.: Government Printing Office, 1969). See also Matsuedo Tsukasa and George Moore, "Japan's Shifting Attitudes toward the Military," *Asian Survey* 7, no. 9 (1967): 597–613.
2. Emphasis supplied.
3. NATO, the North Atlantic Treaty Organization, was formed in 1949; members: Belgium, Canada, Denmark, France, the Federal Republic of Germany, the United Kingdom, Greece, Iceland, Italy, Luxembourg, the Netherlands, Norway, Portugal, Turkey, and the United States.
   OAS, the Organization of American States, was formed in 1948; twenty-three American countries are members, including: Colombia, Mexico, and the United States. (Cuba was suspended in 1962.)
   SEATO, the South-East Asia Treaty Organization, was formed in 1955; members: Australia, France, the United Kingdom, New Zealand, Pakistan, the Philippines, Thailand, and the United States. (n.b., India is not a member.)
   CENTO, the Central Treaty Organization, was formed in 1955; members: the United Kingdom, Iran, Pakistan, and Turkey; associate member: the United States.
4. Warsaw Pact, the Eastern European Mutual Assistance Treaty, was formed in 1955; members: Bulgaria, Czechoslovakia, the Democratic Peoples Republic of Germany, and the Soviet Union.
5. The *New York Times Encyclopedic Almanac, 1971* (New York: *New York Times*, 1970), p. 715.
6. The data for Table 13–1 are from the annual report of the US Arms Control and Disarmament Agency (ACDA) *World Military Expenditures, 1969* (Washington, D.C.: Government Printing Office, 1970). Note that ACDA has given us the dollar amounts in terms of constant 1967 dollars so as to provide a uniform measure of dollar purchasing power for the six-year period, 1964–69.
7. We have avoided the categorization of countries as "developed" and "developing," but in this section we have used the ACDA terminology, since most of the quantitative data are from the ACDA annual reports.
8. Note that Table 13–2 has a different base than Table 13–1. The dollar amounts are in current prices and for a four-year period. Note also that NATO (Eur.) does not include Canada and the United States.

9. Hugh Davis Graham and Ted Robert Gurr, *The History of Violence in America* (New York: Bantam Books, 1969).
10. Graham and Gurr, op. cit. chap. 18, "Social Change and Political Violence: Cross-National Patterns," by Ivo K. Feierabend, Rosalind L. Feierabend, and Betty Nesvold.
11. Note that Feierabend groups Japan with "transitional stable states." We consider Japan highly developed and stable.
12. Graham and Gurr, op. cit. chap. 17, "A Comparative Study of Civil Strife."
13. Ibid., p. 621.
14. Bernard D. Nossiter, 'The GNP: What It Is, and What It Isn't," *Washington Post*, December 22, 1970.
15. Now that you have come to know our typical friends from the various countries, we must tell you that they are models and not real people. Their names are fictitious and any identification with living persons is purely coincidental.
16. US Bureau of the Census, *Statistical Abstract of the United States, 1970*, 91st ed. (Washington, D.C.: Government Printing Office, 1970), p. 329 f.
17. Ibid., p. 327. It should also be noted that 15.7 percent of white families and 6.3 percent of nonwhite families had an income over $15,000 in 1968.
18. Quoted in the *Washington Post*, March 15, 1971, from "News Dispatches, New Delhi."
19. US Department of Health, Education, and Welfare, Social Security Administration, Office of Research and Statistics, *Social Security Programs throughout the World, 1969*, Research Report no. 31 (Washington, D.C.: Government Printing Office, 1970).
20. *Statistical Abstract of the United States, 1970*, p. 62.
21. Frederick L. Pryor, *Public Expenditures in Communist and Capitalist Nations* (Homewood, Ill.: Richard D. Irwin, 1968) analyzes public expenditures in a group of nations with different economic systems including the market system of the United States and the centrally planned economy of the Soviet Union. His analysis covers expenditures for defense, welfare and health, education, and some other budgetary expenditures. Less technical in presentation is Robert J. Osborn *Soviet Social Policies: Welfare, Equality, and Community* (Homewood, Ill.: Dorsey Press, 1970) ; it makes many provocative comparisons between the social policies of the United States and the Soviet Union.
22. Statistical data from *Statistical Abstract of the United States, 1970*, p. 833.
23. Barbara Ward, *The Rich Nations and the Poor Nations* (New York: Norton, 1962), p. 101.
24. Emphasis supplied.
25. Emphasis supplied.
26. Overseas Business Reports, US Department of Commerce, Bureau of International Commerce, *Basic Data on the Economy of Turkey* (December, 1966), p. 11.
27. See Ernst B. Haas, *Human Rights and International Action* (Stanford, Calif.: Stanford University Press, 1970). The focus is on freedom of association, implementation, and issues, 1950–68.
28. *Federal Civil Rights Enforcement Effort: A Report on the United States Commission on Civil Rights, 1970* (Washington, D.C.: Government Printing Office, 1970).
29. Cyril E. Black, "Soviet Society: A Comparative View," in Allen Kassof, ed., *Prospects for Soviet Society* (New York: Praeger, 1968), pp. 38–39. "Since 1955 the professional role of women in the USSR has not been significantly different from that in the advanced countries."
30. "The Pentagon Papers," as published by the *New York Times*, based on in-

vestigative reporting by Neil Sheehan, written by Neil Sheehan, Hedrick Smith, E. W. Kenworthy, and Fox Butterfield (subsequently published by Bantam Books [New York, 1971]).

31. The chief Rabbi of Moscow, Yehuda-Leib Levin, along with three lay leaders of the Moscow Jewish religious community, signed and handed a petition to the American Embassy in Moscow protesting the activities of Jewish militants in the United States, claiming that Soviet Jews do not want such unsolicited protectors. Apparently many Jewish leaders in the Soviet Union feel that Jewish protesters in the United States may open the road to anti-Semitism in the Soviet Union and make it harder for Jews to emigrate (Bernard Gwertzman, *New York Times* News Service, in the *Washington Evening Star*, January 13, 1971).
32. *Washington Post*, February 1, 1971.
33. James F. Clarity, special to the *New York Times*, June 14, 1970. See also *Newsweek*, February 1, 1971, pp. 29–34.
34. The full text of President Brewsters' remarks is to be found in the *Yale Alumni Magazine*, July, 1970.
35. At the date of writing the Soviet authorities had not granted exit permissions to the scientists. News of the day, however, includes the interesting item that Ramsey Clark, a former US attorney general, had applied to the Soviet authorities for permission to observe criminal prosecutions of Jewish defendants if such trials resume. Clark's request was backed by concerned interest groups in the United States, the National Council of Churches, the US Catholic Conference, and the Synagogue Council of America (*Washington Post*, March 25, 1971). Protesting Jews and other political dissenters were rounded up by the KGB (secret police) and detained while the Twenty-fourth Congress of the Soviet Communist party met in Moscow in March, 1971, in order to avoid the kind of political demonstrations that embarrassed the Kremlin when the Twenty-third Party Congress met in 1966.
36. A minority opinion in a US Supreme Court case involving the right of a pacifist (a woman) who refused to bear arms to become a naturalized American citizen. *US* v. *Schwimmer*, 279 US644, 653 (1928).
37. *Area Handbook for India*, Foreign Area Studies Division, American University (Washington, D.C.: Government Printing Office, 1970), p. 714. See also Beatrice Pitney Lamb, *India: a World in Transition*, 3d ed. (New York: Praeger, 1968), esp. chap. 14.
38. James F. Clarity from Moscow, special to the *New York Times*, June 14, 1970.
39. Lloyd Free and Hadley Cantril, *The Political Beliefs of Americans: A Study of Public Opinion* (New York: Simon and Schuster, 1968), pp. 97, 196.

FURTHER READING

DAHL, ROBERT A. *Modern Political Analysis*. 2d ed. Englewood Cliffs, N.J.: Prentice-Hall, 1970.

HUNTINGTON, SAMUEL P. *Political Order in Changing Societies*. New Haven, Conn.: Yale University Press, 1968.

PYE, LUCIEN W., and SIDNEY VERBA, eds. *Political Culture and Political Development*. Princeton, N.J.: Princeton University Press, 1965.

SCHULTZE, CHARLES L., et al. *Setting National Priorities*. Washington, D.C.: Brookings Institution, 1971.

SPIEGEL, STEVEN L., and KENNETH N. WALTZ. *Conflict in World Politics*. Cambridge, Mass.: Winthrop, 1971.

GLOSSARY

administrative court A legal tribunal outside the regular judicial system which hears cases brought by private persons against the government or bureaucracy, common in Continental Europe; technically nonexistent in the United States, although some courts established by Congress to hear suits in special administrative matters are sometimes referred to as administrative courts (Court of Claims and Court of Customs).

allocation The process that decides who gets what. Political theorist David Easton defines the political system as "the authoritative allocation of values." Robert Dahl refers to "the allocation of resources."

anticolonialism A political movement or ideology, usually in colonies or excolonies, aimed at political independence and the withdrawal of the colonial power; sometimes seen as a global movement. Contemporary movements usually include racial overtones, a protest against the white man's world.

apartheid Afrikaans for "apartness," the strict segregation of the races implicitly to the detriment of black persons, as in South Africa.

apparatchik Colloquial Russian for "organization man"; a functionary of the Soviet Communist party apparatus, by implication a stern, conformist, bureaucratic type.

authoritarianism A political system which minimizes demand inputs from the populace at large and concentrates decision-making authority in a small elite group. The ruling elite claims unlimited power to command obedience from the citizens.

back-bencher In Britain's Parliament, a member who does not sit in the front row, which is reserved for government party leaders and members of the cabinet and their counterparts in the opposition party. In present usage, a back-bencher is any relatively unimportant member of a parliament.

bicameral The organization of a legislature into two houses, usually referred to as "the upper house" and "the lower house." The two-house legislature is designed to provide different bases of representation. The lower house is usually selected on a broad popular base (US House of Representatives); the upper house may represent territorial areas, or nationality groups [Russian Council (Soviet) of Nationalities].

bolshevik Left wing of the Russian Social Democratic Labor party. In the spring of 1917 it was still a small minority group. By the fall it had become sufficiently powerful to overthrow the provisional government of Russia and to assume aggressive leadership in the revolutionary movement. The Bolsheviks under Lenin's leadership became the dominant (only) Communist party in the Soviet Union.

bundesrat The upper house of the Federal Republic of Germany, representing the various territorial components of the federal union.

bundestag German for "federal assembly," the lower house of the Parliament of the German Federal Republic.

bureaucracy The permanent, nonelective officials of government and their administrative structure. That part of the political system which is organized to carry out the public policies. German sociologist Max Weber attributed great significance to the bureaucracy, positing a "rational-legal" bureaucracy as the hallmark of a modern state. Carl J. Friedrich describes the vast bureaucratic structures of modern states as "the core of modern government."

caste Hereditary, exclusive social class, as in India. The caste system may be seen as extreme, rigidified social stratification.

centralist A national political system which concentrates decision-making in one locus (the national capital) or one political group.

chancellor Head of government in the Federal Republic of Germany whose position is comparable to that of the British prime minister.

charisma The purely personal (as distinct from institutional) power of a gifted political leader in gaining popular support. Greek for "gift," *charisma* was popularized by the German sociologist Max Weber to characterize a crowd-swaying individual who comes to power by extralegal means. It has since become more general, meaning political drawing power.

citizens Individual members of the political system, who owe allegiance to it and who are entitled to its protection at home and abroad. Citizenship may be acquired by birth within the state (jus soli), by parentage in the state (jus sanguinis) or by naturalization proceedings.

civil service All persons in the public service who are not in the legislative or judicial branches of the government nor in the military service.

coalition The combination of parties in a multiparty parliamentary system to command the vote of a majority of the deputies and thus construct a government in which the participating parties are represented in cabinet positions. *Grand coalition* A coalition of all or most of the big parties in a European-style parliamentary government so that there are few or no parties in opposition to the government.

cold war A period of armed tension and ideological rivalry after World War II—the "bipolarization" of the world, with the Soviet Union heading the Eastern bloc and the United States the Western bloc. The Cold War reached its peak in the 1950s. Scholars (and statesmen) now appear to be divided as to the continuance of the Cold War into the 1960s and its existence in the 1970s.

colonialism The holding of colonies by an imperial power and the attitude that goes with the controlling relationship.

communication In the broad, political-science sense propounded by Karl Deutsch, any link between persons or groups that gives rise to community. This can range from newspapers and radios to highways and jet planes.

competitive In the political-science sense, a system that allows the clash of political forces, usually parties trying to win popular votes, in order to gain control of the government. One-party systems are often considered *noncompetitive.*

constitution The basic law which establishes the political structure, assigns powers and duties to the governmental institutions, and defines the relationships of the governors and the governed.

correlate The mutual or reciprocal linkage of two or more political or social indicators, such as newspaper consumption correlating with literacy.

cross-national The comparison of several countries at once, often by means of statistical data, as opposed to one-country-at-a-time studies.

decision-making An approach to the study of political systems that stresses who makes decisions and why.

de facto Latin for "in fact," used to describe (1) an existing, unvarnished situation, as "the regime had de facto ceased to exist" or (2) the first stage of diplomatic recognition in which one country acknowledges that another country exists, as "the US does not extend de facto recognition to East Germany."

de jure Latin for "in law," used to describe a higher stage of diplomatic recognition than de facto, one of full recognition of the legality of a regime and the presumed willingness to exchange diplomatic representatives.

demands In David Easton's schema of the political system, "articulated statements, directed toward the authorities, proposing that some kind of authoritative allocation ought to be undertaken." Translation: "Gimme!"

demography The statistical study of human population, especially with reference to size, distribution, and such vital statistics as death rate, birthrate, age groups, and occupational groups.

developing nation A people moving toward a modernized (industrial, urban, and secular) society and striving for *political socialization* (see below) of its members.

diet English translation of the name some countries use for their parliaments, such as the Japanese Diet, the Finnish Diet, or in German history, the famous Diet of Worms (1521—the Reformation).

egalitarianism An ideology that stresses the social and economic equality of all citizens, hence a leveling movement aimed at reducing class differences.

election The choosing of governmental officials by popular balloting; hence, the intermittent participation of the population in the affairs of government. *Choosing* implies selecting from a number of candidates for a position. In one-party states, where there is no choice, popular endorsement of the party slate is euphemistically called an "election."

elector In medieval Germany, one of the princes entitled to take part in the selection of the emperor, such as the elector of Brandenburg. In the Holy Roman Empire, the electors, chosen in a rotating system, included both temporal princes and princes of the church.

elite The social class or stratum from which political leaders are habitually chosen. The elite of each country is, of course, different—in Britain, Oxbridge graduates; in Israel, pioneering Zionists from East Europe; in the USSR, Communist party members. Broadly used, *the ruling elite* refers to those who hold the key positions in the social structure, the economy, the military, the academic community, the professions as well as in the political structure.

empirical An approach to the study of politics that emphasizes factual data rather than abstract theorizing. There is no law, however, against combining the two.

executive That branch of government which administers laws. In the United States, the chief executive is the president.

federalism A principle of political organization based on territorial distribution of governmental powers, usually achieved by the delegation of authority by autonomous territorial units to a central (national) government. In a federal union the national government operates directly upon the people in all of the territorial units in common policy areas, but the several territorial components (states in the United States, Länder in the Federal Republic of Germany, republics in the Soviet Union) retain authority over the people in their respective jurisdictions in particular policy areas.

feudalism A political system in which dominion is diffused through powerful landed local lords whose positions are usually inherited. Although characteristic—and even applauded as the best possible system—in the Middle Ages, remnants of feudalism persist unofficially even in many modern countries.

franchise The prerogative or legal right to vote.

function The job which a political institution or individual actually performs within the political system—the emphasis is on the effects or consequences of what is done rather than upon the motives or expectations.

functional Used to describe a social or political institution—sometimes called a "structure"—that is carrying out its job and helping to make the political system work. If it is not doing this, if it is out of kilter, it may be termed *dysfunctional.*

general will A theoretical construct advanced by Jean Jacques Rousseau in the *Social Contract.* The general will (the will for the common good) expresses "a sense of communal belonging." Modern scholars still find the construct useful in explaining the community of a nation. Rousseau differentiated between the general will, which represents the basic desires of all the people, and public opinion, which reflects contemporary interests. The notion of constitutionalism—basic principles and national traditions that transcend current politics—may be likened to the general will.

gross national product Abbreviated GNP; the sum total worth of goods and services produced in a given country in one year. The GNP is taken by many as an indicator of how advanced a country is. It indicates economic, not political, development however.

head of government In most countries, especially those with parliamentary government, the prime minister, the person at the apex of political power.

head of state The official representative of the state, spokesman for all the people —a carry-over from the age of monarchy when a sovereign could claim, "L'état, c'est moi." In modern times the head of state may hold a largely ceremonial and honorific office without great political power, as does the British queen. In some countries, as in the United States, a president combines the offices of head of state and head of government.

histadrut Hebrew for "organization"; the short name for Israel's all-embracing labor union, the General Federation of Labor.

ideology A value system built on political, economic, and social beliefs that underpin a nation's way of life. The ideology of a nation state is determined by the set of beliefs to which the ruling elite subscribe. In a democratic society dissident groups may offer competing ideologies. In a totalitarian system only the official ideology is given expression.

ideological warfare Conflict between rival ideological systems usually involving propaganda, cultural programs, educational projects, and other activities to influence the minds of other peoples. A major aspect of the Cold War of the 1950s was the ideological conflict between the Communist world and the free world.

incrementalism Doing things a little at a time; small changes that added together over a period of time may mean a major shift. In the view of Charles Lindblom, "disjointed incrementalism" is the way a bureaucracy really functions.

industrialization The shift of a country from an agricultural and handicrafts economy to one of factory, mechanized production. This shift is commonly associated with *modernization* and *urbanization* (see below).

infrastructure Originally a term from transportation economics meaning everything in a transportation network that does not move, such as highways, railroad tracks, and repair shops; hence the basic structure needed before things can roll. The term has been broadened in meaning to include political communication as well as material networks, and is frequently applied with reference to developing countries.

institutionalization The process by which political changes, movements, and innovations become fixed, permanent institutions. Mexico's PRI, for example, is the Mexican Revolution institutionalized into a political party. If a political movement is not institutionalized, it dies out.

integration The bringing together of various groups into a communal relationship. Political integration is achieved when the various groups have access to the political system and when the government operates as a cohesive force while meeting plural demands.

intelligentsia A Russian word (from Italian) for the educated class generally, a broader meaning than our use of the word *intellectuals.*

interaction In political-science terms, the mutual effect that two or more social forces or institutions have on each other.

interest group An organized group whose members share common views and objectives, who have joined together to press their demands before government officials. Farmers, industrial workers, business men, professional organizations, etc. form interest groups to influence public opinion and to engage in lobbying. Unlike political parties which seek to control the government generally, interest groups are mainly interested in determining particular policy decisions.

internal passport An identification card required of all adults in some countries —as in the Soviet Union—to assist authorities in keeping track of who is where. The functional equivalent of this in the United States might be the driver's license or social security card which many people use to identify themselves.

judicial review The power of the courts to declare legislative or executive acts unconstitutional.

judiciary A collective term for the courts and judges, whose principal function is to settle disputes between the government and individuals, between governmental agencies, and between private individuals according to the law.

Knesset The Israeli parliament.

kolkhoz Russian abbreviation for "collective farm."

kulak Russian for "fist," used by Stalin to connote the allegedly tight-fisted better-off peasants who were liquidated in order to collectivize Soviet agriculture.

laissez faire French for "let be," an economic doctrine calling for minimal government interference in the supposedly self-regulating mechanisms of the marketplace; or, "hands off" the free economy. The term is most commonly associated with Adam Smith and the classical economics of the nineteenth century.

landed aristocracy The hereditary elite whose members possess large estates. When used to describe current elites, a feudal situation is implied.

latifundio Spanish for a "large, landed estate." The owner of a *latifundio* is a *latifundista,* the target of Latin American revolutionaries and reformers.

legislature That part of a government, usually popularly elected and hence representative, whose principal function is rule-making—the lawmakers.

legitimacy The psychological support a regime gets from its citizens, if they believe the regime is right and ought to be obeyed. A government which fails to establish its right or title to rule is bound to fall.

libertarian A political viewpoint upholding the importance of free expression and clash of opinions, as in a free, uncensored press, in the belief that the best solution will arise after the public has examined all the conflicting views.

mass media Means of communications that reach large audiences, such as newspapers, radio and television; as distinct from personal communications like letters and telephones.

model A theoretical construct, either verbal or graphic, often used by economists, political scientists, and sociologists to depict what they believe the social structures of the real world looks like. Models can at best only approximate reality; none is a verifiably perfect reproduction of reality.

modernization The shift of a country from traditional values and institutions usually grounded in an agrarian economy to a way of life largely determined by a commercial and industrial economy in the Western style.

MP abbreviation for member of Parliament.

nation state A state whose territorial boundaries and legal jurisdiction embrace a *nation*—a people who share common history, traditions, values, interests, and purposes and who have organized as a political community.

nationality Belonging to a particular state by virtue of being born in the state (jus soli) or by virtue of family origin in that state (jus sanguinis).

nationalization The taking of private property—a sector of agriculture, industry, or commerce for public use—the conversion from private to national control.

naturalization The legal process by which an individual changes his nationality and his allegiance from one state to that of another state.

national accounts The statistical data which states report to the United Nations annually. These are the most comprehensive empirical data on which we rely for cross-national comparisons of allocations of national resources for private consumption, expenditures for public services, expenditures for particular purposes, such as, public health or public education.

national budget A comprehensive statement of a nation's finances for a given period—its revenues, expenditures, and obligations. It is also an overall plan for government programs and operations for a given period. The budget of any state is a primary document telling us a great deal about the public policies and the official ordering of national priorities.

national interest That which those in political power deem best for the country as a whole, especially in foreign relations. Virtually all statesmen claim to pursue the national interests of their countries.

oligarchy Greek for "rule of the few"; a political system dominated by a few persons from which the masses are excluded. An oligarchy can be feudal or modernizing, as in the case of some Latin American military regimes.

parliamentary government A government in which the executive and legislative branches are dovetailed. The British parliamentary government is the prime example: the prime minister and his cabinet (the government) hold office as representatives of the majority party in the Parliament and only as long as they can command the confidence of a majority in Parliament.

participatory democracy Strictly speaking a tautology; democracy implies popular participation in the political process. But in present realities the term is useful to connote that not all governments which call themselves "democracies" permit popular participation.

pluralism A political viewpoint acknowledging that there are many groups with diverse, legitimate interests within the political system and that the fair handling of these interests is the basis for liberal democracy.

plurality The most numerous, but not necessarily a majority, vote.

policy The course of action which a government takes (or proposes to take) with regard to specific issues. Policy implies rational courses of action directed toward specific objectives.

political socialization The process by which an individual learns the rules of the political game for his society: how to act, what to expect, what to demand, how to think of the political system and its leaders. In long-established states the process normally begins in childhood and is a function of the educational system. In new and developing states, the process involves the whole people and is part of modernization.

political party Organization of the citizens for participation in the electoral process—the party aims to control the government, to determine who governs.

political stability Not only the absence of revolution or revolt in a political system, but also its ability to adjust to a changing environment and to meet new demands while still maintaining its identity and continuity.

political system The structures and processes related to the authoritative allocation of values and resources in a given society—broadly viewed as the whole set of actors in the political life of a people: citizens, voters, lobbyists, party members, lawmakers, bureaucrats, etc.

prefecture A unit of local administration headed by a prefect, as in France and Japan.

presidential government A government which is designed to separate the executive and legislative branches. The United States is the prime example of presidential government: The president has a mandate separate from the Congress; his tenure does not depend on Congressional support. Actually, the political process in presidential government, as in parliamentary government, calls for a great deal of interaction and cooperative working relations between the executive and the legislature.

proletariat That class of factory workers which emerged with industrialization, described by Karl Marx as the leading class of the future. An individual member of this class is known as a *proletarian.*

proportional representation (PR) An electoral system in which each party is allocated seats in the legislature in proportion to its voting strength. If a party wins 10 percent of the total vote in an election, it gains 10 percent of the seats in the legislature. PR is usually based on a list system with voters indicating party preference rather than individual candidates.

protective tariff A tax placed on imported goods to make their market price higher so as to protect goods of domestic manufacture which may be more expensive and uncompetitive. Most developing countries believe protective tariffs are essential to help their infant industries.

protectorate An almost-colony, a weaker country whose affairs, especially international relations, are at least partly run by a stronger, protecting power.

purge Getting rid of opponents within a political party or government. Stalin ordered massive purges in the Soviet political system in the 1930s that were exceedingly cruel and bloody. But a purge is not necessarily violent; it can simply mean expulsion from the party.

recruitment In the political sense, the process of attracting persons, usually younger, into apprenticeship positions in the bureaucracy or parties; the staffing of the political system.

referendum A mass vote on an issue, such as a new law or constitution, rather than for an individual running for office.

role How an individual is expected to perform, either according to law or in his own mind. (Compare with *function* above.) The emphasis is on political behavior.

secularization A society's shift from traditional, religion-linked values and leaders to modern values and leaders that have no clear religious connection.

single-member constituency The election of a single representative from a territorial unit to sit in the legislature.

stakhanovism A system of differential individual incentives for accelerated production introduced by Stalin in the Soviet Union.

sovereignty A legal term denoting the independence of a state and the supremacy of its authority within its territorial limits. If country X is sovereign, country Y cannot intervene in its affairs. Sovereignty is widely depreciated by some political thinkers as vague, too legalistic, and unrelated to modern national interdependence. Newly sovereign nations, however, take it very seriously.

special interests The interests of particular groups as compared with the interest of the whole society. See *general will* and *pluralism* above.

state A sovereign political unit with full power to allocate resources and to govern the population within its territorial jurisdiction.

stratification The layering of society into classes which have differing amounts of wealth, status, and power.

structure The social institution which performs a *function* or *functions* (see above). A legislature is a structure which performs the function of lawmaking. Some structures have many functions; they are called multifunctional. The cabinet in a parliamentary government is usually multifunctional, performing both executive and legislative functions.

structural-functional The views propounded by social theorist Talcott Parsons and his followers that society is best studied by discerning which structures perform which functions. Parsons holds that there are certain basic functions in all societies which must be performed, although the structures for doing this may be different.

suffrage The right to vote, usually extended historically to more and more social groups, as in the United States or the United Kingdom; but in most new countries granted to everyone all at once.

superpower A nation state with overawing power to make both conventional and nuclear war. At present only the United States and the USSR are unanimously considered superpowers.

supports In David Easton's outline of the political system, the material and psychological inputs from citizens that maintain the system, such as taxes, obedience, and loyalty. Compare with *demands* above.

Supreme Soviet The national legislature of the USSR.

system viability The ability of a political system to adapt itself to a changing environment and to last through time. Considered by some as the only sure test of whether it works.

technocracy A political or social system which relies heavily on scientific and technical expertise, making much use of computers, systems analysis, and costing techniques.

telecommunications Communications that move as electrical impulses such as radio, television, and telegraph. Believed to play a major role in political modernization by linking together the various regions of a country—the nerves of government.

territorial integrity A country's actual possession of all of its real estate, not letting another country intervene within its territorial jurisdiction.

tribalism In premodern political systems, the stress and importance individuals give to tribal membership; an ethnic association sharing common ancestry, language, and culture—larger than the family unit, smaller than a nation.

totalitarianism A political system organized on the basis of monolithic unity, with an all-embracing political ideology, operating through a single party which prescribes on-going policy.

tutelary democracy A political system, usually a modernizing one, that does not yet allow free popular participation. Its leaders purport to be educating the people so they can eventually have complete democracy. Turkey under Atatürk is frequently described as a tutelary democracy.

unicameral A parliament with one house, such as Israel's Knesset. Compare with *bicameral* above.

unitary government A political system which concentrates power in the national (central) government, but delegates authority and administrative functions to local units. The local units are not, however, regarded as autonomous units, as in a federal union. Compare with *federalism* above.

urbanization The movement of persons from the countryside to cities, usually accompanying *industrialization* (see above). A developed country is invariably more urbanized than an underdeveloped country.

value judgment The unverifiable attribution of goodness or badness a political scientist bestows on the system he is examining. Not necessarily wrong or even undesirable, value judgments are best kept strictly separated from objective analyses.

SELECTED BIBLIOGRAPHY

GENERAL READING

ABRAHAM, HENRY J. *The Judicial Process.* 2d ed. New York: Oxford University Press, 1968.
ALMOND, GABRIEL A., and JAMES S. COLEMAN. *The Politics of the Developing Areas.* Princeton, N.J.: Princeton University Press, 1960.
———, and G. BINGHAM POWELL, JR. Comparative Politics: Boston: Little, Brown, 1966.
———, and SIDNEY VERBA. *The Civic Culture.* Boston: Little, Brown, 1965.
APTER, DAVID E. *The Politics of Modernization.* Chicago: University of Chicago Press, 1965.
BAUER, RAYMOND, and KENNETH J. GERGEN, eds. *The Study of Policy Formation.* New York: Free Press, 1968.
BAYLEY, DAVID. *Public Liberties in the New States.* Chicago: Rand McNally, 1964.
BEER, SAMUEL H., and ADAM B. ULAM, eds. *Patterns of Government: The Major Political Systems of Europe.* New York: Random House, 1962.
BROWN, HARRISON, JAMES BONNER, and JOHN WEIR. *The Next Hundred Years.* New York: Viking, 1957.
COLEMAN, JAMES S., ed. *Education and Political Development.* Princeton, N.J.: Princeton University Press, 1965.
COMMISSION ON INTERNATIONAL DEVELOPMENT. *Partners in Development.* New York: Praeger, 1969.
COPLIN, WILLIAM D. *The Functions of International Law.* Chicago: Rand McNally, 1966.
DAHL, ROBERT. *A Modern Political Analysis.* 2d ed. Englewood Cliffs, N.J.: Prentice-Hall, 1970.
———. *Political Oppositions in Western Democracies.* New Haven, Conn.: Yale University Press, 1970.

DEUTSCH, KARL W. *Nationalism and Social Communication.* 2d ed. Cambridge, Mass.: MIT Press, 1966.

———. *The Nerves of Government.* New York: Free Press, 1966.

———. *Politics and Government.* Boston: Houghton Mifflin, 1970.

———, and WILLIAM J. FOLTZ, eds. *Nation-Building.* New York: Atherton, 1966.

DUCHACEK, IVO D. *Comparative Federalism: The Territorial Dimension of Politics.* New York: Holt, Rinehart & Winston, 1970.

DUVERGER, MAURICE. *Political Parties.* New York: John Wiley, 1954.

EARLE, VALERIE, ed. *Federalism: Infinite Variety in Theory and Practice.* Itasca, Ill.: Peacock Publishers, 1968.

EASTON, DAVID. *A Framework for Political Analysis.* Englewood Cliffs, N.J.: Prentice-Hall, 1965.

EPSTEIN, LEON D. *Political Parties in Western Democracies.* New York: Praeger, 1967.

EULAU, HEINZ. *The Behavioral Persuasion in Politics.* New York: Random House, 1963.

FANON, FRANTZ. *The Wretched of the Earth.* New York: Grove Press, 1963.

FRANK, ELKE, ed. *Lawmakers in a Changing World.* Englewood Cliffs, N.J.: Prentice-Hall, 1966.

FRIED, ROBERT C. *Comparative Political Institutions.* New York: Macmillan, 1966.

FRIEDRICH, CARL J. *Constitutional Government and Democracy.* Waltham, Mass.: Blaisdell, 1968.

———. *Man and His Government.* New York: McGraw-Hill, 1963.

GALBRAITH, JOHN KENNETH. *The New Industrial State.* Boston: Houghton Mifflin, 1967.

GANJI, MANOUCHEHR. *International Protection of Human Rights.* Geneva: Libraire E. Droz, 1962.

HAAR, JOHN ENSOR. *The Professional Diplomat.* Princeton, N.J.: Princeton University Press, 1969.

HAAS, ERNST B. *Human Rights and International Action.* Stanford, Calif.: Stanford University Press, 1970.

HEADY, FERREL. *Public Administration: A Comparative Perspective.* Englewood Cliffs, N.J.: Prentice-Hall, 1966.

HOLT, ROBERT T., and JOHN E. TURNER. *The Political Basis of Economic Development.* New York: Van Nostrand, 1966.

HOROWITZ, IRVING. *Three Worlds of Development.* New York: Oxford University Press, 1966.

HUNTINGTON, SAMUEL P. *Political Order in Changing Societies.* New Haven, Conn.: Yale University Press, 1968.

JACOB, PHILIP E., and JAMES V. TOSCANO, eds. *The Integration of Political Communities.* Philadelphia: Lippincott, 1964.

JANOWITZ, MORRIS. *The Professional Soldier.* New York: Free Press, 1960.

KOHN, HANS. *Nationalism: Its Meaning and History.* rev. ed. New York: Van Nostrand, Anvil Books, 1965.

———. *Political Ideologies of the Twentieth Century.* 3d ed. New York: Harper and Row, 1966.

LANE, ROBERT, and DAVID D. SEARS. *Public Opinion.* Englewood Cliffs, N.J.: Prentice-Hall, 1964.

LA PALOMBARA, JOSEPH, and MYRON WEINER, eds. *Political Parties and Political Development.* Princeton, N.J.: Princeton University Press, 1966.

LASSWELL, HAROLD D. *Politics: Who Gets What, When, How.* Cleveland and New York: World Publishing, Meridian Books, 1958.

———, and ABRAHAM KAPLAN. *Power and Society: A Framework for Political Inquiry.* New Haven, Conn.: Yale University Press, 1963.

LEIDEN, CARL, and KARL M. SCHMITT. *The Politics of Violent Revolution in the Modern World.* Englewood Cliffs, N.J.: Prentice-Hall, 1968.

LIJPHART, AREND, ed. *Politics in Europe: Comparisons and Interpretations.* Englewood Cliffs, N.J.: Prentice-Hall, 1969.

LINDBLOM, CHARLES E. *The Policy Making Process.* Englewood Cliffs, N.J.: Prentice-Hall, 1968.

MACIVER, R. M. *The Web of Government.* New York: Macmillan, 1947.

MACRIDIS, ROY C., ed. *Foreign Policy in World Politics.* 3d ed. Englewood Cliffs, N.J.: Prentice-Hall, 1967.

MARTZ, JOHN D., ed. *The Dynamics of Change in Latin American Politics.* Englewood Cliffs, N.J.: Prentice-Hall, 1965.

MOSHER, FREDERICK C. *Democracy and the Public Service.* New York: Oxford University Press, 1968.

MUNGER, FRANK, ed. *Studies in Comparative Politics.* New York: Thomas Y. Crowell, 1967.

MYRDAL, GUNNAR. *Beyond the Welfare State.* New Haven, Conn.: Yale University Press, 1964.

NEUMANN, SIGMUND, ed. *Modern Political Parties.* Chicago: University of Chicago Press, 1955.

PRICE, DON K. *The Scientific Estate.* Cambridge, Mass.: Harvard University Press, Belknap Press, 1965.

PRYOR, FREDERICK L. *Public Expenditures in Communist and Capitalist Nations.* Homewood, Ill.: Richard D. Irwin, 1968.

PYE, LUCIAN W., and SIDNEY VERBA, eds. *Political Culture and Political Development.* Princeton, N.J.: Princeton University Press, 1965.

RIGGS, FRED W. *Administration in Developing Countries: The Theory of Prismatic Society.* Boston: Houghton Mifflin, 1964.

RIKER, W. H. *Federalism: Origin, Operation, Significance.* Boston: Little, Brown, 1964.

ROURKE, FRANCIS E. *Bureaucracy, Politics, and Public Policy.* Boston: Little, Brown, 1969.

RUSSETT, BRUCE M. *Trends in World Politics.* New York: Macmillan, 1965.

SCARROW, HOWARD A. *Comparative Political Analysis: An Introduction.* New York: Harper and Row, 1969.

SCHLEICHER, CHARLES P. *International Relations: Cooperation and Conflict.* Englewood Cliffs, N.J.: Prentice-Hall, 1962.

SPIEGEL, STEVEN L., and KENNETH N. WALTZ, eds. *Conflict in World Politics.* Cambridge, Mass.: Winthrop, 1971.

SPIRO, HERBERT J. *Responsibility in Government: Theory and Practice.* New York: Van Nostrand Reinhold, 1969.

VAN DYKE, VERNON. *International Politics.* 2d ed. New York: Appleton-Century-Crofts, 1966.

WARD, BARBARA. *The Rich Nations and the Poor Nations.* New York: Norton, 1962.

WELCH, CLAUDE E., ed. *Political Modernization: A Reader in Comparative Political Change.* Belmont, Calif.: Wadsworth, 1967.

WHEARE, K. C. *Legislatures.* New York: Oxford University Press, 1963.

COUNTRY STUDIES

Area Handbooks, Foreign Area Studies Division, The American University (Washington, D.C.: Government Printing Office)

Colombia	1970
India	1970
Israel	1970
Ivory Coast	1962
Japan	1969
Kenya	1967
Soviet Union	1971
Turkey	1970

US Department of Commerce, Bureau of International Commerce, *Basic Data on the Economy* (current issue)

Colombia	July, 1966
Federal Republic of Germany	May, 1967
India	December, 1969
Israel	December, 1969
Ivory Coast	April, 1968
Japan	December, 1966
Kenya	November, 1965
Mexico	August, 1967
Turkey	December, 1966
United Kingdom	July, 1966
USSR	April, 1966

US Department of State, *Background Notes*

Colombia	November, 1970
Federal Republic of Germany	January, 1970
India	October, 1969
Israel	December, 1969
Ivory Coast	May, 1970
Japan	September, 1969
Kenya	March, 1970
Mexico	June, 1969
Turkey	May, 1970
United Kingdom	January, 1970
USSR	June, 1971

POLITICS IN THE UNITED STATES

BRZEZINSKI, ZBIGNIEW K., and SAMUEL P. HUNTINGTON. *Political Power: USA/USSR.* New York: Viking, 1963.

BURNS, JAMES MACGREGOR. *The Deadlock of Democracy: Four-Party Politics in America.* Englewood Cliffs, N.J.: Prentice-Hall, 1963.

FREE, LLOYD A., and HADLEY CANTRIL. *The Political Beliefs of Americans: A Study of Public Opinion.* New York: Simon and Schuster, 1968.

GRAHAM, HUGH DAVIS, and TED ROBERT GURR. *The History of Violence in America.* New York: Bantam Books, 1969.
IRISH, MARIAN D., and JAMES W. PROTHRO. *The Politics of American Democracy.* 5th ed. Englewood Cliffs, N.J.: Prentice-Hall, 1971.
JAMES, DOROTHY B. *The Contemporary Presidency.* New York: Pegasus, 1969.
JAMES, JUDSON L. *American Political Parties.* New York: Pegasus, 1969.
LIPSET, SEYMOUR MARTIN. *The First New Nation: The United States in Historical and Comparative Perspective.* New York: Basic Books, 1963.
MITCHELL, W. C. *Public Choice in America.* Chicago: Markham, 1971.
NEUSTADT, RICHARD E. *Presidential Power: The Politics of Leadership.* New York: John Wiley, 1960.
RIVERS, WILLIAM L. *The Opinion Makers.* Boston: Beacon Press, 1965.
SUNDQUIST, JAMES L., and DAVID W. DAVIS. *Making Federalism Work.* Washington, D.C.: Brookings Institution, 1969.

LATIN AMERICAN POLITICS: COLOMBIA AND MEXICO

ALEXANDER, ROBERT S. *Today's Latin America.* Garden City, N.Y.: Doubleday, rev. Anchor book, 1968.
BURNETT, BEN G., and KENNETH F. JOHNSON. *Political Forces in Latin America.* Belmont, Calif.: Wadsworth, 1970.
DIX, ROBERT H. *Colombia: The Political Dimensions of Change.* New Haven, Conn.: Yale University Press, 1966.
FAGEN, RICHARD R., and WAYNE A. CORNELIUS, JR., eds. *Political Power in Latin America.* Englewood Cliffs, N.J.: Prentice-Hall, 1970.
GALBRAITH, W. O. *Colombia.* 2d ed. London: Oxford University Press, 1966.
GILL, CLARK G. *Education in a Changing Mexico.* Washington, D.C.: Government Printing Office, 1969.
HANKE, LEWIS. *Modern Latin America, Continent in Ferment: Mexico and the Caribbean.* Princeton, N.J.: Van Nostrand, 1967.
LIPSET, SEYMOUR MARTIN, and ALDO SOLARI, eds. *Elites in Latin America.* New York: Oxford University Press, 1967.
SCOTT, ROBERT E. *Mexican Government in Transition.* Urbana, Ill.: University of Illinois Press, 1959.
WILKIE, JAMES W. *The Mexican Revolution: Federal Expenditure and Social Change Since 1910.* Berkeley, Calif.: University of California Press, 1970.

WESTERN EUROPEAN POLITICS: UNITED KINGDOM AND THE FEDERAL REPUBLIC OF GERMANY

BEER, SAMUEL H. *British Politics in the Collectivist Age.* New York: Knopf, 1965.
BUTLER, DAVID, and JENNIE FREEMAN. *British Political Facts 1900–1967.* 2d ed. London: Macmillan, 1968.
———, and DONALD STOKES. *Political Change in Britain.* New York: St. Martin's Press, rev. ed. 1971.
CRICK, BERNARD. *The Reform of Parliament.* New York: Doubleday, 1964.
EDINGER, LEWIS. *Politics in Germany.* Boston: Little, Brown, 1968.
HEIDENHEIMER, ARNOLD. *The Governments of Germany.* 2d ed. New York: Thomas Y. Crowell, 1966.

KOHN, HANS. *The Mind of Germany*. New York: Scribner, 1960.
MERKL, PETER H. *The Origin of the West German Republic*. New York: Oxford University Press, 1963.
NEUMANN, ROBERT G. *The Government of the German Federal Republic*. New York: Harper & Row, 1966.
PLISCHKE, ELMER. *Contemporary Governments of Germany*. 2d ed. Boston: Houghton Mifflin, 1961.
ROSE, RICHARD. *England*. Boston: Little, Brown, 1964.
VERNEY, DOUGLAS. *British Government and Politics*. New York: Harper & Row, 1966.

POLITICS IN EAST EUROPE: THE SOVIET UNION

BARGHOORN, FREDERICK C. *Politics in the USSR*. Boston: Little, Brown, 1966.
BERMAN, HAROLD J. *Justice in the USSR*, rev. ed. Cambridge, Mass.: Harvard University Press, 1963.
BRZEZINSKI, ZBIGNIEW K. *Ideology and Power in Soviet Politics*. rev. ed. New York: Praeger, 1967.
BUZEK, ANTONY. *How the Communist Press Works*. New York: Praeger, 1964.
CONQUEST, ROBERT. *The Soviet Police System*. New York: Praeger, 1968.
FAINSOD, MERLE. *How Russia Is Ruled*. 2d ed. Cambridge, Mass.: Harvard University Press, 1963.
FARRELL, R. BARRY, ed. *Political Leadership in Eastern Europe and the Soviet Union*. Chicago: Aldine, 1970.
HAZARD, JOHN N. *The Soviet System of Government*. 4th ed. Chicago: University of Chicago Press, 1968.
INKELES, ALEX. *Public Opinion in Soviet Russia: A Study in Mass Persuasion*. Cambridge, Mass.: Harvard University Press, 1958.
KASSOF, ALLEN. *Prospects for Soviet Society*. New York: Praeger, 1966.
KAUTSKY, JOHN H. *Communism and the Politics of Development*. New York: John Wiley, 1968.
OSBORN, ROBERT J. *Soviet Social Policies: Welfare, Equality, and Community*. Homewood, Ill.: Dorsey Press, 1970.
PIPES, RICHARD. *The Formation of the Soviet Union: Communism and Nationalism, 1917–1923*. Cambridge, Mass.: Harvard University Press, 1954.
RIGBY, T. H., ed. *Stalin*. Englewood Cliffs, N.J.: Prentice-Hall, 1966.
ROMASHKIN, P. S., ed. *Fundamentals of Soviet Law*. Moscow: Foreign Languages Publishing House, n.d.
SCHAPIRO, LEONARD. *The Communist Party of the Soviet Union*. New York: Random House, 1960.
SCHWARTZ, HARRY. *Russia's Soviet Economy*. 2d ed. Englewood Cliffs, N.J.: Prentice-Hall, 1963.
WOLFE, BERTRAM D. *Three Who Made a Revolution*. Boston: Beacon Press, 1955.
YARMOLINSKY, AVRAHM. *The Road to Revolution*. New York: Macmillan, 1959.

POLITICS IN THE MIDDLE EAST: TURKEY AND ISRAEL

BERNSTEIN, MARVER H. *The Politics of Israel, The First Decade of Statehood*. Princeton, N.J.: Princeton University Press, 1957.
FEIN, LEONARD J. *Politics in Israel*. Boston: Little, Brown, 1967.

Frey, Frederick W. *The Turkish Political Elite.* Cambridge, Mass.: MIT Press, 1965.

Karpat, Kemal H. *Turkey's Politics.* Princeton, N.J.: Princeton University Press, 1959.

Kinross, Lord. *Atatürk.* New York: William Morrow, 1965.

Louvish, Misha. *The Challenge of Israel.* Jerusalem: Israel University Press, 1968.

Seligman, Lester A. *Leadership in a New Nation: Political Development in Israel.* New York: Atherton Press, 1964.

AFRICAN POLITICS: IVORY COAST AND KENYA

Adam, Thomas R. *Government and Politics in Africa.* 3d ed. New York: Random House, 1965.

Carter, Gwendolyn M., ed. *African One-Party States.* Ithaca, New York: Cornell University Press, 1962.

Doro, Marion E., and Newell M. Stultz, eds. *Governing in Black Africa.* Englewood Cliffs, N.J.: Prentice-Hall, 1970.

Morgenthau, Ruth Schachter. *Political Parties in French-Speaking Africa.* Oxford: Clarendon, 1964.

Spiro, Herbert J., ed. *Africa: The Primacy of Politics.* New York: Random House, 1966.

———, *Politics in Africa.* Englewood Cliffs, N.J.: Prentice-Hall, 1962.

Zolberg, Aristide R. *One Party Government in the Ivory Coast,* rev. ed. Princeton, N.J.: Princeton University Press, 1969.

ASIAN POLITICS: INDIA AND JAPAN

Bakke, E. Wight. *Revolutionary Democracy: Challenge and Testing in Japan.* Hamden, Conn.: Archon Books, 1968.

Bayley, David H. *The Police and Political Development in India.* Princeton: Princeton University Press, 1969.

Borton, Hugh. *Japan's Modern Century.* New York: Ronald Press, 1955.

Hardgrave, Robert L., Jr. *India: Government and Politics in a Developing Nation.* New York: Harcourt, Brace & World, 1970.

Kubota, Akira. *Higher Civil Servants in Post-War Japan.* Princeton, N.J.: Princeton University Press, 1969.

Lamb, Beatrice Pitney. *India: A World in Transition.* 3d ed. New York: Praeger, 1968.

Langdon, Frank. *Japan.* Boston: Little, Brown, 1967.

Morris-Jones, W. H. *The Government and Politics of India.* London: Hutchinson, 1964.

Palmer, Norman D. *The Indian Political System.* Boston: Houghton Mifflin, 1961.

Park, Richard L. *India's Political System.* Englewood Cliffs, N.J.: Prentice-Hall, 1967.

Pylee, M. V. *India's Constitution.* 2d rev. ed. New York: Asia Publishing House, 1967.

Scalapino, Robert A., and Junnosuke Masumi. *Parties and Politics in Contemporary Japan.* Berkeley, Calif.: University of California Press, 1962.

STORY, RICHARD. *The Double Patriots: A Study of Japanese Nationalism.* Boston: Houghton Mifflin, 1957.

WARD, ROBERT E. *Japan's Political System.* Englewood Cliffs, N.J.: Prentice-Hall, 1967.

———, ed. *Political Development in Modern Japan.* Princeton, N.J.: Princeton University Press, 1968.

WEINER, MYRON. *Party Politics in India.* Princeton, N.J.: Princeton University Press, 1957.

——— and RAGNI KOTHARI, eds. *Indian Voting Behavior: Studies of the 1962 General Elections.* Calcutta: Firma K. L. Mukhopsfsysy, 1965.

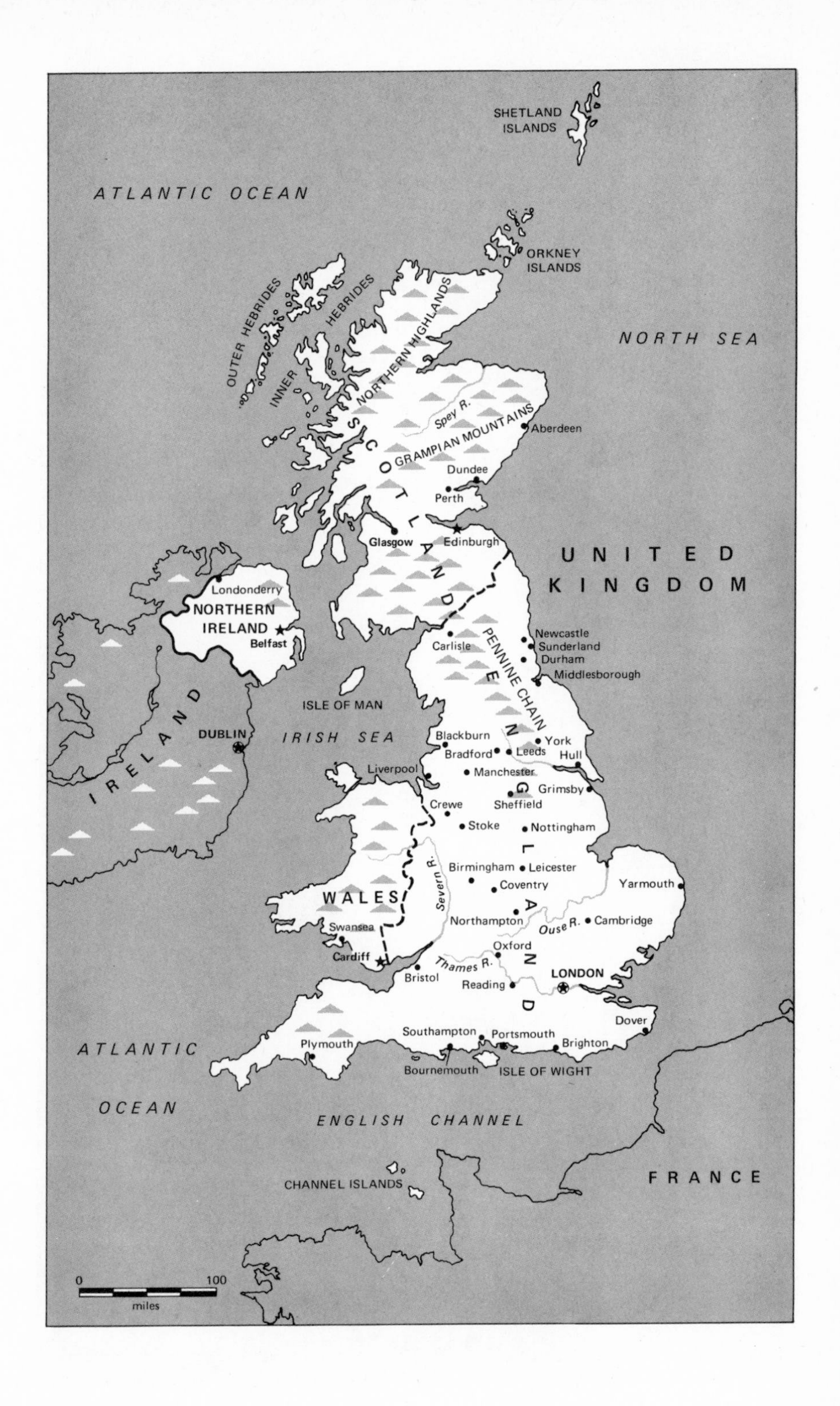

SHETLAND ISLANDS
ATLANTIC OCEAN
ORKNEY ISLANDS
OUTER HEBRIDES
INNER HEBRIDES
NORTHERN HIGHLANDS
NORTH SEA
Spey R.
GRAMPIAN MOUNTAINS
Aberdeen
SCOTLAND
Dundee
Perth
Glasgow
Edinburgh
UNITED KINGDOM
Londonderry
NORTHERN IRELAND
Belfast
Newcastle
Sunderland
Durham
Carlisle
PENNINE CHAIN
Middlesborough
ISLE OF MAN
IRELAND
DUBLIN
IRISH SEA
Blackburn
York
Bradford
Leeds
Hull
Liverpool
Manchester
Grimsby
Crewe
Sheffield
Stoke
Nottingham
ENGLAND
Birmingham
Leicester
Severn R.
Coventry
Yarmouth
WALES
Northampton
Ouse R.
Cambridge
Swansea
Oxford
Cardiff
Thames R.
Bristol
LONDON
Reading
Dover
Southampton
Portsmouth
Brighton
ATLANTIC OCEAN
Plymouth
Bournemouth
ISLE OF WIGHT
ENGLISH CHANNEL
CHANNEL ISLANDS
FRANCE
0
100
miles

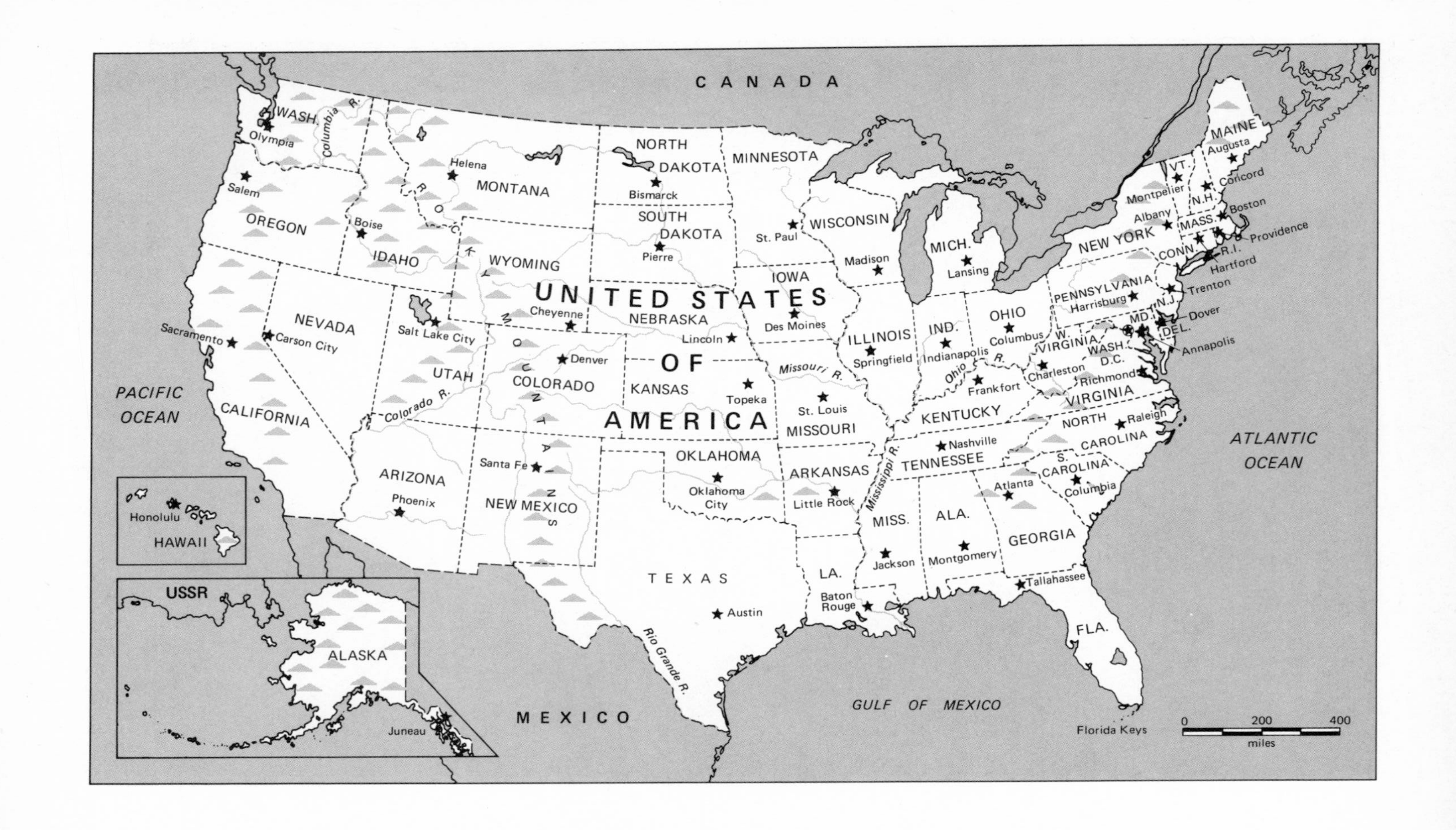

CANADA
UNITED STATES OF AMERICA
ROCKY MOUNTAINS
PACIFIC OCEAN
ATLANTIC OCEAN
GULF OF MEXICO
MEXICO
USSR
WASH.
Olympia
Columbia R.
OREGON
Salem
CALIFORNIA
Sacramento
NEVADA
Carson City
IDAHO
Boise
MONTANA
Helena
WYOMING
Cheyenne
UTAH
Salt Lake City
Colorado R.
COLORADO
Denver
ARIZONA
Phoenix
NEW MEXICO
Santa Fe
NORTH DAKOTA
Bismarck
SOUTH DAKOTA
Pierre
NEBRASKA
Lincoln
KANSAS
Topeka
OKLAHOMA
Oklahoma City
TEXAS
Austin
Rio Grande R.
MINNESOTA
St. Paul
IOWA
Des Moines
Missouri R.
MISSOURI
St. Louis
ARKANSAS
Little Rock
LA.
Baton Rouge
WISCONSIN
Madison
ILLINOIS
Springfield
Mississippi R.
MICH.
Lansing
IND.
Indianapolis
Ohio R.
OHIO
Columbus
KENTUCKY
Frankfort
TENNESSEE
Nashville
MISS.
Jackson
ALA.
Montgomery
GEORGIA
Atlanta
FLA.
Tallahassee
Florida Keys
S. CAROLINA
Columbia
NORTH CAROLINA
Raleigh
VIRGINIA
Richmond
W. VIRGINIA
Charleston
WASH. D.C.
MD.
Annapolis
DEL.
Dover
N.J.
Trenton
PENNSYLVANIA
Harrisburg
NEW YORK
Albany
CONN.
Hartford
R.I.
Providence
MASS.
Boston
VT.
Montpelier
N.H.
Concord
MAINE
Augusta
HAWAII
Honolulu
ALASKA
Juneau
0
200
400
miles

UNION OF
SOVIET SOCIALIST
REPUBLICS
RUSSIAN SOVIET FEDERATED SOCIALIST
ARCTIC OCEAN
BERING SEA
BARENTS SEA
SEA OF OKHOTSK
SAKHALIN
JAPAN
KOREA
CHINA
MONGOLIAN PEOPLE'S REPUBLIC
AFGHANISTAN
PAKISTAN
IRAN
TURKEY
BLACK SEA
ROMANIA
POLAND
FINLAND
CASPIAN SEA
ARAL SEA
URAL MOUNTAINS
KAZAKH SSR
UZBEK SSR
TURKMEN SSR
TADZHIK SSR
KIRGIZ SSR
GEORGIAN SSR
ARMENIAN SSR
AZERBAIJAN SSR
UKRAINIAN SSR
MOLDAVIAN SSR
BELORUSSIAN SSR
LITHUANIAN SSR
RUSSIAN SFSR
LATVIAN SSR
ESTONIAN SSR
MOSCOW
Murmansk
Archangel
Tallin
Riga
Leningrad
Vilna
Minsk
Kiev
Kishinev
Kharkov
Gorki
Voronezh
Rostov
Saratov
Volgograd
Kuybyshev
Ufa
Sverdlovsk
Chelyabinsk
Tiflis
Erivan
Baku
Ashkhabad
Tashkent
Dushanbe
Frunze
Alma Ata
Karaganda
L. Balkhash
Omsk
Novosibirsk
Novokuznetsk
Krasnoyarsk
Irkutsk
Baikal L.
Chita
Yakutsk
Khabarovsk
Vladivostok
Ob R.
Irtysh R.
Yenisey R.
Tunguska R.
Lena R.
Amur R.
Kolyma R.
Ussuri R.
Syr Darya
Amu Darya
0
500
miles

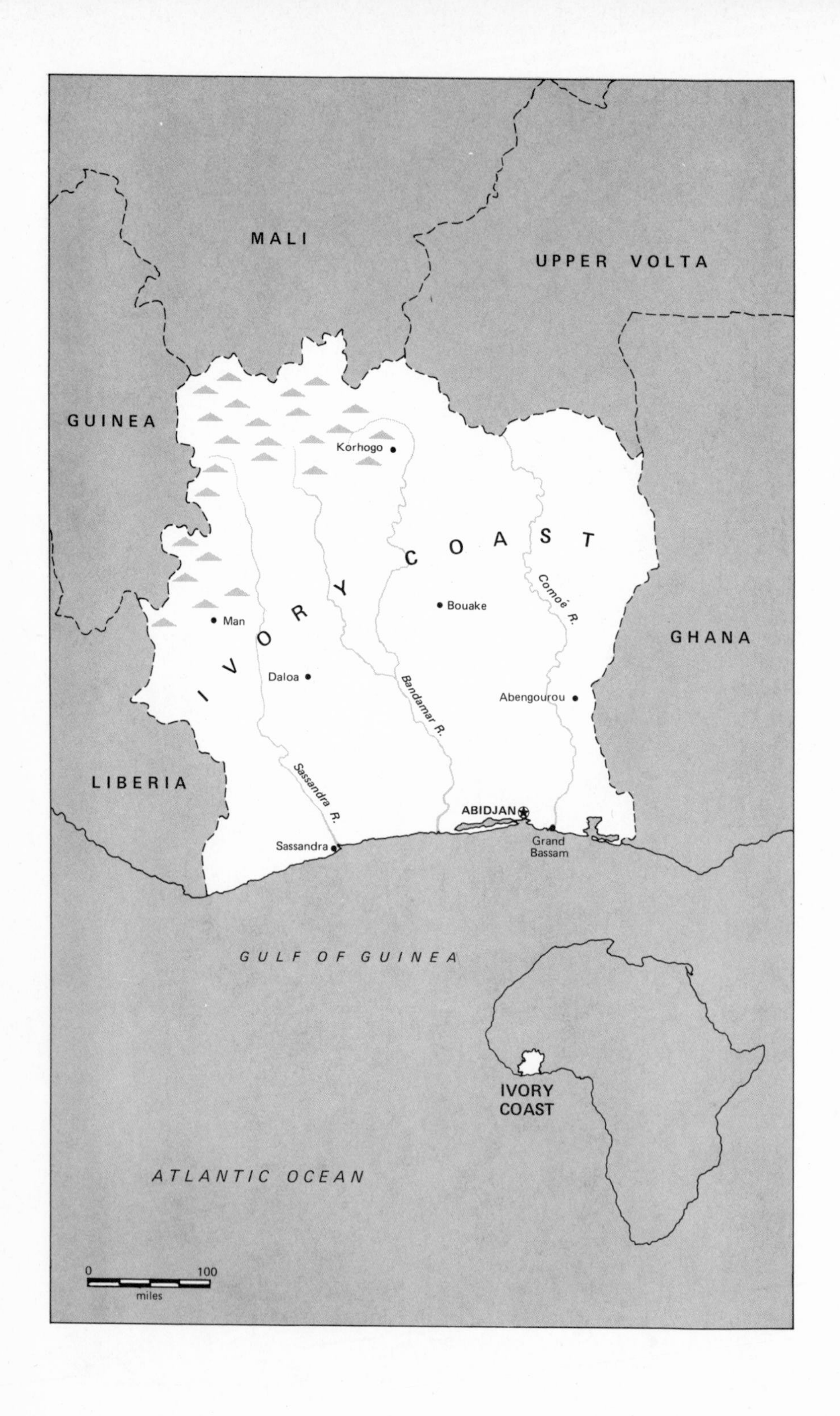
MALI
UPPER VOLTA
GUINEA
Korhogo
IVORY COAST
Man
Bouake
Comoé R.
GHANA
Daloa
Bandamar R.
Abengourou
LIBERIA
Sassandra R.
ABIDJAN
Sassandra
Grand Bassam
GULF OF GUINEA
IVORY COAST
ATLANTIC OCEAN
0
100
miles

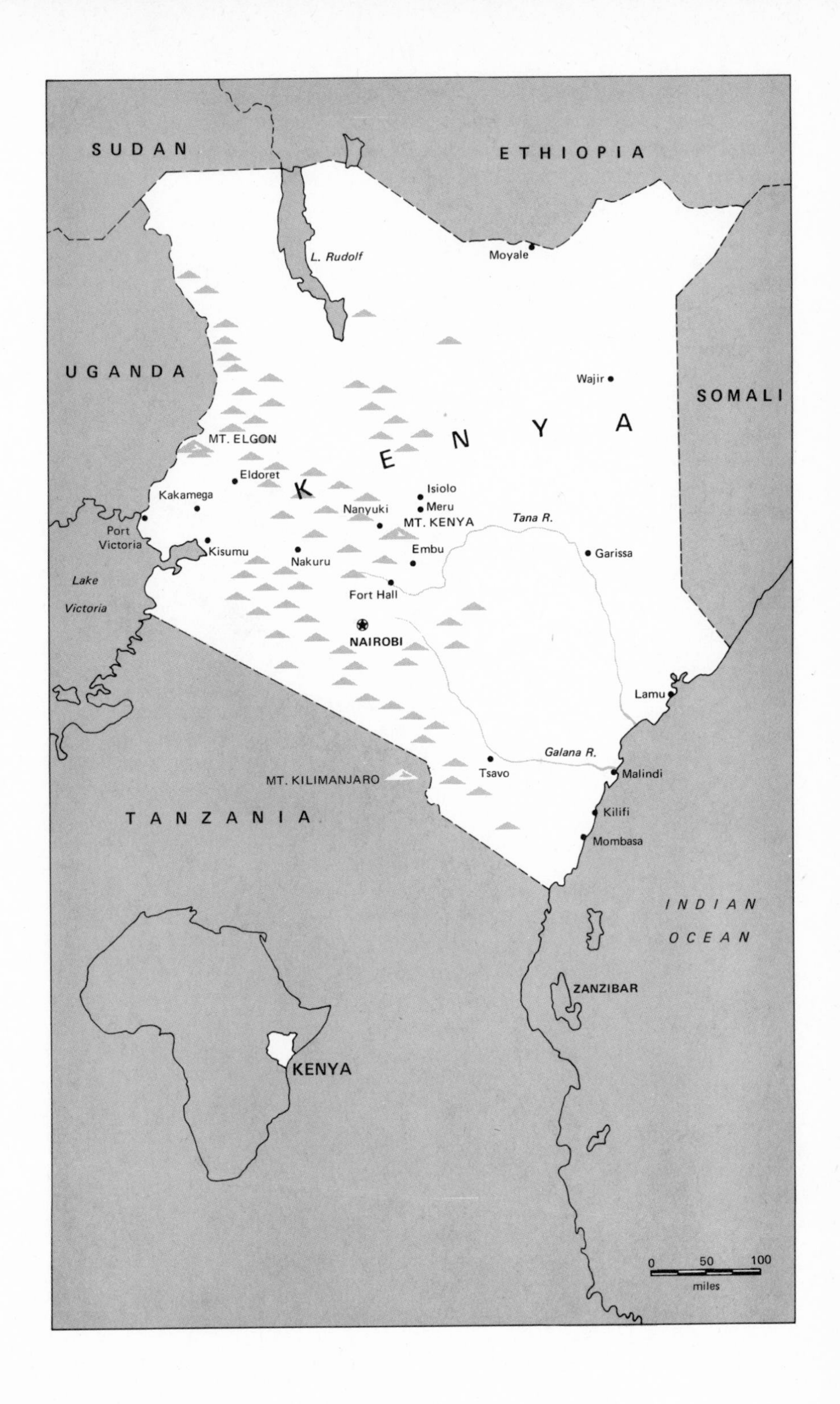
SUDAN
ETHIOPIA
L. Rudolf
Moyale
UGANDA
Wajir
SOMALI
K E N Y A
MT. ELGON
Eldoret
Kakamega
Isiolo
Meru
Nanyuki
MT. KENYA
Tana R.
Port Victoria
Kisumu
Nakuru
Embu
Garissa
Lake Victoria
Fort Hall
NAIROBI
Lamu
Galana R.
Tsavo
Malindi
MT. KILIMANJARO
TANZANIA
Kilifi
Mombasa
INDIAN OCEAN
ZANZIBAR
KENYA
0 50 100
miles

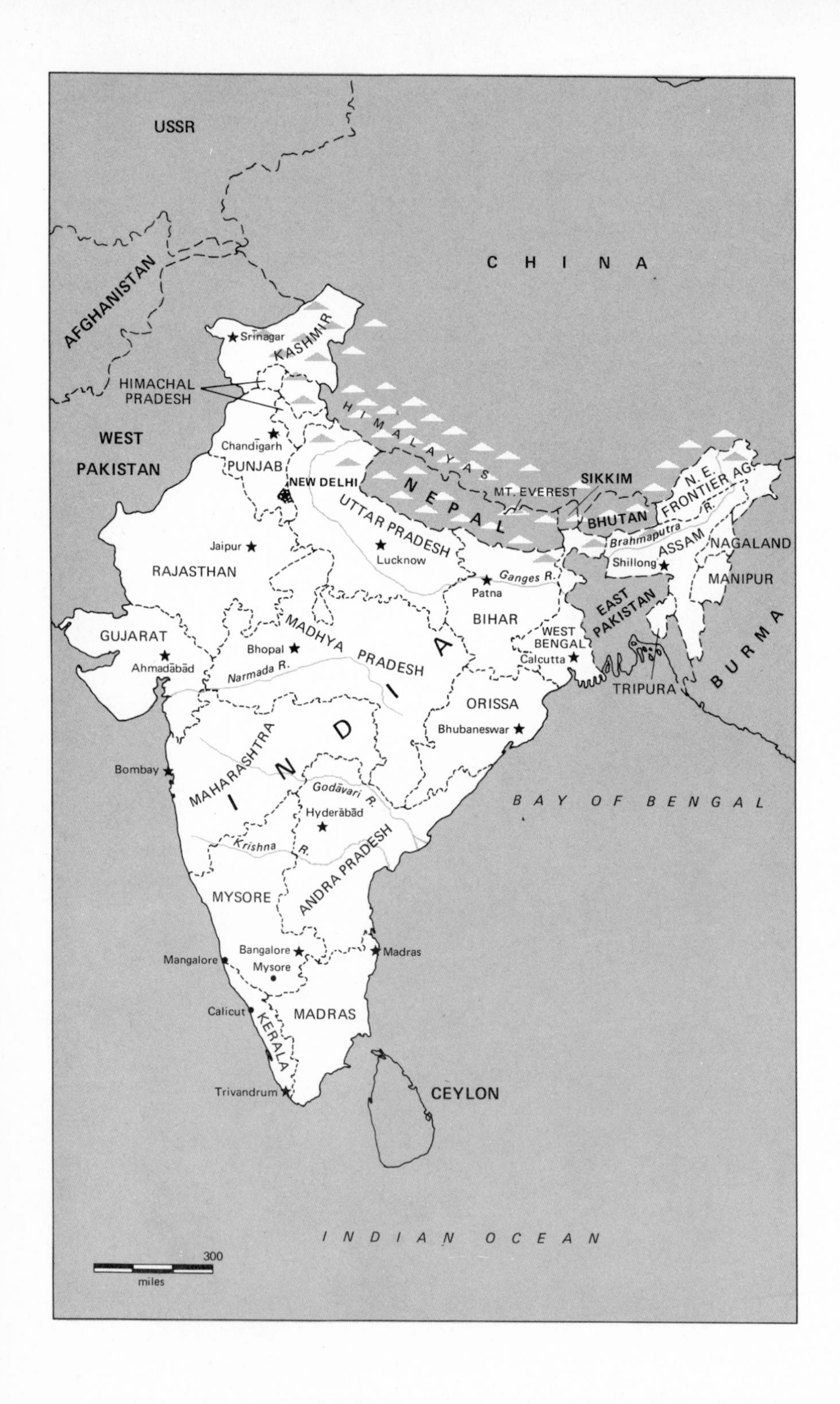
USSR
CHINA
AFGHANISTAN
Srinagar
KASHMIR
HIMACHAL PRADESH
WEST PAKISTAN
Chandigarh
PUNJAB
NEW DELHI
HIMALAYAS
NEPAL
MT. EVEREST
SIKKIM
BHUTAN
N. E. FRONTIER AG.
Brahmaputra R.
ASSAM
NAGALAND
Shillong
MANIPUR
UTTAR PRADESH
Lucknow
Jaipur
RAJASTHAN
Ganges R.
Patna
BIHAR
EAST PAKISTAN
GUJARAT
Ahmadabad
Bhopal
MADHYA PRADESH
WEST BENGAL
Calcutta
TRIPURA
BURMA
Narmada R.
ORISSA
Bhubaneswar
INDIA
MAHARASHTRA
Bombay
Godavari R.
Hyderabad
BAY OF BENGAL
Krishna R.
ANDRA PRADESH
MYSORE
Bangalore
Madras
Mangalore
Mysore
Calicut
KERALA
MADRAS
Trivandrum
CEYLON
INDIAN OCEAN
300
miles

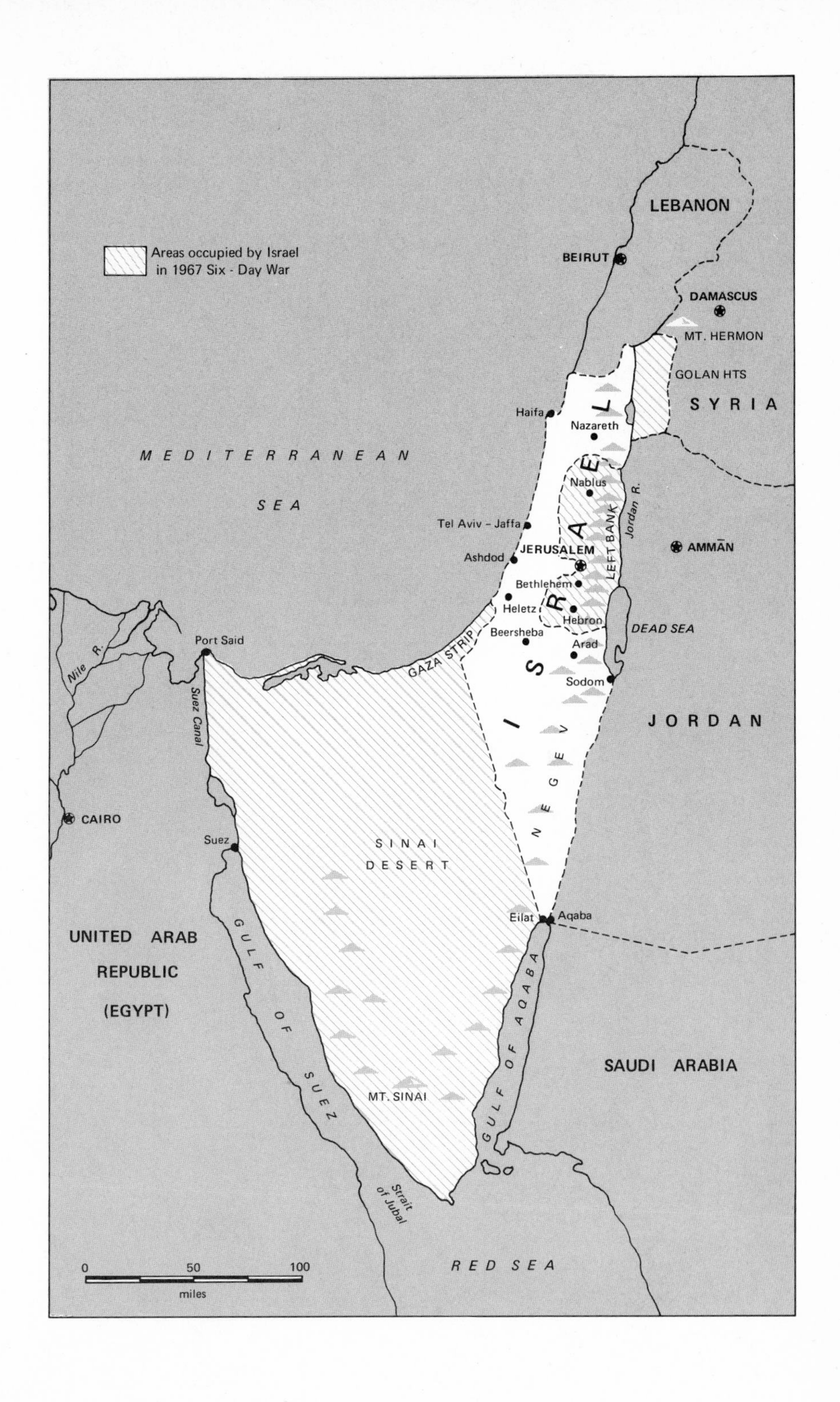

Areas occupied by Israel in 1967 Six - Day War
LEBANON
BEIRUT
DAMASCUS
MT. HERMON
GOLAN HTS
SYRIA
Haifa
Nazareth
MEDITERRANEAN
SEA
Nablus
Jordan R.
Tel Aviv - Jaffa
JERUSALEM
LEFT BANK
AMMĀN
Ashdod
Bethlehem
Heletz
Hebron
DEAD SEA
Beersheba
Port Said
Nile R.
GAZA STRIP
Arad
Sodom
ISRAEL
Suez Canal
JORDAN
NEGEV
CAIRO
Suez
SINAI DESERT
Eilat
Aqaba
UNITED ARAB REPUBLIC (EGYPT)
GULF OF SUEZ
GULF OF AQABA
SAUDI ARABIA
MT. SINAI
Strait of Jubal
RED SEA
0
50
100
miles

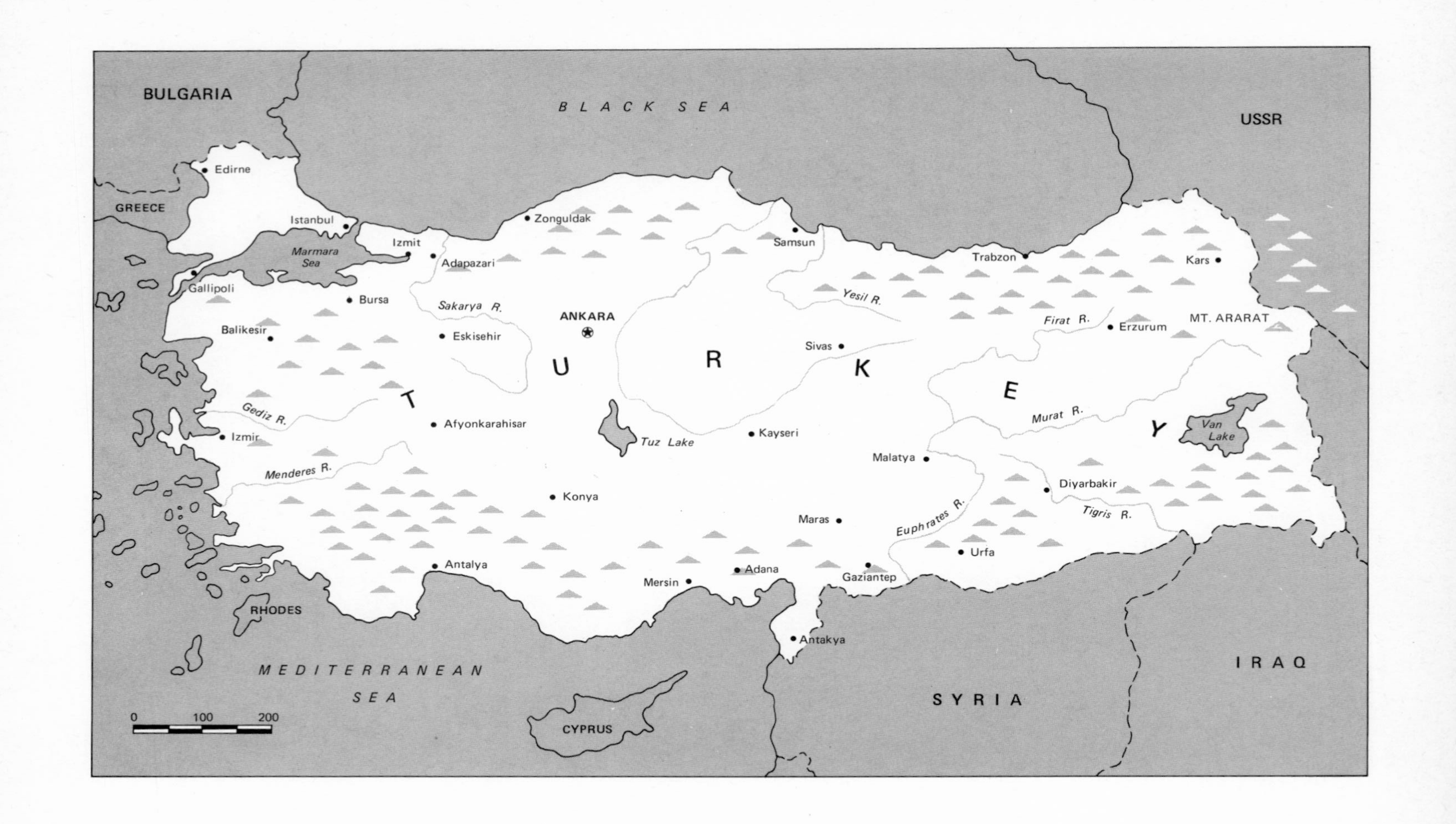
BULGARIA
BLACK SEA
USSR
GREECE
Edirne
Istanbul
Marmara Sea
Gallipoli
Izmit
Adapazari
Zonguldak
Samsun
Trabzon
Kars
Bursa
Sakarya R.
ANKARA
Yesil R.
Firat R.
Erzurum
MT. ARARAT
Balikesir
Eskisehir
Sivas
TURKEY
Murat R.
Van Lake
Gediz R.
Izmir
Afyonkarahisar
Tuz Lake
Kayseri
Malatya
Menderes R.
Diyarbakir
Konya
Tigris R.
Maras
Euphrates R.
Urfa
Antalya
Adana
Mersin
Gaziantep
RHODES
Antakya
MEDITERRANEAN SEA
IRAQ
SYRIA
0
100
200
CYPRUS

UNITED STATES
GULF OF MEXICO
PACIFIC OCEAN
MEXICO
Tijuana
Mexicali
BAJA CALIFORNIA
GULF OF CALIFORNIA
BAJA CALIFORNIA SUR
La Paz
Ciudad Juarez
SONORA
SIERRA MADRE OCCIDENTAL
CHIHUAHUA
Chihuahua
COAHUILA
DURANGO
Durango
SINALOA
Mazatlan
Monterrey
NUEVO LEON
TAMAULIPAS
SIERRA MADRE ORIENTAL
ZACATECAS
SAN LUIS POTOSI
San Luis Potosi
Tampico
QUERETARO
NAYARIT
Aguas-calientes
AGUASCALIENTES
GUANAJUATO
HIDALGO
TLAXCALA
Tlaxco
Vera Cruz
Guadalajara
JALISCO
COLIMA
MICHOACAN
MEXICO CITY
MÉXICO
FEDERAL DISTRICT
GUERRERO
SIERRA MADRE DEL SUR
Acapulco
MORELOS
Puebla
PUEBLA
VERA CRUZ
OAXACA
Oaxaca
TABASCO
CHIAPAS
CAMPECHE
Campeche
YUCATAN
Merida
QUINTANA ROO
Chetumal
BRITISH HONDURAS
GUATEMALA
HONDURAS
0
100
200
miles

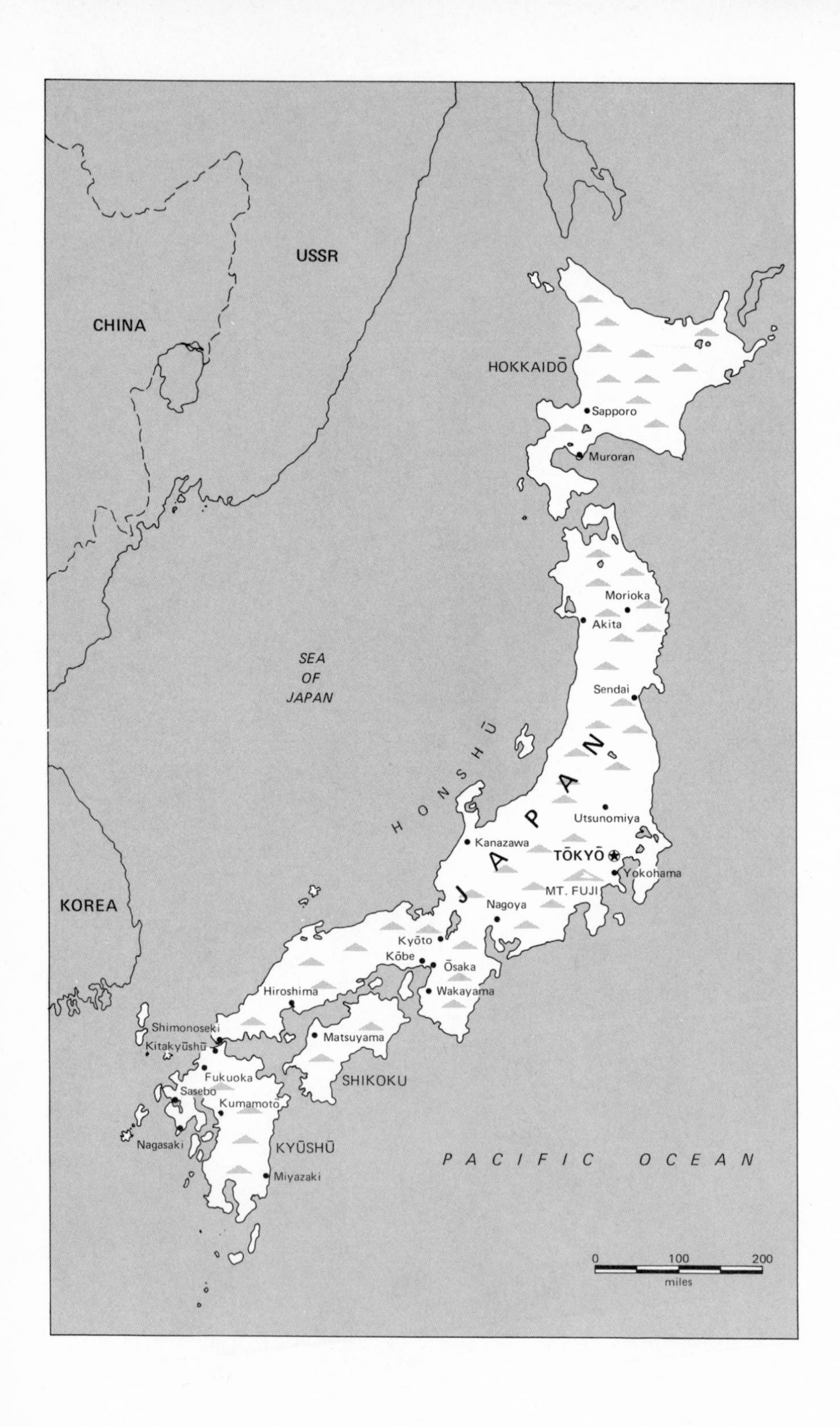
USSR
CHINA
HOKKAIDŌ
Sapporo
Muroran
Morioka
Akita
SEA
OF
JAPAN
Sendai
HONSHŪ
JAPAN
Utsunomiya
Kanazawa
TŌKYŌ
Yokohama
MT. FUJI
KOREA
Nagoya
Kyōto
Kōbe
Ōsaka
Hiroshima
Wakayama
Shimonoseki
Kitakyūshū
Matsuyama
Fukuoka
SHIKOKU
Sasebo
Kumamoto
Nagasaki
KYŪSHŪ
PACIFIC OCEAN
Miyazaki
0
100
200
miles

COPENHAGEN
D E N M A R K
BALTIC SEA
NORTH SEA
Kiel
SCHLESWIG-HOLSTEIN
Lubeck
Hamburg
Wilhelmshaven
Bremerhaven
Oldenburg
Lüneburg
Bremen
Elbe R.
HOLLAND
NIEDERSACHSEN
GERMAN
POLAND
BERLIN
Weser R.
Celle
Hanover
Osnabrück
Braunschweig
Salzgitter
Münster
Bielefeld
DEMOCRATIC
Rhine R.
NORDHEIN-WESTFALEN
Essen
Dortmund
Duisburg
Bochum
Dusseldorf
Kassel
Solingen
REPUBLIC
Cologne
FEDERAL
Aachen
BONN
REPUBLIC OF GERMANY
BELGIUM
HESSEN
Koblenz
RHEINLAND-PFALZ
Frankfurt
Wiesbaden
Main R.
Schweinfurt
PRAGUE
Mainz
Bayreuth
LUX.
Darmstadt
Würzburg
CZECHOSLOVAKIA
Worms
SAARLAND
Mannheim
Saarbrücken
Ludwigshafen
Heidelberg
Nürnberg
BAVARIA
Rhine R.
Karlsruhe
Regensburg
FRANCE
Danube R.
Stuttgart
Baden-Baden
BADEN-WÜRTTEMBERG
Ulm
Augsburg
Munich
Freiburg
ALPS
SWITZERLAND
AUSTRIA
BERN
0
50
100
miles
ITALY

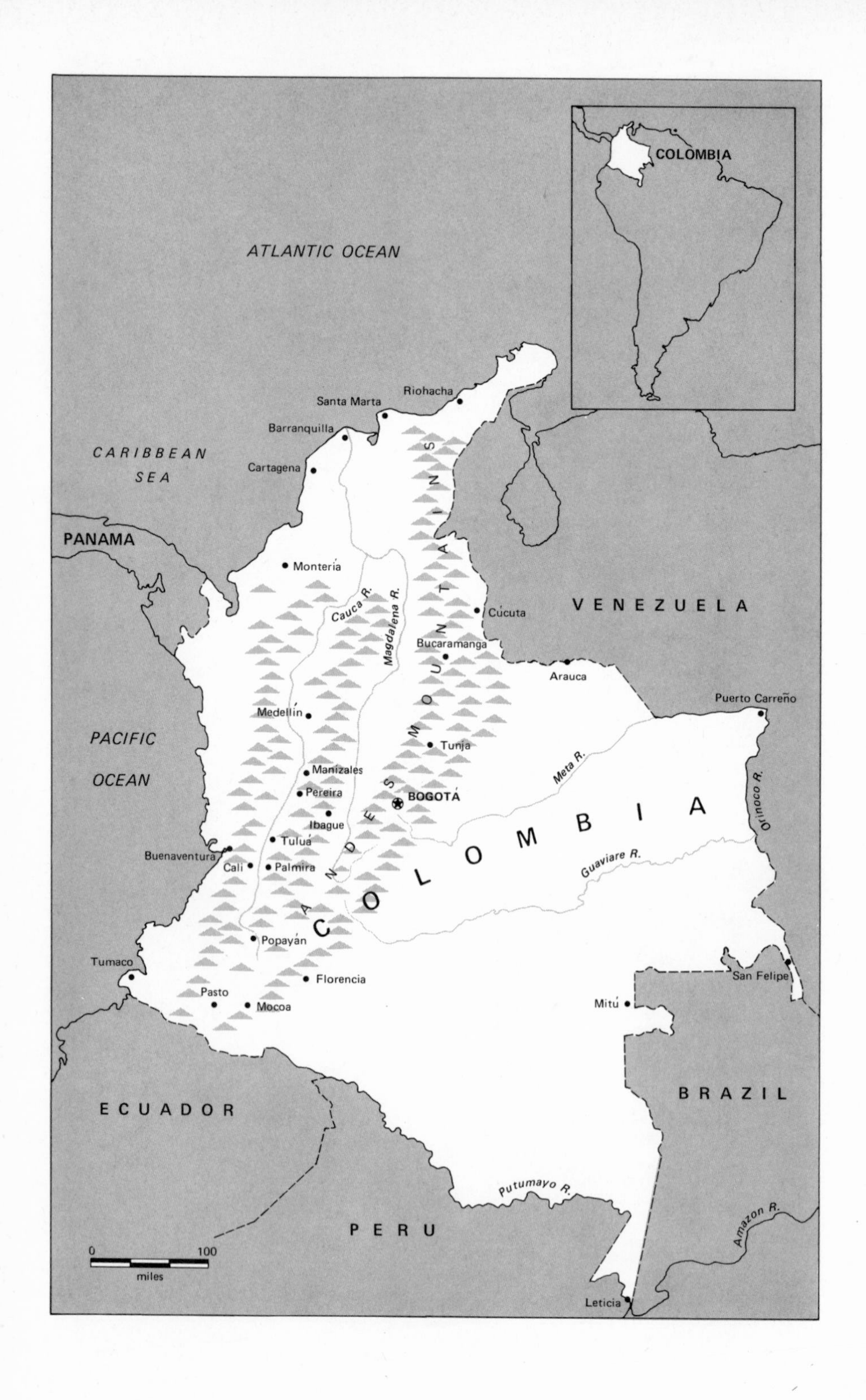
COLOMBIA
ATLANTIC OCEAN
Riohacha
Santa Marta
Barranquilla
CARIBBEAN
SEA
Cartagena
PANAMA
Montería
Cauca R.
Magdalena R.
Cúcuta
VENEZUELA
Bucaramanga
Arauca
Puerto Carreño
Medellín
PACIFIC
OCEAN
Tunja
Meta R.
Manizales
Pereira
BOGOTÁ
Ibagué
Tuluá
Buenaventura
Cali
Palmira
Guaviare R.
Orinoco R.
ANDES MOUNTAINS
COLOMBIA
Popayán
Tumaco
Florencia
San Felipe
Pasto
Mocoa
Mitú
ECUADOR
BRAZIL
Putumayo R.
Amazon R.
PERU
0
100
miles
Leticia

INDEX

	DATE DUE